Thomas Curry

Annual Report of the Comptroller of the Currency

Thomas Curry

Annual Report of the Comptroller of the Currency

ISBN/EAN: 9783741168208

Manufactured in Europe, USA, Canada, Australia, Japa

Cover: Foto ©Thomas Meinert / pixelio.de

Manufactured and distributed by brebook publishing software
(www.brebook.com)

Thomas Curry

Annual Report of the Comptroller of the Currency

OF THE

COMPTROLLER OF THE CURRENCY

TO THE

FIRST SESSION OF THE FORTY-NINTH CONGRESS

OF THE

UNITED STATES.

DECEMBER 1, 1885.

WASHINGTON:
GOVERNMENT PRINTING OFFICE.
1885.

5745 CUR

TREASURY DEPARTMENT,
Document No. 760, 1st ed.
Comptroller of the Currency

TABLE OF CONTENTS.

[A full index will be found at page 247 of this volume.]

REPORT.

4 CONTENTS.

APPENDIX.

REPORT

OF

THE COMPTROLLER OF THE CURRENCY.

TREASURY DEPARTMENT,
OFFICE OF COMPTROLLER OF THE CURRENCY,
Washington, December 1, 1885.

I have the honor to submit for the consideration of Congress, in compliance with section 333 of the Revised Statutes of the United States, the twenty-third annual report of the Comptroller of the Currency. During the year ending November 1, 1885, one hundred and forty-five banks have been organized, with an aggregate capital of $16,938,000; circulating notes have been issued to these new associations amounting to $4,274,910. The following table gives the number of banks organized in each State and Territory during the year ending November 1, 1885, with their aggregate capital and circulation:

States and Territories.	No. of banks.	Capital.	Bonds deposited.	Circulation issued.
Maine	1	$100,000	$25,000	$22,500
New Hampshire	1	50,000	13,000	
Vermont	1	100,000	25,000	22,500
Massachusetts	1	150,000	37,500	33,740
New York	10	1,685,000	790,000	711,000
New Jersey	2	150,000	65,000	58,500
Pennsylvania	6	800,000	182,500	164,240
Delaware	1	210,000	50,000	45,000
Maryland	1	50,000	12,500	
Virginia	1	400,000	50,000	45,000
North Carolina	1	125,000	50,300	45,000
Georgia	2	250,000	71,000	18,900
Florida	2	150,000	55,000	49,500
Mississippi	1	50,000	12,500	11,240
Texas	7	500,000	128,000	115,190
Arkansas	2	300,000	80,000	72,000
Kentucky	3	550,000	140,000	126,000
Tennessee	2	100,000	25,000	22,490
Missouri	3	250,000	155,000	139,500
Ohio	7	1,550,000	546,000	491,400
Indiana	4	1,050,600	675,000	607,500
Illinois	10	2,508,000	312,000	280,780
Michigan	11	1,805,000	365,500	328,880
Wisconsin	3	150,000	65,000	58,490
Iowa	6	350,000	164,500	136,780
Minnesota	1	75,000	19,000	17,100
Kansas	17	965,000	241,300	217,120
Nebraska	14	710,000	180,000	148,390
Oregon	4	275,000	69,000	11,250
Colorado	2	300,000	62,500	56,250
Utah	1	200,000	50,000	45,000
Montana	2	160,000	40,000	36,000
Wyoming	1	50,000	12,500	11,250
Dakota	11	560,000	140,000	81,400
Washington	1	50,000	12,500	11,250
California	2	150,000	37,500	33,750
Total	145	16,938,000	4,959,300	4,274,910

These banks are located by geographical divisions, as follows: Eastern States 4 banks, with capital of $400,000; Middle States, 20, with capital of $2,895,000; Southern States, 21, with capital of $2,425,000; Western States, 76, with capital of $9,473,000; Pacific States, 8, with capital of $725,000; Territories, 16, with capital of $1,020,000.

Since the establishment of the national banking system, on February 25, 1863, there have been organized 3,406 national banks. Of these 432 have gone into voluntary liquidation for the purpose of winding up their affairs; 79 have gone into voluntary liquidation for the purpose of reorganization; 64 are in liquidation by expiration of their charter, of which number 38 have been reorganized; and 104 have been placed in the hands of receivers for the purpose of closing up their affairs; leaving the total number in existence 2,727, on November 1, 1885, which is the largest number that has been in operation at any one time.

The corporate existence of 864 national banks expired during the year ending November 1, 1885, of which 801 have been extended under the act of July 12, 1882. Forty-eight have permitted their corporate existence to expire, and are in liquidation under section 7 of said act (32 of which have been succeeded by other banks located in the same places, and with nearly the same shareholders), and 13 have been placed in voluntary liquidation by vote of shareholders owning two-thirds of their stock, of which 7 were succeeded by other banks. The remaining 2 became insolvent, and were placed in the hands of receivers. The corporate existence of 14 national banks, with an aggregate capital of $4,450,000, will expire during November and December of this year; and the corporate existence of 18 national banks, with an aggregate capital of $3,135,000, will expire during 1886. Four national banks, with an aggregate capital of $600,000, have failed and been placed in the hands of receivers during the year.

Under the provisions of the act of July 12, 1882, national banks with a capital of from $50,000 to $150,000 may be organized upon a minimum deposit of United States bonds equal to 25 per cent. of such capital. The minimum deposit of bonds required by law to be made by banks with a capital of upwards of $150,000 is $50,000. The following table shows the number of banks organized from July 1, 1882, to July 1, 1885, their capital stock, amount of bonds deposited in accordance with law, and the circulation issued thereon:

Year.	Number of banks.	Capital.	Minimum bonds required.	Bonds actually deposited.	Percentage of excess	Circulation issued.
					Per cent.	
July 1, 1882, to July 1, 1883..	251	$26,552,300	$5,155,500	$7,116,400	28	$6,404,760
July 1, 1883, to July 1, 1884..	218	19,944,000	4,016,000	4,676,100	14	4,208,490
July 1, 1884, to July 1, 1885..	142	15,205,000	3,061,250	3,332,800	8	2,999,520

An examination of the foregoing table shows that 611 banks have been organized between the dates above given, with a capital of $61,701,300; that they have deposited $15,125,300 of bonds, upon which circulation to the amount of $13,612,770 has been issued. The minimum deposit of bonds, as required by law for said banks is $12,232,750, and it will be seen that while the actual deposit has in the aggregate exceeded the minimum, yet this excess has steadily decreased during the three years covered by the table. The excess above the required minimum of bonds deposited from July, 1882, to July, 1883, was 28 per cent. of the total deposit. From July, 1883, to July, 1884, this excess was 14 per cent. only of the total deposit, and from July, 1884, to July,

1885, the excess was still further diminished to 8 per cent. This shows conclusively that the banks organized between the periods named have not been induced to enter the system on account of the profit to be derived from the issue of circulating notes, but because it was believed by their managers that they would have a better credit and standing with the public under the national bank act than as State or private banks.

It is also to be noted that the reduction by the act of July 12, 1882, of the minimum amount of bonds to be deposited by national banks of $150,000 capital and under to one-quarter of their capital stock has had a tendency to increase the organization of small banks throughout the country. While the number of banks organized from July 1, 1879, to July 1, 1882, with a capital of $150,000 and under was 232, the number of banks of this class organized from July 1, 1882, to July 1, 1885, was 548. These small banks have in many instances been organized to take the place of private banking firms and small State banks, particularly in the West, Northwest, and Southwest. It is believed that this change is to the advantage of the public, as the majority of these banks were previously carrying on a banking business without being subject to an examination of their affairs, and without the security given by the publication of sworn statements of their condition, to which supervision and requirement they will be subject under the national bank act.

Under the present law, the minimum deposit of bonds required to be made by the 2,714 national banks in operation in the United States on October 1, 1885, would be but $80,970,423 in order to continue as national banking associations. A table has been prepared and will be found in the Appendix, showing for the national banks in each State, Territory, and reserve cities, the minimum amount of bonds required by law, the bonds actually held, and the circulation issued thereon October 1, 1885. This table also shows the increased amount of circulation which the national banks might issue in the event of the passage of a law authorizing them to issue circulation equal to the par value of their bonds on deposit.

It is believed that the national banking system will be continued even if the associations organized under it cannot issue circulation at a profit, inasmuch as the experience under it has shown it is for the best interests of the public, as well as of the banks, that this business should be carried on under a general law having effect throughout all the different States. This statement is made without prejudice to banks organized under the statutes of those States which contain provisions and restrictions similar to those of the national banking law. In many of the States, however, the banking laws are defective, and it is evident that the legislation upon the subject cannot be homogeneous, nor the working of the laws so harmonious and useful under statutes passed by thirty-eight States as under one general law of Congress applicable to all banking institutions.

EXTENSION OF THE CORPORATE EXISTENCE OF NATIONAL BANKS.

The original national currency act of February 25, 1863, provided in section 11 that banks organized under its provisions should have succession for a period of not exceeding twenty years from the date of said act, as follows:

Every association formed pursuant to the provisions of this act may make and use a common seal, and shall have succession by the name designated in its articles of association, and for the period limited therein, not however exceeding twenty years from the passage of this act.

Under the provisions of this act 488 banks were organized, of which 88 had ceased to exist prior to January 1, 1882, leaving 400 still in operation on that date. Of these, 314 were extended under the act of July 12, 1882, 72 were succeeded by other associations with the same or different names, 12 went out by voluntary liquidation or expiration of corporate existence without successors, and 2 were placed in the hands of receivers. The corporate existence of 297 of these banks expired on February 25, 1883, and 270 were then extended; while 103 expired previous to that date, of which 44 were extended.

The national bank act of June 3, 1864, superseding that of February 25, 1863, provides in section 8 that each national bank shall have succession for twenty years from the date of its organization, that is, from the date of its organization certificate. This section was embodied in section 5136, Revised Statutes, now in force, which is as follows:

Upon duly making and filing articles of association and an organization certificate, the association shall become as from the date of execution of its organization certificate a body corporate, and as such and in the name designated in the organization certificate, it shall have power: First, to adopt and use a corporate seal; second, to have succession for a period of twenty years from its organization, unless it is sooner dissolved according to the provisions of its articles of association, or by the act of its shareholders owning two-thirds of its stock, or unless its franchise becomes forfeited by some violation of law.

Anticipating the fact that a large number of national banks would expire by limitation during the years 1882 and 1883, the Comptroller of the Currency, in his annual report for 1881, recommended that an act be passed providing that any national bank might, with the approval of the Comptroller, at any time within two years prior to the date of expiration of its corporate existence, extend its period of succession for twenty years by amending its articles of association.

In accordance with this recommendation, a bill was introduced soon after the assembling of the Forty-seventh Congress, and was referred to the Committee on Banking and Currency, and by that committee reported to the House, and after considerable discussion, passed on May 30, 1882, by a vote of 125 to 67.*

The bill was amended in the Senate in many particulars, and passed that body June 22, 1882, by a vote of 34 to 14.† It subsequently passed the House July 10, 1882, upon a report of conference committee, yeas 110, nays 79, not voting 101,‡ and received the approval of the President July 12, 1882.

Prior to the passage of this act the right of shareholders of national banks whose corporate existence was about to expire, to organize under the national bank act new associations with the same names, in order to retain as far as possible their business and the prestige of their names, which had become known throughout the country, was in doubt, and inasmuch as there was then no statute permitting the extension of their corporate existence, the opinion of the Attorney-General was requested on this point, and on the 23d of February, 1882, an opinion was given, in which he said:

The present national banking laws do not forbid the stockholders of an expiring corporation from organizing a new banking association, nor from assuming the name of the old corporation, with the approval of the Comptroller of the Currency; and in the absence of any prohibition to that effect, no legal obstacle to the formation of a new association by such stockholders, and the adoption of the name of the old association, would in my opinion exist.

---

* Congressional Record, No. 120, p. 25, Forty-seventh Congress.
† *Ibid.*, No. 147, p. 32.
‡ *Ibid.*, July 11, 1882.

As there was some uncertainty in regard to the passage by Congress of the act for the extension of the corporate existence of national banking associations, fifty banks gave notice of liquidation, and in most instances new associations were organized with the same titles and the same stockholders as those which had been placed in liquidation. A proviso attached to section 5 of the act of July 12, 1882, requires that in the organization of any banking association, intended to replace any existing banking association and retaining the name thereof, the holders of stock in the expiring association shall be entitled to preference in the allotment of the shares of the new association in proportion to the number of shares held by them respectively in the expiring association.

Under the act of July 12, 1882, nearly all of the banks then in existence which were organized under the act of February 25, 1863, extended their corporate existence during the following months:

July, 1882	6
August, 1882	9
September, 1882	7
October, 1882	5
November, 1882	4
December, 1882	7
January, 1883	4
February, 1883 *	2
February 25, 1883	270
Total	314

The whole number of banks organized under the act of June 3, 1864, to the date of the act of July 12, 1882, was 2,266, of which 450 had been closed, leaving 1,816 in operation on that date. The following table gives the number of these banks, the original periods of succession of which will terminate during each year from 1886 to 1899 inclusive, with their capital and circulation:

Years.	Number of banks.	Capital.	Circulation.
1886	18	$3,135,000	$1,848,250
1887	5	950,000	925,000
1888	11	1,250,000	719,100
1889	3	600,000	450,000
1890	63	9,290,500	6,419,950
1891	104	13,193,900	9,120,880
1892	103	12,879,600	8,300,870
1893	39	4,740,000	3,849,400
1894	67	7,638,000	5,819,150
1895	81	10,665,000	7,650,000
1896	23	1,968,000	1,525,500
1897	28	2,969,000	2,106,000
1898	27	2,649,000	2,208,600
1899	41	4,820,000	3,811,900
Total	610	76,748,000	54,754,600

On November 1, 1885, 885 banks organized under the act of June 3, 1864, had been extended, making, with the 314 extensions of banks organized under the act of February 25, 1863, 1,199 associations the corporate existence of which has been extended under the act of July 12, 1882. In the Appendix will be found a table showing the distribution and capital of these banks by States. During the year ending November 1, 1885, the periods of succession of 864 banks organized under the act of June 3, 1864, terminated. Of these, 801 have already extended their corporate existence, 5 were placed in voluntary liquidation

---

* Before February 25, 1883.

by the vote of stockholders owning two-thirds of their stock, 15 were permitted by their stockholders to close at the end of their periods of succession, 4 were placed in the hands of receivers, and 39 were succeeded by other associations with different names but with the same shareholders, wholly or in part. From November 1 to December 31, 1885, 14 banks will expire, all of which have applied in due form for extension.

Among the banks extended during the year were 30 in the city of New York, with an aggregate capital of $35,350,000, as well as a large number in Boston, Philadelphia, and other principal cities, being some of the largest banking institutions in the United States. It is also interesting to note that many of the banks extending during the past year were originally organized under the various State laws, and the continuation of their existence under the national banking system indicates their belief that it is for their best interests to do business under the general banking laws of the United States.

The number, capital, and circulation of the national banks whose periods of succession terminated between November 1, 1884, and November 1, 1885, are shown by the following table, which also indicates the number whose corporate existence has been extended, and the number which have expired and have been succeeded by other national banks:

Date.	Number banks that have expired.	Capital.	Circulation.	Number banks that have extended.	Capital.	Circulation.	Number banks succeeded by other banks.	Capital.	Circulation.
1884.									
November.	48	$16,695,150	$9,635,450	46	$16,195,150	$9,545,450	1	$200,000	$45,000
December.	110	40,415,240	22,269,290	106	38,515,240	22,099,640	3	1,850,000	157,500
1885.									
January ..	109	27,549,500	16,420,015	94	25,054,500	14,467,365	11	2,145,000	1,637,650
February .	68	11,576,000	7,921,940	66	11,226,000	7,815,740			
March	126	32,336,350	17,411,510	116	30,946,350	16,507,910	6	855,000	567,000
April.......	85	24,941,970	13,082,085	79	21,266,970	12,704,085	3	275,000	153,000
May	122	28,507,330	18,931,595	116	27,807,340	18,496,845	3	300,000	202,500
June	139	50,094,915	20,418,910	131	47,669,915	19,877,560	3	300,000	176,850
July	24	4,915,000	2,047,800	21	4,265,000	1,522,800	3	650,000	525,000
August ...	14	1,951,000	1,129,500	10	1,516,000	891,000	3	375,000	184,500
September.	12	1,775,000	913,950	9	1,125,000	711,450	3	650,000	202,500
October ..	7	905,000	720,000	7	905,000	720,000			
Total....	864	241,662,455	130,911,045	801	226,492,465	125,367,945	39	7,600,000	3,851,500

It will be seen from the foregoing statements that a larger number of national banks expired by limitation during the year ending November 1, 1885, than have or will expire during any other year between the passage of the act of July 12, 1882, and the year 1900.

The additional labor entailed upon this office by the extension of so large a number of banks in so short a period of time has been very considerable, it being necessary in all instances to carefully examine the original articles of each association as well as the amendments and the signatures of assent of the shareholders thereto. On account of section 6, which provides that new circulating notes shall be issued to each extended association, duplicate accounts have necessarily been opened upon the books of this office with every extended bank, and in accordance with the third section of the act it has been necessary that a special examination should be made of each bank to determine its condition, as before granting a certificate of approval for extension to any association.

the Comptroller must be satisfied that its capital is unimpaired and that it is otherwise in a sound condition.

It appears to be a matter of congratulation to the friends of the national banking system that the associations, the original periods of succession of which have terminated, have up to this time as a rule decided to continue in business, notwithstanding the fact that very little if any profit can be made upon circulation under the present provisions of the law and the prevailing high prices of Government securities.

The provisions of the act for the extension of the corporate existence of national banks in the main appear to be admirably suited for that purpose. Those of the first and second sections, which provide that the period of succession may be extended by simply amending the articles of association, by the consent in writing of shareholders owning not less than two-thirds of the capital stock, are simple and easily carried out by the banks.

Section 3, which provides for a special examination of the association in order to determine its condition, is also well adapted for the purpose. That part of section 4 which provides that the extended bank shall continue to be in all respects the identical association it was before the extension of its period of succession prevents any break or disturbance in its business, enables the bank to retain its surplus fund, and is especially useful in the matter of any litigation for collection of assets, title to property, &c.

It would, however, appear that some of the provisions of section 5 might be amended with advantage to the public. Said section is as follows:

SEC. 5. That when any national banking association has amended its articles of association as provided in this act, and the Comptroller has granted his certificate of approval, any shareholder not assenting to such amendment may give notice in writing to the directors, within thirty days from the date of the certificate of approval, of his desire to withdraw from said association, in which case he shall be entitled to receive from said banking association the value of the shares so held by him, to be ascertained by an appraisal made by a committee of three persons, one to be selected by such shareholder, one by the directors, and the third by the first two; and in case the value so fixed shall not be satisfactory to any such shareholder, he may appeal to the Comptroller of the Currency, who shall cause a reappraisal to be made, which shall be final and binding; and if said reappraisal shall exceed the value fixed by said committee, the bank shall pay the expenses of said reappraisal, and otherwise the appellant shall pay said expenses; and the value so ascertained and determined shall be deemed to be a debt due, and be forthwith paid, to said shareholder, from said bank; and the shares so surrendered and appraised shall, after due notice, be sold at public sale, within thirty days after the final appraisal provided in this section: *Provided*, That in the organization of any banking association intended to replace any existing banking association, and retaining the name thereof, the holders of stock in the expiring association shall be entitled to preference in the allotment of the shares of the new association in proportion to the number of shares held by them respectively in the expiring association.

Provision is thus made to ascertain the value of shares of non-assenting shareholders, by an appraisal to be made by a committee of three persons, one to be selected by the non-assenting shareholder, one by the directors, and a third by the first two. But if the bank does not heed the notice of withdrawal and declines to appoint a person to serve on the committee of appraisal, there is no penalty for such neglect, and apparently the shareholder's only remedy is by a suit in some court of competent jurisdiction. I therefore conclude that some provision should be made for the enforcement of this section. Provision is also made, in case the value of the shares fixed by the committee of appraisal is not satisfactory to the shareholder, that he may appeal to the Comptroller of the Currency, who shall cause a reappraisal to be made, which shall be final and binding. No provision is, however, made for an appeal on the part of the bank, where the valuation fixed by the committee is not satisfactory to it. I have to recommend, therefore, that the section be amended to obviate this defect.

Provision is further made that after the appraised value has been paid to the shareholder, as provided by law, and the shares surrendered, the same shall, after due notice, be sold at public sale within thirty days after the final appraisal. It appears that in many cases thirty days is not sufficient time for the bank to realize a fair price for shares which it is thus compelled under the law to purchase, and inasmuch as section 5201 of the Revised Statutes provides that stock purchased or acquired to prevent loss upon a debt previously contracted in good faith may be sold at any time within six months from the date of its purchase, at public or private sale, it would seem that the law should grant at least as long a period for the sale of the stock which an association is compelled to take from a retiring stockholder under the act of extension, and the Comptroller recommends an amendment to this effect.

Section 6, which relates to the circulation of extended associations, is as follows:

SEC. 6. That the circulating notes of any association so extending the period of its succession which shall have been issued to it prior to such extension shall be redeemed at the Treasury of the United States, as provided in section three of the act of June twentieth, eighteen hundred and seventy-four, entitled "An act fixing the amount of United States notes, providing for redistribution of national-bank currency, and for other purposes," and such notes when redeemed shall be forwarded to the Comptroller of the Currency, and destroyed, as now provided by law; and at the end of three years from the date of the extension of the corporate existence of each bank the association so extended shall deposit lawful money with the Treasurer of the United States sufficient to redeem the remainder of the circulation which was outstanding at the date of its extension, as provided in sections fifty-two hundred and twenty-two, fifty-two hundred and twenty-four, and fifty-two hundred and twenty-five of the Revised Statutes; and any gain that may arise from the failure to present such circulating notes for redemption shall inure to the benefit of the United States; and from time to time, as such notes are redeemed or lawful money deposited therefor as provided herein, new circulating notes shall be issued as provided by this act, bearing such devices, to be approved by the Secretary of the Treasury, as shall make them readily distinguishable from the circulating notes heretofore issued : *Provided, however,* That each banking association which shall obtain the benefit of this act shall reimburse to the Treasury the cost of preparing the plate or plates for such new circulating notes as shall be issued to it.

It is respectfully submitted that more than three years should be granted within which to deposit lawful money to retire the remainder of the circulation outstanding at the date of extension. If this period should be extended to six years the necessary deposit would then be comparatively small. In the natural course of redemption the outstanding circulation of old design of extended associations is constantly being decreased, as all such notes redeemed are retired without regard to their fitness for circulation, notes of a new design, as provided by law, being issued in their place. See tables, pages 114,115.

Upon reference to a statement heretofore made of the extension of the corporate existence of national banks organized under the act of February 25, 1863, it will be noticed that 270 banks, with a circulation of $47,997,430, were extended on February 25, 1883, and therefore lawful money must be deposited under section 6 within thirty days from February 25, 1886, to retire such portion of this circulation as then remains outstanding. From the redemptions of this circulation made in regular course, it has for some time been evident to the Comptroller that the amount of the final deposit required by this law to be made in lawful money during the thirty days succeeding February 25, 1886, would be very large, and that this deposit of lawful money within so short a period would perhaps occasion some temporary disturbance at money centers, particularly as some time would necessarily elapse before new circulation to replace that retired could be issued by the banks. In this connection I desire to call attention to a portion of section 9, which provides that in the aggregate not more than three million dollars of lawful money shall be deposited by national associations during any calendar month in order to withdraw their circulating notes, except when bonds owned by the association shall be called for redemption by the Secretary of the Treasury. It does not appear that lawful money deposits made under section 6 are exempted from the provisions of section 9 referred to, and inasmuch as the deposits under section 6 may at times exceed $3,000,000 in any one month, there is an apparent conflict in the act. I therefore recommend that the time of deposit be extended. I also recommend that section 9 be so amended that its provisions shall not apply to the deposit of lawful money by extended associations.

In anticipation of the difficulty which might arise after February 25, 1886, from the apparent conflict of law referred to, and from the large deposit of lawful money, which, if not made before, would, by the law, be required to be made within thirty days following that date, the Comptroller, early in the present year, began to advise national banks which would be required by section 6 to make deposits of lawful money on or before March 25, 1886, in order to prevent, if possible, any disturbance, to make such deposits in advance, in sums of $10,000 or multiples thereof, extending them over a period of some months. These banks were also advised to order in advance the preparation of notes of new design, that they might be in readiness to be issued to replace the circulation retired by the deposit of lawful money under section 6. Early in August a printed circular letter embodying this advice was sent to all the national banks interested. Many of the banks so addressed have responded, and it is believed that the action of this office has had an excellent effect, and that the amount of lawful money to be deposited within thirty days after February 25, 1886, will be much less than if this action had not been taken.

If the only object of section 6 is to enable the United States to gain the benefit from lost or destroyed notes, this object might have been accomplished by simple enactment to this effect, without the expense of the issuance of new notes and the deposit of lawful money.

The extension of the franchises of expiring associations for the sole purpose of liquidating their affairs until closed, as provided for in section 7, appears to answer its purpose.

The remaining sections of the act are for purposes other than the extension of the corporate existence of national banks, and it is not necessary in this connection to make any statement in regard to their provisions.

At this date but two reappraisals have been made of the stock of non-assenting shareholders, under section five, by the Comptroller of the Currency.

CIRCULATION.

Notwithstanding the fact that 145 new banks were organized during the past year, with a capital of $16,938,000, depositing $4,959,300 of bonds as security for circulating notes, the aggregate of bonds on deposit for that purpose has diminished from $325,316,300 to $308,364,550.

The following table gives the various kinds and amounts of bonds deposited by the banks to secure their circulating notes on November 1, 1883, November 1, 1884, and November 1, 1885.

	1883.	1884.	1885.
Three-and-a-halfs	$632,000		
Threes	201,327,750	$155,604,400	$138,920,650
Four-and-a-halfs	41,319,700	40,537,450	40,547,250
Pacific sixes	3,463,000	3,469,000	3,505,000
Fours	106,164,850	116,705,450	116,391,650
	352,907,300	325,316,300	308,364,550

By reference to this table it will be seen that the aggregate reduction of bonds deposited for the year ending November 1, 1885, was $16,951,750. The changes were as follows: An increase of $36,000 in Pacific currency sixes and of $9,800 in the amount of four-and-a-half per cents deposited, a reduction of $313,800 in the amount of four per cents held, and a reduction of $16,683,750 in the amount of three per cents held, payable at the option of the Government. Of the three per cents $9,586,200 had been called for payment, and interest had ceased on November 1, 1884.*

The following tables show the decrease of national-bank circulation during the years ending November 1, 1883, November 1, 1884, and November 1, 1885, and the amount of lawful money on deposit at each of the dates named:

National-bank notes outstanding November 1, 1882, including notes of national gold banks	$362,727,747	
Less lawful money on deposit at same date, including deposits of gold banks	38,423,404	
		$324,304,343
National-bank notes outstanding November 1, 1883	352,013,787	
Less lawful money on deposit November 1, 1883	35,993,461	
		316,020,326
Net decrease of circulation		8,284,017

National-bank notes outstanding November 1, 1883, including notes of national gold banks	352,013,787	
Less lawful money on deposit at same date, including deposits of national gold banks	35,993,461	
		316,020,326
National-bank notes outstanding November 1, 1884, including notes of national gold banks	333,559,813	
Less lawful money on deposit at same date, including deposits of national gold banks	41,710,163	
		291,849,650
Net decrease of circulation		24,170,676

National-bank notes outstanding November 1, 1884, including notes of national gold banks	333,559,813	
Less lawful money on deposit at same date, including deposits of national gold banks	41,710,163	
		291,849,650
National-bank notes outstanding November 1, 1885, including notes of national gold banks	315,847,168	
Less lawful money on deposit at same date, including notes of national gold banks	39,542,979	
		276,304,189
Net decrease of circulation		15,545,461

* A large proportion of these bonds were replaced by others.

It will be seen that the banks held on November 1, 1884, $155,604,400, and on November 1, 1885, $138,920,650, of three per cents under the act of July 12, 1882, payable at the pleasure of the Government. The Secretary of the Treasury, during the year ending November 1, 1883, paid $105,634,150, and during the year ending November 1, 1884, $105,970,450 of the public debt. In the latter year three per cents only were called. No bonds were called for the year ending November 1, 1885. Reasoning upon the theory that the public debt would, during the year ending November 1, 1885, continue to be reduced by the payment of three per cent. bonds, and that this reduction would occasion the reinvestment of trust and other funds invested in threes, and cause a greater demand for and consequent increase in the price of four per cent. bonds to a point at which it would be more profitable for the national banks to sell them, the Comptroller estimated in his last annual report to Congress, that unless legislation should be secured enabling the banks to issue currency at a fair profit, circulation would be reduced at the rate of at least $40,000,000 per annum. It is believed that this estimate would have been substantially correct had the Government continued during 1885 to call and pay the three per cent. bonds as rapidly as during the two previous years.

The reduction of circulation of national banks during the year ending November 1, 1885, for reasons other than the call of bonds by which it was secured, was greater than anticipated. The causes which have led to this result are small profit remaining to national banks on circulation after paying the tax of 1 per cent. per annum imposed by the Government; reduction in the rates of interest throughout the country, occasioned by the abundance of money in the financial centers; and, doubtless, uneasiness among certain of the bankers of the country as to the outcome of the increase of silver in the Treasury, such increase indicating that possibly the interest on the public debt, and even some portion of the principal, might be paid in standard silver dollars, and that Government bonds might thereby become depreciated in foreign markets, which would undoubtedly affect their price in this country. The credit and standing of this country is deservedly high, and it is not believed that the people desire either the principal or interest on the bonded debt of this country to be paid in anything but gold coin or its equivalent. This matter was discussed at the time the bonds were issued, during the period of the refunding of the debt, and the preparations for the resumption of specie payments, and the conviction is general that the faith and credit of this Government is pledged for the payment of its securities in gold coin or its equivalent.

The Comptroller in his last annual report made the following statement:

The time of the final payment of the debt is, however, yet distant, and with appropriate legislation there will probably be for many years no lack of bonds as a safe basis of circulation. Moreover, no feasible plan with other security has as yet been suggested, affording a sound currency redeemable on demand in specie, and the Comptroller believes that it is extremely doubtful whether, after the experience of the last twenty years, the people would be satisfied with a currency based on any security other than United States bonds.

Public sentiment seems to be in favor of the payment of the public debt as rapidly as possible, and while no doubt this is in general a correct principle, yet as it is apparent that such payment must extend under the most favorable circumstances over a long future period, the interest during which time is as much a portion of the debt as the principal, it is a question if it would not be of ultimate benefit to the country and a payment of the debt to reduce the interest upon it to a minimum rate and defer the payment of the principal, thus giving for many years a safe basis for national-bank circulation. This course would be particularly advantageous if the revenues of the Government are hereafter reduced to a point which, after providing sufficient means for carrying on public business, will necessitate a more gradual reduction of the principal of the debt.

The measures introduced in the Senate and House of Representatives during the last session of Congress to enable national banking associations to issue circulation to the par value of the bonds deposited, and for the funding of the high-rate bonds of the United States into bonds bearing a lower rate of interest, did not become laws, the law taxing circulation was not repealed, and no legislation whatever in relation to the national banks or the refunding of the public debt was enacted.

Unless some measures be taken whereby the banks may be enabled to issue circulation at a reasonable profit to themselves, the contraction of national-bank notes will continue. The profit on circulation may be increased by the removal of the tax and by increasing the amount of currency issued to the par value of the United States bonds deposited; and the Comptroller again respectfully recommends appropriate legislation for that purpose. Even if this be done, the national bank-note circulation is still liable to reduction and final disappearance with the reduction and final payment of the debt of the United States.

Upon examining the various methods of issuing bank notes, adopted in other countries, and which are described elsewhere in the report, it will be seen that a large proportion of the issue of notes under the laws of the different Governments are based upon the credit of the banks—that is to say, they are issued against the general assets of the various institutions, and are not, as a rule, secured by special deposits or securities held in trust, or by coin or bullion set apart specially for the protection of the note-holder.

Irresponsible and illegitimate issues of bank notes have been common to almost all civilized countries, and financial disturbances have again and again resulted from such issues, notwithstanding the attempts which have been made by many different Governments to correct the abuse.

Bank notes, which circulate as money among the people, should either be well secured by special deposit of valuable assets in trust, or they should be issued only by corporations whose assets and management are of such a character as to insure the payment of the notes, and those corporations should be compelled by law to carry a sufficient reserve in the coin of the country for their prompt redemption. Under these circumstances only are bank notes entitled to the confidence of the public. It is, of course, not to be expected that corporations or private bankers will issue bank notes, if the law requires them to be based upon the security of any form of debt and at the same time requires that an amount of coin or bullion equal to the notes issued shall be held by the issuing association for their redemption. There would be absolute loss on such an issue. But as long as a bank note is payable on demand by the issuer thereof, and the public are assured that it rests upon a stable foundation of security, either deposited in trust or vested in the issuer in such a manner as to secure its ultimate payment, and as long as said note is protected by a reserve in proportion to the ordinary demands for coin when needed for dealings with foreign countries or the natural wants of trade, the public will use it as money on account of its greater convenience.

It being conceded that bank notes based upon coin or bullion will not be issued in sufficient quantities for the convenience of the public, banks should be permitted to issue notes upon other securities for the convenience of trade and commerce. The debt of a strong Government is, next to coin or bullion, the most available for this purpose, and in this country up to this time the debt has supplied a safe and satisfactory basis for bank notes, but in view of the anticipated payment of the public debt it becomes a question of interest how far bank notes can safely be issued without other security than the general assets and credit of the banks. If the liability of shareholders on account of notes issued is increased, and note-holders are preferred as against all other creditors, circulating notes might perhaps be issued by joint stock banks, under an improved safety fund system to a certain percentage of their capital, unsecured by a deposit of bonds.

My predecessor, Mr. Knox, in his report for 1883 said:

Experience has shown that if instead of ninety dollars upon each one hundred dollars of bonds, one hundred dollars of circulating notes had been issued upon every seventy dollars of United States bonds deposited, there would not have been any loss to the Government, or to the holders of the circulating notes of any of the national banks which have failed during the last twenty years; but that there might have been an additional loss to the depositors, depending upon the character of the assets held in place of the portion of bonds which on this supposition would have been released If circulation had been issued to these insolvent banks, which had a capital of about twenty millions, to the amount of their capital, the value of the bonds being the same, and there had been just previous to failure a decline in the market of 5 per cent. upon the value of the bonds, the losses would not have exceeded 1 one million of dollars. These possible losses would have fallen upon the holders of the notes of such few banks only as became insolvent, or upon the creditors of these banks or the Government; and if the gain arising from lost notes could have been used as proposed, these possible losses would have been provided for.

He proposed that a safety fund should be accumulated, (1) from the gain arising from the accidental loss or destruction of the circulating notes of national banks; (2) from the tax upon circulation; and (3) from interest to be derived at a low rate upon the fund on deposit in the Treasury for the purpose of redeeming the notes of national banks retiring circulation, which now amounts to more than thirty-nine million dollars.

The amount available for a safety fund from the first source is estimated now to be not less than six million dollars, and the amount derived from the tax of 1 per cent. per annum on circulation during the year 1884 was more than three millions. Even if this tax for safety fund purposes should be fixed at one-half per cent., in the course of three years a safety fund would be in hand amounting to more than ten millions of dollars.

The results of the liquidation of 104 national banks which have failed, and the affairs of which have been liquidated or are in process of liquidation by receivers under the direction of this office, show in a very interesting manner to what extent it may be safe to permit banks under the national system to issue circulation unprotected by a deposit of United States bonds. Of these 104 banks, 70 have been finally closed, and for them the results are absolute. The remaining 34 are still in process of liquidation, but have progressed so far that the final result can be estimated with comparative accuracy.

The dividends paid to the creditors of all these banks from the proceeds of their general assets amount to $28,379,080. They had an aggregate capital of $21,858,900, upon which under the law they could, on deposit of bonds, issue 90 per cent., or $19,673,010 of circulation. It at the time of their failure the law had permitted an issue of circulation to the amount of 90 per cent. of capital, *unsecured except by a first lien on general assets* of the 104 banks mentioned, the note-holders of 58 would have experienced no loss. If the law had authorized an *unsecured* issue equal to 70 per cent. of capital, the notes of 71 of these banks would have been redeemed from the proceeds of their general assets. At 40 per cent., the notes of 90 would have been paid in full, and upon an *unsecured issue* of 25 per cent. of capital.* loss to note holders would have occurred in the case of five banks only, or about $62,000 in all.

The experience with these 104 banks shows almost conclusively that if their issues to the amount of 65 per cent. of their capital had been secured by a deposit of bonds to an equal amount, the remaining 25 per cent. might have been issued without other security than a first lien on the general assets, and if a safety fund had been in existence it would in the case cited have been drawn upon to the extent of $62,000 only upon a circulation amounting to $5,464,700. For a beginning, therefore, it might be safe to authorize banks to issue circulation amounting to 90 per cent. of their capital, 70 per cent. to be secured by an equal amount of United States bonds at par value, the remaining 20 per cent. being issued without other security than a first lien on such assets. But if the law should provide for the accumulation of a safety fund in the manner suggested, then as such safety fund increased, the percentage of circulation unsecured by bonds might be increased, as the diminution of the public debt might require and the safety fund warrant.

Such legislation would have the effect of maintaining bank-note circulation, and prevent its being superseded by Government issues, which an authority as high as Alexander Hamilton has said " are of a nature so liable to abuse, and it may even be affirmed so certain of being abused, that the wisdom of the Government will be shown in never trusting itself with the use of so seducing and dangerous an experiment."

While the bank-note circulation of this country is steadily decreasing, there has been no reduction in the total circulating medium in the United States, the reduction in the national-bank currency outstanding having been more than met by the coinage of the standard silver dollar and the issuance of certificates thereon.

The number of silver dollars coined under the provisions of the act of February 28, 1878, amounted to $213,259,431 on November 1, 1885, of which $163,817,342 remained in the Treasury of the United States, while $49,442,089 were in circulation on that date.

Under section 3 of the act mentioned above, silver certificates have been issued, which are represented by standard silver dollars in the Treasury of the United States, to the amount of $125,053,286. Of the silver certificates so issued $31,906,514 remain in the Treasury of the United States, leaving $93,146,772 of these certificates in circulation on November 1, 1885. Through the operation of the act to authorize the coinage of the standard silver dollar and to restore its legal-tender character, the circulating medium issued by the Government of the United States has been increased in the sum of $213,259,431, of which $49,442,089 in standard silver dollars are in the hands of the people, and $70,670,570 of like coins are in the Treasury of the United States, in addition to $93,146,772 of said standard dollars which are represented by silver certificates in the hands of the people, and which can be converted into

---

* The redemption of the notes from the proceeds of the general assets would of course reduce the amount paid from those assets to the depositors. In the case of the one hundred and four failed banks, if circulation to the amount of 25 per cent. of the capital had been so redeemed, the average dividends to depositors would have been reduced from 67 per cent. to 54 per cent. of the claims proved.

standard dollars at the pleasure of the holder, and are receivable for customs, taxes, and all public debts.

Under section 12 of the act of July 12, 1882, said certificates, when held by any national banking association, are to be counted as a part of its lawful reserve, and national banks are forbidden to be members of any clearing-house in which said certificates shall not be receivable in the settlement of clearing-house balances. These certificates are redeemable in silver dollars, but have no legal-tender quality between individuals or between banks, although national banks are compelled to accept them in settlement of clearing-house balances. It hardly seems just or equitable that national banks should be compelled to receive these certificates under these conditions, when banks organized under State laws, and private individuals, are not compelled to receive them when tendered.

The Comptroller in his last report to Congress stated that he believed the operation of the present law, which compels the coinage of two million standard silver dollars per month, weighing only 412½ grains each, with unlimited legal-tender quality, would eventually bring financial disturbance upon the country, and he is still of the same opinion.

Referring to silver certificates, the following suggestions were also made in the Comptroller's last report:

If it is for the best interests of the United States to issue a circulation based upon silver, the Comptroller believes that the circulation should be issued upon coin or bullion which contains a sufficient number of grains of silver to have an intrinsic value equal in the markets of the world to its nominal value; and that under certain restrictions and regulations it would be far more correct in principle to issue silver certificates based upon a deposit of silver bullion, to be valued in the exact proportion of silver to gold, than to continue the issue of certificates under the present law.

These reflections are upon the theory, held by many, that it is for the best interests of this country to maintain a circulation based upon silver. The Comptroller doubts the correctness of this theory, but it is submitted that the circulation now outstanding based on silver is a depreciated currency, by the issue of which the Government has gained at the expense of the people who now hold the silver dollars and certificates, and that therefore it is incumbent on the Government, if it continues to issue circulation based upon silver, to do so under a plan which will not only provide a sound circulation for the future, but also prevent the holders of the present certificates and dollars from sustaining loss.

As the silver question is more unsettled than it was at the time the foregoing was written, not only in the United States but elsewhere, it seems doubtful if this Government should attempt to issue a circulation based upon silver, even at its bullion value, until the relative value of this metal is more definitely settled throughout the world. The discontinuance of the coinage of the silver dollar by our Government might perhaps have a tendency to bring about some agreement with other nations, and the fixing of a standard for a series of years; it is however evident that the coinage of the standard silver dollar under the present law is in excess of the requirements of the country, and should be discontinued. If we continue to add these dollars to our circulating medium, and they continue to accumulate in the Treasury, the Government must of necessity pay some portion of its obligations in that coin; and if the Government should pay its interest and other obligations and redeem its bonds in standard dollars, the business of the country would immediately go to a silver basis. What effect this would have it is difficult to predict. It would appear, however, that gold would go to a premium, which would compel its being held, to a certain extent, as an article of merchandise, and it would not circulate as money. This would probably occasion contraction in credits and financial disturbance. The effect upon the legal-tender notes, which by the terms of section 12 of the act of July 12, 1882, appear to be redeemable in gold, cannot well be foreseen, but it would be difficult for the Government with its present stock of gold to redeem the outstanding legal-tender notes, or such portion of them as might be presented, if gold was held at a premium. Inasmuch as the national-bank notes are redeemable in legal tender notes, their position would be determined by the status of the latter.

The substitution of standard silver dollars and silver certificates based thereon, in place of bank notes, which is taking place under the provisions of law now in force, evidently requires consideration and appropriate legislation.

BANK-NOTE ISSUES OF OTHER COUNTRIES.

Macleod, in his exhaustive work on the Theory and Practice of Banking, states that—

"The circulating medium of any country is—
(1) Coined money—gold, silver, and copper.
(2) Paper currency, viz, promissory notes and bills of exchange, with all their variety.
(3) Small debts of all sorts, such as credits in bankers' books, called deposits, book debts of traders, and private debts between individuals."

Bank notes come clearly within the second classification, and are merely promises on the part of the bank to pay on demand a sum of money. Unless otherwise provided for, this sum is payable in the coined money of the country where the note is issued. The metallic money in which the note is redeemable on demand is that issued by the government of the country or State, and authenticated as to weight and fineness by its mints.

In the earlier days of banking, promissory notes of joint-stock banks, private bankers, and merchants were all on the same footing as inland bills of exchange, that is to say, they were all transferable by indorsement. Under the present system of issuing bank notes, payable on demand to bearer, they pass in ordinary business transactions from hand to hand as a circulating medium in the same manner as coined money.

The commercial transactions of the world have grown to be so enormous, and the use of bank notes therein so universal, that most Governments, recognizing the necessity of making the security for fulfillment of these promises as substantial as possible, have enacted laws whereby they are issued under certain restrictions and regulations, in order that the public, many of whom are unable to discriminate between the different issues of the banks, may not suffer loss by receiving what is supposed to be an equivalent of money. Either securities are required to be deposited in trust, as under the national bank system, or set aside and held in the bank, as in the case of the Bank of England, or the issues are regulated by the condition of the assets, the amount of capital paid in, and the amount of coin on hand. Very often the law provides that the circulating notes shall be a first lien upon all the assets of the bank, and sometimes a direct guarantee of payment of bank notes is given under conditions by the Government.

Since the passage of the national currency act in 1863, the entire bank-note circulation of the United States has been secured by a deposit of Government bonds with the Treasurer of the United States, and owing to the care with which this precaution has been exercised the general public scarcely realize that these notes are simply promises redeemable on demand, and not money.

As at some time in the future the redemption and payment of the public debt of the United States will probably make it necessary to issue bank notes upon the basis of some other security, it will be useful to examine the various methods of issuing and securing bank notes under the laws of the principal commercial nations of the world, in order that the experience of other countries may be made available for the welfare of our own. A system which is successful in one country or nation may not be adapted to other countries, but from the experience of all, valuable deductions may be drawn.*

ENGLAND.

Bank-note circulation in England is regulated by the act of Parliament of 1844, which provides for the issuance by the Bank of England of £14,000,000 of bank notes through an issue department, to which was to be transferred £14,000,000 in Government securities, and also that the banks of issue, consisting of joint-stock and private banks other than the Bank of England, in existence at the date of the act, should not thereafter be permitted to issue notes except to the amount they then had in circulation, issued by them and outstanding. In other words, the actual circulation to which each of these banks was to be entitled under the act, was to be arrived at by taking the average amount of circulation in each case for twelve weeks prior to April 27 of that year, and under this regulation the maximum issue by provincial banks—that is, banks in England outside of London, not including those of Scotland or Ireland—was then fixed at about eight and three-quarters million pounds. Under certain conditions these banks of issue which were in existence in May, 1844, might cede their privilege of circulation to the Bank of England for a fixed consideration of 1 per cent. per annum to August 1, 1856, and the privilege of issue of any of these banks was forfeited in case of failure to exercise it, of bankruptcy, or certain changes in the constitution of their partnerships. The Bank of England was authorized to issue its own notes for the full amount of the circulation of other banks compounded for, and by order of Crown in council, to two-thirds of the amount of lapsed circulation.

The total amount of issues lapsed or compounded for since 1844 by the country banks is about two and three quarters million pounds, leaving the present authorized circulation of such banks at about six mill ion pounds, or $30,000,000. It is estimated that the actual circulation of these English provincial banks, that is of the banks other than the Bank of England, having privilege of issue, is but four per cent. of their entire liability to the public. By the issue of its own notes in place of the lapsed and surrendered circulation mentioned, the circulation of the the Bank of England, based on Government securities, has been increased

---

* For the facts in reference to foreign banks of issue, the Comptroller is indebted to the paper on "Bank Notes," by John Biddulph Martin, M. A., F. S. S., published in the Journal of the London Institute of Bankers, March, 1880; paper of Mr. Robert W. Barnett, on "Effect of the Development of Banking," Journal London Institute of Bankers, February, 1881; "The Theory and Practice of Banking," Henry Dunning Macleod, M. A., 2 ed., 1866; "The Three Great Banks of Europe," paper by R. H. Inglis Palgrave, in Journal London Institute of Bankers, June, 1879; "Lombard Street," by Walter Bagehot; paper on "Theory and Practice of Banking in Scotland," by James Simpson Fleming, F. R. S., Journal London Institute of Bankers, 1882–1883, read January 17, 1883; "Report of select committee of Parliament on Banks of Issue," ordered printed July 22. 1875; article of Henry May on "The Bank of England," March number, 1885, Fortnightly Review; "Statistique Internationale des Banques d'Émission," published by the Italian Government in 1873; Banking Laws of Great Britain, Canada, and Germany; Notes by Mr. Ernest Seyd, F. S. S., on the German banking law.

from £14,000,000 to over £15,000,000. The circulation of the joint-stock and private banks of issue of England is based entirely upon their general credit; that is to say, it is not based upon securities or bullion specially deposited or held as in the case of the Bank of England, but upon the aggregate assets of the institutions. These banks make weekly returns of their outstanding circulation to the Government, from which it appears that not more than one-half of the notes they are authorized to issue are in actual circulation. The total amount of notes of the Bank of England, issued on the security of the Government debt, is at this time £15,750,000 or about $78,750,000. This bank, in addition, is permitted to issue notes equal in amount to the bullion or coin which is transferred to and held in the vaults of the issue department of said bank. Of the coin and bullion held, 25 per cent. may consist of silver. It is to be noted, however, that very seldom is any circulation of the bank issued upon silver.

The Bank of England is compelled to receive from any person tendering it, bullion in exchange for notes at the rate of £3, 17s. and 9d. per ounce of gold 11-12 fine. Under these provisions the amount in bank notes issued varies from time to time by the receipt or withdrawal of gold. The only tax paid by the bank against its issue of circulation is for the privilege of issuing £15,750,000 against securities of the Government, and for this privilege and the exemption from stamp duty the bank pays to the Government an annual sum of about £200,000.*

Bank of England notes were, by the third section of the act of Parliament of 1833, made legal tender between all parties, except where the bank itself is one, so long, and so long only, as the bank pays them in gold coin on demand.

The act of 1844 declares that the notes of the Bank of England in circulation, including those held by the banking department, shall be deemed to be issued on the credit of such securities (coin and bullion) so appropriated and set apart to the said issue department.

Although the act of 1844 only permits the issue of Bank of England notes under the present situation of country bank issues to the amount of £15,750,000, except on a deposit of coin or bullion, during the crisis of 1857 and in 1866 this statutory provision was suspended and the

---

* The following table, taken from page 553 of appendix to report from the select committee of Parliament on the banks of issue, will give some idea of the profits to the Bank of England from its issue department:

RECEIPTS.

Interest on securities	£458,035
Profit on bullion	32,433
	490,468

PAYMENTS

Composition, in lieu of stamps	60,000
Her Majesty's exchequer	138,578
Country bankers (lapsed issues)	18,860
Bank-note paper	18,022
Wages, pensions, rent, machinery, and general charges	147,500
Balance of profit	107,708
	490,468

The average profits on bullion for the ten years, 1865 to 1874, were £14,900 per annum.

BANK OF ENGLAND, July 27, 1875.

bank was permitted further issue of notes in order to supply a circulating medium to avert financial trouble and distress, and it is believed by many that this course would be pursued again if occasion demanded it.

From information communicated to the State Department by the minister of the United States to Great Britain, it appears that the amount of bank notes outstanding in England on December 31, 1884, was—

Notes of the Bank of England £24,647,000
Other joint-stock banks 1,623,160
Private banks.. 1,507,216

SCOTLAND AND IRELAND.

By the act of Parliament of 1845, the privilege of issuing notes on the part of the existing banks in Scotland and Ireland on their own account was continued to the amount of their outstanding circulation. The privilege of additional issue is granted to these banks upon the basis of gold coin or bullion to the nominal or par value of the notes issued, and in this respect they have the advantage of the English provincial banks. By the terms of the acts under which English, Scotch, and Irish banks were permitted to continue their issue of circulation, unsecured by a deposit of gold or bullion, the liabilities of the individual shareholders of said banks to the general public were unlimited so far as the bank-note circulation was concerned. It seems to be the opinion of all authorities who have examined the subject that Scotch and Irish banks have no securities especially held against their issues.

From information communicated to the State Department by the minister of the United States to Great Britain, it appears tha' the amount of bank notes outstanding in Scotland and Ireland on December 31, 1884, was—

Scotland £6,399,310
Ireland 6,748,027

CANADA.

The general banking act of Canada was passed in 1871, and has since been amended in many particulars. Its effect has been to bring under one uniform system of restrictions and privileges all of the chartered banks in the Dominion, with the exception of a few banks, which, prior to the passage of the general banking act, had been working under special charters. Some of these banks were permitted to retain certain special privileges, which they held under their old charters.

Under the general banking law of Canada none but chartered banks are permitted to issue notes. The bank notes of a bank outstanding at any one time must never exceed its unimpaired paid-up capital. Monthly returns of the condition of each bank are made to the Government, and if these reports show excessive issues, fines are imposed as follows: $100 for an excess of $20,000 or less; $1,000 for an excess between twenty and one hundred thousand dollars; $5,000 for an excess between one hundred and two hundred thousand dollars; and for an excessive issue of over $200,000 a fine of $10,000 is exacted. There is, therefore, some inducement to make small over-issue in stringent times, as the comparatively light penalty might be offset by the profit, while excessive and rash overissues are restrained by penalties virtually prohibitory. No notes can be issued by the banks for less than $5, nor for any denomination except $5 or some multiple thereof.

In case of insolvency, the notes are a first charge upon all the assets of the bank. There appears to be no special security whatever. The shareholders are, however, liable, first, for any amount not paid up on their subscribed stock, and, second, for a further amount equal to their subscribed stock. Suspension of payments in gold or Dominion notes for ninety days constitutes insolvency. The directors may, after payment of notes has been suspended six months, call on the stockholders without regard to assets on hand.

No particular amount of cash reserve is required, this apparently being left to the judgment and discretion of the management; but of the cash reserve kept, one half, if practicable, and never less than 40 per cent., must be in Dominion notes.

The banks may have branches and offices, and notes may be issued and made payable at any of them, but each bank must receive its own notes at any of its different branches or offices, although they need not redeem them in gold or Dominion notes except at the place where the notes are payable. Banks are required to make not less than $60 of any one payment in Dominion notes of denominations of one, two, and four dollars, if so requested.

The Dominion notes mentioned are notes of the Government. The first idea in regard to them appears to have been to have them supplant the use of bank notes, as the first act in regard to Dominion notes was entitled "An act to enable banks in any part of Canada to use notes of the Dominion instead of issuing notes of their own." This act was passed in 1868, but was radically amended in 1870. The act of 1870 authorized the issue of these notes on the security of debentures of the Dominion and specie held for the redemption of the notes by the receiver-general. The portion of specie held was to be not less than 20 per cent. The first amount authorized was $5,000,000, but this might be increased by order in council under certain conditions to $9,000,000, the security for redemption being the same. Debentures or stock were authorized to be issued and delivered to the receiver general, to enable him to keep the required security for the notes issued. To keep the necessary proportion of specie, this officer was authorized to dispose of debentures. If Dominion notes in excess of the amount authorized were at any time outstanding, the receiver-general was required to hold specie to the full extent of this excess in addition to the required security for the authorized issues.

The latest act (1880) permits an increase, when authorized by order of council, to a sum not exceeding $20,000,000. This act fixes the security to be held, at 25 per cent. in specie and Dominion securities guaranteed by the Government in England (not less than 15 per cent., however, to be in specie), and 75 per cent. in Dominion debentures authorized by Parliament. The whole amount outstanding on August 31, 1885, was $17,469,380.83. Of this, over $6,000,000 were in denominations of less than $5, and over $10,700,000 in denominations of $500 and $1,000. The notes are issued in fractional parts of a dollar, and in denominations of $1, $2, $4, $5, $10, $20, $50, $100, $500, and $1,000.

The banks of Canada held on August 31, 1885, $6,823,000 in specie and $12,421,270 in Dominion notes, while at the same date the receiver-general held $3,989,767 in specie as against $17,469,380 Dominion notes outstanding.

ENGLISH AUSTRALASIAN COLONIES.

Banking in Australasia is carried on under the Scotch system, and the only security for circulating notes issued consists of the general assets of the banks. The Australasian banks, however, hold in bullion and specie a larger reserve against their liabilities, including circulation, than is the case in Scotland or England.

In 1840 the council of New South Wales passed an act requiring from all banks of issue a quarterly statement. The other colonies, as they were established, adopted the same law. An article by Nathaniel Cork, in the thirty-seventh volume of the Journal of the London Statistical Society for March, 1874, gives valuable information regarding banking in Australasia and statistics compiled from the quarterly statements, from which it appears that the outstanding bank-note circulation in 1872–'73 of the banks of issue in the colonies of New South Wales, Queensland, New Zealand, South Australia, and Tasmania was £3,410,000. The coin reserve held was over 25 per cent. on all liabilities.

A curious fact connected with the bank-note circulation of the colonies, especially that of Victoria and New South Wales, is the large proportion of £1 notes issued, being 57.2 per cent. of the whole issue in the former and 50.99 per cent. in the latter. It appears that the profits on this circulation are not large, as taxes are imposed on the note issues in circulation in all the colonies excepting South Australia and Western Australia. Edwin Brett, in his article on the history of banking in Australasia, read before the Bankers' Institute, London, October 18, 1882, states the rate of taxation in Queensland to be 3 per cent. and in the other colonies to be 2 per cent. per annum. He also calls attention to the fact that although Australasia is a land of gold, and two branches of the royal mint are actively engaged in converting the precious metals into coin, bank notes still constitute the chief circulating medium in all the colonies.

It appears from the June, 1885, number of the Australasian Insurance and Banking Record, published at Melbourne, that banking in the Australasian colonies has been much extended since 1873, but that the increase in note circulation has been moderate compared with the general increase in the banking business.

A bill was introduced in the New Zealand Parliament, in 1885, providing that bank notes issued in that colony should be a first charge upon the assets, within the colony, of the issuing bank. From appearances, this bill is likely to become a law.

FRANCE.

Bank notes are issued only by the Bank of France, it having in 1848 absorbed all previously existing issues and become the sole issuing bank in France, with branches in the principal towns. The issue of notes of the Bank of France is controlled by the council or directory, who are compelled to report to the Government from time to time. The Government, however, does not appear to interfere with the bank issue, except to see that the legal powers conferred in its charter are not violated. At times, however, the Government has guaranteed or secured a temporary or excessive issue. The notes of the Bank of France are therefore based upon the security of the general assets of the bank, which are at times re-enforced by a loan on the part of the Government of its credit.

The Paris correspondent of the London Economist of June 28, 1879, holds that there is no limitation of the circulation of the bank by its statutes. During the times that specie payments have been suspended, and when the Government has permitted the issue of unconvertible notes or forced currency, a limit is always fixed to such issue.

From information communicated to the State Department by the minister of the United States to France, it appears that notes of the Bank of France are legal tender, and are redeemable at sight, either in gold or silver five-franc coins, at the option of the bank (silver coins of smaller denominations being legal tender only to the extent of 50 francs).

On October 1, 1885, as shown by the returns of the Bank of France, the notes in circulation amounted to 2,786,051,930 francs, the bank holding at that time cash amounting to 2,265,636,853 francs, of which 1,162,987,434 francs was gold and 1,102,649,419 francs silver.

GERMANY.

On the 30th of January, 1875, the existing banking law was passed, and the Imperial or Reichsbank was established. By this act it appears that the Reichsbank, so far as its issue of notes is concerned, takes, to some extent, in Germany, the place that the Bank of Eng and occupied upon the passage of Peel's act of 1844. Under the present banking act of the German Empire, seventeen of the banks in existence on the 30th of January, 1875, were permitted to continue their issue of notes to the aggregate amount of about $27,000,000. In the apportionment of circulation between the Reichsbank, or Imperial Bank of Germany, and the other banks of issue, about $62,000,000 was alloted to the Imperial Bank, and to this was added certain issues of fifteen other banks which had forfeited their right of issue by lapse of charter, voluntary renunciation of the right of issue, or by decision of the Government. Under the present act, banks other than the Reichsbank issuing notes in excess of the limit prescribed, except when protected by cash security, are compelled to pay an annual tax of five per cent. on such excess. The amount of notes free of duty; that is, not incurring this five per cent. tax, is quoted every week in the German papers. The Imperial Bank appears to have the right of unlimited issue under the control of the Imperial Debt Commissioners, and under the present act has practically the control of the issuance of bank notes throughout the Empire. The singular provision in regard to the annual tax of five per cent. on circulation, issued in excess of securities deposited, is, no doubt, intended to permit additional issues in times of financial distress. How far this expedient will meet the end for which it is evidently intended, has never, it is believed, been practically tested. The Imperial Bank is compelled to hold an amount equal to at least one-third of all its issues in German coin, imperial legal-tender notes, gold bars or foreign coin; the remaining two-thirds of its issues must be represented by discounted bills having not more than three months to run.

AUSTRIA.

The exclusive right of note issue of the Empire of Austria was conferred on the Austro-Hungarian Bank, with a charter extending from the 1st of July, 1878, to the 31st of December, 1887. This bank was the outgrowth of the forced currency of the Austrian Empire, Austria having contracted liabilities to the national bank, prior to 1878, in the amount of $40,000,000.

The notes of the Austro-Hungarian Bank are redeemable in the coin of the realm, at its two head offices in Vienna and Budapest, and in case notes are not so redeemed within twenty-four hours after demand the bank forfeits its charter. The bank is authorized to issue $100,000,000 of notes without security being deposited in trust, but is compelled to maintain sufficient reserve to meet demands under the penalty above stated. The bank also has the privilege of issuing additional circulation upon the security of gold or silver bullion, and also appears to be permitted to issue notes against miscellaneous security. The exclusive privileges granted the bank seem to be compensated for by its relations to the Empire. It is compelled at all times to buy the mint pound of silver, coin or bullion, with 45 florins in bank notes, and forward this bullion for coinage. It must also furnish notes of such denominations as are desired by the public in exchange for other denominations of its issue. It is compelled to accept the Government issues of currency as money, these issues forming a debt of the country similar to our legal-tender notes. The bank, however, has the right to issue its own notes on the security of the Government currency, the same as on coin or bullion. The circulation of Austria consists of a trifle less than one-half of notes of the Austro-Hungarian Bank and the balance in notes issued by the Government.

BELGIUM.

The issue of bank notes is confined to the National Bank, which has a charter for thirty years from January 1, 1873. While the Government reserves the right to extend the privilege of issue to other banks, and while theoretically bank notes may be issued by any individual, firm, or company (except a corporation of limited liability), the notes of the National Bank are legal tender to the Government, which controls its issues and business, and on account of this feature the bank really has the monopoly of issuing bank notes. The security to the note-holders rests principally upon the Government supervision of the bank, the investment of a certain portion of its capital and reserve in Government funds, and its being compelled under the act to hold coin or bullion to one-third of its total liabilities to the public (deposits and notes outstanding).

This reserve may, however, under the authority of the Government, be reduced to 25 per cent. of its liabilities. There appears to be no limit to the issue of circulation.

NETHERLANDS.

The Nederlandsche National Bank enjoys the monopoly of issuing bank notes in the Netherlands. This bank was founded in 1814. Its present charter dates from 1864, for a period of twenty-five years. The bank issues two classes of notes, one class amounting to about $4,000,000, covered by the Government debt. This issue is called state notes. Bank notes of the National Bank proper are issued without any fixed maximum limit. The bank, however, is compelled to carry at least 40 per cent. of gold coin or bullion against the aggregate liabilities to the public for deposits on call and bank notes.

DENMARK.

The Bank of Copenhagen has the exclusive privilege of issuing bank notes in Denmark. They may be issued apparently without limit, and rest upon the security of the general assets of the bank. Against the first $8,000,000 of notes issued, the bank must hold good and easily convertible assets to the amount of 50 per cent. of their issue. For any excess over the $8,000,000 the bank must hold a metallic reserve consisting of legal tender, coin, gold bullion, and foreign coin, and may hold silver bullion and silver foreign coin not exceeding one-third of the whole reserve. The metallic reserve is not permitted under the act in any case to fall below three eighths of the whole circulation. From information obtained through the Department of State, the bank notes outstanding in Denmark on December 31, 1884, amounted to 73,000,000 crowns, or about $19,500,000.

NORWAY.

The Bank of Norway (Norgesbank), whose charter dates from 1816, has the exclusive privilege of note issue in Norway. This charter may be annulled by act of the Storthing, confirmed by the King. Modifications of charter have taken place from time to time. The bank has the privilege of issuing unsecured notes in proportion to its capital. It is permitted to issue two and-a-half times its original capital, and also issues twice the amount of an increase of capital made in 1818, and one-and-a-half times its increased capital of 1842 and 1863. It also issues 150 per cent. of notes against its surplus fund, and a further amount of notes equal to its gold on hand. The proportion of secured to unsecured notes is about fifteen to ten. The notes of the Bank of Norway are redeemable in gold and are a full legal tender. In consideration of the privilege of issue the Government participates in the profits, and the bank appears to be practically an institution of the State, and the shareholders have no voice in its management. The Goverment does not guarantee the issue, although it would no doubt protect it, on account of its relations to the bank. Theoretically the notes are secured by the reserve of coin and bullion, the capital, reserve fund, and assets of the bank. From information obtained through the Department of State the bank notes outstanding on December 31, 1884, amounted to 38,983,500 crowns, or over $10,000,000.

SWEDEN.

The Riksbank, or Bank of Sweden, was founded in 1656, and Mr. Palgrave, in his Journal of the Statistical Society, March, 1873, page 117, claims for Sweden the invention of the bank note, the Riksbank being founded, as it will be seen, forty years prior to the Bank of England.

The Bank of Sweden has a circulation of about $10,000,000, which is unsecured, except that the bank is compelled to keep a certain reserve as security to the note-holder. The matter of reserve appears to be well provided for, as its reserve of gold or silver coin or bullion must at no time be less than about $4,100,000, and such gold and silver as is deposited abroad or such cash as it has at call with foreign banks and companies is also held against its circulation This regulation has been at times suspended, in something the same manner as the Peel act of 1844 has been in England. For more than six months in 1869 the reserve was below the minimum required by law, and in 1873 the issue of notes exceeded the prescribed limits. There are other banks of issue in Sweden, known as Enskilda banks, whose organization appears to be in the nature of a private partnership, the liabilities, however, being somewhat limited. They issue circulation under certain regulations and restrictions, being compelled before issuing notes to deposit in a place of public safety 25 per cent. of their capital which has unlimited liability (the partners and shareholders in these banks being divided into unlimited and limited liability shareholders). No notes can be issued against the limited capital until 75 per cent. of such capital is deposited. In addition to the notes issued upon these deposits, bank notes may be issued on coin and notes in hand, gold and silver bullion, upon such balance as the Enskilda Bank may have with the Riksbank or Bank of Sweden, and also upon approved securities. This class of bank notes must not exceed 50 per cent. of the entire capital. The regulations for issue of bank notes in Sweden appear to have been carefully considered. Upon a bank meeting with loss which impairs its capital 10 per cent. and reduces its reserve, the association is compelled to liquidate.

RUSSIA.

Bank notes are issued in Russia exclusively by the Imperial Bank, which was chartered in 1860 with a capital of about $12,000,000. By its charter it has the exclusive issue of bank notes in Russia for twenty-eight years. The Imperial Bank seems to have no limit to its issue of circulation. The increase of its circulation, however, is usually made in response to the requirements of the Government whenever an exigency or a deficit in the annual revenue occurs. The bank appears to furnish a paper circulating medium to the Government in addition to the amount previously issued, which, finding its way into the channels of trade, produces inflation. In 1873 the bank had outstanding upwards of $600,000,000 of bank notes, against which it held as specie reserve only about $43,000,000. On November 1, 1879, it is estimated the circulation was upwards of $900,000,000. This circulating medium was then worth in gold about 60 per cent. of its face or nominal value.

SWITZERLAND.

Notes are issued in Switzerland by banks of two classes—Cantonal and joint-stock banks. (See London Bankers' Magazine, December, 1878.) The issues are unlimited. In 1879 the entire issue of thirty-five banks was about $20,000,000. Notes are received between banks, and business interchanged under an agreement, the interchange being carried on in something like the manner that business of a clearing house is conducted. In some states of Switzerland banking appears to be free from restriction in regard to the issue of bank notes, which are subject to a tax of ½ per cent. per annum. Note-holders of the banks of Switzerland have no preference over other creditors. The present issue of bank notes, as appears from information furnished to the Department of State, was over $25,000,000 on December 31, 1884.

ITALY.

In order to eliminate from the circulating medium of the country the large amount of illegal and badly-secured issues of bank notes which then existed, the law of April 30, 1874, was passed, after an elaborate examination into methods of other countries in dealing with the same subject. This act limited the emission of bank notes to six associated banks, which were required to issue $200,000,000 of notes to the Government of Italy, the Government paying interest on the amount of notes so loaned, and the banks being liable for their payment ratably to their capital. This issue of notes was for the purpose of taking up certain Government loans, and each of the associated banks was permitted in addition, for its own use, to put out a certain amount of circulation which might be regulated by the Government to 40 per cent. of the capital of the bank. The associated circulation is practically the debt of the Government, as Government securities equal in amount thereto were issued to and held as security by the associated banks for the loan of this circulation to the Government. The notes issued by the banks in their individual capacity are redeemable in coin or in the association notes. Banks are compelled to report to the Government full particulars in regard to their issues.

SPAIN.

Bank notes are issued in Spain only by the Bank of Spain, with the head office at Madrid, which has between twenty-five and thirty branches. The bank is permitted to issue notes to three times its capital, which are issued entirely on its credit. The bank is required to keep a reserve of 33 per cent. of its note issue in coin or bullion. The notes, theoretically, are payable in gold on demand, but a considerable proportion of its issue appears to be simply promises to "pay to bearer," the words "on demand" or "presentation" having been left out, and no statement is made as to whether or not the note is payable in gold or silver. The bank does not readily redeem its notes. They have been at a discount in Madrid and the circulation is somewhat limited.

PORTUGAL.

Bank notes are issued in Portugal by the Bank of Portugal, and circulate principally in Lisbon and Oporto. There are other banks of issue also in those cities, as well as in several of the smaller towns, whose circulation is not so generally current in business transactions. The Bank of Portugal has peculiar privileges, and contends that other banks have no right to issue circulation. The charter of this bank expired in 1876, and it exists only under a provisional renewal. Its notes are payable in gold on demand, with the exception of a small portion which are payable in silver and copper. These last circulate in Lisbon only, where copper is legal tender to one-third of all payments. The English sovereign is legal tender in Portugal. Note-holders of the Bank of Portugal are not better secured than the other creditors of the bank. The bank notes outstanding in Portugal on December 31, 1884, as reported to the Department of State, was $6,303,000.

JAPAN.

Bank notes are issued in Japan by banks organized under a national bank act similar in terms to that of the United States. The first regulations of this act were issued in 1872, and were revised and amended in September, 1876. There were, on June 30, 1882, 148 national banks in operation in Japan, with 110 branches. These banks had at that date outstanding circulating notes to the amount of 34,358,868 yen.* There is also one so-called specie bank at Yokohama. This bank has the privilege of issuing "silver notes" to the extent of a million and a

---

* The silver yen is valued at 86.9 cents.

half yen. It apparently had outstanding in 1882, notes to the amount of 294,520 yen. The notes issued by the national banks are secured by a deposit of Government bonds, and the banks are under the supervision of the Banking Bureau of the Imperial Finance Department of Japan. The operation of the national bank act appears to have been of service to the country, and the notes issued by the banks circulate freely throughout the Empire.

On the 27th of June, 1882, the Government of Japan established an institution to be known as the Bank of Japan, with a charter limited to 30 years, and a capital limit of 10,000,000 yen, business to be confined to non-hazardous transactions, and the bank required to transact such Government financial business as it shall be directed to perform. The issue of bank notes is prohibited for a time. The organization of this bank is similar to that of the Belgium State Bank. Its president is appointed directly by the Emperor, the Government subscribing for one-half of its capital. It is evident that the intention is that this bank shall at some time in the future issue circulation under the direction of the Government.

AMOUNT OF INTEREST-BEARING FUNDED DEBT IN THE UNITED STATES AND THE AMOUNT HELD BY NATIONAL BANKS.

The public debt reached its maximum on August 31, 1865, at which time it amounted to $2,845,907,626. More than twelve hundred and seventy-five millions of this debt were in temporary obligations of the Government, of which eight hundred and thirty millions bore interest at 7.30 per cent. per annum. The average rate of interest on seventeen hundred and twenty-five millions of the debt at that date was 6.62 per cent. This large amount of temporary obligations was funded within the three years which followed the close of the war, chiefly into six per cent. bonds. The six per cent. bonds were gradually reduced during the year 1869 and the seven years following, by payment and refunding into five per cents. The six per cents, together with the five per cents, were subsequently rapidly replaced by four and one-half and four per cent. bonds, which were authorized to be issued by the act of July 14, 1870. In the year 1881 all of the unredeemed five and six per cent. bonds, amounting to $579,560,050, were continued payable at the pleasure of the Government, with interest at 3½ per cent., by agreement with the holders. The act of July 12, 1882, authorized the refunding of the three and one-halfs into three per cents.; and since its passage all of these bonds have been converted into three per cents. No call has been made by the Secretary during the year ending November 1 for the payment of any portion of the threes, and the amount of each class of bonds making up the entire interest-bearing funded debt has but slightly changed during the past year. On June 30, 1885, the total registered bonds of the United States amounted to $1,071,460,262, of which sum $11,927,900 only was held in foreign countries.

The report for 1879 and subsequent reports contain tables exhibiting the classification of the unmatured interest-bearing bonded debt of the United States and of the bonds held by the national banks for a series of years, and also tables showing the amount estimated to be held by savings banks, trust companies, etc.

The following table is again presented, and exhibits the amount of the outstanding bonds of the Government, which represent the unmatured interest-bearing bonded debt of the United States and the classification of the same on the dates named:

Date.	Six per cent. bonds.	Five per cent. bonds.	Four and a half per cent. bonds.	Four per cent. bonds.	Total.
Aug. 31, 1865	$908,518,091	$199,792,100			$1,108,310,191
July 1, 1866	1,408,388,469	198,528,435			1,206,916,904
July 1, 1867	1,421,110,719	198,533,435			1,619,644,154
July 1, 1868	1,841,521,800	221,588,400			2,063,110,200
July 1, 1869	1,886,341,300	221,589,300			2,107,930,600
July 1, 1870	1,764,932,300	221,589,300			1,986,521,600
July 1, 1871	1,613,897,300	274,236,450			1,888,133,750
July 1, 1872	1,374,883,800	414,567,300			1,789,451,100
July 1, 1873	1,281,238,650	414,567,300			1,695,805,950
July 1, 1874	1,213,624,700	510,628,050			1,724,252,750
July 1, 1875	1,100,865,550	607,132,750			1,707,998,300
July 1, 1876	984,999,650	711,685,800			1,696,685,450
July 1, 1877	854,621,850	703,266,650	$140,000,000		1,696,888,500
July 1, 1878	738,619,000	703,266,650	240,000,000	$98,850,000	1,780,735,650
July 1, 1879	310,932,500	646,905,500	250,000,000	679,878,110	1,887,716,110
July 1, 1880	235,780,400	484,864,900	250,000,000	739,347,800	1,709,993,100
July 1, 1881	196,378,600	439,841,350	250,000,000	739,347,800	1,625,567,750
July 1, 1882	Continued at 3½ per cent 58,957,150	Continued at 3½ per cent. { 3 per cents. 32,082,600	250,000,000	739,349,350	1,449,810,400
July 1, 1883		{ 304,204,350	250,000,000	737,942,200	1,324,229,150
July 1, 1884		224,612,150	250,000,000	737,661,700	1,212,273,850
July 1, 1885		194,190,500	250,000,000	737,719,850	1,181,910,350
Nov. 1, 1885		194,190,500	250,000,000	737,740,350	1,181,930,850

Pacific sixes amounting to $64,623,512, the Navy pension fund, amounting to $14,000,000 in 3 per cents, the interest upon which is applied to the payment of naval pensions exclusively, and $223,800 of refunding certificates, are not included in the table.

SECURITY FOR CIRCULATING NOTES.

The operations of the Treasury Department for a series of years have largely reduced the amount of interest receivable by the national banks on the bonds owned by them and deposited in trust with the Treasurer of the United States to secure their circulation, owing to the payment of a portion of the public debt and the many changes made in the classes of United States bonds by refunding or extension of the different issues of five and six per cent. bonds to bear interest at 4½, 4, 3½, and 3 per cent. Eighteen years ago the banks had on deposit, as security for circulation, $327,000,000 in United States bonds, of which amount $241,000,000 bore interest at 6 per cent. and $86,000,000 at 5 per cent.; and on July 1, 1882, they held $227,000,000 of three and one-half per cent bonds. The five and six per cent bonds disappeared in the year 1881 from the list of these securities with the exception of $3,500,000 of Pacific sixes, and since that year the three and one-half per cents have entirely disappeared. On November 1, 1885, more than 45 per cent. of the amount pledged for circulation consisted of bonds bearing interest at 3 per cent. only, and the remainder, with the exception of $3,505,000 of Pacifics, bear interest at the rate of four and four and one-half per cent. The average rate of interest now paid by the United States on the bonds deposited as security for circulating notes is a little more than 3.6 per cent. upon their par value.

The amount and classes of United States bonds owned by the banks, including those pledged as security for circulation and for public deposits on the 1st day of July in each year since 1865, and upon November 1 of the present year, is exhibited in the following table:

Date.	United States bonds held as security for circulation.					United States bonds held for other purposes at nearest date.	Grand total.
	6 per cent. bonds.	5 per cent. bonds.	4½ per cent. bonds.	4 per cent. bonds.	Total.		
July 1, 1865....	$170,382,500	$65,576,600			$235,959,100	$155,785,750	$391,744,850
July 1, 1866 ...	241,683,500	86,226,850			327,310,350	121,152,950	448,463,300
July 1, 1867 ...	251,430,400	89,177,100			340,607,500	84,002,650	424,610,150
July 1, 1868 ...	250,726,950	90,764,950			341,495,900	80,922,500	422,418,400
July 1, 1869 ...	255,190,350	87,661,250			342,851,600	55,102,000	397,953,600
July 1, 1870....	247,355,350	94,923,200			342,278,550	43,980,600	386,259,150
July 1, 1871....	220,497,750	139,387,800			359,885,550	39,450,800	399,336,350
July 1, 1872 ...	173,251,450	207,189,250			380,440,700	31,868,200	412,308,900
July 1, 1873 ...	160,923,500	229,487,050			390,410,550	25,724,400	416,134,150
July 1, 1874....	154,370,700	2,6,800,500			391,171,200	25,347,100	416,518,300
July 1, 1875 ...	1,6,955,100	239,359,400			376,314,500	26,900,200	403,214,700
July 1, 1876 ..	109,313,450	232,081,300			341,394,750	45,170,300	386,565,050
July 1, 1877...	87,690,300	206,601,050	$44,372,250		338,714,600	47,315,050	386,028,650
July 1, 1878....	82,421,200	199,514,550	48,448,650	$19,162,000	349,546,400	68,850,900	418,397,300
July 1, 1879 ...	56,042,800	144,616,300	35,056,550	118,538,950	354,254,600	76,603,520	430,858,120
July 1, 1880....	58,656,150	139,758,650	37,760,950	126,076,300	361,652,050	42,831,300	404,483,350
July 1, 1881....	61,901,800	172,348,350	32,600,500	93,637,700	360,488,400	63,849,950	424,338,350
	Continued at 3½ per cent.:	Continued at 3½ per cent.:					
July 1, 1882...	25,142,600	202,487,650	32,752,650	97,429,800	357,812,700	43,122,550	400,935,250
July 1, 1883....	385,700	{ 7,402,800 3 per cents 200,877,850 }	39,408,500	104,954,650	353,029,500	34,094,150	387,123,650
July 1, 1884....	....	172,412,550	46,546,400	111,690,900	330,649,850	31,203,000	361,852,850
July 1, 1885....	Pacifics. 3,520,000	142,240,850	48,483,050	117,901,300	312,145,200	32,195,800	344,341,000
Nov.1, 1885....	3,505,000	138,920,650	49,547,253	116,391,650	308,364,550	31,780,100	340,144,650

The following table shows the authorizing act for each class of bonds held by the Treasurer as security for the circulating notes of the national banks on the 1st day of November, 1885:

Class of bonds.	Authorizing act.	Rate of interest.	Amount.
		Per cent.	
Funded loan of 1891..............	July 14, 1870, and January 20, 1871....	4½	$49,547,250
Funded loan of 1907......	....do ....do.............	4	116,391,650
Funded loan of July 12, 1882............	July 12, 1882......	3	138,920,650
Pacific Railway bonds	July 1, 1862, and July 2, 1864	6	3,505,000
Total			308,364,550

The profits on national bank circulation based on 4 and 4½ per cent. bonds are very small, after paying the annual tax of 1 per cent. Attention is particularly called to carefully prepared tables by Mr. E. B. Elliott, Government Actuary, which appear in the Appendix on page 125, in relation to the average price of the 4 and 4½ per cent. United States securities for the year ending September 30, 1885, and computations based thereon showing the annual profit on circulation during the same period.

5745 CUR——3

COMPARATIVE STATEMENTS OF THE NATIONAL BANKS FOR ELEVEN YEARS.

The following table exhibits the resources and liabilities of the national banks for eleven years, at nearly corresponding dates, from 1875 to 1885, inclusive:

	Oct. 1, 1875.	Oct. 2, 1876.	Oct. 1, 1877.	Oct. 1, 1878.	Oct. 2, 1879.	Oct. 1, 1880.	Oct. 1, 1881.	Oct. 3, 1882.	Oct. 2, 1883.	Sep. 30, 1884.	Oct. 1, 1885.
	2,087 banks.	2,069 banks.	2,080 banks.	2,053 banks.	2,048 banks.	2,090 banks.	2,132 banks.	2,269 banks.	2,501 banks.	2,664 banks.	2,714 banks.
RESOURCES.	Millions.	Millions.	Millions.	Millions.	Millions.	Millions.	Millions.	Millions.	Millions.	Millions.	Millions.
Loans	984.7	931.3	891.9	834.0	878.5	1,041.0	1,173.8	1,243.2	1,309.2	1,245.3	1,306.1
Bonds for circulat'n	370.3	337.2	336.8	347.6	357.3	357.8	363.3	357.6	351.4	327.4	307.7
Other U. S. bonds	28.1	47.8	45.0	94.7	71.2	43.6	56.5	37.4	30.7	30.4	31.8
Stocks, bonds, &c	33.5	34.4	34.5	36.9	39.7	48.9	61.9	66.2	71.1	71.4	77.5
Due from banks	144.7	146.9	129.9	138.9	167.3	213.5	239.8	198.9	208.9	194.2	235.3
Real estate	42.4	43.1	45.2	46.7	47.8	48.0	47.3	46.5	48.3	49.9	51.3
Specie	8.1	21.4	22.7	30.7	42.2	109.3	114.3	102.9	107.8	128.6	174.9
Legal-tender notes	76.5	84.2	66.9	64.4	60.2	56.6	53.2	63.2	79.7	77.0	69.7
Nat'l-bank notes	18.5	15.9	15.6	16.9	16.7	18.2	17.7	20.7	22.7	23.3	23.1
C. H. exchanges	87.9	100.0	74.5	82.4	113.0	121.1	180.2	208.4	96.4	66.3	84.9
U S. cert. of deposit	48.8	29.2	33.4	32.7	26.8	7.7	6.7	8.7	10.0	14.2	18.8
Due from U. S. Treas.	19.6	15.7	16.0	16.5	17.0	17.1	17.5	17.2	16.6	17.7	14.9
Other resources	19.1	19.1	28.7	24.9	22.1	23.0	26.2	28.9	28.9	33.8	36.9
Totals	1,882.2	1,827.2	1,741.1	1,767.3	1,868.8	2,105.8	2,358.4	2,399.8	2,372.7	2,279.5	2,432.9
LIABILITIES.											
Capital stock	504.8	499.8	479.5	466.2	454.1	457.6	463.8	483.1	509.7	524.3	527.5
Surplus fund	134.4	132.2	122.8	116.9	114.8	120.5	128.1	132.0	142.0	147.0	146.6
Undivided profits	53.0	46.4	44.5	44.9	41.3	46.1	56.4	61.2	61.6	63.2	59.4
Circulation	319.1	292.2	291.9	301.9	313.8	317.3	320.2	315.0	310.5	289.8	269.0
Due to depositors	679.4	666.2	630.4	668.4	736.9	887.9	1,083.1	1,134.9	1,063.6	993.0	1,120.1
Due to banks	179.7	179.8	161.6	165.1	201.2	267.0	294.9	259.9	270.4	246.4	299.5
Other liabilities	11.8	10.6	10.4	7.0	6.7	8.5	11.9	13.7	14.9	15.8	10.8
Totals	1,882.2	1,827.2	1,741.1	1,767.3	1,868.8	2,105.8	2,358.4	2,399.8	2,372.7	2,279.5	2,432.9

The different items of resources and liabilities in the preceding table indicate that the business of the national banks during the past seven years has generally increased, having been larger during the past year than at any period since the organization of the national banking system. The items of United States bonds and circulation have decreased. It also appears from the table that the aggregate liabilities of the national banks to depositors and correspondents, which were reduced during the previous year upwards of 94 millions, have increased during the present year more than 180 millions.

The table also shows that during the same period the national banks increased their cash resources by about 46 millions of specie, and decreased the same by about 2½ millions of legal tenders and United States certificates of deposit for same.

The following table is an abstract of the resources and liabilities of the national banks at the close of business on the 1st day of October, 1885, the condition of the New York City, Boston, Philadelphia, Baltimore, and other reserve city banks being tabulated separately from the other banks of the country:

	New York City.	Boston, Philadelphia, and Baltimore.	Other reserve cities.*	Country banks.	Aggregate.
	44 banks.	105 banks.	98 banks.	2,467 banks.	2,714 banks.
RESOURCES.					
Loans and discounts	$236,823,598	$218,424,271	$151,435,438	$694,471,997	$1,301,155,304
Overdrafts	66,314	61,902	322,583	4,537,888	4,988,687
Bonds for circulation	12,566,500	40,009,950	24,070,700	231,009,900	307,657,050
Bonds for deposit	820,000	675,000	4,788,000	11,174,000	17,457,000
United States bonds on hand	4,265,800	419,500	2,510,200	7,133,900	14,329,400
Other stocks and bonds	14,242,734	8,097,293	7,013,425	48,141,778	77,495,230
Due from reserve agents		23,110,458	19,292,151	95,975,906	138,378,515
Due from other national banks	18,846,711	17,059,322	11,580,324	31,475,341	78,967,698
Due from other banks and bankers	2,759,122	1,617,537	4,185,592	9,425,641	17,987,892
Real estate, furniture, and fixtures	19,177,499	6,571,017	4,846,052	29,699,233	51,293,801
Current expenses	787,432	712,308	866,799	4,486,854	6,853,393
Premiums	986,306	1,185,101	1,233,681	9,106,245	12,511,333
Checks and other cash items	2,507,221	1,428,308	658,185	9,663,915	14,347,579
Clearing-house loan certificates	1,110,000				1,110,000
Exchanges for clearing-house	55,453,777	19,718,195	8,265,049	1,489,710	84,926,731
Bills of other national banks	1,507,918	3,028,401	2,954,676	15,481,765	23,062,765
Fractional currency	35,823	42,789	60,593	337,840	477,055
Trade dollars	194,784	338,744	33,717	1,038,519	1,605,764
Specie	91,451,168	22,364,287	19,586,788	41,467,335	174,872,572
Legal-tender notes	16,785,620	9,219,212	14,357,351	29,375,936	69,738,119
United States certificates of deposit	6,920,000	8,805,000	2,575,000	500,000	18,800,000
Five per cent. redemption fund	547,100	1,799,737	1,076,774	10,173,742	13,597,353
Due from United States Treasurer	210,759	157,090	108,035	823,877	1,299,761
Total	479,249,186	384,845,431	281,827,063	1,286,991,322	2,432,913,002
LIABILITIES.					
Capital stock	45,350,000	80,938,510	54,051,500	346,284,400	527,524,410
Surplus fund	23,176,008	23,954,854	13,415,513	87,078,267	146,624,642
Undivided profits	10,487,171	5,983,167	4,839,819	38,025,362	59,335,519
National-bank notes outstanding	9,917,442	34,270,975	20,986,640	203,694,540	268,869,597
State-bank notes outstanding	31,195	20,802		84,901	136,898
Dividends unpaid	232,849	1,208,854	246,253	1,820,370	3,508,326
Individual deposits	250,494,553	176,043,047	126,049,008	549,785,840	1,102,372,450
United States deposits	420,181	454,734	3,435,999	7,241,708	11,552,622
Deposits of United States disbursing officers	47,163	18,188	689,647	1,959,401	2,714,399
Due to national banks	105,687,963	47,853,728	33,823,084	26,176,130	213,534,905
Due to other banks and bankers	34,199,239	14,095,822	22,296,594	15,613,406	86,115,061
Notes and bills rediscounted	205,420		460,006	7,767,367	8,432,793
Bills payable		2,750	723,000	1,465,630	2,191,380
Total	479,249,186	384,845,431	281,827,063	1,286,991,322	2,432,913,002

*The reserve cities, in addition to New York, Boston, Philadelphia, and Baltimore, are Albany, Pittsburgh, Washington. New Orleans, Louisville, Cincinnati, Cleveland, Chicago, Detroit, Milwaukee, Saint Louis, and San Francisco.

The following table exhibits, in the order of their capital, the twenty-five States (exclusive of reserve cities), having the largest amount of capital, together with the amount of circulation, loans and discounts, and individual deposits of each on October 1, 1885:

States.	Capital.	Circulation.	Loans and discounts.	Individual deposits.
Massachusetts	$45, 095, 650	$34, 200, 534	$86, 090, 367	$51, 715, 367
New York	34, 819, 760	23, 989, 591	83, 654, 256	77, 834, 371
Pennsylvania	32, 665, 340	23. 401, 460	65, 239, 486	61, 821, 735
Connecticut	24, 921, 820	15, 932, 600	40, 501, 279	24, 482, 781
Ohio	21, 900, 580	13, 474, 579	40, 660, 917	31, 594, 784
Rhode Island	20, 340, 050	12, 656, 177	30, 974, 846	13, 096, 232
Illinois	13, 673, 600	6, 154, 525	30, 636, 484	27, 693, 720
New Jersey	12, 208, 200	8, 007, 406	29, 343, 068	32, 501, 422
Indiana	12, 180. 500	6, 734, 150	23, 210, 592	19, 815, 317
Minnesota	11, 390. 000	1, 884, 576	28, 076, 758	19, 651, 296
Maine	10, 360, 000	7, 683, 079	16, 577, 506	10, 095, 495
Michigan	10, 194, 600	3, 479. 715	21, 321, 908	18, 575, 061
Iowa	10, 155, 000	3, 813, 858	21, 020, 360	17, 653, 775
Kentucky	9, 648, 900	5, 714, 770	14, 770, 265	8, 234, 931
Vermont	7, 541, 600	5, 355, 913	10, 543, 083	5, 154, 308
Texas	6, 880, 000	1, 739, 250	13, 087, 251	9, 183, 872
New Hampshire	6, 105, 000	5, 149, 045	8, 333, 617	5, 425, 196
Nebraska	5, 949, 250	1, 774, 330	15, 217, 754	11, 316, 707
Tennessee	5, 007, 500	2, 114, 010	11, 468, 980	7, 783, 995
Kansas	4, 995, 720	1, 435, 705	16, 610, 954	10, 080, 067
Wisconsin	3, 785, 000	1, 517, 078	9, 570, 727	10 132, 396
Virginia	3, 576, 300	2, 007, 500	9, 420, 831	8, 876, 663
Missouri	3, 311, 000	1, 251, 648	7, 217, 665	5, 072, 242
Maryland	2, 716, 700	2, 143, 702	5, 695, 512	5, 744, 199
Georgia	2, 472, 345	1, 570, 900	5, 282, 217	3, 335, 352

REDEMPTION.

Since the passage of the act of June 20, 1874, section 3 of which requires the banks at all times to keep on deposit in the Treasury 5 per cent. of their circulation as a redemption fund, that fund, as a rule, has been maintained, and circulating notes of the banks have been promptly redeemed at the Treasury without expense to the Government.

From the passage of the act of June 20, 1874, to November 1, 1885, there was received at the redemption agency of the Treasury $1,594,365,738 of national bank currency for redemption. During the year the receipts amounted to $145,880,327, of which amount $66,974,000, or nearly 46 per cent., was received from the banks in the city of New York, and $29,762,000, or upwards of 20 per cent., from the banks in the city of Boston. The amount received from Philadelphia was $7,446,000, from Chicago $3,943,000, from Cincinnati $2,154,000, from Saint Louis $1,668,000, from Baltimore $3,797,000, from Providence $2,470,000, from New Orleans, $2,514,000, and from Pittsburgh $576,000.

The following table* exhibits the amount of national-bank notes received monthly for redemption by the Comptroller of the Currency during the year ending October 31, 1885, and the amount received during the same period at the redemption agency of the Treasury, together with the total amount received since the passage of the act of June 20, 1874:

* Notes of gold banks are not included in the table.

Months.	Received by the Comptroller of the Currency.					Received at redemption agency.
	From national banks for reissue or surrender.	From redemption agency for reissue.	Act of June 20, 1874.	Notes of national banks in liquidation.	Total.	
1884.						
November	$65,040	$5,279,800	$2,002,195	$060,785	$8,007,820	$11,471,644
December	77,500	5,535,800	1,971,575	041,639	8,229,514	12,240,921
1885.						
January	83,040	6,531,000	2,266,140	798,262	9,678,442	17,882,887
February	11,750	7,343,600	2,072,533	784,537	10,212,420	10,972,096
March	45,000	6,413,300	1,724,795	785,580	8,968,675	10,195,586
April	7,440	6,221,400	1,472,480	819,729	8,521,049	12,549,026
May	20,900	6,591,100	1,527,420	998,910	9,144,330	14,189,983
June	130,250	8,558,600	256,600	107,870	9,053,320	16,652,302
July	10	6,482,500	1,600,415	1,259,814	9,402,739	12,131,083
August	8,690	4,848,900	813,500	807,184	6,477,674	9,893,843
September	60	4,140,900	827,510	799,076	5,767,546	7,588,980
October	22,060	3,675,930	1,981,120	482,794	6,161,904	10,111,976
Total	477,140	71,622,830	18,576,283	8,949,180	99,625,433	145,880,327
Received from June 20, 1874, to October 31, 1884	15,042,450	622,042,055	140,342,018	33,354,329	810,780,852	1,448,485,411
Grand total	15,519,590	693,664,885	158,918,301	42,303,509	910,406,285	1,594,365,738

The amount of notes fit for circulation returned by the redemption agency to the banks of issue during the year was $46,402,730, being an increase over last year of $13,322,430.

The total amount received by the Comptroller of the Currency for destruction, from the agency and from the banks direct, was $72,099,970. Of this amount, $4,953,400 were the issues of banks in the city of New York, $9,557,000 of banks in Boston, $3,018,300 of Philadelphia, $3,463,000 of Providence, $1,812,600 of Baltimore, $1,818,000 of Pittsburgh, $1,033,700 of Cincinnati, $591,500 of Louisville, $415,000 of Albany, $428,700 of New Orleans, and of each of the other principal cities less than $300,000.

The following table exhibits the number and amounts of national-bank notes of each denomination which have been issued and redeemed since the organization of the system, and the number and amount outstanding on November 1, 1885:

Denominations.	Number.			Amount.		
	Issued.	Redeemed.	Outstanding.	Issued.	Redeemed.	Outstanding.
Ones	23,167,077	22,731,963	435,714	$23,107,077	$22,731,963	$435,714
Twos	7,747,519	7,628,877	118,642	15,495,038	15,257,754	237,284
Fives	93,208,400	76,817,000	16,391,374	466,042,000	384,085,330	81,956,670
Tens	39,804,001	29,382,872	10,421,129	398,040,010	293,828,720	104,211,290
Twenties	12,318,173	8,563,797	3,754,376	246,363,460	171,275,940	75,087,520
Fifties	1,758,533	1,345,762	412,771	87,926,650	67,288,100	20,638,550
One hundreds	1,287,686	971,922	315,764	128,768,600	97,192,200	31,576,400
Five hundreds	23,924	22,727	1,197	11,962,000	11,363,500	598,500
One thousands	7,369	7,238	131	7,369,000	7,238,000	131,000
Portion of notes lost or destroyed					−21,890	+21,890
	179,323,282	147,472,224	31,851,058	1,385,134,435	1,070,239,617	314,894,818

A table showing the number and denomination of national-bank notes issued and redeemed, and the number of each denomination outstanding on November 1, for the last thirteen years, will be found in the Appendix.

The following table exhibits the amount of national-bank notes re
ceived at this office and destroyed yearly since the establishment of the
system :

Prior to November 1, 1865	$175,490 00
During the year ending—	
Oct. 31, 1866	1,050,382 00
Oct. 31, 1867	3,401,423 00
Oct. 31, 1868	4,602,825 00
Oct. 31, 1869	8,603,729 00
Oct. 31, 1870	14,305,689 00
Oct. 31, 1871	24,344,047 00
Oct. 31, 1872	30,211,720 00
Oct. 31, 1873	36,433,171 00
Oct. 31, 1874	49,939,741 00
Oct. 31, 1875	137,697,696 00
Oct. 31, 1876	98,672,716 00
Oct. 31, 1877	76,918,963 00
Oct. 31, 1878	57,381 249 00
Oct. 31, 1879	41,101,830 00
Oct. 31, 1880	35,539,660 00
Oct. 31, 1881	54.941,130 00
Oct. 31, 1882	74,917,611 50
Oct. 31, 1883	82,913,766 00
Oct. 31, 1884	93,178,418 00
Oct. 31, 1885	91,048,723 00
Additional amount of. notes of insolvent and liquidating national banks	52,859,636 90
Total	1,070,239,616 40

Notes of gold banks are not included in the above table.

NATIONAL-BANK FAILURES.

The total number of national banks placed in the hands of receivers
to November 1, 1885, has been 104, of which 4 became insolvent and
were placed in this category since November 1, 1884. A full list of
these banks will be found in the appendix, with the amount of capital,
claims proved, and dividends paid. The four which have failed during
the past year are as follows :

Name of bank.	Capital.	Receiver appointed.
Middletown National Bank of Middletown, N. Y	$200,000	Nov. 29, 1884
Farmers' National Bank of Bushnell, Ill.	50,000	Dec. 17, 1884
Schoharie County National Bank of Schoharie, N. Y	50,000	Mar. 23, 1885
Exchange National Bank of Norfolk, Va	300,000	Apr 9, 1885

The affairs of seven banks have been finally closed, and a final dividend has been made to their creditors during the year. These banks,
with the total dividends paid by each, are as follows :

Name of bank.	Total dividends on principal.	Proportion of interest paid.
	Per cent.	Per cent.
Venango National Bank of Franklin, Pa	28.37	....
City National Bank of Chicago, Ill	77.512	....
First National Bank of Georgetown, Colo	37.6483	....
First National Bank of Allentown, Pa	88	....
First National Bank of Dallas, Tex	38.10	....
First National Bank of Newark, N. J.*	100	100
First National Bank of Brattleboro', Vt.†	100	100

*An assessment of 100 per cent. was made on the stock of this bank, but the amount paid was re-
turned to the stockholders; 5 per cent. during the present year.
†An assessment of 25 per cent. was made on the stock of this bank, but 64.625 per cent. of the amount
paid under this assessment was returned to stockholders during the present year.

The affairs of a number of banks in the hands of receivers have been completely liquidated, with the exception of some matters involved in litigation now pending in the courts. Much of this litigation is pending in courts of last resort, and it may be some time before the cases can be heard and decided. This condition of things may delay the final settlement of the affairs of these associations. In such cases, however, the receivers are, as a rule, paid no salary, it being understood that on final settlement of the affairs of the banks they shall be paid only for actual services rendered. The names of the banks in this condition, with the dividends already paid to their creditors, are as follows:

Name of bank.	Dividends paid.
	Per cent.
Scandinavian National Bank of Chicago, Ill	50. 0
New Orleans National Banking Association of New Orleans, La	62. 0
First National Bank of Anderson, Ind	39. 5
Charlottesville National Bank of Charlottesville, Va	62. 0
Fourth National Bank of Chicago, Ill	50. 0
National Bank of the State of Missouri, Saint Louis, Mo	*100. 0
Third National Bank of Chicago, Ill	*100. 0
Central National Bank of Chicago, Ill	60. 0
First National Bank of Waynesburg, Pa	60. 0
People's National Bank of Helena, Mont	40. 0
First National Bank of Bozeman, Mont	85. 0
German-American National Bank of Washington, D. C	50. 0
Second National Bank of Scranton, Pa	†100. 0
First National Bank of Butler Pa	70. 0

*And interest.   † And 50 per cent. of interest.

The following dividends have been paid to the creditors of insolvent banks during the past year, the total dividends paid up to November 1, 1885, being given in each case:

Name of bank.	Dividends paid during the past year.	Total dividends paid to depositors.	Proportion of interest paid to depositors.
	Per cent.	*Per cent.*	*Per cent.*
Venango National Bank of Franklin, Pa	8. 37	23. 37	
New Orleans National Banking Association of New Orleans, La.	2	62	
First National Bank of Anderson, Ind	14. 50	39. 50	
City National Bank of Chicago, Ill	. 512	77. 512	
First National Bank of Georgetown, Colo	15. 1483	37. 6483	
First National Bank of Allentown, Pa	3	88	
First National Bank of Waynesburg, Pa	20	60	
First National Bank of Dallas, Tex	1. 10	38. 10	
Second National Bank of Scranton, Pa	*50	100	50
First National Bank of Newark, N. J	15	100	100
First National Bank of Brattleboro, Vt	‡64. 625	100	100
First National Bank of Buffalo, N. Y	5	38	
Pacific National Bank of Boston, Mass	5	15	
First National Bank of Union Mills, Union City, Pa	10	69	
Vermont National Bank of Saint Albans, Vt	30	42. 50	
First National Bank of Leadville, Colo	5	25	
First National Bank of Saint Albans, Vt	12. 50	12. 50	
First National Bank of Monmouth, Ill	20	90	
Marine National Bank of New York, N. Y	15	40	
Hot Springs National Bank of Hot Springs, Ark	40	70	
Richmond National Bank of Richmond, Ind	36	36	
Logan National Bank of West Liberty, Ohio	30	30	
Middletown National Bank of Middletown, N. Y	40	40	
Farmers' National Bank of Bushnell, Ill	40	40	
Schoharie County National Bank of Schoharie, N. Y	20	20	
Exchange National Bank of Norfolk, Va	20	20	
First National Bank of Jamestown, Dak	100	100	100

*Of interest.
† An assessment of 100 per cent. was made on the stock of this bank, but the amount paid was returned to the stockholders, 5 per cent. during the present year.
‡ An assessment of 25 per cent. was made on the stock of this bank, but 64.625 per cent. of the amount paid under this assessment was returned to the stockholders during the present year.

As has been seen, there have been but four failures of national banks during the year ending November 1, 1885, as against eleven during the previous year. An inspection of the above list will show that each of the four banks failed this year has already paid a dividend to its creditors, two of them 40 per cent. each, and two 20 per cent each.

If receivers, on taking charge of insolvent national banks, discover evidence which appears to indicate that insolvency has been caused by practices in violation of the criminal statutes of the United States, such evidence is at once, by direction of this office, referred through the proper channels to the Department of Justice for appropriate action against those who appear to have rendered themselves liable to the penalties of the law. Prosecutions of officers of many of the insolvent national banks have been instituted by the Department of Justice through the United States attorneys in the districts where the banks were located, and as a rule convictions have been secured where indictments have been found. A number of proceedings of this character are now pending.

Since the commencement of the national banking system 104 banks have been placed in the hands of receivers, 549 banks have voluntarily closed their business by a vote of stockholders owning two-thirds of the stock, under the provisions of sections 5220 and 5221 of the Revised Statutes, and the corporate existence of 26 expired by limitation. Of the banks in the hands of receivers, 9 had been previously placed in liquidation by their stockholders, but failing to pay their depositors, receivers were afterwards appointed by the Comptroller to wind up their affairs. Of the 104 banks placed in the hands of receivers, 70 have been finally closed, leaving 34 in process of settlement, of which, as has been seen, 14 are virtually closed with the exception of pending litigation, leaving 20 receiverships only in active operation.

Since the commencement of the system there has absolutely been no loss to the note-holders of insolvent national banks, every note having been promptly redeemed on presentation at the United States Treasury. The loss to the depositors of these insolvent national banks during the twenty-two years elapsed since the passage of the act of February 25, 1863, as nearly as can be estimated, taking into consideration dividends which will probably hereafter be paid, has been about $9,860,000. The average annual loss to depositors has been therefore about $448,000 in the business of corporations having from year to year an average capital of about $450,000,000, which corporations have been responsible for the safe keeping of deposits in their hands averaging constantly over $800,000,000. The annual average loss to depositors of all the national banks is therefore not in excess of one-twentieth of 1 per cent.

The total amount so far paid to creditors of insolvent national banks has been $25,651,390 upon proved claims amounting to $43,159,252. The amount paid during the year has been $2,151,868.

Assessments amounting to $9,812,750 have been made upon stockholders of the insolvent national banks to enforce their individual liability under section 5151 of the Revised Statutes of the United States. From this source $3,982,627 has been collected; $348,670 of this amount during the past year.

Reference is again made to the tables in the Appendix, showing national banks which have been placed in the hands of receivers, the amount of their capital, of the claims proved, and the rates of dividends paid, and also showing the amount of circulation of such banks issued, redeemed, and outstanding.

As stated in his last report:

"It is the intention of the Comptroller to rigidly enforce the bank act and to call the attention of the Department of Justice to any criminal violations of the same, but experience has proved that it is difficult, not only under the bank act, but generally under criminal statutes, to always obtain sufficient evidence to convict offenders. The Comptroller is of the opinion that, with a few exceptions, the national bank act has adequate provisions for the prosecution and conviction of those who lay themselves liable to its penalties. As stated elsewhere, bank failures are not so much due to the inadequacy of the law as to the failure on the part of the officers and directors to maintain a proper supervision of the affairs of their associations."

TAXATION.

The only United States tax now paid by the national banks is the semi annual duty of one-half of 1 per cent. upon the average amount of their notes in circulation during the preceding six months. The prohibitory tax of 10 per cent. upon State bank circulation paid out, as provided by section 3412 of the Revised Statutes, is also still in force. Section 5173 of the Revised Statutes provides that the expenses of the Bureau of the Comptroller of the Currency, including those of the plates and dies used for the printing of national-bank notes and of the printing of such notes, shall be paid out of the proceeds of the tax on circulation.

The act of June 20, 1874, provides for the redemption of national-bank notes in the office of the Treasurer of the United States; that the cost of such redemptions shall be paid by the banks; and that the cost of the plates for printing, up to that time paid out of the proceeds of the tax on circulation, shall thereafter be paid from the proceeds of an assessment upon the banks. Section 6 of the act of July 12, 1882, for extending the corporate existence of national banking associations, provides that the cost of engraving plates for the issue of circulation of new design, required by the section, should also be paid by the banks. It was the evident intention of the enactors of the original banking law that all the expenses which were incurred by the Government in preparing circulation to be issued to national associations, as well as the expenses of carrying on the Bureau of the Comptroller of the Currency and enforcing the restrictions of the national banking laws, should be defrayed from the tax on circulation. As has been seen, this principle was changed by the act of June 20, 1874, which, without abolishing the tax on circulation, imposed on the banks the expense of the redemption of their notes and preparation of their plates, and this course was also followed in the act of July 12, 1882.

The Comptroller in his last annual report suggested that, inasmuch as the constant contraction of the volume of the national-bank currency was due in great measure to the fact that under present conditions banks can make but a nominal profit from the issue of circulation, a ready and simple way to prevent a further diminution of the volume of national-bank notes would be to abolish this tax, and also that if this tax were abolished the expenses of the Bureau of the Comptroller of the Currency could be paid by a pro rata assessment on the banks, as is now done in the case of the redemption of their notes by the Treasurer of the United States and in the case of the expenses of preparing plates for printing notes.

The total expense of the Office of the Comptroller of the Currency from the date of its organization to June 30, 1885, has been $6,066,227.37, and the expense for the year ending on that date $225,293.38. From the tax on circulation for the year ending June 30, 1885, $2,794,584.01 was realized by the United States Treasury.

The total taxes collected from the national banks to the end of the present fiscal year are shown in the following table:

Years.	On circulation.	On deposits.	On capital.	Totals.
1864	$53, 193 32	$95, 911 87	$18, 432 07	$167, 537 26
1865	733, 247 59	1, 087, 530 86	133, 251 15	1, 954, 029 60
1866	2, 106, 785 30	2, 633, 102 77	406, 947 74	5, 146, 835 81
1867	2, 868, 636 78	2, 650, 180 09	321, 881 36	5, 840, 698 23
1868	2, 946, 343 07	2, 564, 143 44	306, 781 67	5, 817, 268 18
1869	2, 957, 416 73	2, 614, 553 58	312, 918 68	5, 884, 888 99
1870	2, 949, 744 13	2, 614, 767 61	375, 962 26	5, 940, 474 00
1871	2, 987, 021 09	2, 802, 840 85	385, 292 13	6, 175, 154 07
1872	3, 193, 570 03	3, 120, 984 37	389, 356 27	6, 703, 910 67
1873	3, 353, 186 13	3, 196, 569 20	454, 891 51	7, 004, 646 93
1874	3, 404, 483 11	3, 209, 967 72	469, 048 02	7, 083, 498 85
1875	3, 283, 450 89	3, 514, 265 39	507, 417 76	7, 305, 134 04
1876	3, 091, 795 76	3, 50 , 129 64	632, 296 16	7, 229, 221 56
1877	2, 900, 957 53	3, 451, 965 38	660, 784 90	7, 013, 707 81
1878	2, 948, 047 08	3, 273, 111 74	560, 296 83	6, 781, 455 65
1879	3, 009, 647 16	3, 309, 668 90	401, 920 61	6, 721, 236 67
1880	3, 153, 635 63	4, 058, 710 61	379, 424 19	7, 591, 770 43
1881	3, 121, 374 33	4, 940, 945 12	431, 233 10	8, 493, 552 55
1882	3, 190, 981 98	5, 521, 927 47	437, 774 90	9, 150, 684 35
1883	3, 132, 006 73	*2, 773, 790 46	*269, 976 43	6, 175, 773 62
1884	3, 024, 668 24	....	....	3, 024, 668 24
1885	2, 794, 584 01	....	....	2, 794, 584 01
Aggregates	61, 204, 777 22	60, 940, 067 16	7, 855, 887 74	130, 000, 732 12

* Six months to June 1, 1883.

The following table exhibits the taxes upon the circulation, deposits, and capital of banks, other than national, collected by the Commissioner of Internal Revenue, from 1864 to November 1, 1882, the date upon which the taxation of capital and deposits ceased: .

Years.	On circulation.	On deposits.	On capital.	Totals.
1864	$2, 056, 996 30	$780, 723 52	....	$2, 837, 719 82
1865	1, 993, 661 84	2, 043, 841 08	$903, 367 98	4, 940, 870 90
1866	990, 278 11	2, 099, 635 83	374, 074 11	3, 463, 988 05
1867	214, 298 75	1, 355, 395 98	476, 867 73	2, 046, 562 46
1868	28, 669 88	1, 438, 512 77	399, 562 90	1, 866, 745 55
1869	16, 565 05	1, 734, 417 63	445, 071 49	2, 196, 054 17
1870	15, 419 94	2, 177, 576 46	827, 087 21	3, 020, 083 61
1871	22, 781 92	2, 702, 196 84	919, 262 77	3, 644, 241 53
1872	8, 919 82	3, 643, 251 71	976, 057 61	4, 628, 229 14
1873	24, 778 02	3, 009, 302 79	736, 950 05	3, 771, 031 46
1874	16, 738 26	2, 453, 544 26	916, 878 15	3, 387, 160 67
1875	22, 746 27	2, 972, 260 27	1, 102, 241 58	4, 097, 248 12
1876	17, 947 67	2, 999, 550 75	989, 219 61	4, 006, 698 03
1877	5, 430 16	2, 896, 637 93	927, 661 24	3, 829, 729 33
1878	1, 118 72	2, 593, 687 29	897, 225 84	3, 492, 031 85
1879	13, 603 29	2, 354, 911 71	830, 048 56	3, 198, 883 59
1880	28, 771 37	2, 510, 775 43	811, 466 48	3, 350, 985 28
1881	4, 295 08	2, 946, 996 64	811, 006 35	3, 762, 208 07
1882	4, 285 77	4, 096, 102 45	1, 153, 070 25	5, 253, 458 47
1882*	....	1, 993, 026 02	489, 033 53	2, 482, 059 55
Aggregates	5, 487, 608 82	48, 802, 237 39	14, 086, 143 44	69, 275, 989 65

* Six months to November 30, 1882.

STATE TAXATION OF NATIONAL BANKS.

The reports of the Comptroller of the Currency for the years 1877, 1880, 1881, and 1882 contain chapters on the subject of State taxation of national bank shares, in which the decisions of the courts construing the effect of the provisions of the national banking law permitting such taxation were considered.

In view of the recent decision of the United States Supreme Court in the case of Boyer *v.* Boyer, and the action of the New York banks in seeking the protection of the courts against the alleged discriminating taxation of their shares by the city of New York for the year 1885, it is deemed best to give in this report a brief *résumé* of the law authorizing State taxation of national-bank shares, and the most important decisions of the courts construing this law.

The original national currency act of February 25, 1863, contained no provision authorizing the States to tax national banks in any manner whatever. The number of banks organized under this act was, however, comparatively small, and the capital small compared with the capital invested in banks organized under State laws, over which the States had full power of taxation. Much of the opposition to the national system at the time of its inception was manifested by those who regarded it as hostile to the State systems, and as a step toward the removal of one objection, at least, to the State systems becoming merged in the national, Congress seems to have regarded it as necessary to grant to the States the authority to tax national banks. At an early day the Supreme Court of the United States had held that the States had no power to impose taxes on corporations created by Congress, and the same court has since held that the States cannot impose any tax whatever on national banks without the authority of Congress. (Williams *v.* Assessors.)

The power to tax national-bank shares was granted, and the method of imposing such tax indicated by three provisos attached to section 41 of the act of June 3, 1864, by which the original act of February 25, 1863, was superseded. Under this law, shares of national-bank stock were made liable to assessment by State authority at the place where the bank was located, but not at a greater rate than was assessed upon other moneyed capital in the hands of individual citizens of such State, and the tax imposed was not to be at a greater rate than was imposed upon the shares of banks organized under State law. Real estate belonging to a national bank was to be taxed as other real estate was taxed.

The question that appears to have first arisen as to the proper construction of the law permitting State taxation of national bank shares, was in regard to the exemption of United States bonds held by national banks, in arriving at the value of the shares liable to taxation. The Hon. Freeman Clarke, then Comptroller of the Currency, in his report to Congress for the year 1865, took strong ground in favor of the exemption of United States bonds held by the national banks. He claimed that unless such bonds held by a national bank were deducted from its capital in order to arrive at the value of the shares liable to taxation, the States exercised indirectly the right of taxing United States bonds, although such bonds were exempted by law from direct state taxation, and that thus bonds held by national banks were taxed while those held by individuals were exempted. He says, in regard to the ground taken by some, that a tax on the shares was not a tax upon the securities represented by those shares; "that the position assumed by those who favor this hypothesis will be found, upon critical examination, to be fallacious can scarcely admit of a doubt."

The point came before the United States Supreme Court for decision in Van Allen *v.* Assessors (3 Wall., 573), and it was decided by the majority of the court that a share of national bank stock was a distinct thing from the capital of the bank, which capital may be invested in

United States bonds—that the shares are property in the hands of individuals, while the corporation is the legal owner of all the property of the bank, real and personal.

The interest of the shareholder entitles him to participate in the profits of the corporation while the latter is in existence, and also upon its dissolution to receive his proportionate share of such property as may remain after the payment of its debts. It is this entire interest that Congress has left subject to taxation by the States, and not such portion as might remain were the amount invested in United States bonds deducted from capital.

The court also held in this case that a New York statute, assessing shares of national banks for purposes of taxation at the same rate at which other moneyed capital was assessed, the tax not to exceed the par value of the shares, was void, because it was contrary to the provisions of the Federal law—that taxation of national bank shares was not to be at a greater rate than was imposed on State bank shares.

The State banks in New York were not taxed on their shares, but on capital, from which the deduction of the amount invested in United States securities was allowed, while this deduction could not be made to reduce the value of national bank shares. The question then arose in a new form. Inasmuch as the law provides that shares of national banks shall be assessed at the same rate as other moneyed capital in the hands of individual citizens, and inasmuch as United States bonds and securities are exempt in the hands of individual citizens; when the capital of national banks is invested in United States bonds, is not the State tax on their shares invalid? The United States Supreme Court in People v. Commissioners (4 Wall., 244) decided that under such circumstances the State tax on national-bank shares was valid. Under these two decisions it is apparent that no deduction can be made from the value of shares of national banks on account of the exemption from tax of some of the assets in which their capital may be invested. This principle will apply to United States notes and to United States or other securities which may by law be exempt from taxation.

The next important case bearing on this matter decided in the United States Supreme Court was that of Lionberger v. Rouse. This turned upon the construction of that portion of the Federal law providing that the tax on national-bank shares should not be at a greater rate than was imposed on the shares of State banks. The point raised was that the State of Missouri taxed some State banks less than others. These lightly taxed banks, holding an inconsiderable portion of the banking capital of the State, were organized under special charters, granted prior to the commencement of the national system, which the State had no power to change. There was no discrimination as between national-bank shares and those of State banks not so specially exempted. The court construed the clause of the Federal law in question to mean only that the State, as a condition to the exercise of the power to tax the shares of national banks, shall, as far as it has *the capacity*, tax in like manner the shares of banks of its own creation.

The act of February 10, 1868, was passed to further define the place and manner of taxation of national bank shares, amending section 41 of the act of June 3, 1864. It may perhaps be regarded as superseding that section to the extent of dropping out the proviso that shares of national banks shall be taxed at a rate no greater than is imposed on the shares of State banks. This appears to be the view taken by Congress in 1873, when approving the Revised Statutes, as in those statutes this proviso is not included. Section 5219, which now embodies the law on State taxation of national-bank shares, is as follows:

SEC. 5219. Nothing herein shall prevent all the shares in any association from being included in the valuation of the personal property of the owner or holder of such shares, in assessing taxes imposed by authority of the State within which the association is located; but the legislature of each State may determine and direct the manner and place of taxing all the shares of national banking associations located within the State, subject only to the two restrictions, that the taxation shall not be at a greater rate than is assessed upon other moneyed capital in the hands of individual citizens of such State, and that the shares of any national banking association owned by non-residents of any State shall be taxed in the city or town where the bank is located, and not elsewhere. Nothing herein shall be construed to exempt the real property of associations from either State, county, or municipal taxes, to the same extent, according to its value, as other real property is taxed.

The validity of State taxation on national-bank shares, is under this section, to be determined solely by the inquiry whether it is at a greater rate than is assessed upon other moneyed capital in the hands of individual citizens. There has, however, been great difficulty in so regulating the taxation of national-bank shares by the States as to conform strictly to the intent of this law. As a consequence, in many of the States, national bank shares, in the assessment and collection of taxes, have, it is alleged, been in different ways subjected to severe and unjust discrimination, as compared with other moneyed capital. Some of the methods of discrimination are as follows:

(1) Differences are made in the valuation of national-bank shares for purposes of assessing taxes, as compared with the valuation of other moneyed capital for the same purpose.

(2) The individual holders of other moneyed capital have been allowed to make deductions on account of certain exemptions, such as debts owed by such individual holders, when holders of national-bank shares were not permitted to deduct their debts from the value of such shares.

(3) In the different States distinctions are made in the taxation of various kinds of moneyed capital, other than national-bank shares, in the hands of individual citizens, and the standard by which the taxation of national bank shares is to be legally measured becomes thus confused.

Many forms of moneyed capital in the hands of individual citizens are altogether exempted by law from taxation, while national-bank shares are taxed. The difficulty arises in deciding by which class of moneyed capital the tax on national bank shares is to be guided: Whether there is to be no tax, as in case of exempted moneyed capital; a less tax, as in case of the class of moneyed capital taxed at a less rate; or a greater tax, as in case of the class of moneyed capital taxed at a greater rate.

All of these forms of discrimination have been passed on in litigation which has come before the United States Supreme Court.

In Ohio the law provided certain State boards for equalizing the taxation on real estate, on railroad capital, and on capital invested in bank shares; but there was no State board for equalizing the taxation on personal property, other than bank shares, railroad stock, or other moneyed capital. The equalization as to all other personal property assessed ceased with the county boards of equalization, but the county boards throughout the State fixed the valuation of moneyed capital for purposes of taxation at six-tenths of its true value, while the State board fixed the taxable value of bank shares at their actual cash value. The rates of taxation being the same, bank shares were discriminated against to the extent of four-tenths of their value. In New York the law permitted the deduction of just debts of an individual from his personal property, including his moneyed capital, excepting only his bank shares.

In Pelton v. Commercial National Bank of Cleveland (101 U. S., p. 143), and in Cummings v. Merchants' National Bank of Toledo (101 U. S., p. 153), the United States Supreme Court decided the question of discrimination arising under the laws of Ohio. In those cases it was held that a tax upon national-bank shares valued for taxation at a higher rate than other moneyed capital was invalid, and that upon payment of the amount justly assessable a court of equity would enjoin the collection of the residue, but that the bank must pay the portion of the taxes justly due.

In People v. Weaver (100 U. S., p. 539), a case arising under the New York law, the Supreme Court decided that the word *rate* in the provision of section 5219 United States Revised Statutes, that taxation shall not be at a greater rate than is assesssd upon other moneyed capital in the hands of individuals, applies to and *includes as well* the valuation of shares for taxation, as the rate of taxes to be imposed; and that the law of the State of New York, which permitted a party to deduct his just debts from the value of all his personal property, except his national-bank shares, was void as to the taxation of such bank shares. The case of Evansville Bank v. Britton (104 U. S., p. 323), arising under the law of Indiana, taxing national-bank shares, supports the same doctrine. These cases disposed of the first two forms of discriminations already mentioned, and pointed out the proper remedy to be pursued by banks in avoiding the payment of taxes illegally assessed. Supervisors v. Stanley (104 U. S., p. 305) decides questions arising as to the recovery of excessive taxes which have been paid by the shareholders of national banks.

Under the third class of discrimination—where doubt as to the proper taxation of national-bank shares arises from the fact that under State law a discrimination is made in taxing different classes of other moneyed capital in the hands of individual citizens—the important cases decided in United States Supreme Court are Lionberger v. Rouse (9 Wall.), already mentioned; Hepburn v. School Directors (23 Wall., 480), and the recently decided case of Boyer v. Boyer. In Lionberger v. Rouse a discrimination was made by the State in taxing shares of banks organized under its own laws—one class of banks being taxed at a higher rate than another. At that time, as has been seen, the law in force measured the taxation of national-bank shares by the taxation of State-bank shares, and in this case the United States Supreme Court held a tax on national-bank shares to be valid which did not exceed the tax imposed upon the larger bulk of State-bank shares. In Hepburn v. School Directors (23 Wall., 480) it was held by the United States Supreme Court that the exemption by State law from taxation of a small portion of other moneyed capital in the hands of individual citizens was not a reason for exempting national-bank shares from taxation. In this case also it was held that shares of national banks might be taxed at an amount exceeding their par value, if their market value exceeded their par value.

In the case of Boyer v. Boyer, the Supreme Court decided that if the great bulk of moneyed capital in the hands of individual citizens is exempted by State law from municipal taxation, that under the law of Congress national-bank shares must be exempted also. The court says that cases will arise in which it will be difficult to determine whether the exemption of the particular part of moneyed capital in individual hands is so serious or material as to infringe the rules of substantial equality—that a proper construction of the act of Congress forces the conclusion that capital invested in national bank shares was intended to be placed upon the same footing of substantial equality in respect to taxation by State authority, with other moneyed capital in the hands of individual citizens, however invested. The court proceeded to say:

Upon such facts, and in view of the revenue laws of the State, it seems difficult to avoid the conclusion that, in respect of county taxation of national-bank shares, there has been and is such a discrimination in favor of other moneyed capital against capital invested in such shares as is not consistent with the legislation of Congress. The exemptions in favor of other moneyed capital appear to be of such a substantial character in amount as to take the present case out of the operation of the rule that it is not absolute equality that is contemplated by the act of Congress; a rule which rests upon the ground that exact uniformity or equality of taxation cannot in the nature of things be expected or attained under any system. But as substantial equality is attainable, and is required by the supreme law of the land, in respect of State taxation of national-bank shares, when the inequality is so palpable, as to show that the discrimination against capital invested in such shares is serious, the courts have no discretion but to interfere.

Having in view this last decision, the banks of the city of New York, after due investigation of the subject by a committee* appointed for the purpose, have arrived at the conclusion that the valuation of their shares for purposes of taxation is illegal and void, for the reason that the greater portion of moneyed capital in the hands of individual citizens in the city of New York is, under the laws of that State, exempt from municipal taxation.

Suits have been brought in equity, and the bill in each case asks for an injunction from collecting any taxes from the bank or from the individual shareholders until a final hearing of the cause.

The question is frequently asked this office, whether national-bank notes in the hands of individual citizens are liable to State taxation. Section 3707 of the Revised Statutes provides that all stocks, bonds, Treasury notes, and other obligations of the United States shall be exempt from taxation by or under State or municipal or local authority. In section 5413, Revised Statutes, the words "obligation of the United States" is held to include national bank currency. The question of the taxability of national bank currency arose in the case of the Board of Commissioners in Montgomery County v. Elston (32 Ind., 27), and it was decided by the Supreme Court of the State that national-bank currency is not exempt from taxation by the State. The court held that the provision of law making national currency an obligation of the United States, only intended to throw around national currency the same guards against counterfeiting that were by law provided for obligations of the United States, and not to generally define national currency as an obligation of the United States.

In the case of Horne v. Greene, in the Supreme Court of the State of Mississippi (52 Miss., 452), it was decided that the circulating notes of national banks are not subject to State taxes. The question, therefore, still appears to be an open one.

LOANS AND RATES OF INTEREST.

The following table gives the classification of the loans of the banks in the city of New York, in Boston, Philadelphia, and Baltimore, in the

---

* Report of John Jay Knox, Edmund D. Randolph, and W. P. St. John, tax committee, on the recent decision of the Supreme Court of the United States, New York June 9, 1885.

other reserve cities, and in the remaining banks of the country at corresponding dates in each of the last three years:

OCTOBER 2, 1883.

Classification.	48 banks.	103 banks.	97 banks.	2,253 banks.	2,501 banks.
On U. S. bonds on demand	$2,093,526	$344,337	$623,679	$1,972,232	$5,033,774
On other stocks, bonds, &c., on demand	94,321,605	29,638,276	23,099,682	41,518,741	188,578,304
On single-name paper without other security	19,147,049	24,684,110	17,259,584	87,910,589	149,001,332
All other loans	129,546,152	146,149,205	110,381,881	574,760,143	960,837,381
Totals	245,108,332	200,815,928	151,364,826	706,161,705	1,303,450,791

SEPTEMBER 30, 1884.

Classification.	44 banks.	104 banks.	99 banks.	2,417 banks.	2,664 banks.
On U. S. bonds on demand	$2,933,785	$644,017	$268,396	$970,691	$4,816,889
On other stocks, bonds, &c., on demand	69,805,215	25,763,605	18,573,905	34,050,829	148,193,554
On single-name paper without other security	12,559,441	22,458,370	16,239,550	3,816,871	135,074,232
All other loans	120,051,836	150,372,086	107,543,129	574,016,071	951,986,122
Totals	205,353,277	199,238,078	142,624,980	692,854,462	1,240,070,797

OCTOBER 1, 1885.

Classification.	44 banks.	105 banks.	98 banks.	2,467 banks.	2,714 banks.
On U. S. bonds on demand	$3,286,124	$190,195	$585,154	$504,134	$4,565,607
On other stocks, bonds, &c., on demand	80,687,265	33,157,319	25,421,092	34,036,931	173,302,607
On single-name paper without other security	25,331,820	34,806,254	18,480,233	92,873,780	171,492,087
All other loans	127,518,389	150,270,503	106,948,959	567,057,152	951,793,003
Totals	236,823,598	218,424,271	151,435,438	694,471,997	1,301,155,304

In the table below is given a full classification of the loans in New York City alone for the last five years:

Loans and discount.	October 1, 1881.	October 3, 1882.	October 2, 1883.	September 30, 1884.	October 1, 1885.
	48 banks.	50 banks.	48 banks.	44 banks.	44 banks.
On endorsed paper	$112,049,004	$118,692,651	$121,644,204	$116,010,062	$114,013,775
On single-named paper	26,935,878	21,203,573	19,147,051	12,559,443	25,341,820
On U. S. bonds on demand	2,539,928	1,707,687	2,093,527	2,934,785	3,286,124
On other stocks,&c., on demand	97,249,162	89,532,762	94,321,605	69,805,215	89,687,265
On real estate security	236,100	394,732	184,083	163,297	215,385
All other loans	7,747,587	7,600,487	7,717,265	3,881,875	13,280,229
Totals	246,757,659	239,041,892	245,108,332	205,353,277	236,823,598

In previous reports the attention of Congress has been called to the provisions of section 5200 of the Revised Statutes, which place restrictions upon loans, and to the difficulty of enforcing the same. In cities where large amounts of produce are received and stored it is claimed to be impossible for the banks to transact this class of business so long as they are restricted to loans to an amount not exceeding in any case one-tenth of their capital. While it is true that the limitation prescribed does not apply to loans upon produce in transit where the drafts are drawn on existing values, yet if the produce is stored instead of being shipped, loans in excess of the one-tenth limit cannot be made except in violation of law. In such a case the Comptroller has no means of enforcing the law except by bringing suit for forfeiture of charter, which might result in great embarrassment to business, as well as loss to innocent stockholders. It seems evident that the law should be so amended as to permit legitimate loans upon United States bonds, produce or warehouse receipts, and some other classes of collateral security.

RATES OF INTEREST IN NEW YORK CITY AND OF THE BANK OF ENGLAND AND THE BANK OF FRANCE.

The average rate of interest in New York City for each of the fiscal years from 1875 to 1885, as ascertained from data derived from the Journal of Commerce and the Commercial and Financial Chronicle, was as follows:

1875, call loans, 3.0 per cent. ; commercial paper, 5.8 per cent.
1876, call loans, 3.3 per cent. ; commercial paper, 5.3 per cent.
1877, call loans, 3.0 per cent. ; commercial paper, 5.2 per cent.
1878, call loans, 4.4 per cent. ; commercial paper, 5.1 per cent.
1879, call loans, 4.4 per cent. ; commercial paper, 4.4 per cent.
1880, call loans, 4.9 per cent. : commercial paper, 5.3 per cent.
1881, call loans, 3.8 per cent. ; commercial paper, 5 0 per cent.
1882, call loans, 4.4 per cent. : commercial paper, 5.4 per cent.
1883, call loans, 5.7 per cent. ; commercial paper, 5.7 per cent.
1884, call loans, 2.4 per cent. ; commercial paper, 5.6 per cent.
1885, call loans, 2.3 per cent.; commercial paper, 5.5 per cent.*

The average rate of discount of the Bank of England for the same years was as follows:

During the calendar year ending December 31, 1874, 3.69 per cent.
During the calendar year ending December 31, 1875, 3.23 per cent.
During the calendar year ending December 31, 1876, 2.61 per cent.
During the calendar year ending December 31, 1877, 2.91 per cent.
During the calendar year ending December 31, 1878, 3.78 per cent.
During the calendar year ending December 31, 1879, 2.50 per cent.
During the calendar year ending December 31, 1880, 2.76 per cent.
During the calendar year ending December 31, 1881, 3.49 per cent.†
During the calendar year ending December 31, 1882, 4.10 per cent.†
During the calendar year ending December 31, 1883, 3.57 per cent.‡
During the calendar year ending December 31, 1884, 3.18 per cent.§
From December 31, 1884, to September 30, 1885, 2 per cent.§

From December 31, 1884, the rate of discount of the Bank of England was uniform at 2 per cent. The average rate of interest in New York City for the four months previous to November 1, 1885, was, according to the Financial Chronicle, on call loans about 2 per cent. and on commercial paper about 4.3 per cent., and the rate of interest on October 31, 1885, was on call loans 2.5 per cent. and on commercial paper 4.75 per cent. The rate of discount in the Bank of France, which was lowered from 4 to 3½ per cent. on March 23, 1882, was lowered to 3 per cent. on February 23, 1883, and the general council of the bank reported on

* From the Financial Chronicle. Maximum rate.
† From the Financial Chronicle only.
‡ From the London Bankers' Magazine.
§ From the London Economist.

January 29, 1885, as stated in the London Bankers' Magazine, that this rate of discount had stood since the former date, and that they had endeavored for the advantage of business to maintain the position of a fixed rate, and fortunately succeeded in doing so during the year 1884. The number of trade bills admitted to discount in the bank of France during the year 1884* was 5,144,635, representing the sum of $907,870,300. Of this number of bills there were 14,327 bills of $2.08 and under, 661,895 bills from $2.29 to $10, 905,293 bills from $10.21 to $20, and 3,563,120 bills above $20; that is to say, nearly a third in bills under $20.21. The number of trade bills under $20 steadily increases. In 1880 there were 1,014.412 of these small discounted bills, in 1881 1,160,945, in 1882 1,224,326, in 1883 1,349,270, and in 1884 they increased to 1,581,515. The report by the governor of the Bank of France for the year 1884 states that the proportion of the discounts for retail trade in Paris has continually increased during the past year.

DIVIDENDS AND EARNINGS.

The large number of mercantile failures which have occurred during 1884 and 1885 have not apparently injured or weakened the national banks, the aggregate surplus funds and undivided profits having been but slightly reduced. The aggregate surplus of 2,664 banks on September 30, 1884, amounted to $147,055,038, and the undivided profits to $63,234,238.

At the close of business October 1, 1885, the aggregate surplus fund of 2,714 banks amounted to $146,624,642, and the undivided profits to $59,335,519, showing a decrease in surplus of $430,396, and in undivided profits of $3,898,719.

The following table shows the losses of national banks from September 1, 1880, to September 1, 1885, and the ratio of losses to the aggregate capital employed:

Semi-annual dividend periods.	Capital.	Losses.	Ratio.	Number of banks.
September 1, 1880, to March 1, 1881	$456,844,865	$5,007,297	1.10	2,087
March 1, 1881, to September 1, 1881	458,934,485	5,462,713	1.19	2,100
September 1, 1881, to March 1, 1882	460,354,485	3,886,836	0.84	2,137
March 1, 1882, to September 1, 1882	473,947,715	4,412,575	0.93	2,197
September 1, 1882, to March 1, 1883	483,091,312	4,640,865	0.96	2,267
March 1, 1883, to September 1, 1883	494,640,140	6,146,204	1.24	2,359
September 1, 1883, to March 1, 1884	507,969,300	5,593,691	1.10	2,491
March 1, 1884, to September 1, 1884	518,605,725	11,377,203	2.19	2,583
September 1, 1884, to March 1, 1885	522,899,715	9,973,161	1.91	2,650
March 1, 1885, to September 1, 1885	524,599,602	8,739,420	1.67	2,665

The following tables have been compiled in order that comparisons may be made between the annual dividends paid by the national banks of the United States and those paid by banks in foreign countries to their stockholders, and indicate that the average dividends and earnings of

* London Bankers' Magazine, August, 1885, p. 698.

the national banks in the United States are as a rule less than the dividends of joint-stock banks of other countries :

FOREIGN BANKS.

Number of establishments.	Bank.	Paid up capital.	Rate per cent. per annum of dividend on capital.	Number of establishments.	Bank.	Paid up capital.	Rate per cent. per annum of dividend on capital.
	Bank of England	$70, 727, 580	9 3/4				
16	London and partly provincial banks.	75, 096, 763	14 1/8	3	Anglo-Continental banks.	$5, 003, 580	5 8/10
25	Yorkshire and Northern.	27, 325, 763	11 9/10	2	Russian banks	20, 988, 009	9
					Austro-Hungarian	35, 370, 000	7 1/8
16	Lancashire and Cheshire.	30, 314, 936	12 1/2	3	Austro-Hungarian banks.	32, 619, 000	7 1/3
14	Midland and Eastern	18, 667, 260	13 4/10		Banque Nationale	9, 650, 000	13 3/8
7	Welsh and West of England.	9, 384, 324	11	3	Belgian banks	10, 562, 666	11 7/10
	Bank of Scotland	6, 075, 000	14		Banque de France	35, 222, 500	21 1/2
9	Scotch banks	37, 917, 720	12 3/10	8	French banks	114, 352, 500	9 1/2
	Bank of Ireland	13, 458, 457	12		Deutsche Reichs bank	28, 560, 000	6 1/4
10	Irish banks	17, 933, 400	10	6	German banks	52, 407, 600	8 1/4
	Colonial banks.				Banca Nazionale d'Italia.	38, 600, 000	13 1/3
				3	Italian banks	15, 440, 000	9 2/3
24	Australasian	67, 173, 039	12 1/2	6	Swiss banks	8, 202, 500	6 1/3
15	Canadian	47, 332, 316	7 8/10	1	Spanish bank	3, 860, 000	6
9	Eastern	36, 552, 472	8 8/10		Imperial Ottoman	24, 300, 000	8
2.	South African	6, 561, 000	10	6	Turkish banks	18, 715, 512	6 1/8
1	West Indies	2, 916, 000	10				

NATIONAL BANKS IN THE UNITED STATES.

City of Boston	$50, 950, 000	5. 5	Southern States	35, 997, 850	8. 1
New England States	115, 584, 370	7. 1	City of Cincinnati	8, 600, 000	6. 4
City of New York	46, 250, 000	8. 8	City of Cleveland	5, 032, 050	5
City of Albany	1, 775, 000	9. 5	City of Chicago	11, 150, 000	9. 2
City of Philadelphia	18, 058, 000	9. 1	City of Detroit	2, 650, 000	9. 3
City of Pittsburgh	10, 179, 000	7. 4	City of Milwaukee	650, 000	11. 4
City of Baltimore	11. 713, 260	7. 4	City of Saint Louis	3, 250, 000	6. 3
City of Washington	1, 125, 000	6. 8	Western States	95, 518, 140	8. 8
Middle States	83, 958, 888	7. 7	City of San Francisco	1, 500, 000	8
City of New Orleans	3, 525, 000	7. 9	Pacific States and Territories	11, 831, 000	9. 4
City of Louisville	3, 551, 500	6. 8			

The information in regard to the foreign banks has been derived from the London Bankers' Magazine for October, 1885, and is to the latest obtainable date. The principal bank in each country is given separately, and the dividends paid by other banks in the same country are averaged. Similar statements of the national banks of the United States are by geographical divisions, the reserve cities in each being given separately, and the dividends paid by all other banks in the same division are averaged.

Further particulars in relation to dividends paid by the national banks in the United States will be found in a table given in the Appendix.

TRANSACTIONS OF THE NEW YORK CLEARING-HOUSE.

The New York Clearing-House Association is composed of 43 national and 21 State banks and the assistant treasurer of the United States at New York. Through the courtesy of Mr. W. A. Camp, its manager, a statement of the transactions during the year ending October 1, 1885, has been obtained, which shows that the total exchanges were more than $25,000,000,000, while the balances paid in money were over $1,295,000,000. The daily average balances paid were $4,247,069, or about 5.1 per cent. of the amount of the settlements.

The balances paid in money during the year consisted of $120,436,000 in clearing-house certificates of the Bank of America; clearing house certificates for legal-tender notes amounting to $405,900,000; legal-tenders amounting to $212,643,251; and United States gold certificates $556,376,000. Since the date of the issue of the new gold certificates (October 4, 1883), authorized by the act of July 12, 1882, the greater portion of the balances due from the Government, have been paid in these certificates instead of coin, thus dispensing with the movement of large amounts in bags and upon drays from the Treasury to the custody of the banks. During the six months ending November 1, 1884, a portion of the balances due from the Treasury of the United States were paid in legal-tender notes, and during the past year the amount of gold certificates of the United States and of the Bank of America received in payment have decreased, while the balances paid in clearing-house legal-tender certificates and legal-tender notes amount to nearly one-half of the entire money balances paid.

The following table shows the yearly transactions of the New York Clearing-House for the thirty-two years since its organization in 1853, and the amounts and ratios of currency required for the payment of daily balances:

Years.	No. of banks.	Capital.*	Exchanges.	Balances paid in money.	Average daily exchanges.	Average daily balances paid in money.	Ratios.
							Per ct.
1854	50	$47,044,900	$5,750,455,987	$297,411,494	$19,104,505	$988,078	5.2
1855	48	48,884,180	5,362,912,098	289,604,137	17,412,052	940,565	5.4
1856	50	52,883,700	6,906,213,328	334,714,489	22,278,108	1,079,724	4.8
1857	50	64,420,200	8,333,226,718	365,313,902	26,968,371	1,182,246	4.4
1858	46	67,146,018	4,756,664,386	314,238,911	15,393,736	1,016,954	6.6
1859	47	67,921,714	5,448,005,956	363,984,683	20,867,333	1,177,944	5.6
1860	50	69,907,435	7,231,143,057	380,693,438	23,401,757	1,232,018	5.3
1861	50	68,900,605	5,915,742,758	353,383,944	19,269,520	1,151,088	6.0
1862	50	68,375,820	6,871,443,591	415,530,331	22,237,682	1,344,758	6.0
1863	50	68,972,508	14,867,597,849	677,626,483	48,428,657	2,207,252	4.6
1864	49	68,586,763	24,097,196,656	885,719,205	77,984,455	2,866,405	3.7
1865	55	80,363,013	26,032,384,342	1,035,765,108	84,796,040	3,373,828	4.0
1866	58	82,370,200	28,717,146,914	1,066,135,106	93,541,195	3,472,753	3.7
1867	58	81,770,200	28,675,159,472	1,144,963,451	93,401,167	3,747,414	4.0
1868	50	82,270,200	28,484,288,637	1,125,455,237	92,182,164	3,642,250	4.0
1869	59	82,720,200	37,407,028,987	1,120,318,308	121,451,393	3,637,397	3.0
1870	61	83,620,200	27,804,539,406	1,036,484,822	90,274,479	3,365,210	3.7
1871	62	84,420,200	29,300,986,682	1,209,721,029	95,133,074	3,927,666	4.1
1872	61	84,420,200	33,844,369,568	1,428,582,707	109,884,317	4,636,632	4.2
1873	59	83,370,200	35,461,052,826	1,474,508,025	115,885,794	4,818,654	4.1
1874	59	81,635,200	22,855,927,636	1,286,753,176	74,692,574	4,205,076	5.7
1875	59	80,435,200	25,061,237,902	1,408,608,777	81,899,470	4,603,297	5.6
1876	59	81,731,200	21,597,274,247	1,295,042,029	70,349,428	4,218,378	5.9
1877	58	71,085,200	23,289,243,701	1,373,996,302	76,358,176	4,504,906	5.9
1878	57	63,611,500	22,508,438,442	1,307,843,857	73,555,988	4,274,000	5.8
1879	59	60,800,200	25,178,770,691	1,400,111,063	82,015,540	4,560,622	5.6
1880	57	60,475,200	37,182,128,621	1,516,538,631	121,510,224	4,956,009	4.1
1881	60	61,162,700	48,565,818,212	1,776,018,162	159,232,191	5,823,010	3.5
1882	61	60,962,700	46,552,846,161	1,595,000,245	151,637,935	5,195,440	3.4
1883	63	61,162,700	40,293,165,258	1,568,983,196	132,543,307	5,161,129	8.9
1884	61	60,412,700	34,092,037,338	1,524,930,904	111,048,982	4,967,202	4.5
1885	64	58,612,700	25,250,791,440	1,295,355,252	82,789,480	4,247,069	5.1
		†70,014,239	‡744,605,238,867	†32,669,426,493	†75,850,909	†3,327,908	4.4

* The capital is for various dates, the amounts at a uniform date in each year not being obtainable.
† Yearly averages for thirty-two years.   ‡ Totals for thirty-two years.

The total amount of transactions for the thirty-two years given in the table is $744,695,238,867, and the annual average is $23,271,726,214.

The clearing-house transactions of the assistant treasurer of the United States at New York for the year ending October 1, 1885, were as follows:

Exchanges received from clearing-house	$259,935,584 08
Exchanges delivered to clearing-house	114,051,016 05
Balances paid to clearing-house	146,724,869 08
Balances received from clearing-house	840,301 05
Showing that the amount paid by the assistant treasurer to the clearing-house was in excess of the amount received by him	145,884,568 03

A table compiled from statements made by the New York clearinghouse, giving the clearances and balances weekly from September 4. 1880, to October 31, 1885, inclusive, will be found in the Appendix, and is valuable for purposes of comparison.

The following interesting table has been copied from the Commercial and Financial Chronicle of New York City, of November 7, 1885, which gives information concerning the exchanges at New York and other cities having clearing-houses for the week ending October 31, comparing them with those for the corresponding week in 1884, and showing the percentage of differences. The exchanges at the same places for the month ending October 31, 1885, are also given with the percentage of differences resulting from a comparison with the exchanges for the same month of the previous year:

Cities.	Week.			October.		
	1885.	1884.	Per cent.	1885.	1884.	Per cent.
New York	$695,214,387	$458,532,568	+51.6	$3,189,746,196	$2,370,856,125	+34.5
Boston	76,974,841	58,811,408	+30.9	342,121,551	288,641,009	+18.5
Chicago	48,771,241	44,515,792	+ 9.6	234,770,623	204,712,276	+14.7
Philadelphia	47,353,039	39,828,337	+18.9	236,905,761	208,220,032	+13.8
Saint Louis	13,662,131	12,918,575	+ 5.8	66,532,755	63,474,959	+ 4.8
San Francisco	11,512,515	13,365,680	−13.9	51,609,656	54,162,816	− 4.7
New Orleans	10,760,103	8,477,673	+26.9	40,349,600	38,420,300	+ 5.0
Baltimore	10,337,785	11,577,658	−10.7	52,164,929	57,616,449	− 9.5
Cincinnati	8,212,250	8,062,250	+ 1.9	41,952,425	38,736,050	+ 8.3
Pittsburgh	7,407,417	8,461,699	−12.5	32,765,984	37,489,987	−12.6
Providence	5,579,400	4,498,700	+24.0	22,813,000	16,674,200	+36.9
Kansas City	4,771,467	3,602,645	+32.4	25,085,652	17,406,421	+44.1
Milwaukee	4,105,872	3,702,453	+10.9	18,691,227	16,330,797	+14.5
Louisville	3,863,906	3,289,468	+17.5	19,467,445	16,211,381	+20.1
Detroit	2,949,221	2,690,522	+ 9.6	14,591,498	13,279,277	+ 9.9
Cleveland	2,142,899	1,881,996	+13.9	9,858,182	9,397,942	+ 4.9
Memphis	1,582,422	1,383,609	+14.2	6,595,745	5,509,186	+19.9
Hartford	1,534,252	1,179,465	+30.7	8,301,504	6,254,003	+32.7
Columbus	1,386,809	1,192,532	+16.3	6,505,203	6,048,265	+ 7.6
Indianapolis	1,377,473	1,315,327	+ 3.2	6,053,829	5,888,112	+ 2.8
Portland	1,037,815	1,023,975	+ 1.4	4,544,266	4,471,868	+ 1.6
Peoria	936,421	776,746	+20.6	4,454,202	4,079,364	+ 9.2
Worcester	794,964	808,300	− 1.6	4,459,517	3,766,739	+18.4
Springfield	713,723	653,389	+ 9.2	3,499,539	3,291,396	+ 3.6
Saint Joseph	635,979	579,131	+ 9.8	3,323,586	2,666,163	+20.5
Lowell	408,836	456,011	−10.3	2,351,427	2,360,967	− 0.4
Total	964,027,168	693,601,960	+39.0	4,449,431,381	3,495,856,994	+27.3
Outside New York	268,812,781	235,069,401	+14.4	1,259,685,185	1,125,000,869	+11.9

The following table exhibits the transactions of clearing-houses located in twenty-nine cities for the year ending October 1, 1885, from official returns received by the manager of the New York clearing-house:

Clearing-houses.	Exchanges.	Balances.
New York	$25, 250, 791, 440	$1, 295, 355, 253
Boston	3, 365, 702, 730	442, 972, 332
Philadelphia	2, 244, 194, 406	215, 464, 089
Chicago	2, 248, 230, 189	257, 588, 370
Saint Louis	745, 577, 323	122, 057, 237
Baltimore	590, 859, 346	76, 623, 877
San Francisco	562, 610, 183	96, 156, 787
Pittsburgh	358, 517, 850	74, 460, 991
New Orleans	387, 485, 900	46, 712, 200
Cincinnati	439, 634, 000	No record.
Providence	205, 575, 000	No record.
Louisville	208, 714, 120	49, 794, 209
Milwaukee	179, 437, 953	31, 967, 463
Detroit	134, 650, 066	23, 849, 499
Cleveland	101, 305, 282	No record.
Indianapolis	65, 2 45, 339	16, 936, 134
Kansas City	209, 335, 915	34, 309, 955
Hartford	77, 495, 526	23, 484, 960
New Haven	54, 803, 637	12, 542, 686
Columbus	33, 632, 517	10, 905, 258
Memphis	67, 199, 260	16, 008, 332
Peoria	40, 554, 333	11, 370, 217
Worcester	37, 636, 992	11, 358, 664
Springfield	36, 754, 686	10, 396, 230
Lowell	22, 403, 614	8, 578, 929
Syracuse	24, 372, 022	6, 075, 260
Portland	44, 786, 547	8, 556, 421
Omaha	New.	New.
Saint Joseph	33, 784, 703	9, 510, 485
Total	37, 770, 110, 819	2, 905, 629, 837

From the above table it will be seen that the exchanges in New York City amounted to 66.8 per cent. of the whole sum, and the balances in that city were nearly 44.6 per cent. of the total balances.

CLEARING-HOUSE CERTIFICATES.

Section 5192 Revised Statutes, provides that clearing-house certificates representing specie or lawful money specially deposited for the purposes of any clearing-house association, shall also be deemed to be lawful money in the possession of any association belonging to such clearing-house holding and owning such certificates; and section 5193 provides that the Secretary of the Treasury may receive United States notes on deposit, without interest, from any national banking association, in sums not less than $10,000, and issue certificates therefor in denominations of not less than $5,000, which certificates may be counted as part of the lawful money reserve, and may be accepted in the settlement of clearing-house balances at the places where the deposits therefor were made.

The legal-tender note certificates were first issued in the fiscal year 1873. On June 30, 1875, there were outstanding $59,045,000 of these certificates, of which the national banks held $47,310,000. On June 30, 1876, the amount outstanding was $33,140,000, of which the banks held $27,955,000. On June 30, 1879, the amount had been reduced to $29,-330,000, and the banks held on June 14 of the same year $25,180,000. The amount outstanding on September 30, 1885, was $23,185,000, and the national banks held on that day $18,800,000. The issue of the gold certificates was authorized by the fifth section of the act of March 3, 1863, and they were used for clearing-house purposes soon after the passage of the national bank act.

The first issue was made on November 13, 1865. On June 30, 1875, there were outstanding $21,796,300, of which the national banks in New York City held $12,642,180. The issue of these certificates was discontinued on December 1, 1878, and the amount outstanding had decreased on June 30, 1879, to $15,413,700, and on October 1, 1880, to $7,480,100. The amount outstanding on October 3, 1882, was $4,907,440, of which the national banks held $4,594,300. The issue of gold certificates having been discontinued by the Government, and the amount of gold coin having rapidly increased, the banks in New York found it necessary to establish a depository of gold coin for the convenience of the clearinghouse. This depository at the present time is the Bank of America, by which bank certificates of deposit were first issued on October 14, 1879. The amount of such certificates outstanding on January 1, 1880, was $25,610,000, and on October 1, 1883, was $22,955,000. The largest amount of coin on deposit was on January 21, 1882, viz, $45,330,000, the capacity of the vault having been increased since 1880. Of this amount the national banks of New York City held on October 2, 1883, $20,345,000; on September 30, 1884, $15,123,000; and on October 1, 1885, $16,094,000.

These banks on the same date held of gold Treasury certificates issued under the acts of March 3, 1863, and July 12, 1882, $62,249,740. The act of February 28, 1878, authorized any holder of silver dollars of the weight of 412½ grains troy of standard silver to deposit the same with the Treasurer or any assistant treasurer of the United States in sums not less than $10, and receive therefor certificates of not less than $10 each, corresponding with the denomination of the United States notes. It required that the coin deposited or representing the certificates should be retained in the Treasury for the payment of the same on demand, and that said certificates should be receivable for customs, taxes, and all public dues, and also authorized their reissue.

The New York Clearing-House Association issued during July and August, 1885, clearing-house certificates based upon fractional silver specially deposited for such purpose, and on October 1, 1885, the national banks of New York City held $4,825,000 of these certificates.*

It would appear that these certificates could be legally held if desired as a portion of the lawful money reserve of national banks, under section 5192 of the Revised Statutes of the United States, which provides, as heretofore stated, that clearing-house certificates representing specie or lawful money, specially deposited for the purpose in the clearing-house association, shall be deemed lawful money. The fractional silver coin represented by these certificates could also be converted into lawful money at any time, as they are redeemable in lawful money of the United States on presentation at the Treasury.

Section 12, act of July 12, 1882, provides that the Secretary of the Treasury is authorized and directed to receive deposits of gold coin with the Treasurer or assistant treasurers of the United States in sums not less than $20, and to issue certificates therefor in denominations of not less than $20 each, corresponding with the denominations of United States notes. The coin deposited for or representing the certificates of deposit shall be retained in the Treasury for the payment of the same on demand. Said certificates shall be receivable for customs, taxes, and all public dues, and when so received may be reissued; and such certificates, as also silver certificates, when held by any national banking association, shall be counted as part of its lawful reserve, and no national banking association shall be a member of any clearing house

* These certificates were retired during the month of November, the fractional coin which they represented having been presented and redeemed in lawful money.

in which such certificates shall not be receivable in the settlement of clearing-house balances.

The amount of silver certificates on November 1, 1885, was $125,053,-286, and the amount held by the Treasury was $31,906,514, leaving the amount outstanding $93,146,772.

The amount of gold certificates on November 1, 1885, was $140,136,610, and the amount held by the Treasury was $31,115,850, leaving the amount outstanding $109,020,760.

On October 1, 1885, the national banks held $2,274,670 of silver certificates, and $72,986,340 of gold certificates, issued under the acts of March 3, 1863, and July 12, 1882.

In addition to the certificates heretofore mentioned, the national banks of New York City held on October 1, 1885, $1,945,000 clearing-house loan certificates, issued in pursuance of resolutions adopted May 14, 1884, to the Metropolitan National Bank, now in liquidation, and State banks in New York City held $735,000, the total outstanding on that date being $2,680,000. On the 13th of October $130,000 of these certificates were paid by the Metropolitan National Bank, leaving the aggregate amount outstanding on that date $2,550,000. These certificates are secured by a deposit in trust of certain securities and bills receivable with the loan committee of the New York Clearing-House Association, and bear interest at the rate of 5 per cent. per annum. They are carried by the associated banks among their loans, and were more fully described in the report of this office for the year 1884, pages 36 and 37.

RESERVE.

The following table exhibits the amount of net deposits and the reserve required thereon by the act of June 20, 1874, together with the amount and classification of reserve held by the national banks in New York City, in the other reserve cities, and by the remaining banks, at the dates of their reports in October of each year from 1875 to 1883, on September 30, 1884, and on October 1, 1885:

NEW YORK CITY.

	Number of banks.	Net deposits.	Reserve required.	Reserve held.		Classification of reserve.			
				Amount	Ratio to deposits.	Specie.	Other lawful money.	Due from agents.	Redemption fund.
		Millions.	Millions.	Millions.	Per cent.	Millions.	Millions.	Millions.	Millions.
Oct. 1, 1875...	48	202.3	50.6	60.6	29.9	5.0	54.4	....	1.1
Oct. 2, 1876..	47	197.9	49.5	60.7	30.7	14.6	45.3	....	0.8
Oct. 1, 1877	47	174.9	43.7	48.1	27.5	13.0	34.3	....	0.8
Oct. 1, 1878.	47	189.8	47.4	50.9	26.8	13.3	36.5	....	1.1
Oct. 2, 1879...	47	210 2	52.6	53.1	25.3	19.4	32.6	....	1.1
Oct. 1, 1880	47	268.1	67.0	70.6	26.4	58.7	11.0	....	0.9
Oct. 1, 1881	48	268.8	67.2	62.5	23.3	50.6	10.9	....	1.0
Oct. 3, 1882.	50	254.0	63.5	64.4	25.4	44.5	18.9	....	1.0
Oct. 2, 1883.	48	266.9	66.7	70.8	26.5	50.3	19.7	....	0.9
Sept. 30, 1884	44	255.0	63.7	90.8	35.6	63.1	27.0	....	0.7
Oct. 1. 1885.	44	312.9	78.2	115.7	37.0	91.5	23.7	....	0.5

OTHER RESERVE CITIES.

	Number of banks.	Net deposits.	Reserve required.	Reserve held.		Classification of reserve.			
				Amount	Ratio to deposits.	Specie.	Other lawful money.	Due from agents.	Redemption fund.
Oct. 1, 1875	188	223.9	56.0	74.5	33.3	1.5	37.1	32.3	3.6
Oct. 2, 1876..	189	217.0	54.2	76.1	35.1	4.0	37.1	32.0	3.0
Oct. 1, 1877	188	204.1	51.0	67.3	33.0	5.6	34.3	24.4	3.0
Oct. 1, 1878..	184	199.9	50.0	71.1	35.6	9.4	29.4	29.1	3.2
Oct. 2, 1879..	181	228.8	57.2	83.5	36.5	11.3	33.0	35.7	3.5
Oct. 1, 1880..	184	289.4	72.4	105.2	36.2	28.3	25.0	48.2	3.7
Oct. 1, 1881	189	335.4	83.9	100.8	30.0	34.6	21.9	40.6	3.7
Oct. 3, 1882.	193	318.8	79.7	89.1	28.0	28.3	24.1	33.2	3.5
Oct. 2, 1883	200	323.9	81.0	100.6	31.1	26.3	30.1	40.8	3.4
Sept. 30, 1884.	203	307.9	77.0	99.0	32.2	30.3	33.3	32.3	3.1
Oct. 1, 1885.	203	364.5	91.1	122.2	34.5	42.0	34.9	42.4	2.9

STATES AND TERRITORIES.

Oct. 1, 1875	1,851	307.9	46.3	100.1	32.5	1.6	53.3	11.5
Oct. 2, 1876	1,853	291.7	43.8	99.0	34.3	2.7	55.4	10.8
Oct. 1, 1877	1,845	290.1	43.6	95.4	32.9	4.2	46.7	10.7
Oct. 1, 1878... .	1,822	289.1	43.4	106.1	36.7	8.0	56.0	11.0
Oct. 2, 1879	1,820	329.0	49.5	124.3	37.7	11.5	71.3	11.2
Oct. 1, 1880	1,859	410.5	61.6	147.2	35.8	21.2	83.9	11.1
Oct. 1, 1881 ...	1,895	507.2	76.1	15-.3	31.2	27.5	92.4	11.4
Oct. 3, 1882....	2,026	545.8	81.0	150.4	27.5	30.0	80.1	11.4
Oct. 2, 1883 ...	2,253	577.9	86.7	157.5	27.2	31.2	80.8	11.3
Sept. 30, 1884 ..	2,417	535.8	80.4	156.3	29.2	35.2	30.9	79.7	10.6
Oct. 1, 1885	2,467	570.8	85.6	177.5	31.1	41.5	29.9	95.9	10.2

SUMMARY.

Oct. 1, 1875 ...	2,087	734.1	152.2	235.1	32.0	8.1	125.2	85.6	16.2
Oct. 2, 1876. ..	2,089	706.6	147.5	236.7	33.5	21.3	113.4	87.4	14.6
Oct. 1, 1877 ...	2,080	669.1	138.3	210.8	31.5	22.8	100.2	73.3	14.5
Oct. 1, 1878... .,	2,053	678.8	140.8	228.1	33.6	30.7	97.0	85.1	15.3
Oct. 2, 1879. ...	2,048	708.9	159.3	260.9	33.9	42.2	95.9	107.0	15.8
Oct. 1, 1880	2,090	968.0	201.0	323.0	33.4	108.2	64.3	134.6	15.9
Oct. 1, 1881....	2,132	1,111.6	227.2	321.6	28.9	112.7	59.9	133.0	16.1
Oct. 3, 1882.....	2,269	1,118.6	225.1	303.9	27.2	102.8	72.0	113.3	15.8
Oct. 2, 1883 ...	2,501	1,168.7	234.4	328.9	28.1	107.8	80.6	124.9	15.6
Sept. 30, 1884 ..	2,664	1,098.7	221.1	346.1	31.6	128.6	91.2	112.0	14.3
Oct. 1, 1885.....	2,714	1,248.2	254.9	415.4	33.3	175.0	88.5	138.3	13.6

The following table, compiled from returns made to the clearing-house by the national banks in New York City, exhibits the movement of their reserve, weekly, during October, for the last nine years :

Week ending—	Specie.	Legal-tenders.	Total.	Ratio of reserve to—	
				Circulation and deposits.	Deposits.
				Per cent	Per cent
October 7, 1876	$17,682,600	$45,535,600	$63,218,200	30.5	82.4
October 14, 1876	16,233,600	43,004,600	59,238,200	28.8	31.1
October 21, 1876	15,577,500	41,421,700	56,999,200	27.8	30.0
October 28, 1876	14,011,600	41,615,600	55,657,200	28.0	30.3
October 6, 1877	14,665,600	36,168,300	50,833,900	27.0	29.5
October 13, 1877	14,726,500	35,178,900	49,905,400	26.7	29.2
October 20, 1877	14,087,400	35,101,700	49,189,100	26.5	29.0
October 27, 1877	15,209,000	34,367,800	49,576,800	26.8	29.4
October 5, 1878	14,995,800	38,304,900	53,300,700	25.7	28.4
October 12, 1878	12,184,600	37,685,100	49,869,700	24.4	27.0
October 19, 1878	13,531,400	36,576,000	50,107,400	24.7	27.2
October 26, 1878	17,384,200	35,690,500	53,074,700	25.8	28.5
October 4, 1879	18,979,600	34,368,000	53,347,600	23.3	25.8
October 11, 1879	20,901,800	32,820,300	53,722,100	23.4	25.9
October 18, 1879	24,686,500	29,305,200	53,991,700	23.5	26.1
October 25, 1879	25,636,000	26,713,900	52,349,900	23.0	25.5
October 2, 1880	59,823,700	11,129,100	70,952,800	25.4	26.4
October 9, 1880	62,521,300	10,785,000	73,306,300	25.4	27.2
October 16, 1880	62,760,600	10,939,200	73,699,800	25.5	27.1
October 23, 1880	60,888,200	10,988,200	71,876,400	24.8	26.6
October 30, 1880	61,471,600	10,925,000	72,396,600	25.0	26.7
October 1, 1881	54,954,600	12,150,400	67,105,000	23.1	24.8
October 8, 1881	53,287,900	12,153,800	65,441,700	23.1	24.9
October 15, 1881	51,008,300	12,452,700	63,461,000	23.2	23.0
October 22, 1881	54,016,200	12,496,500	66,512,700	24.6	26.6
October 29, 1881	55,961,200	12,947,900	68,909,100	25.6	27.4
October 7, 1882	47,016,000	18,384,500	65,400,500	24.0	26.3
October 14, 1882	48,281,000	18,002,700	66,283,700	24.7	26.6
October 21, 1882	49,518,200	17,023,900	66,542,100	25.0	26.8
October 28, 1882	48,374,200	17,204,700	65,578,900	24.8	26.5
October 6, 1883	51,586,700	20,122,500	71,709,200	25.5	27.0
October 13, 1883	50,894,000	21,145,800	72,039,800	25.4	26.8
October 20, 1883	47,262,900	20,719,700	67,982,600	24.5	25.9
October 27, 1883	46,372,800	20,617,600	66,990,400	24.5	25.9
October 4, 1884	67,470,600	25,817,300	93,287,900	34.5	36.3
October 11, 1884	68,922,500	27,654,100	96,576,600	35.2	36.9
October 18, 1884	67,575,400	27,875,500	95,454,900	34.8	36.5
October 25, 1884	67,638,000	27,354,200	94,992,200	34.6	36.3
October 3, 1885	92,351,600	24,516,600	116,868,200	36.0	37.1
October 10, 1885	93,642,500	23,002,000	116,644,500	35.8	37.0
October 17, 1885	91,945,300	22,221,100	114,166,400	34.9	36.0
October 24, 1885	87,309,100	21,059,800	108,368,900	33.5	34.5
October 30, 1885	84,954,600	21,874,900	106,829,500	33.0	34.1

UNITED STATES LEGAL-TENDER NOTES AND NATIONAL-BANK CIR-CULATION.

The acts of Febuary 25, 1862, July 11, 1862, and March 3, 1863, each authorize the issue of 150 millions of dollars of legal-tender notes, making an aggregate of 450 millions of dollars.

On February 3, 1864, the amount of such notes outstanding was $449,479,222, which was the highest amount outstanding at any one time. The act of June 30, 1864, provided that the total amount of United States notes issued, or to be issued, should not exceed 400 millions of dollars, and such additional sum, not exceeding 50 millions, as might be temporarily required for the redemption of temporary loans.

By the act of June 20, 1874, the maximum amount was fixed at 382 millions. Section 3, act of January 14, 1875, authorized an increase of the circulation of national banks in accordance with existing law, without respect to the limit previously existing, and required the Secretary of the Treasury to retire legal-tender notes, to an amount equal to 80 per cent. of the national bank notes thereafter issued, until the amount of such legal-tender notes outstanding should be 300 millions and no more. Under the operations of this act $35,318,984 of legal-tender notes were retired, leaving the amount in circulation on May 31, 1878, the date of the repeal of the act, $346,681,016, which is the amount outstanding.

In the following table are given the amounts and kinds of the outstanding currency of the United States, and of the national banks on January 1, of each year, from 1866 to 1885, and on November 1, 1885, to which is prefixed the amount on August 31, 1865, when the public debt reached its maximum.

Date.	United States issues.			Notes of national banks, including gold notes.	Aggregate.	Currency price of $100 gold.	Gold price of $100 currency.
	Legal-tender notes.	Old demand notes.	Fractional currency.				
Aug. 31, 1865...	$432,553,012	$402,965	$26,344,742	$176,213,955	$635,515,674	$144 25	$69 82
Jan. 1, 1866	425,839,319	392,670	26,000,420	236,636,998	688,867,907	144 50	69 20
Jan. 1, 1867 ...	380,276,160	221,632	28,732,812	298,588,419	707,819,023	133 00	75 18
Jan. 1, 1868 ...	356,000,000	159,127	31,597,583	299,846,206	647,602,916	133 25	75 04
Jan. 1, 1869 ...	356,000,000	128,098	34,215,715	299,747,569	690,091,382	135 00	74 07
Jan. 1, 1870 ...	356,000,000	113,098	39,762,664	299,629,322	695,505,084	120 00	83 33
Jan. 1, 1871 ...	356,000,000	101,086	39,995,089	306,307,672	702,403,847	110 75	90 29
Jan. 1, 1872 ...	357,500,000	92,801	40,767,877	328,465,481	726,826,109	109 50	91 32
Jan. 1, 1873 ...	358,557,907	84,387	45,722,061	344,582,812	748,947,167	112 00	89 28
Jan. 1, 1874 ...	378,401,702	79,637	48,544,792	350,848,236	777,874,367	110 25	90 70
Jan. 1, 1875 ...	382,000,000	72,317	46,390,598	354,128,250	782,591,165	112 50	88 89
Jan. 1, 1876 ...	371,827,220	69,642	44,147,072	346,479,756	762,523,690	112 75	88 69
Jan. 1, 1877	366,655,084	65,462	26,348,206	321,595,006	714,664,358	107 00	93 46
Jan. 1, 1878	349,943,776	63,532	17,764,109	321,672,505	689,443,922	102 87	97 21
Jan. 1, 1879	346,681,016	62,045	16,108,159	323,791,674	686,642,884	100 00	100 00
Jan. 1, 1880	346,681,016	61,350	15,674,304	342,387,336	704,804,006	100 00	100 00
Jan. 1, 1881 ...	346,681,016	60,745	15,523,464	344,355,203	706,620,428	100 00	100 00
Jan 1, 1882 ..	346,681,016	59,920	15,451,861	362,421,988	724,614,785	100 00	100 00
Jan. 1, 1883 ...	346,681,016	59,205	15,398,008	361,882,791	724,021,110	100 00	100 00
Jan. 1, 1884	346,681,016	58,680	15,365,362	349,949,352	712,054,410	100 00	100 00
Jan. 1, 1885 ...	346,681,016	58,240	15,347,277	329,158,623	691,245,156	100 00	100 00
Nov. 1, 1885 ..	346,681,016	57,825	15,337,096	*315,847,168	677,923,105	100 00	100 00

*Includes $384,269 notes of gold banks and $568,081 mutilated currency in transit.

The act of June 20, 1874, provided that any national banking association might withdraw its circulating notes upon the deposit of lawful money with the Treasurer of the United States, in sums of not less than $9,000. Under this act, and on account of liquidating and insolvent banks, and under the act of July 12, 1882, which provides for a deposit of lawful money to retire the old circulation of national banks whose corporate existence has been extended, $239,347,068 of lawful money has been deposited with the Treasurer. This includes $2,663,720 for the redemption of the notes of national gold banks, and $14,125,820 for the redemption of national-bank notes under section 6 of the act of July 12, 1882. Since June 20, 1874, $203,617,764 of bank notes have been redeemed, destroyed, and retired. This includes $2,279,451 of the notes of national gold banks and $4,425,625 of the notes of national banks whose corporate existence has been extended under the act of July 12, 1882.

The following table shows by States the amount of additional circulation issued during the year ending October 31, 1885, and the total amount of such circulation issued since June 20, 1874. It also shows the amount of circulation retired during the year, and the total amount retired since June 20, 1874:

States and Territories.	Additional circulation issued.	Circulation retired.		
		Act June 20, 1874.	Liquidating banks.	Total.
Maine	$304,750	$69,100	$164,495	$233,595
New Hampshire	150	36,680	69,170	105,850
Vermont	158,220	218,570	329,846	548,416
Massachusetts	926,240	3,928,685	1,765,957	5,694,622
Rhode Island	57,360	763,110	31,611	794,721
Connecticut	140,000	386,733	248,656	653,389
New York	1,687,810	3,457,210	1,968,677	5,425,887
New Jersey	398,760	718,650	196,442	915,092
Pennsylvania	1,107,950	1,664,490	1,074,609	2,739,099
Delaware	49,500	4,100		4,100
Maryland	150,500	513,750	6,740	520,490
District of Columbia		10,790	3,628	14,418
Virginia	45,000	220,070	75,853	295,923
West Virginia	19,310	64,830	5,034	69,864
North Carolina	45,000	116,500	22,525	139,025
South Carolina		36,745		36,745
Georgia	18,900	91,720	7,449	99,169
Florida	49,500			
Alabama	90,000	71,520	23,452	94,972
Mississippi	33,740	5,360	15	5,375
Louisiana	225,800	188,470	4,345	192,815
Texas	191,880	200,630	7,580	208,210
Arkansas	117,000	15,110	9,740	24,850
Kentucky	126,540	561,060	92,482	653,542
Tennessee	22,490	163,100	119,093	282,193
Missouri	308,240	333,645	57,371	391,016
Ohio	1,598,920	1,662,250	1,107,123	2,769,273
Indiana	874,650	494,450	771,032	1,265,482
Illinois	649,010	763,670	414,714	1,178,384
Michigan	374,980	385,890	379,638	765,528
Wisconsin	123,270	175,470	139,994	315,454
Iowa	177,750	588,680	176,026	764,706
Minnesota	50,850	189,410	129,626	319,036
Kansas	291,840	90,010	21,468	111,478
Nebraska	173,320	59,580	42,823	102,403
Nevada			130	130
Oregon	20,250	4,000		4,000
Colorado	83,190	69,990	43,631	113,621
Utah	45,000	56,300	1,064	57,364
Idaho		24,820		24,820
Montana	36,000	65,760	3,280	69,040
Wyoming	11,250	9,250		9,250
New Mexico		22,210		22,210
Dakota	103,470	58,675	15,242	73,817
Washington	101,250	40,410	6,410	46,820
Arizona		2,500	11,370	13,870
California "currency"	135,010	142,770	22,250	165,020
	11,142,650	18,746,593	9,570,591	28,317,184
Surrendered to this office and retired				375,630
		18,746,593	9,570,591	28,692,814
From June 20, 1874, to October 31, 1884	170,074,049	140,163,218	32,857,909	173,021,127
Surrendered to this office same dates				13,878,309
Grand total	181,216,699	158,909,811	42,428,500	215,592,250

In the above table gold notes are excluded.

The amount of additional circulation issued to national banks for the year ending November 1, 1885, was $11,142,650, including $4,297,400 issued to banks organized during the year.

During the year ending November 1, 1885, lawful money to the amount of $26,219,810 was deposited with the Treasurer to retire circulation, of which amount $8,457,295 was deposited by banks in liquidation, $7,772,-165 by banks reducing circulation, under the act of June 20, 1874, and $9,990,350 by banks retiring old circulation, under the act of July 12, 1882. The amount previously deposited under the acts of June 20, 1874, and July 12, 1882, was $171,368,662; by banks in liquidation, $53,339,686; making a total of $250,928,158. Deducting from the total the amount of circulating notes redeemed and destroyed without reissue, $211,769,448, there remained in the hands of the Treasurer on November 1, 1884, $39,158,710 of lawful money for the redemption and retirement of bank circulation.

The portion of lawful money on deposit by insolvent banks, by banks in voluntary liquidation, and by banks reducing or retiring their circulation on the first of each of the last five months was as follows:

	July 1.	August 1.	September 1.	October 1.	November 1.
Insolvent banks	$745,789	$698,584	$715,203	$683,348	$584,960
Liquidating banks	13,569,286	13,796,666	13,774,242	13,565,143	12,778,010
Reducing under act of June 20, 1874	19,784,295	18,699,950	18,029,110	17,443,820	16,095,545
Retiring under act of July 12, 1882	5,003,783	5,889,173	6,685,023	8,181,837	9,700,195
Totals	39,103,153	39,084,373	39,203,578	39,871,143	*39,158,710

* Does not include $384,269 on deposit to retire notes of gold banks.

DENOMINATIONS OF PAPER CIRCULATION OF THE UNITED STATES, THE IMPERIAL BANK OF GERMANY, THE BANK OF FRANCE, AND THE BANK OF ENGLAND.

In accordance with the law, no national-bank notes of a less denomination than five dollars have been issued since January 1, 1879, when the amount outstanding was $7,718,747. Since that date the amount of ones and twos issued by the banks has been reduced $7,283,033, leaving the amount outstanding on November 1, 1885, $435,714, and during the same period the legal-tender notes of these denominations have been increased $5,645,960. The total decrease of the amount of ones and twos outstanding in national-bank and legal-tender notes is $1,637,073.

The following table exhibits by denominations the amount of national-bank and legal-tender notes outstanding on October 31, 1885, and the aggregate amounts of both kinds of notes at the same periods in 1883 and 1884:

| Denominations. | 1885. | | 1884. | 1883 |
	National-bank notes.	Legal-tender notes.	Aggregate.	Aggregate.	Aggregate.
Ones	$435, 714	$22, 703, 459	$23, 139, 173	$27, 258, 839	$30, 785, 265
Twos	237, 284	23, 235, 136	23, 472, 420	27, 067, 206	27, 510, 196
Fives	81, 956, 670	84, 068, 279	166, 024, 949	163, 363, 205	164, 517, 620
Tens	104, 211, 290	71, 003, 390	175, 214, 680	180, 491, 886	189, 275, 406
Twenties	75, 087, 520	56, 941, 267	137, 028, 787	135, 277, 089	142, 382, 409
Fifties	20, 638, 550	22, 896, 595	43, 535, 145	44, 617, 045	46, 278, 145
One hundreds	31, 576, 400	20, 645, 390	61, 221, 790	66, 170, 690	65, 991, 590
Five hundreds	59, 500	15, 152, 000	15, 740, 500	16, 063, 500	15, 895, 500
One thousands	131, 000	21, 910, 500	22, 041, 500	19, 659, 500	15, 429, 500
Five thousands		95, 000	95, 000	105, 000	255, 000
Ten thousands		30, 000	30, 000	60, 000	120, 000
Add for unredeemed fragments of national-bank notes	+21, 890		+21 890	+20, 749	+19, 701
Deduct for legal-tender notes destroyed in Chicago fire		−1, 000, 000	−1, 000, 000	−1, 000, 000	−1, 000, 000
Total	*314, 894, 818	346, 681, 016	661, 575, 834	679, 154, 709	697, 460, 452

* Exclusive of $568,081 due to banks for mutilated notes destroyed and to be replaced by new notes and of $384,269 notes of gold banks.

The amount of one and two dollar national-bank notes outstanding is a little more than one-fifth of 1 per cent. of the whole circulation of the banks; the fives constitute 26 per cent., the tens 33 per cent., the twenties 23.8 per cent., and the fifties and larger notes about 17 per cent. of the entire circulation.

Of the entire amount of national-bank and legal-tender notes outstanding, about 7 per cent. consists of one and two dollar notes; nearly 32.2 per cent. of ones, twos, and fives, 58.6 per cent. is in notes of a less denomination than $20, and about 78.6 per cent. is in notes of a lower denomination than $50. Of the entire issue, about 21.5 per cent. is in denominations of fifties, one hundreds, five hundreds, and one thousands.

There are outstanding nineteen legal-tender notes, of the denomination of $5,000, and three notes of the denomination of $10,000.

The following table * exhibits by denominations the circulation of the Imperial Bank of Germany on December 31, 1884, in thalers and marks, which have been converted into our currency.

| Thalers. | | | | Marks. | | | |
Number of notes.	Denominations.	Value of each note in dollars.	Amount in dollars (thaler = 75 cents).	Number of notes.	Denominations.	Value of each note in dollars.	Amount in dollars (mark = 25 cents).
	Thalers.				Marks.		
76	500	$375 00	$28, 500	266, 959½	1, 000	$250	$66, 739, 875
2, 000	100	75 00	150, 000	128, 771	500	125	16, 096, 375
1, 643½	50	37 50	61, 631	5, 209, 448	100	25	130, 236, 200
8, 302	25	18 75	155, 662				
8, 675½	10	7 50	65, 066				
20, 697			460, 859	5, 605, 178½			213, 072, 450

The circulation of the Imperial Bank of Germany on January 1, 1885, was $213,534,250, showing an increase of $5,751,656 over that of

* London Bankers' Magazine, October, 1885, page 946.

the preceding year, although there was on an average $1,085,000 less in circulation than the average of the previous year. On January 1, 1880, the circulation was $198,201,144, and during the past five years the increase has averaged about $10,000,000.

The following table* gives the circulation of the Bank of France and its branches, with the number of notes and the denominations in francs and in dollars on January 1, 1885:

Number of notes.	Denominations (francs).	Value of each note in dollars.	Amount in francs.	Amount in dollars (francs = 20 cents).
5	5,000	$1,000	25,000	$5,000
1,186,638	1,000	200	1,186,638,000	237,327,600
589,781	500	100	294,890,500	58,978,100
2,619	200	40	523,800	104,760
12,446,499	100	20	1,244,649,900	248,929,980
4,931,340	50	10	246,567,000	49,313,400
20,859	25	5	521,475	104,295
150,046	20	4	3,000,925	600,185
167,163	5	1	835,815	167,163
1,200	Forms out of date.	....	420,175	84,035
19,496,150	....	....	2,978,672,590	595,614,518

The amount of circulation of the Bank of France on January 1, 1884, was 3,161,804,536 francs, or say $632,360,907, showing a decrease of 183,731,946 francs, or $36,746,389, between that time and January 1, 1885, the date of the foregoing table; and since January 30, 1879, an increase of 687,101,760 francs, or $137,420,352.

It will be seen that the Imperial Bank of Germany has in circulation no notes of a less denomination than seven dollars and a half (10 thalers), and issues none of less than $25 (100 marks), and that the Bank of France issues less than a million of dollars in value of notes of a less denomination than $10. The Bank of England issues no notes of less than £5, or $25, and the Irish and Scotch banks none of less than £1, or $5.

DISTRIBUTION OF COIN AND PAPER CURRENCY.

In previous reports tables have been given showing the amount of coin and currency in the country and its distribution, the amount in the Treasury, in the banks, and among the people on January 1, 1879, the date of the resumption of specie payments, and on November 1 of each of the last four years preceding the date of this report. These tables are again presented, the amounts on November 1, 1881, being omitted, while those on November 1, 1885, are added. The amounts of gold and silver in the country available for circulation are based upon the estimates of the Director of the Mint for January 1, 1879. The amounts of gold for the succeeding dates have been obtained by adding the gold production of the country, less the amounts used in the arts, from estimates of the same officer, adding the excess of gold importations during the year, or deducting the excess of gold exportations for the same period, according to the reports of the Bureau of Statistics. The amounts of silver are obtained by adding for each year the amount of silver dollars and fractional silver coined, less amounts recoined. For the year 1885 the silver bullion purchased by the Government for coinage and on hand on November 1 is included.

* London Bankers' Magazine, August, 1885, page 699.

For the year ending November 1, 1885, the production of gold by the mines of the United States is estimated to have been about $30,800,000 During the period from November 1, 1884, to October 1, 1885, the amount of foreign and domestic gold coin and bullion imported in excess of the amount exported has been $12,315,915, making an increase in the stock of gold in the country of $43,115,915. From this amount must be deducted the amount estimated by the Director of the Mint to have been used in the arts during the same period, $12,000,000, leaving $31,115,915 as the increase in the stock of gold coin and bullion in the country.

The total excess of imports of gold over exports of the same from the date of resumption to October 1, 1885, has been $178,028,043, and the total estimated gold product of the mines of the United States for the same period has been about $222,525,000. The total amount of standard silver dollars coined during the year ending November 1, 1885, has been $28,528,602; of subsidiary silver coin, $195,977; and there was of subsidiary coin presented to the mint for recoinage $641,727, thereby reducing the amount of such coin $445,750. The total amount of standard silver dollars coined since the passage of the act of February 28, 1878, authorizing that coinage, up to November 1, 1885, has been $213,259,431. The following table, based upon the estimates and figures given above, shows the amount of coin and currency in the country on January 1, 1879, and on November 1 of the years named:

	January 1, 1879.	November 1, 1882.	November 1, 1883.	November 1, 1884.	November 1, 1885.
Gold coin and bullion	$278,310,126	$547,356,262	$581,970,254	$585,611,872	*$586,727,787
Silver coin	106,573,803	208,744,424	242,701,932	275,735,439	307,658,827
Legal-tender notes	346,681,016	346,681,016	346,681,016	346,681,016	346,681,016
National-bank notes	323,791,674	362,727,747	352,013,787	333,559,813	†315,847,168
Totals	1,055,356,619	1,465,509,449	1,523,366,989	1,541,588,140	1,556,914,798

* In obtaining the amount of gold November 1, 1885, the estimated amount on November 1, 1884, has been reduced by $30,000,000, which amount the Director of the Mint has recently estimated was used in the arts between July 1, 1873, and June 30, 1880, and was not deducted in the original estimate for July 1, 1879.

† The sum of $39,542,979 in lawful money has been deposited by the national banks to retire circulation of a like amount which has not yet been presented for redemption.

There has been no change in the aggregate of legal-tender notes, which still remains as fixed by the act of May 31, 1878. National bank notes have decreased $17,712,645 during the year. The amounts of gold and silver have increased $31,115,915 and $31,923,388, respectively, and the total increase during the year in gold, silver, and currency was $45,326,658. The reduction of former estimates of gold by $30,000,000, as explained in foot-note, has apparently reduced the aggregate increase of gold to $1,115,915, and the aggregate increase of both gold and silver to $33,039,303. The table below gives the portion of the gold, silver, and currency held by the United States Treasury and by the national and State banks. The amounts in the United States Treasury are for the corresponding dates with those in the preceding table. The amounts in the national banks are for the corresponding dates nearest thereto on which returns were made to the Comptroller, viz: January 1, 1879, October 3, 1882, October 2, 1883, September 30, 1884, and October 1, 1885. The amounts in the State banks, trust companies, and savings banks have been compiled in this office from official reports up to the dates nearest to those given in the table.

	January 1, 1879.	November 1, 1882.	November 1, 1883.	November 1, 1884.	November 1, 1885.
GOLD.					
In the Treasury, less certificates	$112,703,342	$148,435,473	$157,353,760	$134,670,790	$142,338,589
In national banks, including certicates	35,039,201	94,127,324	97,570,057	117,185,407	161,657,121
In State banks, including certificates	10,937,812	17,892,500	18,255,300	25,928,757	31,255,789
Total gold	158,680,355	260,455,297	273,179,117	277,784,954	335,251,499
SILVER.					
In the Treasury, standard silver dollars	17,249,740	92,414,977	116,036,450	142,926,725	163,817,342
In the Treasury, bullion	9,121,417	4,012,503	4,936,365	4,646,497	3,840,536
In the Treasury, fractional coin	6,948,194	26,749,482	26,712,424	29,346,757	22,965,536
In national banks	6,460,557	8,234,739	10,247,926	8,092,557	9,120,802
Total silver	38,879,908	131,411,701	157,933,165	185,012,536	199,744,216
CURRENCY.					
n the Treasury, less certificates	44,425,655	26,224,248	30,996,217	26,258,827	27,550,341
In national banks, including certificates	126,491,720	92,544,767	103,316,809	114,507,113	111,600,884
In State banks, including certificates	25,944,485	27,086,482	28,250,062	32,659,605	39,552,017
In savings banks	14,513,779	14,724,978	12,998,594	14,079,452	13,423,064
Total cu. rency	211,375,639	160,580,475	175,570,682	187,504,997	192,126,306
Grand totals	408,935,902	552,447,473	606,682,964	650,302,487	727,122,021

If the aggregates of gold, silver, and currency for the several dates in the above table be deducted from the amounts of the same items at corresponding dates in the table which precedes it, the remainders will be approximately the amounts in the hands of the people at corresponding dates.

	January 1, 1879.	November 1, 1881.	November 1, 1882.	November 1, 1883.	November 1, 1884.	November 1, 1885
Gold	$119,629,771	$256,016,829	$286,900,965	$308,791,137	$307,826,918	$251,476,288
Silver	67,693,895	78,377,937	77,332,723	84,768,767	90,722,903	107,914,611
Currency	459,097,051	567,445,959	548,828,288	523,124,121	492,735,832	470,401,878
Total	646,420,717	901,840,725	913,061,976	916,684,025	891,285,653	*820,792,777

* Included necessarily in these several amounts estimated in the hands of the people are large sums held by private bankers and such State banks and Trust companies as do not make regular reports.

The gold in the Treasury, including bullion in the process of coinage, has increased during the year $7,667,799, and in the banks has increased $44,471,713. The paper currency in the Treasury has increased $1,291,514, and in the banks has decreased $2,906,229. The decrease of gold outside of the Treasury and the banks has been $26,350,629, and in silver coin there has been an increase of $14,240,831. The decrease of paper currency, exclusive of silver certificates, has been $22,334,589. In the foregoing tables the silver certificates issued by the Treasury have not been included, but the standard silver dollars held for their redemption, form a portion of the silver coin in the Treasury. The silver certificates in the hands of the people and the banks at the following dates were as follows:

January 1, 1879	$413,360
November 1, 1880	19,780,240
November 1, 1881	58,838,770
November 1, 1882	65,620,450
November 1, 1883	85,334,381
November 1, 1884	100,741,562
November 1, 1885	93,146,772

It will be seen that the amount of these certificates in circulation has decreased $7,594,790 during the year.

The gold certificates issued under section 12 of the act of July 12, 1882, outstanding in the hands of the people and banks on November 1, 1882, November 1, 1883, November 1, 1884, and November 1, 1885, not including the amount in the Treasury, were $6,962,280, $48,869,940, $85,301,190, and $106,465,420, respectively.

SPECIE IN BANKS AND IN THE TREASURY OF THE UNITED STATES, AND ESTIMATED AMOUNT IN THE COUNTRY—SPECIE IN THE BANK OF ENGLAND AND IN THE BANK OF FRANCE.

The following table exhibits the amount of specie held by the national banks at the dates of their reports for the last twelve years, the coin and coin certificates held by the New York City banks being stated separately:

Dates.	Held by national banks in New York City.				Held by other national banks.	Aggregate.
	Coin.	U. S. gold certificates.	Clearing-house certificates.	Total.		
Sept. 12, 1873..	$1,063,210 55	$13,522,600	....	$14,585,810 55	$5,282,658 90	$19,868,469 45
Dec. 26, 1873..	1,376,170 50	18,325,760	....	19,701,930 50	7,205,107 08	26,907,037 58
Feb. 27, 1874..	1,167,820 09	23,518,640	....	24,686,460 09	8,679,403 49	33,365,863 58
May 1, 1874..	1,530,282 10	23,454,660	....	24,984,942 10	7,585,027 16	32,569,969 26
June 26, 1874..	1,842,525 00	13,671,660	....	15,514,185 00	6,812,022 27	22,326,207 27
Oct. 2, 1874..	1,291,780 56	13,114,480	....	14,406,266 56	6,834,678 67	21,240,945 23
Dec. 31, 1874..	1,443,215 42	14,410,940	....	15,854,155 42	6,582,605 62	22,436,761 04
Mar. 1, 1875..	1,084,555 54	10,622,160	....	11,706,715 54	4,960,390 63	16,667,106 17
May 1, 1875..	930,105 76	5,753,220	....	6,683,325 76	3,937,035 88	10,620,361 64
June 30, 1875..	1,023,015 86	12,642,180	....	13,665,195 86	5,294,386 44	18,959,582 30
Oct. 1, 1875 .	753,904 90	4,201,720	....	4,955,624 90	3,094,704 83	8,050,329 73
Dec. 17, 1875..	869,436 72	12,532,810	....	13,402,246 72	3,668,659 18	17,070,905 90
Mar. 10, 1876..	3,261,131 36	19,086,920	....	22,348,051 36	6,729,294 49	29,077,345 85
May 12, 1876 .	832,313 70	15,183,760	....	16,016,073 70	5,698,520 66	21,714,594 36
June 30, 1876..	1,214,522 92	16,872,780	....	18,087,302 92	7,131,167 00	25,218,469 92
Oct. 2, 1876..	1,120,814 34	13,446,760	....	14,576,574 34	6,785,070 69	21,361,651 03
Dec. 22, 1876..	1,434,701 83	21,602,900	....	23,037,601 83	9,962,046 06	32,999,647 89
Jan. 20, 1877..	669,284 94	33,620,660	....	35,295,944 94	14,410,322 61	40,709,267 55
Apr. 14, 1877..	1,930,725 50	13,889,180	....	15,820,005 50	11,240,132 19	27,070,037 78
June 22, 1877..	1,423,258 17	10,324,320	....	11,747,578 17	9,588,417 89	21,335,996 06
Oct. 1, 1877..	1,538,486 47	11,409,920	....	12,948,406 47	9,710,413 84	22,658,820 31
Dec. 28, 1877..	1,055,716 20	19,119,080	....	21,074,826 20	11,832,924 50	32,907,750 70
Mar. 15, 1878..	2,428,797 44	35,003,220	....	37,432,017 44	17,290,040 58	54,722,058 02
May 1, 1878..	2,688,092 06	25,397,640	....	28,085,732 06	17,938,024 00	46,023,756 06
June 20, 1878..	1,905,705 22	11,954,500	....	13,860,205 22	15,391,264 55	29,251,469 77
Oct. 1, 1878..	1,779,792 43	11,514,810	....	13,294,602 43	17,394,004 16	30,688,606 59
Dec. 6, 1878..	4,009,299 01	12,277,180	....	16,286,479 01	18,068,771 35	34,352,250 36
Jan. 1, 1879..	5,421,552 49	12,739,544	....	18,161,092 49	23,338,664 83	41,499,757 32
Apr. 4, 1879..	5,312,966 90	12,220,940	....	17,533,906 90	23,614,656 51	41,148,563 41
June 14, 1879..	6,058,472 34	12,291,270	....	18,349,742 34	23,983,545 10	42,333,287 44
Oct. 2, 1879..	7,218,967 09	12,130,900	....	19,349,867 09	22,823,873 54	42,173,731 23
Dec. 12, 1879 .	20,096,240 64	8,366,140	$21,509,000 00	50,031,380 64	28,081,651 95	79,013,041 59
Feb. 21, 1880..	12,252,541 44	7,464,650	35,855,000 00	55,572,191 44	33,301,264 55	89,442,651 73
Apr. 23, 1880..	12,505,720 49	6,914,250	25,458,000 00	44,967,970 49	41,461,761 62	86,429,732 21
June 11, 1880..	16,682,226 40	7,810,200	33,337,000 00	57,829,426 40	41,677,078 86	99,506,505 26

Dates.	Held by national banks in New York City.				Held by other national banks.	Aggregate.
	Coin.	U. S. gold certificates.	Clearing-house certificates.	Total.		
Oct. 1, 1880..	$16,104,855 28	$7,480,700	$36,189,000 00	$59,783,555 38	$19,562,954 11	$109,346,509 49
Dec. 31, 1880..	19,773,859 01	6,709,900	28,246,000 00	54,729,759 01	52,443,141 91	107,172,900 92
Mar. 11, 1881..	15,924,683 90	4,825,300	30,809,000 00	51,558,983 90	53,597,211 36	105,156,195 26
May 6, 1881..	26,242,108 60	4,625,900	34,176,000 00	65,044,008 60	57,584,553 48	122,628,562 08
June 30, 1881..	20,822,790 87	4,513,400	41,858,000 00	67,194,190 87	61,444,736 63	128,638,927 50
Oct. 1, 1881..	15,317,168 04	4,486,600	31,721,000 00	51,524,768 04	62,809,968 08	114,334,736 12
Dec. 31, 1881..	16,352,630 49	4,037,600	33,852,000 00	54,242,230 49	59,438,409 11	113,680,639 60
Mar. 11, 1882..	17,093,447 39	4,075,800	29,907,000 00	51,076,247 39	58,907,863 65	109,984,111 04
May 19, 1882..	15,541,956 93	4,034,300	31,783,000 00	51,359,256 93	61,056,549 80	112,415,806 73
July 1, 1882..	14,278,290 77	4,005,100	32,854,000 00	51,137,390 77	60,556,871 77	111,694,262 54
Oct. 3, 1882..	14,391,783 74	3,908,100	26,224,000 00	44,523,883 74	58,333,894 53	102,857,778 27
Dec. 10, 1882..	10,811,726 69	17,720,100	22,020,000 00	50,551,826 69	55,875,332 71	106,427,159 40
Mar. 13, 1883..	10,060,551 05	10,813,320	21,818,000 00	42,691,871 05	55,270,495 29	97,962,366 34
May 1, 1883..	9,891,636 15	16,094,210	21,334,000 00	47,319,846 15	56,287,420 17	103,607,266 32
June 22, 1883..	8,219,744 22	26,477,760	22,139,000 00	56,836,504 22	58,517,800 40	115,354,304 62
Oct. 2, 1883..	9,388,073 82	20,541,100	20,345,000 00	50,274,173 82	57,543,809 71	107,817,983 53
Dec. 31, 1883..	10,703,481 17	20,525,270	21,693,000 00	53,011,751 17	61,274,406 87	114,276,158 04
Mar. 7, 1884..	12,948,002 34	21,582,060	25,912,000 00	60,442,152 34	62,637,974 99	123,080,127 33
Apr. 24, 1884..	8,920,064 27	20,093,380	20,527,000 00	49,549,444 27	65,195,262 82	114,744,707 09
June 20, 1884..	7,466,696 82	20,397,590	15,690,000 00	43,534,286 82	66,127,395 29	109,661,682 11
Sept. 30, 1884..	7,296,178 39	40,765,140	15,052,000 00	63,113,318 39	65,496,156 34	128,609,474 73
Dec. 20, 1884..	11,314,080 57	44,193,870	17,331,000 00	72,838,950 57	66,008,128 96	139,747,079 53
Mar. 10, 1885..	11,802,276 48	61,114,080	17,579,000 00	90,495,356 48	76,620,517 19	167,115,873 67
May 6, 1885..	11,479,763 87	67,646,060	17,374,000 00	96,500,023 87	80,933,095 43	177,433,119 30
July 1, 1885..	14,417,675 25	65,400,390	16,709,000 00	96,527,065 25	81,085,426 77	177,612,492 02
Oct. 1, 1885..	11,290,427 74	62,249,740	17,914,000 00	91,454,167 74	83,418,409 80	174,872,577 54

The amount of silver coin and silver certificates held by the national banks on the dates given in the following table, were as follows:

Date.	Silver coin.	Silver Treasury certificates.	Total.
October 1, 1877	$3,790,703		
October 1, 1878	5,302,628		
October 2, 1879	4,986,493		
October 1, 1880	5,330,357		
October 1, 1881	5,450,387	$1,165,120	$6,495,477
October 3, 1882	6,466,215	1,662,180	7,112,567
October 2, 1883	7,594,896	1,807,600	8,273,815
September 30, 1884	8,092,557	2,658,036	10,247,926
October 1, 1885	*9,120,802	3,331,510	11,424,967
		2,274,650	11,395,452

* This is composed of $6,322,832 standard dollars and $2,797,969.66 fractional silver.

The latest official reports of the State banks in New England, New York, New Jersey, Pennsylvania, Maryland, Virginia, South Carolina, Georgia, Louisiana, Texas, Ohio, Indiana, Michigan, Wisconsin, Iowa, Minnesota, Missouri, Colorado, and the Territory of Montana show that these banks held specie amounting to $20,132,864, of which the banks in New York City held $12,819,217.

The official returns from the State banks of California do not give separately the amount of coin held by them; but it is estimated that the total cash reported, amounting to $11,122,925, consisted almost entirely of coin. The amount of coin held by State banks in the States before mentioned, including California, was, therefore, $31,255,789.

The Director of the Mint, in his report for 1882, estimated the amount of coin in the country on June 30, 1882, at $700,455,545, of which $500,862,185 was gold and $199,573,360 was silver.

His estimate for the fiscal year ending June 30, 1885, is as follows:

United States coin.	Gold.	Silver.	Totals.
Corrected circulation July 1, 1884	$521,632,442	$250,617,357	$772,249,799
Year's coinage	24,861,123	28,848,959	53,710,082
Net imports	1,006,281	535,449	1,541,730
Totals	547,499,846	280,001,765	827,501,611
Less deposits for recoinage	325,210	877,564	1,202,774
Used in the arts	5,000,000	300,000	5,300,000
Total loss	5,325,210	1,177,564	6,502,774
Circulation July 1, 1885	542,174,636	278,824,201	820,998,837
Net gain during the year	20,542,194	28,206,844	48,749,038

From July 1, 1885, to November 1, 1885, there has been coined $8,753,147 of gold and $9,377,159 of silver, making the total stock of coin in the country at the latter date $839,129,143, less such amounts as may have been deposited for recoinage during this period, of which $550,927,783 was gold and $288,201,360 was silver. The amount of bullion in mint and in the New York assay office on October 1, 1885, is stated to have been $71,471,323 of gold and $4,568,057 of silver, making in all $76,039,380, which, added to the amount of coin stated above, gives $915,168,523, of which amount $622,399,106 was gold and $292,769,417 was silver.

The following table shows the amount of gold and silver, including the amount held to protect gold and silver certificates, and the percentage of each in the Treasury of the United States on September 30 of each year from 1876 to 1885, and on November 1, 1885:

Period.	Silver.			Gold coin and bullion.	Total coin and bullion.	Per cent of—	
	Standard dollars.	Other coin and bullion.	Total silver.			Silver.	Gold.
Sept. 30, 1876		$6,029,367	$6,029,367	$55,423,059	$61,452,426	9.8	90.2
Sept. 30, 1877		7,425,454	7,425,454	107,039,529	114,464,983	6.5	93.5
Sept. 30, 1878	$12,155,205	15,777,937	27,933,142	136,036,302	163,969,444	17.0	83.0
Sept. 30, 1879	31,806,774	21,173,023	52,979,797	169,827,571	222,807,368	23.8	76.2
Sept. 30, 1880	47,784,744	30,878,286	78,663,030	135,641,450	214,304,480	36.7	63.3
Sept. 30, 1881	66,092,667	28,915,297	96,037,964	174,361,343	209,399,307	35.3	64.7
Sept. 30, 1882	92,228,649	30,769,705	122,998,354	152,739,106	275,737,460	44.6	55.4
Sept. 30, 1883	114,587,372	31,858,072	146,445,444	206,130,543	352,575,987	41.5	58.5
Sept. 30, 1884	142,058,787	34,408,566	176,467,353	217,904,043	394,371,396	44.7	55.3
Sept. 30, 1885	165,483,721	27,558,016	193,041,737	251,251,114	444,292,851	43.5	56.5
Nov. 1, 1885	163,817,342	26,806,072	190,623,414	251,359,349	441,982,763	43.4	56.6

The bullion in the Bank of England for each year from 1870 to 1885 is shown in the following table, the pound sterling being estimated at five dollars:

1870	$103,900,000	1878	$119,200,000
1871	117,950,000	1879 *	150,942,980
1872	112,900,000	1880 †	141,637,000
1873	113,500,000	1881 †	115,221,870
1874	111,450,000	1882 †	108,689,912
1875	119,600,000	1883 †	121,779,545
1876	143,500,000	1884 ‡	99,161,045
1877	126,850,000	1885 ‖	107,830,670

Below is a similar table, giving the amount of gold and silver, and the percentage of each, in the Bank of France, on December 31 of each year§ from 1870 to 1882, on November 1, 1883, on October 30, 1884, and on October 16, 1885:

Years.	Silver coin and bullion.	Gold coin and bullion.	Total.	Per cent. of—	
				Silver.	Gold.
December 31, 1870	$13,700,000	$85,740,000	$99,440,000	13.8	86.2
December 31, 1871	16,240,000	110,680,000	126,920,000	12.8	87.2
December 31, 1872	26,520,000	131,740,000	158,260,000	16.8	83.2
December 31, 1873	31,260,000	122,260,000	153,520,000	20.4	79.6
December 31, 1874	62,640,000	204,220,000	266,860,000	23.5	76.5
December 31, 1875	101,000,000	234,860,000	335,860,000	30.1	69.9
December 31, 1876	127,720,000	306,080,000	433,800,000	29.4	70.6
December 31, 1877	173,080,000	235,420,000	408,500,000	42.4	57.6
December 31, 1878	211,620,000	196,720,000	408,340,000	51.8	48.2
December 31, 1879	245,520,000	148,320,000	393,840,000	62.3	37.7
December 31, 1880	244,360,000	110,480,000	354,840,000	68.9	31.1
December 31, 1881	231,160,000	129,160,000	360,310,000	64.2	35.8
December 31, 1882	216,553,000	190,981,300	407,594,000	53.1	46.9
November 1, 1883	203,085,000	192,112,000	395,597,000	51.3	48.7
October 30, 1884	205,837,862	210,927,912	416,765,774	49.4	50.6
October 16, 1885	211,500,000	211,005,000	422,505,000	50.1	49.9

NUMBER, CAPITAL, AND DEPOSITS OF STATE AND SAVINGS BANKS AND PRIVATE BANKERS.

Section 333 of the Revised Statutes of the United States requires the Comptroller to present annually to Congress a statement of the condition of the banks and savings banks organized under State laws. Returns of capital and deposits have hitherto been made by these institutions, and by private bankers, semi-annually to this Department for purposes of taxation. From these returns the following table has been compiled, exhibiting in concise form, by geographical divisions, the total average capital and deposits of all the State and savings banks and private bankers of the country for the six months ending November 30, 1882, being the last semi-annual period for which State and

---

* London Economist, November 8, 1879.
† London Bankers' Magazine, October, 1880, 1881, and 1882.
‡ London Economist, November 1, 1884.
‖ London Economist, October 17, 1885.
§ The Bulletin de Statistique, as quoted in the Bankers' Magazine, New York, vol. xiii, page 740; except the items for 1879–'80 and '81, which were obtained from the London Bankers' Magazine for August, 1880, page 661, September, 1881, page 716, and September, 1882, page 739, and the last three items from L'Économiste Français, November 3, 1883, and November 1, 1884.

savings banks and private bankers were required to make returns for taxation purposes.

Geographical divisions.	State banks and trust companies.			Private bankers.			Savings banks with capital.			Savings banks without capital.	
	No.	Capital.	Deposits.	No.	Capital.	Deposits.	No.	Capital.	Deposits.	No.	Deposits.
		Mill's.	Mill's.		Mill's.	Mill's.		Mill's.	Mill's.		Mill's.
New England States..	40	8.30	31.64	94	6.22	6.57	2	0.10	0.89	420	436.25
Middle States	210	40.60	244.02	967	62.42	112.69	8	0.63	5.34	171	486.98
Southern States	248	25.34	45.94	289	6.33	20.68	7	0.56	1.50	2	1.80
Western States and Territories........	563	48.90	168.40	2,062	30.31	149.02	25	2.73	35.74	32	35.23
United States ..	1,061	123.14	490.00	3,412	105.28	288.96	42	4.02	43.47	625	960.26

The capital of the 2,308 national banks in operation on December 30, 1882, being the date of their report nearest to that of the table given above, as will be seen by a table in the Appendix, was $484,883,492, not including surplus, which fund at that date amounted to more than $135,000,000, while the average capital of all the State banks, private bankers, and savings banks for the six months ending November 30, 1882, was but $232,435,330. The latter amount is less than two-fifths of the combined capital and surplus of the national banks at practically the same time. The table below exhibits the capital and net deposits of the national banks on December 30, 1882, together with the aggregate average capital and deposits of all classes of banks other than national for the six months ending November 30, 1882:

Geographical divisions.	State banks, savings banks, private bankers, &c.			National banks.			Total.		
	No.	Capital.	Deposits.	No.	Capital.	Deposits.	No.	Capital.	Deposits.
		Millions.	Millions.		Millions.	Millions.		Millions.	Millions.
New England States	556	14.62	475.35	560	166.23	193 15	1,116	180.85	668.50
Middle States	1,356	103.66	849.03	691	173.19	356.55	2,047	276.85	1,465.58
Southern States .	546	32.23	69.90	214	34.80	68.84	760	67.03	138.74
Western States and Territories	2,682	81.93	388.42	843	110.66	301.28	3,525	192.59	689.70
United States...	5,140	232.44	1,782.70	2,308	484.88	1,119.82	7,448	717.32	2,902.52

The total number of banks and bankers in the country at the date named was 7,448, with a total banking capital of $717,318,822, and total deposits of $2,902,522,245.

In the Appendix will be found similar tables for various periods from 1875 to 1882. On a subsequent page in this report, under the head of "State banks, savings banks, and trust companies," will be found tables showing the resources and liabilities of these corporations for the present year, and in the Appendix similar results for previous years.

A table arranged by States and principal cities, giving the number, capital, and deposits, and the tax thereon, of all banking institutions other than national, and of the private bankers of the country, for the six months ending November 30, 1882, and for previous years, will also be found in the Appendix.

The following table exhibits, for corresponding dates nearest to May 31, in each of the last seven years, and to November 30, 1882, the aggregate amounts of the capital and deposits of each of the classes of banks given in the foregoing table:

Years.	National banks.			State banks, private bankers, &c.			Savings banks with capital.			Savings banks without capital.		Total.		
	No.	Capital.	Deposits.	No.	Capital.	Deposits.	No.	Capital.	Deposits.	No.	Deposits.	No.	Capital.	Deposits.
		Mill's.	Mill's.		Mill's.	Mill's.		Mill's.	Mill's.		Mill's.		Mill's.	Mill's.
1876...	2,091	500.4	713.5	3,803	214.0	480.0	26	5.0	37.2	691	844.6	6,611	719.4	2,075.3
1877...	2,078	481.0	768.2	3,709	218.6	470.5	26	4.9	38.2	676	843.2	6,579	704.5	2,120.1
1878...	2,056	470.4	677.2	3,799	202.2	413.3	23	3.2	26.2	668	803.3	6,450	675.8	1,920.0
1879...	2,048	455.3	713.4	3,639	197.0	397.0	29	4.2	36.1	644	747.1	6,360	656.5	1,893.5
1880...	2,076	455.9	900.8	3,798	190.1	501.5	29	4.0	34.6	629	783.0	6,532	650.0	2,219.9
1881...	2,115	460.2	1,039.9	4,016	206.5	627.5	36	4.2	37.6	629	862.3	6,796	670.9	2,667.3
1882...	2,239	477.2	1,131.7	4,403	231.0	747.6	38	3.9	41.3	622	929.8	7,302	712.1	2,850.4
1882*..	2,308	484.0	1,119.8	4,473	228.4	779.0	42	4.0	43.5	625	960.2	7,448	717.3	2,902.5

* In the last table of the series the returns are given for the six months ending May 31, 1882, and also for the six months ending November 30, of the same year.

It will noticed that the first two tables of this chapter are for the six months ending November 30, while all similar tables in previous reports have been for the six months ending May 31. The law repealing the tax on capital and deposits of State banks and private bankers went into effect on November 30, 1882, in accordance with the opinion of the Attorney-General, and for this reason the Comptroller has given the returns to that date, which was the last data to be obtained from this source.

AMOUNT OF UNITED STATES BONDS HELD BY BANKS ORGANIZED UNDER STATE LAWS.

Through the courtesy of State officers the Comptroller has obtained official reports made to them under State laws by State banks in twenty-six States, by trust companies in five States, and by savings banks in fifteen States, at different dates during the years 1884 and 1885, and from these returns the following table has been compiled:

Held by 975 State banks in twenty-six States........................ $2,994,806
Held by 40 trust companies in five States......................... 25,376,400
Held by 646 savings banks in fifteen States....................... 191,980,698

Total 220,351,904

The interest-bearing funded debt of the United States on November 1, including $64,623,512 Pacific sixes, and excluding $14,000,000 Navy pension fund, was $1,260,778,162. The total amount of bonds held by the national banks, $308,364,550, and by the State savings banks and trust companies, $220,351,904, is about 42 per cent. of the interest-bearing debt. The amount of United States bonds held by State banks, trust companies, and savings banks, is given by geographical divisions for the years 1881, 1882, 1883, 1884, and 1885, as follows:

Geographical divisions.	1881.	1882.	1883.	1884.	1885.
Eastern States.....................	$40,468,340	$42,667,248	$37,399,819	$30,806,938	$30,121,432
Middle States.....................	176,373,889	197,135,239	182,847,588	188,640,523	186,642,288
Southern States	1,073,460	268,350	646,500	96,750	136,071
Western States	5,735,518	3,369,414	3,105,024	2,390,780	3,451,213
Pacific States	14,874,332	20,020,175	17,743,978	(*)	(*)
Total	238,525,539	263,460,426	241,742,909	221,934,991	220,351,904

* The United States bonds held in the Pacific States during the last two years are not included in the above table, as the returns since 1883 do not give United States bonds separately from other bonds held.

In previous reports the Comptroller has given the amount of United States bonds held by banks organized under State laws and by private bankers as returned to the Commissioner of Internal Revenue for purposes of taxation. A table was compiled, for purposes of comparison, from these returns for the six months ending November 30, 1882, and may be found in the report of this office for the year 1884, page 32.

STATE BANKS, TRUST COMPANIES, AND SAVINGS BANKS.

The act of Congress of February 19, 1873, section 333 of the United States Revised Statutes, requires the Comptroller to obtain from authentic sources, and report to Congress, statements exhibiting under appropriate heads the resources and liabilities of such banks and savings banks as are organized under the laws of the several States and Territories. In compliance with this act he has presented annually in the appendices to his reports the resources and liabilities of these corporations, so far as it has been possible to obtain them. Through the courtesy of State officers, returns of State banks, savings banks, and trust and loan companies have, during the past year, been received from twenty-five States. Many of the States and Territories, including West Virginia, North Carolina, Alabama, Arkansas, Tennessee, Illinois, Oregon, and Dakota, do not require periodical returns of the condition of the different classes of banks organized under their laws.

From these returns the following abstract has been compiled, showing the resources and liabilities of State banks and trust companies for the last five years, the number reporting in 1881 being 683; in 1882, 704; in 1883, 788; in 1884, 852; and in 1885, 1,015:

	1881.	1882.	1883.	1884.	1885.
	683 banks.	704 banks.	788 banks.	852 banks.	1,015 banks.
RESOURCES.					
Loans and discounts	$352,725,986	$404,574,420	$462,380,585	$489,067,519	$489,423,169
Overdrafts	1,407,695	1,373,116	1,493,636	1,630,474	1,485,917
United States bonds	27,680,025	25,673,984	22,725,596	25,708,789	28,371,206
Other stocks, bonds, &c	42,330,957	45,658,783	52,405,724	50,331,877	62,395,059
Due from banks	54,662,829	57,973,718	68,270,664	65,354,146	82,521,390
Real estate	21,396,772	19,913,682	20,160,547	21,211,182	24,632,603
Other assets	11,941,741	13,685,205	14,190,044	10,513,813	14,814,705
Expenses	1,136,427	1,193,345	1,131,586	1,235,079	1,432,935
Cash items	16,900,762	18,546,073	35,206,862	28,308,216	26,067,594
Specie	17,925,628	17,902,760	18,255,300	25,929,757	31,255,789
Legal tenders, bank notes, &c	27,391,317	27,322,912	28,259,069	32,659,605	39,552,017
Totals	575,500,139	633,819,998	724,479,613	760,940,457	801,952,444
LIABILITIES.					
Capital stock	112,111,325	113,361,931	125,233,036	133,958,951	151,686,840
Circulation	274,941	286,391	187,978	177,554	98,129
Surplus fund	27,857,976	31,504,352	34,575,461	41,675,486	41,365,559
Undivided profits	12,237,320	14,758,438	18,076,610	22,337,961	20,082,736
Dividends unpaid	576,413	577,419	465,011	499,017	513,177
Deposits	373,032,632	426,677,092	500,374,217	514,111,591	532,725,289
Due to banks	19,105,664	18,409,351	20,918,936	27,886,996	30,148,346
Other liabilities	30,303,868	28,245,024	24,648,364	20,301,901	25,332,368
Totals	575,500,139	633,819,998	724,479,613	760,940,457	801,952,444

The foregoing table was prepared from all the New England States except Maine, from four Middle States, not including Delaware, and from all the Western States, excepting Illinois and Nebraska. The only Southern States from which reports have been received were Virginia,

South Carolina, Georgia, Florida, Louisiana, Kentucky, and Missouri. The only Pacific States were California and Colorado. There are no State banks in Maine, but 1 in New Hampshire, 7 in Vermont, and none in Massachusetts. There are, however, 6 trust and loan companies in the latter State, 1 in Rhode Island, and 6 in Connecticut.

SAVINGS BANKS.

The following table exhibits the aggregate resources and liabilities of the 629 savings banks in 1881 and 1882, 630 in 1883, 636 in 1884, and 646 in 1885:

	1881.	1882.	1883.	1884.	1885.
	629 banks.	629 banks.	630 banks.	636 banks.	646 banks.
RESOURCES.					
Loans on real estate	$307, 096, 158	$307, 089, 227	$328, 197, 858	$358, 636, 040	$389, 953, 928
Loans on personal and collateral security	95, 817, 641	128, 483, 698	155, 874, 522	141, 457, 111	133, 716, 902
United States bonds	210, 845, 514	237, 786, 442	219, 017, 313	196, 226, 202	191, 980, 698
State, municipal, and other bonds and stocks	159, 819, 942	206, 291, 274	190, 629, 915	222, 218, 006	228, 103, 250
Railroad bonds and stocks	27, 069, 048	32, 904, 578	41, 695, 791	50, 994, 579	59, 585, 489
Bank stock	33, 249, 203	35, 365, 717	36, 587, 817	37, 929, 754	38, 460, 603
Real estate	41, 987, 674	39, 882, 429	37, 224, 601	34, 467, 276	32, 174, 810
Other assets	37, 408, 163	11, 047, 346	53, 235, 771	69, 166, 584	68, 445, 304
Expenses	135, 572	132, 204	144, 228	156, 944	166, 636
Due from banks	40, 603, 641	38, 977, 135	43, 184, 629	52, 356, 971	46, 125, 014
Cash	13, 758, 106	14, 932, 015	12, 908, 594	14, 079, 452	13, 423, 064
Totals	967, 790, 662	1, 052, 982, 065	1, 118, 790, 944	1, 177, 740, 919	1, 203, 025, 698
LIABILITIES.					
Deposits	891, 961, 142	960, 797, 081	1, 024, 856, 787	1, 073, 294, 955	1, 095, 172, 147
Surplus fund	60, 289, 905	60, 454, 512	72, 784, 155	82, 395, 717	88, 647, 315
Undivided profits	10, 325, 800	11, 136, 219	15, 738, 223	16, 904, 753	13, 106, 359
Other liabilities	5, 213, 815	5, 594, 253	5, 411, 779	5, 145, 494	6, 099, 877
Totals	967, 790, 662	1, 052, 982, 065	1, 118, 790, 944	1, 177, 740, 919	1, 203, 025, 698

The foregoing table includes the returns from six New England States; from four Middle States, not including Delaware; from the States of Ohio, Indiana, Minnesota, California, and the District of Columbia.

The aggregate of loans in the New England States is $297,220,022 and of deposits $492,373,407. In the Middle States the aggregate of loans is $172,779,215 and of deposits $525,151,161. Some of the largest savings banks in the city of Philadelphia organized under old charters are not required to make reports to any State officer. Returns directly received from four of these banks, having deposits amounting to $35,362,660, are included in the returns from the State of Pennsylvania. The savings-banks deposits, given in the foregoing table for 1885, based upon reports made to the State authorities, are $1,095,172,147, and the deposits of the State banks and trust companies are $532,725,289. These returns do not include bank deposits. The deposits of the national banks on October 1, 1885, exclusive of those due to banks, were $1,102,354,658.

No just comparison of the deposits of national banks with those of savings banks, State banks and trust companies can be made, owing to the fact that the reports of many of the latter classes of banks were made to the State authorities at various dates in 1884 and 1885.

The total population of New England, according to the census of 1880, was 4,010,529, and the number of open deposit accounts of the savings banks in the year 1885 is 1,460,185, which is equal to about 36.4 accounts to each one hundred of the entire population. The average amount of each account is $337.21, or an average of $122.77 per capita. The deposits of the savings banks in the State of New York were $437,107,501, and the population was 5,082,871, showing an average of about $86 per capita.

Tables showing the aggregate resources and liabilities of State banks, trust companies, and savings banks in each State from which returns have been received from the State authorities appear in the Appendix. A table is also there given showing by States the number of savings banks, depositors, and the average amount due to each in 1884 and 1885. Since November 30, 1882, the Comptroller has been entirely dependent for this information upon returns from the officers of the different States, and where the law requires such returns to be made, they are as a rule promptly and courteously forwarded to this office at his request.

PRIVATE BANKERS.

The first official information relating to the private bankers of the country published by this office was contained in a table in the Comptroller's report for 1880, and the last information obtained in reference to them was for the semi-annual period ending November 30, 1882. A table will be found in the Appendix giving information for this and previous years.

APPENDIX.

Tables will be found in the Appendix exhibiting the reserve of the national banks, as shown by their reports, from October 1, 1878, to October 1, 1885; the reserve by States and principal cities for October 1, 1885, and in the States and Territories, in New York City, and in other reserve cities, separately, at three dates in each year from 1881 to 1885.

Special attention is called to the synopsis of judicial decisions contained in the Appendix, to the numerous and carefully prepared tables in both Report and Appendix, and to the index of subjects and list of tables to be found on page 247. At the end of the full volume, of nearly 1,200 pages, is an alphabetical list of the cities and villages in which the national banks are situated.

The Comptroller, in concluding this report, desires to gratefully acknowledge the industry and efficiency of the officers and clerks associated with him in the discharge of official duties, many of whom, in addition to attending to their regular duties, have been compelled, owing to the growth of the national banking system and the extension of the corporate existence of national associations, to perform a large amount of extra work, without regard to office hours.

HENRY W. CANNON,
Comptroller of the Currency.

To THE HONORABLE
THE SPEAKER OF THE HOUSE OF REPRESENTATIVES.

APPENDIX.

NAMES and COMPENSATION of OFFICERS and CLERKS in the OFFICE of the COMPTROLLER OF THE CURRENCY, October 31, 1885.

Name.	Grade.	Salary.
Henry W. Cannon	Comptroller	$5,000 00
John S. Langworthy	Deputy Comptroller	2,800 00
William B. Greene	Chief of division	2,200 00
Frank A. Millor	do	2,200 00
Edward S. Peck	do	2,200 00
Alonzo B. Dickerson	do	2,200 00
David L. Perkins	Superintendent	2,000 00
Watson W. Eldridge	Teller	2,000 00
Theodore O. Ebaugh	Bookkeeper	2,000 00
	Assistant bookkeeper	2,000 00
Charles E. Brayton	Fourth-class clerk	1,800 00
James C. Brown	do	1,800 00
Fernando C. Cate	do	1,800 00
George T. May	do	1,800 00
Edmund E. Schreiner	do	1,800 00
William Sinclair	do	1,800 00
Charles J. Stoddard	do	1,800 00
George H. Wood	do	1,800 00
Edward A. Demaray	Stenographer	1,600 00
Charles H. Cherry	Third-class clerk	1,600 00
John A. Hebrew	do	1,600 00
Washington K. McCoy	do	1,600 00
Isaac C. Miller	do	1,600 00
William D. Swan*	do	1,600 00
Walter Taylor	do	1,600 00
Charles McC. Taylor	do	1,600 00
Edwin D. Tracy	do	1,600 00
William H. Walton	do	1,600 00
Frederick Widdows	do	1,600 00
	do	1,600 00
William E. Colladay	Second-class clerk	1,400 00
J. Edward De Saules	do	1,400 00
Julia R. Donoho	do	1,400 00
Charles B. Hinckley	do	1,400 00
R. Le Roy Livingston	do	1,400 00
Mary L. McCormick	do	1,400 00
Morris M. Ogden	do	1,400 00
Arthur M. Wheeler	do	1,400 00
Eveline C. Bates	First-class clerk	1,200 00
Harriet M. Black	do	1,200 00
Sarah F. Fitzgerald	do	1,200 00
Eliza R. Hyde	do	1,200 00
George H. Koehler	do	1,200 00
Joseph K. Miller	do	1,200 00
Carrie L. Pounock	do	1,200 00
Margaretta L. Simpson	do	1,200 00
Eliza M. Barker	Clerk	1,000 00
Eliza M. Peters	do	1,000 00
Lafayette J. Garner	Engineer	1,000 00
Thomas H. Austin	Clerk	900 00
Ettie J. Broughler	do	900 00
Margaret L. Browne	do	900 00

*Additional as bond clerk, $200.

NAMES and COMPENSATION of OFFICERS and CLERKS, &c.—Continued.

Name.	Grade.	Salary.
Louisa Campbell	Clerk	$900 00
Virginia H. Clarke	do	900 00
Sarah G. Clemens	do	900 00
Mary L. Conrad	do	900 00
Julia De Quindre	do	900 00
Margaret F. Dewar	do	900 00
Annabella H. Finlay	do	900 00
Margaret E. Gooding	do	900 00
William H. Heald	do	900 00
Rebecca C. Hulburd	do	900 00
Alice M. Kennedy	do	900 00
Lucretia W. Knowlton	do	900 00
Emma Lafayette	do	900 00
Edward S. May	do	900 00
Maggie B. Miller	do	900 00
Margaret F. Ogden	do	900 00
Mary E. Oliver	do	900 00
Annie E. Ranney	do	900 00
Emily H. Reed	do	900 00
Marie Richardson	do	900 00
Hannah Sanderson	do	900 00
Eliza Saunders	do	900 00
Fayette C. Snead	do	900 00
Matilda Stoffregen	do	900 00
Amelia P. Stockdale	do	900 00
Sarah A. W Tilley	do	900 00
Therese E. Tilley	do	900 00
Julia C. Townsend	do	900 00
Anna M. Whiteside	do	900 00
Ephraim S. Wilcox	do	900 00
	do	900 00
Abram W. Dyson	Messenger	840 00
Philo L. Bush	Assistant messenger	720 00
William Griffiths	do	720 00
Silas Holmes	do	720 00
Langston W. Allen	Watchman	720 00
Thomas Jackson	do	720 00
John A. McDonald	Fireman	720 00
Mary D. Tarrisse	Laborer	660 00
Lambert A. Whiteley	do	660 00
	do	660 00

Expenses of the office of the Comptroller of the Currency for the fiscal year ending June 30, 1885.

For special dies, plates, printing, &c $123,618 91
For salaries 101,674 47
For salaries reimbursable by national banks 16,756 43

Total expenses of the office of the Comptroller of the Currency from its organization to June 30, 1885, $6,066,227.37.

The contingent expenses of the office are not paid by the Comptroller, but from the general appropriation for contingent expenses of the Treasury Department: and as separate accounts are not kept for the different Bureaus, the amount cannot be stated.

SYNOPSIS of DECISIONS of the SUPREME and CIRCUIT COURTS of the UNITED STATES and of STATE COURTS of LAST RESORT, upon QUESTIONS ARISING UNDER THE NATIONAL BANK ACT and upon COGNATE POINTS of INTEREST to BANKS and to PARTIES HAVING DEALINGS with them. *

ABATEMENT.

I. An action brought by a creditor of a national bank is abated by a decree of a district or circuit court dissolving the corporation and forfeiting its franchises. (*First National Bank of Selma* vs. *Colby*, 21 *Wallace, p.* 609.

II. Suit by the receiver of the *New Orleans National Banking Association* (formerly a State organization called the Bank of New Orleans) against a shareholder to enforce his personal liability. Plea in abatement that " at the date of the appointment of said receiver there was not, nor has there since been, nor is there now, any such corporation as said New Orleans National Banking Association, because said Bank of New Orleans had no power by its charter, nor authority otherwise from the State of Louisiana, to change its organization to that of a national association under the laws of the United States."

On general demurrer this plea was held bad, because no authority from the State was necessary to enable the bank to make such change. The option to do so was given by the forty-fourth section of the banking act of Congress, 13 Statutes, 112. "The power there conferred was ample, and its validity cannot be doubted." (*Casey, Receiver, &c.*, vs. *Galli*, 4 *Otto, p.* 673.)

This plea was also held bad upon the additional ground that " where a shareholder of a corporation is called upon to respond to a liability as such, and where a party has contracted with a corporation, and is sued on his contract, neither is permitted to deny the existence and legal validity of such corporation." (*Ibid.*)

" To hold otherwise," says Mr. Justice Swayne (p. 680), " would be contrary to the plainest principles of reason and good faith, and involve a mockery of justice. Parties must take the consequences of the positions they assume. They are estopped to deny the reality of the state of things which they have made to appear to exist, and upon which others have been led to rely. Sound ethics require that the apparent, in its effects and consequences, should be as if it were real, and the law properly so regards it."

ACCOMMODATION ACCEPTANCES, INDORSEMENTS, AND NOTES.

I. Where bills, indorsed by a national bank for accommodation only, had been negotiated by the bank through its usual channels of communication with its correspondents as its own bills, and the proceeds thereof have been placed to the credit of the bank, which thereupon gave the same credit to the parties for whom it had thus indorsed, and received no benefit therefrom: *Held*, that although an accommodation indorsement by a national bank, in such cases, was void in the hands of holders against whom notice of the character of the indorsement could be concluded, yet that the bank was liable for the same to holders, for value without notice. (*Blair* vs. *First National Bank of Mausfield, Ohio. United States Circuit Court for Ohio, at Cleveland, November term*, 1875, *Emmons, J. Reported in Bankers' Magazine for March*, 1878, *pp.* 721-5.)

II. It is no defense in a suit against the acceptor of a draft which has been discounted, and upon which money has been advanced by plaintiff, that the draft was accepted for the accommodation of the drawer. (*Davis* vs. *Randall*, 115 *Mass., p.* 547.)

III. A national bank discounted a note made by the defendant for the benefit of the payee, and which the payee agreed to take care of at maturity: *Held*, that the bank could recover the note although it had, when it took the note, full notice of the circumstances under which it was given. (*Thatcher* vs. *West River National Bank*, 19 *Mich., p.* 196.) (See, also, Title "EVIDENCE.")

IV. That the accommodation acceptance, indorsement, bill, or note of a corporation is *ultra vires*. (See *Bank of Genesee* vs. *Patchin Bank*, 13 *N. Y., p.* 309, and 19 *N. Y., p.* 312; *Bank of Auburn* vs. *Putnam, jr.*, 1 *Abb. App. Decisions*,

---

* Many of the decisions cited in this synopsis will be found in "Thompson's National Bank Cases," vols. 1 and 2; but in most instances reference is made to the original report, thus indicating the tribunal by which the point was decided.

ACCOMMODATION ACCEPTANCES, INDORSEMENTS, AND NOTES—Continued.

> p. 80; *Monfords* vs. *Farmers & Mechanics' Bank*, 26 *Barb.*, p. 568; *Farmers & Mechanics' Bank* vs. *Troy City Bank*, 1 *Doug.* [*Mich.*], p. 45.)
>
> [NOTE.—In the United States Circuit Court, Western District, Virginia, Judge Bond has recently decided the cases of *Seligman & Co.* vs. *The Charlottesville National Bank,* and *Johnston Brothers & Co.* against the same bank. The first was an action of *covenant* upon a *letter of credit* for £5,000, issued under the seal of the bank, pursuant to a resolution of the board of directors, guaranteeing the drafts of Flannagan & Son to the amount of said letter. The latter was *assumpsit* upon five bills of exchange for $5,000 each, dated April 16, 1875, each drawn by said Charlottesville Bank upon the Citizens' National Bank of Baltimore, payable to the order of Flannagan & Son, acceptance waived, maturing upon days "fixed" within five days of each other, the first, November 20, and the last, December 10 of same year. Said bills were *not* drawn against funds due or to become due from the said Citizens' National Bank, but were a mere loan of the credit of the latter bank (it being without funds) to the said Flannagan & Son, and drawn to be used by the latter, as they were used, as collateral security in part for a loan of $25,000, made by said *Johnston Brothers & Co.* to said Flannagan & Son. Said plaintiffs took said bills as such collateral security, and with full notice of all the facts aforesaid.   *Held,* 1st. That said letter of credit and said bills of exchange were only the accommodation paper of said Charlottesville National Bank, and, as such, void in the hands of the plaintiffs, holding with full notice of their character. 2d. That the incidental powers conferred upon national banks are not such as are conferred upon banks generally, but only such as are necessary to carry on the specific banking business prescribed by the national-bank act. Hence, though such banks may borrow money for certain purposes, they have no power to loan their credit to customers. These cases were reported in the Bankers' Magazine for December, 1879.]

ACTIONS.

I. A national bank may be sued in the proper State court.   (*Bank of Bethel* vs. *Pahquioque Bank*, 14 *Wall.*, pp. 383, 395.)

II. Such banks may sue in Federal courts.   The word "by" was omitted in section 57 of act of 1864 by mistake. (*Kennedy* vs. *Gibson*, 8 *Wall.*, pp. 506–7.)

III. Receivers may also sue in United States courts.   (*Ibid.*)

IV. When the full personal liability of shareholders is to be enforced, the action *must* be at law.   (*Kennedy* vs. *Gibson*, 8 *Wall.*, p. 505; see, also, *Casey, &c.,* vs. *Galli, supra.*)

V. But if contribution only is sought, the proceedings may be in *equity*, joining all the shareholders within the jurisdiction of the court. (*Ibid.*, pp. 505–6.)
   (See, also, Title "SHAREHOLDERS, INDIVIDUAL LIABILITIES OF," VI, *post.*)

VI. But in *Bailey, Receiver, &c.,* vs. *First National Bank of Duluth, U. S. Circuit Court for Minnesota, Nelson, J.* : *Held,* that even where less than the par value was assessed the suit *might* be at law ; and this would seem to be the true theory.
   (See *Bankers' Magazine, April,* 1877, p. 793.)
   [NOTE.—In *Stanton, Receiver, &c.,* vs. *Wilkeson,* 8 *Ben.,* 357, the point was distinctly made before Judge Blatchford. The suit was brought to enforce an assessment of sixty per centum, and defendant insisted that plaintiff should have proceeded by bill in equity ; but the court held that the action at law was the proper remedy, at the option of the receiver.]

VII. A national bank located in one State may bring action in the circuit court of the United States sitting within another State against a citizen thereof. (*Manufacturers' National Bank* vs. *Baack,* 8 *Blatch.*, p. 147.)

VIII. In such action it will be presumed, so far as the question of jurisdiction is concerned, that the stockholders of such bank are citizens of the State where the bank is located.   (*Ibid.*) But in case of *Commercial Bank of Cleveland* vs. *Simmons,* decided in the United States Circuit Court Northern District of Ohio, it was held that a national bank does not sue in the Federal court by virtue of any right conferred by the judiciary act of 1789, but by virtue of the right conferred by its charter, the national bank act, and this would seem to be the true doctrine. (See *Thomp. National Bank Cases,* p. 295. Also *First National Bank of Omaha* vs. *County of Douglas,* 3 *Dillon,* p. 298, decided by Mr. Justice Miller, of the United States Supreme Court.)

IX. National banks can be sued *only* in the courts designated in the national bank act. Therefore a State court of New York has no jurisdiction of an action against a national bank located in Alabama. (*Cadle* vs. *Tracy,* 11 *Blatch.*, p. 101.) To the contrary of this, see *Cooke* vs. *State National Bank,* 52 *N. Y.*, p. 96.

ACTIONS—Continued.

X. Actions in their nature *local*, in the technical legal meaning of that word, may be brought against a national bank in the State court of the proper county. (*Casey* vs. *Adams*, 102 *U. S.*, *p*. 66.)
(See, also, Title "JURISDICTION," *post*.)

XI. An action brought against a national bank in a State court was, upon its petition, removed to the Federal court, and a motion was made to remand it in the United States circuit court for the southern district of New York. Judge Wallace denied the motion on the ground that the right of a national bank, as a corporation created by Congress, to remove a suit brought against it in a State court, is clearly conferred by section 2 of the removal act of 1875. It has been determined that any suit brought by a corporation created by Congress was one arising under the laws of the United States. (*Cruikshank* vs. *Fourth National Bank, June* 19, 1883.)

XII. In a suit brought in the United States circuit court against the stockholders of the Pacific National Bank upon their personal liability, motion was made to dismiss suit for want of jurisdiction, based principally upon the alleged effect of the act of July 12, 1882, placing national banks on the same footing with other banks. The motion was denied.

XIII. The act of July 12, 1882, placed national and other banks on the same footing as to their right to sue in the Federal courts, and, consequently, a national bank cannot, merely in virtue of a corporate right, sue in such courts. But national banks, like other banks and citizens, may sue in such courts whenever the subject-matter of litigation involves some matter of Federal jurisdiction. (*Union National Bank* vs. *Miller, C. C. S. D. Ohio, W. D., March* 26, 1883. *Fed. Rep.*, *vol. xv*, 1703.)

XIV. Under section 1001 of the Revised Statutes no bond for the prosecution of the suit, or to answer in damages and costs, is required on writs of error or appeals issuing from or brought to this court by direction of the Comptroller of the Currency in suits by or against insolvent national banks, or the receivers thereof. (*Pacific National Bank* vs. *Geo. Mixter, U. S. Supreme Court, October Term*, 1884.)

ATTACHMENTS OF ASSETS.

I. When a creditor attaches the property of an insolvent national bank, he cannot hold such property against the claim of a receiver appointed after the attachment suit was commenced. Such creditor must share *pro rata* with all others. (*Bank of Selma* vs. *Colby*, 21 *Wall.*, *p*. 609; see, also, *Harvey* vs. *Allen*, 16 *Blatchf.*, *p*. 29.)
(See, also, Title "JURISDICTION," II, *post*.)

II. Section 5242 Revised Statutes United States prohibits the issuing of an attachment against a national bank by any State, county, or municipal court before final judgment. (*Central National Bank* vs. *Richland National Bank*, 52 *Howard* [*N. Y.*]. *p*. 136.)

III. In *Robinson* vs. *National Bank of New Berne*, 58 *How.*, *p*. 306, the court of appeals decides that a State court can issue attachment process against a *solvent* national bank, located in another State, upon which its funds within the jurisdiction of such court can be seized and subjected to the satisfaction of any claim established by the judgment of such tribunal. But in the supreme court of New York, in *Rhoner* vs. *First National Bank of Allentown*, 14 *Hun.*, *p*. 126, the contrary doctrine is held, in accordance with the ruling in *Central National Bank* vs. *Richland National Bank*, 52 *How.*, *p*. 136, heretofore cited.
[NOTE.—It is submitted that the latter is the correct rule. The currency act favors the policy, on the part of country banks, of keeping a large portion of their *reserve* in certain cities. But if such banks are advised that such reserve funds are there subject, at any moment, to be seized by process of a State court, at the instance or caprice of any resident who may think himself a creditor, such deposits will be made with more or less hesitation, or not at all.]

ATTORNEYS.

I. Section 56 of the currency act is directory only, and it cannot be objected by defense that a suit is brought by a private attorney instead of the United States district attorney. (*Kennedy* vs. *Gibson*, 8 *Wall.*, *p*. 504.)

BY-LAWS.

I. A national bank cannot by its by-laws create a lien on the shares of a stockholder who is a debtor of the association. (*Bullard* vs. *National Bank, &c.*, 18 *Wall.*, *p*. 589.)

80 REPORT OF THE COMPTROLLER OF THE CURRENCY.

BY-LAWS—Continued.

> (See, also, case of *Bank* vs. *Lanier*, 11 *Wall.*, *p.* 369, cited under "LOANS ON SHARES," *post.*)
> [NOTE.—In *Young* vs. *Vough*, 23 *N. J. Equity R.*, *p.* 325, it was held that a national bank could by its by-laws prohibit the transfer of shares by a shareholder while indebted to the bank, and that transfers in violation of such by-laws were void. As it is held by the Supreme Court of the United States that such by-laws can create no lien for indebtedness, it would seem that a regulation prohibiting such transfers can be of little practical use, even if the power exists.]

CHECKS.

The holder of a check on a national bank cannot sue the bank for refusing payment, in the absence of proof that it was accepted by the bank. (*National Bank of the Republic* vs. *Millard*, 10 *Wall.*, *p.* 452.)

II. The relation of banker and customer is that of debtor and creditor. Receiving deposits is an important part of the business of banking, but the moment they are received they become the moneys of the bank, may be loaned as a part of its general fund, and the check of the depositor gives no lien upon them. (*Ibid.*, *p.* 155.)

III. Perhaps, on proof that check had been charged to the drawer, and that the bank had settled with him on that basis, the holder or payee could recover on account for "*money had and received.*" (*Ibid.*, *pp.* 155–6.)

IV. The facts that the bank was a United States depository and the check was drawn by a United States officer to a United States creditor do not vary the rule. (*Ibid.*, *pp.* 155–6.)

V. Where a bank pays a check drawn on it in favor of a party whose indorsement thereon is forged, and the same has passed through several hands, only reasonable diligence is required to be exercised in giving notice to prior holders of the forgery, after its discovery, in order to hold them liable. (*Shrader* vs. *Harvey*, 75 *Ill.*, *p.* 638.)

VI. A clerk of plaintiffs received from their debtors, checks, payable to their (plaintiffs') order, in payment of sums due. The clerk, wrongfully and without authority, indorsed the names of the plaintiffs on these checks and transferred them to other persons, appropriating the proceeds to his own use. Subsequently these checks were deposited with a bank, which in good faith collected them and paid over the proceeds to the depositors. In a suit by plaintiffs against the bank to recover the amount so collected by it: *Held*, that the bank was liable. (*Johnson* vs. *First National Bank*, 13 *N. Y. Sup. Court.*)

VII. Bankers are presumed to know the signatures of their customers, and pay checks purporting to be drawn by them at their peril. (*Weisser* vs. *Dennison*, 10 *N. Y.*, *p.* 68; *National Bank of the Commonwealth* vs. *Grocers' National Bank*, 35 *Howard* [*N. Y. P. R.*,] *p.* 412.) This last case holds that if the bank, the drawee, pays the forged check to the holder, it cannot recover back the money so paid. The same doctrine was held in case of *First National Bank of Quincy* vs. *Ricker*, 71 *Ill.*, *p.* 439; but qualified by holding that it applied only where the presumed negligence was all on the side of the bank, and where the holder or payee had been guilty of no fraud or act to throw the bank off its guard.

VIII. CERTIFYING.—National banks have the power to certify checks; and this power may be exercised by the cashier without any special authorization. The directors can limit this power, but such limitation will be no defense as to parties having no notice. (*Merchants' National Bank* vs. *State National Bank*, 10 *Wall.*, *p.* 604.)

IX. A certificate of a bank that a check is good is equivalent to an acceptance implying that the bank has the funds to pay it, and that they are set apart for that purpose. (*Ibid.*, *p.* 604.)

X. A national bank is liable on a check certified by its cashier to the holder in good faith, although the drawer has no funds in the bank when it was certified. (*Cooke* vs. *State National Bank*, 52 *N. Y.*, *p.* 96.)

XI. The act of Congress of March 3, 1869, making it unlawful for a national bank to certify checks unless the drawer has at the time funds on deposit to an amount equal to the amount specified in the check, does not invalidate a conditional acceptance of a check by such bank, having no funds of the drawer in its hands at the time, but engaging to pay the same when a draft left with it for collection by the drawer shall have been paid. (*First National Bank* vs. *Merchants' National Bank*, 7 *West Va.*, *p.* 544.)

CHECKS—Continued.

XII. A bank is liable to pay a subsequent bona fide purchaser the amount of a check which it has certified, notwithstanding the check was fraudulently raised, if before certification, from a smaller amount. (*Louisiana National Bank* vs. *Citizens' Bank*, 28 *La. Annual*, p. 189.)

XIII. When a bank was chargeable with negligence in certifying a check, which was so drawn as to admit of a fraudulent alteration of the amount being easily made, and the check *was* raised: *Held*, that the bank was liable to a *bona fide* holder, for value, for the increased amount. (*Helwege* vs. *Hibernia National Bank*, 28 *La. Annual*, p. 520.)

[NOTE.—As the above case unquestionably declares the true rule of law, prudence would seem to dictate that cashiers should always insist upon such filling up of checks as to render alteration impracticable, before certifying.]

XIV. A certified check is not deemed dishonored by delay between its date and the time when it is sold to a *bona fide* purchaser, for value, so that the latter takes it as overdue, and subject to equities; because, by certifying, the bank becomes the principal debtor, and liable indefinitely, like an acceptor of a bill of exchange. Hence, one who in good faith, and after making reasonable inquiry, bought a certified check, three or four months after its date, which had been *stolen*, was held entitled to recover its amount. (*Nolan* vs. *The Bank of New York*, 67 *Barb.*, p. 24.)

XV. A check contained on its face this recital: "To hold as collateral for 1,000 P. T. oil, pipage paid to Jan. 4, 1876"; across its face the cashier wrote, "Good when properly indorsed": *Held*, that the check was not drawn in the usual course of banking business, and therefore the certificate of the cashier did not bind the bank. (*Dorsey* vs. *Abrams et al., bankers*, 85 *Pa.*, p. 299. See, further, as to liability on checks, certified or otherwise, *Dodge* vs. *National Exchange Bank*, 30 *O.*, p. 1; *Security Bank* vs. *National Bank of the Republic*, 67 *N. Y.*, p. 458; *Andrews* vs. *German National Bank*, 9 *Heisk.* [*Tenn.*], p. 211.)

BANK CHECK.

XVI. (1.) An order drawn at Kansas City, Mo., on a bank in New York City, to pay money to H. C. or order on demand, without days of grace, is a bank check.

(2.) EQUITABLE ASSIGNMENT OF PART OF DRAWER'S FUND ON DEPOSIT.—Where the depositor of a fund in a bank draws his check for a part of that fund, which is presented in due time, this is an appropriation, and an equitable assignment of so much of the fund as is called for by the check, although no action at law could be maintained upon it.

(3.) EQUITABLE ASSIGNMENT FOR BENEFIT OF CREDITORS.—Where a debtor, having a large fund in bank, drew his checks in favor of certain creditors, and thereafter, before said checks were presented, made a general assignment of all his property for the benefit of his creditors, under a State insolvent law: *Held*, that the check-holders who presented their checks and demanded payment, while the fund remained in the hands of the bank, were entitled to payment as against the assignee. The checks amounted to an appropriation of so much of the fund in which they were drawn, and to that extent it did not pass to the assignee.

(4.) PRESENTATION OF CLAIM TO ASSIGNEE—ELECTION OF REMEDY.—The presentation by the check-holders of their claims to the assignee, and his allowance of them, and their receipt of dividends under the assignment, was not the election by them of a remedy which prevents a recovery in this case. (*First National Bank of Cincinnati et al.* vs. *Kersey Coates et al.* United States circuit court, western district of Missouri, May term, 1881. In equity.)

XVII. B, a banker, in payment of moneys collected by him for C, gave his check on the D bank for a sum less than the amount to his credit in that bank. Before the check was presented for payment B made an assignment for creditors, of which the bank had notice. *Held*, that the check operated as an equitable assignment to C of the deposit to the amount named in the check, and that C was entitled to such amount in preference to the assignee for creditors. (*German Savings Institution* vs. *Adae, United States Circuit Court, Eastern District of Missouri, March*, 1880.)

CIRCULATION

The circulating notes of a national bank are valid without the imprint of the seal of the United States Treasury. (*U. S.* vs. *Bennett* 17 *Blatchf.*, 357.)

CITIZENSHIP.

I. National banks are *citizens* of the State in which they are organized and located, and when sued by national banks of other States have a right to

CITIZENSHIP—Continued.

demand a removal of the suit from a State to the proper Federal court. (*Chatham National Bank* vs. *Merchants' National Bank*, 4 *Thompson & Cook, N. Y. Sup. C.*, *p.* 196, *and* 1 *Hunter* [*N. Y.*], *p.* 702; *Davis* vs. *Cook*, 9 *Nevada*, *p.* 134.) (See also Title "ACTIONS" V and VI, *supra*.)

II. A national bank, being a citizen of the State in which it is located, may be required to give security for costs when suing in another State; and in the State of New York such security may be required, because the bank is regarded as a corporation created by a foreign State. (*National Park Bank* vs. *Gunst*, 1 *Abbott's New Cases*, *p.* 292.)

COLLECTIONS.

I. A bank receiving paper for collection undertakes to use due diligence in making demand at maturity, and giving the proper notices of non-payment. An unreasonable delay will charge the bank with liability for the amount; and proof that the paper would not have been paid, if presented, will constitute no defense. (*Bank of Washington* vs. *Triplett*, 1 *Peters*, *p.* 25; *Bank of New Hanover* vs. *Kenner*, 76 *N. C.*, *p.* 340; *Steele* vs. *Russell*, 5 *Nebr.*, *p.* 211; *Capital State Bank* vs. *Lane*, 52 *Miss.*, *p.* 677; *Fabens* vs. *Mercantile Bank*, 23 *Pick.* [*Mass.*], *p.* 320.)

II. And if the bank receiving paper for collection, upon a sufficient consideration, transmits it to another bank to be collected, the receiving bank will be liable for the misconduct of such other bank, unless there is some agreement to the contrary. (*Montgomery County Bank* vs. *Albany City Bank*, 7 *N. Y.*, *p.* 459; *Commercial Bank* vs. *Union Bank*, 11 *N. Y.*, *p.* 203; *Kent* vs. *Dawson*, 13 *Blatchf.*, *p.* 237; *First National Bank* vs. *First National Bank of Denver.* 4 *Dill.*, *p.* 290.)

III. A bank received a check upon itself for collection, being at the same time a large creditor of the drawer, and failed, without excuse, to notify the depositor of the non-payment of the check: *Held*, that the bank was chargeable for the negligence. (*Bank of New Hanover* vs. *Kenner. supra*.)

IV. A bank holding a check for collection, and accepting the certification of the bank upon which it is drawn, in lieu of payment, assumes the risk and thereby becomes liable to the owner for the amount, with interest from date of certification. (*Essex County National Bank* vs. *Bank of Montreal*, 7 *Bissell*, *p.* 193.)

V. The *Corn Exchange National Bank of Chicago* sent defendant, the *Dawson Bank*, at Wilmington, N. C., a draft drawn upon one *Wiswall*, living at Washington, N. C., for collection. Defendant by letter acknowledged the receipt of the draft, stating that it had been credited to the Corn Exchange Bank and entered for collection. Thereupon defendant sent draft to *Burbank & Gallagher*, bankers at Washington, N. C., for collection. The latter house collected the draft, but failed and passed into bankruptcy before remitting. In a suit brought by the assignee of the Corn Exchange National Bank against the Dawson Bank to recover the proceeds of the draft: *Held*, per Wallace, J., that the latter bank was liable for the amount. (*Kent, assignee, &c.*, vs. *The Dawson Bank*, 13 *Blatchf.*, *p.* 237.) [NOTE.—The court concedes that the authorities are conflicting upon the point involved in this case. In *New York*, *Ohio*, and in *England*, the decisions sustain the conclusions of Judge Wallace, while in *Connecticut*, *Massachusetts*, *Illinois*, and *Pennsylvania* precisely the contrary rule prevails. The point was made in this case that the law of Illinois should control the rights of parties, but it was held otherwise.]

VI. In an action by G against a bank it appeared that a note was made to G's order, indorsed by him, and sent through the house of B, a banker, for collection, and by B indorsed to the defendant bank "for collection and credit": *Held*, that B, by the indorsement, did not become the owner of the note, and had no right to pledge it, or direct its proceeds to be credited to him in payment of his indebtedness to the defendant bank. (*First National Bank* vs. *Gregg*, 79 *Pa.*, *p.* 384.)

VII. In such case, if the defendant bank had made advances, or given new credit to B on the faith of the note, it would have been entitled to retain the amount out of the proceeds (*Ibid.*)

VIII. A bank holding a customer's demand note has a lien upon the proceeds of drafts delivered to it for collection, after the giving of the note, though collected after the filing of a petition in bankruptcy, and can apply such proceeds upon the notes. (*Re Farnsworth*, 5 *Biss.*, *p.* 223.)

COLLECTIONS—Continued.

IX. A collection agent who receives from his principal a bill of lading of merchandise, delivered to order, and attaches to it a time draft, may, in the absence of special instructions, deliver the bill of lading to the drawee of the draft upon the latter's acceptance of the draft. It is not the duty of the agent to hold the bill after such acceptance. (*National Bank of Commerce vs. Merchants' National Bank*, 1 *Otto, p. 92.*)

X. *Woolen & Co.*, bankers at Indianapolis, sent to defendant, a bank at Buffalo, a draft on one Bugbee; also bills of lading for sundry car-loads of lumber. The remittance was by letter, which merely stated that the draft and bills were sent to defendant for collection and remittance of proceeds to plaintiffs, *Woolen & Co.* The draft was drawn by, and to the order of, *Corder & Co.*, indorsed by them, by Mayhew, and the plaintiffs. By the terms of the draft the drawer, indorsers, and acceptor waived presentment for payment and notice of protest and non-payment. It was payable fifteen days after its date, and it was admitted that by ordinary course of *transit* the lumber would reach its destination eight days prior to the maturity of the draft. There had been no business transactions between plaintiffs and defendants, save one collection similar to this. Defendants presented the draft to Bugbee for acceptance, and upon such acceptance delivered to him the bills of lading. Bugbee failed before the draft matured, and plaintiffs sued defendants for delivering the bills of lading to Bugbee before payment of the draft. It was conceded that the draft was drawn for the price or value of the lumber: *Held, per* Wallace, J., that, the draft being on time, it must be presumed that it was the intent of parties that Bugbee should realize from sale of the lumber the funds to meet the draft at maturity. Therefore, upon his acceptance of the draft, he was entitled to the bills of lading, and defendants were not liable for thus delivering them; but if the draft had not been upon time, a different rule might have prevailed. (*Woolen & Webb* vs. *N. Y. and Erie Bank*, 12 *Blatchf., p.* 359.)

XI. L transmitted to a bank a draft indorsed "for collection on his account." The bank provisionally credited the draft, when received, to L, presented it for payment, and surrendered it to the drawee on receipt of his check for the amount. Instead of demanding the money on this check, the bank had it certified "good," and on the same day suspended payment. The next day the check was collected, and the money mingled with the other money in the hands of the receiver: *Held*, that the receiver held the funds in trust for L. (*Levi* vs. *Missouri Bank*, 5 *Dillon, p.* 104.)

XII. The general power of a bank to collect ceases by its suspension as to paper previously deposited therewith. (*Jockusch* vs. *Towsey*, 51 *Tex., p.* 129.)

XIII. As to effect of indorsement "for collection," see *Bank of Metropolis* vs. *First National Bank of Jersey City, U. S. Circuit Court, S. D. N. Y., Bankers' Magazine*, August, 1884.

XIV. A bank in Pittsburgh sent to a bank in New York, for collection, eleven unaccepted drafts, dated at various times through a period of over three months, and payable four months after date. They were all drawn on "Walter M. Couger, secretary Newark Tea Tray Co., Newark, N. J.," and were sent to the New York bank as drafts on the Tea Tray Company. The New York bank sent them for collection to a bank in Newark, and in its letters of transmission recognized them as drafts on the company. The Newark bank took acceptances from Couger individually on his refusal to accept as secretary, but no notice of that fact was given to the Pittsburgh bank until after the first one of the drafts had matured. At that time the drawers and an indorser had become insolvent, the drawers having been in good credit when the Pittsburgh bank discounted the drafts: *Held*, that the New York bank was liable to the Pittsburgh bank for such damages as it had sustained by the negligence of the Newark bank.

The circuit court having on a trial before it without a jury made a finding of facts which did not cover the issue as to damages, and given a judgment for the defendant, this court, on reversing that judgment, remanded the case for a new trial, being unable to render a judgment for the plaintiff for any specific amount of damages. (*Exchange National Bank of Pittsburgh, Pa.*, vs. *The Third National Bank of New York City, U. S. Supreme Court*, 1884, *Bankers' Magazine*, February, 1885, *p.* 611.)

XV. Where a negotiable instrument, indorsed and delivered in blank to a bank, though in fact only for collection, is sent by it to another bank for "collection and credit" before maturity, and the latter receives it without notice that it does not belong to the former, it may lawfully retain the proceeds of the collection to satisfy a claim for a general balance against the

COLLECTIONS—Continued.

other bank, if that balance has been allowed to arise and remain on the faith of receiving payments from such collections pursuant to a usage between the two banks. (*Vickrey* vs. *State Savings Association*, *Federal Reporter*, vol. 21, p. 773.

COMPROMISES.

I. In adjusting and compromising contested claims against it, growing out of a legitimate banking transaction, a national bank may pay a larger sum than would have been exacted in satisfaction of them, so as to thereby obtain a transfer of stocks of railroad and other corporations, in the honest belief that, by turning them into money under more favorable circumstances than then existed, a loss which it would otherwise suffer from the transaction might be averted or diminished. (*First National Bank* vs. *National Exchange Bank*, 2 *Otto*, p. 122.)

II. So, also, it may accept stocks in satisfaction of a doubtful debt, with a view to their subsequent conversion into money, in order to make good or reduce an anticipated loss. (*Ibid.*)
(See, also, Title "ESTATE, REAL," I, *post.*)

III. A court has no power, under section 5234 of the Revised Statutes of the United States, to order the receiver of a national bank to compound debts which are not "bad or doubtful"; and a composition, under such an order, of debts not bad or doubtful, is ineffectual. (*Price, receiver, &c.*, vs. *Yates*, 2 *Thomp. Cases*, p. 204, *U. S. Circuit Court, Western District Pa.*)

IV. A receiver compromised suits with counsel for the United States: *Held*, that the compromise would not be opened after a lapse of years, no fraud being alleged. (*Henderson* vs. *Myers*, 11 *Phil., Pa.*, p. 616.)
[NOTE.—This must have been a compromise made *without* a special order of court.]

COMPTROLLER.

I. The Comptroller appoints the *receiver*, and can therefore remove him. (*Kennedy* vs. *Gibson*, 8 *Wall.*, p. 498.)

II. The Comptroller's certificate, reciting the existence of the facts, of which he is required to be satisfied to justify the appointment of a receiver under section 50 of the national bank act, is sufficient evidence of the validity of such appointment in an action brought by such receiver. (*Platt* vs. *Bebee*, 57 *N. Y.*, p. 339.)

III. The Comptroller must authorize any increase of the capital stock of a national bank; and such increase must be certified by him, as prescribed by section 13 of the act of Congress providing for the organization of national banks. (*Charleston* vs. *People's National Bank*, 5 *S. C.*, p. 103.).

IV. The Comptroller cannot subject the United States Government to the jurisdiction of a court, though he appears and answers to the suit. (*Case* vs. *Terrell*, 11 *Wall.*, p. 199.)
(See, also, Title "SHAREHOLDERS, INDIVIDUAL LIABILITY OF," *post.*)

V. Where a national bank was put into insolvency by the Comptroller of the Currency, and a creditor, whose claim was disputed, recovered judgment seven years after for an amount much larger than the amount of his claim at the time of failure, on account of interest for the interval having been included in the judgment, it was held that dividends must be calculated and paid upon the amount of the claim at the time of the failure of the bank. (*United States ex rel. White* vs. *Knox*, *U. S. Supreme Court*, *May* 5, 1884.)

CONVERSION.

I. The conversion of a State into a national bank works no dissolution, only a change of the original corporation; nor does the latter thereby escape any of its liabilities. (*Maynard* vs. *Bank*, 1 *Brewster, Pa.*, p. 483; *Kelsey* vs. *National Bank of Crawford County*, 69 *Pa.*, p. 426; *Coffey* vs. *National Bank of the State of Missouri*, 46 *Mo.*, p. 140.)

II. The certificate of the Comptroller of the Currency is conclusive as to the regularity of the proceeding by which any bank has been converted into a national bank. (*B. U. Keyser, receiver*, vs. *Jane C. Hitz, Sup. Court, D. C. Decided June* 26, 1883.)

III. Where owners of more than two-thirds of stock consent to the conversion of a bank into a national bank, the conversion may take place without the concurrence of the remaining stockholders. (*Ibid.*)

IV. Although it might be more regular, it is not necessary that, on conversion, a new stock book should be opened, or new certificates of stock issued. (*Ibid.*)

CONVERSION—Continued.

V. A stockholder giving consent to conversion thereby becomes a stockholder in the new bank, even if new certificates of stock are not issued. (*Ibid.*)

CREDITORS OF NATIONAL BANKS.

I. The respective rights and liabilities existing between a national bank and its creditors and debtors become fixed when its *insolvency* occurs. * * * All the property and assets of the association then become a fund, legally dedicated, first, to the satisfaction of any claim of the United States for the redemption of its circulating notes, and, second, for a ratable distribution of the balance among its general creditors upon the principle of equality. (*Balch* vs. *Wilson*, 2 *Thomp. Cases, p.* 276; 25 *Minn., p.* 299.)

II. The United States, as a creditor of a national bank, is not entitled to a priority of payment out of its assets over other creditors. (*Cook Co. National Bank and Aug. H. Burley, receiver of said bank, appellants,* vs. *The United States, U. S. Sup. Court, Oct. term,* 1882.) This suit was appealed from the United States circuit court, northern district Illinois, in the name of the United States, by the bondsmen of McArthur, postmaster of Chicago. The bank was a Government depository, and on its failure the proceeds of its bonds deposited in the United States Treasury to secure deposits were sufficient to refund all the public moneys, except about $20,000 of postal funds. The bondsmen, being liable for any amount the bank might fail to pay if the United States accepted pro rata dividends with other creditors, brought suit for the whole amount, claiming priority of payment under a statute of 1797, providing that in the case of insolvent debtors of the United States, the debt of the United States should first be satisfied from their estate. The court decided that the statute of 1797 was suspended as to national banks by the act authorizing the formation of national banks, by which the United States was placed on the same footing as other creditors. The court said: "We consider that act (national bank act) as constituting by itself a complete system for the establishment and government of national banks." (For further points decided in this case, see "*Set-off.*")

CURRENCY.

I. The word "*currency,*" in a certificate of deposit. means money, including bank notes, which, though not an absolute legal tender, are used as money by authority of law, and are in circulation generally, at the *locus in quo,* on par with coin. (*Klauber* vs. *Biggerstaff,* 47 *Wis., p.* 551.)

CURRENCY ACT.

I. The purpose of the currency act was, in part, to provide a currency for the whole country, and, in part, *to create a market for the Government loans.* (*Per Strong, J.,* in *Tiffany* vs. *National Bank of the State of Missouri,* 18 *Wall., p.* 413.)

II. National banks organized under the act of Congress of June 3, 1864, are the instruments designed to be used to aid the Government in the administration of an important branch of the public service; and Congress, which is the sole judge of the necessity for their creation, having brought them into existence, the States can exercise no control over them, nor in any wise affect their operation, except so far as Congress may see proper to permit. (*Per Swayne, J.,* in *Farmers and Mechanics' National Bank* vs. *Dearing,* 1 *Otto, p.* 29.)

III. The constitutionality of the act of June 3, 1864, is unquestioned. It rests on the same principle as the act creating the second Bank of the United States. The reasoning of Secretary Hamilton and of this court in *McCulloch* vs. *The State of Maryland,* 4 *Wheat., p.* 316, and in *Osborne* vs. *Bank U. S.,* 7 *Wheat., p.* 708, therefore applies.

IV. The power to create carries with it the power to preserve. The latter is a corollary of the former. (*Ibid., per Swayne, J., pp.* 33, 34.)

DEBTORS OF NATIONAL BANKS.

I. Debtors of an insolvent national bank, when sued by the receiver, cannot object that pleadings do not show a compliance with all the steps prescribed by statutes as preliminary to the appointment of such receiver. (*Cadle, receiver, &c.,* vs. *Baker & Co.,* 20 *Wall., p.* 650.)

II. Such ordinary debtors may be sued by receiver without previous order of the Comptroller. (*Bank* vs. *Kennedy,* 17 *Wall., p.* 19.)

DEPOSITS.

I. CERTIFICATES OF.—A certificate of deposit was issued by a bank for a certain sum, subject to the order of the depositor at a certain date, payable on the return of the certificate: *Held*, in an action on said certificate against the bank, brought by an assignee, that there could be no recovery without proof of an actual demand and refusal of payment. (*Brown* vs. *McElroy*, 52 *Ind.*, *p.* 404.)

II. In a suit against the bank upon a stolen certificate of deposit, given by the defendant to the plaintiff, reciting that he had deposited in the bank a certain number of dollars, payable to his order *in current funds*, on the return of the certificate, properly indorsed : *Held*, first, that the instrument should be regarded as the promissory note of the bank, assignable under the statute (of Indiana), but that it was not negotiable as an inland bill of exchange, being made payable not in money, but "in current funds;" second, that the payee could recover on said stolen certificate without giving a bond against a subsequent claim thereunder by another person. (*National State Bank* vs. *Ringel*, 51 *Ind.*, *p.* 393.)

III. Where a bank issues a certificate of deposit, payable on its return, properly indorsed, it is liable thereon to a *bona-fide* holder, to whom it was transferred *seven* years after it was issued, notwithstanding the payment thereof to the original holder. Such certificate is not dishonored until presented. (*National Bank of Fort Edward* vs. *Washington County National Bank*, 5 *Hun.*, *N. Y. Sup. Court*, *p.* 605.)

IV. Under a statute prohibiting the circulation of bills or notes *not* payable on demand, banks have no power to issue time certificates of deposit; and such certificates, if issued, are void. They are equivalent to post notes. (*Bank of Peru* vs. *Farnesworth*, 18 *Ill.*, *p.* 563; *Bank of Orleans* vs. *Merrill*, 2 *Hill* [N. Y.], *p.* 295; *Leavitt* vs. *Palmer*, 3 N. Y. [*Comst.*], *p.* 19.) (See also, "CURRENCY," *supra*.)

V. GENERAL.—The relation between a bank and its depositors is that of debtor and creditor only, and is not fiduciary. Thus, a note deposited for collection, if passed to the credit of the depositor in his general account, then overdrawn, becomes the property of the bank, which becomes indebted to him for the proceeds. Upon the bankruptcy of the bank, the proceeds are assets available to the general creditors. And the fact that the account was made good by other deposits before collection of the note makes no difference. (*In re Bank of Madison*, 5 *Bissell*, *p.* 515.) A national bank may also apply a deposit in payment of a matured note held against the depositors. (*Home Bank* vs. *Newton*, 8 *Ill.*, *App.*, 563.)

VI. A deposit is general, unless the depositor makes it special, or deposits it expressly in some particular capacity. And in case of a general deposit of money with a banker, a previous demand by the depositor, or some other person by his order, is indispensable to the maintenance of an action for the deposit, unless circumstances are shown which amount to a legal excuse. (*Brahm* vs. *Adkins*, 77 *Ill.*, *p.* 263.)

VII. A national bank having become insolvent, a depositor therein assigned his deposit to a debtor of the bank: *Held*, that the latter could not offset such deposit against his debt, in an action thereon (*Venango National Bank* vs. *Taylor*, 56 *Pa.*, *p.* 14.)

VIII. A depositor was also indebted to the bank on bond and mortgage: *Held*, that he could offset his deposit against said indebtedness, the bank being in the hands of a receiver. (*Matter of New Amsterdam Savings Bank* vs. *Gartter*, 54 *How.* [N. Y. P. R.], *p.* 385.)

IX. The claims of depositors in a suspended national bank are, when proved to the satisfaction of the Comptroller of the Currency, on the same footing as if they were reduced to judgments, and from date of such proof bear interest. (*National Bank of the Commonwealth* vs. *Michigan National Bank*, 94 U. S. [4 *Otto*], *p.* 437.)

X. SPECIAL.—The taking of special deposits to keep, merely for the accommodation of the depositor, is not within the authorized business of national banks; and the cashiers of such banks have no power to bind them on any express contract accompanying, or any implied contract arising out of such taking. (*Wiley* vs. *First National Bank*, 47 *Vt.*, *p.* 546.) [NOTE.—To the same effect was the decision of the New York court of appeals in *First Nat. Bank of Lyons* vs. *Ocean Nat. Bank*, 60 N. Y., *p.* 278. But it is to be remembered that in both these cases only the act of the cashier was relied upon to bind the bank. In the latter case it was stated that there was no proof of even implied knowledge or assent on the part of the directory. In the well-reasoned case of *Weckler* vs. *First Nat. Bank of Hagerstown*, 42 *Md.*, *p.* 581, these cases are cited with decided approval; but

DEPOSITS—Continued.

a recent decision of the Supreme Court goes very far towards establishing a different doctrine. In *National Bank* vs. *Graham*, 100 *U. S.*, *p.* 699, the Supreme Court held that section 5228 R. S. U. S. conferred upon a national bank power to receive and take charge of special deposits, such as the public securities of the Government, and that such bank is liable in damages for the loss, *through gross negligence*, of such deposit, when it had been made with the knowledge and acquiescence of its officers and directors. The learned judge who delivered the opinion (Mr. Justice Swayne) cited numerous State decisions, only referring to the cases in Vermont as being in conflict with the weight of adjudications, and based the conclusion of the court upon the doctrine that "gross negligence on the part of a gratuitous bailee, though not a fraud, was equivalent thereto in legal effect, and that the doctrine of *ultra vires* has no application in favor of a corporation when guilty of a wrong."]

XI. A national bank receiving a special deposit for safe-keeping, without reward, is liable only for gross negligence. The burden of proof is on the plaintiff, and gross negligence is not the omission of that care which every attentive and diligent person takes of his own goods, but the omission of that care which the most inattentive takes. (*First National Bank, &c.*, vs. *Rex*, 89 *Penn.*, *p.* 308.)

In *Pattison* vs. *Syracuse Bank*, 80 N. Y., 82, the case of *Nat'l Bank of Lyons* vs. *Ocean National Bank* is substantially overruled, following the ruling in *Nat'l Bank* vs. *Graham*. See also *First National Bank of Mansfield* vs. *Zent* (*supreme court of State of Ohio*).

XII. AUTHORITY OF BANK TO APPLY DEPOSIT IN PAYMENT OF DEBTS.—Where a depositor in a bank is indebted to the bank by bill, note, or other independent indebtedness, the bank has a right to apply so much of the funds of the depositor to the payment of his matured indebtedness as may be necessary to satisfy the same. (*Appellate court, first district, held at Chicago. Home National Bank* vs. *Newton.*)

So, where the bank held the note of a depositor for a certain sum, the bank could, on the morning of the last day of grace upon such note, apply to its payment any money of the depositor then remaining on deposit in such bank.—[Chicago Legal News.]

DIRECTORS OF NATIONAL BANKS.

I. Directors of a national bank may remove the president, both under the law of Congress and the articles of association, where the latter so provide. The power exists if the bank has adopted no by-laws. (*Taylor* vs. *Hutton*, 43 *Barb.*, *N. Y. Sup. Court*, *p.* 195; *S. C.*, 13 *Abb. Pr. R.*, *p.* 16.)

II. In all cases where an act is to be done by a corporate body, a majority of the whole number of directors is necessary to constitute a valid meeting; but at a meeting when a quorum is present the majority of those present may act. A by-law adopted when less than a majority is present is void. (*Lockwood* vs. *American National Bank*, 9 *Rhode Island*, *p.* 308.)

(See Title "OFFICERS," *post.*)

III. The power to compromise or release claims in favor of a bank is in the board of directors and not within the scope of the cashier's authority. (*Chemical Bank* vs. *Kohner*, 8 *Daly* [*N. Y.*], *p.* 530.)

IV. In *Bostwick* vs. *Brinkerhoff* a suit was begun in the supreme court of the State of New York, by a stockholder of the National Bank of Fishkill, to recover damages from the directors for their neglect of their official duties. A demurrer was filed to the complaint, which raised, among others, the question whether such an action could be brought in a State court. The supreme court of the State sustained the demurrer and dismissed the complaint. The judgment was affirmed at general term. An appeal was taken to the court of appeals, where the judgment of the general term was reversed, and the case was remitted to the supreme court to be proceeded upon according to law. A writ of error was taken to the Supreme Court of the United States, which decided that a judgment of reversal by a State court with leave for further proceedings in the court of original jurisdiction is not subject to review in the United States Supreme Court. (*Supreme Court*, 106 *U. S.*)

V. *Ackerman* vs. *Halsey* was a suit brought in the circuit court of Essex County, New Jersey, by a stockholder of the Mechanics' National Bank of Newark, N. J., against a director of that bank, to recover the value of stock lost by the insolvency of the bank through the negligence of directors. The defendant demurred on the ground that directors could not be sued for injury

DIRECTORS OF NATIONAL BANKS—Continued.

by an individual stockholder, but only by the corporation or receiver. Judge Depue sustained the demurrer, stating that such suits should be brought by the receiver in behalf of the corporation, its creditors and stockholders, but that if the receiver refused to bring such suit, any stockholder might do so, joining with himself all other stockholders. This decision was rendered in April, 1882.

VI. *Conway* vs. *Halsey, New Jersey Supreme Court. Bankers' Magazine for November,* 1883, *p.* 378. This was a suit brought by a stockholder of the Mechanics' National Bank of Newark, N. J., against the president and directors, for neglect and mismanagement, &c. It was demurred to on grounds similar to the preceding case, and the demurrer was sustained. The plaintiff also held that he had the right to recover under section 5239 of the Revised Statutes. On this point the judge held that that statute only applied when the charter of the corporation was forfeited on account of willful violation of law on the part of the directors. In this case the plaintiff did not show any willful violation of law by which a direct injury was done to the stockholders. The injuries received were indirect, because the directors were alleged to have permitted, by their negligence, the property of the corporation to be squandered, purloined, or lost.

EMBEZZLEMENT.

I. When the president of a national bank, having charge of its funds, converts them to his own use, he embezzles and abstracts them within section 55 (R. S., sec. 5209) of the national bank act, unless he shows authority for thus using them. (*In the matter of Van Campen*, 2 *Benedict, p.* 419, *per Blatchford, J.*)

II. Although false entries in regard to such embezzlement are made on the books of such bank by the clerk, but by the order of the president, the latter is chargeable as principal; and the intent to defraud the bank is to be inferred from the fact of such embezzlement. (*Ibid.*)

III. The cashier of a national bank was indicted under said section 55 for embezzling and willfully misapplying the moneys of the bank with intent to defraud, &c. On trial it was proved that defendant took the moneys of the bank and used them in stock speculations, carried on in his own name, by depositing the same with a stock broker as "margins" for stock bought on his own account. *Held*, that the intent to injure or defraud was conclusively presumed upon proof of the act charged ; and, therefore, evidence was not admissible to prove that the cashier used the funds with the knowledge and consent of the president and some of the directors of the bank, and on account of and for the benefit of the bank. (*United States* vs. *Taintor*, 11 *Blatchf., p.* 374.)

[NOTE.—This last case was decided in the United States circuit court, southern district of New York, Woodruff, Blatchford, and Benedict, JJ., all concurring in the decision.]

IV. A State court has no jurisdiction of the crime of embezzlement by an officer of a national bank situated within the State. (*Commonwealth* vs. *Felton*, 101 *Mass., p.* 204 ; *State* vs. *Tuller*, 34 *Conn., p.* 280.) But in this latter case it was also held that while a teller of such bank could not be punished for embezzling the funds of the bank, he could be convicted, under the statute of the State, for purloining property deposited with such bank for safekeeping; and in *Commonwealth* vs. *Barry*, 116 *Mass., p.* 1, it was decided that though an officer of a national bank, who has stolen its property, may be subject to punishment for embezzlement under the national law, he may also be punished for the same act, *as a larceny*, under the statute of the State.

ESTATE, REAL.

I. The want of power of a bank, or of its trustee (receiver) in insolvency, to purchase and hold real estate, does not render void an arrangement whereby land subject to a lien in favor of the bank, and to other liens, is discharged of those other liens by funds from the assets of the bank, the land being then sold, and the entire proceeds of such sale realized to the bank assets, provided the title does not pass through the bank or its trustees. (*Zantzingers* vs. *Gunton*, 19 *Wall., p.* 32.)

II. In *Union National Bank et al.* vs. *Mathews*, 98 *U. S., p.* 658, the court recognized the doctrine that, "where a corporation is incompetent by its charter to take a title to real estate, a conveyance to it is not void, but only voidable, and the sovereign alone can object. It is valid unless assailed in a direct proceeding instituted for that purpose."

ESTATE, REAL—Continued.

[NOTE.—Thus it would seem that a mortgage executed to secure a present loan, or any other conveyance of real estate to a national bank, must be held valid until declared void in a direct proceeding instituted for that purpose by the United States Government.]

(See, also, *Wroten's Assignee* vs. *Armat*, 31 *Grattan*, *p.* 238.)

III. The title to real estate taken by a national bank, on adjustment of a liability in its favor, must be held valid until attacked by the United States, in direct proceedings instituted for that purpose. Such title cannot be impeached collaterally, in an ejectment suit. (*Mapes et al.* vs. *Scott et al.*, 94, *Ill.*, *p.* 379; *National Bank* vs. *Whitney*, 106 *U. S.*, *p.* 99; *Graham* vs. *National Bank*, 32 *N. J. Eq.*, *p.* 804; *Warner* vs. *Dewitt*, 4 *Ill. App.*, *p.* 305.)

(See, also, Title "LOANS ON REAL ESTATE," *post.*)

ESTOPPEL.

I. A shareholder in a national bank, who has participated in its transactions as such, and received dividends, is estopped from denying the legality of its incorporation. The same rule applies to one accustomed to deal with a national bank as such, as by giving his promissory note to such bank. (*Wheelock* vs. *Kost*, 77 *Ill.*, *p.* 296; *National Bank of Fairhaven* vs. *Phœnix Warehousing Company*, 6 *Hun.* [*N. Y.*], *p.* 71; *Casey* vs. *Galli*, 94 *U. S.*, *p.* 673, and numerous cases therein cited.)

II. The *Manufacturers' National Bank of Chicago*, defendant, being the city correspondent of the *People's Bank of Belleville*, plaintiff, guaranteed to the latter bank the payment of certain notes of one Picket, pursuant to an agreement that thus guaranteed their amount should be, *as it was, debited to the account of the Belleville Bank.* Such agreement, and the guarantee in pursuance thereof, were made by the vice-president of the defendant bank, with the assent of the president and cashier, but without the assent of the directors. *Held*, that under the circumstances the defendant bank was estopped from setting up, as a defense, that such guarantee was *ultra vires.* (*People's Bank* vs. *National Bank*, 101 *U. S.*, *p.* 181.)

[NOTE.—It will be observed that this decision stops far short of legalizing naked accommodation paper made by a national bank.]

III. A national bank which has wrongfully converted to its own use the property of another, is estopped from denying its liability to account therefor upon the ground that it received and held the property in carrying on the business of a warehousman, outside the powers conferred by its charter. (*German National Bank* vs. *Meadowcroft*, 2 *Thomp. Cases*, *p.* 462. *Sup. Court Ill.*)

EVIDENCE.

I. Even if it be within the authority of the president of a national bank to bind the bank by an agreement with the acceptor of a draft, which is discounted by the bank, not to enforce the draft against him, yet *oral* evidence of such an agreement is not competent in defense of a suit by the bank against the acceptor. (*Davis* vs. *Randall*, 115 *Mass.*, *p.* 547.)

II. The certificate of the Comptroller of the organization of a national bank is conclusive evidence as to the completeness of such organization, in a suit against one of its shareholders. (*Casey* vs. *Galli*, *ante*; *Thatcher* vs. *West River National Bank*, 19 *Mich.*, *p.* 196.)

III. In ordering an assessment for the payment of the debts of an insolvent bank, the stock certificates and stock ledger of the bank must be taken by the Comptroller of the Currency, in the absence of fraud or mistake, as showing who the stockholders were at the time of the failure. (*Davis* vs. *Essex Baptist Society*, 44 *Conn.*, *p.* 582.)

IV. The maker of a certificate of deposit cannot overcome its effect, as proof of a deposit actually made, except by clear and satisfactory evidence. (*First National Bank of Lacon* vs. *Meyers*, 83 *Ill.*, *p.* 507).

INTEREST.

I. Under section 30, act of 1864, a national bank in any State may take as high a rate of interest as by the laws of such State a natural person may stipulate for, although State banks of issue are restricted to a less rate. (*Tiffany* vs. *National Bank of the State of Missouri*, 18 *Wall.*, *p.* 409.)

II. As the action was virtually brought to recover the penalty for *usury*, the statute (section 30) must receive a strict construction. (*Ibid.*, *p.* 409.)

[NOTE.—In Missouri, natural persons may take ten per cent., but State banks are restricted to eight per cent. In this case the national bank had taken nine per cent: *Held*, legal.]

INTEREST—Continued.

III. In a suit by a national bank upon a bill of exchange discounted by it, the acceptor cannot set up by way of counter-claim, or set-off, that the bank in discounting a series of bills of said acceptor, the proceeds of which it used to pay other bills, knowingly took, and was paid, a greater rate of interest than that allowed by law. (*Barnett* vs. *National Bank*, 98 U. S. [8 *Otto*], *p.* 555.)

IV. The act of June 3, 1864 (R. S., sec. 5198), having prescribed that, as a penalty for such taking, the person paying such unlawful interest, or his legal representative, may *in an action of debt* against the bank recover back twice the amount so paid, he can resort to no other mode or form of procedure. (*Brown* vs. *Second National Bank of Erie*, 72 *Pa.*, *p.* 209; *Barnett* vs. *National Bank*, 98 U. S., *p.* 555.)

[NOTE.—The above case of *Barnett* vs. *National Bank*, 98 U. S., *p.* 555, overrules several State adjudications, and settles several points in regard to usurious interests as affecting loans by national banks. It holds that when suit is brought by such bank to recover a loan made at usurious rate, stipulated for, but not paid, the entire interest thus agreed upon, but no part of the principal, is forfeited, and the latter may be recovered in full; that when the usurious interest has been paid, twice its sum may be recovered by the borrower, but this can only be done by a suit directly brought for that purpose, which suit must be in the nature of an action of *debt*, commenced, of course, within the two years specified. Suppose, then, A borrows $1,000 from a national bank on 90 days' time, and for the loan actually pays usurious interest in advance. Suppose his paper is protested and suit is brought upon it. It follows that while A cannot offset twice the usurious interest he has paid, nor any part thereof, in reduction of the face of his paper, the bank can recover from him not only the principal of the loan, but legal interest thereon from the date of maturity of the note or bill.]

(See, also, *Natl. Bank* vs. *Dearing*, 91 U. S., *p.* 29, and Title "USURY," *post*.)

V. ON CLAIMS OF CREDITORS.—Where a national bank is put in charge of a receiver, under section 50 of the original Currency Act (R. S., sec. 5234), and a sufficient sum is realized from its assets to pay all claims against it and leave a surplus, the Comptroller ought to allow interest on the claims during the period of administration, before appropriating the surplus to the stockholders of the bank. An action of assumpsit by the holder of such a claim will not lie against the Comptroller, nor against the receiver, but will lie against the bank. (*Chemical National Bank* vs. *Bailey*, 12 *Blatchf.*, *p.* 480.)

VI. In such action interest is recoverable on all demands originating in contract conditioned for the payment of interest, and on all demands for money due and unpaid, by way of damages for non-payment after such demands became due. And interest is recoverable on a balance due a depositor in such bank, although he has made no formal demand of payment. (*Ibid.*) But, as to this last point, see the ruling of the Supreme Court.

VII. In the case of *National Bank of the Commonwealth* vs. *Mechanics' National Bank*, 4 *Otto*, *p.* 437, the United States Supreme Court decided that a depositor in a national bank, when it suspends payment and a receiver is appointed, is entitled from the date of his demand to interest on the deposit; that the claims of depositors in such bank at date of suspension, for the amount of their deposits, are, when proved to the satisfaction of the Comptroller of the Currency, placed upon the same footing as if reduced to judgments; that is to say, they draw interest from the time of such proof and allowance. It was also decided that, such interest being a liquidated sum at the time of the payment of the deposit, an action lies to recover it, *and interest thereon.*

VIII. When the Comptroller assesses shareholders to pay the debts of an insolvent national bank, such assessment bears interest from the date of the Comptroller's order. (*Casey* vs. *Galli*, *ante.*)

IX. A statute of New York, fixing the rate of interest at 7 per cent., also makes forfeiture of principal and interest the penalty for taking interest at a greater rate. Notwithstanding this statute, the courts of that State have held that the payee of a promissory note may, *in good faith*, sell and indorse it to a third party for a sum agreed upon, amounting as discount to any rate in excess of that prescribed by law; that such purchaser may recover from the maker principal and interest in full, and that if it be necessary to resort to the indorser, the purchaser may recover against him the actual sum paid for the note with interest.

INTEREST—Continued.

Acting upon these adjudications, a national bank in that State discounted for a customer notes (all paid at maturity) for sums aggregating $2,735.36 in excess of the legal rate of interest. Subsequently the seller sued the bank to recover, under sections 5197 and 5198 of the national bank act, the penalties therein prescribed, to wit, double the aggregate paid.

In the State courts the plaintiff had judgment as prayed, and on writ of error to the court of appeals of New York, the Supreme Court of the United States affirmed the judgment below; holding that,

"Although under the laws of New York a contract between natural persons to reserve and pay upon the discount of business paper any stipulated rate of interest (discount) may be valid, such contract, if a national bank be party thereto, and the paper be, in pursuance thereof, transferred to it, is in violation of said sections, if the rate agreed upon exceeds 7 per cent., and subjects such bank to the penalties therein prescribed. (*National Bank* vs. *Johnson*, 104 *U. S.*, 271.)

JUDGMENTS.

I. A judgment against a national bank in the hands of a receiver, upon a claim, only establishes the validity of such claim; the plaintiff can have no execution on such judgment, but must await *pro rata* distribution. (*Bank of Bethel* vs. *Pahquioque Bank*, 14 *Wall.*, p. 383, and *Clifford, J.*, p. 402.)

JURISDICTION.

I. A United States District Court has jurisdiction to authorize a receiver of an insolvent national bank to compromise a debt. (*Matter of Platt*, 1 *Ben.*, p. 534.)

II. A resident (citizen) of Kentucky was a creditor of a national bank located in Alabama, and commenced a suit on his claim against said bank in the supreme court of the State of New York, at the same time attaching certain moneys belonging to said bank, in the hands of the National Park Bank, in New York. Subsequently the receiver of the Alabama bank (which had failed) was, on his own motion, made party defendant to the action pending in the New York supreme court, and pleaded "*want of jurisdiction*," and other defenses. The supreme court overruled his plea to the jurisdiction, rendered judgment against the receiver on the merits, and ordered satisfaction to be made from the moneys attached. Thereupon the receiver filed his bill in chancery in the *United States Circuit Court* for the proper circuit, praying an injunction to restrain the collection of the judgment rendered by said supreme court, and that the moneys attached be paid to him as receiver. *Held*, that, by the provisions of the Currency Act, the State court was deprived of jurisdiction of the attachment proceedings; that the receiver was not estopped by the proceedings in said State court from asserting his rights in said Circuit Court, and that he was entitled to the relief prayed for in his bill. (*Cadle, receiver, &c.*, vs. *Tracy*, 11 *Blatchf.*, p. 101.)

(See, also, Title "RECEIVERS,"VII, *post.*)

III. State courts have no jurisdiction of actions to recover penalties imposed by the national bank act. (*Newell* vs. *National Bank of Somerset*, 12 *Bush.* [*Ky.*], p. 57.)

See, also, Title "EMBEZZLEMENT," IV, *ante.*)

IV. The United States Circuit Court has no jurisdiction of a suit by a private person to restrain or interfere with the Treasurer of the United States or the Comptroller of the Currency in the discharge of their duties in respect to bonds deposited to secure the redemption of circulating notes of a national bank. (*Van Antwerp* vs. *Hubbard, Blatchf.*, p. 426.)

V. An action will not lie against the Comptroller nor the receiver, upon a claim against an insolvent national bank, but will lie against such bank. (*Chemical National Bank* vs. *Bailey, ante.* See, also, *Bank of Bethel* vs. *Pahquioque Bank, ante.*)

VI. A national bank cannot be sued in the United States District Courts outside of the district where it is located. (*Main* vs. *Second Nat. Bank of Chicago*, 6 *Bissell*, p. 26.)

VII. Nor can such action be brought against a national bank in a State court, save in the county or city where it is located. (*Crocker* vs. *Marine National Bank*, 101 *Mass.*, p. 240.)

(See, also, Title "ACTION," VII, *ante*; also "EMBEZZLEMENT," IV, *ante.*

VIII. The provision of section 5198, U. S. Rev. Stats., requiring that suits, actions, and proceedings against a national bank in any State, county, or municipal court must be brought in the county in which such bank is located, is held

JURISDICTION—Continued.

to apply to transitory actions only, and not to such actions as are by law
local in their character. (*Casey, receiver, &c.*, vs. *Adams*, 2 *Thomp. Cases, p.*
102. *U. S. Supreme Court.*)

[NOTE.—The jurisdiction of the local court was sustained in this cause,
although it seemed clear that a complete remedy might have been had in
the U. S. Circuit Court at New Orleans, where the bank was situated.]

IX. National banks are not entitled, by force of the national bank act, to have
any suit in a State court, wherein they are parties defendant, removed to a
Federal court. (*Wilder* vs. *Union Nat. Bank*, 2 *Thomp. Cases, p.* 124.)

X. National banks are not authorized to sue in the Federal courts out of the districts in which they are located when the amount sued for does not exceed
$500. (*St. Louis Bank* vs. *Brinkham*, 1 *McCrary*, 9.)

[NOTE.—As to present jurisdiction of Federal and State courts, see act
of Congress of July 12, 1882, *proviso* to section 4.]

LOANS IN EXCESS.

I. A loan by a national bank in excess of the restriction of section 29 of the act
of 1864 (Revised Statutes, section 5200), which provides that the total liabilities of any person (borrower) shall not exceed ten per centum of the
capital stock, &c., is not void on that account. The loan may be enforced,
though the bank may be liable to proceedings for forfeiture of its privileges,
&c., for making it. (*Stewart* vs. *National Union Bank of Maryland*, 2 *Abb.,
United States, p.* 424. See, also, *O'Hare* vs. *Second National Bank*, 77 *Pa.,
p.* 96.)

II. In *Samuel M. Shoemaker* vs. *The National Mechanics' Bank* and *The same* vs.
The National Union Bank, application for injunction, &c., United States Circuit Court, Baltimore, Md., Judge Giles held, * * * "As to the first
charge in this bill against the defendant, in reference to the amount loaned
to Bayne & Co., in violation of the twenty-ninth section of the act of June
3, 1864, I would only say that the loan made under such circumstances is
not void; it can be enforced as any other loan made by the bank." (*Vide*
31 *Md., p.* 396.)

III. The validity of a loan in excess of the above-named statutory restriction was
established and set at rest by the decision of the United States Supreme
Court in the case of *Gold Mining Company* vs. *Rocky Mountain National
Bank*, 96 *U. S.* [6 *Otto*], *p.* 640.

LOANS ON REAL ESTATE.

I. A executed a note to B, and, to secure payment thereof, also executed a deed
of trust on lands, which was in effect a mortgage, with a power of sale
thereto annexed. A national bank, on the security of the note *and deed,*
loaned money to B, who thereupon assigned them to the bank. The note
not being paid at maturity, the trustee was proceeding to sell the lands
pursuant to the power, when A filed a bill in chancery to enjoin the sale,
upon the ground that by sections 5136–'37, Revised Statutes, the deed did
not inure as a security for a loan made by the bank at the time of the
assignment of said note and deed: *Held*, that the bank was entitled to enforce collection of the note by a sale of the lands pursuant to the power in
the deed of trust. (*Union National Bank of Saint Louis* vs. *Matthews*, 98 U. S.
[8 *Otto*], *p.* 621.) Mr. Justice Miller dissented, holding the note valid, but
that the deed was inoperative as security to the bank.

[NOTE.—It is now well settled that a mortgage given to secure a loan
from a national bank, executed directly to the bank when the loan is made,
is valid, unless set aside by proceedings instituted for that purpose by the
Government. (*National Bank* vs. *Whitney*, 103 *U. S., p.* 99; *Graham* vs.
National Bank, 32 *N. J. Eq., p.* 804; *Warner* vs. *Dewitt*, 4 *Ill. App., p.* 305;
Thornton vs. *Exchange National Bank*, 71 *Mo.*, 221.)]

LOANS ON SHARES.

I. National banks are governed by the act of 1864, which repealed the act of
1863, and cannot, therefore, make loans on the security of their own shares,
unless to secure a pre-existing debt, contracted in good faith. (*Bank, &c.,*
vs. *Lanier*, 11 *Wall., p.* 369.)

II. The placing of funds by one bank on permanent deposit with another bank
is a loan within the spirit of section 35 of act of 1864. (*Ibid., p.* 369.)

III. Loans by such banks to their shareholders do not create a lien on the shares
of such borrowers. (*Ibid., p.* 369.)

(See, also, *Bullard* vs. *Bank*, 18 *Wall., p.* 580; and "BY-LAWS," *supra.*)

LOANS ON SHARES—Continued.

IV. But a national bank has the right to make loans on negotiable notes secured by the stock of another corporation, of marketable values. (*Shoemaker* vs. *National Mechanics' Bank*, 1 *Hugh.*, p. 101.) The same doctrine was also held in the case of *Germania National Bank et al.* vs. *F. F. Case, receiver, &c.*, decided by the United States Supreme Court, 99 *U. S.* [9 *Otto*], p. 628.

LOCATION.

I. Under sections 6, 8, 10, 15, 18, and 44 of the original Currency Act (13 Stat. at Large, 101), respecting the location of banking associations, a national bank is to be regarded as located at the place specified in its organization certificate. If such a place is in a State, the association is located in that State. (*Manufacturers' National Bank* vs. *Baack*, 8 *Blatchf.*, p. 137.)

OFFICERS.

I. CASHIER. The cashier is the general executive officer of a bank, having charge of its funds, notes, bills, and other choses in action. Either directly or through his subordinates he receives all moneys and notes of the bank, delivers up discounted paper when paid, draws checks to withdraw funds of the bank when deposited, and generally, as such executive officer, transacts most of the bank business. (*United States* vs. *City Bank of Columbus*, 21 *How.*, p. 356, and numerous later decisions.)

II. But the cashier can make no declaration binding the bank not within the scope of his general powers. (*Bank of Metropolis* vs. *Jones*, 8 *Pet.*, p. 12; *S. P.*, 3 *Watts & S.*, [*Pa.*], p. 317 ; 3 *Gill* [*Md.*], p. 96.)

III. A cashier who has made sale of corporate property, and holds a balance in his hands, is the agent of the board of directors, and not of the respective stockholders, and cannot be charged by an individual stockholder as holding such balance for his benefit. (*Brown* vs. *Adams*, 5 *Biss.*, p. 181.)

IV. A cashier, without special authority, cannot bind his bank by an official indorsement of his individual note, and the *onus* is on the payee to show such authority. (*West Saint Louis Savings Bank* vs. *Shawnee Co. Bank*, 3 *Dill*, p. 403.)

V. Although the cashier of a bank may, in the ordinary course of business, without the action of the directors, dispose of the negotiable securities of the bank, he has not the power to pledge its assests for the payment of an antecedent debt. (*State of Tennessee* vs. *Davis*, 50 *How.* [*N. Y.*], p. 447.)

VI. A cashier has not the authority to compromise or release a claim of the bank. (*Chemical Bank* vs. *Kohner*, 8 *Daley* [*N. Y.*], p. 530.)

VII. DIRECTORS. It is the duty of directors of a bank to use ordinary diligence in acquiring knowledge of its business. They cannot be heard, when sued, to say that they were not apprised of facts the existence of which is shown by the books, accounts, and correspondence of the bank. They should control the subordinate officers of the bank in all important transactions. Therefore, under the circumstances proved in this particular case, they were held liable for the abstraction and sale of special deposits by the latter. (*United Society, &c.*, vs. *Underwood, 9 Bush* [*Ky.*], p. 609 ; *German Bank* vs. *Wulfekuhler*, 19 *Kansas*, p. 60.)

VIII. The cashier of a national bank, who had executed no bond, embezzled its funds, discovery whereof might have been effected by use of slight diligence on the part of the directory. They, however, published, according to law, a statement of the condition of the bank, which showed that its affairs were being prudently and honestly administered, and from which the public had a right to believe that he was trustworthy. Afterwards, persons who had seen this report became sureties on the official bond of cashier, and for his subsequent embezzlements were sought to be held liable thereon : *Held*, that such sureties, being misled by the statement, were released. They had a right to believe that the directors, before publishing it, investigated the condition of the bank. (*Graves* vs. *Lebanon National Bank*, 10 *Bush* [*Ky.*], p. 23.)

IX. The mere fact that directors of a bank knew of and sanctioned overdrafts will not release from liability the sureties of a teller who causes a loss to the bank by permitting overdrafts ; for the directors of a bank have no power to sanction overdrafts. (*Market Street Bank* vs. *Stumpe*, 2 *Mo.*, *App.*, 545.)

X. PRESIDENT. A guarantee against loss for signing as sureties, given by a bank president without authority from the directors, to those whom he had solicited thus to sign a note, given to the bank to retire a prior note held by it against their principal, is held to be the individual contract of the president, and not binding upon the bank. (*First National Bank* vs. *Bennett*, 33 *Mich.*, p. 520.)

OFFICERS—Continued.

XI. A president of a bank bought the stock of A. for $1,000, and in payment gave up to A. his note for that amount, which the bank held against A: *Held,* that the president exceeded his powers, and that the bank could recover from A. the amount of the note thus surrendered. (*Rhoads* vs. *Webb,* 24 *Minn., p. 292.*)

XII. A president of a bank, who, with the cashier, had the general charge of its business, permitted and directed the drawing of moneys from the bank by one irresponsible, without security, and for a business in which the president was interested with the party drawing the funds. He requested the cashier not to say anything of it to the directors: *Held,* that the president was personally responsible for the moneys thus drawn. (*First National Bank of Sturgis* vs. *Reid, 37 Mich., p. 263.*) *Quere:* Would not an indictment for embezzlement lie under the national bank act?

XIII. The president of a bank, as such, has no authority to release the claims of the bank against any one. Such authority must come from the directors, by vote or implication. (*Olney* vs. *Chadsey, 7 R. I., p. 224.*) Nor can he bind the bank to pay or become liable for a debt by his admission. (*Henry* vs. *Northern Bank, 63 Ala., p. 527.*)

XIV. In reference to what do not constitute offenses under section 5209 of the Revised Statutes (see case of *United States* vs. *Jas. H. Britton, &c., U. S. Sup. Court, October term,* 1882).

XV. A draft indorsed by the president of the Miners' National Bank of Georgetown, Colo., payable to White or order for account of the bank: *Held,* that the bank could not be held on the draft, but that White was entitled to recover the money advanced for the use of the bank, as appeared by the books of the latter, whether it was advanced without consideration or upon the draft as collateral. (*White* vs. *National Bank,* 102 *U. S., p. 658.*)

XVI. AUTHORITY OF BANK CASHIER.

A banking corporation, whose charter does not otherwise provide, may be represented by its cashier in transactions outside of his ordinary duties without his authority to do so being in writing or appearing in the records of the proceedings of the directors.

His authority may be by parol, and collected from circumstances, or implied from the conduct or acquiescence of the directors.

It may be inferred, from the general manner in which, for a period sufficiently long to establish a settled course of business, he has been suffered by the directors, without interference or inquiry, to conduct the affairs of the bank.

When, during a series of years, or in numerous business transactions, he has been permitted, in his official capacity, and without objection, to pursue a particular course of conduct, it may be presumed, as between the bank and those who in good faith deal with it upon the basis of his authority to represent the corporation, that he has acted in conformity with instructions received from those who have the right to control its operations.

That which directors ought, by proper diligence, to have known, as to the general course of the bank's business, they may be presumed to have known in any contest between the corporation and those who are justified by the circumstances in dealing with it upon the basis of that course of business. (*Supreme Court of the United States, October term,* 1883, *Martin* vs. *Webb.*)

XVII. LIABILITY OF CASHIER.

1. Where directors of a corporation appoint one of their number to act as treasurer, secretary, or other ministerial officer of the corporation, he is *prima facie* entitled to reasonable compensation for his services as such officer.

2. Where he assumes the duties of such ministerial officer upon an express contract as to compensation, such contract controls, and this, though the contract is to discharge the duties without any direct compensation in money.

3. An agent of a corporation, who, as an individual, purchases the properties of the corporation from himself as agent, cannot uphold such purchase by proof that he agreed to pay what he thought the property was worth, but is liable to the corporation for the actual value of the property so by him purchased.

4. Ratification implies knowledge, and a party cannot be adjudged to have ratified an act of which he has no knowledge, actual or constructive.

OFFICERS—Continued.

XVII. LIABILITY OF CASHIER—Continued.

5. The doctrine that the directors of a bank are conclusively presumed to know the financial condition of the bank, its general business, and its receipts and expenditures as shown by its regular books, is for the protection of third parties dealing with the bank, and of the bank against prejudicial action of any director, and cannot be invoked to uphold a wrongful appropriation of moneys by the cashier or other officer, which appropriation is made and also entered upon the books of the bank without the actual knowledge of the directors. (*Supreme Court of Kansas; The First National Bank of Fort Scott* vs. *Drake*.)

6. It is no defense to an action brought by a bank against its late cashier for a wrongful appropriation of moneys, that at the time of such appropriation he was the owner of four-fifths of the stock of the bank, and has since that time sold all of said stock to other parties, who are now the officers and managing authority of the bank.

XVIII. A., the president of defendant, a national bank in Vermont, applied to the plaintiff, a banking corporation in Canada, for a loan for his railroad of $50,000 which he had been unable to obtain from defendant. Plaintiff's manager told him the money could not be loaned as an individual loan, as its individual loans were too near the limit allowed by law, but that it would deposit that amount with defendant if desired. A. assented, and they agreed the deposit should draw interest at 6 per cent. while it remained, and that bonds should be deposited as security. Plaintiff drew two drafts for the amount on a Boston bank, delivered them to defendant and received the collaterals, and entered the transaction on its books as a loan to defendant. Defendant indorsed the drafts, forwarded them to the Boston bank, from which it received credit for them, and has always retained their avails. About a year afterwards defendant failed, and a receiver was appointed who rejected the claim of plaintiff when presented for payment, and defendant brought suit. *Held*, that the transaction was not a loan to A. individually, but to defendant; that plaintiff was entitled to a judgment, to be paid by the Comptroller from the assets ratably with other claims; and that the amount due should be adjusted as of the time when the receiver was appointed, and so certified by the receiver to the Comptroller, to be paid in due course of administration. (*Eastern Township Bank* vs. *Vermont Nat. Bank of St. Albans and Another, Federal Reporter, Vol. 22, p. 186.*)

POST-NOTES.

I. Certificates of deposit, payable at a fixed future day, held to be equivalent to post-notes, and therefore void, as prohibited by a State law.

(See, *ante*, Title " DEPOSITS, CERTIFICATES OF," IV, and cases there cited.)

POWER OF ATTORNEY TO COLLECT PAYMENT OF GOVERNMENT BOND.

A power of attorney authorizing an agent to "sell and assign" a Government bond "called" for payment gives authority to the agent to assign to the Secretary of the Treasury for redemption, and to receive in payment a draft drawn by the Treasurer of the United States to the agent by name, who can indorse it for collection or payment. (*Decision by United States Comptroller Lawrence.*)

RECEIVERS.

I. The receiver of a national bank is the instrument of the Comptroller, and may be removed by him. (*Kennedy* vs. *Gibson*, 8 *Wall, p. 505*.)

II. Such receiver is the statutory assignee of the assets of the bank, and may sue to collect the same in his own name, or in the name of the bank for his use. (*Ibid., p. 506*.)

III. In such suit it is not necessary to make the bank or creditors parties. (*Ibid., p. 506*.)

IV. The receiver of a national bank represents such bank and its creditors, but he in no sense represents the United States Government, and cannot subject the Government to the jurisdiction of any court. (*Case* vs. *Terrill*, 11 *Wall., p. 199*.)

V. The decision of a receiver, rejecting a claim against his bank, is not final. Claimant may still sue. (*Bank of Bethel* vs. *Pahquioque Bank*, 14 *Wall., p. 383*.)

VI. The clause of section 50, act of 1864, which prescribes that the receiver shall be "under the direction of the Comptroller," means only that he shall be *subject* to his direction, not that he shall not act without orders. He may and must collect the assets. That is what he is appointed for. (*Bradley, J. in Bank* vs. *Kennedy*, 17 *Wall., pp. 22–3*.)

RECEIVERS—Continued.

VII. Receivers of national banks are officers of the United States, within the meaning of the act of Congress of March 3, 1815, giving United States courts jurisdiction of actions by United States officers, and may sue in such courts. (*Platt, receiver, &c.,* vs. *Beach, 2 Ben., p.* 303.)

[NOTE.—The judge places stress upon the provision of section 31 of the act of 1864, which requires (in that particular instance) that the Secretary of the Treasury shall concur in the appointment of the receiver.]

VIII. Receiver not liable to be sued on a claim against the bank.
(See Title "JURISDICTION," V, *ante*.)

IX. The personal assets and personal property of an insolvent national bank in the hands of a receiver appointed by the Comptroller of the Currency, in accordance with the provision of section 5234 of the Revised Statutes, in legal contemplation still belong to the bank, though in the hands of the receiver to be administered under the law. The bank does not cease to exist on appointment of the receiver. Its corporate capacity continues until its affairs are finally wound up and its assets distributed. (*Rosenblatt* vs. *Johnston, Chief Justice Waite, United States Supreme Court, October term,* 1881.)

X. A new receiver may be substituted as plaintiff and appellant in suits begun by his predecessor. (*Orson Adams, substituted for George E. Bowden, receiver,* vs. *Jacob C. Johnson and Betsey Valentine, United States Supreme Court, October term,* 1882.) This case was appealed from the United States circuit court of New Jersey. When the bill was dismissed in the lower court, a new receiver had been appointed. The appeal was taken in the name of the old receiver, the new receiver becoming surety on the appeal bond. In the Supreme Court a motion on the part of the appellees to dismiss the appeal on the ground that no appeal was lawfully taken was denied, and a motion on the part of appellant to substitute new receiver as plaintiff and appellant was granted.

XI. Under section 1001 of the Revised Statutes no bond for the prosecution of the suit, or to answer in damages and costs, is required on writs of error or appeals issuing from or brought to this court by direction of the Comptroller of the Currency in suits by or against insolvent national banks, or the receivers thereof. (*Pacific National Bank* vs. *George Mixter, United States Supreme Court, October term,* 1884.)

SET-OFF.

I. In an action brought to enfore the individual liabilitiy of a shareholder of an insolvent bank, such shareholder cannot set off against such liability the amount due to him as a creditor of the bank. (*Garrison* vs. *Howe,* 17 *N. Y., p.* 458: *In re Empire City Bank,* 18 *N. Y., p.* 199.)

[NOTE.—Though these cases were decided by a State tribunal (New York court of appeals), and the rulings were based upon provisions of a State constitution and a State statute, yet the principle they enunciate is recognized and fully affirmed in *Sawyer* vs. *Hoag,* 17 *Wall., p.* 610, and *Scammon* vs. *Kimball,* 2 *Otto, p.* 342. See, also, *Venango National Bank* vs. *Taylor,* 56 *Pa., p.* 14.]

II. A creditor of an insolvent national bank, being such at date of its suspension, may set off the amount of his claim against any claim held by the bank against him at the same date; as, for example, his note, even though such note had not then matured. (*Berry* vs. *Brett,* 6 *Bos.* [*N. Y.*]*, p.* 627; *New Amsterdam Savings Bank* vs. *Gartter,* 54 *How.* [*P. R.*]*, p.* 385; *Platt, receiver,* vs. *Bentley,* 11 *Am. Law Register, p.* 171; *Hade, receiver,* vs. *McVay,* 31 *O. St., p.* 231; same case, *Brown's National Bankrupt Cases, p.* 353; and see the cases cited on p. 357, viz, 56 *Maine,* 167; 1 *Paige* [*N. Y.*]*, p.* 444; 12 *Gray* [*Mass.*]*, p.* 233.)

III. Usurious interest *paid* cannot be set off. (*Hade* vs. *McVay,* 31 *O. St., p.* 231; *Barnet* vs. *National Bank,* 98 *U. S., p.* 555.)

IV. The United States cannot set off an indebtedness to itself from a national bank against the surplus proceeds of bonds deposited by said bank as security for its circulation. (*Cook Co. National Bank, and Aug. H. Burley, receiver of said bank, appellants,* vs. *United States. U. S. Supreme Court, October term,* 1882.)

[NOTE.—This was on the grounds that the bonds are a trust, and a trustee cannot set off against the funds held by him in that character, his individual demand against the granter of the trust.]

SHAREHOLDERS.

I. GENERAL RULES.—A person is presumed to be the owner of stock when his name appears on the books of a company as a stockholder; and when he is sued as such the burden of disproving such presumption is cast upon him. (*Turnbull* vs. *Payson*, 95 *U. S.* [5 Otto], p. 418.)

II. Shareholders have no standing in court to interfere for the protection of their company until the board of directors has neglected, or refused on application, to take the proper steps to protect the interests of the company. (*Fifth National Bank, &c.* vs. *Railroad Co.*, 2 Thomp. Cases, p. 190.)

III. Shares of stock in a national bank are salable and transferable like other personal property; and the statute recognizes this transferability by authorizing each association to prescribe the manner of their transfer. (*Johnston* vs. *Laflin*, 103 *U. S.*, per *Field, J.*, on p. 803.)

IV. This power can only go to the extent of prescribing conditions essential to the protection of the association against fraudulent transfers, or such as are designed to evade just responsibility. It must be exercised reasonably. Transfer cannot be clogged with useless restrictions, nor be made dependent on the consent of directors or stockholders. (*Ibid.*)

V. As between the parties to a sale, it is enough that the certificate of stock is delivered, with authority to the purchaser, or any one he may name, to transfer it on the books of the association, and payment of the price. (*Ibid.*, p. 804.)

VI. The entry of the transaction on the books of the association is required, not for the translation of title, but for the protection of parties and others dealing with the bank, to enable the bank to know who are its stockholders, entitled to vote and receive dividends. *It is necessary to protect the seller against subsequent liability as stockholder*, and perhaps also to protect the purchaser against proceedings by creditors of the seller. (*Ibid.*, *Field, J.*, p. 804.)

VII. When a national bank reduces its capital, each shareholder is entitled to a return of his proportional amount, and the bank cannot retain the funds as surplus, or for any other purpose; and having refused to permit shares thus retired to be transferred on its books, the bank is liable for the value of the shares to the holders. (*Seeley* vs. *New York National Exchange Bank*, 4 Abb. New Cases, p. 61.)

VIII. INDIVIDUAL LIABILITY OF.—The Comptroller must decide when and for what amount the personal liability of the shareholders of an insolvent national bank shall be enforced. (*Kennedy* vs. *Gibson*, 8 *Wall.*, p. 505.)

IX. His decision as to this is conclusive. Shareholders cannot controvert it. (*Ibid.*, p. 505; *Casey* vs. *Galli*. 94 *U. S.* [4 Otto], p. 673; *Germania National Bank et al.* vs. *Case, receiver, U. S. Supreme Court*, 99 Otto, p. 628.) [NOTE.—These cases are decisive against the ruling in *Bowden* vs. *Morris*, 1 Hugh., p. 378.]

X. In any suit brought to enforce such personal liability, such decision of the Comptroller must be averred by the plaintiff, and, if put in issue, must be proved. (*Kennedy* vs. *Gibson, supra.*)

XI. The liability of shareholders is several and not joint. (*Ibid.*, p. 505.)

XII. The limit of such liabilities is the par value of the stock held by each one, (*Ibid.*, pp. 505–6.)

XIII. Where the whole amount is sought to be recovered, the proceeding must be at law; where less is required, the proceeding may be in equity, and in such case an interlocutory decree may be taken for contribution, and the case may stand over for the further action of the court, if such action should subsequently prove to be necessary, until the full amount of the liability is exhausted. (*Ibid.*, p. 505.)

XIV. In such equity suit, all shareholders within the jurisdiction of the court should be made parties defendant; but it is no defense that those not within the jurisdiction are not joined. (*Kennedy* vs. *Gibson, supra.*)

XV. Suits to enforce personal liability of shareholders may properly be brought before other assets are exhausted. (*Ibid.*, pp. 505–6.)

XVI. One Stevens bought shares in a national bank, and caused them to be transferred to one Elston, a porter in the office of his New York broker, and irresponsible. At the time of the transfer there was no suspicion of the insolvency of the bank, and it remained in good credit for more than a year afterward: *Held*, that Stevens was liable as stockholder upon the failure of the bank. (*Davis, receiver,* vs. *Stevens,* 2 Thomp. Cases, p. 158, *U. S. Circuit Court Southern District N. Y., per Waite, C. J.*)

XVII. Where, before the failure of a bank, stock was transferred on its books to the name of an irresponsible person, for the purpose of escaping liability,

5745 CUR——7

SHAREHOLDERS—Continued.

and so stood at the time of the appointment of a receiver: *Held*, that the receiver could show who the real owner was, and that the latter was liable for the assessment. (*Ibid.*)

XVIII. RATABLE LIABILITY OF.—Mr. Morse, in his Treatise on Banks, &c., second edition, p. 503, states the law in substance as follows: "The liability of each stockholder is precisely for his ratable proportion of that indebtedness of the bank'which is to be borne by the shareholders. It is for his share of such total indebtedness, not for his proportion of each item thereof. Neither are the solvent shareholders, or those who can be come at for collection, liable to assessment beyond the proportional amount as above stated, by reason of the insolvency or inaccessibility of others of the shareholders. Those who are solvent and accessible have not the burden of paying off the sum which is due from all together; only their own proportionate share." This theory was fully sustained by the United States Supreme Court in the case of *United States* vs. *Knox*, 102 *U. S.*, *p.* 422. See also the cases there cited. When the holder of shares of national-bank stock has information causing apprehension of its failure, and colludes with and transfers his shares to an irresponsible transferee to avoid liability, the transaction will be deemed to be a fraud on the creditors of the bank, and the transferor will be held to his liability. The transfer is good as between the parties, however, and only voidable by election of plaintiff. This case is one of equitable cognizance, and either party may be held liable. (*Orson Adams, substituted for George E. Bowden, receiver*, vs. *Jacob C. Johnson and Betsey Valentine, U. S. Sup. Court, October term,* 1882.)

XIX. LIABILITY OF EXECUTOR, ADMINISTRATOR, AND HEIRS OF.—Where stockholder died, before failure of bank, stock not having been transferred to name of administrator: *Held*, that the stock is not to be regarded as having been at the time of the failure the property of the administrator, in such a sense as to constitute him a shareholder within the meaning of sec. 5152, U. S. Rev. Stat., so as to limit liability of the estate to funds actually in the hands of administrator: *Held*, also, that the provision of the act exempting executors, administrators, and trustee from personal liability was not intended to affect the liability to assessments of estates in process of settlement, but only to prevent a personal liability from running against persons acting in a trust capacity, who had received the stock for the benefit of trust estates. (*Davis* vs. *Weed*, 44 *Conn.*, *p.* 569.)

XX. The liability of a stockholder is in the nature of a *contract*, and as such was a personal liability, for which his estate was holden at his death. (*Davis* vs. *Weed, supra*, citing *Hawthorne* vs. *Calef*, 2 *Wall., p.* 22; *Lowry* vs. *Jamen*, 46 *N. Y.*, *p.* 119; *Bailey* vs. *Hollister*, 26 *N. Y.*, *p.* 112.)

XXI. LIABILITY OF TRUSTEE OF.—To protect trustee of stock from personal liability it must appear upon the books that he held as such trustee. (*Davis* vs. *Essex Baptist Society*, 44 *Conn.*, *p.* 582.)

XXII. Creditors have a right to know who have pledged their personal liability. (*Ibid.*)

XXIII. If a trustee wishes to disclose his trusteeship, there is no difficulty in giving notice upon the books of the bank. If he does not do so, he is guilty of laches, for which others should not suffer. (*Ibid.*)

XXIV. The settlement of the affairs of an insolvent bank would be rendered a matter of great labor, expense, and delay if persons who appeared upon the books of the bank as individual stockholders were permitted to relieve themselves by proof *aliunde* that they held the stock as executors, guardians, or trustees. (*Ibid.*)

[NOTE.—The last-cited case, and *Davis* vs. *Weed, supra*, although reported in the Connecticut Reports, were decided by the United States District Court.]

XXV. LIABILITY OF TRANSFEREE OF.—The transferee of shares, when such transfer is absolute on the books of the bank, is liable to creditors to the amount of such shares, although in fact he holds them as collateral security for a loan to the shareholder who transferred them. (*Hale* vs. *Walker*, 31 *Iowa*, *p.* 614; *Adderly* vs. *Storm*, 6 *Hill*, *p.* 624; *Van Riker's case*, 20 *Wend.*, *p.* 614; *Bowden, receiver*, vs. *Santos et al.*, 1 *Hugh.*, *p.* 158; *Marcy* vs. *Clark*, 17 *Mass.*, *p.* 330.)

[NOTE.—In the *Banker's Magazine* for January, 1875, is a notice of the case of *Mann, receiver*, vs. *Dr. Cheeseman*, decided by Blatchford, J., in the United States Circuit Court in New York, in which the judge held that until there was a transfer of shares *on the books of the bank*, the shareholder whose name there appeared was liable for the debts of the bank; that an actual sale and

SHAREHOLDERS—Continued.

the signing of the ordinary power of attorney on the back of the certificate will not relieve the seller. To the foregoing rulings of State and other subordinate tribunals may now be added the decision of the Supreme Court of the United States in *Germania Bank et al.* vs. *Case, receiver,* already cited. The Germania National Bank of New Orleans discounted a note for the firm of Phelps, McCullough & Co. for $14,000, at ninety days, taking as part security therefor the pledge of 100 shares of the Crescent City National Bank stock, with power of attorney to the Germania cashier to transfer, sell, &c., on default in payment of the note. Phelps, McCullough & Co. failed, and the note was protested at maturity. Prior to the maturity of the note, the Crescent City Bank sustained such heavy losses that it was notoriously in bad repute in New Orleans; and yet, when the note fell due the cashier of the Germania immediately transferred to his own bank, upon the books of the Crescent City Bank, the 100 shares so pledged. Afterwards, on the same day, he transferred 76 of these shares to one Waldo, a clerk of the Germania Bank; and on the day following transferred the remainder to said Waldo. It was proved that Waldo paid nothing, was the mere agent of the Germania Bank, which still owned the 100 shares as security for the payment of said note, and that one of the principal reasons for the transfers to Waldo was the possible liability of the shareholders of the Crescent City Bank for its debts in case of insolvency. Soon after, the Crescent City Bank failed. *Held, per* Strong, J., that the transfers to said Waldo were void as against said receiver, and that although the Germania Bank only held said shares as collateral security for the payment of said discount, it was still liable as owner for the assessment in this case ordered by the Comptroller. The opinion is able and fortified by numerous authorities. In this same case, at a former term, upon a motion to dismiss the appeals of certain of the appellants, the Supreme Court recognized the right of the Comptroller to make an additional assessment, if deemed necessary; and for this reason sustained the appeals, holding that the matter in dispute was, or might be, over $5,000, although the decrees appealed from were severally less than that amount. The assessment was for 70 per cent.]
(See, also, *Pullman* vs. *Upton,* 96 *U. S.* [6 *Otto*], *p.* 323, as to liability of transferee.)

XXVI. Where a shareholder of a corporation is called upon to respond to a liability as such, he is not permitted to deny the existence of such corporation. (*B. U. Keyser, receiver,* vs. *Jane C. Hitz, Supreme Court, D. C., June* 26, 1883.)

XXVII. Under married women's act, D. C., where during marriage a married woman acquires bank stock otherwise than from her husband, both her title and liability are absolute. (*Ibid.*) Where she acquires it from her husband, she holds it with a qualified property in her husband. It is liable, as a *chose in action,* to be reduced to his possession. (*Ibid.*) Where a woman, holding savings-bank stock acquired by deed or gift from her husband, agrees, with his consent, to convert the stock into national-bank stock, and although still holding it subject to his marital rights, she is liable to assessment as a stockholder and must pay such assessment from her estate. (*Ibid.*) If the transfer to her and the subsequent conversion were without her knowledge, it might be otherwise.

XXVIII. The liability incurred by a holder of national-bank stock is statutory and not by contract. Being so it attaches, as an incident of ownership, to all who are capable of such ownership, without reference to any supposed voluntary assumption by contract, express or implied. Therefore when national-bank stock is held by a *feme covert,* either in her own right or subject to the marital rights of her husband, the liability to be assessed affects her alone, and it is not necessary, in an action to enforce collection of an assessment, to join her husband, as would be necessary if it were a common-law obligation or liability of the wife. (*Ibid.*)

XXIX. PLEDGE TO A NATIONAL BANK OF ITS OWN SHARES AS SECURITY.—Where a national bank made a loan upon the pledge of its own shares and afterward sold the shares to obtain payment of the loan which exceeded the amount realized from the shares: *Held,* that the owner of the shares could not, on the ground that the statute forbids a national bank to take its own shares as security, recover from the bank the amount realized upon the sale of the shares. (*Supreme Court of the United States. First National Bank* vs. *Stewart.*)

XXX. The Pacific National Bank of Boston was organized in December, 1877, with a capital of $250,000, with the right to increase it to $1,000,000. In November, 1879, its capital was raised to $500,000; September 13, 1881, the directors voted to increase the capital to $1,000,000. On November 18, 1881, the bank suspended. On December 13, 1881, the directors voted that as $38,700

SHAREHOLDERS—Continued.

of the increase of capital stock had not been paid in, the capital be fixed at $961,300, and the Comptroller of the Currency was notified to that effect, and he notified the bank, under Revised Statutes, section 5205, to pay a deficiency on its capital stock by an assessment of 100 per cent. At the annual meeting the assessment was voted, and on March 18, 1881, with consent of the Comptroller and the approval of the directors and the examiner, the bank resumed business, and continued until May 20, 1881, when it again suspended and was put in the hands of a receiver. Prior to May 20, 1882, $742,800 of the voluntary assessment had been paid in. Complainant was the owner of 25 shares of stock on September 13, 1881, and after the vote to increase the stock, took 25 shares, for which he paid $2,500, on October 1, 1881, and received a certificate. He voted for the assessment at the annual meeting, and in February, 1882, paid the assessment on the old and new stock, and subsequently sought to enjoin the suit at law against him by the receiver to enforce his individual liability as a stockholder, under Revised Statutes, section 5151, on the ground that the increase of capital was illegal and void, and that the voluntary assessment under Revised Statutes, section 5205, relieved the stockholders of individual liability : *Held*, that he was not entitled to relief, and the bill should be dismissed. (*Morrison* vs. *Price. Federal Reporter, vol.* 23, *p.* 217.)

SHAREHOLDER'S RIGHT TO SUE.

I. In an action by a shareholder of a national bank charging the directors with misconduct, if the complainant fails to show a demand on the Comptroller for and his refusal of a direction to the receiver to bring suit, it is bad, and the action must fail; though it is said that if the Comptroller, in a proper case, should thus refuse, probably the stockholders could sue, making the bank a proper party. (*Brinkerhoff* vs. *Bostwick*, 23 *Hun.* [*N. Y.*], 237.)

[NOTE.—In a suit at law in New Jersey, by one *Ackerman*, a shareholder, against *Halsey, president of the Mechanics' National Bank*, it was, by Mr. Justice Depue, *Held*, 1st. That a suit under section 5239 of the national bank act, to enforce the liability of a director for misconduct, should be brought by the corporation, or, when in the hands of a receiver, by him. 2d. That in the event of the improper refusal of the corporation or receiver to sue, one or more shareholders might institute a suit; but in such instances the suit should be for the benefit of all shareholders, making the bank or receiver a proper party, and, of course, the proceedings should be, not at law, but in equity.]

II. ACTION BY SHAREHOLDERS AGAINST BANK OFFICER FOR MISMANAGEMENT.— An action will not lie by a stockholder in a national bank against the president and directors for their neglect and mismanagement of the affairs of the bank, whereby insolvency ensued and the stock became worthless. (*New Jersey Supreme Court. Conway* vs. *Halsey.*)

SHARES OF STOCK.

I. A national bank whose certificates of stock specify that the shares are transferable on the books of the bank on surrender of the certificates, *and not otherwise*, and which suffers a shareholder to transfer without such surrender, is liable to a *bona fide* transferee, for value of same stock, who produces such certificate with usual power of attorney to transfer; and this is so though no notice had been given to the bank of the transfer. (*Bank* vs. *Lanier*, 11 *Wall., p.* 369.)

II. Shares are *quasi* negotiable. (*Ibid., p.* 369.)

III. Stock of an incorporated company is *chose in action*. (*B. U. Keyser* vs. *Jane C. Hitz, Sup. Court D. C., June* 26, 1883.)

IV. The creditors of a shareholder in a national bank sued him in the place where the bank was located, and attached his stock, obtained judgment, sold the shares on execution, and on the sheriff's certificate the bank transferred the stock to purchasers. It appears that a year previous to this action the owner had assigned them to D, with power of attorney to make the transfer, and, January, 1869, D assigned them to S for full consideration, power of attorney, &c. S went to bank to make the transfer. The bank refusing, he brought suit and recovered judgment. The judge held that where there are no positive provisions of law making transfers without public notice void as against attaching creditors, such creditors take their debtor's property subject to honest and *bona fide* liens and equitable transfers. (*Scott* vs. *Pequonnock Nat'l Bank, U. S. Circuit Court, S. D. N. Y.*)

SHARES OF STOCK—Continued.

V. ASSIGNMENT OF BANK STOCK NOT TRANSFERRED ON BANK BOOKS.—The by-laws of the Eliot National Bank provided that its stock should be assignable only on the books, and that when the stock was transferred the certificate should be returned and canceled, and a new one issued. The owner of stock assigned his certificate with power of attorney to the Continental National Bank as collateral security for a loan : *Held*, that this assignment to the latter bank was valid against an attachment of the stock by the former bank in an action by it against the owner of the stock. (*United States Circuit Court, Mass., May 21, 1881; Continental National Bank vs. Eliot National Bank.*)

VI. The payee and indorser of a negotiable promissory note is liable as maker where he knows the maker is a fictitious person; and if he were to be regarded as an indorser, he would be liable on his indorsement without demand or notice. The sale which section 5201 Rev. Stat. requires a national bank to make of its own stock is real and not fictitious. And where the president and cashier of a national bank, which is the owner of some of its own stock, purchase such stock, and execute their note to the bank for the purchase money, in a suit against them on the note by the receiver of such bank they are estopped to set up as a defense that their purchase of the stock was unauthorized, or that their purchase was merely colorable, or to avoid a forfeiture of the bank's charter, or for any other deceptive or illegal purpose. The sale by the president of a national bank to himself and the cashier of the stock of the bank owned by the bank may be ratified by the bank or its legal representative; but a sale by himself to the bank of its own stock, where he acts in the double capacity of seller and buyer, cannot be ratified when the purchase of the stock by the bank is not necessary to prevent loss upon a debt previously contracted. In the one case the sale of the stock is enjoined by law, and its sale by the president may be ratified, however irregular it may have been in the first instance; but the purchase of its own stock by the bank is interdicted by law, and for this act there can be no authorization in advance and no ratification afterwards. (*Bundy, as Receiver, etc.*, vs. *Jackson. Federal Reporter, vol. 24, p. 628.*)

SURPLUS FUND.

I. Where the shares of a national bank are assessed for taxation at their par value, the surplus fund of such bank, in excess of the amount required by law to be kept on hand, is taxable. (*First National Bank vs. Peterborough, 56 N. H., p. 38.*) But when such shares are assessed at their *market* value, and the amount of such surplus is taken into account in estimating such market value, it is not taxable. (*State vs. City of Newark, 10 Vroom [N. J.], p. 380.*)

II. Neither a dividend which has been declared, nor a portion of capital of a national bank remaining after a reduction has been made, can be retained by the directors to constitute a surplus fund. (*Seeley vs. New York National Exchange Bank, 4 Abb. [N. Y.], p. 61.*)

III. The surplus fund which a national bank is required, by section 5199, U. S. Revised Statutes, to reserve from its net profits, is not excluded in the valuation of its shares for taxation. (*Strafford National Bank vs. Dover, 2 Thomp. Cases, p. 296, Sup. Court N. H.*, following *National Bank vs. Commonwealth, 9 Wall., p. 353; People vs. Commissioners, 94 U. S., p. 415.*)

TAXATION.

I. BY LICENSE.—The District of Columbia imposed a *license tax* on all the national banks in the District, the rate being 50 cents annually on each $1,000 of the capital invested. The Citizens' National Bank refused to pay this assessment, and a test case was made in the District criminal court, Mr. Justice MacArthur presiding. This court, after full argument, held the tax illegal and void, as being contrary to the mode of taxation prescribed by Congress, which mode was held to be exclusive. This ruling of Judge MacArthur is fully sustained by the supreme court of Missouri. (*Carthage vs. Carthage National Bank, 71 Mo., 508*; also by *National Bank of Titusville vs. Cadwell, U. S. Dist. Court, West. Dist. Pa., Fed. Reporter, XIII, p. 429.*)

II. OF INSOLVENT BANKS.—A tax levied upon the property of a national bank, subsequent to its insolvency, is subordinate to the rights of a receiver, even though he be appointed after such levy. (*Woodward vs. Ellsworth, 4 Colo., p. 590.*)

(See Title " SURPLUS FUND," *supra*.)

TAXATION—Continued.

III. OF INTEREST AND DIVIDENDS.—Under the internal-revenue act of July, 1870, interest paid and dividends declared during the last five months of 1870 are taxable, as well as those declared during the year 1871. (*Blake* vs. *National Banks*, 23 *Wall.*, *p.* 307.)

IV. OF SHARES OF STOCK.—The act of 1864, rightly construed, subjects the shares of the association in the hands of shareholders to taxation by the States, under certain limitations set forth in section 41, without regard to the fact that part or the whole of the capital of such association is invested in national securities, which are declared by law exempt from State taxation. (*Van Allen* vs. *Assessors*, 3 *Wall.*, 573. Chase, C. J., and other judges dissented.)

V. Act thus construed is constitutional. (*Ibid.*, *p.* 573.)

VI. A certain statute of New York, which taxed *shares* of national-bank stock, was declared void, because *shares* of State banks were not taxed, although their capital was; the act of Congress prescribing that shares of national banks shall be taxed only as *shares* of State banks are. (*Ibid.*, *p.* 573. The ruling as to taxing shares of stock reaffirmed in *Bradley* vs. *People*, 4 *Wall.*, *p.* 459; *National Bank* vs. *Commonwealth*, 9 *Wall.*, *p.* 353.)

VII. In last case, *Held*, that a State law requiring the cashier to pay the tax was valid. *Held*, also, that a certain State tax law virtually taxed "*shares* of moneyed corporations," &c. (*Ibid.*, *p.* 353.)

VIII. Section 5219 of United States Revised Statutes applies to and includes as well the *valuation* of shares for taxation as the *rate* of tax to be imposed, and prohibits a State from discriminating, detrimentally to a national bank, as to either valuation or rate. Therefore, a statute of the State of New York which permitted a party, when being assessed, to deduct his just debts from the value of all his personal property, save such as was invested in shares of national-bank stock, was held void as to taxation of such shares. (*People* vs. *Weaver*, *U. S.*, *p.* 539, overruling the judgment of New York court of appeals in same cause.)

IX. So in another case, where local assessors valued all other property below its cash worth, but assessed shares of national-bank stock at par or their full value: *Held*, that the tax upon shares thus assessed was invalid, and that, upon payment of the amount justly assessable, a court of equity would enjoin collection of the residue. (*Pelton* vs. *Commercial National Bank of Cleveland*, 101 *U. S*, *p.* 143.)

X. Where it appeared that throughout a portion of Ohio, including Lucas County, and perhaps all over the State, a settled rule with the equalizing officers was to value real estate and ordinary personal property at one-third of their worth, while moneyed capital was fixed at three-fifths, and the State board of equalization, without changing the valuation thus made of real estate and ordinary personalty, assessed national bank shares at par: *Held*, that such unequal valuation was in violation of the constitutional rights of such shareholders; and, on payment of the tax justly due, equity would enjoin collection of the residue. (*Cummings* vs. *Merchants' National Bank of Toledo*, 101 *U. S.*, *p.* 153.)

XI. Shares of stock in national banks are personal property, and though in one sense incorporeal, the law which created them could separate them from the person of their owner for taxation, and give them a *situs* of their own. (*Tappan, collector*, vs. *Bank*, 19 *Wall.*, *p.* 490.)

XII. Section 41 did thus separate them and give them a *situs* of their own. (*Ibid.*, *p.* 490.)

XIII. This provision of the national currency act became a law of the property (in shares), and every State in which a bank was located acquired jurisdiction, for taxation, of all the shares, whether owned by residents or non-residents, and power to legislate accordingly. (*Ibid.*, *p.* 490.)

XIV. Under the act of Congress of February 10, 1868, enacting that each State legislature may direct the manner of taxing all shares of stock of national banks located within the State, subject to the restriction that the taxation shall not be greater than the rate assessed *upon other moneyed capital* in the hands of individual citizens of such State, and of a certain act of the legislature of Pennsylvania, which provides that such shares shall be assessed for school, municipal, and local purposes at the same rate as is now or may hereafter be assessed and imposed upon other moneyed capital in the hands of individual citizens of the State: *Held*, that shares of national-bank stock may be valued for taxation for county, school, municipal, and local purposes *at an amount above their par value*. (*Hepburn* vs. *School Directors of the Borough of Carlisle*, 23 *Wall.*, *p.* 480.)

[NOTE.—In this case it appeared that Hepburn owned several thousand dollars of national-bank stock, the par value of which was $100 per share,

TAXATION—Continued.

and that it was valued for taxation, for a school tax, at $150 per share. This assessment was held valid, notwithstanding that by a certain act of the State legislature, applicable to the county of Cumberland, in which the borough of Carlisle was situated, certain specified kinds of moneyed obligations were exempt from taxation except for State purposes.]

XV. The rate of taxation of shares of a national bank by a State should be the same as, or not greater than, that upon the moneyed capital of the individual citizen which is liable to taxation ; that is, no greater in proportion or percentage of tax on the valuation of shares should be levied than upon other moneyed taxable capital in the hands of the citizen. (*People* vs. *The Commissioners*, *&c.*, 4 *Wall.*, *p.* 256.)

XVI. The act of Congress approved June 3, 1864 (R. S., sec. 5219), was not intended to curtail the power of the States on the subject of taxation, or to prohibit the exemption of particular kinds of property, but to protect the corporations formed under its authority from unfriendly discrimination by the States in the exercise of their taxing power. (*Adams* vs. *Nashville*, 95 *U. S.* [5 *Otto*], *p.* 19. See also, *Saint Louis National Bank*, *National Bank of the State of Missouri*, *Third National Bank*, *Valley National Bank*, and *Merchants' National Bank of Saint Louis* vs. *Papin*, in United States circuit court, eastern district of Missouri, September term, 1876. Also, *Gallatin National Bank of New York* vs. *Commissioners of Taxes*, supreme court of New York, first department, general term, November, 1876. These latter cases are published in the *Bankers' Magazine* for December, 1876.)

XVII. OF TOWN AND CITY NOTES, ETC.—Section 3441, U. S. Revised Statutes, which enacts that every national bank, State bank, or banker, or association shall pay a tax of ten per centum on the amount of notes of any town, city, or municipal corporation paid out by them, imposes the taxes thus laid *not* on the notes, *but on their use as a circulating medium*, and is therefore constitutional. (*National Bank* vs. *United States*, 101 *U. S.*, *p.* 1.)

XVIII. When by a State statute the citizen may have the amount of his indebtedness deducted from the total value of his personal property, thus ascertaining the amount of his personal estate subject to taxation, and a subsequent statute relating to taxation of bank shares makes no provision for such deduction, the latter statute is nevertheless the valid rule for assessing such shares in all instances where there are no debts to be deducted. That the latter statute does not authorize a deduction for debts does not invalidate it, except as to that distinct and separable principle.

XIX. Under such statutes assessments of bank shares where there are no debts to deduct are valid. Even in cases of assessments where debts exist, which should be deducted, but are not, the assessments are avoidable only, not void. (*Supervisors of Albany* vs. *Stanley*, U. S. Supreme Court, April, 1882. *Fed. Reporter*, *Vol. XII*, *p.* 82.)

XX. *Johnston* vs. *U. S. Court of Claims*, December 1, 1881. Under section 22 of the act of March 3, 1869, relative to abatement of taxes versus insolvent national banks, semi-annual taxes are expected to come out of profits of the bank, and, thus reducing dividends, they are a tax on the proprietors of the institution, not on the depositors. (*Court of Claims Reports*, *Vol.* 17, 158.)

XXI. In the two following cases, one in California and one in Alabama, it was decided in each instance that the particular form of discrimination under the laws and regulations of the State was contrary to the Federal law permitting the taxation of national-bank shares by States. (*Pollard* vs. *Zuber*, 65 *Ala.*, 635, *Miller* vs. *Heilbrun*, 58 *Cal.*, 133.)

XXII. The former decisions of this court do not sustain the proposition that national-bank shares may be subjected, under the authority of the state, to local taxation, where a very material part, relatively, of other moneyed capital in hands of individual citizens within the same jurisdiction, or taxing district, is exempted from such taxation. While exact uniformity or equality of taxation cannot be expected under any system, capital invested in national-bank shares was intended by Congress to be placed upon the same footing of substantial equality in respect of taxation by State authority as the State establishes for other moneyed capital in the hands of individual citizens, however invested, whether in state bank shares or otherwise. (*Boyer* vs. *Boyer*, *U. S. Supreme Court*, *Bankers' Magazine*, June 1885, *p.* 934.)

TRANSFERS OF ASSETS.

I. A preference of one creditor to another, within the meaning of section 5242 Revised Statutes, is a preference given by the bank to secure or pay a pre existing debt. Where a person, knowing that a national bank is emba

TRANSFERS OF ASSETS—Continued.

rassed, makes to it a loan, taking as security therefor a pledge of part of the assets of the bank, this transfer does not give him the preference prohibited by the statute. (*Casey* vs. *Le Société de Crédit Mobilier*, 2 *Woods, p. 77.*)

II. WHEN NOT BINDING.—Under said section 5242, which declares void transfers of its property by a national bank, made in contemplation of insolvency, and with a view to give a preference to one creditor over another, or with a view to prevent the application of the assets of the bank in the manner prescribed by law, such a transfer is void if the insolvency is in the contemplation of the bank making the transfer, although the party to whom it is made does not know or contemplate the insolvency of the bank. (*Case, Receiver*, vs. *Citizens' Bank*, 2 *Woods. p.* 23.)

III. As to when a *pledge* of assets, even when intended as security for a loan to a national bank, will be held invalid as against general creditors, see the cases of *Casey, Receiver*, vs. *Le Société de Crédit Mobilier; Same* vs. *National Park Bank; Same* vs. *Schuchardt*, 96 *U. S.* [6 *Otto*], *pp.* 467, 492, 494.

IV. After a vote of the directors to close their bank and go into liquidation, any transfer of the assets of the bank to a creditor, whereby that creditor secures a preference, will be presumed to be made with a fraudulent intent. (*National Security Bank* vs. *Price, Receiver, Federal Reporter, Vol.* 22, *p.* 697.)

V. The Pacific National Bank of Boston suspended November 18, 1881, but after examination resumed March 18, 1882, with the consent of the Comptroller of the Currency, and continued to transact business until May 22, 1882, when it again failed. Between March 24, 1882, and April 28, 1882, certain creditors, whose claims had been disputed and placed in a suspense account, attached the property of the bank, whereupon the bank gave bond with the president and a director as sureties, and the attachments were dissolved. The bank transferred to the sureties, March 22, 1882, a certificate of deposit for $100,000 on another bank, which, on April 13, 1882, was exchanged for other property. *Held*, that such transfer was not made after the commission of an act of insolvency by the bank, or in contemplation thereof, and with a view to a preference or to prevent the application of the assets as prescribed by the banking act. (*Price, Receiver*, vs. *Coleman and others, Federal Reporter, Vol.* 22, *p.* 694.)

VI. A bank is in contemplation of insolvency when the fact becomes reasonably apparent to its officers that the concern will presently be unable to meet its obligations, and will be obliged to suspend its ordinary operations. The intent to give a preference is presumed when a payment is made to a creditor by a bank whose officers know of its insolvency, and therefore that it cannot pay all of its creditors in full. Where property is transferred by a bank to a creditor to avoid paying him the amount due him, and thus postpone the failure of the bank, it is none the less fraudulent and void. On rehearing, former opinion (23 Fed. Rep. 311) is overruled, and transfer held fraudulent and set aside. (*Roberts, Receiver, etc.*, vs. *Hill, Adm'r, etc., Federal Reporter, Vol.* 24, *p.* 571.)

TRUSTEES, ETC.

I. A trustee transferred sureties to the Merchants' Bank of Boston as collateral for money advanced and lost in speculation. The Massachusetts supreme court compelled the bank to restore the collateral, some $40,000, to the plaintiff, a lady, on the ground that the stocks and bonds were transferred under such circumstances as to put the bank on inquiry.

ULTRA VIRES.

I. WHAT IS.—National banks cannot sell railroad bonds for third parties on commission, or engage in business of that character. (*Susan Weckler* vs. *First National Bank of Hagerstown*, Court of Appeals of Maryland, 42 Md., *p.* 581.)

II. In an action of deceit against a national bank, for alleged false representations of its teller in the sale to plaintiff of certain railroad bonds: *Held,* that the selling of such bonds on commission was not within the authorized business of a national bank, and being thus beyond the scope of its corporate powers, the defense of *ultra vires* was open to it, and it was not responsible for the deceit of its teller. (*Ibid.*)

III. A national bank has no inherent power to act as agent in the purchase of bonds or stocks for third persons, and its president cannot bind it by an agreement so to act without special authority. (*First National Bank of Allentown* vs. *Hoch*, 89, *Penn.*, *p.* 324.) *Quere:* If the bank has no such inherent power, how can it confer "special authority" on the president ?

[NOTE.—Whether the *purchase* of promissory notes by a bank empowered to discount them is *ultra vires*, is a question upon which the adjudications

ULTRA VIRES—Continued.

are in conflict. That such purchase is valid, see *Pape* vs. *Capital Bank of Topeka*, 20 *Kans.*, p. 440; *Smith* vs. *Exchange Bank*, 26 O., p. 141, &c. Per contra, see *Farmers and Mechanics' Bank* vs. *Baldwin*, 23 *Minn.*, p. 198; *First National Bank of Rochester* vs. *Pierson*, 1 *Thomp. Cases*, p. 673. There is much in the point that if a national bank can *purchase* promissory notes, it can do so for such price as the seller may be willing to take; and thus the prohibitions as to *usury* may be practically nullified. But further, why should not the rule "*expressio unius est exclusio alterius*" control? In *National Bank* vs. *Johnson*, 104 U. S. 271, the United States Supreme Court held that a national bank may purchase business paper (promissory notes) when the transaction amounts in law to a *discount*, but expressly leaves undecided the question whether such bank can buy such paper "indorsed without recourse," or transferred by delivery only. (See the closing paragraph of opinion.)]

IV. WHAT IS NOT.—A national bank took a lien upon real estate to secure a pre-existing debt. Afterward the bank paid $500 to discharge a prior lien upon the land, taking a note and mortgage on land in Kansas to secure this advance. Lien and mortgage held valid and warranted by law. (*Orvin* vs. *Merchants' National Bank*, 16 *Kans.*, p. 341.)

V. *A chattel mortgage* taken by a national bank to secure a pre-existing debt is valid, and will be enforced. (*Spofford* vs. *First National Bank*, 37 *Iowa*, p. 181.)

VI. A bank organized under the national bank act has power to sell any immovable it may own, and may reserve a mortgage and vendor's privilege (lien) thereon. (*New Orleans National Bank* vs. *Raymond*, 29 *La. Annual*, p. 355.)

VII. It would seem that where a national bank had realized the consideration agreed upon for its guarantee of the paper of another, the doctrine of *estoppel in pais* precludes such bank from asserting that such guarantee is *ultra vires*. (*People's Bank* vs. *National Bank*, 101 U. S., p. 181.)

VIII. A national bank has corporate power to enter into an agreement with a customer to exchange for him non-registered for registered United States bonds; and it is bound by an agreement to that effect, made for a sufficient consideration by its cashier. (*Yerkes* vs. *National Bank*, 69 N. Y., p. 382.)

(See, also, Title "DEPOSITS, SPECIAL," *ante*.)

IX. A township in Vermont issued its bonds with interest coupons attached. Each coupon contained an express promise to pay, &c. A national bank bought of these bonds, and sued the township in assumpsit, *on unpaid coupons*: *Held*, that the action was in due form, and that a national bank could legally buy, hold, and sue upon such bonds and upon the coupons. (*North Bennington Bank* vs. *Bennington*, 16 *Blatchf.*, p. 53.)

USURY.

I. State laws relative to usury do not apply to national banks. (*Farmers and Mechanics' National Bank* vs. *Dearing*, 1 *Otto*, p. 29.)

II. The only forfeiture declared by the 30th section of the act of June 3, 1864 (Revised Statutes, section 5198) is of the *entire interest* which the note or bill carries with it, or which has been agreed to be paid thereon, when the rate knowingly reserved or charged by a national bank is in excess of that allowed by that section; and no loss of the entire debt is incurred by such bank as a penalty or otherwise, by reason of the provision of the usury law of a State. (*Farmers and Mechanics' National Bank* vs. *Dearing*, above cited; *National Exchange Bank* vs. *Moore*, 2 *Bond*, p. 170; *Barnett* vs. *National Bank*, 98 U. S. [8 *Otto*], p. 555.)

III. If usurious interest has been *paid* to a national bank, twice the amount of interest thus paid may be recovered from such bank by the person paying the same, or his legal representative; but as this provision of the statute is penal and the same statute prescribes how such recovery may be had, no other remedy can be resorted to. It must be recovered, if at all, in a suit in the nature of an action of debt. That the borrower from a national bank has paid usurious interest can avail him nothing, as a defense, or by way of a set-off, when sued for the amount of the loan by the bank. (*Barnett* vs. *National Bank*, above cited.)

(See Title "INTEREST," *ante*.)

IV. While the national bank act prescribes penalties for usury, it does not make the contract (*c. g.* contract of indorser) void; and for the court so to decide would be to add a penalty not imposed by the statute. This the court will not do. (*Oates* vs. *First National Bank of Montgomery*, 100 U. S., p. 239.)

Usury—Continued.

V. The assignee in bankruptcy of a borrower from a national bank may sue for
and recover the penalty for having received usurious interest. (*Wright* vs.
*First National Bank of Greensburg, 2 Thomp. Cases, p. 138, U. S. Cir. Court,
Indiana.*)

VI. The exacting of usurious interest by a national bank, upon the discount of a
note, works a forfeiture of interest accruing *after*, as well as before, the
maturity of the note. (*National Bank of Uniontown* vs. *Stauffer, 2 Thomp.
Cases, p. 178, U. S. Cir. Court, Western District Penn.*)

VII. There are no State banks of issue in this State entitled to receive more than
six per cent. interest, consequently national banks cannot contract for or
receive a higher rate than six per cent. Where money is recoverable under
a statute that makes no provision for interest none can be recovered.
(*Supreme Court of Pennsylvania, Columbia National Bank* vs. *Bletz.*)

A person who procures the discount by a national bank of promissory notes
of others, held by him, he indorsing the same, at an unlawful rate of interest, may maintain an action to recover back from the bank twice the amount
of such interest, under the provisions of the United States Revised Statutes,
section 5198, giving the right to such an action, and this, notwithstanding
the transaction, would not, under the law of the State where the bank is
located, be usurious if between private persons. (*United States Supreme
Court, December 12, 1881. National Bank of Gloversville* vs. *Johnson.*)

VIII. The provision of the national banking act against usury will be enforced
in favor of the original borrower, or any one who, for a good cause, represents his interest. The bank will be allowed to set off the penalty by expenses of exchange, and by any just debt against the original borrower.
State laws not applicable. (*Barrett* vs. *Shelbyville National Bank, Banker's
Magazine, Vol. 40, p. 212.*)

IX. The Federal statute provides the only remedy, and that by way of penalty,
against a national bank for the taking of usury; thus the plaintiff had
brought a suit in the United States court to recover the penalty prescribed
by the said statute, and had obtained a judgment. *Held*, that he could
not thereafter maintain an action of *assumpsit* in a State court to recover
the excess above the legal interest paid to the bank. (*Phillips Hill* vs. *National Bank of Barre; Vermont Supreme Court, Banker's Magazine, April, 1885,
· p. 775.*)

Visitorial Powers.

I. Section 5241 U. S. Rev. Stats. prohibits a State court from compelling officers
of a national bank to produce the bank books for the purpose of ascertaining facts upon which to impose a State tax upon the deposits of depositors.
(*National Bank of Youngstown* vs. *Hughes, Auditor, &c., 2 Thomp. Cases, p.
176, U. S. Cir. Court, N. Dist. Ohio.*)

Table showing by States the number and capital of national banks, the corporate existence of which was extended prior to November 1, 1885.

State.	No. of banks.	Capital.	State.	No. of banks.	Capital.
Alabama	2	$350,000	Nebraska	2	$250,000
Colorado	1	200,000	New Hampshire	34	4,455,000
Connecticut	73	22,450,820	New Jersey	48	9,783,350
Delaware	11	1,503,185	New York	221	72,572,460
District of Columbia	2	500,000	North Carolina	1	300,000
Georgia	1	150,000	Ohio	82	14,854,000
Illinois	46	6,090,000	Oregon	1	250,000
Indiana	32	4,157,000	Pennsylvania	163	43,779,390
Iowa	23	2,545,000	Rhode Island	59	19,959,800
Kansas	2	200,000	Tennessee	4	1,150,000
Kentucky	10	2,950,000	Texas	1	300,000
Louisiana	1	300,000	Vermont	28	5,156,000
Maine	53	8,630,000	Virginia	7	1,416,000
Maryland	29	12,069,960	West Virginia	11	1,341,000
Massachusetts	199	85,712,500	Wisconsin	19	1,685,000
Michigan	19	1,575,000			
Minnesota	6	2,100,000	Total	1,199	331,885,465
Missouri	8	3,150,000			

National banks whose corporate existence will expire during the year 1886, with the date of the expiration, the amount of capital stock of each bank, the United States bonds on deposit with the Treasurer, and the amount of circulation issued thereon.

No.	Title of bank.	State.	Expiration of corporate existence.	Capital stock.	United States bonds.	Circulation.
			1886.			
1638	The Northfield National Bank	Vt	Jan. 6	$100,000	$100,000	$90,000
1835	The Shenandoah Valley National Bank of Winchester.	Va	Jan. 8	100,000	100,000	90,000
1642	The National Bank of Texas, Galveston	Tex	Jan. 25	100,000	25,000	22,500
1644	The First National Bank of Houston	Tex	Feb. 16	100,000	35,000	31,500
1639	The National Bank of Athens	Ga	Feb. 20	100,000	80,000	72,000
1640	The Merchants' National Bank of Savannah	Ga	Feb. 24	500,000	60,500	54,450
1649	The First National Bank of Helena	Mont	Mar. 17	500,000	100,000	90,000
1648	The Merchants' National Bank of Little Rock.	Ark	Mar. 28	250,000	200,000	180,000
1652	The Rocky Mountain National Bank of Central City.	Col	May 12	60,000	60,000	54,000
1651	The Colorado National Bank of Denver	Col	May 15	200,000	200,000	180,000
1661	The First National Bank of Fort Dodge	Iowa	June 16	50,000	50,000	45,000
1656	The First National Bank of Wilmington	N.C.	June 29	250,000	50,000	45,000
1657	The San Antonio National Bank	Tex	July 6	125,000	50,000	45,000
1664	The National Bank of Lebanon	Tenn	Aug. 30	50,000	12,500	11,250
1662	The Ridgely National Bank of Springfield	Ill	Sept. 11	100,000	50,000	45,000
1663	The Pennsylvania National Bank of Pottsville.	Pa	Sept. 18	200,000	200,000	180,000
1672	The First National Bank of Atchison	Kans	Oct. 4	100,000	80,000	72,000
1666	The Cleveland National Bank	Tenn	Dec. 24	150,000	150,000	135,000

Number of banks organized and in operation, with their capital, bonds on deposit, and circulation issued, redeemed, and outstanding on November 1, 1885.

States and Territories.	Banks.			Capital stock paid in.	U.S. bonds on deposit.	Circulation.		
	Organized.	In liquidation.	In operation.			Issued.	Redeemed.	*Outstanding.
Maine	81	10	71	$10,260,000	$8,724,250	$31,878,550	$23,344,953	$8,533,597
New Hampshire	54	5	49	6,155,000	5,980,800	20,066,655	14,722,096	5,344,559
Vermont	61	14	47	7,541,000	5,744,900	28,262,130	22,515,651	5,746,479
Massachusetts	262	13	249	97,251,800	64,278,250	273,780,315	211,975,698	61,804,617
Rhode Island	64	3	61	20,340,050	13,058,300	57,989,805	44,808,048	13,181,757
Connecticut	94	10	84	24,921,820	18,009,750	75,385,840	58,706,730	16,679,110
Eastern States	616	55	561	166,469,670	115,796,250	487,363,295	376,073,176	111,290,119
New York	415	98	317	83,039,760	41,907,800	249,088,685	204,899,703	44,188,982
New Jersey	82	10	72	12,728,350	9,702,850	44,953,880	35,603,693	9,350,187
Pennsylvania	332	47	285	61,261,140	42,420,600	171,822,155	129,167,320	42,654,835
Delaware	16		16	2,033,985	1,884,200	5,708,885	4,120,145	1,588,740
Maryland	47	3	44	14,429,060	7,791,950	34,270,780	26,125,231	8,145,549
Dist. Columbia	11	5	6	1,377,000	1,060,000	4,603,500	3,734,771	868,729
Middle States	903	163	740	174,870,195	104,766,800	510,447,885	403,650,863	106,797,022
Virginia	37	13	24	3,996,300	2,592,200	10,919,130	8,509,462	2,409,668
West Virginia	26	5	21	2,111,000	1,337,500	6,771,900	5,317,867	1,454,123
North Carolina	18	3	15	2,126,000	1,097,000	5,850,240	4,620,190	1,230,050
South Carolina	14		14	1,936,200	1,216,350	5,018,275	3,946,930	1,069,345
Georgia	23	6	17	2,686,000	1,742,000	7,176,700	5,407,011	1,769,689
Florida	6	1	5	300,000	147,500	221,410	110,260	111,150
Alabama	13	3	10	1,825,000	1,067,500	4,255,670	3,174,947	1,080,723
Mississippi	8	2	6	475,000	175,000	268,890	107,599	161,291
Louisiana	13	4	9	3,625,000	2,225,000	9,507,260	7,038,118	2,469,142
Texas	71	3	68	6,805,900	1,955,500	4,447,660	2,475,301	1,972,359
Arkansas	8	2	6	705,000	360,000	1,032,750	678,600	354,150
Kentucky	81	13	68	13,300,400	8,994,000	31,617,355	22,007,444	9,609,911
Tennessee	47	15	32	5,007,500	2,482,000	9,917,210	7,415,111	2,502,099
Southern States	365	70	295	44,989,300	25,291,550	97,002,540	70,808,840	26,193,700
Missouri	67	25	42	6,631,000	1,708,850	15,316,165	12,646,834	2,669,331
Ohio	279	76	203	36,804,000	22,123,350	90,303,980	65,821,269	24,482,711
Indiana	147	57	90	12,249,500	7,767,300	47,780,855	38,230,733	9,550,122
Illinois	224	59	165	25,362,600	8,234,250	46,484,885	37,383,696	9,101,189
Michigan	138	36	102	13,110,900	4,205,500	25,439,620	19,900,308	5,539,312
Wisconsin	79	30	49	4,485,000	2,235,750	11,320,010	8,761,987	2,558,023
Iowa	167	41	126	10,115,000	4,036,000	19,691,150	14,835,762	4,855,388
Minnesota	66	17	49	11,363,700	2,385,900	10,442,950	8,127,577	2,315,373
Kansas	93	18	75	5,157,100	1,779,800	5,099,260	3,306,989	1,792,271
Nebraska	80	3	77	6,210,000	2,102,500	4,413,120	2,453,065	1,960,055
Western States	1,340	362	978	131,518,800	56,579,400	276,291,995	211,558,220	64,733,775
Nevada	2	1	1	75,000	39,000	198,520	168,418	30,102
Oregon	12		12	935,000	469,000	1,006,190	577,430	428,760
Colorado	34	9	25	2,135,000	1,090,000	3,653,360	2,494,857	1,158,503
Utah	9	3	6	800,000	437,500	1,343,750	912,301	431,449
Idaho	4		4	250,000	67,800	345,430	259,674	85,756
Montana	20	5	15	1,825,000	439,350	1,365,560	890,446	475,114
Wyoming	5		5	800,000	192,500	358,740	217,000	141,740
New Mexico	8		8	650,000	442,500	1,224,890	833,767	390,123
Dakota	48	3	45	2,605,000	810,000	1,354,180	590,915	763,265
Washington	17	2	15	1,005,000	260,000	754,180	269,970	484,210
Arizona	3	3				65,790	29,910	35,880
California	20	3	17	3,850,000	1,643,000	2,359,130	903,830	1,455,300
Pacific States and Territories	182	29	153	15,030,000	5,930,550	14,028,720	8,148,518	5,880,202
Add for mutilated notes								568,081
Total currency banks	3,406	679	2,727	532,877,965	308,364,550	1,385,134,435	1,070,299,617	314,894,818
Add gold banks						3,465,210	3,080,971	384,290
United States	3,406	679	2,727	532,877,965	308,364,550	1,388,599,675	1,073,920,588	315,847,108

* Including $39,542,979 for which lawful money has been deposited with the Treasurer of the United States to retire an equal amount of circulation which has not been presented for redemption.

Number and denominations of national-bank notes issued and redeemed, and the number of each denomination outstanding, on November 1 in each year, from 1873 to 1885.

	Ones.	Twos.	Fives.	Tens.	Twenties.	Fifties.	One hundreds.	Five hundreds.	One thousands.
1873.									
Issued	15,524,189	5,195,111	34,894,456	12,560,399	3,608,219	559,722	416,590	16,496	5,148
Redeemed	9,891,606	3,120,723	9,141,963	2,573,070	053,071	168,976	144,057	9,658	4,530
Outstanding	5,632,583	2,074,388	25,752,493	9,987,329	2,955,148	390,746	272,533	6,838	618
1874.									
Issued	16,548,250	5,530,113	39,243,136	13,337,076	3,962,109	666,950	492,482	17,344	5,240
Redeemed	11,143,606	3,555,019	13,041,605	3,912,707	1,171,608	231,556	196,572	11,676	4,683
Outstanding	5,404,653	1,984,094	26,201,531	9,424,369	2,790,501	435,394	295,910	5,668	557
1875.									
Issued	18,046,176	6,039,752	47,055,184	17,410,507	5,296,064	884,165	645,838	18,476	5,530
Redeemed	14,092,126	4,616,623	24,926,771	7,608,532	2,204,464	381,037	299,428	14,471	5,048
Outstanding	3,954,050	1,423,129	22,128,413	9,801,975	3,091,600	503,128	346,410	4,005	482
1876.									
Issued	18,849,264	6,307,448	51,783,528	20,008,652	6,086,492	985,615	710,900	18,721	5,539
Redeemed	15,556,708	5,124,546	32,382,056	10,369,214	3,052,246	515,784	395,785	16,217	5,272
Outstanding	3,292,556	1,182,902	19,401,472	9,639,438	3,034,246	469,831	315,115	2,504	267
1877.									
Issued	20,616,024	6,896,968	56,816,848	22,266,064	6,776,253	1,079,781	767,317	20,022	5,668
Redeemed	16,815,508	5,555,526	38,115,868	12,434,779	3,703,528	634,679	479,317	17,615	5,411
Outstanding	3,800,456	1,341,442	18,700,980	9,831,285	3,072,725	445,102	288,000	2,407	257
1878.									
Issued	22,478,415	7,517,765	61,191,288	24,157,293	7,344,167	1,147,578	812,903	20,210	6,204
Redeemed	18,194,196	6,026,692	42,683,433	13,859,149	4,133,178	728,222	541,859	18,895	5,900
Outstanding	4,284,219	1,491,073	18,507,855	10,298,144	3,210,989	419,356	271,044	1,315	304
1879.									
Issued	23,167,677	7,747,519	65,578,440	25,904,223	7,869,951	1,211,761	850,720	20,570	6,340
Redeemed	19,600,477	6,501,270	45,996,076	14,930,599	4,437,343	785,263	581,604	19,287	6,057
Outstanding	3,567,200	1,246,249	19,582,364	10,973,624	3,432,608	426,498	269,116	1,283	283
1880.									
Issued	23,167,677	7,747,519	69,131,976	27,203,168	8,266,398	1,253,865	879,490	20,763	6,363
Redeemed	20,875,215	6,943,880	49,149,824	15,821,110	4,684,820	825,499	610,601	19,484	6,124
Outstanding	2,292,462	803,630	19,982,152	11,382,058	3,581,578	428,366	268,889	1,279	239
1881.									
Issued	23,167,677	7,747,519	73,612,504	29,477,519	8,940,817	1,357,574	959,712	21,950	7,144
Redeemed	21,838,565	7,286,434	53,516,488	17,346,635	5,084,992	891,890	660,202	20,495	6,943
Outstanding	1,329,112	461,085	20,096,016	12,130,884	3,855,825	465,684	299,510	1,464	201
1882.									
Issued	23,167,677	7,747,519	78,697,424	32,042,260	9,751,784	1,453,324	1,035,118	22,787	7,187
Redeemed	22,353,877	7,484,140	59,313,233	19,770,934	5,751,707	980,182	719,130	20,880	6,990
Outstanding	813,800	263,379	19,384,191	12,271,326	4,000,077	473,142	315,988	1,907	197
1883.									
Issued	23,167,677	7,747,519	83,447,208	34,544,086	10,578,846	1,556,009	1,114,722	23,163	7,277
Redeemed	22,593,909	7,570,903	65,142,567	22,712,355	6,424,638	1,090,703	789,125	21,367	7,092
Outstanding	573,768	176,616	18,304,641	11,831,731	4,154,208	465,306	325,597	1,796	185
1884.									
Issued	23,167,677	7,747,519	88,101,188	37,182,102	11,442,091	1,661,010	1,199,750	23,736	7,369
Redeemed	22,671,936	7,603,285	71,039,357	26,050,107	7,481,762	1,216,573	874,543	21,981	7,156
Outstanding	495,741	144,234	17,061,831	11,131,995	3,960,329	444,437	325,207	1,755	213
1885.									
Issued	23,167,677	7,747,519	93,208,400	39,804,001	12,318,173	1,758,533	1,287,686	23,924	7,369
Redeemed	22,731,963	7,628,877	76,817,066	29,382,872	8,563,797	1,345,762	971,922	22,727	7,238
Outstanding	435,714	118,642	16,391,334	10,421,129	3,754,376	412,771	315,764	1,197	131

Table showing the losses that would have been incurred by the holders of notes of insolvent of the respective banks, giving results if the issue of such unsecured notes had

	Name and location of bank.	Amount of dividends paid or estimated to be paid.	Capital stock.	Percentage of circulation and amount of loss.		
				Circulation on basis of 90 per cent. of capital.	Loss on circulation if redeemed from avails of assets.	Circulation on basis of 80 per cent. of capital.
1	First National Bank of Attica, N. Y....	$70,811	$50,000	$45,000	....	$40,000
2	Venango National Bank of Franklin, Pa..	101,386	300,000	270,000	$168,614	240,000
3	Merchants' National Bank of Washington, D. C	165,769	230,000	180,000	14,231	160,000
4	First National Bank of Medina, N. Y....	32,305	50,000	45,000	12,295	40,000
5	Tennessee National Bank of Memphis, Tenn	65,335	100,000	90,000	24,665	80,000
6	First National Bank of Selma, Ala......	132,530	100,000	90,000	....	80,000
7	First National Bank of New Orleans, La..	884,663	500,000	450,000	....	400,000
8	National Unadilla Bank, Unadilla, N. Y..	58,661	120,000	108,000	49,339	96,000
9	Farmers and Citizens' National Bank of Brooklyn, N. Y	1,138,871	300,000	270,000	....	240,000
10	Croton National Bank of New York, N. Y..	143,307	200,000	180,000	36,693	160,000
11	First National Bank of Bethel, Conn....	86,738	60,000	54,000	....	48,000
12	First National Bank of Keokuk, Iowa...	134,929	100,000	90,000	....	80,000
13	National Bank of Vicksburg, Miss	16,654	50,000	45,000	28,346	40,000
14	First National Bank of Rockford, Ill....	29,278	50,000	45,000	15,772	40,000
15	First National Bank of Nevada, Austin, Nev	163,982	250,000	225,000	61,018	200,000
16	Ocean National Bank of New York, N. Y.	1,332,473	1,000,000	900,000	....	800,000
17	Union Square National Bank of New York, N. Y	175,920	200,000	180,000	4,080	160,000
18	Eighth National Bank of New York, N. Y.	263,059	250,000	225,000	....	200,000
19	Fourth National Bank of Philadelphia, Pa.	342,946	200,000	180,000	....	160,000
20	Waverly National Bank of Waverly, N. Y.	111,008	106,100	95,400	....	84,800
21	First National Bank of Fort Smith, Ark	21,642	50,000	45,000	23,358	40,000
22	Scandinavian National Bank of Chicago, Ill	124,587	250,000	225,000	100,413	200,000
23	Wallkill National Bank of Middletown, N. Y	175,429	175,000	157,500	....	140,000
24	Crescent City National Bank of New Orleans, La	552,308	500,000	450,000	....	400,000
25	Atlantic National Bank of New York, N. Y	665,180	300,000	270,000	....	240,000
26	First National Bank of Washington, D. C.	1,372,406	500,000	450,000	....	400,000
27	National Bank of the Commonwealth, New York. N. Y	1,024,597	750,000	675,000	....	600,000
28	Merchants' National Bank of Petersburg, Va	261,128	400,000	360,000	98,872	320,000
29	First National Bank of Petersburg, Va..	125,668	200,000	180,000	54,332	160,000
30	First National Bank of Mansfield, Ohio..	102,775	100,000	90,000	....	80,000
31	New Orleans National Banking Association, New Orleans, La	862,181	600,000	540,000	....	480,000
32	First National Bank of Carlisle, Pa......	46,634	50,000	45,000	....	40,000
33	First National Bank of Anderson, Ind ..	57,005	50,000	45,000	....	40,000
34	First National Bank of Topeka, Kans...	31,286	100,000	90,000	58,714	80,000
35	First National Bank of Norfolk, Va	101,540	100,000	90,000	....	80,000
36	Gibson County National Bank of Princeton, Ind	62,647	50,000	45,000	....	40,000
37	First National Bank of Utah, Salt Lake City, Utah	19,003	150,000	135,000	115,997	120,000
38	Cook County National Bank of Chicago, Ill	268,699	500,000	450,000	181,301	400,000
39	First National Bank of Tiffin, Ohio.....	108,318	100,000	90,000	....	80,000
40	Charlottesville National Bank of Charlottesville, Va	224,338	200,000	160,000	....	160,000
41	Miners' National Bank of Georgetown, Colo.	185,797	150,000	135,000	....	120,000
42	Fourth National Bank of Chicago, Ill ...	17,900	200,000	180,000	162,100	160,000
43	First National Bank of Bedford, Iowa...	12,625	30,000	27,000	14,375	24,000
44	First National Bank of Osceola, Iowa ...	34,536	50,000	45,000	10,464	40,000
45	First National Bank of Duluth, Minn ...	92,882	100,000	90,000	....	80,000
46	First National Bank of La Crosse, Wis..	65,846	50,000	45,000	....	40,000
47	City National Bank of Chicago, Ill	516,294	250,000	225,000	....	200,000
48	Watkins National Bank of Watkins, N. Y	67,082	75,000	67,500	418	60,000
49	First National Bank of Wichita, Kans .	59,669	60,000	54,000	....	48,000
50	First National Bank of Greenfield, Ohio.	9,456	50,000	45,000	35,544	40,000
51	National Bank of Fishkill, Fishkill, N. Y.	388,856	200,000	180,000	....	160,000
52	First National Bank of Franklin, Ind ..	182,251	132,000	118,800	....	105,600
53	Northumberland County National Bank of Shamokin, Pa	136,475	67,000	60,300	....	53,600

national banks if such notes had been unsecured, except by a first lien on the general assets been permitted to the extent of 90, 80, 70, 50, and 25 per cent. of the capital.

Percentage of circulation and amount of loss.

Loss on circulation if redeemed from avails of assets.	Circulation on basis of 70 per cent. of capital.	Loss on circulation if redeemed from avails of assets.	Circulation on basis of 50 per cent. of capital.	Loss on circulation if redeemed from avails of assets.	Circulation on basis of 40 per cent. of capital.	Loss on circulation if redeemed from avails of assets.	Circulation on basis of 25 per cent. of capital.	Loss on circulation if redeemed from avails of assets.	Amount of claims proved.	
	$35,000		$25,000		$20,000		$12,500		$122,089	1
$138,614	210,000	$108,164	150,000	$48,614	120,000	$18,614	75,000		434,531	2
	140,000		100,000		80,000		50,000		669,513	3
7,965	35,000	2,695	25,000		20,000		12,500		82,338	4
14,665	70,000	4,665	50,000		40,000		25,000		376,932	5
	70,000		50,000		40,000		25,000		289,467	6
....A..	350,000		250,000		200,000		125,000		1,119,313	7
37,339	84,000	25,339	60,000	1,339	48,000		30,000		127,801	8
	210,000		150,000		120,000		75,000		1,191,500	9
16,698	140,000		100,000		80,000		50,000		170,752	10
	42,000		30,000		24,000		15,000		68,986	11
	70,000		50,000		40,000		25,000		205,256	12
23,346	35,000	18,346	25,000	8,346	20,000	3,346	12,500		33,502	13
10,772	35,000	5,722	25,000		20,000		12,500		69,874	14
36,018	175,000	11,018	125,000		100,000		62,500		170,012	15
	700,000		500,000		400,000		250,000		1,282,254	16
	140,000		100,000		80,000		50,000		157,120	17
	175,000		125,000		100,000		62,500		378,772	18
	140,000		100,000		80,000		50,000		645,558	19
	74,200		53,000		42,400		26,500		79,864	20
18,358	35,000	13,358	25,000	3,358	20,000		12,500		15,142	21
75,413	175,000	50,413	125,000	413	100,000		62,500		249,174	22
	122,500		87,500		70,000		43,750		171,468	23
	350,000		250,000		200,000		125,000		657,020	24
	210,000		150,000		120,000		75,000		574,513	25
	350,000		250,000		200,000		125,000		1,619,965	26
	525,000		375,000		300,000		187,500		796,995	27
58,872	280,000	18,872	200,000		160,000		100,000		992,636	28
34,332	140,000	14,332	100,000		80,000		50,000		167,285	29
	70,000		50,000		40,000		25,000		175,068	30
	420,000		300,000		240,000		150,000		1,429,595	31
	35,000		25,000		20,000		12,500		67,292	32
	35,000		25,000		20,000		12,500		143,765	33
48,714	70,000	38,714	50,000	18,714	40,000	8,714	25,000		55,372	34
	70,000		50,000		40,000		25,000		176,330	35
	35,000		25,000		20,000		12,500		62,646	36
100,997	105,000	85,997	75,000	55,997	60,000	40,997	37,500	$18,497	93,021	37
131,301	350,000	81,301	250,000		200,000		125,000		1,795,992	38
	70,000		50,000		40,000		25,000		237,824	39
	140,000		100,000		80,000		50,000		351,847	40
	105,000		75,000		60,000		37,500		177,512	41
142,100	140,000	122,100	100,000	82,100	80,000	62,100	50,000	32,100	85,801	42
11,375	21,000	8,375	15,000	2,375	12,000		7,500		56,457	43
5,464	35,000	464	25,000		20,000		12,500		34,535	44
	70,000		50,000		40,000		25,000		87,786	45
	35,000		25,000		20,000		12,500		135,952	46
	175,000		125,000		100,000		62,500		703,658	47
	52,500		37,500		30,000		18,750		59,226	48
	42,000		30,000		24,000		15,000		97,464	49
30,544	35,000	25,554	25,000	15,554	20,000	10,554	12,500	3,044	35,023	50
	140,000		100,000		80,000		50,000		352,062	51
	92,400		66,000		52,800		33,000		184,457	52
	40,000		33,500		26,800		16,750		175,952	53

Table showing the losses that would have been incurred by the holders of notes

	Name and location of bank.	Amount of dividends paid or estimated to be paid.	Capital stock.	Percentage of circulation and amount of loss.		
				Circulation on basis of 90 per cent. of capital.	Loss on circulation if redeemed from avails of assets.	Circulation on basis of 80 per cent. of capital.
54	First National Bank of Winchester, Ill..	$85,716	$50,000	$45,000	....	$40,000
55	National Exchange Bank of Minneapolis, Minn .	202,093	100,000	90,000	....	80,000
56	National Bank of the State of Missouri, Saint Louis, Mo .	2,165,388	2,500,000	2,250,000	$84,612	2,000,000
57	First National Bank of Delphi, Ind	81,941	50,000	45,000	....	40,000
58	First National Bank of Georgetown, Colo	53,145	75,000	67,500	14,355	60,000
59	Lock Haven National Bank, Lock Haven, Pa	254,647	120,000	108,000	....	96,000
60	Third National Bank of Chicago, Ill	1,071,774	750,000	675,000	....	600,000
61	Central National Bank of Chicago, Ill ...	177,254	200,000	180,000	2,746	160,000
62	First National Bank of Kansas City, Mo.	267,218	500,000	450,000	182,278	400,000
63	Commercial National Bank of Kansas City, Mo	89,385	100,000	90,000	615	80,000
64	First National Bank of Ashland, Pa.....	33,105	112,500	101,250	68,145	90,000
65	First National Bank of Tarrytown, N.Y	107,575	100,000	90,000	....	80,000
66	First National Bank of Allentown, Pa...	79,725	250,000	225,000	145,275	200,000
67	First National Bank of Waynesburg, Pa	20,062	100,000	90,000	69,938	80,000
68	Washington County National Bank of Greenwich, N.Y	262,887	200,000	180,000	....	160,000
69	First National Bank of Dallas, Tex.....	29,177	50,000	45,000	15,823	40,000
70	People's National Bank of Helena, Mont.	75,000	100,000	90,000	15,000	80,000
71	First National Bank of Bozeman, Mont .	65,000	50,000	45,000	....	40,000
72	Merchant's National Bank of Fort Scott, Kans	16,671	50,000	45,000	28,329	40,000
73	Farmers' National Bank of Platte City, Mo	15,223	50,000	45,000	29,777	40,000
74	First National Bank of Warrensburg, Mo	100,870	100,000	90,000	....	80,000
75	German-American National Bank of Washington, D.C	86,142	130,000	117,000	30,858	104,000
76	German National Bank of Chicago, Ill...	182,570	500,000	450,000	267,430	400,000
77	Commercial National Bank of Saratoga, Springs, N.Y	137,428	100,000	90,000	....	80,000
78	Second National Bank of Scranton, Pa...	151,786	200,000	180,000	28,214	160,000
79	National Bank of Poultney, Poultney, Vt.	88,176	100,000	90,000	1,824	80,000
80	First National Bank of Monticello, Ind...	20,758	50,000	45,000	24,242	40,000
81	First National Bank of Butler, Pa	69,273	50,000	45,000	....	40,000
82	First National Bank of Meadville, Pa...	96,176	100,000	90,000	....	80,000
83	First National Bank of Newark, N.J...	553,409	300,000	270,000	....	240,000
84	First National Bank of Brattleboro, Vt..					
85	Mechanics' National Bank of Newark, N.J					
86	First National Bank of Buffalo, N.Y....					
87	Pacific National Bank of Boston, Mass.					
88	First National Bank of Union Mills, Union City, Pa					
89	Vermont National Bank of Saint Albans, Vt					
90	First National Bank of Leadville, Colo..					
91	City National Bank of Lawrenceburg, Ind					
92	First National Bank of Saint Albans, Vt.					
93	First National Bank of Monmouth, Ill ..					
94	Marine National Bank of New York, N.Y	*8,361,876	3,996,300	3,596,670	347,594	3,197,040
95	Hot Springs National Bank of Hot Springs, Ark					
96	Richmond National Bank of Richmond, Ind					
97	First National Bank of Livingston, Mont					
98	First National Bank of Albion, N.Y....					
99	First National Bank of Jamestown, Dak.					
100	Logan National Bank of West Liberty, Ohio					
101	Middletown National Bank of Middletown, N.Y					
102	Farmers' National Bank of Bushnell, Ill.					
103	Schoharie County National Bank of Schoharie, N.Y					
104	Exchange National Bank of Norfolk, Va					
	Total....................	28,379,080	21,858,900	19,673,010	2,627,996	17,487,040

* Estimated.

of insolvent national banks if such notes had been unsecured, &c.—Continued.

Percentage of circulation and amount of loss.

Loss on circulation if redeemed from avails of assets.	Circulation on basis of 70 per cent. of capital.	Loss on circulation if redeemed from avails of assets.	Circulation on basis of 50 per cent. of capital.	Loss on circulation if redeemed from avails of assets.	Circulation on basis of 40 per cent. of capital.	Loss on circulation if redeemed from avails of assets.	Circulation on basis of 25 per cent. of capital.	Loss on circulation if redeemed from avails of assets.	Amount of claims proved.	
	$35,000		$25,000		$20,000		$12,500		$143,300	54
	70,000		50,000		40,000		25,000		227,355	55
	1,750,000		1,250,000		1,000,000		625,000		1,935,721	56
	35,000		25,000		20,000		12,500		133,112	57
$6,855	52,500		37,500		30,000		18,750		196,365	58
	84,000		60,000		48,000		30,000		254,647	59
	525,000		375,000		300,000		187,500		1,061,598	60
	140,000		100,000		80,000		50,000		298,324	61
132,278	350,000	$82,276	250,000		200,000		125,000		392,394	62
	70,000		50,000		40,000		25,000		75,175	63
56,895	78,750	45,645	56,250	$23,145	45,000	$11,895	28,125		33,105	64
	70,000		50,000		40,000		25,000		118,371	65
120,275	175,000	95,275	125,000	45,275	100,000	20,275	62,500		90,421	66
59,938	70,000	49,938	50,000	29,938	40,000	19,938	25,000	$4,938	33,362	67
	140,000		100,000		80,000		50,000		262,887	68
10,823	35,000	5,823	25,000		20,000		12,500		77,104	69
5,000	70,000		50,000		40,000		25,000		168,048	70
	35,000		25,000		20,000		12,500		69,631	71
23,329	35,000	18,329	25,000	8,329	20,000	3,329	12,500		27,801	72
24,777	35,000	19,777	25,000	9,777	20,000	4,777	12,500		32,449	73
	70,000		50,000		40,000		25,000		156,260	74
17,858	91,000	4,858	65,000		52,000		32,500		282,870	75
217,430	350,000	167,430	250,000	67,430	200,000	17,430	125,000		197,353	76
	70,000		50,000		40,000		25,000		128,832	77
8,214	140,000		100,000		80,000		50,000		132,461	78
	70,000		50,000		40,000		25,000		81,801	79
19,242	35,000	14,242	25,000	4,242	20,000		12,500		21,182	80
	35,000		25,000		20,000		12,500		108,385	81
	70,000		50,000		40,000		25,000		93,625	82
	210,000		150,000		120,000		75,000		580,592	83
										84
										85
										86
										87
										88
										89
										90
										91
										92
										93
217,424	2,797,410	153,920	1,998,150	49,420	1,598,520	12,392	999,075	3,824	16,104,105	94
										95
										96
										97
										98
										99
										100
										101
										102
										103
										104
1,802,950	15,301,160	1,302,944	10,929,400	474,366	8,743,520	234,361	5,464,700	62,421	43,162,549	

National banks that went into voluntary liquidation from January 1, 1879, to January 1, 1881, with the amount of capital, circulation issued, the amount outstanding November 1, 1882, and the percentage unredeemed.

Name and location of bank.	Date of liquidation.	Capital.	Circulation.		
			Issued.	Outstanding November 1, 1882.	Percentage unredeemed.
	1879.				
Corn Exchange National Bank of Chicago, Ill.	Jan. 4	$500,000	$59,160	$20,206	34.16
Franklin National Bank of Columbus, Ohio...	Jan. 4	100,000	93,070	47,347	50.87
Traders' National Bank of Bangor, Me.	Jan. 14	100,000	76,400	38,635	50.57
First National Bank of Gonic, N. H	Jan. 14	60,000	45,597	19,104	41.91
First National Bank of Salem, N. C	Jan. 14	150,000	128,200	64,820	50.55
First National Bank of Granville, Ohio	Jan. 14	50,000	34,365	15,656	45.56
Commercial National Bank of Petersburg, Va.	Jan. 14	120,000	99,800	58,897	59.02
First National Gold Bank of Stockton, Cal ..	Jan. 14	300,000	238,600	112,204	47.03
First National Bank of Sheboygan, Wis	Jan. 14	50,000	45,000	17,912	39.80
First National Bank of Boscobel, Wis	Jan. 21	50,000	43,900	18,832	42.90
National Marine Bank of Oswego, N. Y	Jan. 25	120,000	44,300	14,522	32.78
Central National Bank of Hightstown, N. J..	Feb. 15	100,000	32,400	10,775	33.25
Brookville National Bank, of Brookville, Ind	Feb. 18	100,000	89,000	50,755	57.03
Farmers' National Bank of Centreville, Iowa.	Feb. 27	50,000	41,500	17,908	43.15
First National Bank of Clarinda, Iowa	Mar. 1	50,000	45,000	14,022	31.16
Waterville National Bank of Waterville, Me	Mar. 3	125,000	110,300	41,263	37.41
First National Bank of Tremont, Pa	Mar. 4	75,000	64,600	35,740	55.32
First National Bank of Atlanta, Ill	Apr. 15	50,000	26,500	16,820	62.71
Union National Bank of Aurora, Ill	Apr. 22	125,000	82,000	48,176	58.75
National Bank of Menasha, Wis	Apr. 26	50,000	44,500	17,392	39.08
National Exchange Bank of Jefferson City, Mo.	May 8	50,000	45,000	20,565	45.70
First National Bank of Hannibal, Mo	May 15	100,000	88,200	50,966	57.78
Merchants' National Bank of Winona, Minn..	June 16	100,000	35,000	13,984	39.95
Farmers' National Bank of Keithsburg, Ill...	July 3	50,000	27,000	14,840	54.96
First National Bank of Franklin, Ky	July 5	100,000	54,000	29,375	54.40
National Bank of Salem, Salem, Ind	July 8	50,000	44,400	14,570	32.81
Fourth National Bank of Memphis, Tenn	July 19	125,000	45,000	27,225	60.50
Bedford National Bank of Bedford, Ind	July 21	100,000	87,200	32,193	36.92
First National Bank of Afton, Iowa	Aug. 15	50,000	26,500	14,626	55.19
First National Bank of Deer Lodge, Mont ...	Aug. 16	50,000	45,000	17,085	37.97
First National Bank of Batavia, Ill	Aug. 30	50,000	54,300	20,901	48.27
National Gold Bank and Trust Company, San Francisco, Cal	Sept. 1	750,000	40,000	21,530	53.82
Gainesville National Bank of Gainesville, Ala.	Nov. 25	100,000	90,000	60,342	67.05
First National Bank of Hackensack, N. J	Dec. 6	100,000	90,000	50,495	56.10
	1880.				
National Bank of Delavan, Wis..	Jan. 7	50,000	27,000	16,600	61.48
Mechanics' National Bank of Nashville, Tenn.	Jan. 13	100,000	90,000	53,750	59.72
Manchester National Bank of Manchester, Ohio ...	Jan. 13	50,000	48,303	28,018	58.00
First National Bank of Meyersdale, Pa	Mar. 5	50,000	30,600	12,750	41.67
First National Bank of Mifflinburg, Pa	Mar. 8	100,000	90,000	59,755	66.39
National Bank of Michigan, Marshall, Mich..	May 14	120,000	100,800	62,651	62.15
National Exchange Bank of Houston, Tex....	Sept. 10	100,000	31,500	21,807	69.23
Ascutney National Bank of Windsor, Vt	Oct. 19	100,000	90,000	60,089	66.76
First National Bank of Seneca Falls, N. Y	Nov. 23	60,000	54,000	13,760	25.48
First National Bank of Baraboo, Wis	Nov. 27	50,000	27,000	18,600	68.89
Bundy National Bank of New Castle, Ind	Dec. 6	50,000	45,000	21,882	48.63
Totals and average percentage		4,930,000	2,839,995	1,439,345	50.68

National banks that went into voluntary liquidation from January 1, 1879, to January 1, 1881, with the amount of capital, circulation issued, the amount outstanding November 1, 1885, and the percentage unredeemed.

Name and location of bank.	Date of liquida- tion.	Capital.	Circulation.		
			Issued.	Outstand- ing Novem- ber 1, 1885.	Percent- age unre- deemed.
	1879.				
Corn Exchange National Bank of Chicago, Ill.	Jan. 4	$500,000	$59,160	$9,233	15.61
Franklin National Bank of Columbus, Ohio	Jan. 4	100,000	93,070	10,787	11.59
Traders' National Bank of Bangor, Me	Jan. 14	100,000	76,400	12,415	16.25
First National Bank of Gonic, N. H	Jan. 14	60,000	45,597	5,319	11.66
First National Bank of Salem, N. C	Jan. 14	150,000	128,200	19,640	15.32
First National Bank of Granville, Ohio	Jan. 14	50,000	34,365	4,471	13.01
Commercial National Bank of Petersburg, Va.	Jan. 14	120,000	99,800	17,787	17.82
First National Gold Bank of Stockton, Cal	Jan. 14	300,000	238,600	38,549	16.15
First National Bank of Sheboygan, Wis	Jan. 14	50,000	45,000	3,332	7.40
First National Bank of Boscobel, Wis	Jan. 21	50,000	43,900	3,384	7.71
National Marine Bank of Oswego, N. Y	Jan. 25	120,000	44,300	4,128	9.32
Central National Bank of Hightstown, N. J.	Feb. 15	100,000	32,400	2,085	6.44
Brookville National Bank of Brookville, Ind.	Feb. 18	100,000	89,000	14,800	16.63
Farmers' National Bank of Centreville, Iowa.	Feb. 27	50,000	41,500	2,498	6.02
First National Bank of Clarinda, Iowa	Mar. 1	50,000	45,000	2,018	4.48
Waterville National Bank of Waterville, Me.	Mar. 3	125,000	110,300	12,734	11.54
First National Bank of Tremont, Pa	Mar. 4	75,000	64,600	12,302	19.11
First National Bank of Atlanta, Ill	Apr. 15	50,000	26,500	4,600	17.36
Union National Bank of Aurora, Ill	Apr. 22	125,000	82,000	14,607	17.81
National Bank of Menasha, Wis	Apr. 26	50,000	44,500	3,013	6.77
National Exchange Bank of Jefferson City, Mo.	May 8	50,000	45,000	5,266	11.70
First National Bank of Hannibal, Mo	May 15	100,000	88,200	14,303	16.22
Merchants' National Bank of Winona, Minn	June 16	100,000	35,000	2,673	7.64
Farmers' National Bank of Keithsburg, Ill	July 3	50,000	27,000	4,260	15.80
First National Bank of Franklin, Ky	July 5	100,000	54,000	7,690	14.24
National Bank of Salem, Salem, Ind	July 8	50,000	44,400	2,054	4.63
Fourth National Bank of Memphis, Tenn	July 19	125,000	45,000	8,415	18.70
Bedford National Bank of Bedford, Ind	July 21	100,000	87,200	5,365	6.15
First National Bank of Afton, Iowa	Aug. 15	50,000	26,500	2,671	10.08
First National Bank of Deer Lodge, Mont	Aug. 16	50,000	45,000	2,475	5.50
First National Bank of Batavia, Ill	Aug. 30	50,000	44,300	4,738	10.69
National Gold Bank and Trust Company of San Francisco, Cal	Sept. 1	730,000	40,000	14,140	35.35
Gainesville National Bank of Gainesville, Ala.	Nov. 25	100,000	90,000	19,305	21.45
First National Bank of Hackensack, N J	Dec. 6	100,000	90,000	13,372	14.86
	1880.				
National Bank of Delavan, Wis	Jan. 7	50,000	27,000	4,540	16.81
Mechanics' National Bank of Nashville, Tenn	Jan. 13	100,000	90,000	20,650	22.94
Manchester National Bank of Manchester, Ohio	Jan. 13	50,000	48,303	7,846	16.24
First National Bank of Meyersdale, Pa	Mar. 5	50,000	30,600	2,165	7.08
First National Bank of Mifflinburg, Pa	Mar. 8	100,000	90,000	19,060	21.18
National Bank of Michigan, Marshall, Mich	May 14	120,000	100,800	16,103	15.97
National Exchange Bank of Houston, Tex	Sept. 10	100,000	31,500	6,436	20.43
Ascutney National Bank of Windsor, Vt	Oct. 10	100,000	90,000	16,663	18.63
First National Bank of Seneca Falls, N. Y	Nov. 23	60,000	54,000	3,837	7.18
First National Bank of Baraboo, Wis	Nov. 27	50,000	27,000	4,119	15.25
Bundy National Bank of New Castle, Ind	Dec. 6	50,000	45,000	2,274	5.05
Totals and average percentage		4,930,000	2,839,995	408,122	14.37

Principal liabilities and resources on October 1, 1885, of the national

	States and Territories.	No. of banks.	Capital.	Surplus.	Deposits. Individual.	Other.
1	Maine............................	71	$10,360,000	$2,486,218	$10,095,405	$142,510
2	New Hampshire...............	48	6,105,000	1,220,426	5,425,196	341,317
3	Vermont.........................	47	7,541,000	1,473,839	5,154,308	49,665
4	Boston	54	50,950,000	11,416,551	80,326,965	128,398
5	Massachusetts, other	195	45,095,650	13,515,392	51,715,367	269,727
6	Rhode Island...................	61	20,340,050	3,954,824	13,096,233	128,681
7	Connecticut.....................	84	24,921,820	6,717,781	24,482,781	309,475
	Total Division No. 1......	560	165,313,520	40,785,031	190,296,345	1,369,773
8	New York City	44	45,350,000	22,176,008	250,494,555	487,344
9	Albany	6	1,750,000	1,175,000	7,097,824	84,114
10	New York, other...............	267	34,819,760	8,926,656	77,834,371	718,953
11	New Jersey	72	12,208,200	3,799,945	32,501,422	195,322
12	Philadelphia	34	18,275,250	9,401,803	74,830,558	239,953
13	Pittsburgh	23	10,150,000	3,538,107	19,981,344	268,482
14	Pennsylvania, other...........	228	32,665,340	10,067,362	61,821,735	415,651
	Total Division No. 2	674	155,218,550	50,084,881	524,561,800	2,389,819
15	Delaware.......................	15	1,823,985	683,905	3,986,803	63,879
16	Baltimore	17	11,713,260	3,136,500	20,885,523	104,572
17	Maryland, other...............	27	2,710,700	841,766	5,744,190	....
18	Washington.....................	5	1,125,000	307,000	3,435,468	47,961
19	District of Columbia, other......	1	252,000	60,000	776,518	....
20	Virginia	24	3,576,300	1,143,038	8,376,663	300,519
21	West Virginia	21	2,011,000	512,056	2,529,279	....
	Total Division No. 3	110	23,218,245	6,684,325	45,734,453	516,931
22	North Carolina.................	15	2,063,500	472,379	3,237,572	228,128
23	South Carolina.................	14	1,935,000	802,000	2,723,043	221,282
24	Georgia	16	2,472,345	813,351	3,335,352	71,375
25	Florida	5	300,000	19,923	782,281	37,753
26	Alabama........................	10	1,835,000	290,050	2,143,311	88,011
27	Mississippi	6	475,000	39,100	597,416	....
28	New Orleans	8	3,525,000	1,296,716	8,923,527	....
29	Louisiana	1	100,000	9,000	70,220	....
30	Texas..........................	68	6,880,000	2,002,203	9,183,872	92,044
31	Arkansas	6	705,000	166,170	1,513,893	44,301
32	Louisville......................	9	3,551,500	809,441	3,401,878	782,602
33	Kentucky.......................	59	9,648,900	1,922,323	8,233,931	343,088
34	Tennessee......................	32	5,007,500	908,500	7,783,995	265,803
	Total Division No. 4......	249	38,498,745	9,641,756	51,930,291	2,174,387
35	Cincinnati	12	8,600,000	1,208,000	11,060,894	1,035,000
36	Cleveland	8	6,200,000	620,000	8,998,620	484,882
37	Ohio, other.....................	183	21,909,580	4,502,511	31,594,784	484,580
38	Indiana	90	12,189,500	3,031,908	19,845,317	783,584
39	Chicago........................	12	11,750,000	2,691,600	46,970,739	145,079
40	Illinois, other..................	153	13,673,600	4,195,183	27,693,720	773,176
41	Detroit.........................	5	2,900,000	330,000	7,313,737	389,903
42	Michigan, other................	97	10,194,600	1,864,193	18,575,061	34,827
43	Milwaukee	3	650,000	340,000	5,140,355	486,400
44	Wisconsin, other...............	47	3,785,000	921,008	10,132,390	86,109
	Total Division No. 5......	610	91,852,280	19,774,003	184,325,533	4,703,550
45	Iowa	125	10,155,000	2,290,504	17,053,776	334,524
46	Minnesota	49	11,390,000	1,851,834	19,651,296	380,199
47	St. Louis.......................	6	3,250,000	856,128	5,634,623	401,163
48	Missouri, other	36	3,311,000	623,425	5,972,242	86,339
49	Kansas	74	4,995,720	668,972	10,089,967	262,384
50	Nebraska	75	5,949,250	944,774	11,316,707	352,809
	Total Division No. 6......	365	39,050,970	7,235,637	69,718,611	1,817,478
51	Colorado	25	2,025,000	1,003,190	10,281,553	326,029
52	Nevada	1	75,000	25,000	214,701	....
53	San Francisco..................	1	1,590,000	234,520	1,090,089	....
54	California, other	16	2,345,000	548,415	5,620,030	....
55	Oregon.........................	9	710,000	81,600	2,555,552	414,578
	Total Division No. 7......	52	6,655,000	1,892,635	19,761,925	740,607

banks, by States and reserve cities, arranged in eight principal divisions.

Loans and discounts, including overdrafts.	Gold and gold clearing-house certificates.	Gold Treasury certificates.	Silver.	Silver Treasury certificates.	Legal tenders and United States certificates of deposit.	
$16,604,265	$589,426	$7,699	$72,152	$1,080	$182,196	1
9,371,374	217,329	1,540	63,788	340	139,469	2
16,589,151	238,169	16,290	51,028	2,820	156,953	3
125,331,305	4,538,331	4,218,850	188,084	15,300	4,727,498	4
86,172,244	1,826,290	175,200	414,280	22,540	1,847,817	5
31,992,631	389,363	44,220	125,035	6,840	493,667	6
40,601,465	1,183,543	156,920	218,713	2,980	901,669	7
318,672,435	8,982,451	4,620,710	1,133,080	51,900	8,449,269	
236,889,912	26,463,871	62,249,740	2,157,046	583,510	23,705,620	8
7,130,412	571,094	319,640	30,885	1,250	499,460	9
83,979,729	3,263,280	1,221,050	540,283	29,700	3,456,599	10
29,365,002	1,276,343	327,870	363,279	22,210	1,912,131	11
67,351,230	10,587,757	122,480	483,515	167,340	9,569,351	12
24,871,132	1,807,834	299,560	123,577	64,620	2,167,824	13
65,500,467	3,574,834	180,530	692,611	88,000	3,116,647	14
515,087,884	47,545,013	64,720,850	4,381,196	956,630	44,427,732	
3,906,837	136,721	13,100	44,550	10,190	194,331	15
25,803,638	788,019	1,120,770	127,785	6,950	3,727,363	16
5,738,577	231,287	20,340	83,284	18,810	400,625	17
2,196,158	150,696	264,350	24,531	37,220	469,327	18
322,988	63,383	40,000	6,535	4,500	85,500	19
9,459,575	439,427	15,670	89,547	16,920	786,902	20
3,602,284	189,883	4,100	21,097	14,190	204,795	21
51,030,057	1,999,416	1,478,330	397,329	107,880	5,867,843	
4,871,983	160,900		70,760	80	263,186	22
4,589,643	145,842	910	87,230	1,910	312,239	23
5,383,089	207,125	97,160	116,192	21,100	321,017	24
644,531	6,801		28,801		102,581	25
3,265,790	150,926	8,170	56,272	26,520	167,764	26
1,074,609	22,119	20	20,363	39,850	41,682	27
9,729,590	359,015	70,040	114,956	273,940	1,087,830	28
130,943	1,672		10,071	2,910	2,867	29
13,777,216	462,311	121,700	180,773	118,660	1,002,463	30
1,801,245	51,165	10,770	26,168	31,440	84,711	31
7,788,154	334,489	25,000	20,979	6,000	511,420	32
14,942,400	484,459	29,680	76,822	42,280	402,633	33
11,551,177	473,488	53,540	135,217	34,570	517,389	34
79,353,370	2,860,312	407,990	944,604	599,260	4,817,782	
18,666,707	445,269	318,860	61,958	222,000	3,386,285	35
11,538,041	749,900	115,000	46,325		1,000,000	36
40,932,229	2,290,195	71,370	274,458	84,980	2,850,541	37
22,357,585	1,768,739	63,980	215,033	49,520	1,608,277	38
46,018,906	8,765,476	648,000	199,748	63,680	5,911,100	39
30,947,482	2,072,267	90,180	255,537	22,280	1,647,231	40
8,513,282	944,520		40,217	2,750	662,266	41
21,465,803	1,389,586	41,240	172,291	13,110	795,222	42
3,956,083	595,266	95,000	16,005	2,180	472,621	43
9,663,256	801,029	4,400	99,506	3,910	384,582	44
215,959,374	19,760,246	1,418,970	1,378,078	413,760	18,718,125	
21,324,486	948,588	55,460	182,003	32,800	1,160,047	45
28,172,123	1,430,710	4,610	112,855	3,000	902,453	46
9,202,786	853,215	81,740	17,517	9,700	761,629	47
7,269,132	373,371	44,320	40,938	16,510	577,050	48
10,730,627	720,436	27,420	89,749	32,150	743,148	49
15,432,742	909,131	7,330	116,738	5,260	545,699	50
92,131,896	5,235,451	220,880	568,800	99,450	4,496,026	
7,608,987	883,530	3,990	78,947	11,180	738,561	51
248,248	40,027		5,363	840	2,476	52
2,146,771	442,195	500	15,740		2,589	53
6,051,437	825,040	19,720	49,484	15,840	48,004	54
2,202,226	470,692	2,670	35,310	110	28,764	55
18,257,609	2,561,484	26,880	184,853	27,970	820,391	

Principal liabilities and resources on October 1, 1885, of the national

	States and Territories.	No. of banks.	Capital.	Surplus.	Deposits.	
					Individual.	Other.
56	Dakota....................	41	$2, 402, 100	$500, 573	$3, 725, 522	$151, 117
57	Idaho	4	250, 000	20, 000	416, 655	....
58	Montana	15	1, 810, 000	298, 000	5, 329, 503	162, 622
59	New Mexico	8	650, 000	153, 210	1, 750, 475	177, 278
60	Utah	6	800, 000	274, 500	1, 626, 641	63, 587
61	Washington................... .	15	1, 005, 000	140, 091	1, 450, 206	....
62	Wyoming.....................	5	800, 000	140, 000	1, 744, 353	....
	Total Division No. 8	94	7, 717, 100	1, 526, 374	16, 043, 355	554, 604
	Total for United States....	2, 714	527, 524, 410	146, 624, 642	1, 102, 372, 322	14, 267, 149

REPORT OF THE COMPTROLLER OF THE CURRENCY. 119

banks, by States and reserve cities, arranged in eight principal divisions—Continued.

Loans and discounts, including overdrafts.	Gold and gold clearing-house certificates.	Gold Treasury certificates.	Silver.	Silver Treasury certificates.	Legal tenders and United States certificates of deposit.	
$1,000,272	$173,496	$2,470	$33,268	$1,770	$373,821	56
350,796	37,320	....	3,182	1,600	54,291	57
5,515,195	537,792	3,000	33,309	360	327,458	58
1,423,513	121,207	3,200	17,127	....	70,816	59
1,365,239	141,370	51,130	16,237	6,840	35,040	60
2,035,384	232,644	2,870	22,621	7,230	15,109	61
1,860,906	202,578	....	7,117	....	64,416	62
16,551,305	1,446,407	62,670	132,861	17,800	940,951	
1,306,143,990	90,490,780	72,986,340	9,120,801	2,274,650	88,538,119	

Table, by States, Territories, and reserve cities, exhibiting the number of banks in each with capital of $150,000 and under, and those with capital exceeding $150,000, and showing the amount of bonds deposited to secure circulation on October 1, 1885.

States and Territories.	Banks with capital of $150,000 and under.			Banks with capital over $150,000.			Totals.		
	No. of banks.	Capital.	U. S. bonds.	No. of banks.	Capital.	U. S. bonds.	No. of banks.	Capital.	U. S. bonds.
Maine	57	$5,060,000	$4,645,300	14	$5,390,000	$4,064,000	71	$10,360,000	$8,709,300
New Hampshire	41	4,505,000	4,350,000	7	1,600,000	1,450,000	48	6,105,000	5,800,000
Vermont	34	3,691,000	2,972,000	13	3,850,000	3,045,500	47	7,541,000	6,017,500
Massachusetts	82	9,657,650	7,962,850	113	35,438,000	30,644,000	195	45,095,650	38,606,850
Boston				54	50,950,000	24,614,650	54	50,950,000	24,614,650
Rhode Island	26	2,813,000	2,591,200	35	17,527,050	11,004,200	61	20,340,050	13,595,400
Connecticut	29	3,200,750	2,750,000	55	21,721,070	15,260,100	84	24,921,820	18,010,100
New England States	269	28,927,400	25,271,350	291	136,386,120	90,082,450	560	165,313,520	115,353,800
New York	207	18,726,660	15,201,950	60	16,093,100	12,065,200	267	34,819,760	27,267,150
New York City	1	150,000	150,000	43	45,200,000	12,416,500	44	45,350,000	12,566,500
Albany				6	1,750,000	1,418,000	6	1,750,000	1,418,000
New Jersey	44	3,998,200	3,289,850	28	8,210,000	6,037,000	72	12,208,200	9,326,850
Pennsylvania	172	16,230,390	12,803,000	56	16,434,950	13,826,200	228	32,665,340	26,629,200
Philadelphia	1	150,000	135,000	33	18,125,250	9,192,800	34	18,275,250	9,327,800
Pittsburgh	1	100,000	100,000	22	10,050,000	6,980,500	23	10,150,000	7,080,500
Delaware	12	920,800	865,000	3	903,185	903,200	15	1,823,985	1,768,200
Maryland	23	1,865,000	1,679,000	4	851,700	800,000	27	2,716,700	2,479,000
Baltimore				17	11,713,260	6,667,500	17	11,713,260	6,667,500
District of Columbia				1	232,000	250,000	1	252,000	250,000
Washington	1	100,000	100,000	4	1,925,000	630,000	5	1,125,000	730,000
Middle States	462	42,241,050	34,323,800	277	130,608,445	70,586,900	739	172,849,495	104,910,700
Virginia	16	1,341,000	980,000	8	2,235,300	1,313,350	24	3,576,300	2,293,350
West Virginia	19	1,655,000	1,267,500	2	356,000	202,350	21	2,011,000	1,469,850
North Carolina	10	938,500	737,000	5	1,125,000	425,000	15	2,063,500	1,162,000
South Carolina	11	985,000	811,350	3	950,000	350,000	14	1,935,000	1,161,350
Georgia	12	972,345	731,500	4	1,500,000	1,060,500	16	2,472,345	1,792,000
Florida	5	300,000	147,500				5	300,000	147,500
Alabama	5	410,000	217,000	5	1,425,000	900,000	10	1,835,000	1,117,000
Mississippi	6	475,000	175,000				6	475,000	175,000
Louisiana	1	100,000	100,000				1	100,000	100,000
New Orleans				8	3,525,000	2,125,000	8	3,525,000	2,125,000
Texas	61	4,820,000	1,585,500	7	2,060,000	365,000	68	6,880,000	1,950,500
Arkansas	4	255,000	110,000	2	450,000	250,000	6	705,000	360,000
Kentucky	37	3,863,900	2,110,300	22	5,100,000	4,330,000	59	9,648,900	6,440,300
Louisville				9	3,551,500	2,833,700	9	3,551,500	2,833,700
Tennessee	25	1,907,500	1,036,500	7	3,100,000	1,335,000	32	5,007,500	2,371,500
Southern States	212	18,023,245	10,009,150	82	26,902,800	15,489,900	294	44,086,045	25,499,050
Ohio	149	12,895,580	9,208,700	34	9,014,000	5,086,550	183	21,909,580	15,195,250
Cincinnati				12	8,600,000	5,585,000	12	8,600,000	5,585,000
Cleveland				8	6,200,000	655,000	8	6,200,000	655,000
Indiana	68	6,059,500	4,111,800	22	6,130,000	3,435,000	90	12,189,500	7,546,800
Illinois	142	11,123,600	5,772,500	11	2,556,000	1,140,000	153	13,679,600	6,912,750
Chicago				12	11,750,000	1,183,500	12	11,750,000	1,183,500
Michigan	85	6,434,000	3,128,000	12	3,760,600	830,000	97	10,194,600	3,958,000
Detroit				5	2,900,000	500,000	5	2,900,000	500,000
Wisconsin	44	3,135,000	1,553,250	3	650,000	200,000	47	3,785,000	1,753,250
Milwaukee				3	650,000	500,000	3	650,000	500,000
Iowa	119	8,455,000	3,904,500	6	1,700,000	396,500	125	10,155,000	4,301,000
Minnesota	35	2,390,000	1,078,000	14	9,000,000	1,035,000	49	11,390,000	2,113,000
Missouri	32	2,211,000	1,096,250	4	1,100,000	332,350	36	3,311,000	1,428,600
St. Louis				6	3,250,000	860,000	6	3,250,000	860,000
Kansas	73	4,795,720	1,652,300	1	200,000	50,000	74	4,995,720	1,702,300
Nebraska	68	3,799,250	1,389,000	7	2,150,000	625,000	75	5,949,250	2,014,000
Western States	815	61,298,650	32,894,550	160	69,604,600	23,313,900	975	130,903,250	56,208,450
Colorado	12	1,375,000	682,500	3	650,000	350,000	25	2,025,000	1,032,500
Nevada	1	75,000	40,000				1	75,000	40,000
California	12	1,045,000	560,500	4	1,300,000	400,000	16	2,345,000	960,500
San Francisco				1	1,500,000	600,000	1	1,500,000	600,000
Oregon	8	460,000	173,400	1	250,000	230,000	9	710,000	423,400
Dakota	41	2,402,100	736,500				41	2,402,100	736,500
Idaho	4	250,000	67,800				4	250,000	67,800

Table, by States, Territories, and reserve cities, &c.—Continued.

States and Territories.	Banks with capital of $150,000 and under.			Banks with capital over $150,000.			Totals.		
	No. of banks.	Capital.	U. S. bonds.	No. of banks.	Capital.	U. S. bonds.	No. of banks.	Capital..	U. S. bonds.
Montana	13	$1,060,000	$289,350	2	$750,000	$150,000	15	$1,810,000	$439,350
New Mexico	8	650,000	412,500				8	650,000	412,500
Utah	4	400,000	187,500	2	400,000	250,000	6	800,000	437,500
Washington	15	1,005,000	380,000				15	1,005,000	380,000
Wyoming	3	200,000	55,000	2	600,000	100,000	5	800,000	155,000
Pacific States and Territories	131	8,922,100	3,585,050	15	5,450,000	2,100,000	146	14,372,100	5,685,050
United States	1,889	159,412,445	106,083,900	825	308,111,965	201,573,150	2,714	527,524,410	307,657,050

Table, by States, Territories, and reserve cities, exhibiting the number of banks in each, with their capital, minimum amount of bonds required by law, bonds actually held and circulation outstanding thereon on October 1, 1885, and also showing the increase of circulation which would be authorized in the event of legislation permitting banks to issue circulation to the par value of bonds deposited.

States and Territories.	Number of banks.	Capital.	United States bonds.			Circulation.	
			Minimum	Held October 1, 1885.	Outstanding October 1, 1885.	Increase on bonds now deposited if issue is authorized to par value.	Maximum increase which might occur if issue is authorized to par value.
Maine	71	$10,360,000	$1,965,000	$8,709,300	$7,683,079	$1,026,221	$2,676,921
New Hampshire	48	6,105,000	1,456,250	5,800,000	5,149,045	650,955	955,955
Vermont	47	7,541,000	1,572,750	6,017,500	5,355,913	661,587	2,185,087
Massachusetts	195	45,095,650	8,044,412	38,606,850	34,200,534	4,406,316	10,895,116
Boston	54	50,950,000	2,700,000	24,614,650	21,716,837	2,897,813	29,233,163
Rhode Island	61	20,340,050	2,453,250	13,505,400	12,036,177	1,539,223	8,283,873
Connecticut	84	24,921,820	3,437,500	18,010,100	15,932,600	2,077,500	8,989,220
New England States	560	165,313,520	21,649,162	115,353,800	102,094,185	13,259,615	63,219,335
New York	267	34,819,760	7,681,665	27,267,150	23,989,591	3,277,359	10,830,169
New York City	44	45,350,000	2,187,500	12,586,500	9,917,442	2,649,058	35,432,558
Albany	6	1,750,000	300,000	1,418,000	1,249,790	168,210	500,210
New Jersey	72	12,208,200	2,399,550	9,326,850	8,007,406	1,319,444	4,200,794
Pennsylvania	228	32,605,340	6,857,598	26,629,200	23,401,460	3,227,740	9,263,880
Philadelphia	34	18,275,250	1,687,500	9,327,800	7,797,648	1,530,152	10,477,602
Pittsburgh	23	10,150,000	1,125,000	7,080,500	6,289,780	790,720	3,860,220
Delaware	15	1,823,985	380,200	1,768,200	1,551,029	217,171	272,956
Maryland	27	2,716,700	666,250	2,479,000	2,143,702	335,298	572,998
Baltimore	17	11,713,260	850,000	6,067,500	4,756,490	1,311,010	6,956,770
District of Columbia	1	252,000	50,000	250,000	188,700	61,300	63,300
Washington	5	1,125,000	225,000	730,000	625,850	104,150	490,150
Middle States	739	172,849,495	24,410,263	104,910,700	89,918,888	14,991,812	82,930,607
Virginia	24	3,576,300	735,250	2,293,350	2,007,500	285,850	1,568,800
West Virginia	21	2,011,000	513,750	1,469,850	1,291,705	178,025	719,235
North Carolina	15	2,063,500	484,625	1,162,000	993,415	168,585	1,070,085
South Carolina	14	1,935,000	396,250	1,161,350	1,002,445	158,905	932,555
Georgia	16	2,472,345	443,050	1,792,000	1,570,900	221,100	901,445
Florida	5	300,900	75,000	147,500	120,185	27,315	179,815
Alabama	10	1,835,000	352,500	1,117,000	990,450	126,550	844,550
Mississippi	6	475,000	118,750	175,000	150,999	24,010	324,010
Louisiana	1	100,000	25,000	100,000	90,000	10,000	10,000
New Orleans	8	3,525,000	400,000	2,125,000	1,886,345	238,655	1,038,655
Texas	68	6,880,000	1,555,000	1,950,500	1,739,250	211,250	5,140,750
Arkansas	6	705,000	163,750	360,000	323,300	36,700	381,700
Kentucky	59	9,648,900	2,065,975	6,440,300	5,714,770	725,530	3,934,130
Louisville	9	3,551,500	450,000	2,833,700	2,550,230	283,470	1,001,270
Tennessee	32	5,007,500	826,875	2,371,500	2,114,010	257,490	2,803,490
Southern States	294	44,086,045	8,605,811	25,499,050	22,545,555	2,953,495	21,540,490
Ohio	183	21,909,580	4,923,895	15,195,250	13,474,579	1,720,671	8,435,001
Cincinnati	12	8,600,000	600,000	5,585,000	4,947,120	637,880	3,652,880
Cleveland	8	6,200,000	400,000	655,000	589,410	65,590	5,610,590
Indiana	96	12,189,500	2,614,875	7,546,800	6,734,150	812,650	5,455,350
Illinois	158	13,673,600	3,330,900	6,912,750	6,154,525	758,225	7,519,075
Chicago	12	11,750,000	600,000	1,183,500	722,850	460,650	11,027,150
Michigan	97	10,194,600	2,208,500	3,958,000	3,479,715	478,285	6,714,885
Detroit	5	2,900,000	250,000	500,000	371,265	128,735	2,528,735
Wisconsin	47	3,785,000	933,750	1,753,250	1,517,078	236,172	2,267,922
Milwaukee	3	650,000	150,000	500,000	448,400	51,600	201,600
Iowa	125	10,155,000	2,413,750	4,301,000	3,813,858	487,142	6,341,142
Minnesota	49	11,399,000	1,297,500	2,113,000	1,884,576	228,424	9,505,424
Missouri	36	3,311,000	752,750	1,428,000	1,251,648	176,952	2,059,352
St. Louis	6	3,250,000	300,000	860,000	766,400	93,600	2,483,600
Kansas	74	4,995,720	1,248,030	1,702,300	1,435,705	266,595	3,560,015
Nebraska	75	5,949,250	1,299,812	2,014,000	1,774,330	239,670	4,174,920
Western States	975	130,903,250	23,324,662	56,208,450	49,365,609	6,842,841	81,537,641
Colorado	25	2,025,000	493,750	1,032,500	926,540	105,960	1,098,460
Nevada	1	75,000	18,750	40,000	35,380	4,620	39,620
California	16	2,345,000	461,250	900,500	855,720	104,780	1,489,280
San Francisco	1	1,500,000	50,000	600,000	539,200	60,800	960,800

Table by States, Territories, and reserve cities, &c.—Continued.

States and Territories.	Number of banks.	Capital.	United States bonds.		Circulation.		
			Minimum	Held October 1, 1885.	Outstanding October 1, 1885.	Increase on bonds now deposited if issue is authorized to par value.	Maximum increase which might occur if issue is authorized to par value.
Oregon	9	$710,000	$165,000	$423,400	$546,740	$76,660	$363,260
Dakota	41	2,402,100	600,525	736,500	646,630	89,870	1,755,470
Idaho	4	250,000	62,500	67,800	60,140	7,660	180,860
Montana	15	1,810,000	365,000	439,350	378,250	61,100	1,431,750
New Mexico	8	650,000	162,500	412,500	369,770	42,730	280,230
Utah	6	800,000	200,000	437,500	324,930	112,570	475,070
Washington	15	1,005,000	251,250	380,000	322,560	57,440	682,440
Wyoming	5	800,000	150,000	155,000	139,500	15,500	660,500
Pacific States and Territories	146	14,372,100	2,980,525	5,685,050	4,945,360	739,690	9,426,740
United States	2,714	527,524,410	80,970,423	307,657,050	268,869,597	38,787,453	258,654,813

Statement of monthly increase and decrease of national-bank circulation from November 1, 1881, to October 31, 1885, to which is added the preceding yearly increase and decrease since January 14, 1875.

Months.	National-bank circulation.		Increase.	Decrease.
	Issued.	Retired.		
1881.				
November	$2,730,030	$933,665	$1,797,265	....
December	1,410,820	1,224,639	267,181	....
1882.				
January	1,402,450	1,195,849	206,601	....
February	946,470	1,596,388	....	$649,918
March	1,350,390	1,600,289	....	249,899
April	694,540	1,218,188	....	523,648
May	976,220	1,841,750	....	865,530
June	1,121,530	2,237,820	....	1,116,290
July	1,956,990	1,661,886	295,104	....
August	3,860,000	2,015,043	1,853,957	....
September	3,895,510	1,535,052	2,360,458	....
October	2,028,400	2,061,402	....	33,002
November	1,341,450	1,520,360	....	178,919
December	1,875,420	1,740,379	126,041	....
1883.				
January	1,371,980	1,657,272	....	285,292
February	1,272,780	2,115,551	....	842,771
March	1,290,220	2,798,819	....	1,508,599
April	1,075,650	1,595,875	....	520,225
May	1,107,790	2,076,373	....	968,583
June	1,305,200	2,644,072	....	1,338,872
July	1,114,110	2,147,800	....	1,033,690
August	1,318,770	2,494,194	....	1,175,424
September	642,980	1,883,885	....	1,240,905
October	793,850	1,991,194	....	1,197,344
November	445,240	1,500,866	....	1,055,626
December	1,177,010	1,649,953	....	472,943
1884.				
January	1,126,020	2,021,895	....	895,875
February	500,004	3,373,760	....	2,864,756
March	579,850	2,497,596	....	1,917,746
April	963,440	2,559,448	....	1,596,008
May	733,960	2,829,758	....	2,095,798
June	1,101,050	2,510,737	....	1,409,687
July	943,950	2,543,502	....	1,599,552
August	1,279,030	2,388,946	....	1,109,916
September	943,390	1,744,057	....	800,667
October	569,750	2,700,871	....	2,131,121
November	208,580	2,255,139	....	2,046,559
December	379,930	2,663,801	....	2,283,871
1885.				
January	677,010	2,923,115	....	2,246,105
February	523,560	2,775,207	....	2,251,647
March	548,330	2,990,575	....	2,442,245
April	1,053,370	2,369,330	....	1,315,960
May	403,790	2,442,668	....	2,038,878
June	690,240	484,135	206,105	....
July	1,066,080	2,804,870	....	1,738,790
August	1,160,710	1,505,725	....	345,015
September	1,914,710	1,473,694	411,016	....
October	2,516,340	3,778,735	....	1,262,395
Totals	58,488,794	100,585,137	7,553,728	49,650,071
From January 14, 1875, to October 31, 1875	10,986,675	14,570,305	....	3,583,630
From November 1, 1875, to October 31, 1876	7,093,680	27,506,981	....	20,413,301
From November 1, 1876, to October 31, 1877	16,306,030	18,265,331	....	1,959,301
From November 1, 1877, to October 31, 1878	16,291,685	10,986,116	5,305,569	....
From November 1, 1878, to October 31, 1879	22,933,490	7,040,397	15,593,093	....
From November 1, 1879, to October 31, 1880	13,402,215	6,193,053	7,209,162	....
From November 1, 1880, to October 31, 1881	30,979,630	13,705,250	17,274,371	....
	176,482,199	198,852,570	53,235,923	75,606,303
Circulation surrendered to this office and retired	....	14,253,939	....	....
Grand total	176,482,199	213,106,518	53,235,923	75,606,303

The following tables have been prepared by E. B. Elliott, Esq., Government Actuary:

Average prices (flat and net) of, and rates of interest realized to investors in the U. S. four per cent. securities of 1907, and in the four-and-a-half per cent. securities of 1891, respectively, from October 1, 1884, to September 30, 1885, inclusive.

Months.	Four per cent. securities of 1907		
	Prices, including accrued interest.	Prices, not including accrued interest.	Rates of interest realized to investors.
1884.	*Flat.*	*Net.*	*Per cent.*
October	120.4814	120.3176	2.805
November	122.0025	121.5601	2.737
December	123.4232	122.6032	2.685
1885.			
January	121.9086	121.7330	2.726
February	122.1813	121.6963	2.724
March	122.3260	121.5025	2.731
April	121.8028	121.6435	2.721
May	122.0450	121.5588	2.722
June	123.1625	122.3371	2.679
July	122.6462	122.4777	2.668
August	122.8425	122.3390	2.673
September	123.2331	122.4033	2.666
Average of 12 months	122.3430	121.8484	2.711

Month.	Four-and-a-half per cent. securities of 1891.		
	Prices, including accrued interest.	Prices, not including accrued interest.	Rates of interest realized to investors.
1884.	*Flat.*	*Net.*	*Per cent.*
October	112.6736	112.1163	2.580
November	114.1684	113.2364	2.391
December	113.5810	113.4030	2.343
1885.			
January	112.7788	112.1937	2.505
February	112.7690	111.8233	2.645
March	111.9591	111.7710	2.527
April	112.4350	111.8787	2.488
May	112.8800	111.9599	2.472
June	112.0634	112.4902	2.540
July	112.7525	112.1955	2.365
August	113.0250	112.0917	2.354
September	112.4114	112.2340	2.303
Average of 12 months	112.8414	112.2828	2.359

The following table shows the annual profit on national-bank circulation, computed on the average net prices of the 4 per cent. United States securities of 1907 and the 4½ per cent. United States securities of 1891, respectively, for the year ending September 30, 1885, at rates of interest for bank loans of 5, 6, 7, and 8 per cent., (1st) considering the 5 per cent. redemption fund as not reducing the loanable circulation, (2nd) considering the 5 per cent. redemption fund as reducing the loanable circulation, the tax on circulation of 1 per cent. per annum having been taken into account in each case, as well as an assumed annual charge of .05 of 1 per cent. on the circulation, to be paid the Treasurer of the United States for expenses of redemption:

		Profit with loans at 5 per cent.	Profit with loans at 6 per cent.	Profit with loans at 7 per cent.	Profit with loans at 8 per cent.
		Per cent.	*Per cent.*	*Per cent.*	*Per cent.*
Fours of 1907	1st	0.757	0.530	0.337	0.119
	2nd	0.572	0.328	0.078	loss 0.176
Four-and-a-halfs of 1891	1st	0.540	0.388	0.236	0.082
	2nd	0.340	0.148	loss 0.045	loss 0.239

Table showing, by States, the amount of national-bank circulation issued, the amount of lawful money deposited in the United States Treasury to retire national-bank circulation from June 20, 1874, to November 1, 1885, and the amount remaining on deposit at the latter date.

| States and Territories. | Additional circulation issued since June 20, 1874. | Lawful money deposited to retire national-bank circulation since June 20, 1874. | | | | Lawful money on deposit with the United States Treasurer at date. |
		For redemption of notes of liquidating banks.	To retire circulation under act of July 12, 1882.	To retire circulation under act of June 20, 1874.	Total deposits.	
Maine.................	$2, 216, 994	$786, 500	$372, 750	$1, 110, 500	$2, 269, 750	$622, 437
New Hampshire......	1, 250, 815	465, 083	....	221, 800	687, 783	136, 207
Vermont.............	2. 774, 180	1, 059, 277	`402, 560	2, 614, 990	4, 076, 827	806, 345
Massachusetts	29, 801, 120	1, 746, 400	4, 080, 620	24, 609, 635	30, 436, 655	4, 709, 777
Rhode Island	4, 077, 080	145, 350	54, 700	4, 785, 735	4, 985, 845	975, 843
Connecticut	5, 789, 050	705, 878	488, 135	6, 141, 827	7, 425, 840	1, 094, 096
New York	35, 903, 635	7, 919, 913	2, 890, 530	41, 714, 065	52, 524, 508	6, 864, 303
New Jersey	4, 076, 885	1, 242, 258	384, 000	5, 078, 432	6, 704, 750	1, 019, 076
Pennsylvania........	22, 457, 950	4, 108, 686	2, 122, 142	18, 515, 741	24, 746, 569	4, 235, 658
Delaware....	495, 975	....	....	83, 550	83, 550	....
Maryland	2, 496, 610	166, 600	110, 000	3, 247, 070	3, 523, 670	487, 839
District of Columbia..	457, 000	455, 664	....	530, 060	985, 724	22, 480
Virginia.............	1, 520, 500	937, 369	....	1, 791, 910	2, 729, 279	296, 533
West Virginia.......	351, 860	731, 060	9, 999	582, 885	1, 323, 944	114, 640
North Carolina......	1, 335, 560	212, 009	....	1, 792, 885	2, 004, 885	150, 880
South Carolina.......	201, 000	....	....	1, 355, 005	1, 355, 005	44, 880
Georgia..............	716, 580	330, 925	....	965, 975	1, 296, 900	157, 484
Florida	132, 740	....	....	....	....	....
Alabama	367, 400	135, 000	....	579, 520	714, 520	46, 328
Mississippi..........	195, 740	....	....	38, 150	38, 150	33, 121
Louisiana............	2, 026, 010	666, 413	....	2, 729, 250	3, 395, 663	379, 420
Texas...............	1, 950, 560	78, 590	....	839, 490	918, 080	221, 406
Arkansas	427, 500	11, 250	....	276, 750	288, 000	58, 276
Kentucky	6, 677, 250	1, 025, 417	166, 720	4, 524, 733	5, 716, 870	1, 355, 748
Tennessee	1, 440, 500	767, 841	38, 100	1, 221, 459	2, 027, 400	560, 124
Missouri.............	2, 726, 230	1, 113, 705	....	5, 280, 860	6, 394, 565	547, 572
Ohio	14, 827, 190	6, 607, 018	1, 573, 064	10, 201, 701	18, 382, 983	5, 382, 136
Indiana..............	6, 583, 670	4, 853, 935	328, 760	8, 796, 495	13, 979, 190	2, 585, 807
Illinois..............	6, 145, 905	3, 299, 534	376, 690	9, 989, 056	13, 665, 280	1, 820, 914
Michigan	4, 403, 310	2, 585, 963	122, 780	4, 474, 372	7, 183, 115	1, 482, 857
Wisconsin	2, 193, 680	1, 152, 030	140, 280	1, 931, 009	3, 223, 319	570, 484
Iowa	3, 868, 830	1, 560, 917	96, 130	3, 601, 375	5, 258, 422	1, 000, 581
Minnesota	1, 930, 890	817, 659	208, 340	2, 153, 311	3, 179, 310	352, 032
Kansas	1, 447, 680	803, 701	15, 750	604, 030	1, 423, 481	139, 426
Nebraska	1, 768, 580	56, 240	143, 050	637, 030	836, 320	160, 627
Nevada	36, 000	....	....	....	....	1, 158
Oregon	183, 010	....	....	9, 000	9, 000	....
Colorado.............	1, 087, 580	347, 475	....	368, 650	716, 125	201, 523
Utah	476, 900	161, 191	....	325, 050	486, 241	49, 384
Idaho	33, 990	....	....	63, 000	63, 000	32, 580
Montana.............	601, 440	189, 940	....	272, 250	462, 190	78, 510
Wyoming............	95, 350	....	....	15, 750	15, 750	6, 500
New Mexico	166, 500	....	....	64, 450	64, 450	38, 490
Dakota	915, 180	48, 550	....	222, 800	271, 350	89, 788
Washington	625, 500	24, 750	....	231, 750	256, 500	33, 630
Arizona	53, 090	50, 590	....	2, 500	53, 090	37, 180
California*	1, 905, 750	90, 000	....	409, 500	499, 500	154, 480
Lawful money deposited prior to June 20, 1874, and remaining at that date........	....	....	....	....	3, 813, 675	......
Totals..........	181, 216, 699	47, 552, 172	14, 125, 820	175, 005, 356	240, 497, 023	39, 158, 710

* Exclusive of national gold banks.

National banks that have gone into voluntary liquidation under the provisions of sections 5220 and 5221 of the Revised Statutes of the United States, with the dates of liquidation, the amount of their capital, circulation issued and retired, and circulation outstanding November 1, 1885.

Name and location of bank.	Date of liquidation.	Capital.	Circulation. Issued.	Circulation. Retired.	Circulation. Outstanding.
First National Bank, Penn Yan, N. Y. ‡	Apr. 6, 1864				
First National Bank, Norwich, Conn. *	May 2, 1864				
Second National Bank, Ottumwa, Iowa †	May 2, 1864				
Second National Bank, Canton, Ohio †	Oct. 3, 1864				
First National Bank, Lansing, Mich. †	Dec. 5, 1864				
First National Bank, Columbia, Mo.	Sept. 19, 1864	$100,000	$90,000	$89,875	$125
First National Bank, Carondelet, Mo.	Mar. 15, 1865	30,000	25,500	25,383	117
First National Bank, Utica, N. Y. *	June 9, 1865				
Pittston National Bank, Pittston, Pa.	Sept. 16, 1865	200,000			
Fourth National Bank, Indianapolis, Ind	Nov. 30, 1865	100,000	100,000	99,080	920
Berkshire National Bank, Adams, Mass. ‡	Dec. 8, 1865	100,000			
National Union Bank, Rochester, N. Y.	Apr. 26, 1866	400,000	192,500	191,058	1,442
First National Bank, Leonardsville, N. Y	July 11, 1866	50,000	45,000	44,330	670
Farmers' National Bank, Richmond, Va	Oct. 22, 1866	100,000	85,000	83,018	1,982
Farmers' National Bank, Waukesha, Wis	Nov. 25, 1866	100,000	90,000	89,455	545
National Bank of Metropolis, Washington, D. C	Nov. 28, 1866	200,000	180,000	176,383	3,617
First National Bank, Providence, Pa.	Mar. 1, 1867	100,000	90,000	88,485	1,515
National State Bank, Dubuque, Iowa	Mar. 9, 1867	150,000	127,000	125,480	1,520
First National Bank of Newton, Newtonville, Mass	Mar. 11, 1867	150,000	130,000	128,443	1,557
First National Bank, New Ulm, Minn.	Apr. 18, 1867	60,000	54,000	53,045	955
National Bank of Crawford County, Meadville, Pa	Apr. 19, 1867	300,000	None.		
Kittanning National Bank, Kittanning, Pa.	Apr. 29, 1867	200,000	None.		
City National Bank, Savannah, Ga. †	May 28, 1867	100,000	None.		
Ohio National Bank, Cincinnati, Ohio	July 3, 1867	500,000	450,000	442,840	7,160
First National Bank, Kingston, N. Y.	Sept. 26, 1867	200,000	180,000	177,189	2,811
First National Bank, Bluffton, Ind	Dec. 5, 1867	50,000	45,000	44,521	479
National Exchange Bank, Richmond, Va	Dec. 5, 1867	200,000	180,000	179,850	1,150
First National Bank, Skaneateles, N. Y.	Dec. 21, 1867	150,000	135,000	133,478	1,522
First National Bank, Jackson, Miss.	Dec. 26, 1867	100,000	45,500	45,250	250
First National Bank, Downingtown, Pa	Jan. 14, 1868	100,000	90,000	88,776	1,224
First National Bank, Titusville, Pa.	Jan. 15, 1868	100,000	86,750	85,534	1,216
Appleton National Bank, Appleton, Wis	Jan. 21, 1868	50,000	45,000	44,330	670
National Bank of Whitestown, N. Y.	Feb. 14, 1868	120,000	45,500	45,158	342
First National Bank, New Brunswick, N. J	Feb. 26, 1868	100,000	90,000	88,484	1,516
First National Bank. Cuyahoga Falls, Ohio	Mar. 4, 1868	50,000	45,000	44,377	623
First National Bank, Cedarburg, Wis.	Mar. 23, 1868	100,000	90,000	89,312	688
Commercial National Bank, Cincinnati, Ohio	Apr. 28, 1868	500,000	345,950	342,620	3,330
Second National Bank, Watertown, N. Y	July 21, 1868	100,000	90,000	88,300	1,700
First National Bank, South Worcester, N. Y	Aug. 4, 1868	175,500	157,400	155,551	2,849
National Mechanics' and Farmers' Bank, Albany, N. Y	Aug. 4, 1868	350,000	314,950	311,955	2,995
Second National Bank, Des Moines, Iowa.	Aug. 5, 1868	50,000	42,500	42,097	403
First National Bank, Steubenville, Ohio	Aug. 8, 1868	150,000	135,000	132,432	2,568
First National Bank, Plumer, Pa	Aug. 25, 1868	100,000	87,500	85,797	1,703
First National Bank, Danville, Va	Sept. 30, 1868	50,000	45,000	44,550	450
First National Bank, Dorchester, Mass.	Nov. 23, 1868	150,000	132,500	130,084	2,416
First National Bank, Oskaloosa, Iowa	Dec. 17, 1868	75,000	67,500	66,902	598
Merchants' and Mechanics' National Bank, Troy, N. Y	Dec. 31, 1868	300,000	184,750	168,936	15,814
National Savings Bank, Wheeling, W. Va	Jan. 7, 1869	100,000	90,000	89,175	825
First National Bank, Marion, Ohio	Jan. 12, 1869	125,000	109,850	108,754	1,096
National Insurance Bank, Detroit, Mich	Feb. 26, 1869	200,010	85,000	84,353	647
National Bank of Lansingburg, N. Y.	Mar. 6, 1869	150,000	135,000	133,592	1,408
National Bank of North America, New York, N. Y.	Apr. 15, 1869	1,000,000	333,000	330,082	2,918
First National Bank, Hallowell, Me.	Apr. 19, 1869	60,000	53,350	52,856	494
First National Bank, Clyde, N. Y.	Apr. 23, 1869	50,000	44,000	43,185	815
Pacific National Bank, New York, N. Y.	May 10, 1869	422,700	134,990	133,887	1,103
Grocers' National Bank, New York, N. Y.	June 7, 1869	390,000	85,250	84,736	514
Savannah National Bank, Savannah, Ga.	June 22, 1869	100,000	85,000	84,280	720
First National Bank, Frostburg, Md.	July 30, 1869	50,000	45,000	44,708	292
First National Bank, La Salle, Ill.	Aug. 30, 1869	50,000	45,000	44,440	560
National Bank of Commerce, Georgetown, D. C	Oct. 28, 1869	100,000	90,000	88,945	1,055

* New bank with same title.   † Never completed organization.   ‡ Consolidated with another bank.

National banks that have gone into voluntary liquidation under the provisions of sections 5220 and 5221 of the Revised Statutes of the United States, &c.—Continued.

Name and location of bank.	Date of liquidation.	Capital.	Circulation.		
			Issued.	Retired.	Outstanding.
Miners' National Bank, Salt Lake City, Utah	Dec. 2, 1869	$150,000	$135,000	$133,768	$1,232
First National Bank, Vinton, Iowa	Dec 13, 1869	50,000	42,500	42,264	236
National Exchange Bank, Philadelphia, Pa	Jan. 8, 1870	300,000	175,750	173,185	2,565
First National Bank, Decatur, Ill	Jan. 10, 1870	100,000	85,250	84,149	1,101
National Union Bank, Owego, N. Y	Jan. 11, 1870	100,000	88,250	86,963	1,287
First National Bank, Berlin, Wis.	Jan. 25, 1870	500,000	44,000	43,605	395
Central National Bank, Cincinnati, Ohio.	Mar. 31, 1870	500,000	425,000	420,040	4,960
First National Bank, Dayton, Ohio	Apr. 9, 1870	150,000	135,000	133,537	1,463
National Bank of Chemung, Elmira, N.Y.	June 10, 1870	100,000	90,000	89,413	587
Merchants' National Bank, Milwaukee, Wis	June 14, 1870	100,000	90,000	89,090	910
First National Bank, Saint Louis, Mo.	July 16, 1870	200,000	179,990	178,230	1,760
Chemung Canal National Bank, Elmira, N. Y	Aug. 3, 1870	100,000	90,000	89,011	989
Central National Bank. Omaha, Nebr*	Sept. 23, 1870	100,000			
First National Bank, Clarksville, Va	Oct. 13, 1870	50,000	27,000	26,810	190
First National Bank, Burlington, Vt	Oct. 15, 1870	300,000	270,000	265,638	4,362
First National Bank, Lebanon, Ohio	Oct. 24, 1870	100,000	85,000	84,164	836
National Exchange Bank, Lansingburg, N. Y	Dec. 27, 1870	100,000	90,000	80,178	822
Muskingum National Bank, Zanesville, Ohio	Jan. 7, 1871	100,000	90,000	80,030	970
United National Bank. Winona, Minn	Feb. 15, 1871	50,000	45,000	44,525	475
First National Bank, Des Moines, Iowa.	Mar. 25, 1871	100,000	90,000	80,004	996
Saratoga County National Bank, Waterford, N. Y	Mar. 28, 1871	150,000	135,000	133,771	1,229
State National Bank, Saint Joseph, Mo.	Mar. 31, 1871	100,000	90,000	89,417	583
First National Bank, Fenton, Mich	May 2, 1871	100,000	49,500	48,948	552
First National Bank, Wellsburg, W. Va.	June 24, 1871	100,000	90,000	89,048	952
Clarke National Bank, Rochester, N. Y	Aug. 11, 1871	200,000	180,000	177,879	2,121
Commercial National Bank, Oshkosh, Wis	Nov. 22, 1871	100,000	90,000	89,047	953
Fort Madison National Bank, Fort Madison, Iowa	Dec. 26, 1871	75,000	67,500	66,815	685
National Bank of Maysville, Ky	Jan. 6, 1872	300,000	270,000	267,793	2,207
Fourth National Bank, Syracuse, N. Y.	Jan. 9, 1872	105,500	91,700	90,600	1,100
American National Bank, New York. N. Y	May 10, 1872	500,000	450,000	442,325	7,675
Carroll County National Bank, Sandwich, N. H	May 24, 1872	50,000	45,000	44,127	873
Second National Bank. Portland, Me.	June 24, 1872	100,000	81,000	79,388	1,612
Atlantic National Bank, Brooklyn, N. Y	July 15, 1872	200,000	165,000	163,265	1,735
Merchants' and Farmers' National Bank, Quincy. Ill	Aug. 8, 1872	150,000	135,000	133,385	1,615
First National Bank, Rochester, N. Y.	Aug. 9, 1872	400,000	206,100	203,301	2,799
Lawrenceburg National Bank, Ind	Sept. 10, 1872	200,000	180,000	177,289	2,711
Jewett City National Bank, Jewett City, Conn	Oct. 4, 1872	60,000	48,750	47,967	783
First National Bank, Knoxville, Tenn	Oct. 22, 1872	100,000	80,910	79,715	1,195
First National Bank, Goshen, Ind	Nov. 7, 1872	115,000	103,500	101,987	1,513
Kidder National Gold Bank, Boston, Mass	Nov. 8, 1872	300,000	120,000	120,000	
Second National Bank, Zanesville, Ohio	Nov. 16, 1872	154,700	138,140	135,808	2,332
Orange County National Bank, Chelsea, Vt	Jan. 14, 1873	200,000	180,000	176,290	3,710
Second National Bank, Syracuse, N. Y.	Feb. 18, 1873	100,000	90,000	88,655	1,345
Richmond National Bank, Richmond, Ind.*	Feb. 28, 1873	230,000	207,000	207,000	
First National Bank, Adams, N. Y	Mar. 7, 1873	75,000	66,900	65,779	1,121
Mechanics' National Bank, Syracuse, N. Y.	Mar. 11, 1873	140,000	93,800	92,560	1,240
Farmers' and Mechanics' National Bank, Rochester, N. Y	Apr. 15, 1873	100,000	83,250	82,084	1,166
Montana National Bank, Helena, Mont.	Apr. 15, 1873	100,000	31,500	31,355	145
First National Bank, Havana, N. Y	June 3, 1873	50,000	45,000	44,085	915
Merchants' and Farmers' National Bank, Ithaca, N. Y	June 30, 1873	50,000	45,000	44,118	882
National Bank of Cazenovia, N. Y	July 18, 1873	150,000	116,770	114,896	1,874
Merchants' National Bank, Memphis, Tenn	Aug. 30, 1873	250,000	225,000	221,308	3,692
Manufacturers' National Bank, Chicago, Ill	Sept. 25, 1873	500,000	450,000	442,209	7,791
Second National Bank, Chicago, Ill	Sept. 25, 1873	100,000	97,500	95,571	1,929

* New bank with same title.

National banks that have gone into voluntary liquidation under the provisions of sections 5220 and 5221 of the Revised Statutes of the United States, &c.—Continued.

Name and location of bank.	Date of liquidation.	Capital.	Circulation. Issued.	Circulation. Retired.	Circulation. Outstanding.
Merchants' National Bank, Dubuque, Iowa	Sept. 30, 1873	$200,000	$180,000	$174,562	$5,418
Beloit National Bank, Beloit, Wis	Oct. 2, 1873	50,000	45,000	44,139	861
Union National Bank, Saint Louis, Mo	Oct. 22, 1873	500,000	150,300	147,248	3,052
City National Bank, Green Bay, Wis	Nov. 29, 1873	50,000	45,000	43,819	1,181
First National Bank, Shelbina, Mo	Jan. 1, 1874	100,000	90,000	88,479	1,521
Second National Bank, Nashville, Tenn	Jan. 8, 1874	125,000	92,920	91,010	1,910
First National Bank, Oneida, N. Y	Jan. 13, 1874	125,000	110,500	108,097	2,403
Merchants' National Bank, Hastings, Minn	Feb. 7, 1874	100,000	90,000	87,702	2,298
National Bank of Tecumseh, Mich	Mar. 3, 1874	50,000	45,000	44,100	900
Gallatin National Bank, Shawnectown, Ill	Mar. 7, 1874	250,000	225,000	220,803	4,197
First National Bank, Brookville, Pa	Mar. 26, 1874	100,000	90,000	87,960	2,040
Citizens' National Bank, Sioux City, Iowa	Apr. 14, 1874	50,000	45,000	44,615	385
Citizens' National Bank, Charlottesville, Va	Apr. 27, 1874	100,000	90,000	88,274	1,726
Farmers' National Bank, Warren, Ill	Apr. 28, 1874	50,000	45,000	43,989	1,011
First National Bank, Medina, Ohio	May 6, 1874	75,000	45,000	44,510	490
Croton River National Bank, South East, N. Y	May 25, 1874	200,000	166,550	163,066	3,484
Merchants' National Bank of West Virginia, Wheeling, W. Va	July 7, 1874	500,000	450,000	441,597	8,403
Central National Bank, Baltimore, Md	July 15, 1874	200,000	180,000	177,253	2,747
Second National Bank, Leavenworth, Kans	July 22, 1874	100,000	90,000	87,146	2,854
Teutonia National Bank, New Orleans, La	Sept. 2, 1874	300,000	270,000	264,370	5,630
City National Bank, Chattanooga, Tenn	Sept. 10, 1874	170,000	148,001	143,110	2,891
First National Bank, Cairo, Ill	Oct. 10, 1874	100,000	90,000	87,832	2,168
First National Bank, Olathe, Kans	Nov. 9, 1874	50,000	45,000	44,384	616
First National Bank, Beverly, Ohio	Nov. 10, 1874	102,000	90,000	87,657	2,343
Union National Bank, La Fayette, Ind	Dec. 4, 1874	250,000	224,095	218,915	5,180
Ambler National Bank, Jacksonville, Fla.*	Dec. 7, 1874	42,500			
Mechanics' National Bank, Chicago, Ill	Dec. 30, 1874	250,000	144,900	141,290	3,610
First National Bank, Evansville, Wis	Jan. 9, 1875	55,000	45,000	44,260	740
First National Bank, Baxter Springs, Kans	Jan. 12, 1875	50,000	36,000	35,441	559
Peoples' National Bank, Pueblo, Colo	Jan. 12, 1875	50,000	27,000	26,745	255
National Bank of Commerce, Green Bay, Wis	Jan. 12, 1875	100,000	90,000	88,485	1,515
First National Bank, Millersburg, Ohio	Jan. 12, 1875	100,000	60,400	59,525	875
First National Bank, Staunton, Va	Jan. 23, 1875	100,000	90,000	88,132	1,868
National City Bank, Milwaukee, Wis	Feb. 24, 1875	100,000	60,000	58,345	1,655
Irasburg National Bank of Orleans, Irasburg, Vt	Mar. 17, 1875	75,000	67,500	65,760	1,740
First National Bank, Pekin, Ill	Mar. 25, 1875	100,000	90,000	87,409	2,591
Merchants and Planters' National Bank, Augusta, Ga	Mar. 30, 1875	200,000	180,000	175,890	4,110
Monticello National Bank, Monticello, Iowa	Mar. 30, 1875	100,000	45,000	43,999	1,001
Iowa City National Bank, Iowa City, Iowa	Apr. 14, 1875	125,000	104,800	102,146	2,654
First National Bank, Wheeling, W. Va	Apr. 22, 1875	250,000	225,000	217,895	7,105
First National Bank, Mount Clemens, Mich	May 20, 1875	50,000	27,000	26,765	235
First National Bank, Knob Noster, Mo	May 20, 1875	50,000	45,000	44,459	541
First National Bank, Brodhead, Wis	June 24, 1875	50,000	45,000	44,243	757
Auburn City National Bank, Auburn, N. Y	June 26, 1875	200,000	141,300	137,227	4,073
First National Bank, El Dorado, Kans	June 30, 1875	50,000	45,000	44,288	712
First National Bank, Junction City, Kans	July 1, 1875	50,000	45,000	44,305	695
First National Bank, Chetopa, Kans	July 19, 1875	50,000	36,000	35,448	552
First National Bank, Golden, Colo	Aug. 25, 1875	50,200	27,000	26,705	295
National Bank of Jefferson, Wis	Aug. 26, 1875	60,000	54,000	52,482	1,518
Green Lane National Bank, Green Lane, Pa	Sept. 9, 1875	100,000	90,000	87,950	2,050
State National Bank, Topeka, Kans	Sept. 15, 1875	60,500	30,000	30,282	318
Farmers' National Bank, Marshalltown, Iowa	Sept. 18, 1875	50,000	27,000	26,625	375
Richland National Bank, Mansfield, Ohio	Sept. 25, 1875	150,000	130,300	125,004	5,296
Planters' National Bank, Louisville, Ky.	Sept. 30, 1875	350,000	315,000	299,889	15,111
First National Bank, Gallatin, Tenn	Oct. 1, 1875	75,000	45,000	44,235	765
First National Bank, Charlestown, W. Va	Oct. 2, 1875	100,000	90,000	88,437	1,563
People's National Bank, Winchester, Ill.	Oct. 4, 1875	75,000	67,500	65,688	1,812

Never completed organization.

National banks that have gone into voluntary liquidation under the provisions of sections 5220 and 5221 of the Revised Statutes of the United States, &c.—Continued.

Name and location of bank.	Date of liquidation.	Capital.	Circulation.		
			Issued.	Retired.	Outstanding.
First National Bank, New Lexington, Ohio	Oct. 12, 1875	$50,000	$45,000	$44,309	$691
First National Bank, Ishpeming, Mich..	Oct. 20, 1875	50,000	45,000	43,833	1,167
Fayette County National Bank, Washington, Ohio	Oct. 26, 1875	100,000	81,280	79,576	1,704
Merchants' National Bank, Fort Wayne, Ind	Nov. 8, 1875	100,000	46,820	45,635	1,185
Kansas City National Bank, Kansas City, Mo	Nov. 13, 1875	100,000	90,000	87,922	2,078
First National Bank, Schoolcraft, Mich.	Nov. 17, 1875	50,000	45,000	44,087	913
First National Bank, Curwensville, Pa..	Dec. 17, 1875	100,000	90,000	86,073	3,927
National Marine Bank. Saint Paul, Minn	Dec. 28, 1875	100,000	59,710	57,080	2,630
First National Bank, Rochester, Ind....	Jan. 11, 1876	50,000	45,000	42,720	2,280
First National Bank, Lodi, Ohio	Jan. 11, 1876	100,000	90,000	85,951	4,049
Iron National Bank, Portsmouth, Ohio..	Jan. 19, 1876	100,000	90,000	88,017	1,983
First National Bank, Ashland, Nebr ..	Jan. 26, 1876	50,000	45,000	44,307	693
First National Bank, Paxton, Ill	Jan. 28, 1876	50,000	45,000	43,182	1,818
First National Bank, Bloomfield, Iowa..	Feb. 5, 1876	55,000	49,500	47,925	1,575
Marietta National Bank, Marietta, Ohio.	Feb. 16, 1876	150,000	90,000	86,637	3,363
Salt Lake City National Bank, Salt Lake City, Utah	Feb. 21, 1876	100,000	45,000	43,617	1,383
First National Bank, La Grange, Mo....	Feb. 24, 1876	50,000	45,000	43,862	1,138
First National Bank, Atlantic, Iowa	Mar. 7, 1876	50,000	45,000	43,887	1,113
First National Bank, Spencer, Ind	Mar. 11, 1876	70,000	63,000	61,827	1,173
National Currency Bank, New York, N. Y	Mar. 23, 1876	100,000	45,000	43,135	1,865
Caverna National Bank, Caverna, Ky ...	May 13, 1876	50,000	45,000	44,230	770
City National Bank, Pittsburgh, Pa.....	May 25, 1876	200,000	68,929	65,745	3,184
National State Bank, Des Moines, Iowa.	June 21, 1876	100,000	50,795	48,105	2,690
First National Bank, Trenton, Mo	June 22, 1876	50,000	45,000	43,901	1,099
First National Bank, Bristol, Tenn	July 10, 1876	50,000	45,000	44,225	775
First National Bank, Leon, Iowa........	July 11, 1876	60,000	45,000	42,812	2,188
Anderson County National Bank, Lawrenceburg, Ky. ...	July 29, 1876	100,000	45,000	44,240	760
First National Bank, Newport, Ind......	Aug. 7, 1876	60,000	45,000	42,363	2,637
First National Bank, De Pere, Wis......	Aug. 17, 1876	50,000	31,500	31,021	479
Second National Bank, Lawrence, Kans.	Aug. 23, 1876	100,000	67,500	65,425	2,075
Commercial National Bank, Versailles, Ky	Aug. 26, 1876	170,000	153,000	146,780	6,220
State National Bank, Atlanta, Ga.......	Aug. 31, 1876	200,000	73,725	70,045	3,680
Syracuse National Bank, Syracuse, N. Y.	Sept. 25, 1876	200,000	117,961	110,274	7,687
First National Bank, Northumberland, Pa	Oct. 6, 1876	100,000	62,106	58,718	3,388
First National Bank. Lancaster, Mo	Nov. 14, 1876	50,000	27,000	26,602	398
First National Bank, Council Grove, Kans	Nov. 28, 1876	50,000	26,500	25,840	660
National Bank Commerce, Chicago, Ill..	Dec. 2, 1876	250,000	71,465	68,436	3,029
First National Bank, Palmyra, Mo......	Dec. 12, 1876	100,000	46,140	43,924	2,216
First National Bank, Newton, Iowa.....	Dec. 16, 1876	50,000	45,000	40,809	4,191
National Southern Kentucky Bank, Bowling Green, Ky	Dec. 23, 1876	50,000	27,000	26,395	605
First National Bank, Monroe, Iowa......	Jan. 1, 1877	60,000	35,700	34,260	1,440
First National Bank, New London, Conn	Jan. 9, 1877	100,000	38,300	35,461	2,839
Winona Deposit National Bank, Winona, Minn	Jan. 28, 1877	100,000	63,285	59,125	4,160
First National Bank, South Charleston, Ohio	Feb. 24, 1877	100,000	90,000	85,557	4,443
Lake Ontario National Bank, Oswego, N. Y.	Feb. 24, 1877	275,000	66,405	61,093	5,312
First National Bank, Sidney, Ohio	Feb. 26, 1877	52,000	46,200	43,892	2,308
Chillicothe National Bank, Ohio........	Apr. 9, 1877	100,000	53,825	49,870	3,955
First National Bank, Manhattan, Kans..	Apr. 13, 1877	52,000	44,200	42,671	1,529
National Bank, Monticello, Ky..........	Apr. 13, 1877	60,000	49,500	44,085	5,415
First National Bank, Rockville, Ind	Apr. 25, 1877	200,000	173,090	162,390	10,700
Georgia National Bank, Atlanta, Ga	May 31, 1877	100,000	45,000	42,575	2,425
First National Bank, Adrian, Mich	June 11, 1877	100,000	43,500	40,909	2,591
First National Bank, Napoleon, Ohio....	June 30, 1877	50,000	45,000	42,837	2,163
First National Bank, Lancaster, Ohio ...	Aug. 1, 1877	60,000	54,000	51,015	2,985
First National Bank, Minerva, Ohio	Aug. 24, 1877	50,000	45,000	43,357	1,643
Kinney National Bank, Portsmouth, Ohio	Aug. 28, 1877	100,000	90,000	86,549	3,451
First National Bank, Green Bay, Wis...	Oct. 19, 1877	50,000	45,000	42,525	2,475
National Exchange Bank, Wakefield, R. I	Oct. 27, 1877	70,000	34,650	31,462	3,188
First National Bank, Union City, Ind...	Nov. 10, 1877	50,000	45,000	42,625	2,375
First National Bank, Negaunee, Mich ..	Nov. 13, 1877	50,000	45,000	42,774	2,226
Tenth National Bank, New York, N. Y .	Nov. 23, 1877	500,000	441,000	401,739	39,261
First National Bank, Paola, Kans.......	Dec. 1, 1877	50,000	44,350	41,959	2,391
National Exchange Bank, Troy, N. Y ...	Dec. 6, 1877	100,000	90,000	88,900	6,100
Second National Bank, La Fayette, Ind .	Dec. 20, 1877	200,000	52,167	45,974	6,193
State National Bank, Minneapolis, Minn	Dec. 31, 1877	100,000	82,500	75,721	6,779
Second National Bank, Saint Louis, Mo	Jan. 8, 1878	200,000	53,055	45,680	7,375

National banks that have gone into voluntary liquidation under the provisions of sections 5220 and 5221 of the Revised Statutes of the United States, &c.—Continued.

Name and location of bank.	Date of liquidation.	Capital.	Circulation. Issued.	Retired.	Out- standing.
First National Bank, Sullivan, Ind	Jan. 8, 1878	$50,000	$45,000	$43,255	$1,745
Rockland County National Bank, Nyack, N.Y	Jan. 10, 1878	100,000	89,000	82,751	6,249
First National Bank, Wyandotte, Kans.	Jan. 19, 1878	50,000	45,000	43,053	1,947
First National Bank, Boone, Iowa	Jan. 22, 1878	50,000	32,400	30,285	2,115
First National Bank, Pleasant Hill, Mo	Feb. 7, 1878	50,000	45,000	42,734	2,266
National Bank of Gloversville, N.Y	Feb. 28, 1878	100,000	64,750	59,764	4,986
First National Bank, Independence, Mo.	Mar. 1, 1878	50,000	27,000	23,486	3,514
National State Bank, Lima, Ind	Mar. 2, 1878	100,000	33,471	29,882	3,589
First National Bank, Tell City, Ind.	Mar. 4, 1878	50,000	44,500	43,229	1,271
First National Bank, Pomeroy, Ohio	Mar. 5, 1878	200,000	75,713	69,160	6,553
Eleventh Ward National Bank Boston, Mass	Mar. 14, 1878	200,000	89,400	84,130	5,270
First National Bank, Prophetstown, Ill.	Mar. 19, 1878	50,000	45,000	43,793	1,208
First National Bank, Jackson, Mich	Mar. 26, 1878	100,000	88,400	81,260	7,140
First National Bank, Eau Claire, Wis	Mar. 30, 1878	60,000	38,461	36,280	2,281
First National Bank, Washington, Ohio	Apr. 5, 1878	200,000	69,750	62,410	7,340
First National Bank, Middleport, Ohio	Apr. 20, 1878	80,000	31,500	30,475	1,025
First National Bank, Streator, Ill	Apr. 24, 1878	50,000	40,500	39,205	1,295
First National Bank, Muir, Mich	Apr. 25, 1878	50,000	44,200	42,061	2,139
Kane County National Bank, Saint Charles, Ill	May 31, 1878	50,000	26,300	24,453	1,847
First National Bank, Carthage, Mo	June 1, 1878	50,000	44,500	42,398	2,102
Security National Bank, Worcester, Mass	June 5, 1878	100,000	49,000	45,175	3,825
First National Bank, Lake City, Colo	June 15, 1878	50,000	29,300	28,574	726
People's National Bank, Norfolk, Va	July 31, 1878	100,000	85,705	73,515	12,190
Topeka National Bank, Topeka, Kans	Aug. 7, 1878	100,000	89,300	76,721	12,579
First National Bank, Saint Joseph, Mo.	Aug. 13, 1878	100,000	67,110	57,725	9,385
First National Bank, Winchester, Ind	Aug. 24, 1878	60,000	52,700	46,899	5,801
Muscatine National Bank, Muscatine, Iowa	Sept. 2, 1878	100,000	44,200	36,841	7,359
Traders' National Bank, Chicago, Ohio	Sept. 4, 1878	200,000	43,700	36,235	7,465
Union National Bank, Rahway, N.J	Sept. 10, 1878	100,000	89,200	80,157	9,043
First National Bank, Sparta, Wis	Sept. 14, 1878	50,000	45,000	40,969	4,031
Herkimer County National Bank, Little Falls, N.Y	Oct. 11, 1878	200,000	178,300	157,665	20,635
Farmers' National Bank, Bangor, Me	Nov. 22, 1878	100,000	89,100	78,287	10,813
Pacific National Bank, Council Bluffs, Iowa	Nov. 30, 1878	100,000	45,000	42,600	2,400
First National Bank, Anamosa, Iowa	Dec. 14, 1878	50,000	44,500	37,886	6,614
Smithfield National Bank, Pittsburgh, Pa	Dec. 16, 1878	200,000	90,000	74,950	15,050
First National Bank, Buchanan, Mich	Dec. 21, 1878	50,000	27,000	25,395	1,605
First National Bank, Prairie City, Ill	Dec. 24, 1878	50,000	27,000	20,960	6,040
Corn Exchange National Bank, Chicago, Ill	Jan. 4, 1879	500,000	59,160	49,927	9,233
Franklin National Bank, Columbus, Ohio	Jan. 4, 1879	100,000	93,070	82,283	10,787
Traders' National Bank, Bangor, Me	Jan. 14, 1879	100,000	76,400	63,585	12,815
First National Bank, Gouic, N.H	Jan. 14, 1879	60,000	45,597	40,278	5,319
First National Bank, Salem, N.C	Jan. 14, 1879	150,000	128,200	109,560	18,640
First National Bank, Granville, Ohio	Jan. 14, 1879	50,000	34,365	29,894	4,471
Commercial National Bank, Petersburg, Va	Jan. 14, 1879	120,000	99,800	82,013	17,787
First National Gold Bank, Stockton, Cal.	Jan. 14, 1879	300,000	238,600	200,051	38,549
First National Bank, Sheboygan, Wis.	Jan. 14, 1879	50,000	45,000	41,668	3,332
First National Bank, Boscobel, Wis	Jan. 21, 1879	50,000	43,900	40,516	3,384
National Marine Bank, Oswego, N.Y	Jan. 25, 1879	120,000	44,300	40,172	4,128
Central National Bank, Hightstown, N.J.	Feb. 15, 1879	100,000	32,400	30,315	2,085
Brookville National Bank, Brookville, Ind	Feb. 18, 1879	100,000	89,000	74,200	14,800
Farmers' National Bank, Centreville, Iowa	Feb. 27, 1879	50,000	41,500	39,002	2,498
First National Bank, Clarinda, Iowa	Mar. 1, 1879	50,000	45,000	42,982	2,018
Waterville National Bank, Waterville, Me	Mar. 3, 1879	125,000	110,300	97,566	12,734
First National Bank, Tremont, Pa	Mar. 4, 1879	75,000	64,600	52,298	12,302
First National Bank, Atlanta, Ill	Apr. 15, 1879	50,000	26,500	21,900	4,600
Union National Bank, Aurora, Ill	Apr. 22, 1879	125,000	82,000	67,393	14,607
National Bank of Menasha, Wis	Apr. 26, 1879	50,000	44,500	41,487	3,013
National Exchange Bank, Jefferson City, Mo	May 8, 1879	50,000	45,000	39,734	5,266
First National Bank, Hannibal, Mo	May 15, 1879	100,000	88,200	73,897	14,303
Merchants' National Bank, Winona, Minn.	June 16, 1879	50,000	35,000	32,327	2,673
Farmers' National Bank, Keithsburg, Ill.	July 3, 1879	50,000	27,000	22,740	4,260
First National Bank, Franklin, Ky	July 5, 1879	100,000	54,000	46,310	7,690

National banks that have gone into voluntary liquidation under the provisions of sections 5220 and 5221 of the Revised Statutes of the United States, &c.—Continued.

Name and location of bank.	Date of liquidation.	Capital.	Circulation.		
			Issued.	Retired.	Outstanding.
National Bank of Salem, Salem, Ind	July 8, 1879	$50,000	$44,400	$42,346	$2,054
Fourth National Bank, Memphis, Tenn .	July 10, 1879	125,000	45,000	36,585	8,415
Bedford National Bank, Bedford, Ind...	July 21, 1879	100,000	87,200	81,835	5,365
First National Bank, Afton, Iowa	Aug. 15, 1879	50,000	26,500	23,829	2,671
First National Bank, Deer Lodge, Mont.	Aug. 16, 1879	50,000	45,000	42,525	2,475
First National Bank, Batavia, Ill	Aug. 30, 1879	50,000	44,300	39,562	4,738
National Gold Bank and Trust Company, San Francisco, Cal	Sept. 1, 1879	750,000	40,000	25,860	14,140
Gainesville National Bank, Gainesville, Ala............................	Nov. 25, 1879	100,000	90,000	70,695	19,305
First National Bank, Hackensack, N. J.	Dec. 6, 1879	100,000	90,000	76,628	13,372
National Bank of Delavan, Delavan, Wis	Jan. 7, 1880	50,000	27,000	22,460	4,540
Mechanics' National Bank, Nashville, Tenn......................	Jan. 13, 1880	100,000	90,000	69,350	20,650
Manchester National Bank, Manchester, Ohio	Jan. 13, 1880	50,000	48,303	40,457	7,846
First National Bank, Meyersdale, Pa ...	Mar. 5, 1880	50,000	30,600	28,435	2,165
First National Bank, Mifflinburg. Pa....	Mar. 8, 1880	100,000	90,000	70,940	19,060
National Bank of Michigan, Marshall, Mich.....................	May 14, 1880	120,000	100,800	84,697	16,103
National Exchange Bank, Houston, Tex	Sept. 10, 1880	100,000	31,500	25,064	6,436
Ascutney National Bank, Windsor, Vt...	Oct. 19, 1880	100,000	90,000	73,337	16,663
First National Bank, Seneca Falls, N. Y.	Nov. 23, 1880	60,000	54,000	50,163	3,837
First National Bank, Baraboo, Wis	Nov. 27, 1880	50,000	27,000	22,881	4,119
Bundy National Bank, New Castle, Ind.	Dec. 6, 1880	50,000	45,000	42,723	2,277
Vineland National Bank, Vineland, N. J.	Jan. 11, 1881	50,000	45,000	42,053	2,947
Ocean County National Bank, Tom's River, N. J	Jan. 11, 1881	100,000	119,405	94,915	24,490
Hungerford National Bank, Adams, N. Y.	Jan. 27, 1881	50,000	45,000	36,122	8,878
Merchants' National Bank, Minneapolis, Minn....	Jan. 31, 1881	150,000	98,268	91,195	7,073
Farmers' National Bank, Mechanicsburg, Ohio	Feb. 18, 1881	100,000	30,140	27,320	2,820
First National Bank, Green Spring, Ohio.	Feb. 18, 1881	50,000	45,000	40,196	4,804
First National Bank, Cannon Falls, Minn.	Feb. 21, 1881	50,000	45,000	39,050	5,950
First National Bank, Coshocton, Ohio...	Feb. 21, 1881	50,000	53,058	48,178	4,880
Manufacturers' National Bank, Three Rivers, Mich....................	Feb. 25, 1881	50,000	45,000	40,205	4,795
First National Bank, Lansing, Iowa.....	Feb. 25, 1881	50,000	45,000	40,002	4,998
First National Bank, Watertown, N. Y.	May 26, 1881	100,000	75,510	54,530	20,980
First National Bank, Americus, Ga...	June 17, 1881	60,000	45,000	40,995	4,005
First National Bank, Saint Joseph, Mich.	June 30, 1881	50,000	26,500	21,918	4,582
First National Bank, Logan, Ohio	July 8, 1881	50,000	45,000	40,380	4,620
First National Bank, Rochelle, Ill.....	Aug. 0, 1881	50,000	45,000	38,965	6,035
First National Bank, Shakopee, Minn ...	Aug. 10, 1881	50,000	45,000	36,890	8,110
National State Bank, Oskaloosa, Iowa...	Aug. 13, 1881	50,000	81,665	63,240	18,425
First National Bank, Hobart, N. Y	Aug. 27, 1881	100,000	90,000	79,279	10,721
Attica National Bank, Attica, N. Y	Aug. 30, 1881	50,000	45,000	37,710	7,290
National Bank of Brighton, Boston, Mass.	Oct. 4, 1881	300,000	270,000	212,650	57,350
Clement National Bank, Rutland, Vt.* ..	Aug. 1, 1881	100,000	....	....	....
First National Bank, Lisbon, Iowa.....	Nov. 1, 1881	50,000	45,000	37,950	7,050
First National Bank, Warsaw, Ind	Dec. 1, 1881	50,000	48,500	41,105	7,395
Brighton National Bank, Brighton, Iowa.	Dec. 15, 1881	50,000	45,000	37,815	7,185
Merchants' National Bank, Denver, Colo.	Dec. 24, 1881	120,000	72,000	44,060	27,940
Merchants' National Bank, Holly, Mich..	Dec. 31, 1881	50,000	45,000	39,299	5,701
First National Bank, Alliance, Ohio	Jan. 3, 1882	50,000	45,000	35,040	9,960
National Union Bank, New London, Conn	Jan. 10, 1882	300,000	112,818	82,955	29,863
National Bank of Royalton, Vt	Jan. 10, 1882	100,000	90,000	67,262	22,738
First National Bank, Whitehall, N. Y ...	Jan. 18, 1882	50,000	45,000	33,810	11,190
National Bank of Pulaski, Tenn	Jan. 23, 1882	70,000	43,700	31,605	12,095
First National Bank, Alton, Ill.........	Mar. 20, 1882	100,000	90,000	67,561	22,439
Havana National Bank, Havana, N. Y ...	Apr. 15, 1882	50,000	45,000	37,422	7,578
First National Bank, Brownsville, Pa ...	May 2, 1882	75,000	67,500	47,245	20,255
Second National Bank, Franklin, Ind....	June 20, 1882	100,000	81,000	53,690	27,370
Merchants' National Bank, Georgetown, Colo	June 22, 1882	50,000	45,000	36,698	8,302
Commercial National Bank, Toledo, Ohio.	July 6, 1882	100,000	90,000	68,430	21,570
Harmony National Bank, Harmony, Pa..	July 7, 1882	50,000	45,000	30,990	14,010
First National Bank, Liberty, Ind.......	July 22, 1882	60,000	54,000	39,620	14,380
Manufacturers' National Bank, Amsterdam, N. Y	Aug. 1, 1882	80,000	72,000	55,370	16,630
First National Bank, Bay City, Mich....	Nov. 8, 1882	400,000	156,100	107,110	48,990
First National Bank, Ripley, Ohio.......	Nov. 10, 1882	100,000	69,201	46,001	23,200
National Bank of State of New York, New York, N. Y.................	Dec. 6, 1882	800,000	397,004	295,414	101,590

*New bank with same title.

National banks that have gone into voluntary liquidation under the provisions of sections 5220 and 5221 of the Revised Statutes of the United States, &c.—Continued.

Name and location of bank.	Date of liquidation.	Capital.	Circulation.		
			Issued.	Retired.	Outstanding.
First National Bank, Wellington, Ohio..	Dec. 12, 1882	$100,000	$90,000	$60,906	$29,094
Second National Bank, Jefferson, Ohio ..	Dec. 26, 1882	100,000	90,000	57,910	32,090
First National Bank, Painesville, Ohio ..	Dec. 30, 1882	200,000	162,800	104,460	58,340
Saint Nicholas National Bank, New York, N. Y	Dec. 30, 1882	500,000	450,000	298,530	151,470
Fifth National Bank, Chicago, Ill	Dec. 30, 1882	500,000	29,700	15,310	14,390
First National Bank, Dowagiac, Mich ...	Jan. 3, 1883	50,000	45,000	30,948	14,052
First National Bank, Greenville, Ill	Jan. 9, 1883	150,000	59,400	34,590	24,810
Merchants' National Bank, East Saginaw, Mich	Jan. 9, 1883	200,000	101,100	65,480	35,620
Logan County National Bank, Russellville, Ky	Jan. 9, 1883	50,000	40,050	29,430	10,620
National Bank of Vandalia, Ill	Jan. 11, 1883	100,000	90,000	52,420	37,580
Traders' National Bank, Charlotte, N. C.	Jan. 16, 1883	50,000	38,800	27,570	11,230
First National Bank, Norfolk, Nebr.....	Feb. 3, 1883	45,000	11,240	5,190	6,050
First National Bank, Midland City, Mich*	Feb. 5, 1883	30,000			
Citizens' National Bank, New Ulm, Minn.	Mar. 1, 1883	50,000	27,000	15,790	11,210
National Bank of Owen, Owenton, Ky...	Mar. 5, 1883	56,000	48,900	30,890	18,010
Merchants' National Bank, Nashville, Tenn	June 30, 1883	300,000	141,200	66,190	75,010
Indiana National Bank, Bedford, Ind ...	Aug. 25, 1883	35,000	11,250	11,250	
Stockton National Bank, Stockton, Cal..	Oct. 1, 1883	100,000	90,000	48,850	41,150
Wall Street National Bank, New York, N. Y	Oct. 15, 1883	500,000	102,800	63,150	39,650
Commercial National Bank, Reading, Pa	Oct. 23, 1883	150,000	135,000	69,680	65,320
Corn Exchange National Bank, Chicago, Ill*	Nov. 10, 1883	700,000			
Farmers' National Bank, Sullivan, Ind..	Dec. 24, 1883	50,000	45,000	21,070	23,930
City National Bank, La Salle, Ill	Jan. 8, 1884	100,000	22,500	6,870	15,630
Hunt County National Bank, Greenville, Tex	Jan. 22, 1884	68,250	17,300	5,350	11,950
Waldoboro' National Bank, Waldoboro', Mo	Jan. 31, 1884	50,000	44,000	21,740	22,260
Third National Bank, Nashville, Tenn...	Feb. 20, 1884	300,000	180,000	91,170	88,830
Madison County National Bank, Anderson, Ind ...	Mar. 25, 1884	50,000	45,000	20,850	24,150
First National Bank, Phoenix, Ariz	Apr. 7, 1884	50,000	11,240	4,730	6,510
Cobbossee National Bank, Gardiner, Me.	Apr. 18, 1884	150,000	90,000	40,140	49,860
Mechanics and Traders' National Bank, New York, N. Y	Apr. 24, 1884	200,000	85,400	38,470	46,930
Princeton National Bank, Princeton, N.J.	May 17, 1884	100,000	72,500	36,220	36,280
Kearsarge National Bank, Warner, N. H.	June 30, 1884	50,000	23,586	10,966	12,680
Second National Bank, Lansing, Mich...	July 31, 1884	50,000	40,000	12,400	27,600
First National Bank, Ellensburg, Wash.	Aug.* 9, 1884	50,000	13,500	4,900	8,600
German National Bank, Millerstown, Pa	Aug. 12, 1884	50,000	45,000	12,175	32,825
Exchange National Bank, Cincinnati, Ohio	Aug. 27, 1884	500,000	78,000	18,410	59,590
First National Bank, Rushville, Ill	Sept. 30, 1884	75,000	66,500	15,940	50,560
Mechanics' National Bank, Peoria, Ill...	Oct. 4, 1884	100,000	72,000	19,590	52,410
First National Bank, Freeport, Pa	Oct. 10, 1884	50,000	44,200	11,680	32,520
Genesee County National Bank, Batavia, N. Y	Oct. 11, 1884	50,000	45,000	16,660	28,340
Valley National Bank, Red Oak, Iowa...	Oct. 20, 1884	50,000	22,150	6,280	15,870
Merchants' National Bank, Bismarck, Dak	Oct. 28, 1884	73,000	22,500	3,250	19,250
Manufacturers' National Bank, Minneapolis, Minn	Nov. 1, 1884	300,000	45,000	8,260	36,740
Farmers and Merchants' National Bank, Uhricsville, Ohio	Nov. 10, 1884	50,000	34,600	8,110	26,490
Metropolitan National Bank, New York, N. Y	Nov. 18, 1884	3,000,000	1,447,000	420,270	1,026,730
First National Bank, Grand Forks, Dak.	Dec. 2, 1884	50,000	19,250	5,330	13,920
Freehold National Banking Company, Freehold, N. J	Dec. 10, 1884	50,000	93,000	28,830	64,170
Albia National Bank, Albia, Iowa	Dec. 16, 1884	50,000	11,240	2,390	8,850
First National Bank, Carlinville, Ill	Dec. 16, 1884	50,000	22,450	5,970	16,480
Iron National Bank, Gunnison, Colo.....	Dec. 8, 1884	50,000	11,250	3,030	8,220
Freeman's National Bank, Augusta, Me.	Dec. 26, 1884	100,000	90,000	30,320	59,680
First National Bank, Kokomo, Ind	Jan. 1, 1885	250,000	45,000	9,880	35,120
First National Bank, Sabetha, Kans.....	Jan. 2, 1885	50,000	10,740	2,000	8,740
First National Bank, Wyoming, Ill......	Jan. 13, 1885	50,000	11,200	1,950	9,250
First National Bank, Tarentum, Pa	Jan. 13, 1885	50,000	42,500	7,980	34,520
Farmers' National Bank, Franklin, Tenn.	Jan. 24, 1885	50,000	10,740	1,370	9,370
First National Bank, Walnut, Ill........	Jan. 21, 1885	60,000	36,000	5,680	30,320

* No circulation issued.

National banks that have gone into voluntary liquidation under the provisions of sections 5220 and 5221 of the Revised Statutes of the United States, &c.—Continued.

Name and location of bank.	Date of liquidation.	Capital.	Circulation.		
			Issued.	Retired.	Out-standing.
Citizens' National Bank, Sabetha, Kans.	Jan. 27, 1885	$50, 000	$11, 240	$1, 820	$9, 420
First National Bank, Tucson, Ariz	Jan. 31, 1885	100, 000	28, 100	6, 720	21, 380
Ripon National Bank, Ripon, Wis	Feb. 7, 1885	50, 000	16, 200	1, 960	14, 240
Farmers' National Bank, Franklin, Ohio.	Apr. 1, 1885	50, 000	27, 350	3, 340	24, 010
National Union Bank, Swanton, Vt	Apr. 28, 1885	50, 000	43, 800	5, 030	38, 770
First National Bank, Prescott, Ariz. ...	Apr. 9, 1885	50, 000	11, 250	1, 760	9, 490
German National Bank, Memphis, Tenn.	May 6, 1885	175, 300	120, 100	15, 690	104, 410
First National Bank, Superior, Wis	May 16, 1885	60, 000	18, 900	2, 040	16, 860
Shetucket National Bank, Norwich, Conn	May 18, 1885	100, 000	72, 000	10, 100	61, 900
Cumberland National Bank, Cumberland, R. I.	June 5, 1885	125, 000	112, 500	14, 940	97, 560
Merchants and Farmers' National Bank, Shakopee, Minn	May 12, 1885	50, 000	10, 240	740	9, 500
First National Bank, Columbia, Tenn ...	July 14, 1885	100, 000	66, 800	3, 630	63, 170
Union National Bank, New York, N. Y.	July 21, 1885	1, 200, 000	25, 100	950	24, 150
Manufacturers' National Bank, Appleton, Wis.	Oct. 10, 1885	50, 000	45, 000	None	45, 000
First National Bank, Plankinton, Dak..	Oct. 21, 1885	50, 000	11, 250	None	11, 250
		91, 184, 780	35, 924, 924	30, 820 996	5, 103, 928

National banks that have gone into voluntary liquidation under the provisions of sections 5220 and 5221 of the Revised Statutes of the United States, for the purpose of organizing new associations with the same or different title, with date of liquidation, amount of capital, circulation issued, retired, and outstanding on November 1, 1885.

Name and location of bank.	Date of liquidation.	Capital.	Circulation.		
			Issued.	Retired.	Outstanding.
First National Bank, Rondout, N. Y ...	Oct. 30, 1880	$300,000	$270,000	$216,852	$53,148
First National Bank, Huntington, Ind ..	Jan. 31, 1881	100,000	90,000	80,645	9,355
First National Bank, Indianapolis, Ind..	July 5, 1881	300,000	279,248	215,424	63,824
First National Bank, Valparaiso, Ind ...	Apr. 24, 1882	50,000	45,000	36,015	8,985
First National Bank, Stillwater, Minn ..	Apr. 20, 1882	130,000	83,456	71,477	11,979
First National Bank, Chicago, Ill	Apr. 29, 1882	1,000,000	90,000	75,877	14,123
First National Bank, Woodstock, Ill ...	Apr. 30, 1882	50,000	45,000	34,350	10,650
Second National Bank, Cincinnati, Ohio.	Apr. 28, 1882	200,000	180,000	121,320	58,680
Second National Bank, New York, N. Y.	Apr. 26, 1882	300,000	376,890	274,035	102,855
First National Bank, Portsmouth, N. H.	Apr. 29, 1882	300,000	286,000	214,180	71,820
First National Bank, Richmond, Ind ...	May 5, 1882	200,000	87,400	60,812	26,588
Second National Bank, Cleveland, Ohio.	May 6, 1882	1,000,000	510,800	356,650	154,150
First National Bank, New Haven, Conn.	May 6, 1882	500,000	355,310	264,120	91,190
First National Bank, Akron, Ohio	May 2, 1882	100,000	114,822	78,772	36,050
First National Bank, Worcester, Mass ...	May 4, 1882	300,000	252,000	193,476	58,524
First National Bank, Barre, Mass	May 9, 1882	150,000	135,000	100,893	34,107
First National Bank, Davenport, Iowa..	May 9, 1882	100,000	45,000	29,743	15,257
First National Bank, Kendallville, Ind..	May 12, 1882	150,000	90,000	63,000	27,000
First National Bank, Cleveland, Ohio ...	May 13, 1882	300,000	266,402	181,688	84,774
First National Bank, Youngstown, Ohio.	May 15, 1882	500,000	441,529	321,429	120,100
First National Bank, Evansville, Ind....	May 15, 1882	500,000	442,870	300,040	142,830
First National Bank, Salem, Ohio	May 15, 1882	50,000	110,540	78,950	31,590
First National Bank, Scranton, Pa	May 18, 1882	200,000	45,000	31,705	13,295
First National Bank, Centreville, Ind....	May 18, 1882	50,000	64,525	48,925	15,600
First National Bank, Fort Wayne, Ind ..	May 22, 1882	300,000	45,000	29,861	15,139
First National Bank, Strasburg, Pa	May 22, 1882	100,000	79,200	59,002	20,138
First National Bank, Marietta, Pa	May 27, 1882	100,000	99,000	71,030	27,970
First National Bank, La Fayette, Ind ...	May 31, 1882	150,000	175,060	138,425	36,635
First National Bank, McConnelsville, Ohio	May 31, 1882	50,000	84,640	60,007	24,573
First National Bank, Milwaukee, Wis ...	May 31, 1882	200,000	229,170	159,072	70,098
Second National Bank, Akron, Ohio	May 31, 1882	100,000	102,706	71,932	30,774
First National Bank, Ann Arbor, Mich .	June 1, 1882	100,000	85,078	63,670	21,408
First National Bank, Geneva, Ohio	June 1, 1882	100,000	90,000	61,010	28,990
First National Bank, Oberlin, Ohio ...	June 1, 1882	50,000	58,382	41,298	17,084
First National Bank, Philadelphia, Pa ..	June 10, 1882	1,000,000	799,800	510,920	258,880
First National Bank, Troy, Ohio	June 10, 1882	200,000	180,000	129,093	50,907
Third National Bank, Cincinnati, Ohio..	June 14, 1882	800,000	609,500	422,430	187,070
First National Bank, Cambridge City, Ind..................................	June 15, 1882	50,000	45,000	29,872	15,128
First National Bank, Lyons, Iowa	June 15, 1882	100,000	90,000	55,581	34,419
First National Bank, Detroit, Mich	June 17, 1882	500,000	336,345	249,775	86,570
First National Bank, Wilkes Barre, Pa .	June 20, 1882	375,000	337,500	239,700	97,800
First National Bank, Iowa City, Iowa ..	June 24, 1882	100,000	88,400	63,575	24,825
First National Bank, Nashua, N. H	June 24, 1882	100,000	90,000	66,750	23,250
First National Bank, Johnstown, Pa ...	June 24, 1882	60,000	54,000	37,855	16,145
First National Bank, Pittsburgh, Pa	June 29, 1882	750,000	594,000	402,870	191,139
First National Bank, Terre Hante, Ind..	June 29, 1882	200,000	141,575	101,173	40,402
First National Bank, Hollidaysburg, Pa	June 30, 1882	50,000	45,000	33,250	11,750
First National Bank, Bath, Me	June 30, 1882	200,000	180,000	131,870	48,130
First National Bank, Janesville, Wis ...	June 30, 1882	125,000	121,050	81,110	39,940
First National Bank, Michigan City, Ind	June 30, 1882	100,000	45,000	38,408	6,502
First National Bank, Monmouth, Ill ...	July 3, 1882	75,000	45,000	37,499	7,501
First National Bank, Marion, Iowa	July 11, 1882	50,000	45,000	34,900	10,100
First National Bank, Marlborough, Mass.	Aug. 3, 1882	200,000	180,000	131,270	48,730
National Bank of Stanford, Ky..........	Oct. 3, 1882	150,000	135,000	97,350	37,650
First National Bank, Sandusky, Ohio ...	Oct. 6, 1882	150,000	90,000	56,890	33,110
First National Bank, Sandy Hill, N. Y..	Dec. 31, 1882	50,000	45,000	31,350	13,650
First National Bank, Lawrenceburg, Ind	Feb. 24, 1883	100,000	90,000	58,350	31,650
First National Bank, Cambridge, Ohio ..	Feb. 24, 1883	100,000	80,800	49,100	31,700
First National Bank, Oshkosh, Wis	Feb. 24, 1883	100,000	47,800	35,390	12,410
First National Bank, Grand Rapids, Mich	Feb. 24, 1883	400,000	155,900	117,020	38,880
First National Bank, Delphos, Ohio	Feb. 24, 1883	50,000	45,000	32,300	12,700
First National Bank, Freeport, Ill.......	Feb. 24, 1883	100,000	53,500	41,150	12,350
First National Bank, Elyria, Ohio.......	Feb. 24, 1883	100,000	90,000	54,000	36,000
First National Bank, Troy, N. Y.........	Feb. 24, 1883	900,000	229,550	160,880	68,670
Second National Bank, Detroit, Mich ...	Feb. 24, 1883	1,000,000	363,700	223,880	139,820
Second National Bank, Peoria, Ill.......	Feb. 24, 1883	100,000	90,000	46,440	43,560
National Fort Plain Bank, Fort Plain, N. Y	Feb. 24, 1883	200,000	174,300	111,046	63,254
Logansport National Bank, Logansport, Ind...............................	Dec. 1, 1883	100,000	16,850	9,600	7,250
National Bank of Birmingham, Ala	May 14, 1884	50,000	45,000	20,830	24,170

National banks that have gone into voluntary liquiation under the provisions of sections 5220 and 5221 of the Revised Statutes of the United States, &c.—Continued.

Name and location of bank.	Date of liquidation.	Capital.	Circulation.		
			Issued.	Retired.	Outstanding.
First National Bank, Westfield, N. Y...	June 1, 1884	$50,000	$42,800	$16,180	$26,620
First National Bank, Independence, Iowa	Oct. 31, 1884	100,000	90,000	20,570	69,430
First National Bank, Sturgis, Mich	Dec. 31, 1884	50,000	43,850	10,580	33,270
National Bank, Rutland, Vt............	Jan. 13, 1885	500,000	238,700	72,150	166,550
Kent National Bank, Chestertown, Md..	Feb. 12, 1885	50,000	29,450	14,770	14,680
National Fulton County Bank, Gloversville, N. Y	Feb. 20, 1885	150,000	135,000	28,190	106,810
First National Bank, Centralia, Ill	Feb. 25, 1885	80,000	70,600	9,830	60,770
National Exchange Bank, Albion, Mich.	Feb. 28, 1885	75,000	30,600	6,253	24,347
First National Bank, Paris, Mo	Mar. 31, 1885	100,000	89,155	13,175	75,980
First National Bank, Yakima. Wash....	June 20, 1885	50,000	14,650	1,510	13,140
First National Bank, Flint, Mich	June 30, 1885	200,000	121,500	8,760	112,740
Total................................		17,570,000	12,440,963	8,381,340	4,059,623

Names of banks in liquidation under section 7, act July 12, 1882, with date of expiration of charter, circulation issued, retired, and outstanding November 1, 1885.

Name and location of bank.	Date of liquidation.	Capital.	Circulation.		
			Issued.	Retired.	Outstanding.
First National Bank, Pontiac, Mich.....	Dec. 31, 1881	$50,000	$90,000	$65,370	$24,630
First National Bank, Washington, Iowa.	Apr. 11, 1882	100,000	88,565	60,252	28,313
First National Bank, Fremont, Ohio.....	May 22, 1882	100,000	90,000	63,237	26,763
Second National Bank, Dayton, Ohio....	May 26, 1882	300,000	262,941	181,600	81,341
First National Bank, Girard, Pa.........	June 1, 1882	100,000	90,000	65,775	24,225
First National Bank, Xenia, Ohio........	Feb. 24, 1883	120,000	108,000	64,550	43,450
First National Bank, Peru, Ill...........	Feb. 24, 1883	100,000	45,000	26,300	18,700
First National Bank, Elmira, N. Y.......	Feb. 24, 1883	100,000	90,000	56,570	33,430
First National Bank, Chittenango, N. Y.	Feb. 24, 1883	150,000	135,000	100,040	34,960
First National Bank, Eaton, Ohio........	July 4, 1884	50,000	44,300	13,640	30,660
First National Bank, Leominster, Mass..	July 5, 1884	300,000	244,400	90,690	153,710
First National Bank, Winona, Minn.....	July 21, 1884	50,000	44,200	15,090	29,110
American National Bank, Hallowell, Me.	Sept. 10, 1884	75,000	67,500	25,510	41,990
First National Bank, Attica, Ind........	Oct. 28, 1884	56,000	50,400	19,400	31,000
Citizens' National Bank, Indianapolis, Ind	Nov. 11, 1884	300,000	87,800	24,410	63,390
First National Bank, North East, Pa ...	Dec. 23, 1884	50,000	24,550	3,080	21,470
First National Bank, Galva, Ill.........	Jan. 2, 1885	50,000	36,000	7,800	28,200
First National Bank, Thornton, Ind.....	Jan. 13, 1885	50,000	43,740	10,320	33,420
Muncie National Bank, Muncie, Ind	Jan. 28, 1885				
Merchants' National Bank, Evansville, Ind.............................	Feb. 6, 1885	200,000	161,000	31,900	120,100
Saybrook National Bank, Essex, Conn..	Feb. 20, 1885	250,000	90,800	16,680	74,120
Union National Bank, Albany, N. Y.....	Mar. 7, 1885	100,000	61,200	10,090	51,110
Battenkill National Bank, Manchester, Vt	Mar. 21, 1885	250,000	144,400	39,530	104,870
First National Bank, Owosso, Mich......	Apr. 14, 1885	75,000	57,700	10,850	46,850
Coventry National Bank, Anthony, R. I	Apr. 17, 1885	60,000	53,500	6,990	46,510
State National Bank, Keokuk, Iowa.....	May 23, 1885	100,000	89,000	20,010	68,990
Tolland County National Bank, Tolland, Conn	June 6, 1885	150,000	45,000	4,090	40,010
City National Bank, Hartford, Conn.....	June 9, 1885	100,000	44,100	5,320	38,780
West River National Bank, Jamaica, Vt.	Aug. 17, 1885	550,000	90,000	12,840	77,160
		60,000	54,000	2,850	51,150
Total..............................	....	4,096,000	2,533,096	1,054,784	1,478,312

Names of banks in liquidation under section 7, act July 12, 1882, with date of expiration of charter, circulation issued, retired, and outstanding, succeeded by associations with the same or different title, November 1, 1885.

Name and location of bank.	Date of liqui- dation.	Capital.	Circulation.		
			Issued.	Retired.	Out- standing.
First National Bank, Kittanning, Pa....	July 2, 1882	$200,000	$199,500	$134,360	$65,140
National Bank of Beaver County, New Brighton, Pa...........................	Nov. 12, 1884	200,000	97,300	25,240	72,060
National Bank, Beaver Dam, Wis.......	Dec. 24, 1884	50,000	41,100	9,060	32,040
Merchants' National Bank, Cleveland, O.	Dec. 27, 1884	800,000	228,100	55,230	172,870
Union National Bank, Chicago, Ill	Dec. 29, 1884	1,000,000	62,800	14,070	48,730
First National Bank, Le Roy, N. Y	Jan. 2, 1885	150,000	135,000	38,690	96,310
Evansville National Bank, Indiana.......	Jan. 3, 1885	800,000	543,050	55,430	487,620
National Albany Exchange Bank, Albany, N Y	Jan. 10, 1885	300,000	243,900	70,240	173,660
National Bank, Galena, Ill	Jan. 11, 1885	100,000	55,900	9,850	46,050
National State Bank, La Fayette, Ind....	Jan. 16, 1885	300,000	615,000	519,880	95,120
First National Bank, Knoxville, Ill	Jan. 16, 1885	60,000	43,600	7,700	35,900
Farmers' National Bank, Ripley, Ohio ..	Jan. 17, 1885	100,000	87,400	17,940	69,460
City National Bank, Grand Rapids, Mich.	Jan. 21, 1885	300,000	45,000	11,540	33,460
Lee County National Bank, Dixon, Ill...	Jan. 21, 1885	100,000	41,500	7,660	33,840
Fort Wayne National Bank, Ind	Jan. 25, 1885	350,000	257,300	41,970	215,330
National Exchange Bank, Tiffin, Ohio...	Mar. 1, 1885	125,000	50,500	8,020	42,480
National Bank, Malone, N. Y	Mar. 9, 1885	200,000	65,900	11,910	53,990
Jefferson National Bank, Steubenville, O	Mar. 21, 1885	150,000	132,600	21,780	110,820
First National Bank, Battle Creek, Mich	Mar. 28, 1885	100,000	89,200	10,960	78,240
Central National Bank, Danville, Ky....	Mar. 28, 1885	200,000	180,000	24,720	155,280
Knox County National Bank, Mount Vernon, Ohio...................	Apr. 1, 1885	75,000	53,200	8,000	45,200
First National Bank, Haughton, Mich ..	Apr. 18, 1885	100,000	45,000	5,310	39,690
National Bank, Fort Edward, N. Y......	Apr. 22, 1885	100,000	88,900	16,490	72,410
National Bank, Salem, N. Y.............	May 4, 1885	100,000	86,100	15,480	70,620
National Exchange Bank, Seneca Falls, N. Y...............................	May 6, 1885	100,000	88,400	14,400	74,000
Trumbull Nat'onal Bank, Warren, Ohio.	July 5, 1885	150,000	134,500	7,160	127,340
Attleborough National Bank, North Attleborough, Mass....................	July 17, 1885	100,000	84,300	6,000	78,300
American National Bank, Detroit, Mich.	July 24, 1885	400,000	251,500	9,770	241,730
First National Bank, Paris, Ill..........	Aug. 12, 1885	125,000	111,500	4,520	106,980
First National Bank, Saint John, Mich..	Aug. 14, 1885	50,000	21,000	900	20,100
Second National Bank, Pontiac, Mich...	Sept. 1, 1885	100,000	43,700	1,590	42,110
Raleigh National Bank North Carolina, Raleigh, N. C	Sept. 5, 1885	400,000	123,900	3,590	120,310
First National Bank, Danville, Ky	Sept. 22, 1885	150,000	90,000	6,280	83,720
Total...................	....	7,535,000	4,436,650	1,195,740	3,240,910

National banks that have been placed in the hands of receivers, together with their capital, circulation issued, lawful money deposited with the Treasurer to redeem circulation, the amount redeemed, and the amount outstanding, on November 1, 1885.

Name and location.	Capital.	Lawful money deposited.	Circulation.		
			Issued.	Redeemed.	Outstanding.
First National Bank, Attica, N. Y.	$50,000	$44,000	$44,000	$43,736	$264
Venango National Bank, Franklin, Pa.	300,000	85,000	85,000	84,748	252
Merchants' National Bank, Washington, D. C.	200,000	180,000	180,000	179,259	741
First National Bank, Medina, N. Y.	50,000	40,000	40,000	39,747	253
Tennessee National Bank, Memphis, Tenn.	100,000	90,000	90,000	89,624	376
First National Bank, Selma, Ala.	100,000	85,000	85,000	84,547	453
First National Bank, New Orleans, La.	500,000	180,000	180,000	178,680	1,320
National Unadilla Bank, Unadilla, N. Y.	120,000	100,000	100,000	99,744	256
Farmers and Citizens' National Bank, Brooklyn, N. Y.	300,000	253,900	253,900	252,520	1,380
Croton National Bank, New York, N. Y.	200,000	180,000	180,000	179,580	420
First National Bank, Bethel, Conn.	60,000	26,300	26,300	26,089	211
First National Bank, Keokuk, Iowa	100,000	90,000	90,000	89,569	431
National Bank of Vicksburg, Miss.	50,000	25,500	25,500	25,419	81
First National Bank, Rockford, Ill.	50,000	45,000	45,000	44,663	337
First National Bank of Nevada, Austin, Nev.	250,000	129,700	129,700	128,546	1,154
Ocean National Bank, New York, N. Y.	1,000,000	800,000	800,000	790,457	9,543
Union Square National Bank, New York, N. Y.	200,000	50,000	50,000	49,634	366
Eighth National Bank, New York, N. Y.	250,000	243,393	243,393	240,459	2,934
Fourth National Bank, Philadelphia, Pa.	200,000	179,000	179,000	177,025	1,975
Waverly National Bank, Waverly, N. Y.	106,100	71,000	71,000	69,893	1,107
First National Bank, Fort Smith, Ark.	50,000	45,000	45,000	44,455	545
Scandinavian National Bank, Chicago, Ill.	250,000	135,000	135,000	134,315	685
Walkill National Bank, Middletown, N. Y.	175,000	118,900	118,900	117,249	1,651
Crescent City National Bank, New Orleans, La.	500,000	450,000	450,000	445,715	4,285
Atlantic National Bank, New York, N. Y.	300,000	100,000	100,000	98,483	1,517
First National Bank, Washington, D. C.	500,000	450,000	450,000	439,114	10,886
National Bank of Commonwealth, New York, N. Y.	750,000	234,000	234,000	229,579	4,421
Merchants' National Bank, Petersburg, Va.	400,000	360,000	360,000	352,445	7,555
First National Bank, Petersburg, Va.	200,000	179,200	179,200	174,860	4,340
First National Bank, Mansfield, Ohio	100,000	90,000	90,000	88,122	1,878
New Orleans National Banking Association, New Orleans, La.	600,000	360,000	360,000	353,000	7,000
First National Bank, Carlisle, Pa.	50,000	45,000	45,000	44,110	890
First National Bank, Anderson, Ind.	50,000	45,000	45,000	43,936	1,064
First National Bank, Topeka, Kans.	100,000	90,000	90,000	88,169	1,831
First National Bank, Norfolk, Va.	100,000	95,000	95,000	92,685	2,315
Gibson County National Bank, Princeton, Ind.	50,000	43,800	43,800	43,165	635
First National Bank of Utah, Salt Lake City, Utah	150,000	134,991	134,991	132,747	2,244
Cook County National Bank, Chicago, Ill.	500,000	315,900	315,900	311,053	4,847
First National Bank, Tiffin, Ohio	100,000	68,850	68,850	67,070	1,780
Charlottesville National Bank, Charlottesville, Va.	200,000	146,585	146,585	141,895	4,690
Miners' National Bank, Georgetown, Colo.	150,000	45,000	45,000	43,930	1,070
Fourth National Bank, Chicago, Ill.	200,000	180,000	180,000	175,405	4,595
First National Bank, Bedford, Iowa	30,000	27,000	27,000	24,980	2,020
First National Bank, Osceola, Iowa	50,000	45,000	45,000	44,000	1,000
First National Bank, Duluth, Minn.	100,000	90,000	90,000	88,636	1,364
First National Bank, La Crosse, Wis.	50,000	45,000	45,000	43,618	1,382
City National Bank, Chicago, Ill.	250,000	225,000	225,000	219,486	5,514
Watkins National Bank, Watkins, N. Y.	75,000	67,500	67,500	64,241	3,259
First National Bank, Wichita, Kans.	60,000	52,200	52,200	51,123	1,077
First National Bank, Greenfield, Ohio	50,000	50,000	50,000	48,529	1,471
National Bank of Fishkill, N. Y.	200,000	177,200	177,200	167,253	9,947
First National Bank, Franklin, Ind.	132,000	130,992	130,992	124,422	6,570
Northumberland County National Bank, Shamokin, Pa.	67,000	60,300	60,300	56,870	3,430
First National Bank, Winchester, Ill.	50,000	45,000	45,000	42,587	2,413
National Exchange Bank, Minneapolis, Minn.	100,000	90,000	90,000	81,900	8,100
National Bank of State of Missouri, Saint Louis, Mo.	2,500,000	1,658,800	1,693,660	1,657,670	35,990
First National Bank, Delphi, Ind.	50,000	45,000	45,000	42,990	2,010
First National Bank, Georgetown, Colo.	75,000	45,000	45,000	42,070	2,930
Lock Haven National Bank, Lock Haven, Pa.	120,000	71,200	71,200	64,103	7,097
Third National Bank, Chicago, Ill.	750,000	516,840	597,840	517,602	80,238
Central National Bank, Chicago, Ill.	200,000	45,000	45,000	41,803	3,197
First National Bank, Kansas City, Mo.	500,000	44,940	44,940	38,610	6,330

National banks that have been placed in the hands of receivers, &c.—Continued.

Name and location.	Capital.	Lawful money deposited.	Circulation.		
			Issued.	Redeemed.	Outstanding.
Commercial National Bank, Kansas City, Mo	$100,000	$44,500	$44,500	$39,892	$4,608
First National Bank, Ashland, Pa	112,500	75,554	75,554	65,807	9,747
First National Bank, Tarrytown, N. Y	100,000	89,200	89,200	81,131	8,069
First National Bank, Allentown, Pa	250,000	78,641	78,641	70,463	8,178
First National Bank, Waynesburg, Pa	100,000	69,345	69,345	68,070	1,275
Washington County National Bank, Greenwich, N. Y	200,000	114,220	114,220	105,084	9,136
First National Bank, Dallas, Tex	50,000	29,800	29,800	28,060	1,740
People's National Bank, Helena, Mont	100,000	89,300	89,300	79,975	9,325
First National Bank, Bozeman, Mont	50,000	44,400	41,400	42,420	1,980
Merchants' National Bank, Fort Scott, Kans	50,000	45,000	45,000	42,920	2,080
Farmers' National Bank, Platte City, Mo	50,000	27,000	27,000	25,480	1,520
First National Bank, Warrensburgh, Mo	100,000	45,000	45,000	42,821	2,179
German-American National Bank, Washington, D. C	130,000	62,500	62,500	60,780	1,720
German National Bank, Chicago, Ill	500,000	42,795	42,795	34,085	8,710
Commercial National Bank, Saratoga Springs, N. Y	100,000	86,900	86,900	82,001	4,899
Second National Bank, Scranton, Pa	200,000	91,465	91,465	78,968	12,497
National Bank of Poultney, Vt	100,000	90,000	90,000	82,887	7,113
First National Bank, Monticello, Ind	50,000	27,000	27,000	25,024	1,976
First National Bank, Butler, Pa	50,000	58,165	71,165	57,470	13,695
First National Bank, Meadville, Pa	100,000	89,500	89,500	73,422	16,078
First National Bank, Newark, N. J	300,000	326,643	326,643	281,516	45,127
First National Bank, Brattleboro', Vt	300,000	90,000	90,000	70,117	19,883
Mechanics' National Bank, Newark, N. J	500,000	344,750	450,000	344,813	105,187
First National Bank, Buffalo, N. Y	100,000	75,000	99,500	77,185	22,315
Pacific National Bank, Boston, Mass	961,300	408,000	450,000	391,769	58,231
First National Bank, Union Mills, Pa	50,000	34,000	45,000	30,185	14,815
Vermont National Bank, Saint Albans, Vt	200,000	65,200	65,200	41,767	23,433
First National Bank, Leadville, Colo	60,000	53,000	53,000	27,585	25,415
City National Bank, Lawrenceburg, Ind	100,000	77,000	77,000	27,565	49,435
First National Bank, Saint Albans, Vt	100,000	89,980	89,980	46,258	43,722
First National Bank, Monmouth, Ill	75,000	27,000	27,000	9,120	17,886
Marine National Bank, New York, N. Y	400,000	120,100	260,100	140,081	120,019
Hot Springs National Bank, Hot Springs, Ark	50,000	40,850	40,850	12,480	28,370
Richmond National Bank, Richmond, Ind	250,000	113,900	158,900	61,996	96,904
First National Bank, Livingston, Mont	50,000	11,240	11,240	3,360	7,880
First National Bank, Albion, N. Y	100,000	90,000	90,000	36,559	53,441
First National Bank, Jamestown, Dak	50,000	18,650	18,650	6,662	11,988
Logan National Bank, West Liberty, Ohio	50,000	7,000	23,400	6,685	16,715
Middletown National Bank, Middletown, N. Y	200,000	75,000	176,000	68,672	107,328
Farmers' National Bank. Bushnell, Ill	50,000	20,000	45,000	11,592	33,408
Schoharie County National Bank, Schoharie. N. Y	50,000	27,100	38,350	9,505	28,845
Exchange National Bank, Norfolk, Va	300,000	138,200	228,200	52,118	176,082
	21,858,900	13,723,889	14,455,140	12,942,284	1,512,865

nsolvent national banks, with date of appointment of receivers, amount of capital stock and claims proved, and rate of dividends paid to creditors.

Name and location of bank.	Receiver appointed.	Capital stock.	Proved claims.	Dividends paid.	Remarks.
				Pr.cent.	
First National Bank of Attica, N. Y.	Apr. 14, 1865	$50,000	$122,089	58	Finally closed.
Venango National Bank of Franklin, Pa.	May 1, 1866	300,000	434,531	23.37	Finally closed; 8.37 since last report.
Merchants' National Bank of Washington, D. C.	May 8, 1866	200,000	669,513	24.7	Finally closed.
First National Bank of Medina, N. Y.	Mar. 13, 1867	50,000	82,338	39.15	Finally closed.
Tennessee National Bank of Memphis, Tenn.	Mar. 21, 1867	100,000	376,932	17½	Finally closed.
First National Bank of Selma, Ala.	Apr. 30, 1867	100,000	289,467	46.6	Finally closed.
First National Bank of New Orleans, La.	May 20, 1867	500,000	1,119,313	79	Finally closed.
National Unadilla Bank, Unadilla, N. Y.	Aug. 20, 1867	120,000	127,801	45.9	Finally closed.
Farmers and Citizens' National Bank of Brooklyn, N. Y.	Sept. 6, 1867	300,000	1,191,500	96	Finally closed.
Croton National Bank of New York, N. Y.	Oct. 1, 1867	200,000	170,752	88.5	Finally closed.
First National Bank of Bethel, Conn.	Feb. 28, 1868	60,000	68,986	100	Finally closed.
First National Bank of Keokuk, Iowa.	Mar. 3, 1868	100,000	205,256	68½	Finally closed.
National Bank of Vicksburg, Miss.	Apr. 24, 1868	50,000	33,562	49.2	Finally closed.
First National Bank of Rockford, Ill.	Mar. 15, 1869	50,000	69,874	41.9	Finally closed.
First National Bank of Nevada, Austin, Nev.	Oct. 14, 1869	250,000	170,012	92.7	Finally closed.
Ocean National Bank of New York, N. Y.	Dec. 13, 1871	1,000,000	1,282,254	100	Finally closed; 46 per cent. of interest paid.
Union Square National Bank of New York, N. Y.	Dec. 15, 1871	200,000	157,120	100	Finally closed; 10 per cent. paid to stockholders.
Eighth National Bank of New York, N. Y.	Dec. 15, 1871	250,000	378,772	100	Finally closed.
Fourth National Bank of Philadelphia, Pa.	Dec. 20, 1871	200,000	645,558	100	Finally closed.
Waverly National Bank of Waverly, N. Y.	Apr. 23, 1872	106,100	79,864	100	Finally closed; 32.5 per cent. paid to stockholders.
First National Bank of Fort Smith, Ark.	May 2, 1872	50,000	15,142	100	Finally closed; 13 per cent. paid to stockholders.
Scandinavian National Bank of Chicago, Ill.	Dec. 12, 1872	250,000	249,174	50	
Wallkill National Bank of Middletown, N. Y.	Dec. 31, 1872	175,000	171,468	100	Finally closed; 30 per cent. of interest paid.
Crescent City National Bank of New Orleans, La.	Mar. 18, 1873	500,000	657,020	84.83	Finally closed.
Atlantic National Bank of New York, N. Y.	Apr. 28, 1873	300,000	574,513	100	Finally closed; 50 per cent. of interest paid.
First National Bank of Washington, D. C.	Sept. 19, 1873	500,000	1,619,965	100	Finally closed.
National Bank of the Commonwealth, New York, N.Y.	Sept. 22, 1873	750,000	796,095	100	Finally closed; 35.8 per cent. paid to stockholders.
Merchants' National Bank of Petersburg, Va.	Sept. 26, 1873	400,000	992,636	34	Finally closed.
First National Bank of Petersburg, Va.	Sept. 25, 1873	200,000	167,285	76	Finally closed.
First National Bank of Mansfield, Ohio.	Oct. 18, 1873	100,000	175,068	57.5	Finally closed.
New Orleans National Banking Association, New Orleans, La.	Oct. 23, 1873	600,000	1,429,595	62	2 per cent. since last report.
First National Bank of Carlisle, Pa.	Oct. 24, 1873	50,000	67,292	73.5	Finally closed.
First National Bank of Anderson, Ind.	Nov. 23, 1873	50,000	143,765	39.5	14.5 since last report.
First National Bank of Topeka, Kans.	Dec. 16, 1873	100,000	55,372	58.3	Finally closed.
First National Bank of Norfolk, Va.	June 3, 1874	100,000	176,330	57.5	Finally closed.
Gibson County National Bank of Princeton, Ind	Nov. 28, 1874	50,000	62,646	100	Finally closed.
First National Bank of Utah, Salt Lake City, Utah.	Dec. 10, 1874	150,000	93,021	24.391	Finally closed.
Cook County National Bank of Chicago, Ill.	Feb. 1, 1875	500,000	1,705,092	14.941	Finally closed.
First National Bank of Tiffin, Ohio.	Oct. 22, 1875	100,000	237,824	66	Finally closed.

Insolvent national banks, with date of appointment of receivers, &c.—Continued.

Name and location of bank.	Receiver appointed.	Capital stock.	Proved claims.	Dividends paid.	Remarks.
				Pr.cent.	
Charlottesville National Bank of Charlottesville, Va.	Oct. 28, 1875	$200,000	$351,847	62	
Miners' National Bank of Georgetown, Colo.	Jan. 24, 1876	150,000	177,512	76.5	Finally closed.
Fourth National Bank of Chicago, Ill.*	Fob. 1, 1876	200,000	35,801	50	
First National Bank of Bedford, Iowa.	Feb. 1, 1876	30,000	56,457	22.5	Finally closed.
First National Bank of Osccola, Iowa.	Fob. 25, 1876	50,000	34,535	100	Finally closed.
First National Bank of Duluth, Minn.	Mar. 13, 1876	100,000	87,786	100	Finally closed; interest paid in full.
First National Bank of LaCrosse, Wis.	Apr. 11, 1876	50,000	135,052	48.4	Finally closed.
City National Bank of Chicago, Ill.	May 17, 1876	250,000	703,658	77.512	Finally closed; .512 since last report.
Watkins National Bank of Watkins, N. Y.	July 12, 1876	75,000	59,226	100	Finally closed; 13 per cent. paid to stockholders.
First National Bank of Wichita, Kans.	Sept. 23, 1876	60,000	97,464	70	Finally closed.
First National Bank of Greenfield, Ohio.*	Dec. 12, 1876	50,000	35,023	27	Finally closed.
National Bank of Fishkill, Fishkill, N. Y.	Jan. 27, 1877	200,000	352,062	100	Finally closed; 38.5 per cent. of interest paid.
First National Bank of Franklin, Ind.	Fob. 13, 1877	132,000	184,457	100	Finally closed; interest paid in full.
Northumberland County National Bank of Shamokin, Pa.	Mar. 12, 1877	67,000	175,952	81.59	Finally closed.
First National Bank of Winchester, Ill.	Mar. 16, 1877	50,000	143,300	63.6	Finally closed.
National Exchange Bank of Minneapolis, Minn.	May 24, 1877	100,000	227,355	88.889	Finally closed.
National Bank of the State of Missouri, Saint Louis, Mo.	June 23, 1877	2,500,000	1,935,721	100	Interest paid in full.
First National Bank of Delphi, Ind.	July 20, 1877	50,000	133,112	100	Finally closed; interest paid in full.
First National Bank of Georgetown, Colo.	Aug. 18, 1877	75,000	196,356	37 9663/10000	Finally closed; 15.1483 since last report.
Lock Haven National Bank of Lock Haven, Pa.	Aug. 20, 1877	120,000	254,647	100	Finally closed.
Third National Bank of Chicago, Ill.	Nov. 24, 1877	750,000	1,061,598	100	Interest paid in full.
Central National Bank of Chicago, Ill.	Dec. 1, 1877	200,000	298,324	60	
First National Bank of Kansas City, Mo.	Feb. 11, 1878	500,000	392,394	100	Finally closed.
Commercial National Bank of Kansas City, Mo.	Feb. 11, 1878	100,000	75,175	100	Finally closed; 37.165 per cent. paid to stockholders.
First National Bank of Ashland, Pa.*	Feb. 28, 1878	112,500	33,105	100	Finally closed.
First National Bank of Tarrytown, N. Y.	Mar. 23, 1878	100,000	118,371	90.5	Finally closed.
irst National Bank of Allontown, Pa.*	Apr. 15, 1878	250,000	90,424	88	Finally closed; 3 per cent. since last report.
First National Bank of Waynesburg, Pa.*	May 15, 1878	100,000	33,362	60	20 por cent. since last report.
Washington County National Bank of Greenwich, N. Y.	June 8, 1878	200,000	262,887	100	Finally closed.
First National Bank of Dallas, Tex.	June 8, 1878	50,000	77,104	38.1	Finally closed; 1.1 per cent. since last report.
Peoplo's National Bank of Holena, Mont.	Sept. 13, 1878	100,000	168,048	40	
First National Bank of Bozeman, Mont.	Sopt. 14, 1878	50,000	69,631	85	
Merchants' National Bank of Fort Scott, Kans.*	Sept. 25, 1878	50,000	27,801	60	Finally closed.
Farmers' National Bank of Platte City, Mo.	Oct. 1, 1878	50,000	32,449	100	Finally closed; 18 per cent. paid to stockholders.
First National Bank of Warrensburg, Mo.	Nov. 1, 1878	100,000	156,260	100	Finally closed; interest paid in full.
German American National Bank of Washington, D. C.	Nov. 1, 1878	130,000	282,370	50	

* Formerly in voluntary liquidation.

Insolvent national banks, with date of appointment of receivers, &c.—Continued.

Name and location of bank.	Receiver appointed.	Capital stock.	Proved claims.	Dividends paid.	Remarks.
				Pr.cent.	
German National Bank of Chicago, Ill.*	Dec. 20, 1878	$500,000	$197,353	100	Finally closed; 42.3 per cent. of interest paid.
Commercial National Bank of Saratoga Springs, N. Y.	Feb. 11, 1879	100,000	128,832	100	Finally closed; interest paid in full.
Second National Bank of Scranton, Pa.*	Mar. 15, 1879	200,000	132,461	100	50 per cent. of interest paid since last report.
National Bank of Poultney, Vt....	Apr. 7, 1879	100,000	51,801	100	Finally closed; interest paid in full.
First National Bank of Monticello, Ind.	July 18, 1879	50,000	21,182	98	Finally closed.
First National Bank of Butler, Pa..	July 23, 1879	50,000	108,385	70	
First National Bank of Meadville, Pa.	June 9, 1880	100,000	93,625	100	Finally closed; interest paid in full.
First National Bank of Newark, N. J.	June 14, 1880	300,000	580,592	100	Finally closed; interest paid in full.
First National Bank of Brattleboro', Vt.	June 19, 1880	300,000	104,749	100	Finally closed; interest paid in full.
Mechanics' National Bank of Newark, N. J.	Nov. 2, 1881	500,000	2,703,285	60	
First National Bank of Buffalo, N. Y.	Apr. 22, 1882	100,000	891,431	38	5 per cent. since last report.
Pacific National Bank of Boston, Mass.	May 22, 1882	961,300	2,330,990	15	5 per cent. since last report.
First National Bank of Union Mills, Union City, Pa.	Mar. 24, 1883	50,000	186,993	60	10 per cent. since last report.
Vermont National Bank of Saint Albans, Vt.	Aug. 9, 1883	200,000	401,492	42.5	30 per cent. since last report.
First National Bank of Leadville, Colo.	Jan. 24, 1884	60,000	189,618	25	5 per cent. since last report.
City National Bank of Lawrenceburg, Ind.*	Mar. 11, 1884	100,000	38,951	....	
First National Bank of Saint Albans, Vt.	Apr. 22, 1884	100,000	282,384	12.5	Since last report.
First National Bank of Monmouth, Ill.	Apr. 22, 1884	75,000	230,671	90	20 per cent. since last report.
Marine National Bank of New York, N. Y.	May 13, 1884	400,000	4,463,578	40	15 per cent. since last report.
Hot Springs National Bank of Hot Springs, Ark.	June 2, 1884	50,000	36,496	70	40 per cent. since last report.
Richmond National Bank of Richmond, Ind.	July 23, 1884	250,000	322,515	36	Since last report.
First National Bank of Livingston, Mont.	Aug. 25, 1884	50,000	18,091	....	
First National Bank of Albion, N. Y.	Aug. 26, 1884	100,000	153,229	....	
First National Bank of Jamestown, Dak.	Sept. 13, 1884	50,000	8,131	....	100 per cent. and interest in full since last report.
Logan National Bank of West Liberty, Ohio.	Oct. 18, 1884	50,000	77,598	30	Since last report.
Middletown National Bank of Middletown, N. Y.	Nov. 29, 1884	200,000	636,482	40	
Farmers' National Bank of Bushnell, Ill.	Dec. 17, 1884	50,000	77,290	40	
Schoharie County National Bank of Schoharie, N. Y.	Mar. 23, 1885	50,000	137,315	20	
Exchange National Bank of Norfolk, Va.	Apr. 9, 1885	300,000	2,812,906	20	
Totals....................		21,858,900	43,162,549	....	

* Formerly in voluntary liquidation.

Classification of the loans and discounts of the national banks in New York City, in Boston, Philadelphia, and Baltimore, in the other reserve cities, and in the States and Territories, on October 1, 1885.

Cities, States, and Territories.	No. of banks.	On single-name paper.	On U. S. bonds.	On other stocks.	All other loans.	Total.
New York City......	44	$25,331,820	$3,286,124	$80,687,265	$127,518,389	$236,823,598
Boston..............	54	19,654,817	111,829	17,539,160	87,950,446	125,276,252
Philadelphia........	34	8,957,740	66,466	12,300,258	46,021,061	67,345,525
Baltimore	17	6,193,697	11,900	3,297,901	16,298,996	25,802,494
Totals.........	105	34,806,254	190,195	33,157,319	150,270,503	218,424,271
Albany.............	6	397,089	1,080	2,073,615	4,653,733	7,126,117
Pittsburgh	23	1,344,386	....	1,897,658	21,572,649	24,814,093
Washington........	5	5,576	31,205	442,328	1,713,373	2,192,482
New Orleans........	8	151,631	....	2,180,731	7,333,398	9,665,760
Louisville	9	4,365	900	331,381	7,387,970	7,724,616
Cincinnati	12	3,268,373	130,550	2,502,567	12,695,212	18,656,702
Cleveland..........	8	855,921	....	1,255,193	9,405,175	11,516,289
Chicago	12	10,226,583	33,400	10,967,875	24,761,567	45,989,425
Detroit	5	404,473	....	1,081,401	7,017,743	8,503,617
Milwaukee	3	508,128	....	999,501	2,438,095	3,945,724
St. Louis..........	6	124,550	388,019	1,197,060	7,473,788	9,182,417
San Francisco	1	1,189,558	....	431,782	496,256	2,117,596
Totals.........	98	18,480,233	585,154	25,421,092	106,948,959	151,435,438
Maine	71	954,206	4,850	837,706	14,780,744	16,577,506
New Hampshire......	48	647,112	1,675	1,021,824	6,663,006	8,333,617
Vermont............	47	597,321	152,144	315,117	9,478,501	10,543,083
Massachusetts.......	195	14,451,073	27,544	5,124,328	66,487,421	86,090,366
Rhode Island	61	5,428,897	100	665,702	24,880,147	30,974,846
Connecticut	84	5,823,219	3,475	2,523,973	32,150,612	40,501,279
New York	267	6,360,935	91,780	6,447,882	70,753,658	83,654,255
New Jersey.........	72	2,191,600	50,447	3,915,963	23,230,058	29,343,068
Pennsylvania.......	228	4,384,621	44,750	1,480,741	59,399,374	65,259,486
Delaware	15	92,695	100	6,500	3,806,072	3,905,367
Maryland .*........	27	418,923	....	184,110	5,092,479	5,695,512
District of Columbia..	1	....	2,137	123,815	196,690	322,672
Virginia...........	24	379,236	....	446,787	8,600,809	9,420,832
West Virginia.......	21	83,977	....	9,450	3,492,931	3,586,358
North Carolina	15	310,236	....	64,784	4,249,468	4,624,488
South Carolina......	14	136,476	20,000	303,591	4,083,915	4,543,982
Georgia............	16	469,917	....	640,160	4,172,141	5,282,218
Florida	5	48,565	....	35,139	545,750	629,454
Alabama	10	409,712	....	386,574	2,440,538	3,236,824
Mississippi	6	203,929	....	79,172	750,231	1,033,032
Louisiana..........	1	....	....	4,888	126,055	130,943
Texas..............	68	2,330,286	30,895	404,100	10,321,970	13,087,251
Arkansas...........	6	103,894	7,000	46,196	1,634,401	1,791,491
Kentucky	59	821,746	6,150	257,230	13,685,138	14,770,264
Tennessee	32	2,163,480	1,645	2,026,748	7,277,107	11,468,980
Ohio	183	3,372,875	4,050	976,075	36,308,117	40,661,117
Indiana	90	2,436,643	9,249	785,320	19,979,381	23,210,593
Illinois	153	5,579,182	2,500	1,041,472	24,013,330	30,636,484
Michigan...........	97	3,466,240	....	320,216	17,535,443	21,321,908
Wisconsin..........	47	1,243,139	....	172,332	8,155,255	9,570,726
Iowa...............	125	3,603,549	5,175	455,123	16,956,513	21,020,360
Minnesota..........	49	9,835,243	2,800	1,235,955	17,002,761	28,076,759
Missouri...........	36	1,044,511	....	277,599	5,895,555	7,217,665
Kansas............	74	1,412,569	1,604	102,230	9,004,550	10,610,953
Nebraska..........	75	2,521,332	5,000	354,574	12,336,849	15,217,755
Colorado	25	2,432,813	....	247,502	4,812,634	7,492,949
Nevada............	1	114,041	....	20,498	110,200	244,739
California..........	16	1,602,736	2,000	303,428	4,067,274	5,975,438
Oregon	9	958,448	....	397	1,234,751	2,193,596
Dakota	41	535,072	16,906	124,871	3,252,491	3,929,340
Idaho	4	73,161	....	6,084	258,117	337,063
Montana...........	15	1,890,106	....	85,952	3,406,468	5,382,526
New Mexico.........	8	421,753	....	40,174	935,350	1,397,277
Utah	6	567,588	....	59,271	712,017	1,338,876
Washington........	15	359,696	4,158	77,811	1,548,800	1,990,465
Wyoming...........	5	695,318	....	2,987	1,139,080	1,837,385
Totals.........	2,467	92,875,780	504,134	34,036,991	567,057,152	694,471,097
United States...	2,714	171,492,087	4,565,607	173,302,607	951,795,003	1,301,155,304

Liabilities of the national banks, and the reserve required and held at three dates in each year from 1882 to 1885.

STATES AND TERRITORIES EXCLUSIVE OF RESERVE CITIES.

Date.	No. of banks.	Net deposits.	Reserve required.	Reserve held.			Classification of reserve.		
				Amount.	Ratio to deposits.	Specie.	Other lawful money.	Due from agents.	Redemption fund.
	Millions.	*Millions.*	*Millions.*	*Millions.*	*Per cent.*	*Millions.*	*Millions.*	*Millions.*	*Millions.*
May 19, 1882	1,981	519.2	77.9	154.7	29.8	30.0	28.7	84.7	11.3
July 1, 1882	1,996	527.6	79.1	151.9	28.8	30.1	27.5	83.2	11.1
Oct. 3, 1882	2,026	545.8	81.9	150.4	27.5	30.0	30.0	80.1	11.3
May 1, 1883	2,128	556.3	83.4	118.9	26.7	31.4	31.0	75.2	11.3
June 22, 1883	2,164	560.7	84.1	157.7	28.1	31.1	29.6	85.8	11.2
Oct. 2, 1883	2,253	577.9	86.7	157.5	27.2	31.2	30.8	84.1	11.3
Apr. 24, 1884	2,340	576.0	86.4	162.5	28.2	36.4	31.5	83.7	10.9
June 20, 1884	2,376	544.7	81.7	146.0	26.8	36.4	32.0	66.8	10.7
Sept 30, 1884	2,417	535.8	80.4	156.3	29.2	35.2	30.9	79.7	10.5
May 6, 1885	2,432	540.3	81.1	171.0	31.6	40.7	30.2	90.0	10.1
July 1, 1885	2,442	552.2	82.8	170.3	30.8	40.1	28.1	92.1	10.0
Oct. 1, 1885	2,467	570.8	85.6	177.5	31.1	41.5	29.9	95.9	10.2

NEW YORK CITY.

Date.	No. of banks.	Net deposits.	Reserve required.	Amount.	Ratio to deposits.	Specie.	Other lawful money.	Due from agents.	Redemption fund.
May 19, 1882	50	267.3	66.8	70.5	26.4	50.5	19.0	....	1.0
July 1, 1882	50	277.4	69.3	72.1	26.0	50.5	20.6	....	1.0
Oct. 3, 1882	50	254.0	63.5	64.4	25.4	44.5	18.9	....	1.0
May 1, 1883	48	253.7	63.4	64.6	25.5	47.3	16.5	....	0.8
June 22, 1883	48	279.3	69.8	80.5	28.8	56.8	22.8	....	0.8
Oct. 2, 1883	48	266.9	66.7	70.8	26.5	50.3	19.7	....	0.9
Apr. 24, 1884	47	282.2	70.5	75.2	26.6	49.5	24.9	....	0.8
June 20, 1884	45	231.8	57.9	69.1	29.8	43.5	24.9	....	0.7
Sept. 30, 1884	44	254.9	63.7	90.8	35.6	63.1	27.0	....	0.7
May 6, 1885	44	297.7	74.4	123.5	41.5	96.5	26.4	....	0.6
July 1, 1885	45	312.7	78.2	132.8	42.5	96.5	37.5	....	0.6
Oct. 1, 1885	44	312.9	78.2	115.7	37.0	91.5	23.7	....	0.5

OTHER RESERVE CITIES.

Date.	No. of banks.	Net deposits.	Reserve required.	Amount.	Ratio to deposits.	Specie.	Other lawful money.	Due from agents.	Redemption fund.
May 19, 1882	192	323.5	80.9	102.4	31.6	30.7	28.6	39.5	3.6
July 1, 1882	193	327.0	81.8	95.9	29.3	30.2	27.0	35.2	3.5
Oct. 3, 1882	193	318.8	79.7	89.1	28.0	28.3	24.1	33.2	3.5
May 1, 1883	199	314.6	78.7	91.8	29.2	24.9	29.2	31.1	3.6
June 22, 1883	200	342.0	83.0	103.9	31.3	27.5	32.1	40.8	3.6
Oct. 2, 1883	200	323.9	81.0	100.6	31.0	26.3	30.1	40.8	3.4
Apr. 24, 1884	202	338.0	84.5	104.1	30.8	28.8	33.3	38.8	3.2
June 20, 1884	204	302.8	75.7	91.1	30.1	29.7	29.9	28.4	3.1
Sept. 30, 1884	203	308.0	77.0	99.0	32.2	30.3	33.3	32.3	3.1
May 6, 1885	202	316.5	86.6	124.0	35.8	40.2	30.9	40.9	3.0
July 1, 1885	202	356.5	89.1	123.4	34.6	41.0	38.8	40.7	2.9
Oct. 1, 1885	203	364.5	91.1	122.2	33.5	41.9	35.0	42.4	2.9

SUMMARY.

Date.	No. of banks.	Net deposits.	Reserve required.	Amount.	Ratio to deposits.	Specie.	Other lawful money.	Due from agents.	Redemption fund.
May 19, 1882	2,223	1,110.0	225.6	327.6	29.5	111.2	76.3	124.2	15.9
July 1, 1882	2,239	1,132.0	230.2	319.9	28.3	110.8	75.1	118.4	15.6
Oct. 3, 1882	2,269	1,118.6	225.1	303.9	27.2	102.8	72.0	113.3	15.8
May 1, 1883	2,375	1,124.6	225.5	303.3	27.1	103.6	76.7	109.3	15.7
June 22, 1883	2,417	1,172.0	236.9	342.1	29.2	115.4	84.5	124.6	15.6
Oct. 2, 1883	2,501	1,168.7	234.4	328.9	28.1	107.8	80.6	124.9	15.6
Apr. 24, 1884	2,589	1,196.2	241.4	341.8	28.6	114.7	89.7	122.5	14.9
June 20, 1884	2,625	1,079.3	215.3	306.2	28.4	109.6	86.8	95.2	14.5
Sept. 30, 1884	2,664	1,098.7	221.1	346.1	31.6	128.6	91.2	112.0	14.3
May 6, 1885	2,678	1,184.5	242.1	418.5	35.3	177.4	96.5	130.9	13.7
July 1, 1885	2,689	1,221.4	250.1	426.5	34.9	177.6	102.6	132.8	13.5
Oct. 1, 1885	2,714	1,248.2	254.9	415.4	33.3	174.9	88.6	138.3	13.6

Dividends and earnings of the national banks, arranged by geographical divisions, for semi-annual periods from September 1, 1876, to September 1, 1885.

Geographical divisions.	No. of banks	Capital.	Surplus.	Dividends.	Net earnings.	Dividends to capital.	Dividends to capital and surplus.	Earnings to capital and surplus.
						Pr. ct.	*Pr. ct.*	*Pr. ct.*
Sept., 1876, to March, 1877:								
New England States ..	542	$168,178,520	$43,109,865	$6,501,179	$6,128,206	3.9	3.1	2.9
Middle States	631	190,272,820	53,430,368	8,328,761	6,787,978	4.4	3.4	2.8
Southern States	175	32,120,440	5,678,226	1,387,478	1,470,475	4.3	3.7	3.9
Western States	732	106,079,800	28,653,706	5,586,551	5,206,303	5.3	4.1	3.9
Totals	2,080	496,651,580	130,872,165	21,803,969	19,502,962	4.4	3.5	3.1
March, 1877, to Sept., 1877:								
New England States	541	167,237,820	41,370,408	6,147,573	3,744,799	3.7	2.9	1.8
Middle States	631	185,468,951	51,871,038	7,686,267	6,185,157	4.1	3.2	2.6
Southern States	175	32,599,989	5,571,362	1,299,476	1,207,343	4.0	3.4	3.2
Western States	725	101,018,100	25,536,446	6,983,800	4,136,729	6.9	5.5	3.3
Totals	2,072	486,324,860	124,349,254	22,117,116	15,274,028	4.5	3.6	2.5
Sept., 1877, to March, 1878:								
New England States	544	166,546,320	40,560,405	5,903,213	4,985,926	3.5	2.9	2.4
Middle States	631	178,149,931	51,551,601	7,261,608	6,283,445	4.1	3.2	2.7
Southern States	176	32,166,800	5,482,012	1,217,880	1,174,220	3.8	3.2	3.1
Western States	722	98,746,700	24,779,543	4,599,669	4,503,105	4.7	3.7	3.7
Totals	2,074	475,609,751	122,373,561	18,982,390	16,946,696	4.0	3.2	2.8
March 1878, to Sept., 1878:								
New England States	543	166,587,820	38,956,874	5,459,786	3,846,183	3.3	2.7	1.9
Middle States	629	176,694,576	50,182,622	6,674,618	4,999,505	3.8	2.9	2.2
Southern States	176	31,491,800	5,684,035	1,115,865	951,995	3.5	3.0	2.6
Western States	699	95,457,700	23,863,603	4,708,954	3,861,210	4.9	4.0	3.2
Totals	2,047	470,231,896	118,687,134	17,959,223	13,658,893	3.8	3.0	2.3
Sept., 1878, to March, 1879:								
New England States	544	165,645,820	38,037,115	5,295,347	3,658,989	3.2	2.6	1.8
Middle States	630	173,979,676	50,084,782	6,876,398	5,826,662	4.0	3.1	2.6
Southern States	175	30,882,800	5,240,054	1,077,333	961,734	3.5	3.0	2.7
Western States	694	93,905,700	23,382,183	4,291,976	4,231,275	4.6	3.6	3.6
Totals	2,043	464,413,996	116,744,134	17,541,054	14,678,660	3.8	3.0	2.5
March, 1879, to Sept., 1879:								
New England States	542	164,450,120	37,441,984	5,257,526	4,761,422	3.2	2.6	2.4
Middle States	640	169,645,635	49,779,783	6,890,394	7,128,979	3.9	3.0	3.2
Southern States	175	30,281,800	5,198,481	1,056,594	979,496	3.5	3.0	2.7
Western States	688	90,754,200	22,729,103	4,397,353	4,003,303	4.8	3.9	3.5
Totals	2,045	455,132,056	115,149,351	17,401,867	16,873,200	3.8	3.1	3.0
Sept., 1879, to March, 1880:								
New England States	546	164,820,020	37,869,312	5,409,351	5,610,287	3.3	2.7	2.8
Middle States	640	169,399,170	51,306,583	7,151,166	9,220,826	4.2	3.2	4.2
Southern States	175	30,432,700	5,210,198	1,246,470	1,278,695	4.1	3.5	3.6
Western States	685	89,428,200	22,840,408	4,314,286	5,042,976	4.8	3.8	4.5
Totals	2,046	454,080,090	117,226,501	18,121,273	21,152,784	4.0	3.2	3.7
March, 1880, to Sept., 1880:								
New England States	548	165,380,242	38,450,297	5,858,484	7,413,622	3.5	2.9	3.6
Middle States	654	169,343,870	52,762,674	7,120,204	9,805,448	4.2	3.2	4.1
Southern States	176	30,443,700	5,516,335	1,139,203	1,434,102	3.7	3.2	4.0
Western States	694	89,067,250	23,416,343	4,172,359	5,380,078	4.7	3.7	4.8
Totals	2,072	454,215,062	120,145,619	18,290,200	24,033,250	4.0	3.2	4.2
Sept., 1880, to March, 1881:								
New England States	550	165,623,120	38,944,841	5,900,861	6,757,787	3.6	2.9	3.3
Middle States	657	170,739,045	53,536,248	6,974,934	9,162,771	4.1	3.1	4.1
Southern States	178	30,448,700	5,808,107	1,261,398	1,905,600	4.2	3.5	5.2
Western States	702	90,034,000	24,192,592	4,737,324	6,625,773	5.3	4.2	5.8
Totals	2,087	456,844,865	122,481,788	18,877,517	24,452,021	4.1	3.3	4.2

Dividends and earnings of the national banks, &c.—Continued.

Geographical divisions.	No. of banks	Capital.	Surplus.	Dividends.	Net earnings.	Ratios.		
						Dividends to capital.	Dividends to capital and surplus.	Earnings to capital and surplus.
						Pr. ct.	*Pr. ct.*	*Pr. ct.*
March, 1881, to Sept., 1881:								
New England States ..	550	$165,373,120	$39,878,448	$6,005,608	$8,166,022	3.6	2.9	4.0
Middle States.........	660	171,560,315	55,747,501	7,558,407	11,925,784	4.4	3.3	5.3
Southern States	181	30,673,950	6,530,604	1,282,120	2,300,624	4.1	3.4	6.1
Western States	709	91,027,100	25,061,751	4,653,833	6,778,112	5.1	3.9	5.8
Totals	2,100	458,934,485	127,208,394	19,499,908	29,170,542	4.3	3.3	5.0
Sept., 1881, to March, 1882:								
New England States ..	553	162,660,870	40,703,776	5,952,275	7,123,339	3.7	2.9	3.5
Middle States	666	171,488,315	57,470,278	7,367,409	10,210,373	4.3	3.2	4.5
Southern States	188	31,672,700	6,928,882	1,333,715	1,981,226	4.2	3.5	5.1
Western States........	730	94,542,600	26,188,953	5,261,076	7,768,661	5.6	4.3	6.4
Totals	2,137	460,354,485	131,291,889	19,915,375	27,083,599	4.3	3.4	4.6
March, 1882, to Sept., 1882:								
New England States...	555	165,515,870	41,033,296	5,729,842	6,732,530	3.5	2.8	3.3
Middle States.........	678	173,270,315	58,491,606	7,194,528	9,704,251	4.1	3.1	4.2
Southern States.......	194	32,212,700	7,503,078	1,289,362	2,062,960	4.0	3.2	5.2
Western States........	770	102,948,830	26,542,862	6,602,821	7,737,893	6.5	5.1	6.0
Totals	2,197	473,947,715	133,570,931	20,896,553	26,237,635	4.4	3.4	4.3
Sept., 1882, to March, 1883:								
New England States ..	557	165,653,070	41,341,246	5,819,093	6,200,443	3.5	2.8	3.0
Middle States	687	174,375,472	62,118,694	7,542,146	9,900,021	4.3	3.2	4.2
Southern States.......	207	33,963,000	8,228,309	1,405,019	2,198,993	4.1	3.3	5.2
Western States	816	109,099,800	25,881,856	5,518,844	8,133,477	5.1	4.1	6.0
Totals	2,267	483,091,342	137,570,105	20,285,102	26,432,934	4.2	3.3	4.2
March, 1883, to Sept., 1883:								
New England States...	562	166,793,070	41,727,679	5,861,182	6,651,595	3.5	2.8	3.2
Middle States.........	698	173,915,465	63,453,454	7,556,795	9,060,635	4.3	3.2	4.2
Southern States	224	35,685,300	9,084,011	1,415,529	2,433,336	4.0	3.2	5.4
Western States	875	118,246,305	26,967,043	5,560,070	8,528,648	4.7	3.8	5.9
Totals	2,350	494,640,140	141,232,187	20,393,576	27,574,214	4.1	3.2	4.3
Sept., 1883, to March, 1884:								
New England States...	565	167,478,070	41,863,161	5,726,356	6,095,915	3.4	2.7	2.9
Middle States..........	715	175,317,315	64,841,178	7,639,670	9,529,978	4.4	3.2	4.0
Southern States.......	248	38,214,310	9,854,923	1,700,113	2,950,096	4.4	3.5	6.1
Western States	963	126,959,605	29,041,587	6,016,667	9,418,775	4.7	3.9	6.0
Totals	2,491	507,969,300	145,600,849	21,082,806	27,994,764	4.1	3.2	4.3
March, 1884, to Sept., 1884:								
New England States ..	568	167,600,370	41,905,905	5,551,603	5,738,456	3.3	2.6	2.7
Middle States	723	175,767,355	64,580,406	7,089,673	8,198,912	4.0	2.9	3.4
Southern States	264	40,638,300	10,726,209	1,601,520	2,747,018	4.2	3.3	5.3
Western States	1,027	134,599,700	30,808,955	5,838,871	7,083,633	4.3	3.5	4.7
Totals	2,582	518,605,725	147,721,475	20,171,667	24,368,019	3.9	3.0	3.7
Sept., 1884, to March, 1885:								
New England States...	587	167,400,370	41,413,826	5,661,537	4,388,812	3.4	2.7	2.1
Middle States.........	732	173,212,145	64,741,009	7,156,680	7,474,752	4.1	3.0	3.1
Southern States	258	42,648,400	11,527,942	1,790,726	2,426,858	4.2	3.3	4.5
Western States	1,073	139,648,800	31,088,344	5,828,707	7,310,780	4.2	3.4	4.3
Totals	2,650	522,899,715	148,771,121	20,437,650	21,601,202	3.9	3.0	3.2
March, 1885, to Sept., 1885:								
New England States ..	562	165,668,370	40,786,007	5,391,401	4,725,395	3.3	2.6	2.3
Middle States	731	172,907,352	64,247,888	6,953,332	7,297,159	4.0	2.9	3.1
Southern States	287	43,500,300	11,505,477	1,655,261	2,282,782	3.8	3.0	4.2
Western States........	1,085	142,523,580	30,364,123	6,218,477	7,718,959	4.5	3.6	4.5
Totals	2,665	524,599,602	146,903,495	20,218,471	22,024,295	3.9	3.0	3.8
General averages	2,222	481,030,371	130,440,555	19,660,432	22,174,983	4.1	3.2	3.6

Abstract of reports of dividends and earnings of national banks

	States and Territories.	Number of banks.	Capital stock.	Surplus.	Capital and surplus.
1	Maine	69	$10,210,000 00	$2,463,328 61	$12,673,328 61
2	New Hampshire	48	6,105,000 00	1,207,094 92	7,312,094 92
3	Vermont	50	8,011,000 00	1,616,102 20	9,627,102 20
4	Massachusetts	195	45,627,500 00	13,720,777 82	59,348,277 82
5	Boston	54	50,950,000 00	11,524,034 93	62,474,034 93
6	Rhode Island	63	20,540,050 00	4,045,952 79	24,586,002 79
7	Connecticut	88	25,956,820 00	6,836,535 14	32,793,355 14
	New England States	567	167,400,370 00	41,413,826 41	208,814,196 41
8	New York	267	35,170,410 00	9,108,688 68	44,279,098 68
9	New York City	44	46,250,000 00	22,669,264 18	68,919,264 18
10	Albany	7	1,800,000 00	1,400,000 00	3,200,000 00
11	New Jersey	69	12,053,350 00	3,783,638 91	15,836,988 91
12	Pennsylvania	224	32,074,840 00	10,036,275 22	42,111,115 22
13	Philadelphia	33	18,058,000 00	9,326,244 58	27,384,284 58
14	Pittsburgh	23	10,179,400 00	3,587,222 57	13,766,822 57
15	Delaware	15	1,823,985 00	670,000 00	2,493,985 00
16	Maryland	27	2,711,700 00	790,521 32	3,502,221 32
17	Baltimore	17	11,713,200 00	3,004,673 00	14,717,923 00
18	District of Columbia	1	252,000 00	60,000 00	312,000 00
19	Washington	5	1,125,000 00	304,500 00	1,429,500 00
	Middle States	732	173,212,145 00	64,741,008 46	237,953,154 46
20	Virginia	24	3,545,300 00	1,335,087 69	4,880,387 69
21	West Virginia	21	2,011,000 00	524,108 74	2,534,108 74
22	North Carolina	15	2,401,000 00	547,496 84	2,948,496 84
23	South Carolina	14	1,935,000 00	778,000 00	2,713,000 00
24	Georgia	15	2,436,200 00	855,790 95	3,292,090 95
25	Florida	3	150,000 00	17,922 70	167,922 70
26	Alabama	10	1,735,000 00	260,100 00	1,995,100 00
27	Mississippi	4	325,000 00	18,400 00	343,400 00
28	Louisiana	1	100,000 00	7,000 00	107,000 00
29	New Orleans	8	3,525,000 00	1,257,132 42	4,782,132 42
30	Texas	59	6,034,100 00	1,932,907 31	7,967,007 31
31	Arkansas	4	405,000 00	156,584 52	561,584 52
32	Kentucky	58	9,458,900 00	1,936,318 21	11,395,218 21
33	Louisville	9	3,551,500 00	806,955 29	4,358,455 29
34	Tennessee	33	5,035,300 00	1,095,137 23	6,130,437 23
	Southern States	278	42,648,400 00	11,327,941 90	54,176,341 90
35	Ohio	183	22,014,000 00	4,586,320 36	26,600,320 36
36	Cincinnati	12	8,600,000 00	1,150,500 00	9,750,500 00
37	Cleveland	8	5,664,100 00	705,000 00	6,369,100 00
38	Indiana	93	13,199,000 00	3,691,751 46	16,991,251 46
39	Illinois	151	13,284,600 00	4,194,191 59	17,478,791 59
40	Chicago	12	10,550,000 00	2,890,000 00	13,440,000 00
41	Michigan	95	9,929,600 00	2,238,127 20	12,167,727 20
42	Detroit	5	2,650,000 00	260,000 00	2,910,000 00
43	Wisconsin	47	3,780,000 00	880,561 47	4,660,561 47
44	Milwaukee	3	650,000 00	340,000 00	990,000 00
45	Iowa	121	10,055,000 00	2,293,472 37	12,348,472 37
46	Minnesota	49	11,215,006 00	1,798,878 87	13,013,878 87
47	Missouri	34	3,005,000 00	641,348 16	3,706,348 16
48	St. Louis	6	3,250,000 00	852,874 15	4,102,874 15
49	Kansas	60	3,895,000 00	601,099 99	4,496,099 99
50	Nebraska	63	4,745,000 00	706,447 87	5,451,447 87
	Western States	942	126,646,800 00	27,839,573 49	154,486,373 49
51	Colorado	22	1,757,000 00	1,034,500 00	2,791,500 00
52	Nevada	1	75,000 00	25,000 00	100,000 00
53	California	14	2,050,000 00	499,779 96	2,549,779 96
54	San Francisco	1	1,500,000 00	228,850 49	1,728,850 49
55	Oregon	8	695,000 00	64,000 00	759,000 00
56	Arizona	2	150,000 00	2,842 19	152,842 19
57	Dakota	34	2,135,000 00	464,674 35	2,599,674 35
58	Idaho	4	250,000 00	20,000 00	270,000 00
59	Montana	13	1,650,000 00	292,500 00	1,942,500 00
60	New Mexico	8	645,000 00	136,575 88	781,575 88
61	Utah	5	605,000 00	206,250 00	800,250 00
62	Washington	15	960,000 00	101,798 54	1,061,798 54
63	Wyoming	4	525,000 00	112,900 00	637,900 00
	Pacific States and Territories	131	12,892,000 00	3,248,770 41	16,240,770 41
	United States	2,650	522,899,715 00	148,771,120 67	671,670,835 67

in the United States from September 1, 1884, to March 1, 1885.

Dividends.	Net earnings.	Ratios.			Charged off.		
		Dividend to capital.	Dividend to capital and surplus.	Earnings to capital and surplus.	Premiums.	Losses.	
		Per cent.	*Per cent.*	*Per cent.*			
$418,200 00	$372,864 13	4.10	3.30	2.94	$25,732 13	$174,410 46	1
227,800 00	207,203 74	3.78	3.12	3.66	15,484 94	45,407 93	2
288,355 00	196,899 70	3.69	3.09	2.04	12,205 17	145,813 06	3
1,678,653 08	1,307,949 98	3.64	2.79	2.20	103,590 31	739,808 13	4
1,435,443 00	851,953 21	2.82	2.30	1.36	19,729 04	1,103,481 00	5
679,813 75	529,846 18	3.31	2.77	2.15	43,485 98	389,966 77	6
953,289 70	863,174 06	3.67	2.91	2.63	39,992 17	352,006 27	7
5,661,536 53	4,388,812 00	3.38	2.71	2.10	266,288 82	2,941,654 22	
1,308,657 71	1,262,034 25	3.72	2.96	2.85	79,273 99	951,851 45	8
2,067,510 00	1,968,179 04	4.47	3.00	2.86	145,722 94	1,049,177 13	9
112,460 00	131,628 10	6.25	3.51	4.11	15,500 00	10,017 87	10
543,136 00	524,146 51	4.51	3.43	3.31	51,940 61	375,411 85	11
1,226,399 10	1,547,475 44	3.82	2.91	3.67	113,892 85	411,034 04	12
826,675 00	747,365 75	4.58	3.02	2.73	10,959 73	511,805 32	13
382,888 00	457,600 59	3.76	2.78	3.32	10,448 80	147,031 16	14
87,918 48	124,780 32	4.82	3.53	5.00	4,860 00	3,452 15	15
113,543 00	124 918 07	4.19	3.24	3.57	-8,154 77	28,364 72	16
439,163 08	554,335 62	3.75	2.98	3.77	1,661 25	88,409 35	17
10,080 00	11,109 43	4.00	3.23	3.56	3,565 17	....	18
38,250 00	21,178 73	3.40	2.68	1.48	1,078 12	36,223 04	19
7,156,680 37	7,474,752 48	4.13	3.01	3.14	447,056 23	4,212,778 08	
148,742 00	187,170 10	4.20	3.05	3.84	28,862 86	31,060 06	20
78,730 00	78,260 62	3.91	3.11	3.09	4,041 25	17,542 98	21
107,330 00	108,877 00	4.47	3.64	3.69	8,823 75	26,049 80	22
82,850 00	89,361 04	4.28	3.05	3.29	4,690 35	56,132 68	23
90,125 00	126,521 72	3.70	2.74	3.84	664 38	7,852 98	24
4,500 00	7,752 35	3.00	2.68	4.02	....	1,573 92	25
78,000 00	97,555 84	4.50	3.91	4.89	3,923 58	15,439 81	26
17,500 00	18,403 22	5.38	5.10	5.36	454 19	1,561 87	27
4,000 00	4,530 80	4.00	3.74	4.23	375 00	....	28
144,000 00	137,037 28	4.09	3.01	2.87	1,250 00	122,538 46	29
331,343 33	640,579 70	5.49	4.16	8.04	7,021 14	71,606 21	30
18,000 00	29,063 10	4.44	3.20	5.18	....	1,713 86	31
343,316 00	470,763 51	3.63	3.01	4.13	20,231 36	19,215 32	32
115,560 00	108,374 91	3.25	2.65	2.49	13,892 71	62,416 41	33
226,730 00	322,606 31	5.30	4.35	5.26	12,699 48	48,067 01	34
1,790,726 33	2,426,857 50	4.20	3.31	4.48	107,530 05	483,460 37	
832,237 46	928,907 20	3.78	3.13	3.49	67,196 96	265,030 07	35
265,000 00	325,363 36	3.08	2.72	3.23	1,325 00	53,220 26	36
129,000 00	136,646 66	2.26	2.03	2.15	....	168,114 21	37
486,010 00	566,281 20	3.65	2.86	3.33	32,858 20	251,928 76	38
644,330 00	867,414 24	4.85	3.69	4.96	31,587 40	116,225 48	39
521,000 00	209,678 40	4.94	3.88	1.56	38,500 00	659,987 87	40
479,085 13	527,243 85	4.82	3.94	4.34	10,846 78	106,742 01	41
122,500 00	170,233 28	4.02	4.21	5.85	7,000 00	11,434 50	42
179,507 51	222,015 67	4.75	3.84	4.75	4,711 74	69,387 63	43
42,000 00	12,907 17	6.46	4.24	1.30	15,000 00	32,164 49	44
447,634 45	604,379 22	4.45	3.62	4.90	41,388 37	29,515 06	45
434,239 77	602,542 61	3.87	3.34	4.63	5,166 92	108,184 26	46
108,650 00	204,419 32	3.47	2.87	5.52	845 43	6,192 66	47
112,500 00	151,383 06	3.46	2.74	3.69	....	12,197 01	48
158,450 00	335,326 41	3.94	3.41	7.46	6,117 15	15,625 75	49
229,920 00	406,529 48	4.85	4.22	7.16	5,570 11	15,363 39	50
5,187,064 32	6,271,171 33	4.09	3.36	4 06	268,144 21	1,981,314 61	
168,000 00	224,669 75	9.60	6.04	8.05	4,888 08	97,133 75	51
7,500 00	8,481 04	10.00	7.50	8.48	....	3,495 20	52
92,000 00	193,519 00	4.49	3.61	7.59	4,446 65	58,777 01	53
60,000 00	35,405 89	4.00	3 53	2.05	600 00	38,200 22	54
40,500 00	74,080 28	5.83	5.34	9.76	5,013 50	22,268 82	55
....	2,082 76	....	....	1.36	756 00	830 92	56
105,667 57	102,858 08	4.95	4.06	3.96	8,831 40	55,557 08	57
35,000 00	29,351 20	14.00	12.96	10.87	125 00	1,665 50	58
13,000 00	150,215 81	0.77	0.67	7.73	3,056 22	23,012 43	59
39,500 00	20,304 85	6.12	5.05	2.60	170 30	36,330 58	60
23,500 00	60,809 85	3.92	2.71	7.02	1,656 25	2,202 90	61
37,750 00	89,984 89	3.93	3.56	8.47	....	2,844 99	62
18,625 00	47,844 99	3.55	2.92	7.51	520 00	11,484 33	63
641,642 57	1,039,608 39	4.92	3.95	6.40	30,673 40	353,893 82	
20,437,650 12	21,601,201 70	3.61	3.04	3.20	1,119,692 71	9,973,101 10	

Abstract of reports of dividends and earnings of national banks

	States and Territories.	Number of banks.	Capital stock.	Surplus.	Capital and surplus.
1	Maine	71	$10,360,000 00	$2,482,751 95	$12,842,751 95
2	New Hampshire	48	6,105,000 00	1,218,055 99	7,323,055 99
3	Vermont	48	7,551,000 00	1,471,221 78	9,022,221 78
4	Massachusetts	195	45,140,500 00	13,499,376 70	58,639,876 70
5	Boston	54	50,950,000 00	11,345,587 69	62,295,587 69
6	Rhode Island	62	20,440,050 00	4,034,242 52	24,474,292 52
7	Connecticut	84	25,121,820 00	6,734,819 96	31,856,639 96
	New England States	562	165,668,370 00	40,786,006 59	206,454,376 59
8	New York	266	34,785,557 00	8,831,332 06	43,616,889 06
9	New York City	44	46,250,000 00	22,401,007 68	68,651,007 68
10	Albany	6	1,750,000 00	1,175,000 00	2,925,000 00
11	New Jersey	70	12,103,350 00	3,788,453 86	15,891,803 86
12	Pennsylvania	224	32,150,340 00	10,122,979 06	42,273,319 06
13	Philadelphia	33	18,058,000 00	9,401,803 08	27,459,803 08
14	Pittsburgh	23	10,179,600 00	3,538,106 84	13,717,706 84
15	Delaware	15	1,823,985 00	678,905 00	2,502,890 00
16	Maryland	27	2,716,260 00	838,847 30	3,555,107 30
17	Baltimore	17	11,713,260 00	3,104,453 00	14,817,713 00
18	District of Columbia	1	252,000 00	60,000 00	312,000 00
19	Washington	5	1,125,000 00	367,000 00	1,432,000 00
	Middle States	731	172,907,352 00	64,247,888 48	237,155,240 48
20	Virginia	23	3,246,300 00	1,193,097 85	4,439,397 85
21	West Virginia	21	2,011,000 00	509,534 62	2,520,534 62
22	North Carolina	15	2,401,000 00	552,378 71	2,953,378 71
23	South Carolina	14	1,935,000 00	802,000 00	2,737,000 00
24	Georgia	15	2,436,000 00	873,223 88	3,309,223 88
25	Florida	4	200,000 00	19,922 70	219,922 70
26	Alabama	10	1,835,000 00	289,650 00	2,124,650 00
27	Mississippi	5	425,000 00	39,100 00	464,100 00
28	Louisiana	1	100,000 00	9,000 00	109,000 00
29	New Orleans	8	3,525,000 00	1,296,715 70	4,821,715 70
30	Texas	65	6,670,600 00	2,050,517 33	8,721,117 33
31	Arkansas	6	705,000 00	166,170 32	871,170 32
32	Kentucky	58	9,458,900 00	1,877,224 34	11,336,124 34
33	Louisville	9	3,551,500 00	809,441 26	4,360,941 26
34	Tennessee	33	5,000,000 00	1,017,499 82	6,017,499 82
	Southern States	287	43,500,300 00	11,505,476 53	55,005,776 53
35	Ohio	183	21,964,000 00	4,573,529 29	26,537,529 29
36	Cincinnati	12	8,600,000 00	1,208,000 00	9,808,000 00
37	Cleveland	8	6,200,000 00	620,000 00	6,820,000 00
38	Indiana	89	11,789,500 00	3,035,401 57	14,824,901 57
39	Illinois	150	13,519,600 00	4,221,370 32	17,740,970 32
40	Chicago	12	11,750,000 00	2,681,600 00	14,431,600 00
41	Michigan	97	10,260,700 00	1,893,656 18	12,154,356 18
42	Detroit	5	2,650,000 00	275,000 00	2,925,000 00
43	Wisconsin	46	3,735,000 00	903,187 94	4,638,187 94
44	Milwaukee	3	650,000 00	340,000 00	990,000 00
45	Iowa	124	10,200,000 00	2,320,348 82	12,520,348 82
46	Minnesota	50	11,340,000 00	1,849,226 08	13,189,226 08
47	Missouri	35	3,265,000 00	577,925 08	3,842,925 08
48	St. Louis	6	3,250,000 00	856,128 29	4,106,128 29
49	Kansas	62	4,229,728 00	720,702 32	4,950,482 32
50	Nebraska	66	5,450,000 00	911,897 95	6,361,897 95
	Western States	948	128,853,580 00	27,005,974 44	155,859,554 44
51	Colorado	24	1,965,000 00	998,100 00	2,963,100 00
52	Nevada	1	75,000 00	25,000 00	100,000 00
53	California	15	2,150,000 00	517,936 33	2,667,936 33
54	San Francisco	1	1,500,000 00	234,520 48	1,734,520 48
55	Oregon	9	745,000 00	77,466 04	822,466 04
56	Dakota	37	2,230,000 00	503,073 85	2,733,073 85
57	Idaho	4	250,000 00	20,000 00	270,000 00
58	Montana	14	1,750,000 00	298,000 00	2,048,000 00
59	New Mexico	8	650,000 00	152,094 75	802,094 75
60	Utah	5	600,000 00	274,000 00	874,000 00
61	Washington	14	955,000 00	117,957 67	1,072,957 67
62	Wyoming	5	800,000 00	140,000 00	940,000 00
	Pacific States and Territories	137	13,670,000 00	3,358,148 62	17,028,148 62
	Total United States	2,665	524,590,602 00	146,903,494 66	671,503,096 66

in the United States from March 1, 1885, to September 1, 1885.

Dividends.	Net earnings.	Ratios.			Charged off.		
		Dividend to capital.	Dividend to capital and surplus.	Earnings to capital and surplus.	Premiums.	Losses.	
		Per cent.	Per cent.	Per cent.			
$446,750 00	$422,132 61	4.31	3.48	3.29	$10,535 92	$121,540 72	1
225,800 00	223,912 73	3.70	3.08	3.04	9,921 94	72,259 52	2
241,155 50	203,565 10	3.19	2.67	2.26	20,240 25	114,146 54	3
1,548,850 00	1,453,543 69	3.43	2.64	2.48	101,570 22	933,206 27	4
1,389,250 00	1,632,470 15	2.71	2.22	1.66	25,827 90	758,764 66	5
654,782 50	619,980 45	3.20	2.67	2.54	6,447 00	255,649 54	6
803,812 70	769,890 20	3.56	2.80	2.41	30,922 39	439,702 29	7
5,391,400 70	4,725,394 93	3.25	2.61	2.29	205,465 02	2,695,269 54	
1,284,700 10	1,414,204 40	3.69	2.97	3.24	52,047 81	607,262 04	8
1,996,050 00	2,002,586 92	4.32	2.91	3.00	40,465 70	1,371,660 94	9
57,000 00	29,416 52	3.26	1.95	1.01	55,499 42	48,880 27	10
533,544 00	509,522 40	4.41	3.36	3.21	31,475 14	372,933 16	11
1,195,624 10	1,302,531 31	3.72	2.83	3.08	56,434 74	523,817 21	12
833,235 00	921,791 80	4.04	3.03	3.36	8,585 46	107,501 27	13
369,740 00	355,510 06	3.63	2.70	2.59	2,847 56	165,745 39	14
89,317 97	109,103 86	4.88	3.56	4.36	2,350 00	15,694 82	15
111,579 80	125,322 24	4.10	3.14	3.53	10,058 34	27,727 13	16
434,711 22	394,963 60	3.71	2.93	2.67	14,000 00	140,223 44	17
10,980 00	11,129 51	4.09	3.23	3.57	2,900 00	....	18
38,250 00	60,895 39	3.40	2.67	4.25	44 77	18,004 87	19
6,953,332 19	7,297,158 61	4.02	2.93	3.08	276,708 94	3,519,510 54	
130,262 00	209,077 91	4.01	2.94	4.71	6,658 25	39,977 52	20
73,700 00	61,699 78	3.66	2.92	2.45	1,585 00	50,579 68	21
58,750 00	86,902 06	3.70	3.01	2.94	....	109,632 42	22
83,250 00	100,071 85	4.30	3.04	3.87	5,106 74	92,462 68	23
88,125 00	142,621 56	3.62	2.66	4.31	881 25	34,503 19	24
4,500 00	16,030 88	2.25	2.04	7.29	....	2,211 00	25
81,000 00	128,374 18	4.41	3.81	6.04	2,160 00	26,036 98	26
13,000 00	42,028 66	3.06	2.80	9.19	1,625 00	127 03	27
4,000 00	5,850 68	4.00	3.07	5.37	100 00	....	28
136,250 00	203,635 77	3.87	2.83	4.22	1,552 50	137,275 50	29
217,298 00	375,520 16	3.26	2.49	4.31	11,788 00	194,523 49	30
26,500 00	37,482 77	3.76	3.04	4.30	....	1,392 90	31
301,316 00	441,435 91	3.82	3.19	3.89	15,960 90	60,512 35	32
125,560 00	133,689 09	3.54	2.88	3.07	2,430 00	56,482 25	33
221,750 00	291,760 37	4.44	3.69	4.85	13,661 73	42,502 34	34
1,655,261 00	2,282,781 63	3.81	3.01	4.16	63,510 33	848,219 42	
814,791 45	761,534 89	3.71	3.07	2.87	68,020 30	381,724 61	35
285,000 00	336,438 67	3.31	2.91	3.43	6,000 00	51,587 78	36
172,000 00	275,734 85	2.77	2.52	4.04	7,343 75	25,175 53	37
538,110 00	542,877 95	4.56	3.63	3.68	18,564 50	130,346 88	38
658,615 00	781,841 65	4.87	3.71	4.41	17,559 09	147,334 76	39
509,386 00	750,164 12	4.26	3.47	5.10	11,900 00	125,225 50	40
465,555 00	493,174 95	4.54	3.83	4.06	14,437 38	137,004 03	41
125,000 00	144,125 35	4.72	4.27	4.93	3,000 00	40,518 68	42
153,475 00	216,868 27	4.11	3.31	4.67	5,120 10	45,082 31	43
32,000 00	53,826 55	4.92	3.23	5.44	....	2,003 16	44
512,450 00	587,571 03	5.02	4.09	4.69	13,982 44	71,294 81	45
464,050 00	527,399 68	4.09	3.52	4.00	3,454 32	114,278 50	46
283,817 18	246,620 20	8.69	7.39	6.42	10,343 72	19,557 34	47
91,500 00	149,413 64	2.82	2.23	3.64	....	92,580 39	48
241,273 27	403,126 01	5.59	4.77	8.13	5,307 98	33,164 22	49
287,175 00	456,236 58	5.27	4.51	7.19	8,133 37	29,023 97	50
5,625,226 90	6,726,956 39	4.37	3.61	4.32	192,567 55	1,450,697 52	
137,800 00	152,082 29	7.01	4.65	5.13	11,151 05	65,104 44	51
6,000 00	8,584 25	8.00	6.00	8.58	....	79 88	52
92,000 00	174,558 84	4.28	3.45	6.54	798 40	5,112 47	53
60,000 00	56,699 87	4.00	3.46	3.20	600 00	12,509 43	54
41,500 00	96,402 77	5.57	5.05	11.73	710 50	12,419 65	55
89,750 00	115,972 22	4.02	3.28	4.24	7,650 46	64,385 02	56
....	16,140 08	....	....	5.98	125 00	....	57
29,500 00	106,406 02	1.69	1.44	5.20	160 94	32,623 45	58
36,000 00	45,610 45	5.54	4.49	5.69	....	10,199 37	59
33,500 00	30,204 43	5.58	3.83	3.47	3,773 08	22,119 38	60
37,200 00	108,369 82	3.89	3.47	10.10	217 40	1,733 78	61
30,000 00	80,821 90	3.75	3.19	8.60	363 98	818 50	62
593,250 00	992,002 94	4.34	3.48	5.83	25,550 81	227,105 37	
20,218,470 79	22,024,294 50	3.85	3.01	3.28	763,803 25	8,740,862 39	

Table, by States and reserve cities, of the ratios to capital, and to capital and surplus, of

	States, Territories, and reserve cities.	Ratio of dividends to capital for six months ending—										Ratio of	
		March 1, 1881.	Sept. 1, 1881.	March 1, 1882.	Sept. 1, 1882.	March 1, 1883.	Sept. 1, 1883.	March 1, 1884.	Sept. 1, 1884.	March 1, 1885.	Sept. 1, 1885.	March 1, 1881.	Sept. 1, 1881.
		Pr. ct	Pr. ct.	Pr. ct.	Pr. ct.	Pr. ct.	Pr. ct.	Pr. ct.	Pr. ct.	Pr. ct.	Pr. ct.	Pr. ct.	Pr. ct.
1	Maine	4.4	4.4	4.4	4.3	4.3	4.2	4.1	4.1	4.1	4.3	3.6	3.5
2	New Hampshire	3.9	3.7	3.9	3.6	3.8	3.9	3.7	3.7	3.7	3.7	3.3	3.1
3	Vermont	4.1	5.3	4.1	3.4	3.8	4.2	3.9	3.8	3.6	3.2	3.3	4.4
4	Massachusetts	3.9	3.9	4.1	3.6	3.7	3.7	3.6	3.3	3.6	3.4	3.1	3.0
5	Boston	2.9	2.8	2.9	2.8	2.9	2.9	2.7	2.8	2.8	2.7	2.4	2.3
6	Rhode Island	3.3	3.4	3.4	3.4	3.4	3.5	3.4	3.3	3.3	3.2	2.8	2.8
7	Connecticut	3.8	4.1	4.0	4.1	4.0	4.0	3.9	3.8	3.7	3.6	3.0	3.3
8	New York	3.7	4.1	4.1	4.0	4.0	4.4	4.2	3.9	3.7	3.7	3.0	3.3
9	New York City	4.5	5.0	4.8	4.5	4.7	4.6	4.7	4.3	4.5	4.3	3.3	3.6
10	Albany	6.2	4.2	6.0	4.6	6.1	4.2	6.2	4.2	6.2	3.3	3.5	2.4
11	New Jersey	4.2	4.2	4.4	4.2	4.7	4.6	4.7	4.4	4.5	4.4	3.3	3.2
12	Pennsylvania	3.8	4.1	3.9	4.1	3.9	3.9	4.0	3.5	3.8	3.7	3.0	3.3
13	Philadelphia	4.4	4.4	4.4	4.0	4.9	4.7	4.7	4.6	4.6	4.6	3.0	3.0
14	Pittsburgh	3.4	3.7	3.7	3.7	3.8	3.7	3.8	3.7	3.8	3.7	2.6	2.8
15	Delaware	4.4	4.4	4.4	4.4	4.5	4.8	4.6	4.8	4.8	4.9	3.4	3.4
16	Maryland	4.6	5.6	4.4	4.4	4.7	4.4	4.4	4.5	4.2	4.1	3.6	4.3
17	Baltimore	3.8	4.0	3.7	3.9	3.6	3.8	3.7	3.8	3.8	3.7	3.1	3.3
18	District of Columbia	4.0	4.0	4.0	4.0	4.0	4.0	4.0	4.0	4.0	4.0	3.2	3.2
19	Washington	2.6	2.4	2.6	2.4	2.4	3.3	3.4	3.4	3.4	3.4	2.1	2.0
20	Virginia	4.3	4.1	4.3	4.3	4.2	4.1	5.7	4.0	4.2	4.0	3.3	3.2
21	West Virginia	4.7	4.6	4.5	4.3	4.3	4.1	4.1	3.7	3.9	3.7	3.8	3.6
22	North Carolina	3.7	3.7	3.6	3.8	3.9	3.4	3.9	3.3	4.5	3.7	3.3	3.2
23	South Carolina	5.1	3.6	3.5	4.0	4.0	4.1	4.3	4.0	4.3	4.3	4.2	2.0
24	Georgia	3.8	3.9	3.5	3.3	3.7	3.4	3.5	3.2	3.7	3.6	3.1	3.2
25	Florida	5.0	2.5	2.5	2.5	7.6	2.5	2.5	2.5	3.0	2.3	4.7	2.4
26	Alabama	3.5	3.7	4.1	4.0	4.0	3.5	3.8	3.6	4.5	4.4	3.0	3.2
27	Mississippi					8.0		7.4	2.8	5.4	3.1		
28	Louisiana					5.0	5.0	4.0	4.0	4.0	4.0		
29	New Orleans	4.2	4.1	4.1	4.1	4.1	4.2	6.6	3.6	4.1	3.9	3.5	3.2
30	Texas	3.8	5.8	6.9	3.6	5.3	3.9	5.0	5.7	5.5	3.3	3.1	4.7
31	Arkansas	6.3	3.7	6.3	3.8	5.9	4.0	5.8	4.4	4.4	3.8	5.3	3.0
32	Kentucky	3.7	3.8	3.7	3.8	3.6	3.8	3.6	4.1	3.6	3.8	3.2	3.2
33	Louisville	3.6	4.2	3.7	3.9	3.4	3.9	3.5	3.8	3.3	3.5	3.1	3.6
34	Tennessee	5.6	5.1	5.6	4.9	5.4	5.0	5.0	4.7	5.3	4.4	4.7	4.3
35	Ohio	4.3	4.4	4.5	5.8	4.3	4.1	4.0	4.0	3.8	3.7	3.5	3.7
36	Cincinnati	4.5	3.8	4.6	10.5	3.5	3.8	3.3	3.2	3.1	3.3	3.9	3.3
37	Cleveland	4.1	4.1	4.1	5.2	4.1	4.1	3.8	4.1	2.3	2.8	3.4	3.4
38	Indiana	4.7	5.1	4.7	5.9	5.1	4.6	4.1	3.9	3.7	4.6	3.6	3.9
39	Illinois	6.4	5.7	7.0	6.9	6.0	5.7	5.7	5.0	4.9	4.9	4.8	4.2
40	Chicago	9.5	4.9	9.6	14.7	5.0	3.9	3.7	4.7	4.9	4.3	6.0	3.0
41	Michigan	5.2	4.9	5.9	5.6	5.6	5.3	5.9	4.4	4.8	4.5	4.1	3.9
42	Detroit	4.9	5.1	5.1	3.1	4.2	3.7	4.2	4.2	4.6	4.7	3.6	3.7
43	Wisconsin	6.5	5.4	5.5	4.6	4.3	4.5	7.0	5.3	4.8	4.1	5.0	4.2
44	Milwaukee	4.0	4.0	4.0	3.1	4.3	4.9	4.9	6.5	6.5	4.9	3.2	2.9
45	Iowa	5.3	5.2	5.6	7.0	5.3	4.9	4.9	4.4	4.5	5.0	4.2	4.1
46	Minnesota	4.6	8.0	5.1	4.9	5.3	5.1	5.2	3.1	3.9	4.1	3.9	6.7
47	Missouri	7.8	4.3	4.6	3.5	9.7	4.1	4.2	4.1	3.5	8.7	3.3	3.5
48	St. Louis	3.7	3.7	3.5	2.6	2.7	3.9	3.6	3.0	3.5	2.8	2.9	2.9
49	Kansas	3.4	3.6	8.3	4.2	6.1	5.9	7.4	8.8	3.9	5.6	2.8	2.9
50	Nebraska	7.6	7.4	7.6	13.8	4.9	4.9	5.9	4.9	4.9	5.3	5.9	5.6
51	Colorado	10.7	9.6	15.6	8.4	12.0	7.2	7.0	10.0	9.6	7.0	8.2	7.0
52	Nevada	5.0	5.0	12.0	10.0	10.0	10.0	12.0	10.0	10.0	8.0	4.8	4.5
53	California	4.6	4.2	4.7	4.7	5.2	5.6	7.9	3.5	4.5	4.3	4.1	3.7
54	San Francisco	4.0	4.0	4.0	4.0	4.0	4.0	4.0	4.0	4.0	4.0	3.6	3.6
55	Oregon	12.0	32.0	12.0	18.3	14.2	19.3	10.8	6.0	5.8	5.6	10.0	26.7
56	Arizona					5.0	7.0	7.0	3.3				
57	Dakota	3.6	5.0	6.0	4.0	3.3	1.9	3.0	4.6	4.0	4.0	3.1	5.2
58	Idaho	18.0	28.0	22.0	15.0	20.0	15.0	22.5		14.0		15.0	23.3
59	Montana			7.5			10.9		4.1	0.8	1.7		
60	New Mexico	6.4	4.9	7.7	5.3	12.2	7.3	8.9	7.8	6.1	5.5	6.4	3.3
61	Utah	6.0	6.0	6.0	4.0	4.6	3.6	5.2	4.7	3.9	5.6	4.4	4.0
62	Washington			3.0	3.7	9.5	4.2	1.6	3.1	3.9	3.9		
63	Wyoming	20.0		11.1	1.2	6.9	3.4	22.5	3.0	3.6	3.7	15.0	
	Averages	4.1	4.2	4.3	4.4	4.2	4.1	4.2	3.9	3.9	3.8	3.3	3.3

NOTE.—Figures printed in bold-faced type in column

the dividends and earnings of national banks, from March 1, 1881, to September 1, 1885.

dividends to capital and surplus for six months ending—								Ratio of earnings to capital and surplus for six months ending—										
March 1, 1882	Sept. 1, 1882	March 1, 1883	Sept. 1, 1883	March 1, 1884	Sept. 1, 1884	March 1, 1885	Sept. 1, 1885	March 1, 1881	Sept. 1, 1881	March 1, 1882	Sept. 1, 1882	March 1, 1883	Sept. 1, 1883	March 1, 1884	Sept. 1, 1884	March 1, 1885	Sept. 1, 1885	
Pr. ct.	Pr. ct.	Pr. ct.	Pr. ct.	Pr. ct.	Pr. ct.	Pr. ct.	Pr. ct.	Pr. ct.	Pr. ct.	Pr. ct.	Pr. ct.	Pr. ct.	Pr. ct.	Pr. ct.	Pr. ct.	Pr. ct.	Pr. ct.	
3.5	3.5	3.4	3.3	3.3	3.3	3.3	3.5	4.1	5.1	3.9	3.6	3.5	3.6	2.4	2.3	2.9	3.3	1
3.3	3.0	3.2	3.2	3.1	3.1	3.1	3.1	3.3	3.8	3.4	3.4	2.9	3.9	3.9	2.0	3.7	3.0	2
3.4	2.7	3.1	3.4	3.2	3.2	3.0	2.7	3.2	3.6	3.7	3.2	3.2	3.4	3.3	2.6	2.0	2.3	3
3.1	2.8	2.9	2.8	2.6	2.5	2.8	2.6	3.5	4.4	3.7	3.5	2.9	3.5	2.9	3.0	2.2	2.5	4
2.4	2.3	2.3	2.3	2.2	2.3	2.3	2.2	3.0	3.4	3.2	2.7	2.7	2.7	2.5	2.4	1.4	1.7	5
2.9	2.8	2.8	2.9	2.9	2.7	2.8	2.7	2.0	4.0	3.6	3.4	2.7	3.6	3.3	3.3	2.2	2.5	6
3.2	3.2	3.1	3.1	3.1	3.0	2.9	2.8	4.1	4.1	3.6	3.6	3.7	2.9	3.3	2.7	2.1	2.4	7
3.4	3.2	3.2	3.1	3.2	2.9	3.0	3.0	4.0	4.5	4.1	4.4	4.1	4.3	3.5	4.0	2.9	3.2	8
3.4	2.6	3.4	2.4	3.5	2.4	3.5	2.0	4.1	3.9	3.4	2.1	5.1	3.3	4.1	2.4	4.1	1.0	10
3.4	3.3	3.6	3.5	3.6	3.3	3.4	3.4	3.9	4.5	3.8	4.0	4.7	4.4	4.7	4.0	3.3	3.2	11
3.0	3.2	3.1	3.1	3.1	2.7	2.9	2.8	3.8	4.4	4.4	4.5	3.8	4.5	4.5	3.9	3.7	3.1	12
2.9	2.7	3.3	3.1	3.1	3.0	3.0	3.0	3.7	4.3	6.2	3.2	3.9	3.8	4.4	4.1	2.7	3.4	13
2.8	2.8	2.9	2.8	2.9	2.7	2.7	2.7	3.7	4.6	3.5	0.3	3.8	3.7	4.3	3.9	3.3	2.6	14
3.4	3.4	3.4	3.5	3.4	3.6	3.5	3.6	4.2	5.9	3.1	4.9	4.6	5.1	4.9	3.8	5.0	4.4	15
3.4	3.4	3.6	3.4	3.4	3.2	3.1	3.2	4.5	4.0	4.2	4.2	4.5	4.4	4.4	4.4	3.6	3.5	16
3.0	3.2	2.9	3.1	3.0	3.0	3.0	2.9	4.9	4.3	4.4	4.9	3.5	3.9	3.5	3.9	3.9	3.8	17
3.2	3.2	3.2	3.2	3.2	3.2	3.2	3.2	4.1	3.6	3.9	4.3	3.9	4.5	5.5	2.8	3.6	3.6	18
2.1	2.0	2.0	2.6	2.7	2.7	2.7	2.7	0.3	2.0	3.6	1.9	2.5	3.8	4.4	3.7	1.5	4.3	19
3.2	3.2	3.1	3.1	4.3	3.0	3.0	2.9	4.8	5.5	6.7	4.3	4.5	5.1	6.3	5.2	3.8	4.7	20
3.6	3.4	3.4	3.3	3.2	3.0	8.1	2.9	4.2	4.6	4.3	4.0	3.9	3.7	3.9	3.9	3.1	2.5	21
3.1	3.3	3.3	2.8	3.2	2.7	3.6	3.0	4.7	4.8	7.8	3.3	3.3	4.9	4.2	4.6	3.7	2.9	22
2.9	3.1	2.9	2.9	3.1	2.8	3.0	3.0	9.4	7.2	7.3	8.8	5.0	6.4	6.6	6.7	3.3	3.9	23
2.8	2.7	3.0	2.7	2.7	2.4	2.7	2.7	5.5	5.5	4.5	4.8	4.8	5.5	4.8	3.8	4.3	24	
2.3	2.3	6.8	2.2	2.2	2.2	2.7	2.0	8.2	10.4	2.7	14.7	2.0	11.6	6.2	6.9	4.6	7.3	25
3.5	3.4	3.4	2.9	3.2	3.0	3.9	3.8	5.0	5.1	2.3	6.3	2.7	2.8	3.9	3.3	4.9	6.0	26
				7.7			7.0	2.6	5.1	2.8			0.3	5.2	8.5	5.8	8.9	5.4	9.2	27
			5.0	4.9	3.8	3.8	3.7	3.7					0.1	5.8	6.6	6.3	5.9	4.2	5.4	28
3.1	3.1	3.0	3.0	4.8	2.7	3.0	2.8	6.1	7.6	5.8	5.4	5.3	6.3	6.5	5.1	2.9	4.2	29
5.5	2.8	4.0	2.9	3.7	4.3	4.2	2.5	5.2	10.0	8.8	7.5	11.9	10.8	12.3	8.5	8.0	4.3	30
5.2	3.1	4.9	3.4	5.0	3.3	3.2	3.0	5.6	6.6	4.0	8.1	10.1	5.3	8.4	12.0	5.2	4.3	31
3.2	3.2	3.1	3.2	3.0	3.5	3.0	3.2	4.2	5.2	3.3	4.2	4.5	4.5	4.4	4.4	4.1	3.9	32
3.2	3.3	2.8	3.2	2.8	3.1	2.7	2.9	4.3	7.9	4.0	4.8	4.9	4.4	4.4	3.8	2.5	3.1	33
4.7	4.1	4.6	4.2	4.2	4.0	4.3	3.7	6.1	6.0	6.4	5.4	6.7	5.5	7.8	5.4	5.3	4.9	34
3.8	4.8	3.6	3.4	3.3	3.1	3.0	4.6	4.9	4.8	4.5	5.0	4.7	4.5	3.4	3.5	2.9	35	
4.1	9.4	3.1	3.4	3.0	2.9	2.7	2.9	5.5	5.1	7.7	5.8	4.5	3.5	3.7	2.9	3.2	3.4	36
3.3	4.5	3.5	3.5	3.3	3.6	2.0	2.5	4.2	5.0	6.3	8.6	5.8	4.3	5.0	2.4	2.2	4.0	37
3.6	4.6	4.0	3.6	3.2	3.1	2.9	3.6	4.4	4.8	4.7	4.8	4.6	4.7	4.2	3.4	3.3	3.7	38
5.2	5.2	4.6	4.3	4.3	3.8	3.7	3.7	5.5	6.3	6.6	5.8	5.8	5.1	5.2	5.0	4.4	39	
5.4	8.7	3.8	3.1	2.9	3.6	3.9	3.5	8.8	9.8	10.2	8.3	10.8	7.8	6.1	5.7	1.6	5.2	40
4.6	4.5	4.4	4.3	4.8	3.6	3.9	3.8	5.5	6.2	6.2	6.0	6.0	6.2	6.3	4.0	4.3	4.1	41
3.7	2.4	3.8	3.4	3.9	4.2	4.3	4.5	6.5	4.2	8.3	0.7	7.4	6.7	5.0	5.9	4.9	42	
4.3	3.7	3.4	3.7	5.7	4.3	3.8	3.3	6.1	6.1	6.0	5.4	5.7	6.2	6.5	5.0	4.8	4.7	43
2.9	2.2	3.0	3.4	3.2	4.2	4.2	3.2	11.1	5.6	9.4	18.5	9.5	8.9	6.0	5.6	1.3	5.4	44
4.4	5.6	4.3	4.0	4.0	3.6	3.6	4.1	5.7	3.2	6.6	5.5	6.6	6.0	5.9	5.1	4.9	4.7	45
4.2	4.3	4.4	4.2	4.3	2.6	3.3	3.5	7.0	7.0	4.2	5.1	6.9	5.7	7.9	4.3	4.6	4.0	46
3.7	2.9	8.0	3.4	3.5	3.4	2.9	7.4	5.5	5.5	6.6	4.5	5.2	5.5	6.6	5.5	5.5	6.4	47
2.9	2.2	2.2	3.2	2.9	2.4	2.7	2.2	5.0	3.7	4.6	4.8	0.9	5.7	5.0	3.8	3.7	3.6	48
6.7	3.4	5.3	4.9	6.2	7.7	3.4	4.8	6.8	7.4	9.3	7.2	8.6	8.5	10.7	9.2	7.5	8.1	49
5.5	10.4	4.1	4.1	5.0	4.2	4.2	4.5	16.5	6.7	12.1	12.4	8.0	11.3	7.3	7.5	7.2	50	
10.8	5.9	8.0	4.8	4.8	6.5	6.0	4.7	15.7	11.8	18.9	10.9	12.2	9.8	15.4	8.7	8.1	5.1	51
10.6	8.4	8.0	7.9	9.0	7.6	7.5	6.0	8.7	11.2	16.0	12.4	12.9	11.2	12.4	12.6	8.5	6.6	52
4.0	4.0	4.3	4.6	6.6	2.7	3.6	3.5	6.7	5.1	8.9	6.1	6.7	6.8	7.7	6.1	7.6	6.5	53
3.6	3.5	3.5	3.5	3.5	3.5	3.5	3.5	5.6	5.1	4.3	4.4	4.8	5.2	4.6	3.5	2.1	3.3	54
10.0	13.0	12.0	16.5	9.6	5.4	5.3	5.1	13.6	16.7	14.5	20.9	14.4	24.6	19.5	16.0	9.8	11.7	55
		5.0	6.9	6.8	3.3							5.5	7.7	9.0	1.8	1.4		56
5.3	3.4	2.8	1.6	2.4	3.8	4.1	3.3	17.1	14.6	10.0	8.7	11.2	9.5	7.6	3.2	4.0	4.2	57
18.3	12.5	16.7	12.5	20.4		13.0		14.6	23.1	18.4	12.7	17.0	12.0	22.7	10.4	10.0	6.0	58
6.2			9.5		3.4	0.7	1.4	11.3	16.6	27.6	11.2	16.3	10.1	9.8	9.2	7.7	5.2	59
5.9	4.2	9.8	5.8	7.0	6.0	5.1	4.5	12.5	7.0	9.1	8.6	8.6	8.6	7.7	7.2	2.6	5.7	60
3.7	2.8	3.2	2.6	3.5	3.4	2.7	3.8	7.5	19.9	4.4	7.4	5.9	7.8	9.1	6.5	7.0	3.5	61
2.7	3.2	8.2	3.9	1.5	2.9	3.6	3.5	11.1	17.2	12.5	16.9	16.5	8.8	11.1	8.4	8.5	10.1	62
8.3	1.0	5.6	2.7	19.4	2.6	2.9	3.2	12.8	5.0	16.1	4.2	8.8	8.3	11.4	7.0	7.5	8.6	63
3.4	3.4	3.3	3.2	3.2	3.0	3.0	3.0	4.2	5.0	4.6	4.3	4.2	4.3	4.3	3.7	3.2	3.3	

for 1884 signify percentage of loss.

Clearings and balances of the banks of New York City for the weeks ending at the dates given.

Week ending—	Clearings	Balances.
Sept. 4, 1880	$603, 877, 203 02	$33, 414, 325 94
Sept. 11, 1880	625, 650, 183 37	26, 812, 778 80
Sept. 18, 1880	623, 375, 055 48	30, 733, 842 94
Sept. 25, 1880	573, 355, 801 73	30, 070, 332 13
Oct. 2, 1880	705, 598, 706 46	32, 827, 400 90
Oct. 9, 1880	651, 169, 020 35	28, 586, 849 16
Oct. 16, 1880	693, 917, 360 86	27, 875, 042 64
Oct. 23, 1880	872, 895, 695 57	32, 910, 082 09
Oct. 30, 1880	785, 361, 021 85	31, 018, 354 80
Nov. 6, 1880	866, 393, 048 37	33, 236, 599 77
Nov. 13, 1880	896, 540, 451, 06	34, 579, 373 05
Nov. 20, 1880	868, 076, 513 35	34, 404, 649 13
Nov. 27, 1880	1, 072, 680, 747 81	32, 472, 796 33
Sept. 3, 1881	857, 413, 203 85	37, 132, 230 86
Sept. 10, 1881	639, 907, 979 97	28, 808, 004 38
Sept. 17, 1881	925, 116, 460 37	36, 408, 897 13
Sept. 24, 1881	773, 401, 695 57	29, 389, 049 98
Oct. 1, 1881	758, 155, 052 10	26, 349, 314 58
Oct. 8, 1881	1, 154, 052, 466 33	35, 187, 686 23
Oct. 15, 1881	975, 722, 717 38	31, 678, 440 10
Oct. 22, 1881	953, 850, 125 23	35, 159, 491 42
Oct. 29, 1881	881, 124, 243 74	32, 450, 957 70
Nov. 5, 1881	1, 021, 882, 159 85	37, 173, 439 72
Nov. 12, 1881	796, 664, 256 97	27, 635, 753 35
Nov. 19, 1881	892, 319, 707 29	31, 043, 351 43
Nov. 26, 1881	892, 475, 593 06	23, 882, 022 31
Sept. 2, 1882	787, 790, 346 16	27, 396, 924 64
Sept. 9, 1882	806, 102, 117 62	29, 786, 386 41
Sept. 16, 1882	1, 010, 634, 205 97	30, 418, 411 78
Sept. 23, 1882	950, 962, 831 49	27, 978, 458 28
Sept. 30, 1882	1, 011, 393, 333 57	34, 393, 848 91
Oct. 7, 1882	1, 124, 300, 247 43	30, 742, 717 31
Oct. 14, 1882	999, 817, 864 93	35, 772, 217 86
Oct. 21, 1882	1, 044, 396, 226 21	33, 623, 283 86
Oct. 28, 1882	857, 816, 086 35	26, 633, 506 70
Nov. 4, 1882	991, 296, 926 46	37, 122, 701 71
Nov. 11, 1882	950, 469, 956 50	26, 969, 785 92
Nov. 18, 1882	1, 054, 384, 065 67	33, 258, 877 77
Nov. 25, 1882	1, 246, 998, 567 95	26, 657, 750 01
Sept. 1, 1883	645, 021, 546 86	26, 472, 986 85
Sept. 8, 1883	730, 732, 907 18	31, 195, 746 55
Sept. 15, 1883	732, 316, 071 00	30, 914, 820 30
Sept. 22, 1883	700, 082, 400 54	30, 061, 000 19
Sept. 29, 1883	763, 567, 336 28	30, 260, 285 71
Oct. 6, 1883	759, 872, 865 58	32, 844, 144 42
Oct. 13, 1883	833, 965, 948 88	31, 363, 439 92
Oct. 20, 1883	919, 608, 026 44	31, 917, 847 51
Oct. 27, 1883	906, 319, 847 51	31, 844, 418 48
Nov. 3, 1883	817, 996, 284 43	29, 708, 441 71
Nov. 10, 1883	622, 487, 973 40	28, 478, 167 32
Nov. 17, 1883	783, 094, 622 25	33, 519, 486 15
Nov. 24, 1883	682, 451, 400 44	28, 333, 263 64
Sept. 6, 1884	463, 912, 628 57	21, 278, 921 75
Sept. 13, 1884	422, 613, 919 74	22, 793, 210 60
Sept. 20, 1884	492, 009, 873 06	21, 412, 397 53
Sept. 27, 1884	491, 337, 861 20	22, 028, 068 11
Oct. 4, 1884	554, 662, 698 69	32, 658, 517 10
Oct. 11, 1884	496, 582, 476 56	26, 358, 572 40
Oct. 18, 1884	518, 575, 214 89	28, 696, 794 93
Oct. 25, 1884	605, 195, 931 55	27, 673, 214 95
Nov. 1, 1884	458, 532, 568 11	23, 225, 190 59
Nov. 8, 1884	477, 210, 695 35	28, 269, 591 59
Nov. 15, 1884	527, 541, 755 74	26, 823, 261 26
Nov. 22, 1884	555, 711, 569 01	26, 496, 903 13
Nov. 29, 1884	450, 294, 007 66	21, 392, 407 63
Sept. 5, 1885	476, 800, 526 79	22, 990, 787 52
Sept. 12, 1885	484, 537, 657 96	23, 969, 307 46
Sept. 19, 1885	480, 733, 380 21	24, 410, 868 93
Sept. 26, 1885	471, 632, 048 41	22, 978, 969 63
Oct. 3, 1885	572, 076, 277 97	30, 158, 232 32
Oct. 10, 1885	659, 560, 540 70	28, 462, 678 38
Oct. 17, 1885	702, 060, 829 74	29, 632, 037 42
Oct. 24, 1885	828, 373, 048 53	30, 475, 583 77
Oct. 31, 1885	695, 214, 389 87	29, 590, 574 77
Nov. 7, 1885	775, 416, 616 98	30, 751, 563 50
Nov 14, 1885	779, 244, 286 61	27, 323, 721 40

Average weekly deposits, circulation, and reserve of the national banks of New York City, as reported to the New York Clearing House, for the months of September and October in each year from 1878 to 1885.

Week ending—	Liabilities.			Reserve.			Ratio to liabilities.
	Circulation.	Net deposits.	Total.	Specie.	Legal-tenders.	Total.	
	Dollars.	Dollars.	Dollars.	Dollars.	Dollars.	Dollars.	Per cent.
Sept. 7, 1878	19,037,000	191,650,200	210,687,200	14,583,200	43,260,300	57,843,500	27.45
Sept. 14, 1878	19,453,000	191,090,500	210,543,500	15,929,300	41,673,400	57,602,700	27.30
Sept. 21, 1878	19,591,000	190,268,100	209,259,100	15,590,400	41,894,700	57,485,100	27.40
Sept. 28, 1878	19,592,500	189,872,700	209,425,200	16,373,300	39,762,000	55,135,300	26.33
Oct. 5, 1878	19,552,200	187,568,400	207,120,600	14,995,600	38,304,900	53,300,700	25.73
Oct. 12, 1878	19,567,800	184,825,400	204,393,200	12,184,600	37,685,100	49,869,700	24.40
Oct. 19, 1878	19,575,900	183,627,600	203,203,500	13,531,400	36,576,000	50,107,400	24.66
Oct. 26, 1878	19,864,400	186,082,100	205,946,500	17,384,200	35,690,500	53,074,700	25.77
Sept. 6, 1879	21,354,100	201,608,400	222,962,500	18,502,900	36,275,800	54,778,700	24.57
Sept. 13, 1879	21,585,300	201,071,200	222,656,500	18,538,000	36,181,600	54,719,600	24.58
Sept. 20, 1879	21,366,700	203,326,900	224,693,600	18,670,400	37,781,100	56,451,500	25.12
Sept. 27, 1879	21,513,700	204,964,400	226,478,100	18,731,600	35,901,900	54,633,500	24.12
Oct. 4, 1879	21,914,200	206,866,800	228,781,000	18,970,000	34,368,000	53,317,600	23.32
Oct. 11, 1879	22,061,900	207,663,500	229,716,400	20,901,800	32,820,300	53,722,100	23.38
Oct. 18, 1879	22,268,600	207,290,200	229,468,800	24,686,500	29,305,200	53,991,700	23.53
Oct. 25, 1879	22,430,500	205,496,800	227,927,300	25,636,000	26,713,900	52,349,900	22.97
Sept. 4, 1880	19,324,200	267,791,300	287,115,500	61,269,200	12,545,900	73,815,100	25.71
Sept. 11, 1880	19,345,500	267,792,600	287,128,100	60,716,000	11,952,000	72,668,000	25.31
Sept. 18, 1880	19,326,400	268,244,300	287,570,700	61,522,200	11,407,100	72,929,300	25.36
Sept. 25, 1880	18,864,400	264,358,200	283,222,600	60,026,600	11,090,500	71,116,100	25.11
Oct. 2, 1880	18,618,000	263,755,000	282,373,600	59,823,700	11,129,100	70,952,800	25.37
Oct. 9, 1880	18,555,600	260,993,400	280,549,000	62,521,300	10,785,000	73,306,300	25.42
Oct. 16, 1880	17,611,000	271,907,700	289,518,700	62,760,600	10,939,200	73,699,800	25.46
Oct. 23, 1880	18,682,500	269,708,600	288,391,100	60,888,200	10,988,200	71,876,400	24.92
Oct. 30, 1880	18,628,400	271,230,700	289,859,100	61,471,600	10,925,000	72,396,600	24.98
Sept. 3, 1881	19,669,400	278,241,700	297,911,100	57,816,100	13,226,600	71,042,700	23.85
Sept. 10, 1881	19,764,500	277,011,700	296,776,200	59,991,600	12,591,300	72,582,900	24.46
Sept. 17, 1881	19,708,100	279,404,900	299,173,000	61,224,100	11,979,000	73,203,100	24.47
Sept. 24, 1881	19,747,500	277,268,600	297,016,100	60,476,000	12,451,300	72,927,300	24.55
Oct. 1, 1881	19,841,400	270,727,100	290,568,500	54,954,600	12,150,400	67,105,000	23.09
Oct. 8, 1881	19,849,400	263,081,600	282,931,000	53,287,900	12,153,800	65,441,700	23.13
Oct. 15, 1881	19,878,400	254,224,700	274,103,100	51,008,300	12,452,700	63,461,000	23.15
Oct. 22, 1881	19,901,400	250,299,000	270,200,400	54,016,200	12,496,500	66,512,700	24.61
Oct. 29, 1881	19,930,400	251,480,300	271,410,700	55,961,200	12,947,900	68,909,100	25.61
Sept. 2, 1882	18,278,400	271,999,400	290,277,800	49,775,400	19,953,100	69,728,500	24.02
Sept. 9, 1882	18,307,000	265,566,900	283,873,900	47,148,500	19,448,800	66,597,300	23.46
Sept. 16, 1882	18,357,500	263,736,700	282,094,200	48,571,500	18,681,500	67,263,000	23.84
Sept. 23, 1882	18,622,700	260,205,800	278,828,500	47,114,000	17,993,700	65,107,700	23.35
Sept. 30, 1882	18,768,100	251,858,100	270,644,200	41,925,500	18,389,000	63,314,500	23.25
Oct. 7, 1882	18,894,800	260,136,800	279,031,600	47,016,000	18,384,500	65,400,500	24.03
Oct. 14, 1882	18,732,000	249,629,700	268,361,700	48,281,000	18,002,700	66,283,700	24.70
Oct. 21, 1882	18,749,400	247,974,400	266,723,800	49,518,200	17,023,900	66,542,100	24.97
Oct. 28, 1882	18,764,500	247,575,400	266,339,900	48,374,200	17,204,700	65,578,900	24.77
Sept. 1, 1883	15,622,600	269,961,900	285,584,500	53,529,000	21,729,000	75,258,000	26.35
Sept. 8, 1883	15,527,600	268,805,500	284,332,500	52,601,400	21,074,500	73,675,900	25.91
Sept. 15, 1883	15,519,700	272,325,100	287,844,800	53,397,400	20,662,700	74,060,100	25.73
Sept. 22, 1883	15,394,600	271,728,200	287,122,800	49,360,600	22,443,300	71,803,900	25.01
Sept. 29, 1883	15,184,800	268,496,600	283,681,400	50,067,900	20,566,800	70,634,700	24.90
Oct. 6, 1883	15,069,100	265,592,500	280,661,600	51,586,700	20,122,500	71,709,200	25.51
Oct. 13, 1883	15,164,200	268,942,000	284,106,200	50,894,000	21,145,800	72,039,800	25.36
Oct. 20, 1883	15,252,000	262,635,700	277,888,600	47,262,900	20,719,700	67,982,600	24.47
Oct. 27, 1883	15,336,200	258,589,600	273,925,800	46,372,800	20,617,000	66,990,400	24.46
Sept. 6, 1884	14,221,000	251,527,200	265,748,200	64,899,900	25,060,800	89,960,700	33.85
Sept. 13, 1884	14,132,300	251,654,700	265,787,000	64,288,200	25,191,800	89,480,000	33.67
Sept. 20, 1884	14,081,400	254,141,200	268,222,600	65,409,500	25,268,000	90,677,500	33.81
Sept. 27, 1884	14,083,300	252,765,500	266,848,800	64,302,000	25,375,700	89,677,700	33.61
Oct. 4, 1884	13,578,400	256,696,800	270,275,200	67,470,000	25,817,300	93,287,900	34.52
Oct. 11, 1884	12,884,700	261,801,600	274,686,300	68,922,500	27,654,100	96,576,600	35.16
Oct. 18, 1884	12,752,700	261,527,700	274,280,400	67,579,400	27,875,500	95,454,900	34.80
Oct. 25, 1884	12,910,900	261,405,400	274,316,300	67,638,000	27,356,200	94,992,200	34.63
Sept. 5, 1885	9,701,700	321,859,000	331,563,700	102,921,100	28,701,900	131,623,000	39.70
Sept. 12, 1885	9,753,300	320,910,000	330,663,300	100,255,300	28,842,300	129,097,600	39.04
Sept. 19, 1885	9,735,800	319,060,800	328,796,600	95,037,900	26,014,800	121,052,100	38.01
Sept. 26, 1885	9,808,000	316,767,000	326,575,000	95,037,900	26,014,800	121,052,100	37.07
Oct. 3, 1885	9,902,900	315,502,600	321,905,500	94,951,600	24,516,600	116,868,200	35.97
Oct. 10, 1885	9,921,200	315,596,200	325,517,400	93,642,500	23,002,000	116,644,500	35.83
Oct. 17, 1885	9,954,600	317,296,700	327,250,700	91,945,800	22,221,100	114,166,400	34.89
Oct. 24, 1885	10,006,000	313,767,200	323,773,200	87,309,100	21,059,800	108,368,900	33.47
Oct. 31, 1885	9,989,800	313,399,700	323,389,500	84,954,600	21,874,900	106,829,500	33.03

State of the lawful-money reserve of the national banks as

STATES AND

	Dates.	No. of banks.	Net deposits.	Reserve required.
1	Oct. 2, 1879	1, 820	$329, 874, 452	$49, 535, 540
2	Dec. 12, 1879	1, 824	348 834, 775	52, 379, 535
3	Feb. 21, 1880	1, 831	375, 281, 538	56, 446, 827
4	Apr. 23, 1880	1, 844	384, 765, 183	57, 766, 633
5	June 11, 1880	1, 845	385, 168, 252	57, 801, 806
6	Oct. 1, 1880	1, 859	410, 522, 448	61, 502, 298
7	Dec 31, 1880	1, 863	439, 354, 304	65, 922, 995
8	Mar. 11, 1881	1, 860	447, 410, 923	67, 131, 602
9	May 6, 1881	1, 868	460, 478, 466	69, 091, 733
10	June 30, 1881	1, 880	484, 089, 521	72, 633, 329
11	Oct. 1, 1881	1, 895	507, 247, 143	76, 196, 945
12	Dec. 31, 1881	1, 926	518, 701, 965	77, 809, 257
13	Mar. 11, 1882	1, 945	515, 198, 159	77, 283, 686
14	May 19, 1882	1, 981	519, 247, 650	77, 891, 110
15	July 1, 1882	1, 996	527, 588, 049	79. 142, 169
16	Oct. 3, 1882	2, 026	545, 842, 660	81. 880, 361
17	Dec. 30, 1882	2, 065	554, 245, 520	83, 140, 390
18	Mar. 13, 1883	2, 097	550, 802, 283	82, 637, 104
19	May 1, 1883	2, 128	556, 309, 464	83, 449, 581
20	June 22, 1883	2, 169	560, 731, 879	84. 112, 683
21	Oct. 2, 1883	2, 253	577, 880, 812	86, 685, 688
22	Dec. 31, 1883	2, 280	579, 512, 711	86, 930, 753
23	Mar. 7, 1884	2, 314	573, 619, 524	86, 046, 715
24	Apr. 24, 1884	2, 340	575, 995, 025	86, 399, 263
25	June 20, 1884	2, 376	544, 660, 331	81, 699, 049
26	Sept. 30, 1884	2, 417	535, 807, 406	80, 371, 111
27	Dec. 20, 1884	2, 417	520, 283, 576	78, 042, 536
28	Mar. 10, 1885	2, 425	537, 613, 418	80, 642, 012
29	May 6, 1 85	2. 432	540, 281, 214	81, 042, 182
30	July 1, 1885	2, 412	552, 196, 593	82, 829, 489
31	Oct. 1, 1885	2, 467	570, 838, 327	85, 625, 749

RESERVE

1	Oct. 2, 1879	228	439, 009. 954	109, 752, 489
2	Dec. 12, 1879	228	458, 944, 779	114. 736, 195
3	Feb. 21, 1880	230	498, 980, 548	124, 745, 187
4	Apr. 23, 1880	231	482, 230, 794	120, 557, 698
5	June 11, 1880	231	516, 491, 857	129, 122, 964
6	Oct. 1, 1880	231	557, 508, 975	130, 377. 244
7	Dec. 31, 1880	232	544, 501, 717	130, 125, 429
8	Mar. 11, 1881	234	536, 112, 658	134, 028, 165
9	May 6, 1881	234	588, 714, 401	147. 178, 600
10	June 30, 1881	235	655, 815. 066	163, 953, 766
11	Oct. 1, 1881	237	604, 438, 599	151, 109, 650
12	Dec. 31, 1881	238	577, 163, 351	144, 290, 838
13	Mar. 11, 1882	242	564, 058, 531	141, 014, 632
14	May 19, 1882	242	590, 883, 075	147. 720, 769
15	July 1, 1882	243	604, 391, 647	151, 097, 911
16	Oct. 3, 1882	243	572, 791, 257	143, 197, 814
17	Dec. 30, 1882	243	565, 948, 445	141, 487, 111
18	Mar. 13, 1883	246	559, 431, 070	139, 857, 768
19	May 1, 1883	247	568, 267, 546	142. 066, 886
20	June 22, 1883	248	611, 259, 171	152. 814, 793
21	Oct. 2, 1883	248	590, 785, 930	147, 696, 483
22	Dec. 31, 1883	249	612, 621, 435	153, 155, 359
23	Mar. 7, 1884	249	642, 682, 644	160. 670, 660
24	Apr. 24, 1884	249	620, 221, 832	155, 055, 456
25	June 20, 1884	249	534, 629, 056	133 637, 263
26	Sept. 30, 1884	247	562, 888, 105	140. 722, 026
27	Dec. 20, 1884	247	588, 299, 710	147. 074, 927
28	Mar. 10, 1885	246	626, 616, 971	156, 654, 242
29	May 6, 1885	246	644, 259, 607	161, 064, 902
30	July 1, 1885	247	669, 199, 214	167, 299, 805
	Oct. 1, 1885	247	677, 332, 060	169, 333, 265

shown by their reports from October 2, 1879, to October 1, 1885.

TERRITORIES.

Reserve held.		Classification of reserve held.					
Amount.	Ratio to liabilities.	Specie.	Legal tenders.	United States certificates of deposit.	Due from reserve agents.	Redemption fund with Treasurer.	
Per cent.							
$124,315,513	37.7	$11,474,961	$29,628,096	$735,000	$71,302,887	$11,184,569	1
124,666,178	35.7	13,267,825	29,357,057	670,000	70,017,269	11,304,027	2
139,489,054	37.2	15,931,268	28,471,133	670,000	83,134,250	11,282,454	3
133,966,543	34.8	18,523,230	30,138,708	645,000	73,296,236	11,363,369	4
138,632,303	36.0	18,988,961	28,650,254	605,000	79,126,763	11,262,285	5
147,105,244	35.8	21,115,738	27,613,370	640,000	86,371,229	11,334,907	6
155,406,303	35.4	25,108,888	29,063,892	630,000	89,258,930	11,344,083	7
150,919,415	33.7	26,660,882	26,783,131	585,000	86,060,705	10,829,697	8
155,258,632	33.7	27,842,501	28,672,789	585,000	87,109,924	11,048,428	9
170,055,750	35.1	27,635,215	27,416,230	575,000	103,297,184	11,132,121	10
158,209,642	31.2	27,509,821	26,473,092	620,000	92,335,036	11,361,183	11
159,060,717	30.7	30,283,767	28,905,001	595,000	87,745,656	11,551,203	12
150,725,091	29.3	29,161,734	26,897,694	610,000	82,599,924	11,455,739	13
154,776,359	29.8	30,036,477	28,160,627	535,000	84,721,909	11,322,286	14
151,908,107	28.8	30,089,064	26,857,620	620,000	83,221,970	11,119,453	15
159,351,513	27.5	30,024,289	28,318,646	610,000	80,064,196	11,334,382	16
158,882,406	28.7	31,095,496	31,638,111	635,000	84,783,917	11,279,882	17
155,131,167	28.2	30,072,360	28,871,031	565,000	84,431,394	11,191,382	18
148,836,606	26.7	31,414,155	30,367,252	585,000	75,216,795	11,253,404	19
157,728,089	28.1	31,055,220	29,053,116	575,000	85,825,601	11,219,153	20
157,493,584	27.2	31,253,191	30,245,600	585,000	84,119,738	11,290,152	21
167,741,690	28.6	33,178,829	32,695,209	610,000	88,057,473	11,200,089	22
167,008,672	29.1	33,471,053	29,859,216	595,000	92,267,704	10,815,097	23
162,496,064	28.2	36,352,084	30,944,464	550,000	83,664,761	10,954,155	24
145,997,562	26.8	36,407,051	31,448,254	575,000	66,843,814	10,723,443	25
156,304,733	29.2	35,238,175	30,392,840	500,000	79,652,119	10,521,590	26
161,864,287	31.1	34,587,231	29,943,391	505,000	86,489,195	10,279,470	27
175,620,558	32.6	38,852,692	30,134,197	665,000	95,289,830	10,088,839	28
171,011,853	31.6	40,736,669	29,508,036	635,000	89,991,054	10,141,074	29
176,245,483	30.8	4,065,640	27,473,329	645,000	92,068,593	10,002,921	30
177,470,804	31.1	41,467,335	29,375,956	500,000	95,954,541	10,172,992	31

CITIES.

136,610,443	31.1	30,698,771	39,557,866	26,035,000	35,720,660	4,598,146	1
138,648,047	30.2	65,527,137	25,362,067	10,180,000	32,725,183	6,843,660	2
149,451,113	30.0	73,215,503	26,749,506	10,090,000	34,657,128	4,738,976	3
140,898,106	29.2	67,410,642	30,889,350	7,225,000	30,667,994	4,705,120	4
169,206,207	32.8	80,023,104	35,821,472	11,895,000	36,808,905	4,657,726	5
175,852,502	31.5	87,035,651	29,023,558	7,015,000	48,191,549	4,586,834	6
157,721,336	29.0	80,609,813	30,150,982	5,520,000	36,896,084	4,544,457	7
147,308,032	27.5	77,490,354	25,371,178	5,525,000	34,759,986	4,161,514	8
18,221,803	30.6	94,555,721	34,842,177	7,460,000	40,862,229	4,531,676	9
197,889,047	30.2	100,058,123	31,308,173	8,965,000	52,961,453	4,596,298	10
164,348,053	27.0	85,162,735	26,67,602	6,120,000	40,633,147	4,754,569	11
161,410,332	28.0	82,253,632	31,188,493	7,335,000	35,784,810	4,848,307	12
157,802,939	28.0	79,620,297	29,725,208	8,835,000	34,852,796	4,769,548	13
172,827,165	29.2	81,177,310	37,797,247	9,850,000	39,467,976	4,534,632	14
167,963,478	27.8	80,731,158	37,153,139	10,425,000	35,233,042	4,461,199	15
153,557,856	26.8	72,883,489	34,904,871	8,035,000	33,213,032	4,481,464	16
162,987,772	28.7	75,361,663	37,440,310	7,840,000	37,282,190	4,493,609	17
148,706,922	26.6	67,890,006	31,977,037	7,840,000	36,592,761	4,407,118	18
156,419,122	27.5	72,193,111	37,889,216	7,835,000	34,090,027	4,411,768	19
161,362,255	30.2	84,299,176	44,779,342	10,070,000	40,821,353	4,392,424	20
171,448,008	29.0	76,561,789	40,437,397	9,375,000	40,798,990	4,371,832	21
182,221,554	29.7	81,097,329	47,864,497	10,230,000	38,042,133	4,087,595	22
198,511,843	30.9	88,609,073	45,987,877	13,450,000	46,437,308	4,027,585	23
179,371,793	28.9	78,392,093	46,768,164	11,410,000	38,827,197	3,944,410	24
160,231,029	30.0	73,254,631	45,468,958	9,295,000	28,403,338	3,849,102	25
189,859,706	33.7	93,371,209	46,651,819	13,700,000	32,340,900	3,786,688	26
208,349,105	35.4	105,159,848	46,126,164	18,475,000	34,672,781	3,615,312	27
235,974,313	37.7	128,261,181	40,883,125	22,095,000	41,172,443	3,560,564	28
247,455,812	38.1	136,678,750	47,828,063	18,560,000	40,912,019	3,535,850	29
256,223,121	38.3	137,546,852	52,228,023	22,285,000	40,661,809	3,501,437	30
237,894,989	35.1	133,405,237	40,362,183	18,300,000	42,402,609	3,424,960	31

Lawful money reserve of the national banks, as shown by the reports

STATES AND

	Cities, States, and Territories.	No. of banks.	Deposits.	Reserve required.	Reserve held.	Ratio of reserve.
				15 *per cent.*		*Per ct.*
1	Maine	71	$10,193,112	$1,528,967	$4,075,398	39.98
2	New Hampshire	48	6,271,243	940,686	2,423,330	38.64
3	Vermont	47	5,229,319	784,398	1,708,605	32.67
4	Massachusetts	195	53,596,198	8,039,430	14,543,979	27.14
5	Rhode Island	61	14,643,995	2,196,599	4,019,836	27.45
6	Connecticut	84	24,856,645	3,728,497	7,045,166	30.76
7	New York	267	79,493,208	11,923,981	24,016,615	30.21
8	New Jersey	72	33,374,140	5,006,121	12,580,433	37.70
9	Pennsylvania	228	62,410,870	9,361,630	19,573,910	31.36
10	Delaware	15	4,060,680	609,102	1,656,136	40.78
11	Maryland	27	5,774,469	866,170	1,897,394	32.86
12	District of Columbia	1	781,158	117,174	364,649	46.68
13	Virginia	24	8,740,810	1,311,122	2,643,742	30.25
14	West Virginia	21	2,551,850	382,778	777,006	30.45
15	North Carolina	15	3,608,690	541,305	906,742	25.13
16	South Carolina	14	3,125,974	468,896	771,195	24.67
17	Georgia	16	3,605,469	540,820	943,425	26.17
18	Florida	5	820,034	123,005	201,271	24.54
19	Alabama	10	2,236,670	335,501	569,345	25.45
20	Mississippi	6	700,148	105,022	152,259	21.75
21	Louisiana	1	70,368	10,546	25,559	36.35
22	Texas	68	9,498,471	1,424,771	3,266,400	34.39
23	Arkansas	6	1,575,731	236,360	472,135	29.97
24	Kentucky	59	8,603,990	1,290,598	2,542,188	29.55
25	Tennessee	32	8,743,371	1,311,506	2,023,880	23.15
26	Ohio	183	32,080,769	4,812,115	10,303,089	32.11
27	Indiana	90	20,591,521	3,088,728	7,479,260	36.32
28	Illinois	153	28,482,359	4,272,354	9,735,237	34.18
29	Michigan	97	18,633,927	2,795,089	6,735,176	36.14
30	Wisconsin	47	10,219,341	1,532,901	3,224,593	31.55
31	Iowa	125	17,519,419	2,627,913	5,306,828	30.29
32	Minnesota	49	21,980,913	3,297,137	5,000,386	23.02
33	Missouri	36	6,609,697	991,455	1,966,995	29.76
34	Kansas	74	10,367,841	1,555,176	3,055,981	29.48
35	Nebraska	75	13,697,320	2,054,598	3,769,537	27.52
36	Colorado	25	10,610,175	1,591,526	4,216,167	39.74
37	Nevada	1	234,829	35,224	53,548	22.80
38	California	16	5,622,200	843,330	1,555,425	27.67
39	Oregon	9	3,005,240	450,786	809,865	26.95
40	Dakota	41	3,890,878	583,632	1,031,699	26.52
41	Idaho	4	416,055	62,408	122,586	29.42
42	Montana	15	5,492,154	823,823	1,328,900	24.20
43	New Mexico	8	1,927,994	289,199	554,326	28.75
44	Utah	6	1,693,399	254,010	405,695	23.96
45	Washington	15	1,450,781	217,617	451,030	31.09
46	Wyoming	5	1,744,353	261,653	525,994	30.15
	Total	2,467	570,838,327	85,625,749	177,492,919	31.09

RESERVE

				25 *per cent.*		
1	Boston	54	102,057,664	25,514,416	28,726,398	28.15
2	Albany	6	8,918,686	2,229,672	3,480,862	39.03
3	Philadelphia	34	77,989,267	19,497,317	28,843,991	36.98
4	Pittsburgh	23	21,433,579	5,358,395	7,086,072	33.06
5	Baltimore	17	21,235,138	5,308,784	7,728,299	36.39
6	Washington	5	3,485,363	871,341	1,336,120	38.32
7	New Orleans	8	8,889,186	2,222,296	2,496,237	28.08
8	Louisville	9	6,295,248	1,573,812	1,457,011	23.14
9	Cincinnati	12	19,524,163	4,881,041	6,921,954	35.45
10	Cleveland	8	9,784,273	2,446,068	3,101,341	31.70
11	Chicago	12	50,071,218	14,767,804	22,261,245	37.68
12	Detroit	5	9,533,423	2,383,356	3,323,592	34.86
13	Milwaukee	3	5,077,343	1,494,336	1,909,330	31.94
14	St. Louis	6	9,303,829	2,325,957	3,026,315	32.53
15	San Francisco	1	976,175	244,044	488,024	49.99
	Total	203	364,474,555	91,118,639	122,186,751	33.52
16	New York	44	312,858,505	78,214,626	115,706,868	36.98
	United States	2,714	1,248,171,387	254,959,014	415,386,538	33.28

NOTE.—Prior to June 20, 1874, the required reserve in States and Territories was 15 per centum, centum of the deposits only.

of their condition at the close of business on October 1, 1885.

TERRITORIES.

Cash reserve.			Classification of reserve held.				
Required.	Held.	Specie.	Legal tenders.	U. S. certificates of deposit.	Due from reserve agents.	Redemption fund with Treasurer.	
$458,579	$852,544	$670,348	$182,196		$2,840,335	$382,519	1
272,285	422,465	282,996	139,469		1,740,890	259,975	2
207,620	465,260	308,307	156,953		975,997	265,348	3
2,524,229	4,286,128	2,438,311	1,672,817	$175,000	8,528,992	1,728,850	4
638,332	1,059,124	565,457	493,667		2,359,942	600,770	5
1,172,642	2,463,824	1,562,155	901,669		4,384,449	796,893	6
4,281,613	8,510,992	5,054,293	3,191,699	265,000	14,285,673	1,219,950	7
1,836,211	3,891,833	1,979,702	1,902,131	10,000	8,273,007	415,593	8
3,271,589	7,652,623	4,535,976	3,106,647	10,000	10,738,628	1,182,659	9
212,284	397,892	204,561	173,331	20,000	1,179,851	78,393	10
306,471	754,346	353,721	400,625		1,043,055	99,993	11
42,370	199,918	114,418	85,500		153,481	11,250	12
483,921	1,348,466	561,564	786,902		1,193,956	101,320	13
127,992	434,065	229,270	204,795		280,143	62,798	14
197,824	494,927	231,741	263,186		365,075	46,745	15
166,655	548,131	235,892	312,239		170,895	52,259	16
184,450	762,594	441,577	321,017		101,136	79,695	17
46,923	138,183	35,602	102,581		57,389	5,699	18
115,553	409,652	241,888	167,764		113,074	46,619	19
39,739	124,034	82,352	41,682		22,551	5,674	20
2,418	17,520	14,653	2,867		3,539	4,500	21
534,806	1,885,906	883,443	1,002,463		1,292,963	87,531	22
88,064	204,254	119,543	84,711		251,681	16,200	23
406,398	1,026,874	624,241	402,633		1,240,710	274,604	24
482,218	1,214,204	696,815	517,389		703,715	105,961	25
1,664,851	5,521,543	2,671,002	2,850,541		4,131,559	649,987	26
1,106,090	3,705,549	2,097,272	1,598,277	10,000	3,450,208	323,503	27
1,589,082	4,087,495	2,440,264	1,637,231	10,000	5,348,093	299,649	28
1,049,295	2,411,448	1,616,226	795,222		4,151,875	171,853	29
581,960	1,293,427	908,845	384,582		1,853,155	78,001	30
978,567	2,385,498	1,218,851	1,166,647		2,739,834	181,496	31
1,282,381	2,453,627	1,551,174	902,453		2,515,574	91,185	32
372,009	861,219	484,169	377,050		1,044,343	61,433	33
593,675	1,612,903	869,755	743,148		1,372,090	70,988	34
786,243	1,583,558	1,038,459	545,099		2,096,988	88,901	35
618,226	1,716,208	977,647	738,561		2,453,997	45,962	36
13,370	48,706	46,230	2,476		3,042	1,800	37
320,043	958,088	910,084	48,004		554,115	43,222	38
172,695	537,552	508,791	28,761		253,263	19,050	39
220,460	584,825	211,004	373,821		414,412	32,462	40
23,780	96,393	42,102	54,291		23,144	3,049	41
321,893	901,919	574,461	327,458		407,898	19,092	42
108,740	212,350	141,534	70,816		324,626	17,350	43
93,729	250,618	215,578	35,040		135,390	19,687	44
80,567	280,475	265,366	15,109		154,355	16,200	45
101,871	274,111	209,695	64,416		244,908	6,975	46
30,180,803	71,343,271	41,467,335	29,375,936	500,000	95,975,906	10,173,742	

CITIES.

12,263,597	13,688,063	8,960,565	3,542,498	1,185,000	13,931,113	1,107,222	1
1,082,932	1,422,329	922,860	189,469	310,000	1,994,666	63,807	2
9,548,916	20,930,449	11,361,092	4,234,351	5,335,000	7,494,463	419,485	3
2,523,183	4,463,416	2,295,592	2,167,824		2,310,620	312,030	4
2,517,877	5,769,987	2,642,624	1,442,363	2,285,000	1,685,282	273,030	5
419,920	946,124	476,797	469,327		358,496	31,500	6
1,063,586	1,903,781	817,951	1,087,830		495,351	95,125	7
723,149	897,888	386,468	511,420		431,609	127,514	8
2,314,335	4,434,372	1,048,087	1,976,285	1,410,000	2,235,212	252,370	9
1,208,296	1,911,225	911,225	985,000	15,000	1,160,641	29,475	10
7,356,774	15,584,354	9,673,254	5,191,100	720,000	6,622,634	54,257	11
1,180,428	1,649,754	987,488	662,266		1,651,338	22,500	12
735,918	1,119,071	646,450	472,621		767,779	22,500	13
1,143,631	1,723,801	962,172	641,629	120,000	1,263,819	38,695	14
108,522	461,024	458,435	2,589			27,000	15
44,121,064	76,907,632	41,951,069	23,576,563	11,380,000	42,402,609	2,876,510	
77,667,526	115,159,788	91,454,168	16,785,620	6,920,000		547,109	16
151,969,393	263,410,691	174,872,572	69,738,119	18,800,000	138,378,515	13,597,352	

and in reserve cities 25 per centum of circulation and deposit; since that date 15 per centum and 25 per

Number of State banks and trust companies, private bankers, and savings banks, with the
months ending

States and Territories.	State banks and trust companies.				Private		
	Banks	Capital.	Deposits.	Invested in U. S. bonds.	Banks.	Capital.	Deposits.
1 Maine	1		$2,340	$8,314	5	$47,319	$120,155
2 New Hampshire	1	$50,000	36,003	5,202	5	1,000	61,240
3 Vermont	5	350,000	1,607,553	36,984	1	3,790	16,025
4 Massachusetts	3	260,000	1,323,634	185,063	4	250,000	434,415
5 Boston	3	644,349	6,120,679	568,043	42	4,483,750	1,636,216
6 Rhode Island	15	3,074,385	3,611,242	630,543	7	234,119	334,718
7 Connecticut	12	2,476,896	3,767,165	254,312	10	140,000	1,146,936
New England States	40	6,855,630	16,408,616	1,668,460	74	5,159,888	3,743,705
8 New York	49	7,001,542	19,581,388	1,944,768	163	1,524,193	11,492,788
9 New York City	31	18,148,114	86,794,593	7,624,691	452	31,187,192	30,532,744
10 Albany	2	550,000	1,390,139	354,521	3	91,000	71,649
11 New Jersey	11	1,255,373	2,973,119	268,883	6	29,180	920
12 Pennsylvania	85	4,411,401	10,072,689	478,606	185	4,378,527	18,727,565
13 Philadelphia	15	762,175	25,234,689	81,876	42	1,346,729	4,104,001
14 Pittsburgh	21	3,270,897	5,215,545	653,938	6	334,382	1,474,866
15 Delaware	5	673,689	917,742	20,000	1	2,000	1,824
16 Maryland	4	455,841	441,036	251,189	3	98,508	143,185
17 Baltimore	11	2,447,511	2,274,006	106,863	18	667,256	2,072,366
18 Washington					6	357,060	2,988,231
Middle States	234	38,976,546	154,894,971	11,782,335	885	40,005,937	71,510,139
19 Virginia	54	2,321,590	5,137,229	270,208	20	374,472	2,061,637
20 West Virginia	17	1,177,128	3,089,199	87,468	3	70,000	915,514
21 North Carolina	9	747,894	1,477,46		4	42,427	119,216
22 South Carolina	4	295,000	611,067	52,333	9	216,499	47,745
23 Georgia	27	3,634,625	4,341,983		29	433,054	683,840
24 Florida					8	81,830	272,706
25 Alabama	6	615,000	1,012,426		20	425,241	1,287,221
26 Mississippi	17	644,205	1,441,669	123,758	16	439,485	1,193,246
27 Louisiana					3	126,265	87,343
28 New Orleans	3	2,723,698	4,632,122	643,013	8	53,333	
29 Texas	18	1,939,276	2,280,131	3,000	87	1,761,804	4,052,620
30 Arkansas	2	133,000	412,310	71,017	13	112,110	165,318
31 Kentucky	49	5,705,038	5,902,969	218,553	22	394,628	1,795,145
32 Louisville	12	5,040,444	5,116,149	471,197	3	206,584	087,524
33 Tennessee	23	1,697,764	3,050,686	112,388	7	71,464	172,054
Southern States	241	26,694,662	38,505,356	2,055,955	252	4,809,796	13,541,159
34 Ohio	31	1,278,058	3,132,931	163,656	213	4,361,082	17,001,516
35 Cincinnati	4	626,769	1,350,032	20,882	8	775,472	3,042,679
36 Cleveland	3	940,924	4,198,909	623,837	5	105,000	826,104
37 Indiana	27	1,201,244	2,169,517	88,268	103	3,164,190	9,590,096
38 Illinois	25	987,034	3,228,683	117,717	286	3,042,881	13,282,590
39 Chicago	10	3,681,114	8,816,734	2,398,878	23	586,381	3,736,770
40 Michigan	31	1,337,700	3,378,821	88,073	124	1,009,099	3,727,131
41 Detroit	5	710,000	4,819,999	329,602	8	206,041	8,6,455
42 Wisconsin	28	785,614	2,654,682	112,477	81	793,229	3,309,346
43 Milwaukee	5	473,201	6,252,203	13,480	4	161,500	1,536,607
44 Iowa	60	2,521,985	6,100,307	222,112	245	2,533,754	7,017,806
45 Minnesota	22	971,307	1,911,978	51,924	70	933,068	2,814,325
46 Missouri	95	3,167,050	10,308,654	325,025	75	1,083,125	4,946,562
47 St. Louis	18	5,250,582	10,074,610	849,920	10	454,973	614,089
48 Kansas	31	767,707	1,810,416	47,883	117	796,437	3,066,734
49 Nebraska	12	192,032	480,354		71	461,458	1,539,460
50 Colorado	7	259,250	545,512		31	325,667	2,934,365
Western States	414	25,151,600	70,346,491	5,454,733	1,474	20,845,757	70,805,653
51 Nevada	4	108,000	98,560	...	9	256,457	735,988
52 California	58	8,283,006	11,269,822	197,341	20	466,913	818,952
53 San Francisco	5	7,901,233	18,199,412	3,319,780	12	2,083,317	7,912,530
54 Oregon					14	1,203,466	974,571
55 Arizona					5	112,032	243,673
56 Dakota					18	127,511	396,279
57 Idaho					2	5,358	18,308
58 Montana					13	416,700	724,031
59 New Mexico					5	6,967	181,925
60 Utah					11	206,809	1,231,952
61 Washington					4	257,900	525,119
62 Wyoming					4	128,054	271,201
Pacific States and Territories	67	16,292,239	29,567,794	3,517,121	117	5,300,583	14,036,579
United States	996	113,970,677	318,783,228	24,498,604	2,802	76,121,961	182,657,235

average amount of their capital, deposits, and investments in United States bonds, for the six May 31, 1880.

bankers. Invested in U.S. bonds.	Banks.	Capital.	Deposits.	Invested in U.S. bonds.	Banks.	Capital.	Deposits.	Invested in U.S. bonds.	
	58	....	$21,599,469	$3,284,637	64	$47,319	$21,721,964	$3,292,950	1
....	65	....	28,204,308	919,297	71	51,000	28,301,540	924,499	2
....	16	....	6,907,562	653,862	22	353,700	8,531,140	690,846	3
$93,550	154	....	142,510,224	13,633,993	161	510,000	144,208,273	13,857,606	4
1,964,018	12	....	56,796,871	6,499,110	57	5,128,099	64,553,706	9,051,771	5
7,045	34	....	39,188,748	4,570,369	56	3,308,504	43,184,708	5,207,937	6
18,420	83	....	73,549,860	8,131,932	105	2,616,896	78,457,961	8,404,664	7
2,043,033	422	....	368,757,040	37,693,200	536	12,015,518	388,969,361	41,430,293	
353,430	91	....	131,291,297	45,993,290	303	8,525,645	162,275,473	48,203,488	8
7,525,342	23	....	174,560,730	73,737,079	506	49,335,306	291,914,072	88,890,112	9
3,000	7	....	12,289,861	2,552,905	12	641,000	13,751,649	2,910,426	10
800	34	$40,000	17,417,079	5,871,992	51	1,324,558	20,391,118	6,141,675	11
274,180	1	....	270,878	70,000	271	8,789,931	29,071,132	822,786	12
117,527	4	....	22,157,680	8,472,097	61	2,108,904	51,496,370	6,471,500	13
7,425	4	458,300	7,961,178	1,679,366	31	4,053,579	74,651,589	2,340,729	14
....	2	....	1,207,860	....	8	673,689	2,127,426	20,000	15
....	5	10,085	235,793	13,538	12	564,434	819,944	264,727	16
293,037	9	20,075	21,467,697	9,890,353	38	3,134,842	25,814,319	10,200,253	17
280,758	1	....	317,044	20,535	7	357,060	3,305,875	310,293	18
8,782,499	181	528,460	389,183,857	146,301,155	1,300	79,510,943	615,618,967	166,865,989	
24,000	2	340,912	558,336	....	76	3,046,974	7,757,202	294,208	19
50,000	....	....	....	....	20	1,247,128	4,054,743	137,488	20
....	....	....	....	....	13	790,321	1,596,632	....	21
....	....	....	....	....	13	511,499	658,812	52,333	22
18,050	2	....	885,004	1,000	58	4,088,279	5,910,827	19,050	23
....	1	2,000	14,583	....	9	83,870	287,289	....	24
742	....	....	....	....	26	1,040,241	2,269,647	742	25
85,600	....	....	....	....	33	1,083,690	2,634,915	209,338	26
45,000	....	....	....	....	3	126,265	887,313	45,000	27
....	....	....	....	....	11	2,777,031	4,632,122	643,013	28
160,133	....	....	....	....	105	3,701,080	1,332,751	163,133	29
1,085	....	....	....	....	15	245,110	577,628	75,102	30
88,426	....	....	....	....	71	6,099,666	7,608,114	300,979	31
....	....	....	....	....	15	5,267,028	5,803,673	471,197	32
13,000	....	....	....	....	30	1,760,228	3,222,740	125,988	33
486,036	5	342,912	1,457,923	1,000	498	31,547,370	53,504,438	2,542,991	
703,819	4	65,000	697,202	86,959	248	5,704,140	20,834,648	954,434	34
254,789	....	....	....	....	12	1,402,241	4,392,711	275,671	35
54,532	....	....	8,940,548	2,151,270	9	1,045,924	13,905,571	2,829,610	36
419,685	14	....	1,413,171	42,061	144	4,305,434	13,172,783	550,014	37
557,889	5	62,400	550,515	60,000	316	4,092,314	17,061,788	735,606	38
160,945	1	5,000	10,570	....	34	4,272,405	12,581,083	2,559,823	39
65,921	....	....	....	....	155	2,316,799	7,105,952	154,891	40
16,050	1	150,000	1,867,594	134,267	14	1,606,041	7,514,048	480,000	41
72,384	....	....	....	....	109	1,578,848	5,964,028	184,781	42
2,425	....	....	....	....	9	634,731	7,788,900	15,914	43
97,704	4	48,167	208,018	....	309	5,153,996	13,726,191	319,876	44
68,044	3	....	273,847	....	95	1,906,375	5,000,150	119,968	45
103,183	....	....	....	....	170	4,250,175	15,307,216	428,208	46
23,455	....	....	....	....	28	885,555	18,688,609	873,395	47
42,514	....	....	....	....	148	1,564,144	4,871,150	90,397	48
39,492	....	....	....	....	83	653,890	2,019,814	39,492	49
....	....	....	....	....	34	584,917	3,470,877	....	50
2,682,821	33	330,567	13,961,465	2,474,537	1,921	46,327,924	173,113,609	10,612,111	
100,000	....	....	....	....	17	364,457	814,548	100,000	51
....	....	7	680,710	2,839,944	85	9,430,029	14,928,718	197,241	52
120,272	....	9	2,119,796	41,385,352	2,711,604	26	12,101,546	67,497,201	6,160,656	53
113,423	....	1	41,742	58,532	6,300	15	1,245,208	1,053,103	118,723	54
25,000	....	....	....	....	5	112,932	243,673	25,000	55
....	....	....	....	....	18	127,511	398,279	....	56
....	....	....	....	....	2	5,358	18,368	....	57
....	....	....	....	....	33	446,708	724,631	....	58
....	....	....	....	....	5	6,607	181,925	....	59
....	....	....	....	....	11	266,000	1,233,952	....	60
....	....	....	....	....	4	257,000	525,109	....	61
....	....	....	....	....	4	128,054	271,201	....	62
366,695	17	2,842,248	44,283,828	2,717,904	201	24,435,070	87,888,201	6,601,720	
14,366,684	658	4,044,187	817,644,113	186,187,816	4,456	194,136,825	1,319,094,576	228,053,104	

Number of State banks and trust companies, private bankers, and savings banks, with the months ending

States and Territories.	State banks and trust companies.				Private		
	Banks.	Capital.	Deposits.	Invested in U. S. bonds.	Banks.	Capital.	Deposits.
1 Maine	2	...	$77,409	......	7	$53,200	$169,764
2 New Hampshire	1	$50,000	25,658	$1,375	4	1,000	45,234
3 Vermont	6	350,000	2,057,666	113,748	1	2,804	17,267
4 Massachusetts	3	260,000	1,977,822	167,614	3	50,000	539,028
5 Boston	3	790,633	8,153,354	592,798	47	4,065,097	2,570,068
6 Rhode Island	15	3,361,608	4,212,867	909,584	7	358,181	462,268
7 Connecticut	11	2,451,600	4,463,846	132,725	12	168,500	1,359,079
New England States.	41	7,263,841	20,968,622	1,917,844	80	4,698,782	5,162,708
8 New York	48	7,211,333	25,277,222	1,832,351	163	1,531,347	12,699,067
9 New York City	31	20,527,888	105,898,639	6,987,938	508	45,482,515	45,414,376
10 Albany	2	66,000	182,579	......	3	550,000	1,611,470
11 New Jersey	10	1,167,685	3,487,561	323,675	5	26,231	1,560
12 Pennsylvania	73	3,718,015	11,500,119	388,685	172	4,140,679	19,978,585
13 Philadelphia	18	768,280	33,648,619	48,033	52	1,890,614	6,174,785
14 Pittsburgh	18	2,922,125	3,943,543	623,348	7	563,910	2,025,477
15 Delaware	4	604,501	844,743	10,009	1	5,000	19,183
16 Maryland	4	447,812	548,605	256,675	2	49,177	43,742
17 Baltimore	10	1,846,816	2,346,610	36,189	19	773,657	2,389,032
18 Washington					6	364,000	3,747,703
Middle States	218	39,280,513	189,777,240	10,506,894	938	55,397,130	94,104,080
19 Virginia	53	2,280,452	6,371,435	208,136	18	369,792	2,103,077
20 West Virginia	16	1,158,983	3,313,510	66,790	3	70,000	992,802
21 North Carolina	9	463,807	1,063,523	59	4	40,833	102,240
22 South Carolina	4	305,000	1,553,145	45,000	8	229,956	53,921
23 Georgia	22	2,959,758	3,961,950	......	30	478,910	1,308,131
24 Florida					6	90,079	521,660
25 Alabama	6	615,000	1,109,300	......	21	564,085	1,372,342
26 Mississippi	17	675,293	1,311,167	122,693	11	314,579	833,326
27 Louisiana					3	146,329	35,812
28 New Orleans	7	2,237,808	5,147,188	395,161	5	32,000	
29 Texas	13	1,487,013	1,777,789	......	107	2,560,951	7,033,240
30 Arkansas	3	130,236	495,204	65,230	11	87,066	184,305
31 Kentucky	52	5,683,563	7,065,484	91,177	23	368,731	1,936,815
32 Louisville	12	4,907,554	5,903,321	249,922	3	178,000	728,464
33 Tennessee	20	1,748,019	3,356,247	199,763	5	48,517	118,240
Southern States	240	24,712,481	42,429,163	1,443,922	258	5,588,828	17,323,504
34 Ohio	28	1,225,363	3,390,421	162,308	213	4,119,220	19,931,774
35 Cincinnati	4	562,150	1,558,046	60,004	8	812,167	3,864,817
36 Cleveland	3	1,004,667	4,876,469	491,161	4	55,000	969,898
37 Indiana	24	1,301,220	2,291,526	40,190	106	3,130,268	11,570,164
38 Illinois	14	320,682	1,301,320	26,383	310	4,183,346	21,856,149
39 Chicago	7	1,051,600	8,793,445	1,001,700	24	2,004,197	10,455,069
40 Michigan	22	1,150,704	3,404,975	42,227	137	1,213,796	5,218,413
41 Detroit	6	732,772	5,587,273	300,367	7	161,256	945,660
42 Wisconsin	29	982,117	5,204,809	95,256	79	848,746	4,901,883
43 Milwaukee	4	373,231	6,954,542	1,717	4	64,667	530,047
44 Iowa	58	2,635,731	7,975,671	291,564	276	2,975,737	10,388,843
45 Minnesota	20	2,196,744	4,475,937	23,774	89	679,227	2,772,567
46 Missouri	101	3,245,850	14,816,825	339,742	81	1,120,294	6,843,267
47 St. Louis	19	5,501,723	24,807,740	339,419	11	261,302	304,976
48 Kansas	40	920,390	2,342,089	30,937	135	1,001,172	4,676,393
49 Nebraska	12	269,072	607,795	......	86	675,300	2,053,586
50 Colorado	8	355,613	1,159,507	5,000	51	547,827	2,705,441
Western States	399	24,757,047	99,847,750	3,251,769	1,621	23,853,472	109,481,990
51 Nevada	6	89,000	617,119	......	9	92,85	637,530
52 California	57	7,778,073	12,405,968	254,290	22	387,709	1,022,592
53 San Francisco	7	8,796,011	18,816,574	4,219,649	9	1,275,018	8,271,600
54 Oregon	4	436,344	461,049	6,500	12	436,500	973,519
55 Arizona	4	80,000	108,669	50,000	5	67,319	436,587
56 Dakota					37	216,263	484,345
57 Idaho					2	6,561	19,697
58 Montana					14	512,706	904,498
59 New Mexico					8	13,333	459,518
60 Utah	2	51,000	97,808		10	157,225	1,484,711
61 Washington					9	284,050	657,015
62 Wyoming					4	135,208	421,310
Pacific States and Territories	86	17,180,428	32,597,187	4,530,239	141	3,785,643	15,772,372
United States	978	113,194,310	385,619,962	21,650,668	3,038	93,328,855	241,845,554

average amount of their capital, deposits, and investments in United States bonds, for the six
May 31, 1881.

bankers.					Savings banks.		Total.			
Invested in U. S. bonds.	Banks.	Capital.	Deposits.	Invested in U. S. bonds.	Banks.	Capital.	Deposits.	Invested in U. S. bonds.		
$9,906	57	....	$24,116,117	$4,049,652	64	$53,200	$24,363,290	$4,056,618	1
....	67	$25,000	32,099,232	738,716	72	76,000	32,189,124	740,091	2
....	16	....	7,971,977	584,777	22	352,804	10,046,950	622,525	3
16,667	157	....	102,120,082	14,485,728	163	310,000	164,637,832	14,670,009	4
1,003,343	12	....	59,921,155	5,720,483	62	4,855,730	70,644,577	7,316,624	5
32,613	33	....	38,364,066	4,228,338	55	3,719,789	43,049,201	5,170,535	6
8,963	83	....	78,466,347	6,909,101	106	2,620,101	84,289,272	7,049,889	7
1,067,652	425	25,000	403,052,876	36,640,795	546	11,987,623	429,184,206	39,626,291	
304,268	89	....	149,650,176	54,828,091	300	8,762,680	183,626,465	37,094,710	8
9,670,751	24	....	192,417,560	83,257,940	563	66,010,403	347,830,575	99,916,629	9
351,000	7	....	13,981,392	2,964,825	11	646,000	15,775,441	3,315,825	10
333	33	45,000	20,388,409	7,729,081	48	1,238,914	23,877,530	8,053,089	11
288,461	1	....	369,457	67,850	246	7,858,694	31,947,161	744,996	12
224,208	4	....	25,007,693	6,534,649	74	2,658,804	64,831,097	6,806,890	13
20,374	5	533,300	9,918,603	2,372,208	30	4,019,335	17,887,623	3,015,930	14
.. ....	2	....	1,435,466	....	7	609,561	2,299,392	10,000	15
....	5	10,055	295,395	10,976	11	507,074	887,742	267,651	16
195,384	10	20,225	23,123,778	10,749,845	39	2,640,698	27,859,420	10,981,418	17
287,029	1	....	397,172	31,585	7	364,000	4,144,875	318,614	18
11,401,808	181	608,610	433,085,101	168,617,050	1,327	95,280,253	716,907,321	190,525,752	
35,000	3	418,741	813,449	21,689	74	3,068,985	9,286,961	264,825	19
35,617	....	....	....	....	19	1,228,983	4,306,402	102,407	20
....	....	....	....	....	13	504,640	1,165,763	50	21
....	2	15,000	307,201	....	14	549,956	1,914,267	45,000	22
7,000	2	....	929,082	....	54	3,438,668	6,199,163	7,000	23
....	1	2,000	17,750	....	7	101,079	539,449	....	24
800	....	....	....	....	27	1,179,085	2,481,642	800	25
48,280	....	....	....	....	28	989,872	2,144,493	170,973	26
80,000	....	....	....	....	3	146,329	35,812	30,000	27
....	1	2,129	2,397	....	13	2,271,932	5,149,585	395,161	28
14,000	....	....	....	....	120	4,047,964	8,811,029	14,000	29
1,250	....	....	....	....	14	217,302	679,509	66,480	30
80,000	....	....	....	....	75	6,052,294	9,002,299	171,177	31
....	....	....	....	....	15	5,145,554	6,631,685	240,922	32
11,833	....	....	....	....	31	1,796,536	3,474,487	211,506	33
263,780	9	437,870	2,069,879	21,689	507	30,739,179	61,822,546	1,729,391	
636,222	5	165,000	4,173,782	118,369	246	5,509,583	24,495,977	936,899	34
280,295	....	....	....	....	13	1,374,317	5,421,863	340,299	35
8,307	1	....	10,021,320	2,133,583	8	1,059,607	15,861,757	2,633,711	36
571,929	15	....	1,716,510	122,645	145	4,433,488	15,878,206	734,834	37
1,248,738	6	75,350	946,035	85,234	330	4,579,374	23,903,504	1,357,305	38
172,589	2	10,000	67,515	24,648	33	3,905,197	10,316,023	1,198,937	39
74,461	2	75,000	393,671	550	161	2,415,500	9,017,659	117,241	40
7,533	1	150,000	2,586,087	202,292	14	1,014,028	9,419,629	509,992	41
111,960	....	....	....	....	108	1,830,863	10,106,752	207,194	42
359	....	....	....	....	8	437,898	7,484,589	2,067	43
67,287	3	40,000	228,281	2,125	337	5,671,468	18,592,795	360,976	44
45,848	3	....	506,510	....	112	2,875,971	7,751,414	69,622	45
134,142	....	....	....	....	182	4,366,103	21,660,092	478,884	46
44,406	....	....	....	....	30	5,761,025	25,112,676	383,825	47
82,000	....	....	....	....	175	1,921,571	6,418,482	63,537	48
14,070	....	....	....	....	98	944,372	2,661,291	14,070	49
15,000	....	....	....	....	59	903,440	3,864,948	20,000	50
3,483,180	38	515,350	17,639,717	2,689,446	2,058	49,125,869	226,969,457	9,424,395	
100,000	....	....	....	....	15	381,851	1,254,649	100,000	51
....	4	681,965	2,233,524	....	52	8,847,747	15,662,084	254,290	52
104,074	8	1,951,243	41,892,395	6,911,198	24	11,953,172	68,980,629	11,234,921	53
250,000	....	....	....	....	16	892,844	1,431,568	256,300	54
....	....	....	....	....	9	147,319	635,256	50,000	55
....	....	....	....	....	37	216,203	484,345	....	56
....	....	....	....	....	2	6,561	19,097	....	57
....	....	....	....	....	14	512,706	904,498	....	58
....	....	....	....	....	8	13,333	459,518	....	59
....	....	....	....	....	12	208,225	1,582,519	....	60
....	....	....	....	....	9	284,050	657,015	....	61
....	....	....	....	....	4	135,208	421,310	....	62
454,074	12	2,633,208	44,125,919	6,911,198	233	23,599,279	92,493,478	11,895,511	
16,670,494	665	4,220,038	899,973,492	214,880,178	4,681	210,738,203	1,527,439,008	253,201,340	

Number of State banks and trust companies, private bankers, and savings banks, with the months ending

States and Territories.	State banks and trust companies.				Private.		
	Banks.	Capital.	Deposits.	Invested in U. S. bonds.	Banks.	Capital.	Deposits.
1 Maine	1	.....	$9,272	....	10	$88,125	$224,909
2 New Hampshire	1	$50,000	25,541	....	2	....	256
3 Vermont	6	450,000	2,629,483	$210,000	1	....	22,001
4 Massachusetts	3	200,000	2,156,705	4,405	3	64,167	618,206
5 Boston	4	1,850,000	10,828,462	555,325	64	6,088,250	5,980,301
6 Rhode Island	14	3,174,035	4,379,082	810,417	8	412,496	553,489
7 Connecticut	11	2,540,308	4,934,177	83,377	16	477,158	2,018,460
New England States	40	8,324,343	24,966,722	1,663,524	104	7,130,196	9,417,712
8 New York	52	7,431,333	31,281,778	1,788,506	162	1,753,420	15,152,959
9 New York City	31	21,355,841	130,220,901	7,239,463	536	51,654,464	56,364,207
10 Albany	2	550,000	1,674,602	351,000	3	91,000	85,707
11 New Jersey	10	1,183,491	4,047,185	418,644	4	16,710	341
12 Pennsylvania	63	3,760,025	13,329,320	616,576	203	4,295,918	24,780,177
13 Philadelphia	16	728,105	35,300,119	42,900	50	2,040,877	6,097,791
14 Pittsburgh	16	2,834,696	5,770,173	626,174	10	785,754	3,278,514
15 Delaware	4	554,686	958,305	6,667	1	5,000	7,132
16 Maryland	4	456,835	480,104	244,075	2	37,837	31,386
17 Baltimore...........	7	1,707,780	2,445,706	38,202	35	1,104,268	2,942,802
18 Washington	....	......	......	......	8	408,517	4,338,716
Middle States......	205	40,562,792	225,506,253	11,372,207	1,014	62,193,765	113,079,792
19 Virginia	54	2,369,397	7,779,008	197,686	19	410,590	2,378,429
20 West Virginia	18	1,145,057	3,970,727	104,500	3	40,000	1,195,100
21 North Carolina	10	510,534	1,154,273	....	5	56,667	110,750
22 South Carolina......	4	405,000	1,774,087	51,667	8	189,577	63,432
23 Georgia.............	22	2,970,333	4,517,393	....	30	561,667	951,045
24 Florida	....	......	......	....	9	131,521	884,965
25 Alabama............	6	615,000	2,046,648	....	23	576,175	1,792,676
26 Mississippi	17	659,824	1,620,183	111,583	10	372,537	1,017,893
27 Louisiana..........	....	......	......	....	3	132,286	80,235
28 New Orleans........	4	2,213,700	5,586,109	557,302	10	71,000	1,082
29 Texas	15	1,978,679	3,357,246	26,619	123	2,708,364	7,224,606
30 Arkansas..........	5	112,167	206,712	17,981	16	176,676	529,125
31 Kentucky	52	5,577,074	6,530,576	73,311	25	662,368	2,779,621
32 Louisville	13	5,090,596	6,858,511	465,185	3	180,500	709,290
33 Tennessee	26	1,725,292	3,063,792	29,981	6	99,773	312,193
Southern States ...	246	25,372,053	48,465,265	1,635,815	293	6,369,701	19,931,042
34 Ohio	22	996,856	3,667,715	121,135	221	4,294,085	23,709,057
35 Cincinnati	2	300,000	1,156,458	64,156	11	686,994	2,869,514
36 Cleveland	2	1,053,435	5,545,652	400,000	5	77,000	1,509,202
37 Indiana............	22	1,333,696	2,582,609	197,814	118	3,286,507	14,069,359
38 Illinois	14	605,876	2,581,150	73,167	207	3,735,378	24,328,452
39 Chicago	7	2,697,573	11,914,114	1,158,567	27	8,604,848	10,916,243
40 Michigan..........	19	975,372	4,954,348	55,100	149	1,407,597	6,390,293
41 Detroit	6	805,164	6,934,957	216,383	7	161,541	1,095,922
42 Wisconsin	31	942,930	5,773,209	74,999	85	780,952	4,317,006
43 Milwaukee	5	473,231	9,072,025	3,366	4	160,000	2,362,465
44 Iowa	53	2,290,823	7,578,034	204,390	315	4,186,651	16,703,207
45 Minnesota	23	2,291,842	6,495,137	22,200	109	992,068	4,446,316
46 Missouri	118	4,306,632	17,706,715	528,940	89	1,263,396	6,961,756
47 St. Louis ...'	19	5,081,333	28,527,263	47,229	11	295,351	246,285
48 Kansas	54	1,216,801	2,742,402	35,929	164	1,639,912	5,046,452
49 Nebraska..........	28	555,731	1,301,035	....	126	931,366	3,046,989
50 Colorado...........	14	558,401	2,477,522	10,000	48	629,939	2,469,192
Western States...	439	26,486,256	120,170,435	3,213,375	1,786	33,127,362	131,117,831
51 Nevada............	5	97,363	359,627	....	7	215,445	779,056
52 California	53	7,190,822	13,811,198	976,635	25	352,006	1,309,128
53 San Francisco	10	8,540,142	16,959,847	4,349,874	12	2,630,465	10,863,554
54 Oregon	3	88,175	515,184	....	17	863,367	2,370,681
55 Arizona	4	47,167	326,019	....	11	81,889	536,727
56 Dakota	5	39,435	29,249	....	61	392,789	810,324
57 Idaho	....	......	......	....	6	11,575	57,390
58 Montana............	....	......	......	....	15	579,858	1,433,947
59 New Mexico........	....	......	......	....	11	25,927	793,359
60 Utah	2	57,994	860,577	....	9	278,464	1,259,082
61 Washington	....	......	......	....	15	418,957	1,408,857
62 Wyoming	....	......	......	....	5	193,426	772,078
Pacific States and Territories	82	16,061,068	52,891,701	5,326,509	194	5,434,868	21,995,783
United States........	1,012	116,806,512	452,002,376	23,211,430	3,391	114,255,892	295,622,160

average amount of their capital, deposits, and investments in United States bonds, for the six
May 31, 1882.

bankers.	Savings banks.				Total.				
Invested in U. S. bonds.	Banks.	Capital.	Deposits.	Invested in U. S. bonds.	Banks.	Capital.	Deposits.	Invested in U. S. bonds.	
$15,113	56	.....	$27,172,630	$5,293,227	67	$58,125	$27,406,711	$5,314,340	1
....	65	$94,250	36,630,394	602,414	65	141,250	36,656,791	602,414	2
....	16	.....	9,249,045	502,598	23	450,000	11,900,529	712,598	3
34,309	153	.....	161,344,850	12,587,172	159	321,167	164,119,761	12,625,886	4
871,395	14	.....	64,187,146	7,309,254	82	7,938,250	80,945,999	8,726,974	5
52,983	33	.....	41,647,644	4,504,880	55	3,586,531	46,580,215	5,368,280	6
7,571	83	.....	81,938,327	6,256,080	110	3,017,466	88,894,964	6,341,028	7
981,371	420	94,250	422,126,536	37,046,625	561	15,548,789	456,504,970	39,601,520	
493,976	89	.....	159,564,970	68,542,916	303	9,184,753	205,999,707	65,825,398	8
7,846,422	24	.....	209,919,780	89,965,526	591	73,010,305	396,504,448	105,051,411	9
....	7	.....	15,416,751	4,185,189	12	641,000	17,177,120	4,536,189	10
73	32	55,000	26,304,884	10,111,406	46	1,255,201	30,442,410	10,530,123	11
227,954	1	.....	453,744	65,700	267	8,955,943	38,563,241	910,230	12
77,738	4	.....	28,788,501	7,453,283	70	2,768,982	70,186,411	7,573,021	13
54,712	3	526,383	10,945,882	3,249,803	31	4,146,833	19,994,569	3,940,689	14
....	2	.....	1,597,886	.....	7	559,486	2,563,323	6,667	15
....	5	10,085	325,989	10,976	11	504,757	837,479	255,051	16
177,107	10	20,350	24,437,120	11,159,458	52	2,832,398	29,825,628	11,374,767	17
326,634	2	225	483,205	31,585	10	408,742	4,821,921	358,219	18
9,204,616	181	612,043	478,328,212	189,775,842	1,400	103,368,000	816,916,257	210,352,065	
40,000	3	411,783	1,083,348	.....	76	3,191,770	11,240,785	237,686	19
32,108	.....	.....	.....	.....	21	1,185,057	5,105,817	136,608	20
....	.....	.....	.....	.....	15	567,201	1,265,023	.....	21
....	1	30,000	4,332	.....	13	624,577	1,841,852	51,667	22
6,000	2	.....	1,146,692	.....	54	3,532,000	6,615,730	6,000	23
....	1	2,000	62,477	.....	10	133,521	897,412	.....	24
500	.....	.....	.....	.....	29	1,191,175	3,839,324	500	25
36,907	.....	.....	.....	.....	27	1,032,361	2,638,076	148,490	26
....	.....	.....	.....	.....	3	132,286	80,235	.....	27
....	1	83,727	79,486	.....	15	2,368,427	5,666,677	557,302	28
11,175	.....	.....	.....	.....	138	4,686,443	10,581,852	37,794	29
62,911	.....	.....	.....	.....	21	288,843	735,837	80,022	30
21,083	.....	.....	.....	.....	77	6,239,442	9,310,197	94,394	31
....	.....	.....	.....	.....	16	5,271,096	7,567,801	465,185	32
16,417	.....	.....	.....	.....	32	1,825,065	3,375,985	46,398	33
227,131	8	527,510	2,376,336	.....	547	32,269,264	70,822,643	1,862,946	
784,737	6	189,029	1,520,154	198,924	249	5,480,570	28,896,926	1,104,796	34
203,858	1	.....	81,654	.....	14	986,994	4,107,626	268,014	35
14,210	1	.....	11,452,182	1,739,022	8	1,130,435	18,597,036	2,153,232	36
706,965	14	.....	1,990,547	76,100	154	4,620,203	18,642,315	980,879	37
634,845	6	42,500	1,651,672	118,233	317	4,383,254	28,561,274	826,245	38
235,787	2	9,000	132,257	38,455	36	11,311,191	22,902,614	1,432,807	39
147,207	2	30,000	206,322	2,150	170	2,412,969	11,190,963	201,457	40
5,750	1	150,000	3,189,367	181,828	14	1,117,705	11,280,247	403,961	41
69,816	.....	.....	.....	.....	116	1,723,882	10,090,305	144,815	42
3,812	.....	.....	.....	.....	9	633,281	11,424,490	7,178	43
321,310	3	40,000	274,612	.....	371	6,517,474	24,555,913	525,700	44
18,413	4	.....	942,701	.....	136	3,283,910	11,924,154	40,613	45
218,696	.....	.....	.....	.....	207	5,570,028	24,668,471	747,636	46
45,825	.....	.....	.....	.....	30	5,376,684	28,773,518	93,054	47
435,531	.....	.....	.....	.....	218	2,850,780	7,788,854	471,460	48
38,237	.....	.....	.....	.....	154	1,487,097	4,348,024	38,237	49
1,500	.....	.....	.....	.....	62	1,188,310	4,946,714	11,500	50
3,886,499	40	461,129	21,441,468	2,354,710	2,265	60,074,747	272,759,734	9,454,584	
100,000	.....	.....	.....	.....	12	312,778	1,139,283	100,000	51
....	3	428,057	2,128,976	25,699	81	7,970,885	17,249,302	1,602,334	52
152,956	8	1,744,583	44,678,418	12,825,906	30	12,315,190	72,501,819	17,328,736	53
265,250	.....	.....	.....	.....	20	951,512	2,915,865	265,250	54
2,667	.....	.....	.....	.....	15	129,056	862,746	2,667	55
....	.....	.....	.....	.....	66	432,224	839,573	.....	56
....	.....	.....	.....	.....	6	11,575	57,390	.....	57
....	.....	.....	.....	.....	15	570,858	1,434,947	.....	58
....	.....	.....	.....	.....	11	25,927	793,359	.....	59
47,755	.....	.....	.....	.....	11	336,458	2,119,659	47,755	60
2,500	.....	.....	.....	.....	15	418,657	1,008,857	2,500	61
....	.....	.....	.....	.....	5	193,426	772,078	.....	62
571,128	11	2,172,040	46,807,394	12,851,605	287	23,668,576	101,694,878	18,749,242	
14,870,745	600	3,867,572	971,073,946	242,928,782	5,063	284,929,976	1,718,698,482	230,110,957	

Number of State banks and trust companies, private bankers, and savings banks, with the months ending

States and Territories.	State banks and trust companies.				Private		
	Banks.	Capital.	Deposits.	Invested in U. S. bonds.	Banks.	Capital.	Deposits.
1 Maine					9	$83,343	$256,080
2 New Hampshire	1	$50,000	$26,099				
3 Vermont	6	450,600	2,959,123	$175,233	1		20,097
4 Massachusetts	3	260,000	2,310,348	7,015	3	68,333	572,673
5 Boston	4	1,850,000	11,895,403	555,249	61	5,439,589	3,621,863
6 Rhode Island	13	2,809,444	9,005,582	800,000	7	406,539	577,740
7 Connecticut	13	2,870,600	5,503,432	42	13	217,893	1,519,857
New England States	40	8,296,044	31,637,987	1,537,539	94	6,215,637	6,568,310
8 New York	53	7,661,046	31,456,891	1,738,697	116	1,742,899	15,556,555
9 New York City	33	21,030,532	143,742,564	6,649,176	506	51,758,575	55,565,884
10 Albany	2	550,000	1,769,771	951,800	3	91,000	17,592
11 New Jersey	10	1,219,175	4,172,632	405,075	4	16,026	1,119
12 Pennsylvania	65	3,877,327	14,841,439	424,189	189	4,248,463	24,174,291
13 Philadelphia	16	760,271	37,026,174	42,900	44	2,206,728	6,738,522
14 Pittsburgh	17	2,794,971	7,030,947	618,348	8	755,312	2,922,571
15 Delaware	4	506,686	1,061,025		1	5,000	8,519
16 Maryland	3	436,793	447,027	240,625	3	39,025	36,149
17 Baltimore	7	1,707,780	2,469,845	38,202	35	1,126,748	3,037,799
18 Washington					8	428,450	4,611,745
Middle States	210	40,604,581	244,017,706	10,507,612	967	62,418,206	112,690,656
19 Virginia	65	2,244,559	7,664,815	119,741	17	381,991	2,914,803
20 West Virginia	18	1,150,314	4,035,793	36,291	3	40,000	1,158,647
21 North Carolina	11	566,026	936,711		5	58,333	83,728
22 South Carolina	4	415,000	1,959,169	59,000	9	177,207	58,122
23 Georgia	21	2,845,433	3,176,132		29	652,177	1,117,969
24 Florida					9	153,874	962,202
25 Alabama	7	717,500	1,906,695		22	514,500	1,530,913
26 Mississippi	17	614,590	1,175,794	31,500	11	423,615	949,095
27 Louisiana	1	7,500	3,667		4	158,536	55,907
28 New Orleans	4	2,213,700	4,628,934	202,025	11	85,667	692
29 Texas	14	1,785,590	3,283,417		124	2,881,555	8,251,624
30 Arkansas	6	256,973	493,801	117,038	16	118,568	249,633
31 Kentucky	53	5,756,800	6,721,715	22,250	22	395,396	2,244,248
32 Louisville	13	5,109,877	7,331,686	445,740	3	181,000	732,766
33 Tennessee	24	1,653,144	2,620,008	6,229	5	111,591	344,952
Southern States	248	25,337,055	45,938,357	1,040,714	289	6,334,090	20,675,301
34 Ohio	26	1,257,300	4,346,189	132,587	215	4,135,645	22,482,648
35 Cincinnati	2	300,000	1,693,727	26,254	11	673,496	2,600,855
36 Cleveland	3	1,118,333	6,330,405	405,369	5	52,000	1,359,130
37 Indiana	24	1,731,445	4,286,990	212,266	117	2,910,130	12,151,432
38 Illinois	13	754,186	3,235,214	100,548	337	3,654,239	24,591,579
39 Chicago	11	5,466,586	15,302,803	1,334,825	22	1,473,408	10,660,525
40 Michigan	19	1,007,120	4,029,014	48,376	152	1,424,515	7,064,720
41 Detroit	5	823,149	7,417,295	190,500	9	205,708	1,192,947
42 Wisconsin	32	976,762	5,964,034	25,256	87	764,904	4,405,467
43 Milwaukee	5	478,231	9,588,726	1,070	4	160,000	2,453,626
44 Iowa	61	2,740,674	9,393,150	303,796	321	4,200,584	11,580,124
45 Minnesota	26	2,554,115	7,779,219	25,583	116	1,000,781	4,770,307
46 Missouri	125	4,484,020	16,502,648	592,122	83	1,195,967	6,052,673
47 St. Louis	19	5,736,675	28,751,842	368,760	9	220,412	18,729
48 Kansas	59	1,404,849	2,967,604	30,587	161	1,323,412	5,595,708
49 Nebraska	37	740,328	1,521,620	50,556	149	1,044,974	3,369,134
50 Colorado	14	615,754	2,433,417	10,000	47	774,735	2,423,305
Western States	481	32,143,538	130,943,897	3,818,404	1,845	25,243,810	125,751,709
51 Nevada	5	77,300	262,382		7	191,434	724,663
52 California	60	7,835,590	16,832,311	1,290,652	27	364,260	1,701,252
53 San Francisco	6	8,530,333	19,010,692	3,902,369	10	1,509,102	8,910,782
54 Oregon	3	90,300	823,557		17	868,709	2,752,552
55 Arizona	1	25,000	149,865		10	105,248	679,988
56 Dakota	5	52,254	81,645		79	567,104	1,299,323
57 Idaho					10	39,947	181,471
58 Montana					17	525,727	1,546,824
59 New Mexico					13	25,417	929,000
60 Utah	2	143,682	296,891		9	216,103	2,274,675
61 Washington					13	466,414	1,221,654
62 Wyoming					5	214,805	1,061,393
Pacific States and Territories	82	16,754,459	37,460,443	5,193,021	217	5,094,490	23,271,602
United States	1,061	123,135,677	490,064,370	22,097,290	3,412	105,276,233	288,957,578

average amount of their capital, deposits, and investments in United States bonds, for the six November 30, 1882.

bankers. Invested in U.S. bonds.	Banks.	Capital	Deposits.	Invested in U.S. bonds.	Banks.	Capital.	Deposits.	Invested in U.S. bonds.	
$10,137	57	....	$29,009,220	$5,339,575	66	$83,343	$29,205,309	$5,349,712	1
....	65	$100,000	38,472,971	521,145	66	150,000	38,490,070	521,145	2
....	16	....	9,949,218	467,798	23	450,000	12,928,438	643,031	3
60,693	154	....	166,502,943	11,694,434	160	328,333	169,385,964	11,762,142	4
878,590	14	....	65,912,931	6,122,503	79	7,289,589	81,338,197	7,556,342	5
7,480	33	....	42,983,717	4,341,253	53	3,215,983	52,567,039	5,148,739	6
7,052	83	....	84,340,264	5,787,491	109	3,094,433	91,363,553	5,794,585	7
963,958	422	100,000	437,141,273	34,274,190	556	14,611,681	475,347,570	36,775,696	
446,821	89	....	161,154,094	58,824,572	308	9,403,935	211,167,540	61,009,490	8
7,926,345	23	....	216,964,102	87,280,284	562	72,789,107	416,272,550	101,856,005	9
....	7	....	15,914,020	3,889,173	12	641,000	17,701,383	4,249,153	10
61	30	57,500	25,654,735	8,591,146	44	1,292,701	29,827,886	8,996,282	11
218,107	2	....	767,743	99,633	256	8,125,790	39,783,464	741,320	12
73,914	4	....	29,747,052	6,367,917	64	2,966,999	73,531,748	6,484,731	13
54,878	4	525,000	11,307,805	3,026,942	29	4,075,283	21,351,353	3,700,168	14
....	2	....	1,670,800	....	7	571,686	2,749,353	....	15
....	6	30,135	358,070	10,976	12	505,953	841,246	251,601	16
183,365	10	20,396	25,122,461	11,010,351	52	2,854,914	30,660,015	11,231,918	17
324,037	2	399	553,743	31,585	10	428,819	5,145,488	355,622	18
9,227,728	179	633,400	492,323,664	179,131,959	1,356	103,656,187	849,032,026	198,867,299	
20,000	3	399,806	1,148,041	....	75	3,026,396	11,748,559	139,741	19
14,325	....	....	....	....	21	1,190,314	5,194,440	50,616	20
....	....	....	....	....	16	624,359	1,020,439	....	21
....	1	30,000	5,235	....	14	622,297	2,022,526	59,000	22
6,000	3	30,000	1,947,620	....	53	3,527,610	6,241,721	6,000	23
....	1	2,000	69,603	....	10	155,874	1,031,805	....	24
....	....	....	....	....	29	1,232,000	3,437,608	....	25
....	....	....	....	....	28	1,038,205	2,124,889	31,500	26
....	....	....	....	....	5	166,036	59,574	....	27
....	1	100,000	117,973	....	16	2,399,367	4,747,599	202,925	28
10,075	....	....	....	....	137	4,667,145	11,335,041	16,675	29
2,500	....	....	....	....	22	375,541	743,434	119,538	30
28,167	....	....	....	....	75	6,152,255	8,965,963	50,417	31
....	....	....	....	....	16	5,290,877	8,064,452	445,740	32
19,500	....	....	....	....	29	1,764,735	2,964,960	25,729	33
107,167	9	561,806	3,289,372	....	546	32,283,011	69,903,010	1,147,881	
557,442	6	235,000	1,702,765	166,011	247	5,625,145	28,531,602	856,040	34
143,683	1	....	85,255	....	14	973,096	3,779,835	169,336	35
11,525	1	....	11,754,444	1,606,872	9	1,170,333	19,443,079	2,023,766	36
516,395	18	....	2,192,977	101,558	159	4,641,575	18,541,399	830,129	37
640,121	5	42,500	1,636,303	78,033	355	4,450,925	20,403,096	818,702	38
153,249	2	8,500	112,047	38,600	35	6,948,496	26,105,415	1,546,674	39
131,803	2	53,000	454,622	....	173	2,486,644	11,528,356	180,179	40
5,933	1	150,000	3,374,985	152,044	15	1,178,857	11,985,237	348,477	41
92,435	....	....	....	....	119	1,741,666	10,360,501	117,695	42
3,614	....	....	....	....	9	633,231	12,021,752	4,684	43
216,551	4	48,333	394,814	....	386	6,089,591	24,368,088	514,347	44
14,997	4	....	1,110,140	....	146	3,554,896	13,650,696	40,550	45
121,165	1	10,000	34,288	....	209	5,658,087	22,589,009	653,287	46
35,838	....	....	....	....	28	5,957,087	28,770,571	404,598	47
36,685	....	....	....	....	220	2,728,261	8,563,312	67,272	48
35,512	....	....	....	....	186	1,745,362	4,890,754	86,068	49
....	....	....	....	....	61	1,390,489	4,656,722	10,000	50
2,710,262	45	549,333	22,772,688	2,143,118	2,371	57,906,681	279,468,204	8,671,784	
105,000	....	....	....	....	12	268,734	987,075	105,000	51
7,987	3	428,748	2,214,169	55,000	90	8,628,599	20,717,792	1,354,619	52
149,637	8	1,746,873	45,969,257	14,375,007	24	11,766,368	73,899,731	18,377,013	53
270,000	....	....	....	....	20	959,900	3,576,109	270,000	54
....	....	....	....	....	11	130,248	829,953	....	55
....	....	....	....	....	84	619,358	1,380,968	....	56
....	....	....	....	....	10	39,047	184,471	....	57
....	....	....	....	....	17	525,727	1,540,824	....	58
....	....	....	....	....	13	25,417	920,000	....	59
56,124	....	....	....	....	11	350,785	2,571,566	56,124	60
....	....	....	....	....	13	466,414	1,221,654	....	61
....	1	3,200	26,664	....	5	218,165	1,088,062	....	62
588,728	12	2,178,821	48,210,090	14,380,007	311	24,027,770	108,948,135	20,161,756	
13,597,843	667	4,023,420	1,003,737,087	229,929,283	5,140	232,435,330	1,782,609,035	265,624,416	

Number of State banks, savings banks, trust companies, and private bankers, with their average capital and deposits, and the tax thereon, for the six months ending November 30, 1882.

States and Territories.	Banks.	Capital.	Deposits.	Tax. On capital.	Tax. On deposits.	Tax. Total.
Maine	66	83,343	$29,265,309	$183 02	$784 18	$967 20
New Hampshire	66	150,000	38,499,071	375 00	1,707 70	2,082 70
Vermont	23	450,000	12,928,488	686 91	7,582 26	8,269 17
Massachusetts	100	328,333	109,385,964	651 55	7,425 74	8,077 29
Boston	79	7,289,589	81,338,196	14,639 40	38,579 64	53,219 04
Rhode Island	53	3,215,983	52,567,039	6,021 23	31,667 62	37,688 85
Connecticut	109	3,094,433	91,363,553	7,718 35	24,147 39	31,865 74
New England States ...	556	14,611,681	475,347,570	30,275 46	111,894 53	142,169 99
New York	208	9,403,935	211,167,540	18,047 50	118,701 18	136,748 68
New York City	562	72,789,107	416,272,550	145,543 41	498,400 93	643,943 34
Albany	12	641,000	17,701,382	725 00	4,472 23	5,197 23
New Jersey	44	1,292,702	29,827,886	2,075 19	10,587 45	12,662 64
Pennsylvania	256	8,125,790	39,783,464	18,708 71	98,214 02	116,922 73
Philadelphia	64	2,966,999	73,531,748	7,125 46	109,411 92	116,537 17
Pittsburgh	29	4,075,283	21,351,354	8,437 79	27,216 30	35,654 09
Delaware		571,686	2,749,353	1,429 21	2,712 25	4,141 46
Maryland	12	505,953	841,246	663 32	1,324 79	1,988 11
Baltimore	52	2,854,913	30,660,015	6,583 39	14,048 11	20,631 50
Washington	10	428,819	5,145,488	261 95	11,527 37	11,791 32
Middle States	1,356	103,656,187	849,032,026	209,590 93	896,027 34	1,106,218 27
Virginia	75	3,026,396	11,748,589	7,216 60	26,981 11	34,197 71
West Virginia	21	1,190,314	5,194,440	2,849 24	12,986 07	15,835 31
North Carolina	16	624,359	1,020,439	1,560 89	2,551 07	4,111 96
South Carolina	14	622,297	2,022,526	1,408 24	5,048 83	6,457 07
Georgia	53	3,527,610	6,241,720	8,803 92	13,611 08	22,415 00
Florida	10	155,874	1,031,866	389 66	2,417 90	2,807 56
Alabama	29	1,232,000	3,437,608	3,080 00	8,593 97	11,673 97
Mississippi	28	1,038,205	2,124,889	2,516 73	5,312 13	7,828 86
Louisiana	5	166,086	59,574	415 09	148 83	564 00
New Orleans	16	2,999,307	4,747,599	5,491 10	11,574 14	17,065 24
Texas	137	4,607,145	11,535,041	11,626 13	28,837 54	40,463 67
Arkansas	22	375,541	743,434	440 00	1,858 53	2,498 53
Kentucky	75	6,152,255	8,905,963	15,254 55	22,414 75	37,669 30
Louisville	16	5,290,877	8,064,452	12,112 86	20,161 12	32,273 98
Tennessee	29	1,764,735	2,964,960	4,347 40	7,412 34	11,759 83
Southern States	546	32,233,011	69,903,010	77,712 50	169,909 51	247,622 01
Ohio	247	5,628,145	28,531,603	12,207 16	67,261 32	79,468 48
Cincinnati	14	973,096	3,779,835	2,009 40	9,241 37	11,250 77
Cleveland	9	1,170,333	19,443,970	1,883 60	19,223 84	21,107 44
Indiana	150	4,041,575	18,541,399	9,782 43	41,338 13	51,120 56
Illinois	355	4,450,925	29,463,096	9,269 34	69,999 63	79,268 97
Chicago	35	6,948,496	26,105,415	13,593 55	64,910 26	78,503 81
Michigan	173	2,486,644	11,528,356	5,766 03	27,826 75	33,592 78
Detroit	15	1,178,857	11,985,237	2,356 05	23,102 31	25,548 36
Wisconsin	119	1,741,060	10,369,501	4,059 86	25,923 61	29,983 47
Milwaukee	9	633,231	12,021,752	1,571 36	30,054 37	31,625 73
Iowa	386	6,989,591	24,368,088	16,187 89	60,036 28	76,224 17
Minnesota	146	3,554,896	13,639,066	8,785 90	31,724 62	40,510 52
Missouri	209	5,688,087	22,589,009	12,586 93	56,472 25	69,059 18
St. Louis	28	5,957,087	28,770,571	13,881 21	71,926 42	85,807 63
Kansas	220	2,728,261	8,563,312	6,052 44	21,408 09	28,000 53
Nebraska	186	1,745,302	4,890,753	4,148 05	12,226 69	16,374 74
Colorado	61	1,390,489	4,856,722	3,451 23	12,141 74	15,592 97
Western States	2,371	57,906,681	279,468,294	128,192 43	644,907 68	773,100 11
Nevada	12	266,734	987,065	409 33	2,467 64	2,876 97
California	90	8,628,598	20,747,732	18,187 42	48,039 28	66,226 70
San Francisco	24	11,786,369	73,899,731	16,972 22	86,126 64	103,098 86
Oregon	20	959,009	5,576,110	1,722 52	8,940 26	10,662 78
Arizona	11	130,248	829,953	325 61	2,074 86	2,400 47
Dakota	84	619,358	1,390,908	1,548 36	3,452 30	5,000 66
Idaho	10	39,947	184,471	99 86	461 17	561 03
Montana	17	525,726	1,540,824	1,314 31	3,852 03	5,166 34
New Mexico	13	25,417	9,0,000	63 55	2,299 99	2,363 54
Utah	11	359,785	2,571,566	759 14	6,428 92	7,188 06
Washington	13	466,444	1,221,654	1,166 02	3,054 10	4,220 12
Wyoming	6	218,165	1,088,061	545 41	2,684 13	3,229 54
Pacific States and Territories	311	24,027,770	108,948,135	43,113 75	169,881 32	212,995 07
Grand totals	5,140	232,435,330	1,782,699,045	488,885 07	1,993,220 38	2,482,105 45

Table, by geographical divisions, of the number, average capital and deposits, of State banks, private bankers, and trust and loan companies, and of savings banks with and without capital—

FOR SIX MONTHS ENDING NOVEMBER 30, 1875.

Geographical divisions.	State banks, private bankers, and trust companies.			Savings banks with capital.			Savings banks without capital.		Total.		
	No.	Capital.	Depos-its.	No.	Capital.	Depos-its.	No.	Depos-its.	No.	Capital.	Depos-its.
		Mill'ns.	*Mill'ns.*		*Mill'ns.*	*Mill'ns.*		*Mill'ns.*		*Mill'ns.*	*Mill'ns.*
New England States	126	11.6	24.0	2	0.3	5.2	436	413.9	564	11.9	443.1
Middle States	1,270	90.8	232.4	3	0.2	0.8	218	382.8	1,491	91.0	616.0
Southern States	517	36.0	42.6	3	0.4	0.5	3	1.9	523	36.4	45.0
Western States and Territories	1,853	70.9	188.0	19	4.1	32.6	38	47.0	1,910	75.0	267.6
United States	3,766	209.3	487.0	27	5.0	39.1	695	845.6	4,488	214.3	1,371.7

FOR SIX MONTHS ENDING MAY 31, 1876.

	No.	Capital.	Depos.	No.	Capital.	Depos.	No.	Depos.	No.	Capital.	Depos.
New England States	135	11.7	23.6	1	0.2	4.4	436	415.1	572	11.9	443.1
Middle States	1,256	89.2	223.4	3	0.3	1.2	212	382.5	1,471	89.5	607.1
Southern States	516	35.7	44.9	3	0.4	0.6	4	2.0	523	36.1	47.5
Western States and Territories	1,896	77.4	188.1	19	4.1	31.0	39	45.0	1,954	81.5	264.1
United States	3,803	214.0	480.0	26	5.0	37.2	691	844.6	4,520	219.0	1,361.8

FOR SIX MONTHS ENDING NOVEMBER 30, 1876.

	No.	Capital.	Depos.	No.	Capital.	Depos.	No.	Depos.	No.	Capital.	Depos.
New England States	131	11.34	22.76	1	0.20	4.15	438	422.99	570	11.54	449.90
Middle States	1,213	88.34	226.40	2	0.16	0.77	211	385.82	1,426	88.50	612.09
Southern States	505	35.40	42.40	4	0.48	0.64	3	2.04	512	35.88	45.08
Western States and Territories	1,015	82.14	192.49	17	4.21	32.38	35	44.68	1,067	86.35	269.55
United States	3,764	217.22	484.05	24	5.05	37.94	687	855.53	4,475	222.27	1,377.53

FOR SIX MONTHS ENDING MAY 31, 1877.

	No.	Capital.	Depos.	No.	Capital.	Depos.	No.	Depos.	No.	Capital.	Depos.
New England States	117	11.07	19.99	1	0.20	3.94	439	428.60	557	11.27	452.62
Middle States	1,202	84.87	215.87	2	0.16	0.88	200	368.81	1,404	85.03	585.56
Southern States	517	34.58	46.17	3	0.42	0.52	4	2.12	524	35.00	48.81
Western States and Territories	1,963	88.11	188.51	20	4.09	32.83	33	43.54	2,016	92.20	264.88
United States	3,799	218.63	470.54	26	4.87	38.17	676	843.16	4,501	223.50	1,351.87

FOR SIX MONTHS ENDING MAY 31, 1878.

	No.	Capital.	Depos.	No.	Capital.	Depos.	No.	Depos.	No.	Capital.	Depos.
New England States	113	11.05	18.29	1	0.07	1.14	441	403.43	555	11.12	422.86
Middle States	1,133	76.93	184.02	3	0.16	1.37	190	358.68	1,326	77.09	544.07
Southern States	513	34.98	44.35	4	0.88	1.28	3	2.14	520	35.56	47.77
Western States and Territories	1,950	79.49	166.65	15	2.13	22.39	34	39.05	1,999	81.62	228.09
United States	3,709	202.15	413.31	23	3.24	26.18	668	803.30	4,400	205.39	1,242.70

Table, by geographical divisions, of the number, average capital and deposits of State banks and trust companies, private bankers, and savings banks with and without capital, for the six months ending May 31, 1878, the private bankers being given separately.

Geographical divisions.	State banks and trust companies.			Private bankers.			Savings banks with capital.			Savings banks without capital.	
	No.	Capital.	Deposits.	No.	Capital.	Deposits.	No.	Capital.	Deposits.	No.	Deposits.
		Mill'ns.	*Mill'ns.*		*Mill'ns.*	*Mill'ns.*		*Mill'ns.*	*Mill'ns.*		*Mill'ns.*
New England States	42	8.19	15.06	71	2.88	3.23	1	0.07	1.14	441	403.43
Middle States	217	42.45	122.10	916	34.48	61.92	3	0.16	1.37	190	358.68
Southern States	233	27.38	30.67	280	7.30	13.68	4	0.83	1.28	3	2.14
Western States and Territories	361	46.33	61.65	1,589	33.16	105.00	15	2.13	22.39	34	39.05
United States ..	853	124.35	229.48	2,856	77.80	183.83	23	3.24	26.18	668	803.30

Table, by geographical divisions, of the number, average capital and deposits of State banks, private bankers, savings banks, and trust and loan companies, for the six months ending May 31, 1878, and of the number, capital, and deposits of the national banks on June 29, 1878.

Geographical divisions.	State banks. savings banks, private bankers, and trust companies.			National banks.			Total.		
	No.	Capital.	Deposits.	No.	Capital.	Deposits.	No.	Capital.	Deposits.
		Millions.	*Millions.*		*Millions.*	*Millions.*		*Millions.*	*Millions.*
New England States.	555	11.12	422.86	542	166.52	128.83	1,097	177.64	551.69
Middle States	1,326	77.09	544.07	634	177.18	374.89	1,960	254.27	918.96
Southern States ..	520	35.55	47.77	176	31.49	35.94	696	67.04	83.71
Western States and Territories	1,999	81.62	228.09	704	95.20	137.50	2,703	176.82	365.59
United States ..	4,400	205.38	1,242.79	2,056	470.39	677.16	6,456	675.77	1,919.95

Table, by geographical divisions, of the number, average capital and deposits of State banks and trust companies, private bankers, and savings banks with and without capital, for the six months ending May 31, 1879, the private bankers being given separately.

Geographical divisions.	State banks and trust companies.			Private bankers.			Savings banks with capital.			Savings banks without capital.	
	No.	Capital.	Deposits.	No.	Capital	Deposits.	No.	Capital.	Deposits.	No.	Deposits.
		Mill'ns.	*Mill'ns.*		*Mill'ns.*	*Mill'ns.*		*Mill'ns.*	*Mill'ns.*		*Mill'ns.*
New England States..	40	7.10	14.39	70	3.72	3.92	....	....	....	426	306.46
Middle States	239	40.72	121.64	853	34.54	54.53	6	0.51	2.44	182	350.95
Southern States	251	27.43	32.60	247	5.64	11.80	3	0.86	0.83	3	1.69
Western States and Territories	475	52.02	85.44	1,474	25.85	70.18	20	2.85	32.80	33	27.96
United States ..	1,005	127.27	257.07	2,644	69.75	139.92	29	4.22	36.07	644	747.06

Table, by geographical divisions, of the number, average capital and deposits of State banks, private bankers, savings banks, and trust and loan companies, for the six months ending May 31, 1879, and of the number, capital, and deposits of the national banks on June 14, 1879.

Geographical divisions.	State banks, savings banks, private bankers, &c.			National banks.			Total.		
	No.	Capital.	Deposits.	No.	Capital.	Deposits.	No.	Capital.	Deposits.
		Millions.	*Millions.*		*Millions.*	*Millions.*		*Millions.*	*Millions.*
New England States	536	10.83	384.17	544	164.43	126.72	1,080	175.26	510.89
Middle States	1,280	75.77	582.56	640	170.21	393.42	1,920	245.98	925.68
Southern States ...	494	33.92	47.02	176	30.40	37.93	670	64.32	84.95
Western States and Territories	2,002	80.72	216.37	688	90.20	155.63	2,690	170.92	372.00
United States..	4,312	201.24	1,180.12	2,048	455.24	713.40	6,360	656.48	1,893.52

Table, by geographical divisions, of the number, average capital and deposits of State banks and trust companies, private bankers, and savings banks with and without capital, for the six months ending May 31, 1880, the private bankers being given separately.

Geographical divisions.	State banks and trust companies.			Private bankers.			Savings banks with capital.			Savings banks without capital.	
	No.	Capital.	Depos. its.	No.	Capital.	Depos. its.	No.	Capital.	Depos. its.	No.	Depos. its.
		Mill'ns.	*Mill'ns.*		*Mill'ns.*	*Mill'ns.*		*Mill'ns.*	*Mill'ns.*		*Mill'ns.*
New England States ...	40	6.86	16.47	74	5.16	3.74				422	368.70
Middle States	234	38.98	154.89	885	40.01	71.54	6	0.53	3.19	175	386.00
Southern States	241	26.09	38.51	252	4.84	13.54	3	0.34	0.57	2	.85
Western States and Territories	481	41.44	108.91	1.591	26.14	93.85	20	3.17	30.85	30	27.39
United States ...	996	113.97	318.78	2,802	76.12	182.67	29	4.04	34.61	629	783.03

Table, by geographical divisions, of the number, average capital and deposits of State banks, private bankers, savings banks, and trust and loan companies, for the six months ending May 31, 1880, and of the number, capital, and deposits of the national banks on June 11, 1880.

Geographical divisions.	State banks, savings banks, private bankers, &c.			National banks.			Total.		
	No.	Capital.	Deposits.	No.	Capital.	Net deposits.	No.	Capital.	Deposits.
		Millions.	*Millions.*		*Millions.*	*Millions.*		*Millions.*	*Millions.*
New England States	536	12.02	388.97	548	165.60	161.96	1,084	177.62	550.93
Middle States	1,300	79.51	615.62	654	170.44	480.06	1,954	249.55	1,095.68
Southern States	498	31.85	53.50	177	30.79	45.90	675	62.64	99.40
Western States and Territories	2,122	70.76	261.00	697	89.08	212.87	2,819	159.84	473.87
United States .	4,456	194.14	1,319.09	2,076	455.91	900.79	6,532	650.05	2,219.88

Table, by geographical divisions, of the number, average capital and deposits of State banks and trust companies, private bankers, and savings banks with and without capital, for the six months ending May 31, 1881, the private bankers being given separately.

Geographical divisions.	State banks and trust companies.			Private bankers.			Savings banks with capital.			Savings banks without capital.	
	No.	Capital.	Depos-its.	No.	Capital.	Depos-its.	No.	Capital.	Depos-its.	No.	Depos-its.
		Mill'ns.	*Mill'ns.*		*Mill'ns.*	*Mill'ns*		*Mill'ns.*	*Mill'ns.*		*Mill'ns.*
New England States ..	41	7.26	20.97	80	4.70	5.16	1	0.02	0.19	424	402.80
Middle States	218	39.28	189.78	938	55.40	94.11	7	0.61	4.68	174	428.40
Southern States........	240	24.71	42.43	258	5.59	17.32	6	0.44	0.84	3	1.24
Western States and Territories...............	479	41.94	132.44	1,762	27.64	125.26	22	3.15	31.90	28	29.86
United States	978	113.19	385.62	3,038	93.33	241.85	36	4.22	37.61	629	862.36

Table, by geographical divisions, of the number, average capital and deposits of State banks, private bankers, savings banks, and trust and loan companies, for the six months ending May 31, 1881, and of the number, capital, and deposits of the national banks on June 30, 1881.

Geographical divisions.	State banks, savings banks, private bankers, &c.			National banks.			Total.		
	No.	Capital.	Deposits.	No.	Capital.	Net deposits.	No.	Capital.	Deposits.
		Millions.	*Millions.*		*Millions.*	*Millions.*		*Millions.*	*Millions.*
New England States.	546	12.0	420.2	552	165.9	177.9	1,098	177.9	637.8
Middle States	1,337	95.3	717.0	664	171.7	599.7	2,001	267.0	1,316.7
Southern States	507	30.7	61.8	184	31.1	59.5	691	61.8	121.3
Western States and Territories	2,291	72.7	319.4	715	91.5	272.1	3,006	164.2	591.5
United States ...	4,681	210.7	1,527.4	2,115	460.2	1,139.9	6,796	670.9	2,667.3

Table, by geographical divisions, of the number, average capital and deposits of State banks and trust companies, private bankers, and savings banks with and without capital, for the six months ending May 31, 1882, the private bankers being given separately.

Geographical divisions.	State banks and trust companies.			Private bankers.			Savings banks with capital.			Savings banks without capital.	
	No.	Capital.	Depos-its.	No.	Capital.	Depos-its.	No.	Capital.	Depos-its.	No.	Depos-its.
		Mill'ns.	*Mill'ns.*		*Mill'ns.*	*Mill'ns.*		*Mill'ns.*	*Mill'ns.*		*Mill'ns.*
New England States	40	8.32	24.96	104	7.13	9.42	2	0.09	0.77	418	421.35
Middle States	205	40.56	225.51	1,014	62.19	113.08	8	0.61	5.07	173	478.26
Southern States. .	246	25.37	48.47	293	6.37	19.98	6	0.53	1.23	2	1.15
Western States and Territories	521	42.54	153.06	1,980	38.56	153.14	22	2.63	34.17	29	34.07
United States ...	1,012	116.79	452.00	3,391	114.25	295.62	38	3.86	41.24	622	929.83

Table, by geographical divisions, of the number, average capital and deposits of State banks, private banks, savings banks, and trust and loan companies, for the six months ending May 31, 1882, and of the number, capital, and deposits of the national banks on July 1, 1882.

Geographical divisions.	State banks, savings banks, private bankers, &c.			National banks.			Total.		
	No.	Capital.	Deposits.	No.	Capital.	Net deposits.	No.	Capital.	Deposits.
	Millions.	*Millions.*		*Millions.*	*Millions.*		*Millions.*	*Millions.*	
New England States.	564	15. 5	456. 5	557	165. 7	191. 4	1, 121	181. 2	647. 9
Middle States	1, 400	103. 4	816. 9	686	173. 3	572. 8	2, 086	276 7	1, 389. 7
Southern States	547	32. 3	70. 8	200	32. 9	62 0	747	65. 2	132. 8
Western States and Territories	2, 552	83. 7	374. 5	796	105. 3	305. 5	3, 348	189. 0	680. 0
United States ...	5, 063	234. 9	1, 718. 7	2, 239	477. 2	1, 131. 7	7, 302	712. 1	2, 850. 4

Table, by geographical divisions, of the number, average capital and deposits of State banks and trust companies, private bankers, and savings banks with and without capital, for the six months ending November 30, 1882, the private bankers being given separately.

Geographical divisions.	State banks and trust companies.			Private bankers.			Savings banks with capital.			Savings banks without capital.	
	No.	Capital.	Deposits.	No.	Capital.	Deposits.	No.	Capital.	Deposits.	No.	Deposits.
	Mill'ns.	*Mill'ns.*		*Mill'ns.*	*Mill'ns.*		*Mill'ns.*	*Mill'ns.*			*Mill'ns.*
New England States .	40	8. 30	31. 64	94	6. 22	6. 57	2	0. 10	0. 89	420	436. 25
Middle States	210	40. 60	244. 02	967	62. 42	112. 09	8	0. 63	5. 34	171	486. 98
Southern States	248	25. 34	43. 94	289	6. 33	20. 68	7	0. 56	1. 50	2	1. 80
Western States and Territories	563	48. 90	168. 40	2, 062	30. 31	149. 02	25	2. 73	35. 74	32	35. 22
United States ..	1, 061	123. 14	490. 00	3, 412	105. 28	288. 96	42	4. 02	43. 47	625	960. 26

Table, by geographical divisions, of the number, average capital and deposits of State banks, private bankers, savings banks, and trust and loan companies, for the six months ending November 30, 1882, and of the number, capital, and deposits of the national banks on December 30, 1882.

Geographical divisions.	State banks, savings banks, private bankers, &c.			National banks.			Total.		
	No.	Capital.	Deposits.	No.	Capital.	Deposits.	No.	Capital.	Deposits.
	Millions.	*Millions.*		*Millions.*	*Millions.*		*Millions.*	*Millions.*	
New England States.	556	14. 62	475. 35	560	166. 23	193. 15	1, 116	180. 85	668. 50
Middle States	1, 356	107. 66	840 03	691	173. 19	556. 55	2, 047	276. 85	1, 405. 58
Southern States	546	32. 23	69. 90	214	34. 80	68. 84	760	67. 03	138. 74
Western States and Territories	2, 682	81. 93	388. 42	843	110. 66	301. 28	3, 525	192. 59	689. 70
United States .	5, 140	232. 44	1, 782. 70	2, 308	484. 88	1, 119. 82	7, 448	717. 32	2, 902. 52

Table of resources and liabilities of State banks at various dates.

Resources and liabilities.	New Hampshire, Jan. 1, 1885.	Vermont, June 30, 1885.	Rhode Island, Nov. 18, 1884.	Connecticut, Oct. 1, 1884.	New York, Sept. 12, 1885.	New York City, Sept. 12, 1885.
	1 bank.	8 banks.	10 banks.	6 banks.	64 banks.	28 banks.
RESOURCES.						
Loans and discounts	$82,009	$1,804,989	$2,601,005	$3,515,980	$32,140,274	$68,736,634
Overdrafts					69,859	22,418
United States bonds		75,522				
Other stocks, bonds, &c	12,400	852,178	182,327	298,872	2,910,942	2,103,288
Due from banks		261,086	102,338	685,991	8,697,169	4,890,908
Real estate	1,854	5,190	219,554	142,954	685,987	2,243,427
Other assets		68,513	3,834		91,958	631,561
Expenses			3,337		177,035	212,048
Cash items					717,353	21,735,694
Specie			13,928		807,984	12,819,217
Legal tenders, bank notes, &c	469	39,756	132,264	304,934	1,763,267	6,210,476
Total	96,732	3,107,234	3,318,587	4,948,731	48,061,828	119,605,671
LIABILITIES.						
Capital stock	50,000	455,000	1,785,831	1,850,000	8,103,000	14,187,700
Circulation	1,130		5,416	19,356	5,470	2,005
Surplus fund	17,673	5,000			2,381,584	4,512,639
Undivided profits		115,520	186,544	390,322	1,761,879	2,949,673
Dividends unpaid	1,155		6,642			
Deposits	17,961	2,480,946	1,172,366	2,284,865	31,278,723	85,495,205
Due to banks	8,813		102,788	395,388	2,898,032	11,510,231
Other liabilities		50,768			1,573,060	947,008
Total	96,732	3,107,234	3,318,587	4,948,731	48,061,748	119,605,751

Resources and liabilities.	New Jersey, Jan. 1, 1885.	Pennsylvania, Nov. 1, 1884.	Maryland, Oct. 1, 1885.	Virginia, July 1, 1885.	South Carolina, Sept. 30, 1884.	Georgia, June 30, 1885.
	9 banks.	81 banks.	10 banks.	52 banks.	5 banks.	21 banks.
RESOURCES.						
Loans and discounts	$3,852,274	$23,737,720	$4,410,145	$8,042,406	$1,710,779	$7,621,508
Overdrafts	220		1,978	104,541		5,914
United States bonds	281,000	1,093,100	55,000	11,406	50,000	
Other stocks, bonds, &c	280,210	4,683,316	431,773	1,146,065	928,975	6,334,586
Due from banks	461,481	3,958,064	393,665	1,241,734	123,796	444,043
Real estate	129,021	2,039,437	430,890	387,658	103,741	348,422
Other assets	32,800	1,327,407	31,371	98,870	1,246	266,834
Expenses	11,043	181,641	21,977	79,993	11,470	62,990
Cash items	3,947		182,451	320,989		70,035
Specie	4,875	838,754	43,384	143,235		305,811
Legal tenders, bank notes, &c	270,961	1,855,307	291,751	586,860	237,739	721,382
Total	5,327,832	39,714,836	6,294,385	12,163,357	3,167,746	16,181,615
LIABILITIES.						
Capital stock	1,299,350	8,050,205	2,006,805	2,881,439	500,000	7,921,950
Circulation			233			
Surplus fund	366,660	1,521,252	242,160	556,011	46,000	1,274,890
Undivided profits	154,801	844,776	180,468	234,371	122,281	28,954
Dividends unpaid	15,172		32,745	41,185	200	
Deposits	3,409,800	28,101,754	3,651,156	7,846,492	2,341,354	5,271,567
Due to banks	52,049	540,082	149,860	208,818	59,706	610,028
Other liabilities	30,000	596,767	30,958	395,041	98,255	1,073,646
Total	5,327,832	39,714,836	6,294,385	12,163,357	3,167,746	16,181,615

Table of resources and liabilities of State banks at various dates—Continued.

Resources and liabilities.	Florida, Apr. 30, 1885.	Louisiana, July, 1885.	Texas, June 30, 1884.	Kentucky. June 30, 1885.	Missouri, Aug. 31, 1885.
	1 bank.	4 banks.	6 banks.	69 banks.	187 banks.
RESOURCES.					
Loans and discounts	$70,765	$4,036,049	$1,728,998	$21,538,357	$43,041,286
Overdrafts			19,868	36,155	506,650
United States bonds				5,965	996,053
Other stocks, bonds, &c	12,500	998,292	3,680	1,282,920	4,368,017
Due from banks	1,236	505,434	408,701	3,251,720	10,722,815
Real estate	6,583	567,127	71,010	777,919	1,689,607
Other assets	3,882	238,110	12,683	444,249	236,015
Expenses		3,414	34,909	14,890	
Cash items		418,717	2,086	17,034	1,793,191
Specie	7,133		16,604	106,323	2,987,898
Legal tenders, bank notes, &c.	15,754	2,355,865	398,482	2,318,943	6,203,353
Total	117,853	9,121,008	2,697,221	29,794,475	72,544,885
LIABILITIES.					
Capital stock	50,000	2,582,200	643,971	11,309,391	13,011,423
Circulation		8,617		55,302	
Surplus fund	3,386	200,000	142,880	1,537,794	6,419,827
Undivided profits	225	144,548	139,554	906,740	
Dividends unpaid	5,000	20,297		200,243	32,956
Deposits	48,568	5,816,536	1,500,763	14,548,675	46,859,759
Due to banks	5,674	348,810	260,044	943,917	6,220,920
Other liabilities	5,000		10,000	172,413	
Total	117,853	9,121,008	2,697,221	29,794,475	72,544,885

Resources and liabilities.	Ohio, Apr. 4, 1885.	Indiana, Nov. 1, 1884.	Michigan, July 6, 1885.	Wisconsin. July 6, 1885.	Iowa, Apr. 24, 1885.
	38 banks.	27 banks.	44 banks.	50 banks.	82 banks.
RESOURCES.					
Loans and discounts	$6,934,285	$2,980,308	$16,752,755	$15,404,522	$12,719,492
Overdrafts	30,279	55,598	43,870	106,202	205,113
United States bonds	155,310	26,950	241,000		
Other stocks, bonds, &c	697,143	23,190	1,192,225	1,782,266	
Due from banks	848,093	413,929	3,005,640	4,271,498	2,417,901
Real estate	446,839	172,888	393,602	402,495	722,233
Other assets	98,742	42,164	94,694		
Expenses	48,188	24,903	53,681	18,050	
Cash items	41,851		137,204	382,783	
Specie	138,479		117,480	383,462	
Legal tenders, bank notes, &c.	889,837	431,679	1,187,856	1,418,770	992,902
Total	10,328,046	4,201,609	23,310,077	24,169,958	17,057,641
LIABILITIES.					
Capital stock	2,537,000	1,449,200	3,494,170	2,462,200	4,366,043
Circulation					
Surplus fund	344,904	261,944	502,542	782,175	571,154
Undivided profits	157,190	80,370	628,641		425,281
Dividends unpaid	1,127	2,611	30,003		
Deposits	6,880,201	2,360,961	18,357,108	16,026,614	11,524,620
Due to banks	215,160	3,533	119,912		170,543
Other liabilities	192,464	34,651	177,701	4,898,969	
Total	10,328,046	4,201,609	23,310,077	14,169,958	17,057,641

Resources and liabilities of State banks at various dates—Continued.

Resources and liabilities.	Minnesota, June 30, 1885.	Kansas, June 30, 1885.	Colorado, July 1, 1885.	Montana, October 1, 1884.	California July 1, 1885.
	34 banks.	54 banks.	8 banks.	3 banks.	73 banks.
RESOURCES.					
Loans and discounts...............	$9, 814, 476	$4, 184, 206	$928, 375	$181, 245	$40, 309, 586
Overdrafts.....	86, 707	37, 357	6, 912	10, 357	....
United States bonds.............	3, 100	800	....	....	....
Other stocks, bonds, &c...........	263, 840	34, 862	10, 064	48, 731	1, 753, 158
Due from banks..................	2, 048, 220	907, 1r7	371, 580	43, 737	8, 404, 424
Real estate.....................	450, 968	248. 407	14, 000	8, 076	3, 164, 513
Other assets	2, 707	128, 419	103, 773	478	1, 830, 741
Expenses......................	122, 734	38, 154	4, 409	6, 017	....
Cash items...................	148, 631	403	....	493	....
Specie........................	....	6, 230	....	3, 792	11, 122, 025
Legal tenders, bank notes, &c.....	930, 974	1, 150, 647	260, 722	25, 271	....
Total..................	13, 872, 372	6, 736, 672	1, 708, 844	328, 197	75, 585, 349
LIABILITIES.					
Capital stock..................	3, 854, 500	2, 149, 221	390, 000	75, 000	27, 672, 641
Circulation...................	....	....	....	....	....
Surplus fund.................	427, 434	97, 271	78, 301	....	9, 650, 975
Undivided profits.............	431, 605	307, 733	65, 703	54, 762	....
Dividends unpaid.............	13, 334	1, 327	945	....	....
Deposits....................	8, 310, 120	4, 035, 429	1, 160, 451	179, 344	33, 286, 788
Due to banks...............	793, 509	47, 854	9, 414	9, 417	4, 205, 321
Other liabilities.............	41, 870	97, 837	4, 000	9, 674	769, 624
Total..................	13, 872, 372	6, 736, 672	1, 708, 844	328, 197	75, 585, 349

Aggregate resources and liabilities of State banks from 1881 to 1885.

Resources and liabilities.	1880-'81.	1881-'82.	1882-'83.	1883-'84.	1884-'85.
	652 banks.	672 banks.	754 banks.	817 banks.	975 banks.
RESOURCES.					
Loans and discounts...............	$250, 819, 420	$272, 520, 217	$322, 358, 227	$331, 049, 510	$347, 880, 520
Overdrafts......	1, 335, 310	1, 196, 369	1, 392, 961	1, 262, 725	1, 340, 998
United States bonds.............	12, 048, 452	8, 739, 172	5, 287, 606	2, 337, 705	2, 994, 806
Other stocks, bonds, &c...........	24, 904, 903	19, 780, 527	22, 083, 304	31, 452, 019	32, 641, 839
Due from banks	46, 657, 328	40, 919, 183	58, 709, 516	48, 836, 689	59, 062, 403
Real estate....................	13, 914, 238	13, 037, 939	13, 592, 791	15, 058, 411	15, 873, 313
Other assets	10, 542, 266	12, 306, 578	9, 943, 706	7, 671, 876	5, 791, 111
Expenses......................	965, 327	999, 944	918, 403	1, 025, 237	1, 130, 883
Cash items...................	16, 900, 325	18, 546, 073	35, 118, 379	28, 219, 414	25, 972, 022
Specie........................	17, 071, 445	17, 201, 489	17, 429, 817	25, 376, 565	29, 807, 724
Legal tenders, bank notes, &c.....	23, 797, 016	24, 586, 682	25, 302, 316	28, 787, 615	30, 994, 221
Total..................	418, 956, 060	438, 834, 173	512, 137, 026	521, 077, 766	553, 562, 761
LIABILITIES.					
Capital stock...................	92, 922, 525	91, 808, 213	102, 454, 861	110, 020, 351	125, 258, 240
Circulation	274, 941	286, 391	187, 978	177, 554	98, 129
Surplus fund.................	20, 970, 187	23, 148, 050	25, 762, 738	31, 483, 942	30, 680, 575
Undivided profits.............	7, 943, 466	8, 902, 579	11, 287, 623	12, 718, 894	11, 574, 736
Dividends unpaid.............	567, 171	481, 858	442, 652	473, 735	493, 926
Deposits	261, 362, 303	281, 835, 496	334, 995, 702	325, 365, 669	344, 307, 996
Due to banks...............	18, 870, 406	18, 262, 172	20, 651, 930	27, 125, 108	29, 9 0, 453
Other liabilities.............	16, 039, 021	14, 109, 414	16, 353, 542	13, 712, 513	11, 209, 706
Total..................	418, 956, 060	438, 834, 173	512, 137, 026	521, 077, 766	553, 562, 761

Resources and liabilities of trust and loan companies at various dates.

Resources and liabilities.	Massachusetts, October 31, 1884.	Rhode Island, November, 18, 1884.	Connecticut, October 1. 1884.	New York, January 1, 1885.	Pennsylvania, September 1, 1885.
	6 banks.	1 bank.	6 banks.	18 banks.	9 banks.
RESOURCES.					
Loans and discounts	$16, 676, 100	$4, 130, 156	$2, 117, 530	$91, 594, 743	$27, 024, 120
Overdrafts				1, 136	134, 783
United States bonds	1, 340, 200	800, 000		22, 518, 850	717, 350
Other sources, bonds, &c	1, 779, 454	2, 295, 100	397, 123	9, 780, 935	15, 497, 588
Due from banks	3, 009, 402	100, 000	517, 707	13, 253, 474	6, 598, 402
Real estate	56, 250		305, 782	5, 626, 103	3, 371, 151
Other assets	580, 303	258, 241		8, 058, 159	126, 971
Expenses	72, 829		23, 815	10, 327	195, 581
Cash items					94, 672
Specie					1, 388, 065
Legal tenders, bank notes, &c	766, 707	784, 792	116, 856	5, 714, 960	1, 174, 481
Total	24, 280, 745	8, 368, 289	3, 478, 813	155, 938, 672	56, 323, 164
LIABILITIES.					
Capital stock	3, 300, 000	800, 000	976, 600	12, 977, 000	8, 375, 000
Circulation					
Surplus fund	585, 500			6, 578, 907	3, 532, 077
Undivided profits	552, 185	28, 836	199, 800	5, 469, 388	2, 257, 791
Dividends unpaid	633		3, 449		15, 169
Deposits	19, 640, 061	7, 539, 453	2, 168, 619	121, 759, 836	37, 309, 424
Due to banks			130, 415	67, 478	
Other liabilities	202, 896			9, 086, 003	4, 833, 703
Total	24, 280, 745	8, 368, 289	3, 478, 813	155, 938, 672	56, 323, 164

Aggregate resources and liabilities of trust and loan companies from 1881 to 1885.

Resources and liabilities.	1880–'81.	1881–'82.	1882–'83.	1883–'84.	1884–'85.
	31 banks.	32 banks.	34 banks.	35 banks.	40 banks.
RESOURCES.					
Loans and discounts	$101, 906, 566	$132, 054, 203	$140, 022, 358	$158, 018, 009	$141, 542, 649
Overdrafts	72, 385	176, 747	100, 675	367, 749	135, 919
United States bonds	15, 631, 573	16, 934, 812	17, 437, 990	23, 371, 084	25, 376, 400
Other stocks, bonds, &c	17, 426, 054	25, 878, 256	30, 322, 420	27, 879, 858	29, 750, 200
Due from banks	8, 005, 501	8, 054, 535	9, 561, 148	16, 517, 457	23, 458, 985
Real estate	7, 482, 534	6, 877, 743	6, 567, 756	6, 152, 771	8, 750, 291
Other assets	1, 309, 475	1, 378, 627	4, 246, 338	2, 841, 937	9, 623, 654
Expenses	171, 100	193, 401	213, 183	209, 842	302, 052
Cash items	437		88, 483	88, 802	94, 672
Specie	854, 183	701, 271	825, 483	552, 102	1, 388, 065
Legal tenders, bank notes, &c	3, 594, 271	2, 736, 230	2, 950, 753	3, 871, 900	8, 557, 796
Total	156, 544, 079	194, 985, 825	212, 342, 587	239, 871, 691	248, 389, 683
LIABILITIES.					
Capital stock	19, 188, 800	21, 553, 718	22, 778, 175	23, 938, 600	26, 428, 600
Circulation					
Surplus fund	6, 881, 809	8, 350, 302	8, 812, 723	10, 191, 544	10, 695, 984
Undivided profits	4, 293, 854	5, 855, 859	6, 788, 987	9, 619, 067	8, 508, 000
Dividends unpaid	9, 242	95, 561	22, 359	25, 282	19, 251
Deposits	111, 670, 329	144, 841, 596	165, 378, 515	188, 745, 922	188, 417, 203
Due to banks	235, 198	147, 179	267, 006	761, 888	197, 893
Other liabilities	14, 264, 847	14, 135, 610	8, 294, 822	6, 589, 388	14, 122, 662
Total	156, 544, 079	194, 985, 825	212, 342, 587	239, 871, 691	248, 389, 683

Table, by geographical divisions, of the resources and liabilities of State banks and trust companies, 1884-'85.

Resources and liabilities.	New England States.	Middle States.	Southern States.	Western States.	Pacific States.	Aggregate.
	38 banks.	219 banks.	158 banks.	516 banks.	84 banks.	1,015 banks.
RESOURCES.						
Loans and discounts.....	$30,927,769	$251,495,910	$44,748,952	$111,831,330	$50,419,208	$489,423,169
Overdrafts	....	230,394	166,478	1,071,776	17,269	1,485,917
United States bonds	2,215,722	24,665,300	66,971	1,423,213	....	28,371,206
Other stocks, bonds, &c...	5,817,454	35,688,082	10,707,018	8,361,552	1,820,952	62,395,059
Due from banks	4,736,524	38,233,163	5,976,664	24,755,289	8,819,750	82,521,390
Real estate	731,584	13,920,021	2,262,460	4,525,949	3,186,589	24,642,603
Other assets	910,891	10,300,267	1,065,874	602,741	1,934,992	14,814,765
Expenses	99,481	800,652	207,666	305,710	10,426	1,432,935
Cash items	....	22,734,117	828,861	2,504,123	493	26,067,594
Specie	13,928	15,902,279	579,306	3,633,559	11,126,717	31,255,789
Legal tenders, bank notes, &c.	2,145,778	17,281,203	6,633,025	13,206,018	285,998	39,552,017
Total	47,599,131	431,266,388	73,243,275	172,221,260	77,622,390	801,952,444
LIABILITIES.						
Capital stock	9,237,431	55,059,060	25,948,951	33,323,757	28,137,641	151,686,840
Circulation	25,902	8,308	63,919	....	....	98,129
Surplus fund	607,673	19,135,279	2,486,080	9,407,251	9,729,276	41,365,559
Undivided profits	1,481,207	13,618,776	2,822,559	2,039,729	120,465	20,082,736
Dividends unpaid	11,879	64,086	355,879	81,388	945	513,177
Deposits	35,303,971	311,065,968	37,373,935	114,354,812	34,626,583	532,725,269
Due to banks	697,404	15,217,792	2,437,597	7,571,431	4,224,182	30,148,346
Other liabilities	253,664	17,098,159	1,754,355	5,442,893	783,298	25,332,368
Total	47,599,131	431,266,388	73,243,275	172,221,260	77,622,390	801,952,444

Resources and liabilities of savings banks organized under State laws at various dates.

Resources and liabilities.	Maine, November 1, 1884.	New Hampshire, January 1, 1885.	Vermont, June 30, 1885.	Massachusetts, October 31, 1884.	Rhode Island, November 18, 1884.
	54 banks.	68 banks.	18 banks.	168 banks.	38 banks.
RESOURCES.					
Loans on real estate	$5,438,608	$16,785,954	$6,639,933	$98,979,283	$19,601,188
Loans on personal and collateral security	4,608,680	9,182,952	1,662,424	74,952,754	9,722,367
United States bonds	4,739,840	552,384	209,830	14,553,600	3,803,500
State, municipal, and other bonds and stocks	10,912,591	9,070,910	1,927,440	25,956,713	6,189,029
Railroad bonds and stocks	4,363,382	7,968,544	....	13,808,173	6,138,750
Bank stock	1,583,537	1,752,463	163,537	25,874,045	2,594,349
Real estate	1,124,088	770,901	163,856	6,562,474	3,417,271
Other assets....................	1,579,049	210,175	320,543	3,159,313	339,556
Expenses	....	....	....	....	....
Due from banks	....	884,529	550,201	9,488,904	733,193
Cash	751,869	136,720	85,114	581,579	963,827
Totals	35,101,644	47,315,532	11,782,968	273,916,918	53,503,030
LIABILITIES.					
Deposits	32,913,805	43,827,356	11,218,285	262,720,147	51,079,161
Surplus fund	1,200,405	1,950,954	237,464	5,692,504	....
Undivided profits	887,170	1,515,443	312,446	5,247,371	2,413,681
Other liabilities	100,234	21,779	14,773	256,896	10,188
Totals......	35,101,644	47,315,532	11,782,968	274,916,918	53,503,030

Resources and liabilities of savings banks organized under State laws, &c.—Continued.

Resources and liabilities.	Connecticut, Oct. 1, 1884.	New York, Jan. 1, 1885.	New Jersey, Jan. 1, 1885.	Pennsylvania, Sept. 1, 1885.	Maryland, July 1, 1885.
	84 banks.	126 banks.	30 banks.	4 banks.	18 banks.
RESOURCES.					
Loans on real estate	$39,202,431	$141,944,250	$8,482,062	$4,598,312	$3,833,853
Loans on personal and collateral security	10,443,448	6,402,850	1,226,910	6,290,978	
United States bonds	3,986,556	134,628,660	10,040,519	6,767,332	10,540,477
State, municipal, and other bonds and stocks	13,532,805	128,211,340	3,398,059	5,757,481	2,635,016
Railroad bonds and stocks	13,720,975			12,587,566	998,099
Bank stock	6,224,960				264,722
Real estate	4,907,204	8,116,813	931,118	830,387	658,091
Other assets	599,967	51,327,579	759,957		9,732,825
Expenses				105,444	
Due from banks	2,402,711	29,400,725	749,222	3,236	
Cash	484,040	5,889,279	297,044	2,066,581	
Totals	95,625,157	505,927,496	25,884,891	39,007,317	28,663,083
LIABILITIES.					
Deposits	90,614,623	437,107,501	24,017,917	35,362,660	28,663,083
Surplus fund	2,973,224	68,669,001	1,674,104	2,551,612	
Undivided profits	1,352,813			989,045	
Other liabilities	684,497	150,994	192,870	104,000	
Totals	95,625,157	505,927,496	25,884,891	39,007,317	28,663,083

Resources and liabilities.	District of Columbia, Oct. 1, 1885.	Ohio, Apr. 4, 1885.	Indiana, Nov. 1, 1884.	Minnesota, June 30, 1885.	California, July 1, 1885.
	1 bank.	4 banks.	6 banks.	6 banks.	21 banks.
RESOURCES.					
Loans on real estate	$181,470	$3,677,303	$1,826,264	$1,859,056	$30,903,901
Loans on personal and collateral security	184,086	1,315,113		642,139	7,082,201
United States bonds	70,000	1,925,000	103,000		
State, municipal, and other bonds and stocks	233,500	6,147,226	97,547	267,075	14,656,518
Railroad bonds and stocks			3,000		
Bank stock	30,596	101,143	104,724	25,939	4,370,145
Real estate	22,188	19,389	7,492	43,296	323,975
Other assets	2,131	12,895	4,246	41,920	
Expenses	545	481,358	101,192	487,373	775,645
Due from banks					
Cash	16,101	140,903	112,291	137,092	1,760,624
Total	740,617	13,820,330	2,359,756	3,503,890	65,873,009
LIABILITIES.					
Deposits	731,733	12,605,008	2,171,009	3,195,926	58,943,903
Surplus fund		1,000,000	136,140	40,317	2,521,590
Undivided profits	8,884	215,035	52,607	111,864	
Other liabilities			287	*165,783	†4,407,576
Total	740,617	13,820,330	2,359,756	3,503,890	65,873,009

* Includes $150,000 capital stock.   † Includes $3,851,437 capital stock.

Aggregate resources and liabilities of savings banks from 1881 to 1885.

Resources and liabilities.	1880–'81. 629 banks.	1881–'82. 629 banks.	1882–'83. 630 banks.	1883–'84. 636 banks.	1884–'85. 646 banks.
RESOURCES.					
Loans on real estate	$307,096,158	$307,089,227	$328,197,858	$358,686,040	$389,953,928
Loans on personal and collateral security	95,817,641	128,483,698	155,874,522	141,457,111	133,716,902
United States bonds	210,845,514	237,786,442	219,017,313	196,226,202	191,980,698
State, municipal, and other bonds and stocks	150,819,942	206,291,274	190,629,915	222,218,006	228,993,250
Railroad bonds and stocks	27,069,048	32,994,578	41,695,701	50,994,579	59,585,489
Bank stock	33,249,203	35,365,717	36,587,817	37,929,754	38,460,603
Real estate	41,987,674	39,882,429	37,224,601	34,467,276	32,174,810
Other assets	37,408,163	11,047,346	53,235,771	69,166,584	68,445,304
Expenses	135,572	132,204	144,223	156,944	166,636
Due from banks	40,603,641	38,977,135	43,184,629	52,358,971	46,125,014
Cash	13,758,106	14,932,015	12,998,504	14,079,452	13,423,064
Totals	967,790,662	1,052,982,065	1,118,790,944	1,177,740,919	1,203,025,698
LIABILITIES.					
Deposits	891,961,142	966,797,081	1,024,856,787	1,073,294,955	1,095,172,147
Surplus fund	60,289,905	69,454,512	72,784,155	82,395,717	88,647,315
Undivided profits	10,325,800	11,136,219	15,738,223	16,994,753	13,106,359
Other liabilities	5,213,815	5,594,253	5,411,779	5,145,494	6,099,877
Total	967,790,662	1,052,982,065	1,118,790,944	1,177,740,919	1,203,025,698

Table, by States, of the aggregate deposits of savings banks, with the number of their depositors and the average amount due to each in 1884 and 1885.

States.	1883–'84. Number of depositors.	1883–'84. Amount of deposits.	1883–'84. Average to each depositor.	1884–'85. Number of depositors.	1884–'85. Amount of deposits.	1884–'85. Average to each depositor.
Maine	101,822	$31,371,869	$308 10	105,680	$32,913,835	$311 44
New Hampshire	117,317	42,091,597	358 77	121,216	43,827,356	361 56
Vermont	38,574	11,061,056	286 75	39,284	11,218,285	285 57
Massachusetts	806,010	252,607,593	313 40	826,068	262,720,147	318 06
Rhode Island	120,482	50,127,806	416 07	115,782	51,079,161	441 29
Connecticut	246,652	88,098,384	357 18	252,245	90,614,023	359 28
New York	1,147,588	431,080,010	375 64	1,165,174	437,107,501	375 14
New Jersey	98,760	29,323,428	296 92	87,356	24,017,917	274 94
Pennsylvania	130,381	34,031,154	261 01	135,953	35,362,660	260 11
Maryland	*77,212	28,336,934	367 00	*78,101	28,663,083	367 00
District of Columbia	6,180	622,304	100 70	6,735	731,733	108 64
Ohio	34,558	12,969,666	375 33	54,836	12,605,008	361 84
Indiana	*9,131	2,108,428	230 91	*9,402	2,171,009	230 91
Minnesota				11,753	3,195,926	271 92
California	*80,489	59,464,726	738 70	*82,000	58,943,909	718 83
Total	3,015,151	1,073,294,955	355 96	3,071,495	1,095,172,147	356 56

* Estimated.

Statement showing the amount of national bank and of legal-tender notes outstanding on June 20, 1874, January 14, 1875, May 31, 1878, and November 1, 1885, and the increase or decrease in each.

NATIONAL-BANK NOTES.

Amount outstanding June 20, 1874	$340, 894, 182
Amount outstanding January 14, 1875	351, 861, 450
Amount outstanding May 31, 1878	322, 555, 965
Amount outstanding November 1, 1885*	315, 402, 899
Decrease in circulation during the last month	1, 559, 905
Decrease in circulation since November 1, 1884	17, 562, 835

LEGAL-TENDER NOTES.

Amount outstanding June 20, 1874	382, 000, 000
Amount outstanding January 14, 1875	382, 000, 000
Amount retired under act of January 14, 1875, to May 31, 1878	35, 318, 984
Amount outstanding on and since May 31, 1878	346, 681, 016
Amount on deposit with the Treasurer U. S. to redeem notes of insolvent and liquidating banks, and banks retiring circulation under act of June 20, 1874	39, 158, 710
Decrease in deposit during the last month	715, 433
Decrease in deposit since November 1, 1884	2, 097, 374

* The notes of national gold banks located in the State of California, amounting to $384,269, not included.

AGGREGATE RESOURCES AND LIABILITIES

OF

THE NATIONAL BANKS

FROM

OCTOBER, 1863, TO OCTOBER, 1885.

Aggregate resources and liabilities of the National

1863.

Resources.	JANUARY.	APRIL.	JULY.	OCTOBER 5.
				66 banks.
Loans and discounts				$5,466,088 33
U. S. bonds and securities				5,662,600 00
Other items				106,009 12
Due from nat'l and other b'ks				2,625,597 05
Real estate, furniture, &c				177,565 69
Current expenses				53,898 92
Premiums paid				2,503 69
Checks and other cash items				492,138 58
Bills of nat'l and other banks				764,725 00
Specie and other lawful mon'y				1,446,607 62
Total				16,797,644 00

1864.

	JANUARY 4.	APRIL 4.	JULY 4.	OCTOBER 3.
	130 banks.	307 banks.	467 banks.	508 banks.
Loans and discounts	$10,666,095 60	$31,593,943 43	$70,746,513 33	$93,238,657 92
U. S. bonds and securities	15,112,250 00	41,175,150 00	92,530,500 00	108,064,400 60
Other items	74,571 48	432,050 05	842,017 73	1,434,739 76
Due from national banks		4,699,479 56	15,935,730 13	19,965,729 47
Due from other b'ks and b'k'rs	*4,786,124 58	8,537,908 94	17,337,558 66	14,651,396 31
Real estate, furniture, &c	381,144 00	755,696 41	1,694,049 46	2,202,318 29
Current expenses	118,854 43	352,729 77	502,341 31	1,021,569 02
Checks and other cash items	577,507 92	2,651,916 96	5,057,122 90	7,640,169 14
Bills of nat'l and other banks	895,521 00	1,660,000 00	5,344,172 00	4,687,727 00
Specie and other lawful mon'y	5,018,622 57	22,961,411 64	42,283,798 23	44,801,497 48
Total	37,630,691 58	114,820,287 66	232,273,803 75	297,108,195 30

1865.

	JANUARY 2.	APRIL 3.	JULY 3.	OCTOBER 2.
	638 banks.	907 banks.	1,294 banks.	1,513 banks.
Loans and discounts	$166,448,718 00	$252,404,208 07	$362,442,743 08	$487,170,136 29
U. S. bonds and securities	176,578,750 00	277,619,990 00	391,744,850 00	427,731,300 00
Other items	3,294,883 27	4,275,769 51	12,569,129 38	19,048 513 15
Due from national banks	30,820,175 44	40,963,243 47	76,977,539 59	89,978,980 55
Due from other b'ks and b'k'rs	19,836,072 83	22,354,636 57	26,078,028 01	17,393,262 25
Real estate, furniture, &c	4,083,226 12	6,525,118 80	11,231,237 28	14,703,281 77
Current expenses	1,054,725 34	2,298,625 65	2,338,775 56	4,539,525 11
Premiums paid	1,323,023 56	1,823,291 84	2,243,210 31	2,585,501 06
Checks and other cash items	17,837,496 77	29,681,394 13	41,314,904 50	72,309,854 44
Bills of nat'l and other banks	14,275,153 00	13,710,370 00	21,651,826 00	16,247,241 00
Specie	4,481,937 68	6,659,660 47	9,437,060 40	18,672,012 59
Legal tenders and fract'l cur'y	72,535,504 07	112,999,329 59	168,426,166 55	189,988,496 28
Total	512,566,666 66	771,514,939 10	1,126,455,481 66	1,359,768,074 49

* Including amount due from national banks.

Banks from October, 1863, to October, 1885.

1863.

Liabilities.	JANUARY.	APRIL.	JULY.	OCTOBER 5.
				66 banks.
Capital stock				$7, 188, 393 00
Undivided profits..........				128, 030 06
Individual and other deposits.				8, 497, 681 34
Due to nar'l and other banks*.				981, 178 59
Other items................				2, 360 51
Total				16, 797. 644 00

1864.

	JANUARY 4.	APRIL 4.	JULY 4.	OCTOBER 3.
	139 banks.	307 banks.	467 banks.	508 banks.
Capital stock	$14, 740, 522 00	$42, 204, 474 00	$75, 213, 945 00	$86, 782, 802 00
Surplus fund...............			1, 120, 910 22	2, 010, 286 10
Undivided profits...........	432, 827 81	1, 625, 656 87	3, 094, 330 11	5, 982, 392 22
National b'k notes outstanding	30, 155 00	9, 797, 975 00	25, 825, 665 00	45, 266, 504 00
Individual and other deposits.	19, 450, 492 53	51, 274, 914 01	119, 414, 239 03	122, 106, 536 40
Due to nat'l and other banks*.	2, 153, 770 38	6, 814, 930 40	27, 382, 605 37	34, 862, 384 81
Other items................	822, 914 86	3, 102, 337 38	213, 708 02	43, 289 77
Total...............	37, 630, 691 58	114, 820, 287 66	252, 273, 863 75	297, 108, 193 30

1865.

	JANUARY 2.	APRIL 3.	JULY 3.	OCTOBER 2.
	638 banks.	907 banks.	1,294 banks.	1,513 banks.
Capital stock	$135, 618, 674 00	$213, 326, 623 00	$325, 834, 552 00	$393. 157. 206 00
Surplus fund...............	8 668, 811 99	17. 318, 942 05	51, 000, 565 04	39, 719, 380 72
Undivided profits...........	12, 183, 812 65	17. 809, 307 14	23, 159, 408 17	32, 350. 278 19
National b'k notes outstanding	66, 760, 375 00	98, 896, 488 00	131, 452, 158 00	171. 321. 903 00
Individual and other deposits.	183, 479, 636 98	262, 961, 473 13	398, 357, 559 59	500. 910, 873 22
United States deposits.......	37, 764, 729 77	57, 630, 141 01	58. 032, 720 67	48. 170, 381 31
Due to national banks	30, 619, 175 57	41. 301, 031 16	78, 261, 945 64	90. 044, 837 08
Due to other b'ks and bankers*	37, 104, 130 62	53, 692, 581 64	79, 591, 594 93	84. 155, 161 27
Other items................	265. 620 87	578, 951 37	462, 871 02	944, 053 70
Total	512 568, 666 68	771, 514, 939 10	1, 126, 455, 481 66	1, 359, 768, 074 49

* Including State bank circulation outstanding.

Aggregate resources and liabilities of the National

1866.

Resources.	JANUARY 1. 1,582 banks.	APRIL 2. 1,612 banks.	JULY 2. 1,634 banks.	OCTOBER 1. 1,644 banks.
Loans and discounts	$500,650,109 19	$528,080,526 70	$550,353,094 17	$603,314,704 83
U.S. b'ds dep'd to secure circ'n	298,376,850 00	315,850,300 00	326,483,350 00	331,843,200 00
Other U.S. b'ds and securities.	142,003,500 00	125,625,750 00	121,152,950 00	94,974,650 00
Oth'r stocks, b'ds, and mortg's	17,483,753 18	17,379,738 92	17,565,911 46	15,887,400 06
Due from national banks	93,254,551 02	87,564,329 71	96,696,482 66	107,650,174 18
Due from other b'ks and b'k'rs	14,658,229 87	13,682,345 12	13,982,613 23	15,211,117 16
Real estate, furniture, &c ...	15,436,296 16	15,895,564 46	16,730,923 62	17,134,002 58
Current expenses	3,193,717 78	4,927,599 79	3,632,716 27	5,311,253 35
Premiums paid..............	2,423,912 02	2,253,516 31	2,398,872 26	2,493,773 47
Checks and other cash items.	89,837,684 50	105,490,619 36	96,077,134 53	103,684,249 21
Bills of national and other b'ks	20,406,442 00	18,279,816 00	17,860,742 00	17,437,779 00
Specie.....................	19,205,018 75	17,529,778 42	12,629,376 30	9,226,831 82
Legal tenders and fract'l cur'y	187,846,548 82	189,867,852 52	201,425,041 63	205,793,578 76
Total..............	1,404,776,619 29	1,442,407,737 31	1,476,305,208 13	1,526,962,804 42

1867.

	JANUARY 7. 1,648 banks.	APRIL 1. 1,642 banks.	JULY 1. 1,656 banks.	OCTOBER 7. 1,642 banks.
Loans and discounts	$608,771,799 61	$597,648,280 53	$588,450,396 12	$609,675,214 61
U.S. b'ds dep'd to secure circ'n	339,570,700 00	338,863,650 00	337,684,250 00	338,640,150 00
U.S. b'ds dep'd to sec're dep'ts	36,185,950 00	38,465,800 00	38,368,950 00	37,862,100 00
U.S. b'ds and sec'ties on hand.	52,949,300 00	46,639,400 00	45,653,700 00	42,460,800 00
Oth'r stocks, b'ds, and mortg's	15,073,737 45	20,196,875 21	21,452,615 43	21,505,881 42
Due from national banks	92,552,206 29	94,121,186 21	92,308,911 87	95,217,610 14
Due from other b'ks and b'k'rs	12,996,157 49	16,737,392 00	9,663,322 82	8,389,226 47
Real estate, furniture, &c....	18,925,315 51	19,625,893 81	19,800,905 86	20,639,708 23
Current expenses	2,822,675 18	5,693,784 17	3,249,153 34	5,207,494 13
Premiums paid...	2,860,398 85	3,411,325 56	3,338,600 37	2,764,186 35
Checks and other cash items.	101,430,220 18	87,951,405 13	128,312,177 70	134,603,231 51
Bills of national banks	19,263,718 00	12,873,785 00	16,138,700 00	11,841,104 00
Bills of other banks.........	1,176,142 00	825,748 00	531,267 00	333,209 00
Specie	19,726,043 20	11,444,529 15	11,128,672 98	12,798,044 40
Legal tenders and fract'l cur'y	104,872,371 64	92,801,254 17	102,534,613 46	100,550,849 91
Compound interest notes	82,047,250 00	84,065,790 00	75,488,220 00	56,888,230 00
Total..............	1,511,222,985 40	1,465,451,105 84	1,494,084,526 01	1,499,469,000 17

1868.

	JANUARY 6. 1,642 banks.	APRIL 6. 1,643 banks.	JULY 6. 1,640 banks.	OCTOBER 5. 1,643 banks.
Loans and discounts	$616,603,479 89	$628,029,347 65	$655,729,546 42	$657,668,847 83
U.S. b'ds dep'd to secure circ'n	339,064,200 00	339,686,650 00	339,560,100 00	340,487,950 00
U.S. b'ds dep'd to sec're dep'ts	37,315,750 00	37,446,000 00	37,883,150 00	37,360,150 00
U.S. b'ds and sec'ties on hand.	44,164,500 00	45,958,550 00	43,068,350 00	36,817,600 00
Oth'r stocks, b'ds, and mortg's	19,365,864 77	19,874,384 33	20,007,327 42	20,693,406 40
Due from national banks....	99,311,446 60	95,900,606 35	114,424,097 93	102,278,547 77
Due from other b'ks and b'k'rs	8,480,199 74	7,074,297 44	8,642,456 72	7,848,822 24
Real estate, furniture, &c ...	21,125,665 68	22,082,570 33	22,699,829 70	22,747,875 18
Current expenses	2,986,893 86	5,428,460 25	2,958,519 04	5,278,911 22
Premiums paid..............	2,464,536 96	2,660,106 09	2,432,074 37	1,819,815 50
Checks and other cash items.	109,390,260 37	114,993,036 23	124,076,097 71	143,241,394 99
Bills of national banks	16,655,572 00	12,573,514 00	13,210,179 00	11,842,974 00
Bills of other banks.........	261,269 00	196,106 00	342,550 00	222,668 00
Fractional currency..........	1,927,876 78	1,825,640 16	1,863,358 91	2,262,791 97
Specie......	20,981,601 45	18,373,943 22	20,735,919 04	13,009,713 39
Legal-tender notes	111,306,491 00	84,396,219 00	100,166,100 00	92,453,915 00
Compound interest notes	39,997,030 00	38,917,490 00	19,473,420 00	4,513,730 00
Three per cent. certificates.	8,245,000 00	24,255,000 00	44,905,000 00	59,080,000 00
Total..............	1,502,647,644 10	1,499,668,920 97	1,572,167,076 26	1,559,621,773 49

Banks from October, 1863, to October, 1885—Continued.

1866.

Liabilities.	JANUARY 1. 1,582 banks.	APRIL 2. 1,612 banks.	JULY 2, 1,634 banks.	OCTOBER 1. 1,644 banks.
Capital stock	$403, 357, 346 00	$409, 273, 534 00	$414, 270, 493 00	$415, 472, 369 00
Surplus fund	43, 000, 370 78	44, 687, 810 54	50, 151, 991 77	53, 359, 277 64
Undivided profits	28, 972, 493 70	30, 964, 422 73	29, 286, 175 45	32, 593, 480 69
National b'k notes outstanding	213, 239, 530 00	248, 886, 282 00	267, 798, 678 00	280, 253, 818 00
State bank notes outstanding	45, 449, 155 00	33, 800, 865 00	19, 996, 163 00	9, 748, 025 00
Individual deposits	522, 507, 829 27	534, 734, 950 33	533, 338, 174 25	564, 616, 777 64
U. S. deposits	29, 747, 236 15	29, 150, 729 82	36, 938, 183 03	30, 420, 819 80
Dep'ts of U.S. disb'sing officers			3, 060, 892 22	2, 979, 955 77
Due to national banks	94, 709, 074 15	89, 067, 501 54	96, 496, 726 42	110, 531, 957 31
Due to other b'ks and bankers.	23, 793, 584 24	21, 841, 641 35	25, 951, 728 99	26, 986, 317 57
Total	1, 404, 776, 619 29	1, 442, 407, 737 31	1, 476, 395, 208 13	1, 526, 962, 804 42

1867.

	JANUARY 7. 1,648 banks.	APRIL 1. 1,642 banks.	JULY 1. 1,636 banks.	OCTOBER 7. 1,642 banks.
Capital stock	$420, 229, 739 00	$419, 309, 484 00	$418, 558, 148 00	$420, 073, 415 00
Surplus fund	59, 902, 874 57	60, 206, 013 58	63, 232, 811 12	66, 695, 587 01
Undivided profits	26, 961, 382 60	31, 131, 034 39	30, 656, 222 84	33, 751, 446 21
National b'k notes outstanding	291, 436, 749 00	292, 788, 572 00	291, 769, 553 00	293, 887, 941 00
State bank notes outstanding.	6, 961, 499 00	5, 460, 312 00	4, 484, 112 00	4, 092, 153 00
Individual deposits	358, 699, 768 06	512, 046, 182 47	539, 590, 076 10	540, 797, 837 51
U. S. deposits	27, 284, 876 93	27, 473, 005 66	29, 838, 391 53	23, 062, 119 92
Dep's of U.S. disb'sing officers	2, 477, 509 48	2, 650, 981 39	3, 474, 192 74	4, 352, 379 43
Due to national banks	92, 761, 998 43	91, 156, 890 89	89, 821, 751 60	93, 111, 240 89
Due to other b'ks and bankers	24, 416, 588 33	23, 138, 629 46	22, 659, 267 08	19, 644, 940 20
Total	1, 511, 222, 985 40	1, 465, 451, 105 84	1, 494, 084, 526 01	1, 499, 469, 060 17

1868.

	JANUARY 6. 1,642 banks.	APRIL 6. 1,643 banks.	JULY 6. 1,640 banks.	OCTOBER 5. 1,643 banks.
Capital stock	$420, 260, 790 00	$420, 676, 210 00	$420, 105, 011 00	$420, 634, 511 00
Surplus fund	70, 585, 125 70	72, 349, 119 60	75, 840, 118 94	77, 095, 761 40
Undivided profits	31, 899, 877 57	32, 861, 597 08	33, 543, 223 35	36, 095, 883 98
National b'k notes outstanding	294, 377, 390 00	295, 336, 044 00	294, 908, 264 00	295, 760, 489 00
State bank notes outstanding.	3, 792, 013 00	3, 310, 177 00	3, 163, 771 00	2, 906, 352 00
Individual deposits	534, 704, 709 00	532, 011, 480 36	575, 842, 070 12	589, 949, 820 85
U. S. deposits	24, 305, 638 02	22, 750, 742 77	24, 660, 670 86	17, 573, 250 64
Dep'ts of U.S. disb'sing officers	3, 208, 783 63	4, 976, 682 31	3, 499, 380 99	4, 570, 478 16
Due to national banks	98, 144, 669 61	94, 073, 631 25	113, 306, 346 34	99, 414, 397 28
Due to other b'ks and bankers	21, 867, 648 17	21, 323, 636 00	27, 355, 204 56	23, 720, 820 18
Total	1, 502, 647, 644 10	1, 499, 668, 920 97	1, 572, 167, 076 26	1, 559, 621, 773 49

Aggregate resources and liabilities of the National

1869.

Resources.	JANUARY 4. 1,628 banks.	APRIL 17. 1,620 banks.	JUNE 12. 1,619 banks.	OCTOBER 9. 1,017 banks.
Loans and discounts	$644, 945, 039 53	$662, 084, 813 47	$686, 347, 755 81	$682, 883, 106 97
U. S. bonds to secure circ'lat'n	338, 539, 950 00	338, 379, 250 00	338, 609, 750 00	339, 480, 100 00
U. S. bonds to secure deposits.	34, 538, 350 00	29, 721, 350 00	27, 625, 350 00	18, 704, 000 00
U. S. b'ds and sec'ties on hand.	35, 010, 600 00	30, 226, 550 00	27, 476, 650 00	25, 903, 950 00
Oth'r stocks, b'ds, and mortg'a	20, 127, 732 96	20, 074, 435 69	20, 777, 560 53	22, 250, 697 14
Due from redeeming agents..	65, 727, 070 80	57, 554, 382 55	62, 912, 636 82	56, 660, 562 84
Due from other national banks	36, 067, 316 84	36, 520, 527 89	35, 556, 504 53	35, 393, 563 47
Due from State b'ks and b'k'rs	7, 715, 719 34	8, 075, 595 60	9, 140, 919 24	8, 790, 418 57
Real estate, furniture, &c....	22, 289, 838 28	23, 768, 188 13	23, 859, 271 17	25, 169, 188 95
Current expenses...........	3, 265, 990 81	5, 641, 195 01	5, 820, 577 87	5, 646, 382 96
Premiums paid.............	1, 654, 352 70	1, 716, 210 13	1, 809, 070 01	2, 092, 364 85
Checks and other cash items.	142, 605, 984 92	154, 137, 191 23	161, 614, 852 66	108, 809, 817 37
Bills of other national banks.	14, 684, 799 00	11, 725, 239 00	11, 524, 447 00	10, 776, 023 00
Fractional currency	2, 280, 471 06	2, 088, 545 18	1, 804, 855 53	2, 000, 727 38
Specie.....................	29, 626, 750 26	9, 944, 532 15	18, 455, 090 48	23, 002, 405 83
Legal-tender notes	88, 239, 300 00	80, 875, 161 00	80, 934, 119 00	83, 719, 295 00
Three per cent. certificates..	52, 075, 000 00	51, 190, 000 00	49, 815, 000 00	45, 845, 000 00
Total..................	1, 540, 394, 266 50	1, 517, 753, 167 03	1, 564, 174, 410 65	1, 497, 226, 604 33

1870.

	JANUARY 22. 1,615 banks.	MARCH 24. 1,615 banks.	JUNE 9. 1,612 banks.	OCTOBER 8. 1,615 banks.	DECEMBER 28. 1,648 banks.
Loans and discounts .	$688, 875, 203 70	$710, 848, 609 39	$719, 341, 186 06	$715, 028, 079 81	$725, 515, 538 49
Bonds for circulation	339, 350, 750 00	339, 251, 350 00	338, 845, 200 00	340, 857, 450 00	344, 104, 200 00
Bonds for deposits ..	17, 502, 000 00	16, 102, 000 00	15, 704, 000 00	15, 381, 500 00	15, 189, 500 00
U. S. bonds on hand ..	24, 677, 100 00	27, 292, 150 00	28, 276, 600 00	22, 323, 800 00	23, 893, 300 00
Other stocks and b'ds	21, 082, 412 00	20, 524, 294 55	23, 300, 681 87	23, 614, 721 25	22, 686, 358 59
Due from red'g ag'nts	71, 641, 480 05	73, 435, 117 98	74, 635, 405 61	66, 275, 668 92	64, 805, 062 88
Due from nat'l banks	31, 994, 609 26	29, 510, 688 11	36, 128, 750 66	33, 048, 805 65	37, 478, 166 49
Due from State banks	9, 319, 560 54	10, 238, 219 85	10, 488, 731 32	9, 202, 496 71	9, 824, 144 18
Real estate, &c	26, 002, 713 01	26, 330, 701 24	26, 503, 357 00	27, 470, 746 97	28, 021, 637 44
Current expenses ...	3, 469, 588 00	6, 683, 189 54	6, 324, 955 47	5, 871, 750 02	6, 905, 073 32
Premiums paid......	2, 439, 591 41	2, 680, 882 39	3, 076, 456 74	2, 491, 222 11	3, 251, 648 72
Cash items	111, 024, 822 00	11, 267, 703 12	11, 407, 534 13	12, 536, 613 57	13, 229, 403 34
Clear'g-house exch'gs	....	75, 317, 992 22	83, 936, 515 64	79, 089, 688 30	76, 208, 707 00
National bank notes .	15, 840, 669 00	14, 226, 817 00	16, 342, 582 00	12, 512, 927 00	17, 001, 846 00
Fractional currency .	2, 476, 966 75	2, 285, 499 02	2, 184, 714 39	2, 078, 178 05	2, 159, 522 89
Specie	48, 345, 383 72	37, 096, 543 44	31, 099, 437 78	18, 460, 011 47	26, 307, 251 59
Legal-tender notes ..	87, 708, 502 00	82, 485, 978 00	94, 573, 751 00	79, 324, 577 00	80, 580, 745 00
Three per cent. cert'fs	43, 820, 000 00	48, 570, 000 00	43, 465, 000 00	43, 345, 000 00	41, 845, 000 00
Total............	1, 546, 261, 357 44	1, 529, 147, 735 85	1, 565, 756, 909 67	1, 510, 713, 236 92	1, 538, 998, 105 93

1871.

	MARCH 13. 1,688 banks.	APRIL 29. 1,707 banks.	JUNE 10. 1,723 banks.	OCTOBER 2. 1,767 banks.	DECEMBER 16. 1,790 banks.
Loans and discounts.	$767, 858, 490 59	$779, 321, 828 11	$789, 416, 568 13	$831, 552, 210 00	$818, 026, 311 74
Bonds for circulation	351, 556, 700 00	354, 427, 200 00	357, 388, 950 00	364, 475, 800 00	366, 844, 200 00
Bonds for deposits ..	15, 231, 500 00	15, 236, 500 00	15, 250, 500 00	28, 087, 500 00	23, 155, 150 00
U. S. bonds on hand .	23, 911, 350 00	22, 487, 950 00	24, 200, 300 00	17, 753, 650 00	17, 675, 500 00
Other stocks and b'ds	22, 763, 869 20	22, 414, 659 05	23, 132, 871 05	24, 517, 059 35	23, 061, 184 20
Due from red'g ag'nts	83, 809, 188 02	85, 061, 016 31	92, 369, 246 71	86, 878, 608 84	77, 985, 609 53
Due from nat'l banks	30, 201, 119 99	38, 332, 679 74	39, 636, 579 35	43, 525, 362 05	43, 313, 344 78
Due from State banks	10, 271, 605 34	11, 478, 174 71	11, 853, 308 60	12, 772, 669 83	13, 069, 361 40
Real estate, &c	28, 805, 814 79	29, 242, 762 79	29, 637, 999 30	30, 080, 783 85	30, 079, 380 57
Current expenses....	6, 694, 014 17	6, 764, 159 73	6, 295, 099 46	6, 153, 370 29	7, 336, 424 12
Premiums paid.....	3, 939, 905 20	4, 414, 755 40	5, 026, 385 97	5, 500, 890 17	5, 956, 073 74
Cash items	11, 642, 644 74	12, 749, 289 84	13, 101, 497 95	14, 058, 268 86	13, 784, 424 76
Clear'g-house exch'gs	100, 683, 917 54	130, 855, 698 15	102, 091, 311 75	101, 165, 854 52	114, 536, 539 93
National bank notes .	13, 137, 006 00	16, 632, 323 00	19, 101, 389 00	14, 197, 653 00	13, 085, 904 00
Fractional currency .	2, 103, 298 16	2, 135, 763 00	2, 134, 249 00	2, 093, 685 89	2, 061, 669 89
Specie	25, 769, 166 64	22, 732, 027 02	19, 924, 955 16	13, 262, 998 17	20, 595, 299 56
Legal-tender notes ..	91, 072, 349 00	106, 219, 126 00	122, 137, 660 00	109, 414, 735 00	93, 942, 707 00
Three per cent. cert'fs	37, 570, 000 00	33, 935, 000 00	30, 690, 000 00	25, 075, 000 00	21, 400, 000 00
Total	1, 627, 032, 030 28	1, 694, 440, 912 94	1, 703, 415, 335 65	1, 730, 566, 899 72	1, 715, 861, 897 22

Banks from October, 1863, to October, 1885—Continued.

1869.

Liabilities.	JANUARY 4. 1,628 banks.	APRIL 17. 1,620 banks.	JUNE 12. 1,619 banks.	OCTOBER 9. 1,617 banks.
Capital stock	$419,040,931 00	$420,818,721 00	$422,659,260 00	$426,399,151 00
Surplus fund	81,160,936 52	82,653,989 19	82,218,576 47	86,165,334 32
Undivided profits	35,318,273 71	37,488,314 82	43,812,898 70	40,687,300 92
Nat'l bank notes outstanding	294,476,702 00	292,457,098 00	292,753,286 00	293,593,645 00
State bank notes outstanding	2,734,669 00	2,615,387 00	2,558,874 00	2,454,697 00
Individual deposits	568,530,934 11	547,922,174 91	574,307,382 77	511,400,196 63
U. S. deposits	13,211,850 19	10,114,328 32	10,301,907 71	7,112,646 67
Dep'ts U.S.disbursing officers	3,472,884 90	3,665,131 61	2,454,948 99	4,510,648 12
Due to national banks	95,453,139 33	92,662,648 49	100,033,910 03	95,067,802 83
Due to State banks and b'k'rs	26,984,945 74	23,018,610 62	28,046,771 30	23,849,371 62
Notes and bills re-discounted		2,464,849 81	2,302,205 61	3,839,357 10
Bills payable		1,870,913 26	1,735,289 07	2,140,363 12
Total	1,540,394,266 50	1,517,753,167 03	1,564,174,410 65	1,497,226,604 33

1870.

	JANUARY 22. 1,615 banks.	MARCH 24. 1,615 banks.	JUNE 9. 1,612 banks.	OCTOBER 8. 1,615 banks.	DECEMBER 28. 1,648 banks.
Capital stock	$426,074,954 00	$427,504,247 00	$427,235,701 00	$430,399,301 00	$435,356,004 00
Surplus fund	90,174,281 14	90,229,954 59	91,689,834 12	94,061,488 95	94,705,740 34
Undivided profits	34,300,430 89	43,109,471 62	42,861,712 59	38,608,618 91	46,056,428 55
Nat'l bank circulat'n	292,838,935 00	292,509,149 00	291,183,614 00	291,798,640 00	296,205,446 00
State bank circulat'n	2,351,998 00	2,279,469 00	2,222,793 00	2,138,548 00	2,091,799 00
Dividends unpaid	2,290,296 27	1,483,416 15	1,517,595 18	2,462,591 31	2,242,556 49
Individual deposits	546,236,881 57	516,058,085 26	542,261,563 18	501,407,586 90	507,368,618 67
U. S. deposits	6,750,139 19	6,424,421 25	10,677,873 92	6,807,978 49	6,074,407 90
Dep'ts U.S.dis.officers	2,592,001 21	4,778,225 93	2,592,967 54	4,550,142 68	4,155,304 25
Due to national banks	108,351,300 33	109,667,715 95	115,456,491 84	100,348,292 45	106,090,414 53
Due to State banks	28,904,849 14	29,767,575 21	33,012,162 78	29,693,910 80	29,200,587 29
Notes re-discounted	3,842,542 30	2,462,647 49	2,741,843 53	3,843,577 67	4,612,131 08
Bills payable	1,543,758 49	2,873,357 40	2,302,756 99	4,592,669 76	4,836,667 83
Total	1,546,261,357 44	1,529,147,735 85	1,565,756,909 67	1,510,713,236 92	1,538,998,105 93

1871.

	MARCH 18. 1,688 banks.	APRIL 29. 1,707 banks.	JUNE 10. 1,723 banks.	OCTOBER 2. 1,767 banks.	DECEMBER 16. 1,790 banks.
Capital stock	$444,232,771 00	$446,925,493 00	$450,330,841 00	$458,255,696 00	$460,225,866 00
Surplus funds	96,862,081 66	97,620,099 28	98,322,203 80	101,112,671 01	101,573,159 62
Undivided profits	43,883,857 64	44,776,930 71	45,535,227 79	42,008,714 38	48,630,925 81
Nat'l bank circulation	301,713,460 00	306,131,393 00	307,793,880 00	315,519,117 00	318,265,481 00
State bank circulation	2,035,800 00	1,982,580 00	1,968,058 00	1,921,056 00	1,886,538 00
Dividends unpaid	1,263,767 70	2,235,248 46	1,408,628 25	4,540,104 70	1,303,427 98
Individual deposits	561,190,830 41	611,025,174 10	602,110,758 16	600,868,486 55	596,586,487 54
U. S. deposits	6,314,957 81	6,521,572 92	6,205,167 94	20,511,935 98	14,820,525 65
Dep'ts U.S.dis.officers	4,813,016 66	3,757,873 84	4,893,907 25	5,393,598 89	5,399,108 34
Due to national banks	118,904,805 84	128,037,469 17	135,167,847 69	131,730,713 04	118,657,614 16
Due to State banks	37,311,519 13	36,113,290 67	41,219,802 96	40,211,971 67	38,116,950 67
Notes re-discounted	3,256,896 42	3,573,723 02	3,120,030 09	3,964,552 57	4,922,455 78
Bills payable	5,248,206 01	5,740,964 77	5,278,973 72	4,528,191 12	5,374,362 67
Total	1,627,032,080 28	1,694,440,912 94	1,703,415,335 65	1,730,566,899 72	1,715,861,897 22

Aggregate resources and liabilities of the National

1 8 7 2 .

Resources.	FEBRUARY 27.	APRIL 19.	JUNE 10.	OCTOBER 3.	DECEMBER 27.
	1,814 banks.	1,843 banks.	1,853 banks.	1,919 banks.	1,940 banks.
Loans and discounts.	$839,665,077 91	$844,902,253 49	$871,531,448 67	$877,197,923 47	$885,653,449 62
Bonds for circulation	370,324,700 00	374,428,450 00	377,029,700 00	382,046,400 00	384,458,500 00
Bonds for deposits..	15,870,000 00	15,169,000 00	15,409,950 00	15,479,750 00	16,304,750 00
U. S. bonds on hand.	21,323,150 00	19,292,100 00	16,458,250 00	12,142,550 00	10,306,100 00
Other stocks and b'ds	22,838,338 80	21,536,914 06	22,270,610 47	23,533,151 73	23,160,557 29
Due from red'g ag'nts	89,548,329 93	82,120,017 24	91,564,269 53	80,717,071 30	86,401,459 44
Due from nat'l banks	38,282,905 86	36,607,592 81	39,468,323 39	34,486,503 87	42,707,613 54
Due from State banks	12,269,822 68	12,299,716 94	13,014,265 26	12,976,878 61	12,008,813 54
Real estate, &c	30,637,076 75	30,800,274 98	31,123,843 21	32,276,498 17	33,014,796 83
Current expenses...	6,265,655 15	7,026,041 23	6,719,794 90	6,310,428 79	8,454,803 97
Premiums paid	6,308,821 86	6,544,279 20	6,616,174 75	6,546,818 52	7,097,847 86
Cash items	12,143,403 12	12,461,171 40	13,458,753 80	14,916,784 34	13,696,723 85
Clear'g-house exch'gs	93,154,319 74	114,195,966 36	88,592,800 16	110,086,315 37	90,145,482 72
National-bank notes	15,552,087 00	18,492,832 00	16,253,560 00	15,787,296 00	19,070,322 00
Fractional currency.	2,278,143 24	2,143,249 29	2,069,464 12	2,151,747 88	2,270,576 32
Specie	25,507,825 32	24,433,899 46	24,256,644 14	10,229,756 79	19,647,336 45
Legal-tender notes..	97,865,400 00	105,732,455 00	122,994,417 00	105,121,104 00	102,922,369 00
U.S. cert'fs of deposit	....	....	....	6,716,000 00	12,650,000 00
Three per cent. cert'fs	18,980,000 00	15,365,000 00	12,605,000 00	7,140,000 00	4,185,000 00
Total	1,719,415,657 34	1,743,652,213 55	1,770,637,269 40	1,755,857,098 24	1,773,556,532 43

1 8 7 3 .

	FEBRUARY 28.	APRIL 25.	JUNE 13.	SEPTEMBER 12.	DECEMBER 26.
	1,947 banks.	1,962 banks.	1,968 banks.	1,976 banks.	1,976 banks.
Loans and discounts.	$913,265,189 67	$912,064,267 31	$925,557,682 42	$944,220,116 34	$856,816,555 05
Bonds for circulation	384,675,050 00	386,763,800 00	388,080,300 00	388,330,400 00	389,384,400 00
Bonds for deposits..	15,035,000 00	16,235,000 00	15,935,000 00	14,805,000 00	14,815,200 00
U. S. bonds on hand.	10,436,950 00	9,613,550 00	9,789,400 00	8,824,850 00	8,630,850 00
Other stocks and b'ds	22,063,306 20	22,449,146 04	22,912,415 63	23,709,034 53	24,358,125 06
Due from red'g ag nts	95,773,077 10	88,815,557 80	97,143,326 94	96,134,120 66	73,032,046 87
Due from nat'l banks	39,483,700 09	38,671,088 63	43,328,792 29	41,413,080 06	40,404,757 97
Due from State banks	13,595,079 17	12,883,353 37	14,073,287 77	12,022,873 41	11,185,253 08
Real estate, &c......	34,023,057 77	34,216,875 07	34,820,562 77	34,661,823 21	35,556,746 48
Current expenses ...	6,977,831 35	7,410,045 87	7,154,211 69	6,985,436 99	8,678,270 39
Premiums paid	7,205,259 67	7,559,987 67	7,890,962 14	7,752,843 87	7,987,107 14
Cash items	11,761,711 50	11,425,209 00	13,036,482 58	11,433,913 22	12,321,072 80
Clear'g-house exch'gs	131,383,860 95	94,132,125 24	91,918,526 59	88,926,003 53	62,884,342 16
National bank notes.	15,998,779 00	19,310,202 00	20,894,772 00	16,103,842 00	21,403,179 00
Fractional currency.	2,289,680 21	2,198,973 37	2,197,559 84	2,302,775 26	2,287,454 03
Specie	17,777,673 53	16,868,808 74	27,950,086 72	18,868,409 45	26,907,937 58
Legal-tender notes..	97,141,900 00	100,605,287 00	106,381,491 00	92,522,663 00	103,719,500 00
U.S. cert'fs of deposit	18,460,000 00	18,370,000 00	22,365,000 00	20,610,000 00	24,010,000 00
Three per cent. cert'fs	1,865,000 00	710,000 00	305,000 00	....	....
Total	1,839,152,715 21	1,800,303,280 11	1,851,234,860 38	1,830,627,845 53	1,729,380,303 61

1 8 7 4 .

	FEBRUARY 27.	MAY 1.	JUNE 26.	OCTOBER 2.	DECEMBER 31.
	1,975 banks.	1,978 banks.	1,983 banks.	2,004 banks.	2,027 banks.
Loans and discounts	$897,859,600 46	$923,347,030 79	$926,195,671 70	$954,394,791 59	$953,862,586 51
Bonds for circulation	389,614,700 00	389,240,100 00	390,281,700 00	388,254,800 00	382,976,200 00
Bonds for deposits ..	14,600,200 00	14,890,200 00	14,890,200 00	14,691,700 00	14,714,000 00
U. S. bonds on hand.	11,043,400 00	10,152,000 00	10,456,900 00	13,313,550 00	15,290,300 00
Other stocks and b'ds	25,305,736 24	25,460,460 20	27,010,727 48	27,867,826 92	28,313,473 12
Due from res'vo ag'ts	101,502,861 53	94,017,603 31	97,871,517 06	83,885,126 94	80,488,831 45
Due from nat'l banks	36,624,001 39	41,201,015 24	45,770,715 59	39,695,309 47	48,106,842 02
Due from State banks	11,496,711 47	12,374,391 28	12,469,592 33	11,196,611 73	11,655,573 07
Real estate, &c......	36,043,741 50	36,708,066 39	37,270,876 51	38,112,926 52	39,190,683 04
Current expenses ...	6,998,875 79	7,547,203 05	7,550,125 24	7,058,738 82	5,510,566 47
Premiums paid	8,741,028 77	8,680,370 84	8,568,202 27	8,376,659 07	8,626,112 16
Cash items	10,269,055 50	11,949,020 71	10,496,257 00	12,296,416 77	14,005,517 33
Clear'g-house exch'gs	62,768,119 19	94,877,796 52	63,896,271 31	97,388,687 11	112,095,317 55
National bank notes.	20,003,251 00	20,673,452 00	23,527,991 00	18,450,013 00	22,532,336 00
Fractional currency.	2,309,919 73	2,187,186 69	2,283,808 92	2,324,949 12	2,392,668 74
Specie	33,365,863 58	32,569,969 26	22,320,207 27	21,240,915 23	22,436,701 04
Legal-tender notes..	102,717,563 00	101,692,930 00	103,108,350 00	80,021,946 00	82,604,791 00
U.S. cert'fs of deposit	37,235,000 00	40,135,000 00	47,780,000 00	42,825,000 00	33,670,000 00
Dep. with U. S. Treas	....	....	91,250 00	20,349,950 15	21,043,084 36
Total	1,808,500,529 16	1,867,802,796 28	1,851,840,913 64	1,877,180,942 44	1,902,409,638 46

Banks from October, 1863, to October, 1885—Continued.

1872.

Liabilities.	FEBRUARY 27.	APRIL 19.	JUNE 10.	OCTOBER 3.	DECEMBER 27.
	1,814 banks.	1,848 banks.	1,853 banks.	1,919 banks.	1,940 banks.
Capital stock	$464,081,744 00	$467,924,318 00	$470,543,301 00	$479,629,174 00	$482,666,252 00
Surplus fund	103,787,082 62	104,312,525 81	105,181,943 28	110,257,516 45	111,410,248 98
Undivided profits	43,310,344 46	46,428,590 90	50,234,298 32	46,623,784 50	56,762,411 89
Nat'l bank circulation	321,634,675 00	325,305,752 00	327,092,752 00	333,495,027 00	336,289,285 00
State bank circulation	1,830,563 00	1,763,885 00	1,700,935 00	1,567,143 00	1,511,396 00
Dividends unpaid	1,451,746 29	1,561,914 45	1,454,044 06	3,149,749 61	1,356,934 48
Individual deposits	593,645,666 16	620,775,265 78	618,801,619 49	613,290,671 45	598,114,679 26
U. S. deposits	7,114,893 47	6,355,722 95	6,993,014 77	7,853,772 41	7,863,894 93
Dep'ts U.S. dis. officers	5,024,699 44	3,416,371 16	5,463,953 48	4,568,833 79	5,136,597 74
Due to national banks	128,627,494 44	120,755,565 86	132,804,924 02	110,047,347 67	124,218,392 83
Due to State banks	39,025,165 44	35,005,127 84	39,878,826 42	33,789,083 82	34,794,963 37
Notes re-discounted	3,818,686 91	4,925,622 04	4,745,178 22	5,549,431 88	6,545,059 78
Bills payable	6,662,896 91	5,821,551 76	5,942,479 34	6,040,562 66	6,946,416 17
Total	1,719,415,657 34	1,743,652,213 55	1,770,857,269 40	1,755,857,098 24	1,773,556,532 43

1873.

	FEBRUARY 28.	APRIL 25.	JUNE 13.	SEPTEMBER 12.	DECEMBER 26.
	1,947 banks.	1,962 banks.	1,968 banks.	1,976 banks.	1,976 banks.
Capital stock	$484,551,811 00	$487,891,251 00	$490,109,801 00	$491,072,616 00	$490,266,611 00
Surplus fund	114,681,048 73	115,803,574 57	116,847,454 62	120,314,400 20	120,961,267 91
Undivided profits	48,578,045 28	52,415,348 46	55,306,151 69	54,515,131 76	58,375,169 43
Nat'l bank circulation	336,292,459 00	338,163,804 00	338,788,504 00	339,081,790 00	341,320,256 00
State bank circulation	1,366,271 00	1,280,208 00	1,224,470 00	1,188,853 00	1,130,585 00
Dividends unpaid	1,465,993 60	1,462,336 77	1,400,491 90	1,402,547 89	1,269,474 74
Individual deposits	656,187,551 61	646,848,358 25	641,121,775 27	622,625,563 29	540,510,602 78
U. S. deposits	7,044,848 34	7,880,057 73	8,691,001 95	7,829,327 73	7,680,375 20
Dep'ts U.S. dis. officers	5,885,696 60	4,425,750 14	6,416,275 10	8,098,560 13	4,705,593 36
Due to national banks	134,231,842 95	126,631,926 24	137,856,085 67	133,672,732 94	114,996,666 54
Due to State banks	38,124,803 85	35,036,433 18	40,741,788 47	39,298,148 14	36,598,076 29
Notes re-discounted	5,117,810 50	5,463,043 38	5,515,900 67	5,987,512 36	3,811,487 89
Bills payable	5,672,582 75	7,059,128 29	7,215,157 04	5,480,554 09	7,754,137 41
Total	1,839,152,715 21	1,800,303,280 11	1,851,234,860 38	1,830,627,845 53	1,729,380,303 61

1874.

	FEBRUARY 27.	MAY 1.	JUNE 26.	OCTOBER 2.	DECEMBER 31.
	1,975 banks.	1,978 banks.	1,933 banks.	2,004 banks.	2,027 banks.
Capital stock	$490,859,101 00	$490,077,001 00	$491,003,711 00	$493,765,121 00	$495,802,481 00
Surplus fund	123,497,347 20	125,561,081 23	126,230,308 44	128,958,106 84	100,405,611 37
Undivided profits	50,236,919 88	54,331,713 13	58,332,965 71	51,484,437 32	51,477,629 33
Nat'l bank circulation	339,602,955 00	340,267,649 00	338,598,743 00	333,225,298 00	331,193,159 00
State bank circulation	1,078,988 00	1,049,286 00	1,009,021 00	964,567 00	860,417 00
Dividends unpaid	1,291,055 63	2,259,129 91	1,242,474 81	3,516,276 99	6,088,845 01
Individual deposits	595,350,334 90	649,286,298 95	622,863,154 44	669,068,995 88	682,816,007 45
U. S. deposits	7,276,959 87	7,904,422 27	7,322,830 85	7,302,153 58	7,492,307 78
Dep'ts U.S. dis. officers	5,034,624 46	3,297,689 24	3,238,630 20	3,927,828 27	3,379,722 94
Due to national banks	138,435,388 39	135,640,418 24	143,083,822 26	125,102,049 93	129,188,671 42
Due to State banks	48,112,223 40	49,772,426 18	50,227,426 18	50,718,007 87	51,629,002 36
Notes re-discounted	3,448,828 92	4,581,420 38	4,436,256 22	4,197,372 25	6,365,652 97
Bills payable	4,275,002 51	4,772,662 59	4,352,560 57	4,950,727 51	5,398,900 83
Total	1,808,500,520 16	1,867,802,796 28	1,851,840,913 64	1,877,180,042 44	1,902,409,638 46

Aggregate resources and liabilities of the National

1875.

Resources.	MARCH 1. 2,029 banks.	MAY 1. 2,046 banks.	JUNE 30. 2,076 banks.	OCTOBER 1. 2,088 banks.	DECEMBER 17. 2,086 banks.
Loans and discounts	$956,485,939 35	$971,835,298 74	$972,026,532 14	$984,691,434 40	$962,571,807 70
Bonds for circulation	380,682,650 00	378,026,900 00	375,127,900 00	370,321,700 00	363,618,100 00
Bonds for deposits	14,492,200 00	14,372,200 00	14,147,200 00	14,097,200 00	13,981,500 00
U. S. bonds on hand	18,062,150 00	14,207,650 00	12,753,000 00	13,989,950 00	16,009,550 00
Other stocks and b'ds	28,268,841 09	29,102,197 10	32,010,316 18	33,505,045 15	31,657,000 52
Due from res've ag'ts	89,091,175 34	80,620,878 75	89,768,903 73	85,701,259 82	81,462,682 27
Due from nat'l banks	44,720,394 11	46,039,597 57	48,513,388 86	47,028,760 18	44,831,891 48
Due from State banks	12,724,243 07	12,094,086 39	11,625,647 15	11,963,768 00	11,895,551 08
Real estate, &c.	39,430,952 12	40,312,285 99	40,069,920 40	42,366,647 65	41,583,311 94
Current expenses	7,790,581 86	7,706,700 42	4,992,044 34	7,841,213 05	9,218,455 47
Premiums paid	9,006,880 92	8,434,453 14	8,742,393 83	8,670,091 18	9,442,801 54
Cash items	11,734,762 42	13,122,145 88	12,433,100 43	12,758,872 03	11,238,725 72
Clear'g-house exch'gs	81,127,796 39	116,970,819 05	88,924,025 93	75,142,863 45	67,886,967 04
Bills of other banks	18,909,397 00	19,504,640 00	24,261,961 00	18,528,837 00	17,166,190 00
Fractional currency	3,008,592 12	2,702,326 44	2,620,504 26	2,595,631 78	2,901,023 10
Specie	16,667,106 17	10,620,361 64	18,950,582 30	8,050,329 73	17,070,905 90
Legal-tender notes	78,508,170 00	84,015,928 00	87,492,895 00	76,458,734 00	70,725,077 00
U. S. cert'fs of deposit	37,200,000 00	38,615,000 00	47,330,000 00	48,810,000 00	31,005,000 00
Due from U. S. Treas	21,007,919 76	21,454,422 20	19,640,785 52	19,686,960 30	19,202,256 68
Total	1,869,819,753 22	1,909,847,891 40	1,913,239,201 16	1,882,209,307 62	1,823,469,752 44

1876.

	MARCH 10. 2,091 banks.	MAY 12. 2,089 banks.	JUNE 30 2,091 banks.	OCTOBER 2. 2,089 banks.	DECEMBER 22. 2,082 banks.
Loans and discounts	$950,205,555 62	$939,895,085 34	$933,686,530 45	$931,304,714 06	$929,066,408 42
Bonds for circulation	354,547,750 00	344,537,350 00	339,141,750 00	337,170,400 00	336,705,300 00
Bonds for deposits	14,216,500 00	14,128,000 00	14,328,000 00	14,698,000 00	14,757,000 00
U. S. bonds on hand	25,910,650 00	26,577,000 00	30,842,300 00	33,142,150 00	31,937,950 00
Other stocks and b'ds	30,425,430 43	30,905,105 82	32,482,805 75	34,445,157 16	31,565,914 50
Due from res've ag'ts	99,068,360 35	86,709,083 97	87,989,000 90	87,326,950 48	83,789,174 65
Due from nat'l banks	42,341,542 67	44,328,609 40	47,417,029 03	47,525,689 98	44,011,064 97
Due from State banks	11,180,562 15	11,262,193 96	10,989,507 95	12,061,283 08	12,415,341 97
Real estate, &c.	41,937,617 25	42,183,058 78	42,722,415 27	43,121,942 01	43,408,445 49
Current expenses	8,206,207 85	6,820,573 35	5,025,549 38	6,987,644 46	9,818,422 88
Premiums paid	10,046,713 15	10,414,847 28	10,021,634 03	10,715,251 16	10,811,300 66
Cash items	9,517,808 86	9,603,186 37	11,724,592 67	12,043,139 68	10,658,709 26
Clear'g-house exch'gs	58,863,182 43	56,806,632 63	75,328,878 84	87,870,817 06	68,027,016 40
Bills of other banks	18,536,502 00	20,347,964 00	20,308,422 00	15,910,315 00	17,521,663 00
Fractional currency	3,215,594 30	2,771,886 26	1,987,897 44	1,447,203 66	1,146,741 94
Specie	20,077,345 85	21,714,594 36	25,218,469 02	21,360,767 42	32,999,647 89
Legal-tender notes	76,768,446 00	79,858,661 00	90,836,876 00	84,250,847 00	66,221,400 00
U. S. cert'fs of deposit	30,805,000 00	27,380,000 00	27,955,000 00	29,170,000 00	26,095,000 00
Due from U. S. Treas	18,479,112 79	16,911,680 20	17,063,407 65	16,743,695 40	16,350,491 73
Total	1,834,360,941 70	1,793,306,002 78	1,825,760,967 28	1,827,265,367 61	1,787,407,093 76

1877.

	JANUARY 20. 2,083 banks.	APRIL 14. 2,073 banks.	JUNE 22. 2,078 banks.	OCTOBER 1. 2,080 banks.	DECEMBER 28. 2,074 banks.
Loans and discounts	$929,561,018 65	$911,946,833 88	$901,731,416 03	$891,920,593 54	$881,856,744 87
Bonds for circulation	337,590,700 00	339,658,100 00	337,754,100 00	336,810,950 00	343,849,550 00
Bonds for deposits	14,782,000 00	15,084,000 00	14,071,000 00	14,903,000 00	13,538,000 00
U. S. bonds on hand	31,988,650 00	32,964,050 00	32,344,050 00	30,088,700 00	28,479,800 00
Other stocks and b'ds	31,819,930 20	32,554,594 44	35,655,755 20	34,435,995 21	32,169,401 03
Due from res've ag'ts	88,698,308 85	84,942,718 41	82,132,099 96	73,284,133 12	75,960,087 27
Due from nat'l banks	44,844,616 88	42,027,778 81	44,567,308 63	45,217,246 82	44,123,924 97
Due from State b'nks	13,680,990 81	11,911,437 36	11,246,340 70	11,415,761 60	11,479,945 65
Real estate, &c.	43,704,335 47	44,736,509 49	44,818,722 07	45,229,983 25	45,311,932 25
Current expenses	4,131,516 48	7,842,296 86	7,910,864 84	6,915,792 50	8,958,903 60
Premiums paid	10,991,714 50	10,494,505 12	10,320,674 34	9,219,174 02	8,841,939 09
Cash items	10,295,404 19	10,410,621 87	10,099,988 46	11,674,587 50	10,265,059 49
Clear'g-house exch'gs	81,117,889 04	85,159,422 74	57,861,481 13	74,525,215 89	64,660,415 01
Bills of other banks	18,418,727 00	17,942,693 00	20,182,948 00	15,531,487 00	20,312,602 00
Fractional currency	1,238,226 08	1,114,820 09	1,055,128 61	900,805 47	776,084 78
Specie	49,709,267 55	27,070,037 78	21,335,096 08	22,058,820 31	32,907,750 70
Legal-tender notes	72,689,710 00	72,351,573 00	78,004,386 00	66,920,604 00	70,568,248 00
U. S. cert'fs of deposit	25,470,000 00	32,100,000 00	44,430,000 00	32,410,000 00	26,515,000 00
Due from U. S. Treas	16,441,509 98	16,291,040 84	17,932,574 60	16,021,753 01	16,493,577 08
Total	1,818,174,517 68	1,796,603,275 29	1,774,352,833 81	1,741,084,663 84	1,737,295,145 79

Banks from October, 1863, *to* October, 1885—Continued.

1875.

Liabilities.	MARCH 1.	MAY 1.	JUNE 30.	OCTOBER 1.	DECEMBER 17.
	2,029 banks.	2,046 banks.	2,076 banks.	2,083 banks.	2,086 banks.
Capital stock	$496,272,901 00	$498,717,143 00	$501,568,563 50	$504,829,760 00	$505,485,865 00
Surplus fund	131,240,079 47	131,604,608 66	133,169,094 79	134,356,676 41	133,985,422 30
Undivided profits	51,650,243 62	55,907,619 95	52,100,104 68	52,964,933 50	59,204,957 81
Nat'l bank circulation	324,525,349 00	323,321,230 00	318,148,406 00	318,350,379 00	314,079,451 00
State bank circulation	824,876 00	815,220 00	786,844 00	772,348 00	752,722 00
Dividends unpaid	1,001,255 48	2,501,742 39	6,105,519 34	4,003,534 90	1,353,396 80
Individual deposits	647,735,879 69	695,347,677 70	686,478,630 48	664,579,019 39	618,517,245 74
U. S. deposits	7,971,932 75	6,797,972 00	6,714,328 70	6,507,331 59	6,652,556 07
Dep'ts U.S. dis. officers	5,330,414 16	2,766,387 41	3,459,001 80	4,271,195 19	4,232,550 87
Due to national banks	137,735,121 44	127,280,034 02	138,914,828 39	129,810,681 60	119,843,665 44
Due to State banks	55,294,663 84	53,037,582 89	55,714,055 18	49,918,530 95	47,048,174 56
Notes re-discounted	4,841,600 20	5,671,031 44	4,261,464 45	5,254,453 66	5,257,100 61
Bills payable	4,786,436 57	6,079,632 94	5,758,209 85	6,590,234 43	7,056,583 64
Total	1,869,819,753 22	1,909,847,891 40	1,913,239,201 16	1,882,209,307 62	1,823,469,752 44

1876.

	MARCH 10.	MAY 12.	JUNE 30.	OCTOBER 2.	DECEMBER 22.
	2,091 banks.	2,080 banks.	2,091 banks.	2,089 banks.	2,082 banks.
Capital stock	$504,818,660 00	$500,982,006 00	$500,393,796 00	$499,802,232 00	$497,482,016 00
Surplus fund	133,091,739 50	131,795,199 94	131,807,197 21	132,202,282 00	131,390,664 07
Undivided profits	51,177,031 26	49,039,278 75	46,609,341 51	46,445,215 59	52,327,715 08
Nat'l bank circulation	307,476,155 00	300,252,085 00	294,444,678 00	291,544,020 00	292,011,575 00
State bank circulation	714,539 00	607,060 00	658,938 00	626,847 00	608,548 00
Dividends unpaid	1,405,829 06	2,325,523 51	6,116,679 30	3,848,705 64	1,286,540 28
Individual deposits	620,674,211 05	612,355,096 50	641,432,886 08	651,385,210 19	619,350,223 06
U. S. deposits	6,606,394 90	8,493,878 18	7,667,722 97	7,256,601 42	6,727,153 14
Dep'ts U.S. dis. officers	4,313,915 45	2,596,273 30	3,392,939 48	3,746,781 58	4,749,615 39
Due to national banks	139,407,880 06	127,880,045 04	131,702,164 87	131,535,969 04	122,351,813 09
Due to State banks	54,002,131 54	46,706,060 52	51,403,995 59	48,250,111 63	48,685,392 14
Notes re-discounted	4,631,882 57	4,653,460 08	3,867,622 24	4,464,407 31	4,553,158 76
Bills payable	6,049,566 31	5,650,126 87	6,173,006 03	6,154,784 21	5,882,672 15
Total	1,834,369,941 70	1,793,306,002 78	1,825,760,967 28	1,827,265,367 61	1,787,407,093 76

1877.

	JANUARY 20.	APRIL 14.	JUNE 22.	OCTOBER 1.	DECEMBER 28.
	2,083 banks.	2,073 banks.	2,078 banks.	2,080 banks.	2,074 banks.
Capital stock	$493,634,611 00	$489,684,645 00	$481,044,771 00	$479,467,771 00	$477,128,771 00
Surplus fund	130,224,469 02	129,793,326 52	124,714,072 93	122,776,124 24	121,618,455 32
Undivided profits	37,456,550 32	45,609,418 27	50,508,351 70	44,572,078 72	51,530,910 18
Nat'l bank circulation	292,851,351 00	294,710,713 00	290,602,057 00	291,874,236 00	299,240,475 00
State bank circulation	581,242 00	535,963 00	521,611 00	481,738 09	470,543 00
Dividends unpaid	2,448,909 70	1,853,974 79	1,398,101 52	3,623,703 43	1,464,178 34
Individual deposits	659,691,969 76	641,772,525 08	636,267,529 26	616,403,987 12	604,512,544 52
U. S. deposits	7,234,490 00	7,584,207 72	7,187,431 67	7,972,714 75	6,329,031 90
Dep'ts U.S. dis. officers	3,105,316 55	3,076,878 70	3,710,167 20	2,376,983 02	3,780,754 40
Due to national banks	130,293,566 36	125,422,444 43	121,443,601 23	115,028,954 38	115,773,660 58
Due to State banks	49,965,770 27	48,604,820 69	48,352,583 90	46,577,430 88	44,807,958 79
Notes re-discounted	4,000,067 82	3,935,450 75	2,953,128 58	3,791,219 47	4,054,784 51
Bills payable	6,483,820 92	5,569,241 94	6,249,426 88	6,137,416 83	5,843,107 03
Total	1,816,174,517 68	1,796,603,273 29	1,774,352,833 81	1,741,084,663 84	1,737,205,145 79

Aggregate resources and liabilities of the National

1 8 7 8.

Resources.	MARCH 15. 2,063 banks.	MAY 1. 2,059 banks.	JUNE 29. 2,056 banks.	OCTOBER 1. 2,053 banks.	DECEMBER 6. 2,055 banks.
Loans and discounts.	$854,750,708 87	$847,620,392 49	$835,078,133 13	$833,988,450 59	$826,017,451 87
Bonds for circulation	343,871,350 00	345,256,350 00	347,332,100 00	347,556,650 00	347,812,300 00
Bonds for deposits ..	13,320,000 00	19,536,000 00	28,371,000 00	47,936,850 00	49,110,500 00
U. S. bonds on hand.	34,881,600 00	33,615,700 00	40,479,900 00	46,785,600 00	44,255,850 00
Other stocks and b'ds	34,674,307 21	34,697,320 53	36,694,996 24	36,859,534 82	35,816,810 47
Due from res've ag'ts	86,016,900 78	71,331,219 27	78,875,055 92	85,083,418 51	81,733,137 00
Due from nat'l banks	39,692,105 87	40,545,522 72	41,897,858 89	41,492,918 75	43,144,220 68
Due from State banks	11,683,050 17	12,413,579 10	12,232,316 30	12,314,698 11	12,259,856 69
Real estate, &c......	45,792,363 73	45,001,536 93	46,153,409 35	46,702,476 26	46,728,147 36
Current expenses ...	7,786,572 42	7,239,365 78	4,718,618 66	6,272,566 73	7,608,128 83
Premiums paid	7,806,252 00	7,574,255 95	7,335,454 49	7,134,735 68	6,978,768 71
Cash items..........	10,107,583 76	10,989,440 78	11,525,376 07	10,982,432 89	9,985,004 21
Clear'g house exch'gs	697,398 86	95,525,134 23	87,493,287 82	82,372,537 88	61,999,286 11
Bills of other banks.	16,250,560 00	18,363,395 00	17,063,576 00	16,929,721 00	19,392,281 00
Fractional currency.		661,044 69	610,084 25	515,661 04	496,864 34
Specie	54,729,558 02	46,023,756 06	29,251,469 77	30,688,606 50	34,355,250 36
Legal-tender notes..	64,034,972 00	67,245,975 00	71,643,402 00	64,428,600 00	64,672,762 00
U.S. cert'fs of deposit	20,605,000 00	20,995,000 00	36,905,000 00	32,690,000 00	32,520,000 00
Due from U. S. Treas.	16,257,608 98	16,364,036 47	16,798,667 62	16,543,674 36	17,946,918 34
Total	1,720,465,956 90	1,741,898,959 05	1,750,464,706 51	1,767,279,133 21	1,742,826,837 37

1 8 7 9.

Resources.	JANUARY 1. 2,051 banks.	APRIL 4. 2,048 banks.	JUNE 14. 2,048 banks.	OCTOBER 2. 2,048 banks.	DECEMBER 12. 2,052 banks.
Loans and discounts.	$823,906,765 08	$814,653,422 69	$835,875,012 36	$878,503,097 45	$933,543,661 93
Bonds for circulation	347,118,300 00	348,487,700 00	352,208,600 00	357,343,300 00	364,272,700 00
Bonds for deposits ..	66,507,350 00	309,348,450 00	257,038,200 00	18,204,650 00	14,788,800 00
U. S. bonds on hand.	44,257,250 00	54,601,750 00	62,180,300 00	52,942,100 00	40,677,500 00
Other stocks and b'ds	35,569,400 93	36,747,129 43	37,017,015 13	39,671,916 50	38,836,369 80
Due from res've ag't's	77,925,086 68	74,003,830 40	93,443,463 05	107,623,546 81	102,742,452 54
Due from nat'l banks	44,161,948 46	39,143,388 90	48,192,531 93	46,692,994 78	55,352,459 82
Due from State banks	11,892,540 26	10,535,252 99	11,268,543 45	13,630,772 63	14,428,072 00
Real estate, &c ...	47,091,964 70	47,461,614 54	47,796,106 26	47,817,169 36	47,992,332 99
Current expenses ...	4,033,024 67	6,603,668 43	5,013,420 46	6,111,256 56	7,474,082 10
Premiums paid	6,366,648 85	6,609,390 80	5,674,497 80	4,332,419 63	4,159,526 17
Cash items........	13,564,550 25	10,011,204 64	10,209,982 43	11,306,132 48	10,377,272 77
Clear'g house exch'gs	109,035,237 82	68,712,445 55	88,152,359 49	112,964,964 25	112,172,677 95
Bills of other banks.	19,535,588 00	17,068,505 00	16,685,484 00	16,707,550 00	16,406,213 00
Fractional currency	475,516 50	467,177 47	468,217 26	396,065 00	374,227 62
Specie	41,499,757 32	41,148,563 41	42,333,287 44	42,173,731 23	79,013,041 59
Legal-tender notes	70,561,233 00	64,461,221 00	67,059,152 00	69,496,696 00	54,715,096 00
U.S. cert'fs of deposit	28,915,000 00	21,885,000 00	25,180,000 00	26,770,000 00	10,860,000 00
Due from U. S. Treas	17,175,433 13	17,029,121 31	16,620,986 20	17,929,065 45	17,034,816 40
Total	1,800,592,062 25	1,984,068,936 53	2,019,884,549 16	1,868,787,428 19	1,925,229,617 08

1 8 8 0.

Resources.	FEBRUARY 21. 2,061 banks.	APRIL 23. 2,075 banks.	JUNE 11. 2,076 banks.	OCTOBER 1. 2,090 banks.	DECEMBER 31. 2,095 banks.
Loans and discounts	$974,295,360 70	$992,970,823 10	$994,712,646 41	$1,040,977,267 53	$1,071,356,143 79
Bonds for circulation	364,901,700 00	361,274,650 00	359,512,050 00	357,789,350 00	358,042,650 00
Bonds for deposits..	14,917,000 60	14,722,000 00	14,727,000 00	14,827,000 00	14,726,500 00
U. S. bonds on hand	36,798,600 00	29,569,600 00	28,605,800 00	28,763,400 00	25,010,349 00
Other stocks and b'ds	41,923,582 33	42,494,927 73	44,947,345 75	48,863,150 22	48,628,372 77
Due from res've ag'ts	177,791,385 81	193,994,229 84	115,935,668 27	134,562,778 70	126,155,014 49
Due from nat'l banks	53,230,634 03	54,493,463 99	56,578,444 60	63,023,796 84	69,079,824 15
Due from State banks	14,501,432 54	13,293,775 94	14,881,582 77	15,881,197 74	17,111,241 03
Real estate, &c	47,845,915 77	47,808,207 09	47,079,244 53	48,015,532 54	47,744,461 47
Current expenses...	6,404,713 54	7,007,404 10	5,778,820 19	6,306,182 01	4,442,440 82
Premiums paid	3,908,059 27	3,791,703 33	3,702,354 60	3,488,470 11	3,288,602 63
Cash items	10,520,274 51	9,857,615 34	9,980,179 32	12,720,062 19	14,713,979 92
Clear'g house exch'gs	166,736,402 64	99,357,056 41	122,306,460 45	131,095,249 72	229,733,961 59
Bills of other banks.	15,369,257 00	21,064,504 00	21,908,193 00	18,216,043 00	21,849,367 00
Fractional currency	397,187 23	395,747 67	387,226 13	367,171 73	389,021 75
Specie	89,442,051 75	86,429,732 21	99,595,505 26	100,946,599 49	107,172,909 92
Legal tender notes.	55,229,408 00	61,048,841 00	64,476,717 00	56,640,458 00	59,216,934 00
U.S. cert'fs of deposit	10,760,000 00	7,890,000 00	12,510,000 00	7,655,000 00	6,150,000 00
Due from U.S. Treas	16,994,381 37	17,226,060 01	16,999,083 78	17,103,860 00	17,125,822 37
Total	2,658,066,498 46	1,974,600,472 95	2,035,493,280 15	2,105,786,625 82	2,241,683,829 91

Banks from October, 1863, *to October*, 1885—Continued.

1878.

Liabilities.	MARCH 15.	MAY 1.	JUNE 29.	OCTOBER 1.	DECEMBER 6.
	2,063 banks.	2,050 banks.	2,056 banks.	2,053 banks.	2,055 banks.
Capital stock	$473,952,541 00	$471,971,627 00	$470,393,366 00	$466,147,436 00	$464,874,996 00
Surplus fund	120,870,290 10	119,291,126 13	118,178,530 75	116,897,779 98	116,402,118 84
Undivided profits	45,040,851 85	43,938,961 98	40,482,522 64	40,936,213 58	44,040,171 84
Nat'l bank circulat'n	300,926,284 00	301,884,704 00	299,621,059 00	301,888,092 00	303,324,733 00
State bank circulat'n	439,339 00	426,504 00	417,808 00	413,913 00	400,715 00
Dividends unpaid	1,207,472 68	1,930,609 58	5,466,350 52	3,118,389 91	1,473,784 86
Individual deposits	602,882,585 17	625,479,771 12	621,672,166 06	620,236,176 82	598,805,775 56
U. S. deposits	7,243,234 29	13,811,474 14	22,686,619 67	41,654,812 08	40,269,825 72
Dep's U.S. dis. officers	3,004,064 90	2,392,281 61	2,903,531 99	3,342,794 73	3,451,436 56
Due to national banks	123,229,448 50	109,720,396 70	117,845,495 88	122,496,513 92	120,261,774 54
Due to State banks	43,979,299 39	44,006,531 05	43,366,527 86	42,636,703 42	41,767,755 07
Notes re-discounted	2,465,390 79	2,834,012 00	2,453,839 77	3,007,324 85	3,228,192 93
Bills payable	4,215,196 23	4,270,879 74	5,022,894 37	4,502,082 92	4,525,617 45
Total	1,729,465,956 90	1,741,898,959 05	1,750,464,706 51	1,767,279,133 21	1,742,826,837 37

1879.

	JANUARY 1.	APRIL 4.	JUNE 14.	OCTOBER 2.	DECEMBER 12.
	2,051 banks.	2,048 banks.	2,048 banks.	2,048 banks.	2,052 banks.
Capital stock	$462,031,396 00	$455,611,362 00	$455,244,415 00	$454,667,365 00	$454,498,515 00
Surplus fund	116,200,863 52	114,823,316 49	114,321,375 87	114,786,528 10	115,429,031 93
Undivided profits	36,836,269 21	40,812,777 59	45,802,845 82	41,300,941 40	47,573,820 75
Nat'l bank circulat'n	303,506,470 00	304,407,139 00	307,328,605 00	313,786,342 00	321,949,154 00
State bank circulat'n	388,308 00	352,452 00	339,027 00	325,954 00	322,502 00
Dividends unpaid	5,816,348 82	2,158,516 79	1,300,059 13	2,658,337 46	1,305,480 45
Individual deposits	643,337,745 26	598,822,694 02	618,934,141 42	719,737,508 89	755,459,966 01
U. S. deposits	59,701,222 00	303,463,595 09	243,421,340 25	11,013,862 74	6,923,323 97
Dep's U.S. dis. officers	3,556,801 25	2,689,189 44	3,082,320 67	3,469,600 02	3,898,217 43
Due to national banks	118,311,635 60	110,481,176 98	137,360,091 60	149,200,257 16	152,484,079 44
Due to State banks	44,035,787 56	43,709,770 14	50,403,064 54	52,022,453 99	50,232,301 93
Notes re-discounted	2,926,434 95	2,224,491 91	2,226,306 89	2,205,015 54	2,116,484 47
Bills payable	3,942,659 18	4,452,544 48	4,510,876 47	4,208,201 89	4,041,649 70
Total	1,800,592,002 25	1,984,068,936 53	2,019,884,549 16	1,868,737,428 19	1,925,229,817 08

1880.

	FEBRUARY 21.	APRIL 23.	JUNE 11.	OCTOBER 1.	DECEMBER 31.
	2,061 banks.	2,075 banks.	2,076 banks.	2,090 banks.	2,095 banks.
Capital stock	$454,548,585 00	$456,097,035 00	$455,909,565 00	$457,553,985 00	$458,540,085 00
Surplus fund	117,044,441 03	117,299,350 00	118,102,014 11	120,518,583 43	121,524,029 03
Undivided profits	42,863,804 95	48,226,087 61	50,443,635 45	46,130,690 24	47,946,741 04
Nat'l bank circulat'n	320,303,874 00	320,759,472 00	318,088,562 00	317,350,026 00	317,484,496 00
State bank circulat'n	303,452 00	299,790 00	290,738 00	271,045 00	258,499 00
Dividends unpaid	1,365,001 91	1,542,447 98	1,330,179 85	3,452,504 17	6,196,288 38
Individual deposits	843,926,599 96	791,555,959 63	833,701,034 20	873,637,637 07	1,000,452,852 82
U. S. deposits	7,835,791 07	7,925,988 37	7,630,905 40	7,548,533 67	7,898,100 94
Dep's U.S. dis. officers	3,069,880 74	3,220,600 61	3,026,757 31	3,344,386 62	5,489,561 01
Due to national banks	170,245,961 08	157,299,750 14	171,462,131 23	192,124,705 10	192,413,205 78
Due to State banks	65,429,334 51	63,317,107 96	67,088,795 35	75,735,677 06	71,185,817 08
Notes re-discounted	1,918,788 88	2,616,900 53	2,258,544 72	3,178,232 50	3,354,697 18
Bills payable	4,181,280 53	4,529,967 08	5,290,417 43	5,031,604 96	4,636,876 05
Total	2,038,066,498 46	1,974,600,472 95	2,035,493,280 15	2,105,786,625 82	2,241,683,829 91

Aggregate resources and liabilities of the National

1881.

Resources.	MARCH 11. 2,094 banks.	MAY 6. 2,102 banks.	JUNE 30. 2,115 banks.	OCTOBER 1. 2,132 banks.	DECEMBER 31. 2,164 banks.
Loans and discounts	$1,073,786,749 70	$1,095,649,382 16	$1,144,978,949 45	$1,173,796,683 69	$1,169,177,557 16
Bonds for circulation	339,811,950 00	352,678,500 00	358,287,500 00	363,385,500 00	368,735,700 00
Bonds for deposits	14,851,500 00	15,240,000 00	15,295,000 00	15,548,000 00	15,715,000 00
U. S. bonds on hand	46,626,150 00	41,116,500 00	48,584,950 00	40,866,750 00	31,884,000 00
Other stocks and b'ds	49,545,154 92	52,908,123 98	58,949,292 63	61,952,402 95	62,663,218 93
Due from res'g ng'ts	120,820,691 00	128,017,627 03	156,258,637 05	132,968,183 12	123,530,465 75
Due from nat'l banks	62,295,517 34	63,176,225 67	75,763,599 78	78,505,446 17	77,633,902 77
Due from State banks	17,022,261 64	16,958,734 56	18,550,775 34	19,396,826 62	17,644,704 62
Real estate, &c	47,525,790 02	47,791,348 36	47,834,080 20	47,329,111 16	47,445,050 46
Current expenses	7,810,930 33	6,096,109 78	4,235,911 19	6,731,936 48	4,647,101 04
Premiums paid	3,530,516 71	4,034,763 60	4,115,980 01	4,138,485 71	3,581,728 72
Cash items	10,144,682 87	11,826,603 16	13,531,227 31	14,831,879 30	17,337,904 78
Clear'g-house exch'gs	147,761,543 96	196,683,558 01	143,980,236 84	180,222,255 95	217,214,627 10
Bills of other banks	17,753,632 00	25,120,925 00	21,031,932 00	17,792,712 00	24,190,534 90
Fractional currency	386,569 63	356,950 21	372,140 23	373,915 96	366,361 52
Specie	165,156,195 24	122,628,502 08	128,038,927 59	114,334,736 12	113,080,639 60
Legal-tender notes	52,156,439 00	62,516,296 00	58,758,713 00	53,158,441 00	60,104,387 00
U. S. cert's of deposit	6,120,000 00	8,045,000 00	9,540,000 00	6,740,000 00	7,930,000 00
Due from U. S. Treas	17,015,269 83	18,456,600 14	17,251,868 22	17,472,505 96	18,097,923 40
Total	2,140,110,944 78	2,270,226,817 76	2,325,832,700 75	2,358,387,591 59	2,381,890,866 85

1882.

	MARCH 11. 2,187 banks.	MAY 19. 2,224 banks.	JULY 1. 2,239 banks.	OCTOBER 3. 2,269 banks.	DECEMBER 30. 2,308 banks.
Loans and discounts	$1,182,661,609 53	$1,189,094,830 35	$1,208,932,665 92	$1,243,203,210 08	$1,230,456,213 97
Bonds for circulation	367,333,700 00	360,153,800 00	355,789,550 00	357,631,750 00	357,047,650 00
Bonds for deposits	16,093,000 00	15,920,000 00	15,920,000 00	16,111,000 00	16,344,000 00
U. S. bonds on hand	28,523,450 00	29,062,700 00	27,242,550 00	21,334,750 00	15,462,150 00
Other stocks and b'ds	64,430,686 18	65,274,993 32	66,691,399 56	66,168,916 64	66,908,620 36
Due from res'v ag't's	117,451,719 75	124,189,945 23	118,455,012 48	119,277,227 87	122,066,106 75
Due from nat'l banks	68,301,645 12	66,883,512 75	75,366,970 74	63,516,841 06	76,073,227 76
Due from State banks	15,921,432 07	16,890,174 92	16,344,688 66	17,105,468 44	18,405,748 49
Real estate, &c	47,075,247 45	46,956,574 28	46,425,351 40	46,537,066 41	46,969,408 41
Current expenses	8,494,036 21	6,774,571 86	3,930,164 69	7,298,270 17	5,130,505 53
Premiums paid	3,762,382 59	5,062,314 52	5,494,234 35	6,512,153 03	6,472,585 82
Cash items	13,808,120 70	12,205,256 96	20,166,927 33	14,784,625 21	16,281,815 07
Clear'g-house exch'g's	162,058,077 94	107,279,094 71	159,114,220 08	208,346,510 08	155,951,114 81
Bills of other banks	19,440,089 00	25,226,186 00	21,405,758 00	20,088,425 00	23,344,775 00
Fractional currency	369,508 07	390,236 36	372,745 83	396,367 64	401,314 70
Specie	109,984,111 04	112,415,866 73	111,694,262 54	102,857,778 27	100,427,159 40
Legal-tender notes	56,633,572 00	65,969,522 00	64,019,518 00	63,318,517 00	68,478,421 00
U.S. cert's of deposit	9,445,000 00	10,395,000 00	11,045,000 00	8,615,000 00	8,475,000 00
Due from U. S. Treas	17,720,701 07	17,099,385 34	16,830,407 40	17,161,367 94	17,954,669 42
Total	2,309,057,088 72	2,277,924,911 13	2,354,342,026 90	2,399,833,676 84	2,360,793,467 09

1883.

	MARCH 13. 2,343 banks.	MAY 1. 2,375 banks.	JUNE 22. 2,417 banks.	OCTOBER 2. 2,501 banks.	DECEMBER 31. 2,529 banks.
Loans and discounts	$1,249,181,879 43	$1,262,389,961 87	$1,285,591,902 19	$1,309,244,781 64	$1,307,491,256 34
Bonds for circulation	354,716,500 00	354,480,250 00	354,002,900 00	351,412,850 00	345,505,800 00
Bonds for deposits	16,769,000 00	16,949,000 00	17,116,600 00	17,081,000 00	16,846,000 00
U. S. bonds on hand	17,850,100 00	15,870,600 00	16,978,100 00	13,503,050 00	15,151,250 00
Other stocks and b'ds	68,429,085 67	68,349,500 79	68,532,973 03	71,114,031 11	71,099,421 62
Due from res've ag't's	121,024,154 69	109,306,823 23	126,646,954 62	124,918,728 71	126,809,606 92
Due from nat'l banks	67,203,503 86	68,477,918 02	66,194,658 21	65,714,229 44	77,902,785 97
Due from State banks	16,993,541 72	19,382,129 33	19,451,498 16	18,266,275 05	19,402,047 12
Real estate, &c	47,062,365 08	47,175,909 80	47,562,193 52	48,337,665 02	49,510,760 35
Current expenses	8,910,615 28	7,754,956 86	6,829,278 36	6,898,327 30	4,876,318 44
Premiums paid	7,420,932 84	7,798,443 04	8,079,726 01	8,061,073 80	8,647,252 98
Cash items	11,366,721 07	15,461,050 16	11,100,701 18	13,581,049 94	17,491,804 43
Clear'g-house exch'g's	107,790,065 17	145,990,968 18	90,792,679 08	96,353,211 76	131,545,273 98
Bills of other banks	19,739,526 00	22,655,833 00	26,279,856 00	22,075,447 00	28,809,600 00
Fractional currency	431,931 15	416,318 94	443,725 83	443,951 12	427,754 55
Specie	97,962,366 34	103,607,266 32	115,354,391 62	107,817,983 53	114,270,158 04
Legal-tender notes	60,848,060 00	68,256,468 00	73,822,458 00	70,672,997 00	80,590,700 00
U. S. cert's of deposit	8,405,000 00	8,420,000 00	10,685,000 00	9,970,000 00	10,840,000 00
Due from U. S. Treas	16,726,451 30	17,407,694 31	17,407,906 20	16,586,712 60	16,865,938 85
Total	2,298,918,165 11	2,360,192,285 85	2,364,853,122 44	2,372,656,364 82	2,446,580,917 40

Banks from October, 1863, to October, 1885—Continued.

1881.

Liabilities.	MARCH 11. 2,094 banks.	MAY 6. 2,102 banks.	JUNE 30. 2,115 banks.	OCTOBER 1. 2,132 banks.	DECEMBER 31. 2,164 banks.
Capital stock........	$458,254,935 00	$450,039,205 00	$160,227,835 00	$463,821,985 00	$465,859,835 00
Surplus fund	122,470,996 73	124,405,926 91	126,679,517 97	128,140,617 73	129,867,493,92
Undivided profits ...	54,072,225 49	54,906,090 47	54,684,137 16	56,372,190 92	54,221,816 16
Nat'l bank circulation	298,590,802 00	309,737,193 00	312,223,352 00	320,200,009 00	325,018,161 00
State bank circulat'n	252,765 00	252,647 00	242,967 00	244,399 00	241,701 00
Dividends unpaid ...	1,402,118 43	2,617,134 37	5,871,595 59	3,836,445 84	6,372,737 13
Individual deposits..	933,392,430 75	1,027,040,514 10	1,031,731,043 42	1,070,997,431 71	1,102,079,163 71
U. S. deposits.......	7,381,149 25	9,504,081 25	8,971,826 73	8,476,689 74	8,796,078 73
Dep's U.S.dis. officers	3,839,324 77	3,371,512 48	3,272,610 45	3,631,803 41	3,595,720 83
Due to national banks	181,677,285 37	191,250,091 90	223,503,034 19	205,862,945 80	197,252,326 01
Due to State banks..	71,579,477 47	80,700,506 06	91,035,599 65	89,047,471 00	79,380,429 38
Notes re-discounted.	2,616,203 05	2,908,370 45	2,220,053 02	3,091,165 30	4,122,472 79
Bills payable.......	4,581,231 47	4,493,544 77	5,169,128 57	4,664,077 12	4,482,325 25
Total...........	2,140,110,944 78	2,270,226,817 76	2,325,832,700 75	2,358,387,391 59	2,381,890,866 85

1882.

	MARCH 11. 2,187 banks.	MAY 19. 2,224 banks.	JULY 1. 2,239 banks.	OCTOBER 3. 2,269 banks.	DECEMBER 30. 2,308 banks.
Capital stock.......	$469,390,232 00	$473,810,124 00	$477,184,390 00	$483,104,217 00	$484,883,492 00
Surplus fund	130,924,139 66	129,273,358 24	131,079,251 16	131,977,450 77	135,930,969 31
Undivided profits ...	60,475,764 98	62,345,199 19	52,128,817 73	61,180,310 53	55,343,816 94
Nat'l bank circulation	325,651,577 00	315,671,236 00	308,921,898 00	314,721,215 00	315,230,925 00
State bank circulation	241,527 00	241,319 00	235,173 00	221,177 00	207,273 00
Dividends unpaid ...	1,418,119 12	1,950,554 88	6,634,372 20	3,153,836 30	6,805,057 82
Individual deposits..	1,036,595,098 20	1,001,687,693 74	1,069,707,248 75	1,122,472,682 46	1,066,901,719 85
U. S. deposits	8,853,242 16	9,741,133 36	9,817,224 44	8,817,411 21	9,622,303 56
Dep's U.S.dis. officers	3,372,363 96	3,493,252 88	2,867,385 63	3,627,846 72	3,786,202 20
Due to national banks	187,433,824 90	192,067,865 26	194,668,025 46	180,075,749 77	194,491,260 00
Due to State banks..	78,359,675 85	78,911,787 20	84,066,023 66	79,885,652 22	77,031,165 82
Notes re-discounted .	3,912,902 38	3,754,044 38	4,195,210 98	5,747,614 68	6,703,164 45
Bills payable........	4,428,531 51	3,908,343 00	5,637,865 88	4,848,517 18	3,856,056 54
Total...........	2,309,057,088 72	2,277,924,911 13	2,344,342,686 90	2,399,833,676 84	2,360,793,467 09

1883.

	MARCH 13. 2,343 banks.	MAY 1. 2,375 banks.	JUNE 22. 2,417 banks.	OCTOBER 2. 2,501 banks.	DECEMBER 31. 2,529 banks.
Capital stock........	$490,456,072 00	$493,963,009 00	$500,298,312 00	$509,699,787 00	$511,837,575 00
Surplus fund	136,922,884 44	137,775,004 39	138,331,902 06	141,991,789 18	144,800,252 19
Undivided profits ...	59,340,913 64	66,739,878 85	68,354,157 15	61,560,652 04	58,787,945 91
Nat'l bank circulation	312,778,055 00	313,540,999 00	311,965,302 00	310,517,857 00	304,044,131 00
State bank circulation	206,779 00	198,162 00	189,253 00	184,357 00	181,121 00
Dividends unpaid....	1,389,092 96	2,819,629 87	1,454,232 01	3,229,226 31	7,082,682 28
Individual deposits..	1,004,111,400 55	1,067,962,238 35	1,043,137,763 11	1,049,437,760 57	1,100,453,008 23
U. S. deposits	9,613,873 33	11,624,894 57	10,130,757 88	10,183,196 95	10,626,777 79
Dep's U. S. dis. officers	3,787,225 31	3,618,114 79	3,743,320 56	3,980,259 28	3,768,862 04
Due to national banks	191,296,859 14	180,445,876 92	194,150,076 43	186,828,676 27	200,867,280 06
Due to State banks ..	80,251,968 26	78,544,128 82	84,744,666 35	83,602,073 01	84,776,421 60
Notes re-discounted.	5,101,458 69	5,557,183 69	5,197,514 12	7,387,537 40	8,248,562 67
Bills payable	3,600,724 79	3,364,061 00	3,187,259 77	4,053,252 81	4,106,297 72
Total...........	2,208,918,165 11	2,360,192,235 85	2,364,833,122 44	2,372,656,364 82	2,445,880,917 40

Aggregate resources and liabilities of the National

1884.

Resources.	MARCH 7.	APRIL 24.	JUNE 20.	SEPTEMBER 30.	DECEMBER 20.
	2,563 banks.	2,589 banks.	2,625 banks.	2,664 banks.	2,664 banks.
Loans and discounts.	$1,321,548,289 62	$1,333,433,230 54	$1,269,862,935 96	$1,245,294,093 37	$1,234,202,226 44
Bonds for circulation	339,816,150 00	337,342,900 00	334,346,350 00	327,435,000 00	317,586,050 00
Bonds for deposits ..	16,850,000 00	17,135,000 00	17,960,000 00	16,810,000 00	16,740,000 00
U S. bonds on hand..	18,672,250 00	15,560,400 00	14,143,000 00	13,579,600 00	12,305,900 00
Other stocks and b'ds	73,155,984 60	73,424,815 97	72,572,306 93	71,363,477 46	73,449,352 02
Due from res'vo ng'ts	138,795,012 74	122,401,957 98	95,247,152 62	111,993,619 65	121,161,976 80
Due from nat'l banks	64,638,322 58	68,031,209 90	64,891,670 13	66,335,544 57	69,450,884 45
Due from State banks	17,937,976 35	18,145,827 61	16,306,500 01	15,833,982 98	18,329,912 01
Real estate, &c	49,418,805 02	49,667,126 87	50,149,083 90	49,900,886 91	49,889,936 00
Current expenses ..	7,813,880 56	8,054,206 82	8,866,558 09	6,913,508 85	9,670,996 14
Premiums paid	9,742,601 42	9,826,386 76	10,605,343 49	11,632,631 08	11,923,447 13
Cash items	11,383,792 57	11,237,975 71	11,382,292 69	13,103,098 55	11,924,152 89
Cl'g-house loan cert's			10,335,000 00	1,690,000 00	
Clear'g-house exch'gs	68,403,373 30	83,531,472 58	69,498,913 13	66,257,118 15	75,195,955 95
Bills of other banks..	23,485,124 00	26,525,120 00	23,388,695 00	23,258,854 00	22,377,965 00
Fractional currency	491,067 76	489,802 51	473,046 66	469,023 89	456,778 26
Specie	122,080,127 33	114,744,707 49	109,66',682 11	128,690,474 73	130,747,079 53
Legal-tender notes ..	75,847,095 00	77,712,628 00	76,917,212 00	77,044,659 00	76,369,555 00
U. S. cert's of deposit	14,045,000 00	11,990,000 00	9,870,000 00	14,200,000 00	19,040,000 00
Due from U. S. Treas.	16,465,785 66	17,468,976 58	17,022,999 34	17,739,906 28	15,442,306 52
Total	2,390,500,638 51	2,396,813,834 92	2,282,598,742 96	2,279,493,880 07	2,297,143,474 27

1885.

Resources.	MARCH 10.	MAY 6.	JULY 1.	OCTOBER 1.
	2,671 banks.	2,678 banks.	2,689 banks.	2,714 banks.
Loans and discounts	$1,232,327,453 69	$1,241,450,649 79	$1,257,655,547 02	$1,306,143,990 40
Bonds for circulation	313,106,200 00	312,168,500 00	310,102,200 00	307,657,050 00
Bonds for deposits	16,815,000 00	16,740,000 00	17,607,000 00	17,457,000 00
U. S. bonds on hand	14,607,650 00	14,769,250 00	14,588,800 00	14,329,400 00
Other stocks and bonds	75,152,010 35	75,019,208 99	77,249,159 42	77,495,230 20
Due from reserve agents	136,462,273 26	130,903,101 77	132,733,904 34	138,378,515 13
Due from national banks	66,442,054 87	67,866,656 57	77,220,972 29	78,967,607 80
Due from State banks	17,572,822 65	17,348,938 11	17,180,008 46	17,987,801 44
Real estate, &c	49,399,501 42	49,886,378 87	50,729,896 08	51,293,801 10
Current expenses	7,877,320 27	7,096,268 00	3,533,759 49	6,853,392 72
Premiums paid	12,380,437 60	12,558,982 70	12,690,663 41	12,511,383 41
Cash items	11,228,856 82	11,276,626 48	17,214,373 52	14,347,579 53
Clearing-house loan certif't's.	1,530,000 00	1,430,000 00	1,380,000 00	1,110,000 00
Clearing-house exchanges....	59,085,781 99	72,259,129 39	113,158,675 32	84,926,730 70
Bills of other banks	22,013,314 00	26,217,171 00	23,465,388 00	23,062,765 00
Fractional currency	519,529 96	513,200 12	489,927 18	477,055 17
Trade dollars				1,605,763 66
Specie	167,115,873 07	177,433,119 30	177,612,492 02	174,872,572 54
Legal-tender notes	71,017,322 00	77,336,999 00	79,701,352 00	69,738,119 00
U. S. cert's of deposit	22,760,000 00	19,135,000 00	22,920,000 00	18,800,000 00
Due from U. S. Treasurer	15,079,935 80	15,473,270 84	14,617,897 02	14,897,114 24
Total	2,312,744,247 35	2,346,682,452 99	2,421,852,016 47	2,432,913,002 28

Banks from October, 1863, to October 1, 1885—Continued.

1884.

Liabilities.	MARCH 7, 2,563 banks.	APRIL 24, 2,589 banks.	JUNE 20, 2,625 banks.	SEPTEMBER 30, 2,664 banks.	DECEMBER 20, 2,664 banks.
Capital stock	$515,725,005 08	$518,471,844 00	$522,515,996 00	$524,271,345 00	$524,089,065 00
Surplus fund	145,741,679 90	146,647,936 07	145,763,416 17	147,055,037 85	146,867,119 06
Undivided profits	63,044,861 56	67,450,159 00	70,597,487 21	63,234,237 62	70,711,369 95
Nat'l bank circulation	298,791,610 00	297,506,243 00	295,175,334 00	289,775,123 00	280,197,043 00
State bank circulation	180,589 00	180,576 00	179,666 00	179,653 00	174,645 00
Dividends unpaid	1,422,901 91	1,415,889 58	1,384,686 71	3,686,160 33	1,331,421 54
Individual deposits	1,046,059,107 90	1,069,778,388 06	979,020,349 68	975,243,795 14	987,849,055 68
U. S. deposits	9,956,875 24	11,233,495 77	10,530,759 44	10,367,009 92	10,655,803 72
Dep'ts U.S.dis.officers	3,856,461 66	3,583,980 50	3,664,326 13	3,703,804 34	3,749,969 86
Due to national banks	207,461,179 63	192,868,942 31	155,785,354 44	173,979,149 80	187,296,348 30
Due to State banks	88,466,363 89	86,778,138 85	70,480,617 11	72,408,206 83	72,572,384 43
Notes re-discounted	6,234,202 32	7,299,284 58	11,343,505 55	11,008,595 07	8,433,724 67
Bills payable	2,068,740 50	3,193,635 20	4,262,244 57	4,580,862 15	3,415,524 07
Cl'g-house loan cert's			11,895,000 00		
Total	2,390,500,638 51	2,396,813,834 92	2,282,598,742 96	2,279,493,880 07	2,297,143,474 27

1885.

Liabilities.	MARCH 10, 2,671 banks.	MAY 6, 2,678 banks.	JULY 1, 2,689 banks.	OCTOBER 1, 2,714 banks.
Capital stock	$524,235,151 00	$525,195,577 00	$526,273,602 00	$527,524,410 00
Surplus fund	145,907,800 02	145,103,770 01	146,523,799 94	146,624,642 06
Undivided profits	60,296,432 56	60,181,358 12	52,220,946 61	59,335,519 11
National bank circulation	274,054,157 00	273,703,047 00	269,147,690 00	268,869,597 00
State bank circulation	162,581 00	144,498 00	144,489 00	136,898 00
Dividends unpaid	1,301,937 73	2,577,236 08	6,414,263 98	3,508,324 36
Individual deposits	996,501,647 40	1,035,802,188 56	1,106,376,516 80	1,102,372,450 35
U. S. deposits	11,006,919 47	11,690,707 52	10,995,974 68	11,552,621 98
Dep'ts U. S. disbursing officers	3,039,646 40	3,330,522 70	3,027,218 02	2,714,399 37
Due to national banks	203,877,203 09	199,081,104 40	203,932,800 05	213,531,905 08
Due to State banks	82,190,567 43	81,966,092 25	88,847,454 78	86,115,061 25
Notes re-discounted	6,299,722 15	5,736,012 02	5,864,000 85	8,432,792 64
Bills payable	1,850,462 10	2,167,333 33	2,074,259 76	2,191,380 16
Total	2,312,744,247 35	2,346,682,452 99	2,421,852,010 47	2,432,913,002 96

ABSTRACT

OF

REPORTS OF THE CONDITION

OF

THE NATIONAL BANKS

ON

DECEMBER 20, 1884, MARCH 10, MAY 6, JULY 1, AND OCTOBER 1, 1885.

Arranged by States, Territories, and Reserve Cities.

NOTE.—The abstract of each State is exclusive of any reserve city therein.

Abstract of reports since September 30, 1884,

MAINE.

Resources.	DECEMBER 20. 71 banks.	MARCH 10. 71 banks.	MAY 6. 71 banks.	JULY 1. 71 banks.	OCTOBER 1. 71 banks.
Loans and discounts	$17,377,324 26	$16,712,572 44	$16,898,143 95	$16,871,587 96	$16,604,265 52
Bonds for circulation	8,892,300 00	8,809,300 00	8,809,300 00	8,809,300 00	8,792,800 00
Bonds for deposits	170,000 00	170,000 00	170,000 00	170,000 00	170,000 00
U. S. bonds on hand	22,500 00	22,500 00	21,300 00	20,300 00	24,650 00
Other stocks and b'ds	612,380 98	616,821 78	713,307 89	805,741 39	751,130 60
Due from res've ag'ts	1,910,755 33	2,169,471 72	2,027,711 76	1,967,566 39	2,849,384 70
Due from nat'l banks	376,880 96	368,790 90	398,072 67	406,776 81	607,381 37
Due from State banks	20,941 22	7,641 02	18,522 39	13,169 51	19,314 05
Real estate, &c	543,281 33	538,992 55	539,731 36	535,126 65	521,809 01
Current expenses	69,845 60	47,184 39	57,278 70	24,466 66	51,181 25
Premiums paid	206,065 85	197,183 64	189,885 40	187,013 80	184,019 55
Cash items	223,780 02	221,103 98	194,151 69	234,709 67	270,604 04
Clear'g-house exch'gs	59,216 26	104,514 63	84,488 51	110,690 41	124,319 53
Bills of other banks	347,524 00	265,609 00	330,551 00	328,625 00	362,040 00
Fractional currency	3,646 65	3,376 96	3,494 46	5,418 58	2,894 72
Trade dollars					339 80
Specie	641,132 37	611,738 47	612,157 23	630,198 83	670,348 15
Legal-tender notes	180,747 00	192,560 00	177,460 00	237,602 00	182,190 00
U. S. cert's of deposit					
Due from U. S. Treas	407,053 50	409,318 50	409,418 50	430,718 50	487,218 50
Total	32,061,373 33	31,498,679 98	31,556,068 51	31,789,012 16	32,590,547 52

NEW HAMPSHIRE.

	48 banks.	48 banks.	48 banks.	48 banks.	48 banks.
Loans and discounts	$8,353,301 75	$8,177,857 71	$8,292,611 96	$8,284,316 17	$8,371,374 04
Bonds for circulation	5,815,000 00	5,800,000 00	5,800,000 00	5,800,000 00	5,800,000 00
Bonds for deposits	372,000 00	372,000 00	372,000 00	372,000 00	372,000 00
U. S. bonds on hand	14,100 00	14,750 00	13,350 00	13,350 00	15,200 00
Other stocks and b'ds	1,394,220 57	1,386,773 15	1,312,693 74	1,394,744 75	1,522,334 16
Due from res've ag'ts	1,263,057 15	1,244,284 93	1,303,952 84	1,429,740 04	1,746,889 70
Due from nat'l banks	58,779 72	57,776 59	85,346 48	89,486 50	139,529 97
Due from State banks	22,309 67	55,337 05	68,966 49	50,942 05	41,132 45
Real estate, &c	180,108 22	174,756 45	173,874 14	177,017 53	181,709 52
Current expenses	58,169 67	54,608 06	41,771 87	24,540 10	52,201 97
Premiums paid	177,623 70	193,146 60	188,859 13	203,383 75	201,031 11
Cash items	139,424 19	106,157 45	114,296 25	183,271 74	165,046 87
Clear'g-house exch'gs					
Bills of other banks	229,424 00	231,032 00	222,587 00	267,800 00	236,834 00
Fractional currency	6,955 73	6,358 66	5,903 06	6,644 71	6,577 15
Trade dollars					105 00
Specie	235,964 21	252,276 72	242,434 97	248,230 57	282,996 08
Legal-tender notes	115,837 00	105,449 00	113,242 00	117,374 00	139,469 00
U. S. cert's of deposit					
Due from U. S. Treas	268,750 00	267,275 00	267,075 00	285,375 00	260,475 00
Total	18,705,025 88	18,499,833 37	18,618,964 93	18,948,236 91	19,528,966 02

VERMONT.

	50 banks.	50 banks.	48 banks.	48 banks.	47 banks.
Loans and discounts	$11,397,743 07	$10,327,260 62	$10,240,263 59	$10,206,764 14	$10,589,150 33
Bonds for circulation	6,463,500 00	6,256,000 00	6,126,000 00	6,142,500 00	6,017,500 00
Bonds for deposits	50,000 00	50,000 00	50,000 00	50,000 00	50,000 00
U. S. bonds on hand	68,650 00	75,150 00	122,700 00	217,750 00	232,350 00
Other stocks and b'ds	900,355 13	877,089 49	848,461 44	902,771 66	931,044 89
Due from res've ag'ts	1,019,339 72	1,021,750 95	879,407 43	1,104,694 24	977,996 78
Due from nat'l banks	169,683 49	124,975 70	167,032 91	187,300 33	185,893 38
Due from State banks	19,002 74	13,342 39	5,998 46	35,726 55	26,009 59
Real estate, &c	276,927 01	214,986 27	210,956 99	211,664 16	216,559 26
Current expenses	57,915 92	25,769 71	47,955 21	18,400 10	35,594 90
Premiums paid	92,661 08	113,179 08	136,404 67	151,522 79	154,098 96
Cash items	46,765 64	48,778 67	74,729 92	81,880 60	79,720 27
Clear'g-house exch'gs					
Bills of other banks	140,904 00	136,313 00	151,432 00	180,133 00	122,596 00
Fractional currency	3,202 90	4,361 85	4,267 90	3,082 50	3,255 02
Trade dollars					4,595 80
Specie	248,221 65	207,583 65	272,272 07	293,551 10	308,307 94
Legal-tender notes	184,689 00	161,873 00	166,550 00	151,564 00	156,953 00
U. S. cert's of deposit					
Due from U. S. Treas	279,904 50	257,320 50	252,220 50	264,622 50	287,347 50
Total	21,419,617 95	19,976,643 88	19,756,662 09	20,203,927 67	20,379,573 42

arranged by States and reserve cities.

MAINE.

Liabilities.	DECEMBER 20.	MARCH 10.	MAY 6.	JULY 1.	OCTOBER 1.
	71 banks.	71 banks.	71 banks.	71 banks.	71 banks.
Capital stock	$10,360,000 00	$10,360,000 00	$10,360,000 00	$10,360,000 00	$10,360,000 00
Surplus fund.... ...	2,443,544 72	2,460,665 15	2,464,253 19	2,481,306 15	2,486,217 94
Undivided profits. ..	1,403,413 21	1,093,707 12	1,159,646 37	977,810 09	1,142,139 04
Nat'l bank circulation	7,844,170 00	7,729,337 00	7,797,819 00	7,797,294 00	7,683,079 00
State bank circulation	1,427 00				
Dividends unpaid....	38,611 57	48,505 98	65,698 58	263,419 58	79,426 17
Individual deposits ..	8,907,147 85	9,132,727 89	8,944,584 12	9,144,271 62	10,095,495 13
U. S. deposits.......	73,878 61	78,361 47	78,603 40	73,916 70	85,018 85
Dep'ts U.S.dis.officers	56,213 87	60,608 07	73,280 61	66,192 85	57,491 19
Due to national banks	693,591 39	341,645 77	484,029 83	450,234 19	442,044 95
Due to State banks ..	164,011 01	151,061 53	88,153 41	123,254 89	114,532 48
Notes re-discounted..	73,364 10	42,000 00	40,000 00	50,000 00	45,103 10
Bills payable				1,312 00	
Total	32,061,373 33	31,498,679 98	31,556,068 51	31,789,012 16	32,590,547 53

NEW HAMPSHIRE.

	48 banks.	48 banks.	48 banks.	48 banks.	48 banks.
Capital stock	$6,105,000 00	$6,105,000 00	$6,105,000 00	$6,105,000 00	$6,105,000 00
Surplus fund.......	1,193,316 76	1,195,189 54	1,187,832 14	1,216,855 90	1,220,425 93
Undivided profits ...	656,791 47	576,027 62	584,849 99	499,095 05	581,752 04
Nat'l bank circulation	5,122,238 00	5,108,256 00	5,113,570 00	5,125,810 00	5,149,045 00
State bank circulation	6,838 00	6,838 00	6,838 00	6,838 00	6,838 00
Dividends unpaid...	17,313 53	18,276 59	35,807 09	06,517 65	30,780 80
Individual deposits	4,682,832 47	4,415,333 45	4,624,045 15	4,833,418 61	5,425,196 24
U. S. deposits.....	228,978 37	193,064 74	217,782 62	230,822 75	234,006 71
Dep'ts U.S.dis.officers	100,560 81	121,359 03	103,928 16	88,059 47	106,710 48
Due to national banks	358,689 88	365,086 05	308,661 05	323,441 93	326,554 34
Due to State banks...	206,456 49	372,579 96	320,140 73	395,361 66	328,056 60
Notes re-discounted..	18,010 10	13,622 39	10,510 00	12,913 22	14,000 00
Bills payable........	8,000 00	7,700 00		8,102 58	
Total	18,705,025 88	18,499,833 37	18,618,864,93	18,948,236 91	19,528,960 02

VERMONT.

	50 banks.	50 banks.	48 banks.	48 banks.	47 banks.
Capital stock	$8,053,000 00	$7,671,000 00	$7,531,000 00	$7,551,000 00	$7,541,000 00
Surplus fund........	1,626,485 21	1,511,840 24	1,477,010 60	1,485,105 74	1,473,839 48
Undivided profits....	789,009 47	478,200 47	578,497 26	436,777 97	501,204 06
Nat'l bank circulation	5,731,892 00	5,509,808 00	5,437,518 00	5,419,203 00	5,355,913 00
State bank circulation	3,500 00	3,500 00	3,500 00	3,500 00	3,500 00
Dividends unpaid....	9,234 63	14,761 17	11,004 63	93,864 38	13,284 36
Individual deposits ..	4,821,597 31	4,535,747 47	4,381,085 50	4,870,534 97	5,154,308 13
U. S. deposits......	33,560 64	37,150 49	42,783 15	35,493 31	36,720 06
Dep'ts U.S.dis.officers	10,427 38	6,769 91	5,962 91	7,604 24	12,943 97
Due to national banks	173,813 15	94,057 26	144,284 50	140,753 29	151,316 13
Due to State banks .	37,106 64	34,593 95	56,382 21	94,178 27	63,139 24
Notes re-discounted .	107,979 90	58,101 00	60,522 34	51,521 96	62,894 83
Bills payable........	21,110 93	21,110 93	21,110 93	14,390 54	9,509 00
Total	21,419,617 35	19,976,643 88	19,756,662 09	20,203,927 67	20,379,573 43

Abstract of reports since September 30, 1884, arranged

MASSACHUSETTS.

Resources.	DECEMBER 20. 195 banks.	MARCH 10. 195 banks.	MAY 6. 195 banks.	JULY 1. 195 banks.	OCTOBER 1. 195 banks.
Loans and discounts	$82, 898, 870 20	$82, 608, 208 90	$83, 508, 226 94	$83, 000, 007 30	$86, 172, 243 64
Bonds for circulation	39, 831, 350 00	39, 228, 350 00	39, 094, 350 00	38, 749, 350 00	38, 606, 850 00
Bonds for deposits	300, 000 00	300, 000 00	300, 000 00	300, 000 00	350, 000 00
U. S. bonds on hand	386, 950 00	249, 950 00	267, 550 00	270, 950 00	249, 500 00
Other stocks and b'ds	3, 732, 902 57	3, 981, 504 55	4, 203, 219 58	4, 410, 318 00	4, 357, 382 99
Due from res've ag'ts	8, 048, 929 29	8, 755, 246 63	8, 073, 745 93	9, 306, 605 50	8, 528, 991 60
Due from nat'l banks	869, 860 37	1, 114, 184 13	796, 251 52	695, 644 53	840, 487 73
Due from State banks	85, 336 88	138, 300 50	131, 116 72	136, 950 71	183, 497 23
Real estate, &c	2, 046, 362 27	2, 002, 606 63	1, 998, 611 57	2, 026, 823 00	2, 044, 992 41
Current expenses	542, 492 33	592, 414 59	291, 984 85	209, 936 28	257, 033 75
Premiums paid	1, 180, 155 72	1, 173, 087 08	1, 119, 300 63	1, 120, 633 00	1, 120, 747 33
Cash items	677, 218 43	689, 418 71	696, 743 79	983, 402 44	807, 484 65
Clear'g-house exch'gs	33, 652 12	40, 822 48	29, 465 22	70, 113 15	66, 984 03
Bills of other banks	1, 149, 235 00	1, 188, 343 00	1, 251, 022 00	1, 231, 021 00	1, 379, 501 00
Fractional currency	34, 175 33	38, 256 93	33, 179 06	29, 785 68	31, 626 79
Trade dollars					15, 243 75
Specie	1, 931, 291 85	2, 054, 319 47	2, 069, 225 88	2, 256, 383 16	2, 438, 310 74
Legal-tender notes	1, 478, 722 00	1, 488, 443 00	1, 512, 348 00	1, 507, 587 00	1, 672, 817 00
U. S. cert's of deposit	165, 000 00	155, 000 00	165, 000 00	170, 000 00	175, 000 00
Due from U. S. Treas	1, 807, 843 73	1, 810, 385 00	1, 783, 499 00	1, 748, 448 75	1, 791, 626 40
Total	147, 200, 355 09	117, 609, 051 62	148, 194, 835 69	148, 230, 679 65	151, 190, 29 13

CITY OF BOSTON.

	54 banks.	54 banks.	54 banks.	54 banks.	54 banks.
Loans and discounts	$117, 388, 982 92	$114, 820, 830 89	$116, 935, 654 72	$122, 729, 511 49	$125, 331, 305 35
Bonds for circulation	26, 606, 150 00	25, 876, 150 00	25, 694, 650 00	25, 559, 650 00	24, 614, 650 00
Bonds for deposits	175, 000 00	175, 000 00	175, 000 00	175, 000 00	175, 000 00
U. S. bonds on hand	76, 800 00	71, 200 00	72, 550 00	263, 250 00	46, 400 00
Other stocks and b'ds	2, 276, 917 68	2, 538, 223 91	2, 890, 122 25	3, 008, 544 53	3, 031, 822 75
Due from res've ag'ta	10, 037, 135 92	14, 102, 248 43	15, 222, 650 80	13, 547, 054 86	13, 931, 112 86
Due from nat'l b'nks	9, 084, 695 45	7, 665, 963 20	8, 651, 671 60	9, 823, 208 94	10, 154, 928 37
Due from State banks	706, 404 84	305, 855 94	325, 072 13	415, 190 34	243, 996 14
Real estate, &c	3, 007, 972 09	2, 972, 825 63	2, 976, 522 64	2, 975, 795 58	2, 072, 149 53
Current expenses	742, 923 35	1, 159, 011 96	178, 492 44	430, 918 59	27, 379 02
Premiums paid	782, 970 35	738, 094 05	716, 994 98	817, 587 62	874, 438 83
Cash items	380, 471 50	380, 146 14	1, 603, 329 31	1, 665, 329 31	649, 521 05
Clear'g-house exch'gs	6, 421, 272 80	6, 477, 522 82	6, 822, 949 17	11, 314, 625 65	9, 558, 729 20
Bills of other banks	1, 967, 748 00	1, 582, 391 00	1, 745, 068 00	2, 103, 743 00	2, 034, 077 00
Fractional currency	11, 778 79	11, 111 91	7, 809 86	9, 677 60	7, 895 66
Trade dollars					397 00
Specie	7, 956, 418 48	8, 386, 727 10	8, 650, 666 77	8, 978, 450 12	8, 960, 565 17
Legal-tender notes	3, 912, 020 00	3, 452, 339 00	3, 376, 482 00	3, 949, 267 00	3, 642, 498 00
U. S. cert's of deposit	1, 335, 000 00	1, 305, 000 00	780, 000 00	1, 395, 000 00	1, 185, 000 00
Due from U. S. Treas	1, 596, 152 82	1, 278, 551 75	1, 305, 191 75	1, 155, 349 25	1, 154, 071 75
Total	194, 466, 815 08	193, 397, 064 82	197, 051, 392 53	209, 626, 649 88	208, 495, 842 68

RHODE ISLAND.

	63 banks.	63 banks.	62 banks.	61 banks.	61 banks.
Loans and discounts	$30, 641, 179 97	$30, 524, 144 93	$30, 238, 892 51	$30, 213, 023 98	$31, 602, 030 77
Bonds for circulation	13, 820, 400 00	13, 820, 400 00	13, 627, 400 00	13, 595, 400 00	13, 595, 400 00
Bonds for deposits	150, 000 00	150, 000 00	150, 000 00	150, 000 00	150, 000 00
U. S. bonds on hand	152, 400 00	152, 800 00	153, 750 00	153, 650 00	251, 200 00
Other stocks and b'ds	1, 353, 381 78	1, 392, 354 47	1, 447, 779 38	1, 476, 464 89	1, 466, 908 69
Due from res've ag'ts	2, 289, 793 31	2, 138, 567 27	2, 629, 834 21	2, 538, 637 23	2, 350, 941 96
Due from nat'l banks	775, 694 60	688, 214 19	518, 064 00	572, 712 92	688, 405 81
Due from State banks	68, 419 43	41, 001 10	56, 559 09	29, 244 03	37, 519 44
Real estate, &c	798, 846 08	738, 423 42	700, 543 80	674, 665 87	687, 029 83
Current expenses	129, 494 36	120, 169 43	121, 298 43	81, 375 20	109, 684 05
Premiums paid	435, 969 71	405, 874 74	405, 979 51	428, 151 80	430, 760 95
Cash items	163, 215 40	146, 485 67	136, 687 52	178, 836 74	144, 191 72
Clear'g-house exch'gs	312, 300 04	266, 684 26	266, 765 64	714, 259 25	298, 659 32
Bills of other banks	378, 111 00	304, 052 00	355, 094 00	314, 829 00	359, 239 00
Fractional currency	11, 463 96	13, 096 37	13, 250 99	13, 631 56	11, 038 45
Trade dollars					339 00
Specie	445, 706 04	489, 253 54	473, 197 23	490, 909 87	565, 457 48
Legal-tender notes	505, 529 00	480, 187 00	496, 374 00	458, 430 00	493, 697 00
U. S. cert's of deposit					
Due from U. S. Treas	643, 935 27	570, 896 00	636, 640 00	695, 565 00	637, 715 00
Total	53, 075, 965 85	52, 455, 498 86	52, 428, 049 87	52, 720, 442 30	53, 290, 948 82

by States and reserve cities—Continued.

MASSACHUSETTS.

Liabilities.	DECEMBER 20. 195 banks.	MARCH 10. 195 banks.	MAY 6. 195 banks.	JULY 1. 195 banks.	OCTOBER 1. 195 banks.
Capital stock	$45,677,500 00	$45,667,500 00	$45,217,500 00	$45,117,500 00	$45,095,656 00
Surplus fund	13,646,123 61	13,592,155 35	13,475,857 62	13,524,622 47	13,545,392 18
Undivided profits	4,497,302 31	4,917,608 52	3,949,782 28	4,150,393 57	3,551,604 11
Nat'l bank circulation	35,151,022 00	34,499,177 00	34,350,814 00	33,954,639 00	34,200,534 00
State bank circulation					
Dividends unpaid	114,694 74	107,177 94	205,582 47	378,343 98	791,574 44
Individual deposits	42,713,969 74	46,232,755 84	48,474,915 94	40,132,964 05	51,715,367 00
U. S. deposits	240,293 81	213,760 72	212,559 88	289,547 52	259,377 38
Dep'ts U.S.dis.officers	29,656 20	42,669 78	43,056 97	16,187 17	16,349 62
Due to national banks	2,256,741 65	1,572,068 68	1,664,149 13	1,397,004 21	1,612,390 62
Due to State banks	132,226 00	120,167 26	158,636 07	265,214 06	214,582 72
Notes re-discounted	578,494 74	290,010 58	176,900 33	81,000 00	153,945 51
Bills payable	190,000 00	45,000 00	39,000 00	43,263 62	89,526 55
Total	147,200,355 09	147,009,951 62	148,194,855 60	148,239,670 05	151,190,293 13

CITY OF BOSTON.

	54 banks.	54 banks.	54 banks.	54 banks.	54 banks.
Capital stock	$50,950,000 00	$50,950,000 00	$50,950,000 00	$50,950,000 00	$50,950,000 00
Surplus fund	11,418,270 35	11,324,141 37	11,345,536 80	11,345,536 80	11,416,551 48
Undivided profits	3,366,106 71	4,596,112 41	2,787,718 25	3,568,185 03	2,897,141 82
Nat'l bank circulation	23,301,482 00	22,957,375 00	22,505,170 00	22,370,171 00	21,716,837 00
State bank circulation					
Dividends unpaid	51,337 81	36,389 06	100,636 80	62,096 55	1,111,741 05
Individual deposits	70,812,461 44	70,142,264 22	74,707,502 60	81,075,250 34	80,326,965 06
U. S. deposits	106,227 70	193,633 51	113,154 51	110,945 30	110,260 14
Dep'ts U.S.dis.officers	29,424 06	26,427 21	22,750 71	17,810 55	18,188 86
Due to national banks	27,101,674 06	25,980,442 98	25,336,780 69	30,560,153 61	30,512,185 09
Due to State banks	6,904,829 15	7,154,719 48	8,762,142 08	9,555,466 61	9,933,273 20
Notes re-discounted					
Bills payable	425,000 00	117,439 58	420,000 00	1,095 00	2,750 00
Total	194,466,815 08	195,307,964 83	107,051,392 53	209,626,640 88	208,495,842 68

RHODE ISLAND.

	63 banks.	63 banks.	62 banks.	61 banks.	61 banks.
Capital stock	$20,510,050 00	$20,540,050 00	$20,465,050 00	$20,340,050 00	$20,340,050 00
Surplus fund	4,021,095 66	4,020,220 84	4,011,602 23	3,861,833 06	3,954,823 93
Undivided profits	1,710,289 58	1,455,990 49	1,448,187 08	1,297,580 33	1,208,408 09
Nat'l bank circulation	12,310,203 00	12,180,863 00	12,085,574 00	12,019,254 00	12,056,177 00
State bank circulation	8,658 00	7,001 00	2,795 00	2,795 00	2,790 00
Dividends unpaid	81,907 59	92,690 82	132,007 87	243,592 31	196,513 57
Individual deposits	11,422,794 44	11,977,368 58	12,069,262 63	12,586,981 15	13,006,232 40
U. S. deposits	37,144 20	47,247 14	99,835 36	32,505 63	71,092 66
Dep'ts U.S.dis.officers	65,055 72	84,180 72	91,750 47	107,188 45	57,589 25
Due to national banks	1,982,832 03	1,307,358 07	1,054,718 00	1,281,192 31	1,315,925 88
Due to State banks	892,615 63	726,512 70	1,035,266 53	945,400 42	937,285 95
Notes re-discounted					
Bills payable					
Total	53,075,965 85	52,455,498 36	52,428,049 37	52,720,442 83	53,290,948 82

Abstract of reports since September 30, 1884, arranged
CONNECTICUT.

Resources.	DECEMBER 20. 88 banks.	MARCH 10. 87 banks.	MAY 6. 87 banks.	JULY 1. 84 banks.	OCTOBER 1. 84 banks.
Loans and discounts	$40,480,025 27	$40,346,387 20	$40,242,199 97	$40,510,342 71	$40,601,465 01
Bonds for circulation	18,319,100 00	18,252,100 00	18,240,100 00	18,010,100 00	18,010,100 00
Bonds for deposits	360,000 00	360,000 00	360,000 00	360,000 00	360,000 00
U.S. bonds on hand	162,450 00	268,500 00	271,450 00	270,500 00	531,400 00
Other stocks and b'ds	2,678,909 41	2,716,284 94	2,759,474 36	2,851,305 49	3,178,167 93
Due from res've ag'ts	4,679,244 63	5,817,393 41	6,369,524 15	5,260,268 50	4,384,449 32
Due from nat'l banks	2,006,890 69	2,223,624 31	1,959,872 60	2,718,200 47	2,865,559 25
Due from State banks	275,030 13	216,437 21	197,488 17	229,719 14	151,762 79
Real estate, &c	1,595,900 12	1,455,280 79	1,416,947 61	1,424,118 80	1,434,863 30
Current expenses	283,904 53	172,037 63	248,076 41	48,157 05	204,904 53
Premiums paid	515,688 10	542,996 73	543,692 63	546,787 10	559,388 13
Cash items	385,977 74	474,619 24	384,211 26	452,321 72	401,232 78
Clear'g-house exch'gs	194,861 76	207,008 33	187,242 44	331,905 24	224,692 88
Bills of other banks	714,181 00	787,401 00	937,820 00	896,288 00	762,670 00
Fractional currency	15,723 47	17,897 76	14,472 72	13,437 35	13,769 50
Trade dollars					35,212 39
Specie	1,331,908 63	1,371,499 91	1,436,312 59	1,505,629 16	1,562,155 22
Legal-tender notes	808,542 00	777,505 00	904,552 00	883,715 00	901,660 00
U.S. cert's of deposit					
Due from U.S. Treas	794,013 35	856,851 35	847,342 75	827,232 25	856,892 40
Total	75,504,391 13	76,863,630 81	77,342,688 15	77,170,100 04	77,041,238 04

NEW YORK.

	266 banks.	266 banks.	265 banks.	266 banks.	267 banks.
Loans and discounts	$84,276,886 19	$82,629,206 69	$83,860,625 39	$83,214,057 04	$83,979,728 98
Bonds for circulation	27,898,650 00	27,492,150 00	27,362,150 00	27,392,150 00	27,257,150 00
Bonds for deposits	775,000 00	775,000 00	775,000 00	892,000 00	892,000 00
U.S. bonds on hand	1,473,950 00	1,610,600 00	1,587,000 00	1,543,050 00	1,486,800 00
Other stocks and b'ds	7,185,686 67	7,214,736 10	6,836,124 34	6,846,954 33	7,202,547 53
Due from res've ag'ts	13,663,909 95	15,679,869 32	13,603,123 04	13,611,766 38	14,285,672 97
Due from nat'l banks	2,353,126 45	2,137,313 33	2,500,969 96	2,846,764 47	2,797,892 77
Due from State banks	1,275,642 45	641,909 18	663,624 14	808,355 70	670,772 16
Real estate, &c	3,356,754 17	3,237,623 91	3,167,294 78	3,257,084 38	3,250,720 56
Current expenses	671,336 40	463,195 94	550,304 48	224,178 82	444,269 93
Premiums paid	1,163,289 89	1,156,598 09	1,202,013 47	1,266,955 35	1,288,108 04
Cash items	1,443,862 20	1,309,115 60	1,278,151 76	3,248,824 98	1,797,882 48
Clear'g house exch'gs	33,426 36	34,467 36	48,213 27	61,715 44	60,482 61
Bills of other banks	1,188,055 00	4,152,167 00	1,225,986 00	1,137,599 00	1,204,478 00
Fractional currency	33,087 31	38,182 52	37,368 63	34,289 04	33,037 55
Trade dollars					243,814 40
Specie	3,961,563 01	4,486,115 13	4,814,533 19	4,870,057 05	5,034,293 02
Legal-tender notes	3,834,901 00	3,683,640 00	3,363,679 00	2,823,560 00	3,191,690 00
U.S. cert's of deposit	325,000 00	425,000 00	403,000 00	403,000 00	265,000 00
Due from U.S. Treas	1,259,692 21	1,284,731 00	1,247,659 60	1,295,447 10	1,296,586 65
Total	156,173,909 29	155,482,712 17	154,543,646 05	155,785,818 68	156,628,718 04

CITY OF NEW YORK.

	44 banks.	44 banks.	44 banks.	45 banks.	44 banks.
Loans and discounts	$210,385,727 11	$224,283,771 51	$211,897,611 98	$216,409,219 45	$236,589,011 33
Bonds for circulation	14,177,500 00	13,669,500 00	13,609,500 00	12,895,500 00	12,596,500 00
Bonds for deposits	820,000 00	820,000 00	820,000 00	820,000 00	820,000 00
U.S. bonds on hand	4,498,150 00	5,800,250 00	5,366,500 00	5,387,250 00	4,205,800 00
Other stocks and b'ds	13,686,446 11	14,254,892 28	14,462,710 71	15,468,258 85	14,242,731 53
Due from res've ag'ts					
Due from nat'l banks	19,546,175 74	15,031,685 56	15,651,528 07	19,420,625 12	18,846,713 33
Due from State banks	2,752,540 28	2,377,141 76	2,341,448 65	2,550,676 35	2,759,121 81
Real estate, &c	9,874,271 63	10,160,145 56	10,203,273 14	10,230,972 04	10,177,498 07
Current expenses	1,731,068 11	653,906 60	933,453 49	184,329 80	757,433 42
Premiums paid	1,195,887 21	1,312,859 67	1,318,040 63	1,358,394 08	990,395 71
Cash items	1,792,170 51	1,851,001 91	2,142,102 04	2,374,359 50	2,597,221 04
C.H. loan certificates	1,870,000 00	1,520,000 00	1,440,000 00	1,250,000 00	1,110,000 00
Clear'g-house exch'gs	53,927,631 33	38,206,796 88	51,393,979 14	77,451,807 67	55,451,777 33
Bills of other banks	2,654,849 00	4,353,898 00	2,336,784 00	2,684,458 80	1,595,018 60
Fractional currency	38,918 00	35,463 74	48,651 88	44,578 93	35,852 21
Trade dollars					104,783 90
Specie	72,808,908 97	90,495,336 48	96,500,028 87	96,527,005 25	91,464,167 74
Legal-tender notes	23,265,272 00	18,602,546 00	20,428,591 00	27,164,671 00	16,785,620 00
U.S. cert's of deposit	8,005,000 00	8,360,000 00	5,970,000 00	8,540,000 00	6,920,000 00
Due from U.S. Treas	1,086,864 85	1,078,613 87	1,483,637 32	837,654 52	757,858 72
Total	443,488,192 48	439,292,149 82	457,902,849 26	501,707,358 03	479,249,180 24

CONNECTICUT.

Liabilities.	DECEMBER 20. 88 banks.	MARCH 10. 87 banks.	MAY 6. 87 banks.	JULY 1. 34 banks.	OCTOBER 1 84 banks.
Capital stock	$26,050,820 00	$25,850,820 00	$25,071,820 00	$24,921,820 00	$24,921,820 00
Surplus fund	6,246,700 57	6,826,373 78	6,772,236 28	6,715,073 30	6,717,780 44
Undivided profits	2,197,911 07	1,673,555 91	1,915,264 11	1,257,521 42	1,732,755 09
Nat'l bank circulation	16,176,757 00	15,928,602 00	16,065,952 00	15,717,275 00	15,932,600 00
State bank circulation	38,007 00	20,162 00	24,558 00	24,558 00	18,675 00
Dividends unpaid	57,501 85	75,749 19	74,302 04	530,756 38	93,081 94
Individual deposits	20,565,254 07	22,678,676 81	23,420,993 66	25,246,464 78	24,482,789 55
U. S. deposits	282,245 31	294,990 63	205,428 33	251,828 59	289,431 76
Dep'ts U.S.dis.officers	16,243 68	10,604 45	16,813 14	19,076 00	20,043 25
Due to national banks	2,539,915 14	2,729,969 97	2,315,489 91	1,843,427 63	1,007,596 19
Due to State banks	527,691 65	639,497 45	702,831 17	576,265 98	653,674 36
Notes re-discounted	179,631 79	120,428 27	42,896 51	36,023 05	5,000 00
Bills payable	27,500 00	5,000 00	15,000 00		200,000 00
Total	75,504,301 13	76,863,630 81	77,342,688 15	77,170,100 04	77,041,238 94

NEW YORK.

	266 banks.	266 banks.	265 banks.	266 banks.	267 banks.
Capital stock	$35,004,160 00	$34,714,160 00	$34,582,260 00	$34,748,357 00	$34,819,760 00
Surplus fund	9,985,597 21	8,814,099 92	8,729,535 36	8,840,334 05	8,926,655 46
Undivided profits	6,618,687 27	3,348,375 61	5,790,196 67	5,013,794 62	5,614,629 77
Nat'l bank circulation	24,811,412 00	24,128,811 00	24,106,386 00	23,876,591 00	23,989,591 00
State bank circulation	30,626 00	30,626 00	30,626 00	30,624 00	30,623 00
Dividends unpaid	50,552 35	71,280 80	73,639 66	344,630 62	62,367 42
Individual deposits	74,592,081 38	77,430,640 92	75,775,909 50	78,059,538 33	77,814,371 10
U. S. deposits	520,918 41	568,779 28	626,915 20	487,101 47	617,988 34
Dep'ts U.S.dis.officers	113,767 13	84,618 60	115,856 09	132,727 70	160,964 46
Due to national banks	3,351,953 74	2,917,491 49	3,184,527 15	2,480,612 30	2,953,653 94
Due to State banks	1,071,444 87	890,930 14	871,776 29	906,782 08	1,207,402 03
Notes re-discounted	647,722 92	378,776 43	466,966 62	494,716 06	315,104 44
Bills payable	274,980 01	114,121 98	131,051 51	360,922 45	155,607 88
Total	156,173,909 29	155,482,712 17	154,549,646 05	155,785,818 63	156,628,718 84

CITY OF NEW YORK.

	44 banks.	44 banks.	44 banks.	45 banks.	44 banks.
Capital stock	$46,250,000 00	$46,250,000 00	$46,250,000 00	$46,522,500 00	$45,350,000 00
Surplus fund	22,582,580 00	22,430,264 18	22,304,264 18	22,435,654 65	22,176,007 68
Undivided profits	12,138,436 21	10,088,278 01	10,603,375 33	9,340,280 34	10,487,170 66
Nat'l bank circulation	11,897,617 00	11,899,992 00	10,961,242 00	9,952,392 00	9,917,442 00
State bank circulation	32,870 00	32,400 00	32,837 00	32,830 00	31,197 00
Dividends unpaid	250,545 15	136,455 80	217,479 91	1,039,830 58	282,849 10
Individual deposits	201,634,524 42	189,906,120 43	218,066,568 64	247,364,935 53	226,925,990 62
Certified checks	25,356,371 64	19,626,365 63	25,933,735 47	28,592,960 74	23,568,335 80
U. S. deposits	413,400 64	434,962 70	425,544 04	423,465 48	420,181 03
Dep'ts U.S.dis.officers	240,547 40	211,444 80	180,492 46	36,113 74	47,102 59
Due to national banks	92,017,629 63	101,381,214 80	98,761,129 95	90,927,194 70	105,037,933 50
Due to State banks	30,674,133 51	31,096,072 36	32,167,703 29	36,139,270 37	34,199,239 26
Notes re-discounted					205,420 00
Bills payable					
Total	443,488,192 48	439,202,149 82	457,902,849 26	501,707,358 03	479,249,186 24

Abstract of reports since September 30, 1884, arranged

CITY· OF ALBANY.

Resources.	DECEMBER 20. 7 banks.	MARCH 10. 6 banks.	MAY 6. 6 banks.	JULY 1. 6 banks.	OCTOBER 1. 6 banks.
Loans and discounts	$7,132,627 08	$7,213,719 74	$7,613,299 96	$7,402,069 18	$7,130,411 94
Bonds for circulation	1,518,000 00	1,218,000 00	1,318,000 00	1,418,000 00	1,418,000 00
Bonds for deposits	100,000 00	100,000 00	100,000 00	100,000 00	100,000 00
U.S. bonds on hand	300 00	100 00	100 00	100 00	100,100 00
Other stocks and b'ds	313,606 15	364,105 06	421,650 00	491,665 00	479,175 00
Due from res've ag'ts	1,819,963 42	1,976,384 68	2,636,741 74	2,543,559 47	1,994,663 65
Due from nat'l banks	747,804 54	789,584 60	989,597 30	1,034,858 64	1,056,328 06
Due from State banks	126,835 21	91,591 35	82,275 68	34,891 55	68,280 77
Real estate, &c	321,256 45	275,500 00	281,500 00	281,500 00	281,500 00
Current expenses					
Premiums paid	22,500 00	66,296 66	88,122 00	95,296 00	89,796 00
Cash items	48,718 33	77,982 72	98,585 64	55,245 98	67,904 78
Clear'g-house exch'gs	137,864 48	102,093 05	141,331 87	216,682 60	135,967 65
Bills of other banks	150,528 00	152,478 00	126,563 00	141,160 00	187,311 00
Fractional currency	3,376 30	1,564 20	828 53	1,372 81	1,352 77
Trade dollars					600 00
Specie	682,323 82	816,902 80	817,997 50	869,410 50	922,889 50
Legal-tender notes	226,368 00	149,860 00	170,860 00	205,960 00	189,460 00
U.S. cert's of deposit	310,000 00	310,000 00	310,000 00	310,000 00	310,000 00
Due from U.S. Treas	71,047 47	66,040 27	63,842 47	65,907 50	75,393 70
Total	13,731,109 25	13,672,149 31	15,255,195 69	15,262,653 23	14,559,110 85

NEW JERSEY.

	70 banks.	70 banks.	70 banks.	70 banks.	72 banks.
Loans and discounts	$29,107,283 36	$28,236,623 24	$29,438,576 64	$29,189,183 07	$29,365,001 57
Bonds for circulation	9,286,850 00	9,286,850 00	9,286,850 00	9,286,850 00	9,326,850 00
Bonds for deposits	250,000 00	250,000 00	250,000 00	250,000 00	250,000 00
U.S. bonds on hand	972,050 00	913,700 00	775,250 00	788,850 00	912,350 00
Other stocks and b'ds	2,554,686 10	2,797,439 28	2,696,145 29	2,681,185 16	3,000,237 61
Due from res've ag'ts	7,257,914 65	7,276,854 32	6,222,966 23	6,779,312 60	8,273,007 32
Due from nat'l banks	1,324,982 33	1,141,370 06	1,161,549 69	1,082,288 30	1,343,336 36
Due from State banks	180,387 13	150,604 59	192,979 74	206,933 98	171,471 33
Real estate, &c	1,594,951 74	1,585,651 72	1,592,541 16	1,587,192 33	1,602,887 57
Current expenses	275,368 51	161,213 37	198,174 46	92,570 60	179,542 08
Premiums paid	318,050 54	424,593 30	385,527 29	383,225 18	391,160 62
Cash items	868,035 91	738,983 57	644,129 26	805,375 10	1,041,367 91
Clear'g-house exch'gs					
Bills of other banks	441,477 00	463,364 00	514,084 00	469,409 00	457,065 00
Fractional currency	18,198 17	17,630 68	16,536 67	15,569 37	18,446 80
Trade dollars					60,163 20
Specie	1,278,893 53	1,454,955 56	1,533,633 92	1,629,861 08	1,979,701 70
Legal-tender notes	1,680,786 00	1,833,971 00	1,823,798 00	1,689,259 00	1,902,131 00
U.S. cert's of deposit	20,000 00	20,000 00		10,000 00	10,000 00
Due from U.S. Treas	422,968 00	426,068 00	421,187 40	449,668 00	448,923 00
Total	57,252,841 97	57,188,871 78	57,189,819 75	57,395,732 81	60,733,643 07

PENNSYLVANIA.

	224 banks.	223 banks.	224 banks.	225 banks.	228 banks.
Loans and discounts	$66,378,981 51	$64,630,467 72	$65,378,864 59	$34,973,905 55	$65,596,407 02
Bonds for circulation	26,784,600 00	26,747,100 00	26,640,200 00	26,599,200 00	26,630,200 00
Bonds for deposits	480,000 00	480,000 00	480,000 00	480,000 00	480,000 00
U.S. bonds on hand	1,004,100 00	819,700 00	1,124,450 00	1,183,100 00	1,321,500 00
Other stocks and b'ds	8,050,306 03	8,873,908 96	8,493,469 66	8,671,461 05	8,587,405 51
Due from res've ag'ts	9,955,973 78	10,910,284 79	10,136,767 03	9,642,133 23	10,738,628 28
Due from nat'l banks	2,076,473 62	2,369,275 71	2,257,317 66	2,721,787 84	3,632,510 77
Due from State banks	892,528 60	1,063,818 92	959,660 15	1,464,844 51	1,054,605 07
Real estate, &c	3,468,758 16	3,481,280 39	3,341,706 16	3,548,389 04	3,576,021 78
Current expenses	358,974 52	371,888 72	483,733 40	281,493 26	500,004 81
Premiums paid	1,007,979 65	1,041,489 20	1,012,970 65	1,024,835 71	1,061,676 92
Cash items	717,973 05	625,387 80	679,308 35	848,657 65	664,982 15
Clear'g-house exch'gs	76,891 52	10,544 91	40,844 90	27,126 22	19,022 82
Bills of other banks	954,147 00	982,606 00	1,314,915 00	1,317,724 00	1,378,596 00
Fractional currency	42,262 49	50,205 20	54,814 54	52,652 07	46,337 43
Trade dollars					562,351 91
Specie	4,187,727 22	4,426,686 48	4,083,119 42	4,828,201 64	4,565,935 40
Legal-tender notes	2,737,575 00	2,585,385 00	3,079,506 00	2,906,336 00	3,106,647 00
U.S. cert's of deposit	10,000 00	10,000 00	10,000 00	10,000 00	10,000 00
Due from U.S. Treas	1,176,447 07	1,204,307 50	1,197,185 91	1,149,213 30	1,275,649 83
Total	129,081,798 22	130,775,437 39	132,351,902 31	131,409,484 56	134,107,127 39

by States and reserve cities—Continued.

CITY OF ALBANY.

Liabilities.	DECEMBER 20. 7 banks.	MARCH 10. 6 banks.	MAY 6. 6 banks.	JULY 1. 6 banks.	OCTOBER 1. 6 banks.
Capital stock	$1,800,000 00	$1,750,000 00	$1,750,000 00	$1,750,000 00	$1,750,000 00
Surplus fund	1,400,000 00	1,150,000 00	1,150,000 00	1,150,000 00	1,175,000 00
Undivided profits ...	377,967 65	268,922 23	234,550 34	227,785 48	205,058 46
Nat'l bank circulation	1,336,690 00	1,006,190 00	1,122,330 00	1,184,330 00	1,249,790 00
State bank circulation					
Dividends unpaid....	499 00	397 94	2,553 00	9,951 50	8,958 00
Individual deposits ..	5,571,415 50	5,985,343 72	7,637,978 87	7,984,454 75	7,097,824 43
U. S. deposits	61,887 26	80,401 10	99,990 40	79,115 08	82,966 63
Dep'ts U.S.dis.officers	16,184 24	5,011 22	1,519 22	654 61	1,147 52
Due to national banks	2,515,868 19	2,824,182 71	2,666,315 75	2,169,098 83	2,365,764 85
Due to State banks ..	650,597 41	601,700 39	589,958 11	707,202 98	622,600 96
Notes re-discounted..					
Bills payable... ..					
Total............	13,731,109 25	13,672,149 31	15,255,195 09	15,262,653 23	14,559,110 85

NEW JERSEY.

	70 banks.	70 banks.	70 banks.	70 banks.	72 banks.
Capital stock	$12,103,350 00	$12,103,350 00	$12,103,350 00	$12,103,350 00	$12,208,200 00
Surplus fund........	3,738,069 26	3,761,638 91	3,751,397 63	3,804,353 86	3,799,944 97
Undivided profits....	2,068,153 91	1,720,968 05	1,873,278 62	1,587,593 13	1,820,748 66
Nat'l bank circulation	8,229,171 00	8,213,221 00	8,228,171 00	8,042,886 00	8,007,406 00
State bank circulation	8,450 00	8,450 00	8,396 00	8,396 00	8,396 00
Dividends unpaid....	32,302 04	55,153 50	49,817 56	269,627 50	87,982 92
Individual deposits ..	28,720,619 16	28,885,845 24	28,614,228 76	29,176,693 67	32,501,421 62
U. S. deposits........	178,306 96	165,708 09	178,333 39	164,529 84	166,974 18
Dep'ts U.S.dis.officers	16,706 37	29,862 01	41,742 29	24,547 89	28,347 48
Due to national banks	1,802,502 40	1,938,417 07	1,895,827 36	1,908,242 88	1,797,166 11
Due to State banks...	275,910 87	224,957 91	287,102 25	254,387 04	300,755 13
Notes re-discounted..	3,000 00	25,000 00	81,874 89	29,825 00	
Bills payable	76,300 00	56,300 00	76,300 00	21,300 00	6,300 00
Total..........	57,252,841 97	57,188,871 78	57,189,819 75	57,395,732 81	60,733,643 07

PENNSYLVANIA.

	224 banks.	223 banks.	224 banks.	225 banks.	226 banks.
Capital stock	$32,084,840 00	$32,050,340 00	$32,150,340 00	$32,270,340 00	$32,665,340 00
Surplus fund........	9,938,413 09	9,807,900 07	9,970,766 01	10,080,212 91	10,067,362 42
Undivided profits....	3,140,118 18	3,178,037 04	3,130,705 26	2,824,083 54	3,479,814 40
Nat'l bank circulation	23,697,930 00	23,503,307 00	23,522,007 00	23,255,802 00	23,401,460 00
State bank circulation	18,317 00	18,296 00	9,079 00	9,079 00	9,079 00
Dividends unpaid....	175,670 09	158,682 09	432,814 94	313,508 24	166,916 54
Individual deposits ..	56,907,478 74	58,453,050 20	59,792,797 96	60,205,543 98	61,821,734 86
U. S. deposits........	362,516 62	363,815 64	435,466 06	377,260 59	403,400 43
Dep'ts U.S.dis.officers	15,707 36	8,548 76	14,027 46	12,002 48	12,250 73
Due to national banks	2,509,474 88	2,218,605 41	2,139,813 28	1,445,024 92	1,570,363 02
Due to State banks ..	357,442 01	324,058 67	314,961 72	229,577 85	212,867 18
Notes re-discounted..	525,399 97	451,245 43	398,675 27	345,558 77	270,048 44
Bills payable........	248,490 28	112,499 28	43,445 45	32,490 28	26,490 28
Total	129,981,798 22	130,773,437 39	132,354,902 31	131,409,484 56	134,107,127 39

Abstract of reports since September 30, 1884, arranged

CITY OF PHILADELPHIA.

Resources.	DECEMBER 20. 33 banks.	MARCH 10. 33 banks.	MAY 6. 33 banks.	JULY 1. 33 banks.	OCTOBER 1. 34 banks.
Loans and discounts	$60,443,482 53	$62,075,220 63	$61,209,044 83	$62,993,900 08	$67,351,229 73
Bonds for circulation	9,427,800 00	9,427,800 00	9,427,800 00	9,327,800 00	9,327,800 00
Bonds for deposits ..	300,000 00	300,000 00	300,000 00	300,000 00	300,000 00
U. S. bonds on hand..	148,100 00	148,100 00	148,100 00	248,100 00	298,100 00
Other stocks and b'ds	4,333,993 85	4,288,195 79	4,578,698 84	4,374,490 59	4,295,046 24
Due from res've ag'ts	6,049,861 57	6,104,202 98	6,942,984 00	6,604,155 71	7,494,063 01
Due from nat'l banks	4,816,942 72	4,410,475 70	4,628,277 60	5,855,981 93	5,681,881 85
Due from State banks	925,830 64	984,643 24	1,010,324 82	941,365 33	1,221,724 28
Real estate, &c	2,769,910 61	2,807,797 15	2,787,912 65	2,809,015 49	2,820,894 67
Current expenses....	213,798 08	488,323 62	92,138 79	285,616 45	533,762 26
Premiums paid	216,718 44	208,472 10	201,442 10	214,360 59	252,384 25
Cash items	514,382 84	395,394 34	460,032 67	754,615 91	681,040 35
Clear'g-house exch'gs	5,339,723 84	6,241,034 16	5,298,511 55	10,468,009 82	8,186,845 09
Bills of other banks..	645,754 00	705,723 00	977,909 00	745,618 00	702,533 00
Fractional currency .	24,159 86	25,473 05	18,308 19	19,611 27	28,007 08
Trade dollars........					250,165 00
Specie	8,055,463 00	10,205,812 79	10,870,262 51	11,364,871 70	11,361,091 75
Legal-tender notes ..	3,946,475 00	3,496,773 00	3,765,546 00	4,187,944 00	4,234,351 00
U. S. cert's of deposit	5,815,000 00	7,230,000 00	6,280,000 00	6,240,000 00	5,335,000 00
Due from U. S. Treas	465,040 71	481,650 50	481,932 50	493,916 50	479,124 50
Total..........	114,452,437 69	120,025,092 05	119,479,226 05	128,229,382 37	130,835,104 06

CITY OF PITTSBURGH.

	23 banks.	23 banks.	23 banks.	23 banks.	23 banks.
Loans and discounts	$25,720,804 65	$25,370,191 95	$25,505,311 12	$25,765,926 65	$24,871,131 54
Bonds for circulation	7,080,500 00	7,080,500 00	7,080,500 00	7,080,500 00	7,080,500 00
Bonds for deposits...	250,000 00	250,000 00	250,000 00	250,000 00	250,000 00
U. S. bonds on hand..	101,100 00	103,450 00	104,700 00	151,600 00	150,.50 00
Other stocks and b'ds	1,042,347 71	1,011,768 04	436,629 66	438,355 13	463,170 68
Due from res've ag'ts	2,046,500 82	2,323,115 36	1,805,357 95	1,789,070 44	2,310,626 11
Due from nat'l banks	882,523 74	878,719 60	782,106 07	667,201 75	1,215,728 19
Due from State banks	302,433 15	160,796 81	246,338 00	179,307 11	239,179 72
Real estate, &c	1,410,992 31	1,432,485 76	1,441,431 24	1,451,804 30	1,469,407 98
Current expenses....	144,326 19	148,921 23	125,033 91	42,436 21	161,646 03
Premiums paid	74,514 88	73,370 47	73,449 38	81,319 26	84,503 38
Cash items	181,153 44	147,448 79	159,672 69	213,392 37	187,859 68
Clear'g-house exch'gs	1,115,573 17	770,866 51	937,848 01	1,249,998 73	859,811 44
Bills of other banks..	374,325 00	456,580 00	601,258 00	302,013 00	564,218 00
Fractional currency .	12,420 58	15,758 74	14,595 56	13,354 62	11,126 46
Trade dollars........					11,881 00
Specie	2,049,590 05	2,053,895 52	2,163,369 95	2,122,272 77	2,295,591 64
Legal-tender notes ..	1,988,760 00	1,962,349 00	2,500,034 00	2,012,687 00	- 2,167,824 00
U. S. cert's of deposit					
Due from U. S. Treas	346,080 41	329,496 14	331,291 14	343,735 95	328,530 00
Total..........	45,123,946 10	44,569,713 92	44,558,926 68	44,154,975 29	44,723,285 85

DELAWARE.

Resources.	15 banks.	15 banks.	15 banks.	15 banks.	15 banks.
Loans and discounts	$3,918,072 90	$3,919,311 37	$3,938,850 80	$3,850,314 40	$3,906,837 13
Bonds for circulation	1,763,200 00	1,763,200 00	1,763,200 00	1,763,200 00	1,768,200 00
Bonds for deposits	60,000 00	60,000 00	60,000 00	60,000 00	60,000 00
U. S. bonds on hand.	3,000 00	3,000 00	3,000 00	3,000 00	3,000 00
Other stocks and b'ds	230,907 91	232,382 91	285,974 95	290,307 40	262,307 40
Due from res've ag'ts	806,173 93	779,228 47	648,660 97	668,505 47	1,179,851 39
Due from nat'l banks	158,936 01	132,229 54	164,523 71	158,388 63	248,049 09
Due from State banks	46,533 64	58,752 74	62,203 34	53,614 42	55,807 93
Real estate, &c	199,070 00	199,881 92	199,947 51	208,317 13	218,135 09
Current expenses....	27,755 98	15,995 03	22,971 26	22,723 68	33,971 57
Premiums paid	115,005 71	108,309 55	106,284 55	105,334 55	104,545 80
Cash items	63,862 45	70,984 31	73,548 18	91,869 79	74,465 59
Clear'g-house exch'gs					
Bills of other banks..	102,971 00	94,386 00	109,704 00	98,595 00	114,189 00
Fractional currency .	2,308 45	2,833 72	3,334 51	3,665 31	3,526 11
Trade dollars					24,436 75
Specie	187,404 07	225,295 75	222,120 87	246,954 30	204,560 49
Legal-tender notes ..	108,253 00	159,456 00	161,837 00	182,640 00	171,331 00
U. S. cert's of deposit	20,000 00	20,000 00	20,000 00	20,000 00	20,000 00
Due from U. S. Treas.	79,263 33	80,892 50	84,492 50	89,292 50	91,092 50
Total.........	7,952,718 38	7,926,139 81	7,930,654 15	7,910,722 58	8,546,206 84

by States and reserve cities—Continued.

CITY OF PHILADELPHIA.

Liabilities.	DECEMBER 20.	MARCH 10.	MAY 6.	JULY 1.	OCTOBER 1.
	33 banks.	33 banks.	33 banks.	33 banks.	34 banks.
Capital stock	$18,058,000 00	$18,058,000 00	$18,058,000 00	$18,058,000 00	$18,275,250 00
Surplus fund	9,353,303 08	9,388,303 08	9,381,803 08	9,381,803 08	9,401,803 08
Undivided profits	1,746,695 52	2,079,623 30	1,392,678 68	1,772,539 39	2,280,684 44
Nat'l bank circulation	8,315,020 00	8,034,000 00	8,049,390 00	7,746,090 00	7,797,648 00
State bank circulation					
Dividends unpaid	55,457 56	42,614 81	472,306 21	57,001 46	42,440 06
Individual deposits	63,304,343 03	65,572,832 17	66,130,388 53	74,014,361 98	74,830,558 33
U. S. deposits	229,424 07	236,433 82	226,266 00	225,837 19	239,952 55
Dep'ts U.S.dis.officers					
Due to national banks	10,663,586 25	13,137,264 49	12,669,769 88	13,366,688 34	14,312,281 48
Due to State banks	2,723,608 18	3,466,020 38	3,088,623 67	3,607,060 93	3,654,486 12
Notes re-discounted					
Bills payable		10,000 00	10,000 00		
Total	114,452,437 69	120,025,092 05	119,479,226 05	128,229,382 37	130,835,104 06

CITY OF PITTSBURGH.

	23 banks.	23 banks.	23 banks.	23 banks.	23 banks.
Capital stock	$10,150,000 00	$10,150,000 00	$10,150,000 00	$10,150,000 00	$10,150,000 00
Surplus fund	3,434,375 91	3,501,813 75	3,516,813 75	3,538,106 84	3,538,106 84
Undivided profits	978,279 86	853,927 79	883,688 62	694,594 46	977,101 04
Nat'l bank circulation	6,296,950 00	6,240,195 00	6,245,660 00	6,257,295 00	6,280,780 00
State bank circulation					
Dividends unpaid	58,564 75	53,629 75	151,509 25	236,716 50	92,129 50
Individual deposits	20,660,439 88	20,319,784 04	20,335,534 69	20,025,037 97	19,981,344 30
U. S. deposits	178,497 19	199,455 79	151,655 87	213,011 90	162,266 71
Dep'ts U.S.dis.officers	74,735 50	48,138 87	103,802 37	43,503 21	106,214 93
Due to national banks	2,008,627 99	1,988,167 47	1,876,556 49	1,709,007 94	2,182,686 37
Due to State banks	1,050,880 67	1,146,482 88	1,111,382 13	1,275,747 95	1,223,656 16
Notes re-discounted	232,594 35	68,117 68	32,323 51	9,953 52	20,000 00
Bills payable					
Total	45,123,946 10	44,569,713 92	44,558,926 68	44,154,075 29	44,723,285 85

DELAWARE.

Liabilities.	15 banks.	15 banks.	15 banks.	15 banks.	15 banks.
Capital stock	$1,823,985 00	$1,823,985 00	$1,823,985 00	$1,823,985 00	$1,823,985 00
Surplus fund	647,540 00	670,000 00	675,000 00	677,000 00	683,005 00
Undivided profits	248,187 35	185,884 19	206,522 50	225,833 83	207,611 20
Nat'l bank circulation	1,574,309 00	1,561,949 00	1,564,199 00	1,557,759 00	1,551,029 00
State bank circulation	624 00	624 00	624 00	624 00	624 00
Dividends unpaid	7,207 70	11,455 96	11,216 30	21,233 49	9,996 26
Individual deposits	3,240,856 01	3,284,567 70	3,285,879 61	3,328,322 64	3,986,802 91
U. S. deposits	45,858 80	46,600 84	55,361 12	41,875 95	61,769 15
Dep'ts U.S.dis.officers	2,038 57	1,292 87	2,142 36	2,178 37	2,109 90
Due to national banks	333,264 69	299,321 04	266,723 06	144,770 03	200,176 08
Due to State banks	13,847 76	23,174 21	6,374 26	7,944 91	17,584 34
Notes re-discounted		17,285 00	32,626 85	42,106 36	612 00
Bills payable	15,000 00			37,000 00	
Total	7,952,718 38	7,926,130 81	7,930,654 15	7,910,722 58	8,546,206 84

Abstract of reports since September 30, 1884, arranged

MARYLAND.

Resources.	DECEMBER 20. 27 banks.	MARCH 10. 27 banks.	MAY 6. 27 banks.	JULY 1. 27 banks.	OCTOBER 1. 27 banks.
Loans and discounts	$5,991,624 44	$5,625,244 51	$5,612,412 51	$5,664,090 49	$5,738,577 08
Bonds for circulation	2,499,000 00	2,479,000 00	2,479,000 00	2,479,000 00	2,479,000 00
Bonds for deposits					
U. S. bonds on hand	167,450 00	140,850 00	140,650 00	141,150 00	215,450 00
Other stocks and b'ds	438,019 22	433,368 95	445,584 39	455,726 25	516,730 75
Due from res've ag'ts	801,547 24	721,286 54	582,799 60	526,607 17	1,043,054 94
Due from nat'l banks	371,998 42	378,649 23	360,875 32	357,455 13	455,047 21
Due from State banks	49,184 59	48,844 68	39,092 28	35,800 68	75,831 32
Real estate, &c	280,880 14	280,084 57	267,628 53	274,837 43	269,767 43
Current expenses	58,477 89	39,412 96	53,578 31	14,638 74	54,337 88
Premiums paid	107,786 13	104,903 19	105,157 44	102,036 41	113,709 20
Cash items	39,701 36	40,098 10	53,671 76	69,320 96	57,036 12
Clear'g-house exch'gs					
Bills of other banks	48,423 00	58,667 00	91,242 00	84,601 00	97,180 00
Fractional currency	3,432 88	3,848 48	4,185 45	4,094 41	4,048 13
Trade dollars					11,133 34
Specie	293,028 62	315,597 82	334,089 07	318,035 76	353,721 37
Legal-tender notes	305,250 00	368,826 00	412,018 00	304,822 00	400,625 00
U. S. cert's of deposit					
Due from U. S. Treas	109,703 38	100,892 50	103,190 75	112,890 00	102,142 50
Total	11,565,507 31	11,139,574 53	11,085,775 41	10,945,106 43	11,987,392 27

CITY OF BALTIMORE.

	17 banks.	17 banks.	17 banks.	17 banks.	17 banks.
Loans and discounts	$24,808,695 06	$25,393,279 78	$24,268,354 02	$24,409,481 34	$25,803,638 28
Bonds for circulation	6,212,000 00	6,167,500 00	6,167,500 00	6,067,500 00	6,067,500 00
Bonds for deposits	200,000 00	200,000 00	200,000 00	200,000 00	200,000 00
U. S. bonds on hand				75,000 00	75,000 00
Other stocks and b'ds	68,773 48	81,569 71	312,016 24	771,452 14	770,423 04
Due from res've ag'ts	2,185,818 04	1,455,213 15	1,005,942 21	1,691,159 89	1,685,282 05
Due from nat'l banks	1,108,558 68	1,312,046 54	1,142,275 81	1,487,250 55	1,222,511 30
Due from State banks	270,948 27	133,292 22	160,529 76	142,735 68	151,816 42
Real estate, &c	784,289 25	779,847 47	779,660 27	779,413 55	777,972 59
Current expenses	168,517 08	98,452 70	151,702 47	31,609 21	151,167 09
Premiums paid	50,611 25	57,950 00	57,950 00	58,278 13	58,278 13
Cash items	70,819 75	50,550 71	59,124 61	102,854 18	97,746 93
Clear'g-house exch'gs	1,297,551 83	1,211,778 57	1,313,793 32	3,021,443 73	1,972,626 21
Bills of other banks	455,001 00	577,155 00	667,978 00	622,399 00	201,796 00
Fractional currency	6,262 19	6,930 84	6,564 64	6,124 69	6,926 96
Trade dollars					88,182 00
Specie	1,026,763 30	1,312,955 12	1,660,063 63	1,852,530 97	2,042,624 45
Legal-tender notes	1,760,680 00	1,720,061 00	1,691,843 00	1,300,655 00	1,442,363 00
U S. cert's of deposit	1,510,000 00	2,585,000 00	2,965,000 00	3,760,000 00	2,285,000 00
Due from U. S. Treas	303,507 50	300,530 00	308,530 00	283,630 00	323,630 00
Total	42,297,796 68	43,444,112 81	43,518,827 98	46,063,718 06	45,514,484 45

DISTRICT OF COLUMBIA.

	1 bank.	1 bank.	1 bank.	1 bank.	1 bank.
Loans and discounts	$275,365 94	$231,664 17	$249,092 26	$274,633 85	$322,987 83
Bonds for circulation	250,000 00	250,000 00	250,000 00	250,000 00	250,000 00
Bonds for deposits					
U. S. bonds on hand	151,200 00	151,200 00	151,200 00	151,200 00	151,200 00
Other stocks and b'ds	155,930 00	162,930 00	162,930 00	162,930 00	170,930 00
Due from res've ag'ts	85,800 35	140,946 34	165,410 03	162,628 43	153,480 88
Due from nat'l banks	10,994 33	19,233 34	8,794 05	7,228 22	6,636 91
Due from State banks	1,591 11	6,983 85	679 06		1,949 59
Real estate, &c	20,000 00	20,000 00	20,000 00	20,000 00	20,000 00
Current expenses	5,647 54	2,373 42	4,568 00	34 10	3,402 38
Premiums paid	35,919 10	32,380 93	32,380 93	29,480 93	29,993 43
Cash items	3,310 00	5,160 00	3,811 00	15,182 00	8,851 02
Clear'g-house exch'gs					
Bills of other banks	12,253 00	13,934 00	19,003 00	9,952 00	5,639 00
Fractional currency	21 14	31 26	8 55	8 19	5 69
Trade dollars					
Specie	112,908 00	138,799 50	120,610 00	111,294 00	114,418 00
Legal-tender notes	50,400 00	80,500 00	113,000 00	68,780 00	85,500 00
U. S. cert's of deposit					
Due from U. S. Treas	11,250 00	11,250 00	11,250 00	11,250 00	11,250 00
Total	1,182,590 51	1,267,406 81	1,312,736 88	1,274,536 72	1,336,244 78

by States and reserve cities—Continued.

MARYLAND.

Liabilities	DECEMBER 20.	MARCH 10.	MAY 6.	JULY 1.	OCTOBER 1.
	27 banks.	27 banks.	27 banks.	27 banks.	27 banks.
Capital stock	$2,711,700 00	$2,691,700 00	$2,709,090 00	$2,709,090 00	$2,716,700 00
Surplus fund	784,579 86	780,521 32	780,521 32	838,696 32	841,766 51
Undivided profits	377,005 22	290,901 95	334,841 60	178,311 27	254,045 82
Nat'l bank circulation	2,199,909 00	2,168,413 00	2,166,183 00	2,119,517 00	2,143,702 00
State bank circulation					
Dividends unpaid	26,607 48	21,826 45	13,450 70	51,206 70	30,270 06
Individual deposits	5,124,242 30	4,902,972 95	4,811,566 10	4,796,647 06	5,744,199 08
U. S. deposits					
Dept's U.S.dis.officers					
Due to national banks	215,228 08	169,941 11	190,562 39	150,696 15	215,514 05
Due to State banks	36,836 57	34,956 96	29,065 92	36,485 65	36,022 43
Notes re-discounted	89,398 80	78,340 79	50,494 36	64,456 28	5,172 32
Bills payable					
Total	11,565,507 31	11,139,574 53	11,085,775 41	10,945,106 43	11,987,392 27

CITY OF BALTIMORE.

	17 banks.	17 banks.	17 banks.	17 banks.	17 banks.
Capital stock	$11,713,260 00	$11,713,260 00	$11,713,260 00	$11,713,260 00	$11,713,260 00
Surplus fund	3,012,300 00	3,086,710 00	3,091,710 00	3,136,500 00	3,136,500 00
Undivided profits	1,603,400 39	1,294,662 77	1,489,389 14	928,116 92	1,305,340 66
Nat'l bank circulation	5,255,141 00	5,169,731 00	5,122,590 00	4,808,540 00	4,756,490 00
State bank circulation	20,852 00	20,851 00	20,849 00	20,843 00	20,802 00
Dividends unpaid	46,636 71	54,251 59	43,343 03	317,616 62	54,672 64
Individual deposits	17,607,262 64	18,374,491 13	18,735,146 83	22,084,581 29	20,885,522 82
U. S. deposits	112,730 84	111,618 30	113,738 48	107,323 96	104,572 01
Dep'ts U.S.dis.officers					
Due to national banks	2,517,603 04	3,160,939 66	2,762,812 23	2,974,797 81	3,029,202 01
Due to State banks	406,610 06	457,597 36	425,987 27	572,132 46	508,062 31
Notes re-discounted					
Bills payable					
Total	42,297,796 68	43,444,112 81	43,518,827 98	46,663,718 06	45,514,484 45

DISTRICT OF COLUMBIA.

	1 bank.	1 bank.	1 bank.	1 bank.	1 bank.
Capital stock	$252,000 00	$252,000 00	$252,000 00	$252,000 00	$252,000 00
Surplus fund	60,000 00	60,000 00	60,000 00	60,000 00	60,000 00
Undivided profits	57,425 09	47,450 35	53,941 82	44,189 31	53,186 97
Nat'l bank circulation	225,000 00	214,400 00	208,400 00	197,100 00	188,700 00
State bank circulation					
Dividends unpaid	3,692 00	4,916 00	3,960 00	8,120 00	4,610 00
Individual deposits	574,756 30	676,123 94	720,396 19	690,194 81	776,518 17
U. S. deposits					
Dep'ts U.S.dis.officers					
Due to national banks	8,445 05	12,275 47	12,990 70	17,835 73	1,049 07
Due to State banks	1,272 07	241 05	1,048 17	5,096 82	150 57
Notes re-discounted					
Bills payable					
Total	1,182,590 51	1,267,406 81	1,312,736 88	1,274,536 72	1,336,344 78

Abstract of reports since September 30, 1884, arranged

CITY OF WASHINGTON.

Resources.	DECEMBER 20. 5 banks.	MARCH 10. 5 banks.	MAY 6. 5 banks.	JULY 1. 5 banks.	OCTOBER 1. 5 banks.
Loans and discounts	$2,104,911 61	$2,056,812 90	$2,009,793 64	$2,185,985 80	$2,196,157 88
Bonds for circulation	730,000 00	730,000 00	730,000 00	730,000 00	730,000 00
Bonds for deposits	100,000 00	100,000 00	100,000 00	100,000 00	100,000 00
U. S. bonds on hand	159,100 00	182,550 00	321,700 00	386,300 00	401,550 00
Other stocks and b'ds	180,806 83	197,915 85	213,562 52	216,747 63	226,306 00
Due from res've ag'ts	221,064 30	284,872 28	425,952 36	365,830 00	358,496 02
Due from nat'l banks	154,819 33	184,352 01	187,892 72	162,295 38	165,033 25
Due from State banks	6,754 92	9,376 69	16,238 06	20,016 26	15,068 90
Real estate, &c	402,638 78	366,648 03	366,648 03	361,198 03	353,954 45
Current expenses	41,726 00	17,618 10	32,029 62	5,451 15	21,731 09
Premiums paid	37,426 85	41,016 74	66,386 14	79,957 73	82,285 73
Cash items	98,823 27	130,309 58	109,203 82	128,948 15	141,570 54
Clear'g-house exch'gs					
Bills of other banks	32,143 00	53,442 00	32,069 00	15,174 00	18,669 00
Fractional currency	5,981 37	5,861 24	5,974 24	5,733 49	5,355 59
Trade dollars					5,493 00
Specie	325,503 75	517,308 25	500,514 25	442,616 25	476,797 00
Legal-tender notes	288,920 00	416,068 00	484,187 00	354,114 00	469,327 00
U. S. cert's of deposit	30,000 00	200,000 00	20,000 00		
Due from U. S. Treas	41,500 00	31,500 00	29,500 00	31,500 00	31,500 00
Total	4,961,214 01	5,525,651 67	5,651,642 40	5,591,867 87	5,799,295 45

VIRGINIA.

	24 banks.	24 banks.	23 banks.	23 banks.	24 banks.
Loans and discounts	$11,321,295 77	$11,407,475 51	$8,717,214 70	$9,212,167 93	$9,459,574 82
Bonds for circulation	2,358,350 00	2,358,350 00	2,258,350 00	2,243,350 00	2,293,350 00
Bonds for deposits	525,000 00	525,000 00	350,000 00	350,000 00	350,000 00
U. S. bonds on hand	25,050 00	25,350 00	20,100 00	300 00	600 00
Other stocks and b'ds	520,878 84	551,139 88	346,975 34	338,458 87	363,837 59
Due from res've ag'ts	1,153,578 01	997,541 53	673,810 35	596,921 77	1,193,955 47
Due from nat'l banks	550,613 34	369,200 41	374,373 49	335,987 75	493,770 82
Due from State banks	478,545 13	413,596 72	201,243 74	226,495 44	249,635 86
Real estate, &c	434,755 48	429,410 08	363,589 22	360,474 94	397,616 73
Current expenses	136,267 14	57,545 92	91,084 13	4,250 54	77,094 36
Premiums paid	129,920 74	136,904 90	136,397 74	122,616 99	129,196 02
Cash items	202,651 89	246,747 87	264,190 78	296,587 59	162,463 27
Clear'g-house exch'gs	25,951 25	42,333 62			37,585 58
Bills of other banks	249,398 00	295,387 00	280,576 00	229,937 00	385,179 00
Fractional currency	4,113 33	5,299 56	6,184 44	4,626 05	3,768 28
Trade dollars					7,938 55
Specie	441,295 57	461,904 71	527,085 06	516,688 16	561,564 20
Legal-tender notes	851,741 00	785,396 00	691,900 00	612,475 00	786,902 00
U. S. cert's of deposit					
Due from U. S. Treas	112,334 50	127,075 00	108,443 63	108,576 19	122,149 88
Total	19,521,739 99	19,235,658 80	15,411,518 62	15,559,914 22	17,076,182 43

WEST VIRGINIA.

	21 banks.	21 banks.	21 banks.	21 banks.	21 banks.
Loans and discounts	$3,606,072 89	$3,616,272 54	$3,664,268 56	$3,602,628 60	$3,602,283 67
Bonds for circulation	1,459,450 00	1,469,850 00	1,469,850 00	1,469,850 00	1,469,850 00
Bonds for deposits					
U. S. bonds on hand	8,600 00	10,000 00	9,200 00	10,300 00	9,300 00
Other stocks and b'ds	140,741 81	139,741 81	136,541 81	130,541 81	133,141 81
Due from res've ag'ts	317,061 55	256,183 12	218,640 63	245,301 48	280,143 38
Due from nat'l banks	201,385 23	147,434 73	156,344 91	184,780 21	187,580 05
Due from State banks	46,591 80	44,026 89	40,896 10	40,976 55	93,882 45
Real estate, &c	223,754 99	215,082 71	216,887 53	217,576 27	226,807 27
Current expenses	56,970 88	24,352 15	34,826 12	13,422 07	20,299 27
Premiums paid	36,274 30	32,548 21	32,382 87	32,406 14	32,283 99
Cash items	22,166 37	19,341 46	15,227 76	19,067 74	19,019 22
Clear'g-house exch'gs					
Bills of other banks	75,213 00	70,919 00	95,379 00	78,619 00	94,074 00
Fractional currency	2,658 46	3,387 08	3,655 40	3,354 87	2,903 18
Trade dollars					8,723 29
Specie	246,901 59	227,565 98	197,330 57	220,189 62	229,369 87
Legal-tender notes	265,740 00	260,355 00	184,651 00	162,458 00	204,795 00
U. S. cert's of deposit					
Due from U. S. Treas	64,492 59	63,748 00	69,649 12	65,842 64	69,245 44
Total	6,774,078 46	6,600,750 68	6,545,731 38	6,497,315 00	6,692,551 89

by States and reserve cities—Continued.

CITY OF WASHINGTON.

Liabilities.	DECEMBER 20. 5 banks.	MARCH 10. 5 banks.	MAY 6. 5 banks.	JULY 1. 5 banks.	OCTOBER 1. 5 banks.
Capital stock	$1,125,000 00	$1,125,000 00	$1,125,000 00	$1,125,000 00	$1,125,000 00
Surplus fund	302,000 00	304,500 00	304,500 00	305,500 00	307,000 00
Undivided profits	129,700 82	62,300 32	99,459 14	81,438 82	119,826 43
Nat'l bank circulation	623,300 00	618,000 00	610,100 00	607,600 00	625,850 00
State bank circulation					
Dividends unpaid	1,974 00	1,911 50	1,401 00	13,717 00	1,933 50
Individual deposits	2,550,778 10	3,184,412 78	3,358,118 17	3,323,316 34	3,435,467 92
U. S. deposits	49,828 10	73,663 69	22,040 05	33,828 60	47,961 44
Dep'ts U.S.dis.officers					
Due to national banks	149,593 18	138,382 00	97,934 39	83,961 58	115,738 20
Due to State banks	29,039 81	17,480 38	33,089 65	17,505 53	20,517 96
Notes re-discounted					
Bills payable					
Total	4,961,214 01	5,525,651 67	5,651,642 40	5,591,867 87	5,799,295 45

VIRGINIA.

	24 banks.	24 banks.	23 banks.	23 banks.	24 banks.
Capital stock	$3,545,300 00	$3,546,300 00	$3,246,300 00	$3,246,300 00	$3,576,300 00
Surplus fund	1,262,321 91	1,332,112 94	1,177,112 94	1,189,978 50	1,143,097 75
Undivided profits	776,846 91	531,471 93	502,866 42	323,000 64	474,982 48
Nat'l bank circulation	2,112,300 00	2,114,780 00	2,021,060 00	2,002,980 00	2,007,500 00
State bank circulation					
Dividends unpaid	4,005 16	6,534 15	3,680 15	48,433 65	5,214 15
Individual deposits	10,140,338 13	10,174,861 77	7,344,627 99	7,669,044 60	8,376,662 67
U. S. deposits	361,233 09	364,108 90	288,650 10	262,158 95	260,119 14
Dep'ts U.S.dis.officers	116,305 66	69,912 65	16,405 41	29,674 63	40,399 42
Due to national banks	604,298 82	498,137 71	290,836 01	215,355 81	352,222 65
Due to State banks	477,026 96	437,788 31	303,976 93	322,852 45	374,232 52
Notes re-discounted	73,703 35	50,650 44	154,952 67	184,134 99	369,451 65
Bills payable	54,000 00	109,000 00	61,000 00	66,000 00	96,000 00
Total	19,521,739 99	19,235,658 80	15,411,518 62	15,550,914 22	17,076,182 43

WEST VIRGINIA.

	21 banks.	21 banks.	21 banks.	21 banks.	21 banks.
Capital stock	$2,011,000 00	$2,011,000 00	$2,011,000 00	$2,011,000 00	$2,011,000 00
Surplus fund	513,888 97	505,892 97	506,740 13	505,107 58	512,056 40
Undivided profits	196,882 58	130,261 62	155,136 64	106,978 19	135,691 22
Nat'l bank circulation	1,281,620 00	1,260,165 00	1,300,200 00	1,300,015 00	1,291,765 00
State bank circulation					
Dividends unpaid	17,480 00	20,494 00	18,871 00	47,647 00	22,571 00
Individual deposits	2,543,488 15	2,465,980 74	2,315,141 49	2,342,461 31	2,529,278 85
U. S. deposits					
Dep'ts U.S.dis.officers					
Due to national banks	163,292 01	116,008 69	108,430 33	71,815 03	104,380 96
Due to State banks	35,781 16	55,247 66	47,914 37	42,997 95	58,170 96
Notes re-discounted	10,645 59	22,700 00	77,297 42	64,292 94	27,637 50
Bills payable		4,000 00	5,000 00	5,000 00	
Total	6,774,078 46	6,600,750 68	6,545,731 38	6,497,315 00	6,692,551 89

Abstract of reports since September 30, 1884, arranged

NORTH CAROLINA.

Resources.	DECEMBER 20. 15 banks.	MARCH 10. 15 banks.	MAY 6. 15 banks.	JULY 1. 15 banks.	OCTOBER 1. 15 banks.
Loans and discounts.	$4,612,146 86	$4,605,100 99	$4,704,366 14	$4,904,277 33	$4,671,983 29
Bonds for circulation.	1,262,000 00	1,262,000 00	1,262,000 00	1,162,000 00	1,162,000 00
Bonds for deposits...	200,000 00	200,000 00	200,000 00	250,000 00	250,000 00
U. S. bonds on hand..	20,150 00	20,150 00	20,150 00	20,150 00	5,000 00
Other stocks and b'ds	477,721 59	461,356 35	447,028 37	459,661 14	335,698 84
Due from res've ng'ts.	750,359 88	742,522 75	359,974 64	293,007 90	365,075 43
Due from nat'l banks	335,374 56	251,691 54	208,915 79	215,053 20	202,063 10
Due from State banks	76,295 99	56,132 96	52,830 40	47,491 41	53,242 21
Real estate, &c	275,852 78	252,186 68	280,087 04	267,823 20	259,738 74
Current expenses....	48,001 16	17,844 11	33,732 86	18,450 56	33,539 17
Premiums paid	51,224 34	51,224 34	51,224 34	47,974 34	82,541 84
Cash items	50,724 58	33,053 54	57,695 52	28,451 94	36,525 04
Clear'g-house exch'gs					
Bills of other banks..	158,790 00	151,182 00	87,962 00	90,719 00	144,443 00
Fractional currency .	1,720 95	2,598 34	3,534 62	2,975 34	3,911 25
Trade dollars........					124,00
Specie	168,113 45	281,094 14	275,854 92	234,477 07	231,740 79
Legal-tender notes ..	327,088 00	382,140 00	404,911 00	257,175 00	263,186 00
U. S. cert's of deposit.					
Due from U. S. Treas	56,148 14	56,741 09	59,483 17	49,513 49	49,560 34
Total..........	8,872,312 25	8,826,938 83	8,509,770 81	8,349,200 92	8,150,373 04

SOUTH CAROLINA.

	14 banks.	14 banks.	14 banks.	14 banks.	14 banks.
Loans and discounts.	$3,417,181 04	$3,772,092 91	$4,217,382 24	$4,255,164 21	$4,589,642 74
Bonds for circulation.	1,247,600 00	1,247,600 00	1,247,600 00	1,161,350 00	1,161,350 00
Bonds for deposits...	250,000 00	250,000 00	250,000 00	250,000 00	250,000 00
U. S. bonds on hand .	3,100 00	3,100 00	3,100 00	3,100 00	3,100 00
Other stocks and b'ds	562,546 79	534,602 20	515,584 51	515,674 48	520,717 73
Due from res've ng'ts.	1,147,444 92	811,834 81	430,253 67	248,346 13	170,805 04
Due from nat'l banks	856,558 74	749,379 44	601,930 71	417,452 27	312,948 59
Due from State banks	141,783 13	103,879 00	64,337 61	73,568 01	51,504 32
Real estate, &c	206,934 15	205,325 21	202,347 44	198,847 44	198,847 44
Current expenses ...	82,192 99	30,269 50	70,273 05	25,466 84	42,099 60
Premiums paid	31,530 60	26,562 95	26,562 95	28,926 70	25,676 70
Cash items	54,794 84	40,920 80	18,117 39	17,310 27	34,999 03
Clear'g-house exch'gs					
Bills of other banks..	223,304 00	186,808 00	142,015 00	80,039 00	194,605 00
Fractional currency .	1,309 38	1,462 82	1,725 81	1,485 19	1,269 37
Trade dollars........					
Specie	164,054 05	311,520 35	323,681 80	266,094 66	235,892 36
Legal-tender notes ..	490,474 00	436,187 00	319,548 00	286,204 00	312,239 00
U. S. cert's of deposit.					
Due from U. S. Treas	59,937 60	57,945 05	58,183 05	57,880 65	60,513 25
Total..........	8,940,746 23	8,769,470 04	8,492,643 23	7,883,909 85	8,166,210 17

GEORGIA.

	15 banks.	15 banks.	15 banks.	15 banks.	16 banks.
Loans and discounts.	$4,580,275 10	$4,453,865 36	$4,529,423 56	$4,704,799 00	$5,383,089 49
Bonds for circulation.	1,861,000 00	1,861,000 00	1,861,000 00	1,801,000 00	1,792,000 00
Bonds for deposits ..	110,000 00	110,000 00	110,000 00	110,000 00	110,000 00
U. S. bonds on hand .		50,000 00	50,000 00	50,000 00	
Other stocks and b'ds	198,154 94	295,768 24	275,748 24	264,130 74	229,290 74
Due from res've ng'ts	496,867 57	309,435 01	112,745 28	166,476 45	101,136 43
Due from nat'l banks	311,823 41	183,828 69	124,133 20	125,126 41	116,732 94
Due from State banks	153,936 44	123,667 13	94,912 61	105,990 41	147,546 82
Real estate, &c	417,426 42	418,143 98	432,693 88	439,974 71	460,980 12
Current expenses....	89,218 39	37,096 49	73,594 35	11,371 43	45,760 39
Premiums paid	48,617 81	54,634 68	54,134 68	52,659 68	53,950 47
Cash items	106,777 92	93,748 56	113,071 82	122,267 76	126,945 09
Clear'g-house exch'gs					
Bills of other banks..	352,155 00	243,260 00	232,412 00	199,277 00	248,663 00
Fractional currency .	2,408 25	3,744 06	3,590 73	4,370 51	4,570 27
Trade dollars					
Specie	366,657 43	534,055 93	506,139 68	492,345 50	441,577 07
Legal-tender notes ..	443,075 00	332,295 00	238,563 00	271,612 00	321,617 00
U. S. cert's of deposit.					
Due from U. S. Treas.	97,404 66	97,102 26	90,002 26	88,379 20	83,573 20
Total..........	9,635,797 44	9,206,654 39	8,916,865 19	9,009,480 80	9,666,842 03

by States and reserve cities—Continued.

NORTH CAROLINA.

Liabilities.	DECEMBER 20. 15 banks.	MARCH 10. 15 banks.	MAY 6. 15 banks.	JULY 1. 15 banks.	OCTOBER 1. 15 banks.
Capital stock	$2,401,000 00	$2,401,000 00	$2,401,000 00	$2,401,000 00	$2,063,500 00
Surplus fund	532,591 92	547,496 84	547,496 84	549,496 84	472,378 71
Undivided profits	386,637,56	317,377 29	362,414 76	274,408 82	235,799 45
Nat'l bank circulation	1,112,185,00	1,101,050 00	1,094,085 00	1,010,290 00	993,415 00
State bank circulation					
Dividends unpaid	4,908 50	6,344 50	4,748 00	29,756 50	2,999 00
Individual deposits	3,883,602 64	3,932,513 13	3,610,360 10	3,310,159 39	3,237,571 76
U. S. deposits	155,830 18	170,620 32	156,060 69	179,243 74	210,815 50
Dep'ts U.S.dis.officers	25,220 74	24,963 14	31,751 84	32,266 67	17,312 74
Due to national banks	195,676 75	131,641 36	90,870 02	80,663 27	229,266 13
Due to State banks	35,171 05	45,311 47	42,931·37	24,268 31	22,050 32
Notes re-discounted	126,987 91	148,620 78	148,052 19	316,647 38	525,264 43
Bills payable	12,500 00		20,000 00	140,000 00	140,000 00
Total	8,872,312 25	8,826,938 83	8,509,770 81	8,349,200 92	8,150,373 04

SOUTH CAROLINA.

	14 banks.	14 banks.	14 banks.	14 banks.	14 banks.
Capital stock	$1,935,000 00	$1,935,000 00	$1,935,000 00	$1,935,000 00	$1,935,000 00
Surplus fund	772,500 00	778,000 00	778,000 00	802,000 00	802,000 00
Undivided profits	719,256 87	635,280 02	730,877·86	550,685 56	589,698 49
Nat'l bank circulation	1,096,110 00	1,068,345 00	1,053,525 00	953,970 00	1,002,445 00
State bank circulation					
Dividends unpaid	7,866 50	11,250 75	9,194 50	42,626 50	9,342 50
Individual deposits	3,682,568 98	3,602,983 05	3.261,106 42	2,900,397 90	2,723,042 58
U. S. deposits	156,207 99	199,635 77	182,385 10	177,372 62	187,431 58
Dep'ts U.S.dis.officers	69,635 13	33,836 05	48,566 90	39,297 88	33,850 06
Due to national banks	214,475 39	160,575 31	174,226 76	143,744 52	212,879 76
Due to State banks	293,125 37	344,564 09	272,259 18	150,128 53	179,880 23
Notes re-discounted			32,501 51	125,686 34	346,639 97
Bills payable			15,000 00	63,000 00	144,000 00
Total	8,940,746 23	8,769,470 04	8,492,643 23	7,883,909 85	8,166,210 17

GEORGIA.

	15 banks.	15 banks.	15 banks.	15 banks.	16 banks.
Capital stock	$2,436,000 00	$2,436,000 00	$2,436,000 00	$2,436,000 00	$2,472,345 00
Surplus fund	815,355 00	855,790 95	855,790 95	887,969 21	813,350 93
Undivided profits	406,280 80	322,176 34	405,925 73	270,491 15	336,807 05
Nat'l bank circulation	1,648,180 00	1,642,300 00	1,646,780 00	1,645,555 00	1,570,900 00
State bank circulation					
Dividends unpaid	2,650 00	2,696 00	1,945 00	30,200 50	2,482 50
Individual deposits	3,679,967 49	3,455,526 11	3,045,369 40	3,103,363 78	3,335,351 73
U. S. deposits	57,959 13	42,898 96	44,776 16	67,783 80	35,076 93
Dep'ts U.S.dis.officers	38,007 17	57,181 84	31,509 97	15,878 86	36,297 58
Due to national banks	177,461 65	176,912 75	152,790 73	123,358 55	247,298 22
Due to State banks	190,328 91	179,187 99	113,452 84	95,170 98	137,242 07
Notes re-discounted	73,607 29	25,983 45	127,524 41	263,718 97	603,690 02
Bills payable	110,000 00	10,000 00	55,000 00	70,000 00	76,000 00
Total	9,635,797 44	9,206,654 39	8,916,865 19	9,009,480 80	9,666,842 03

Abstract of reports since September 30, 1884, arranged

FLORIDA.

Resources.	DECEMBER 20. 4 banks.	MARCH 10. 4 banks.	MAY 6. 5 banks.	JULY 1. 5 banks.	OCTOBER 1. 5 banks.
Loans and discounts	$453,695 82	$443,130 86	$530,415 29	$581,170 76	$644,531 03
Bonds for circulation	122,500 00	122,500 00	147,500 00	147,500 00	147,500 00
Bonds for deposits				50,000 00	50,000 00
U. S. bonds on hand				1,300 00	5,700 00
Other stocks and b'ds	61,771 14	72,020 94	68,527 11	75,418 62	82,198 37
Due from res've ag'ts	35,714 59	206,787 55	243,687 54	190,737 97	57,388 82
Due from nat'l banks	8,252 88	11,150 11	28,445 05	88,156 09	35,705 73
Due from State banks	27,555 66	29,328 88	49,085 86	51,420 75	32,954 29
Real estate, &c	28,074 85	37,416 98	41,774 30	43,682 43	43,086 37
Current expenses	18,802 05	14,330 03	21,175 34	22,606 92	18,767 02
Premiums paid	1,725 00	1,725 00	3,086 12	9,333 12	9,979 99
Cash items	6,417 36	7,910 26	5,738 59	5,472 98	7,307 82
Clear'g-house exch'gs					
Bills of other banks	21,752 00	53,926 00	72,184 00	54,835 00	54,983 00
Fractional currency	554 61	321 55	433 15	496 99	504 76
Trade dollars					
Specie	16,095 95	42,804 90	42,025 70	54,056 55	35,601 80
Legal-tender notes	77,745 00	97,662 00	134,516 00	107,759 00	102,581 00
U. S. cert's of deposit					
Due from U. S. Treas	3,548 15	7,574 15	5,099 15	6,199 15	5,699 15
Total	884,205 66	1,148,589 21	1,394,283 20	1,490,146 33	1,334,489 15

ALABAMA.

	10 banks.	10 banks.	10 banks.	10 banks.	10 banks.
Loans and discounts	$2,872,066 75	$2,574,250 22	$2,703,625 70	$2,874,125 51	$3,265 790 12
Bonds for circulation	1,017,000 00	1,067,000 00	1,117,000 00	1,117,000 00	1,117,000 00
Bonds for deposits	100,000 00	100,000 00	100,000 00	100,000 00	100,000 00
U. S. bonds on hand					
Other stocks and b'ds	345,591 22	344,774 84	381,261 85	414,132 60	477,774 50
Due from res've ag'ts	444,732 46	493,988 70	196,716 16	263,445 10	113,073 51
Due from nat'l banks	239,287 63	418,253 78	513,092 21	380,415 75	189,943 47
Due from State banks	136,043 54	187,530 30	204,752 45	93,427 71	101,087 47
Real estate, &c	178,667 92	184,039 89	189,581 25	189,035 58	192,705 58
Current expenses	59,045 54	37,402 54	60,102 60	1,516 95	30,175 37
Premiums paid	81,528 54	84,126 00	90,251 00	88,289 14	71,332 00
Cash items	18,935 34	57,378 73	34,017 29	28,155 22	35,286 06
Clear'g-house exch'gs					
Bills of other banks	130,551 00	228,864 00	121,072 00	124,468 00	95,543 00
Fractional currency	1,121 51	1,601 35	1,404 92	1,924 95	1,378 78
Trade dollars					
Specie	238,632 31	339,807 91	274,017 66	245,510 15	241,887 90
Legal-tender notes	236,328 00	244,858 00	206,769 00	239,153 00	167,764 00
U. S. cert's of deposit					
Due from U. S. Treas	42,114 21	47,978 11	46,971 96	50,258 76	47,368 76
Total	6,141,643 97	6,411,854 37	6,243,656 05	6,210,858 42	6,248,171 12

MISSISSIPPI.

	5 banks.	5 banks.	6 banks.	6 banks.	6 banks.
Loans and discounts	$501,887 34	$445,662 88	$545,798 33	$720,838 62	$1,074,609 22
Bonds for circulation	205,000 00	205,000 00	217,500 00	217,500 00	175,000 00
Bonds for deposits					
U. S. bonds on hand	1,600 00	1,600 00	1,600 00	1,600 00	1,600 00
Other stocks and b'ds	58,118 38	47,891 24	50,163 46	91,553 25	85,806 29
Due from res've ag'ts	37,615 37	183,708 65	71,100 27	72,203 09	22,550 89
Due from nat'l banks	200,424 38	249,285 40	249,980 54	62,151 27	24,087 65
Due from State banks	36,155 32	91,120 11	53,688 78	26,356 62	8,761 65
Real estate, &c	31,615 32	34,547 32	39,644 65	40,285 40	44,018 25
Current expenses	15,483 44	10,646 31	17,169 54	10,149 61	13,374 74
Premiums paid	24,581 87	23,255 43	25,921 31	24,562 31	12,900 94
Cash items	1,257 40	6,753 91	5,099 11	2,209 77	9,292 48
Clear'g-house exch'gs					
Bills of other banks	6,887 00	8,491 00	13,875 00	14,502 00	26,161 00
Fractional currency	65 59	735 71	531 02	505 68	336 87
Trade dollars					
Specie	101,526 85	177,102 78	105,471 65	108,670 65	82,352 00
Legal-tender notes	32,172 00	47,503 00	68,380 00	46,184 00	41,682 00
U. S. cert's of deposit					
Due from U. S. Treas	6,800 00	10,825 00	12,625 00	14,293 35	6,247 40
Total	1,351,190 26	1,543,478 74	1,478,548 66	1,453,565 62	1,628,781 87

*by States and reserve cities—*Continued.

FLORIDA.

Liabilities.	DECEMBER 20. 4 banks.	MARCH 10. 4 banks.	MAY 6. 5 banks.	JULY 1. 5 banks.	OCTOBER 1. 5 banks.
Capital stock	$200,000 00	$200,000 00	$300,000 00	$300,000 00	$300,000 00
Surplus fund	16,422 70	17,922 70	19,922 70	19,922 70	19,922 70
Undivided profits	19,731 57	17,005 07	26,304 59	30,409 63	36,298 34
Nat'l bank circulation	81,840 00	88,415 00	89,385 00	88,540 00	120,165 00
State bank circulation					
Dividends unpaid					
Individual deposits	514,063 01	810,867 85	932,499 43	958,306 78	782,280 90
U. S. deposits				41,883 96	35,037 55
Dep'ts U.S.dis.officers				1,026 86	2,715 28
Due to national banks	3,225 38	3,619 29	14,196 06	35,254 70	14,178 47
Due to State banks	45,423 00	5,669 30	9,975 42	8,741 70	23,870 91
Notes re-discounted	3,500 00	5,000 00	2,000 00	6,000 00	
Bills payable					
Total	884,205 66	1,148,569 21	1,394,283 20	1,490,146 33	1,334,489 15

ALABAMA.

	10 banks.	10 banks.	10 banks.	10 banks.	10 banks.
Capital stock	$1,735,000 00	$1,835,000 00	$1,835,000 00	$1,835,000 00	$1,835,000 00
Surplus fund	256,100 00	282,000 00	282,000 00	285,500 00	290,650 00
Undivided profits	271,976 12	209,686 73	271,992 16	203,096 59	212,571 67
Nat'l bank circulation	914,400 00	943,900 00	989,500 00	990,050 00	990,450 00
State bank circulation					
Dividends unpaid	2,166 00	5,540 00	1,178 00	29,010 00	5,347 20
Individual deposits	2,501,009 91	2,843,863 80	2,496,710 73	2,421,074 06	2,143,811 12
U. S. deposits	84,254 06	84,550 41	95,146 09	91,644 92	82,326 79
Dep'ts U.S.dis.officers	8,144 61	4,966 48	9,107 01	212 76	5,684 48
Due to national banks	54,638 32	47,969 73	67,016 53	32,795 22	106,537 18
Due to State banks	85,864 05	53,073 02	52,981 03	33,925 87	39,221 08
Notes re-discounted	108,090 90	81,304 20	123,024 50	286,539 00	537,071 60
Bills payable	30,000 00	20,000 00	20,000 00		
Total	6,141,643 97	6,411,854 37	6,243,656 05	6,210,858 42	6,248,171 12

MISSISSIPPI.

	5 banks.	5 banks.	6 banks.	6 banks.	6 banks.
Capital stock	$425,000 00	$425,000 00	$450,000 00	$475,000 00	$475,000 00
Surplus fund	10,824 35	18,400 00	19,400 00	20,100 00	39,100 00
Undivided profits	48,042 30	35,674 71	56,881 34	55,615 56	38,003 50
Nat'l bank circulation	165,100 00	103,350 00	164,900 00	175,340 00	150,990 00
State bank circulation					
Dividends unpaid		200 00	200 00	5,200 00	320 00
Individual deposits	639,266 99	875,317 75	772,829 48	690,847 73	597,416 08
U. S. deposits					
Dep'ts U.S.dis.officers					
Due to national banks	42,915 57	8,650 55	9,339 01	10,612 16	101,934 53
Due to State banks	4,941 05	16,885 73	4,998 83	10,850 17	33,327 00
Notes re-discounted	15,100 00				192,690 76
Bills payable				10,000 00	
Total	1,351,190 26	1,543,478 74	1,478,548 66	1,453,565 62	1,628,781 87

Abstract of reports since September 30, 1884, arranged

LOUISIANA.

Resources.	DECEMBER 20. 1 bank.	MARCH 10. 1 bank.	MAY 6. 1 bank.	JULY 1. 1 bank.	OCTOBER 1. 1 bank.
Loans and discounts.	$131,977 43	$136,557 08	$133,280 28	$133,170 77	$130,942 38
Bonds for circulation	100,000 00	100,000 00	100,000 00	100,000 00	100,000 00
Bonds for deposits...					
U. S. bonds on hand..					
Other stocks and b'ds	9,187 90	9,207 49	9,207 49	9,387 90	9,187 90
Due from res've ag'ts	9,430 70	4,033 68	388 46	5,117 57	3,539 45
Due from nat'l banks	110 21	1,505 92	917 06	563 95	344 16
Due from State banks	2,817 87	28 78	268 31	1,105 36	213 86
Real estate, &c	986 70	986 70	986 70	986 70	1,144 80
Current expenses....	3,552 38	1,812 23	2,819 28	66 60	2,448 88
Premiums paid......	3,375 00	3,000 00	3,000 00	3,000 00	3,000 00
Cash items					
Clear'g-house exch'gs					
Bills of other banks..	282 00	1,589 00	1,662 00	280 00	890 00
Fractional currency.	44 88	92 36	20 10	6 63	30 36
Trade dollars......					
Specie	17,628 00	17,792 50	19,174 00	13,283 00	14,653 50
Legal-tender notes...	3,125 00	6,195 00	2,880 00	5,752 00	2,867 00
U. S. cert's of deposit					
Due from U. S. Treas.	4,500 00	4,500 00	4,500 00	4,500 00	4,500 00
Total	287,018 16	287,300 74	279,112 68	277,220 57	273,763 38

CITY OF NEW ORLEANS.

	8 banks.	8 banks.	8 banks.	8 banks.	8 banks.
Loans and discounts	$9,666,389 20	$8,681,060 42	$9,277,862 82	$9,166,022 83	$9,729,589 78
Bonds for circulation.	2,225,000 00	2,225,000 00	2,225,000 00	2,025,000 00	2,125,000 00
Bonds for deposits ..					
U. S. bonds on hand..	7,300 00	516,750 00	507,150 00	70,400 00	7,450 00
Other stocks and b'ds	812,749 99	967,673 18	1,040,192 98	1,117,822 02	1,016,860 36
Due from res've ag'ts	583,532 66	1,652,965 92	1,110,123 26	1,142,681 84	495,351 38
Due from nat'l banks	317,205 87	269,238 94	197,071 36	151,341 89	154,150 92
Due from State banks	456,303 90	576,177 27	452,943 06	405,520 63	297,378 19
Real estate, &c	402,756 49	400,924 62	401,374 87	409,842 63	427,461 46
Current expenses....	150,900 41	77,947 60	135,232 56	2,830 91	92,867 69
Premiums paid	54,013 00	90,663 00	90,423 00	71,971 80	62,903 83
Cash items	1,975 55	2,143 43	813 43	106 86	696 87
Clear'g-house exch'gs	1,753,592 50	900,894 59	640,383 09	658,505 53	808,367 16
Bills of other banks..	106,760 00	217,603 00	194,354 00	132,025 00	124,032 00
Fractional currency .	4,404 65	7,461 46	8,089 95	8,822 51	10,965 61
Trade dollars.......					
Specie	905,747 60	2,024,499 00	1,945 147 00	1,020,479 75	817,950 50
Legal-tender notes ..	751,183 00	1,651,830 00	1,918,701 00	1,658,359 00	1,087,830 00
U. S. cert's of deposit.					
Due from U. S. Treas	101,625 00	104,625 00	104,625 00	100,480 00	100,175 00
Total..........	18,310,439 82	20,307,457 43	20,279,687 40	18,142,303 20	17,359,030 75

TEXAS.

	61 banks.	65 banks.	66 banks.	68 banks.	68 banks.
Loans and discounts	$11,651,514 55	$12,329,782 84	$12,785,262 97	$13,083,748 87	$13,777,215 51
Bonds for circulation.	1,866,750 00	1,957,000 00	1,962,000 00	1,960,000 00	1,950,500 00
Bonds for deposits ..	125,000 00	125,000 00	125,000 00	125,000 00	125,000 00
U. S. bonds on hand..	260,000 00		500 00	1,000 00	
Other stocks and b'ds	239,092 12	156,739 36	201,768 80	180,259 74	263,343 88
Due from res've ag'ts	1,319,593 77	1,140,463 61	1,099,302 30	1,088,126 87	1,292,962 99
Due from nat'l banks	681,816 41	698,297 27	793,953 65	892,823 52	886,802 36
Due from State banks	604,462 24	599,917 97	653,997 03	726,597 01	694,445 90
Real estate, &c	637,077 05	668,027 18	684,932 89	695,536 76	735,164 89
Current expenses....	230,007 84	159,226 66	204,412 83	91,566 42	140,072 00
Premiums paid......	136,571 42	155,140 48	156,305 88	152,875 81	153,917 80
Cash items	107,184 94	106,783 75	97,314 38	103,043 38	233,156 32
Clear'g-house exch'gs					
Bills of other banks..	576,879 00	460,385 00	462,935 00	430,747 00	485,615 00
Fractional currency .	10,338 15	12,965 93	17,399 97	20,807 91	13,567 43
Trade dollars.......					6 00
Specie	731,169 91	1,037,537 82	922,520 50	971,174 13	883,443 15
Legal-tender notes ..	1,339,867 00	1,099,212 00	1,097,842 00	1,159,363 00	1,002,463 00
U. S. cert's of deposit.					
Due from U. S. Treas	81,614 53	80,032 35	88,078 79	93,897 66	95,461 53
Total..........	20,552,328 93	20,666,361 32	21,353,546 99	21,752,468 08	23,733,137 76

by States and reserve cities—Continued.

LOUISIANA.

Liabilities	DECEMBER 20. 1 bank.	March 10. 1 bank.	MAY 1. 1 bank.	JULY 1. 1 bank.	OCTOBER 1. 1 bank.
Capital stock	$100,000 00	$100,000 00	$100,000 00	$100,000 00	$100,000 00
Surplus fund	6,000 00	7,000 00	7,000 00	9,000 00	9,000 00
Undivided profits	8,713 02	4,698 63	7,218 86	874 54	4,455 10
Nat'l bank circulation	90,000 00	90,000 00	90,000 00	90,000 00	90,000 00
State bank circulation					
Dividends unpaid		8 00	4 00	1,312 00	88 00
Individual deposits	82,305 14	85,594 11	69,614 18	72,191 85	70,220 28
U.S deposits					
Dep't's U.S.dis.officers					
Due to national banks			5,275 64	3,842 18	
Due to State banks					
Notes re-discounted					
Bills payable					
Total	287,018 16	287,300 74	279,112 68	277,220 57	273,763 38

CITY OF NEW ORLEANS.

	8 banks.	8 banks.	8 banks.	8 banks.	8 banks.
Capital stock	$3,525,000 00	$3,525,000 00	$3,525,000 00	$3,525,000 00	$3,525,000 00
Surplus fund	1,195,000 00	1,257,132 42	1,257,132 42	1,296,715 70	1,296,715 70
Undivided profits	735,731 34	486,953 82	603,540 87	300,974 38	501,887 45
Nat'l bank circulation	1,980,930 00	1,965,050 00	1,954,595 00	1,553,545 00	1,886,345 00
State bank circulation					
Dividends unpaid	18,115 48	20,977 03	18,147 03	85,151 08	11,244 75
Individual deposits	9,514,184 70	10,991,687 17	11,081,315 07	10,174,445 44	8,923,526 74
U.S. deposits					
Dep't's U.S.dis.offices					
Due to national banks	440,156 43	1,030,735 58	1,002,055 48	391,474 07	385,633 55
Due to State banks	895,321 87	1,029,921 41	837,301 53	754,997 53	828,677 56
Notes re-discounted					
Bills payable					
Total	18,310,439 82	20,307,457 43	20,279,687 40	18,142,303 20	17,359,030 75

TEXAS.

	61 banks.	65 banks.	66 banks.	68 banks.	68 banks.
Capital stock	$6,142,100 00	$6,551,800 00	$6,676,100 00	$6,805,000 00	$6,880,000 00
Surplus fund	1,712,710 76	1,916,160 28	1,948,460 28	2,016,411 54	2,002,202 91
Undivided profits	1,159,198 39	653,076 16	840,426 99	626,324 82	844,255 44
Nat'l bank circulation	1,653,495 00	1,700,465 00	1,729,595 00	1,686,755 00	1,739,250 00
State bank circulation					
Dividends unpaid	1,300 00	6,898 25	1,097 00	80,520 00	2,148 00
Individual deposits	8,285,515 30	8,308,815 12	8,499,433 89	8,873,131 96	9,183,872 32
U.S. deposits	44,452 50	27,739 13	69,849 27	36,597 66	51,481 19
Dep'ts U.S.dis.officers	72,084 21	57,436 96	62,320 75	74,472 53	40,563 01
Due to national banks	315,978 95	403,775 31	472,013 10	436,695 83	482,185 98
Due to State banks	577,237 32	513,577 17	490,274 58	534,532 71	542,718 68
Notes re-discounted	303,528 36	396,867 94	412,226 13	415,276 03	744,053 58
Bills payable	384,758 14	129,750 00	151,750 00	106,750 00	220,406 65
Total	20,652,328 93	20,666,361 32	21,353,546 99	21,752,468 08	22,733,137 76

Abstract of reports since September 30, 1884, arranged

ARKANSAS.

Resources.	DECEMBER 20. 4 banks.	MARCH 10. 5 banks.	MAY 6. 6 banks.	JULY 1. 6 banks.	OCTOBER 1. 6 banks.
Loans and discounts	$994,441 24	$920,789 33	$1,431,618 29	$1,533,162 21	$1,801,245 41
Bonds for circulation	230,000 00	260,000 00	310,000 00	310,000 00	360,000 00
Bonds for deposits	100,000 00	100,000 00	100,000 00	200,000 00	100,000 00
U. S. bonds on hand		40,000 00	40,200 00	40,200 00	40,200 00
Other stocks and b'ds	64,037 47	67,793 19	57,597 04	57,409 04	51,256 18
Due from res've ag'ts	270,708 92	329,675 41	495,976 50	347,158 47	251,680 95
Due from nat'l banks	33,680 61	85,711 82	98,072 27	41,670 85	11,776 05
Due from State banks	21,226 19	31,946 76	73,272 64	52,506 25	25,306 31
Real estate, &c	17,600 59	18,425 28	23,682 66	23,682 66	23,682 66
Current expenses	4,110 15	2,339 47	6,823 06	4,306 52	2,309 70
Premiums paid	5,143 45	6,343 45	7,880 45	11,005 45	11,005 45
Cash items	2,845 44	21,046 70	10,589 04	7,200 53	2,804 52
Clear'g-house exch'gs					
Bills of other banks	54,705 00	41,977 00	74,569 00	42,336 00	32,975 00
Fractional currency	799 19	1,115 92	2,415 93	3,403 00	3,556 60
Trade dollars					
Specie	75,537 05	116,592 85	160,468 75	120,980 00	119,545 30
Legal-tender notes	128,191 00	69,520 00	105,211 00	84,250 00	84,711 00
U. S. cert's of deposit					
Due from U. S. Treas.	10,350 00	10,660 00	14,841 40	14,098 40	16,256 00
Total	2,013,376 30	2,123,887 18	3,013,218 03	2,893,373 38	2,938,309 13

KENTUCKY.

	58 banks.	59 banks.	59 banks.	59 banks.	59 banks.
Loans and discounts	$14,871,270 47	$15,053,997 01	$15,444,770 18	$15,401,401 04	$14,942,400 23
Bonds for circulation	6,939,700 00	6,964,700 00	6,815,300 00	6,615,300 00	6,440,300 00
Bonds for deposits	450,000 00	450,000 00	450,000 00	450,000 00	450,000 00
U. S. bonds on hand	7,050 00	4,500 00	4,200 00	3,350 00	8,200 00
Other stocks and b'ds	824,035 69	826,881 25	660,574 27	693,795 33	722,801 95
Due from res've ag'ts	1,259,028 70	1,198,141 81	948,944 52	1,024,025 83	1,240,709 77
Due from nat'l banks	618,433 83	686,864 49	610,958 46	570,020 28	748,704 05
Due from State banks	239,790 65	208,657 98	183,276 26	139,033 67	200,415 98
Real estate, &c	536,250 25	531,509 06	520,138 39	501,204 44	501,174 80
Current expenses	151,760 38	82,039 00	104,190 26	33,662 15	127,064 10
Premiums paid	316,970 96	305,655 83	314,870 95	301,174 49	295,379 36
Cash items	67,392 37	65,643 84	66,365 74	110,154 74	57,224 92
Clear'g-house exch'gs					
Bills of other banks	242,533 00	278,661 00	317,474 00	278,909 00	278,553 00
Fractional currency	4,275 46	4,490 07	4,113 01	4,565 60	4,608 78
Trade dollars					6,851 10
Specie	471,632 80	508,747 54	564,118 46	562,195 52	624,241 25
Legal-tender notes	421,422 00	457,298 00	418,009 00	397,748 00	402,633 00
U. S. cert's of deposit					
Due from U. S. Treas	299,692 03	286,780 65	278,800 00	255,906 00	278,154 20
Total	27,721,238 59	27,974,517 53	27,706,202 50	27,342,446 09	27,329,417 39

CITY OF LOUISVILLE.

	9 banks.	9 banks.	9 banks.	9 banks.	9 banks.
Loans and discounts	$7,753,348 22	$7,747,851 62	$7,984,844 56	$7,753,925 50	$7,788,153 55
Bonds for circulation	3,033,700 00	3,033,700 00	3,033,700 00	3,033,700 00	2,833,700 00
Bonds for deposits	900,000 00	900,000 00	900,000 00	900,000 00	900,000 00
U. S. bonds on hand	6,450 00	6,450 00	1,450 00	3,950 00	1,350 00
Other stocks and b'ds	144,412 75	291,156 96	280,189 23	364,975 10	340,230 90
Due from res've ag'ts	441,397 44	387,202 37	410,912 50	551,595 01	431,609 55
Due from nat'l banks	247,135 69	181,782 24	188,153 49	206,021 82	267,913 77
Due from State banks	148,908 25	176,675 11	137,004 24	116,821 49	126,333 34
Real estate, &c	118,620 80	124,046 05	132,524 81	173,524 23	173,439 45
Current expenses	38,229 46	58,440 86	28,840 20	17,908 49	81,384 00
Premiums paid	165,584 62	163,800 87	163,628 37	170,005 73	162,096 87
Cash items	47,191 63	37,128 85	29,895 17	52,989 89	58,859 72
Clear'g-house exch'gs	69,119 67	36,901 70	26,651 19	34,905 88	50,365 44
Bills of other banks	42,448 00	48,920 00	43,423 00	46,994 00	71,997 00
Fractional currency	512 75	546 14	570 83	416 53	1,030 12
Trade dollars					1,170 00
Specie	265,104 90	427,516 80	259,045 15	311,723 05	386,468 49
Legal-tender notes	295,550 00	378,890 00	323,800 00	333,430 00	511,420 00
U. S. cert's of deposit					
Due from U. S. Treas	138,514 00	137,513 50	138,513 75	142,014 00	130,514 00
Total	13,856,234 18	14,138,523 07	14,083,205 99	14,214,900 72	14,313,086 20

by States and reserve cities—Continued.

ARKANSAS.

Liabilities.	DECEMBER 20. 4 banks.	MARCH 10. 5 banks.	MAY 6. 6 banks.	JULY 1. 6 banks.	OCTOBER 1. 6 banks.
Capital stock	$405,000 00	$505,000 00	$705,000 00	$705,000 00	$705,000 00
Surplus fund	148,273 81	160,584 52	163,880 84	166,170 32	166,170 32
Undivided profits	44,354 70	28,711 33	45,230 57	39,071 31	47,839 71
Nat'l bank circulation	205,700 00	204,700 00	256,100 00	277,700 00	323,300 00
State bank circulation					
Dividends unpaid	890 00	1,703 00	1,286 00	12,816 00	2,553 00
Individual deposits	1,057,051 46	1,102,701 98	1,690,962 65	1,548,000 70	1,513,893 06
U. S. deposits	55,298 49	61,338 57	58,404 34	58,144 98	32,923 25
Dp'ts U.S.dis.officers	15,388 81	13,456 56	19,208 96	8,469 31	11,378 08
Due to national banks	2,299 70	5,933 09	15,668 47	33,217 59	20,581 43
Due to State banks	13,697 24	35,258 13	51,088 03	34,464 00	31,484 96
Notes re-discounted	55,422 00	4,500 00	6,319 17	10,319 17	83,185 32
Bills payable	10,000 00				
Total	2,013,376 30	2,123,887 18	3,013,218 03	2,893,373 38	2,938,309 13

KENTUCKY.

	58 banks.	59 banks.	59 banks.	59 banks.	59 banks.
Capital stock	$9,458,900 00	$9,620,500 00	$9,628,900 00	$9,708,900 00	$9,648,900 00
Surplus fund	1,849,084 49	1,909,968 77	1,814,453 76	1,937,585 68	1,922,323 18
Undivided profits	818,027 97	586,610 26	717,443 96	460,410 17	695,237 61
Nat'l bank circulation	6,192,860 00	6,214,710 00	6,110,720 00	5,914,200 00	5,714,770 00
State bank circulation					
Dividends unpaid	15,627 50	21,106 50	16,385 50	129,895 50	26,970 00
Individual deposits	8,245,429 05	8,400,947 20	8,057,589 61	8,049,297 71	8,233,931 88
U. S. deposits	321,933 39	337,709 16	334,674 11	315,339 71	333,738 14
Dep'ts U.S.dis.officers	3,821 07	13,458 01	17,593 66	11,137 59	9,350 22
Due to national banks	424,628 11	400,583 11	424,503 11	267,860 67	350,489 31
Due to State banks	293,037 21	331,695 97	319,579 44	304,654 98	269,188 73
Notes re-discounted	53,385 00	81,191 20	208,828 73	231,229 18	124,518 82
Bills payable	44,504 80	56,037 35	58,530 62	12,024 90	
Total	27,721,238 59	27,974,517 53	27,706,202 50	27,342,446 09	27,329,417 39

CITY OF LOUISVILLE.

	9 banks.	9 banks.	9 banks.	9 banks.	9 banks.
Capital stock	$3,551,500 00	$3,551,500 00	$3,551,500 00	$3,551,500 00	$3,551,500 00
Surplus fund	791,603 68	793,603 68	803,474 48	809,441 20	809,441 26
Undivided profits	221,514 08	263,935 08	215,893 10	184,547 80	312,680 28
Nat'l bank circulation	2,730,004 00	2,723,804 00	2,721,704 00	2,730,180 00	2,550,230 00
State bank circulation					
Dividends unpaid	9,624 00	5,690 00	27,973 50	42,546 50	5,304 00
Individual deposits	2,870,826 27	2,914,171 79	2,986,974 09	3,216,983 57	3,401,878 31
U. S. deposits	649,536 04	698,810 27	633,394 81	609,450 61	603,970 84
Dep'ts U.S.dis.officers	154,470 54	84,841 36	148,751 27	153,560 20	178,631 12
Due to national banks	1,221,048 96	1,451,698 54	1,415,927 43	1,473,796 74	1,335,832 28
Due to State banks	1,108,052 98	1,281,962 66	1,154,756 63	1,146,748 01	1,214,244 25
Notes re-discounted	472,053 63	281,305 69	372,856 08	266,146 03	349,323 86
Bills payable	85,000 00	85,000 00	50,000 00	30,000 00	
Total	13,856,234 18	14,138,523 07	14,083,205 99	14,214,900 72	14,313,036 02

Abstract of reports since September 30, 1884, arranged

TENNESSEE.

Resources.	DECEMBER 20. 33 banks.	MARCH 10. 33 banks.	MAY 6. 32 banks.	JULY 1. 33 banks.	OCTOBER 1. 32 banks.
Loans and discounts.	$11,080,448 17	$11,461,722 43	$11,240,560 85	$11,030,213 33	$11,554,177 46
Bonds for circulation.	2,534,000 00	2,534,000 00	2,484,000 00	2,496,500 00	2,371,500 00
Bonds for deposits ...	350,000 00	350,000 00	350,000 00	350,000 00	350,000 00
U. S. bonds on hand..	5,700 00	24,100 00	25,950 00	26,900 00	4,650 00
Other stocks and b'ds	460,199 04	462,749 62	461,150 71	488,078 56	459,878 24
Due from res've mg'ts.	1,034,901 71	964,611 19	806,649 64	893,546 40	703,714 57
Due from nat'l banks	520,210 26	827,142 63	575,489 33	426,382 63	429,219 08
Due from State banks	141,407 18	177,110 52	160,468 37	162,478 68	146,608 30
Real estate, &c	430,676 79	436,746 15	411,416 20	416,227 49	403,947 51
Current expenses....	116,982 91	120,112 53	110,864 57	20,049 24	57,469 64
Premiums paid	136,943 63	152,154 88	151,903 38	140,923 53	144,143 91
Cash items	217,406 30	165,128 38	188,912 70	295,421 45	173,109 52
Clear'g-house exch'gs	94,927 56	69,842 53	56,549 40	22,856 87	37,104 63
Bills of other banks..	412,983 00	386,140 00	339,473 00	292,359 00	233,090 00
Fractional currency .	2,514 89	3,375 29	3,429 23	4,552 65	2,906 31
Trade dollars.......					2,161 50
Specie..............	662,455 61	860,559 54	799,069 25	779,611 78	696,815 02
Legal-tender notes ..	493,426 00	564,320 00	559,135 00	455,787 00	517,389 00
U. S. cert's of deposit					
Due from U. S. Treas.	123,216 08	131,939 67	125,647 42	110,856 92	111,408 05
Total..........	18,818,399 13	19,691,755 36	18,850,669 05	18,418,745 53	18,397,783 34

OHIO.

	183 banks.	184 banks.	183 banks.	183 banks.	183 banks.
Loans and discounts.	$41,005,521 02	$40,559,087 89	$40,828,297 02	$41,241,136 76	$40,932,229 44
Bonds for circulation.	15,589,750 00	15,500,250 00	15,362,250 00	15,327,350 00	15,195,250 00
Bonds for deposits ..	500,000 00	450,000 00	450,000 00	525,000 00	525,000 00
U. S. bonds on hand..	304,500 00	442,000 00	339,750 00	363,600 00	381,800 00
Other stocks and b'ds	2,343,982 59	2,265,075 19	2,263,195 40	2,172,516 59	2,070,628 87
Due from res've ag'ts.	3,383,744 08	4,325,580 64	3,393,669 51	3,946,287 42	4,131,559 24
Due from nat'l banks	1,260,280 95	1,373,646 56	1,323,750 54	1,361,325 33	1,286,986 81
Due from State banks	388,063 80	442,350 73	388,699 17	448,072 02	478,449 33
Real estate, &c	1,683,898 52	1,690,454 12	1,696,001 05	1,704,909 10	1,770,944 62
Current expenses....	250,224 90	380,426 27	234,406 52	194,981 38	403,951 50
Premiums paid......	429,130 51	460,881 57	442,529 77	441,158 19	446,725 22
Cash items	398,340 10	351,631 82	354,665 02	420,765 05	350,951 93
Clear'g-house exch'gs	16,945 37	25,224 53	23,724 29	20,512 06	63,588 20
Bills of other banks..	989,427 00	1,329,675 00	1,182,529 00	989,848 00	1,459,125 00
Fractional currency .	24,206 88	29,185 97	29,326 40	26,051 64	25,904 62
Trade dollars					27,368 20
Specie..............	2,323,566 35	2,549,036 42	2,644,709 61	2,345,811 32	2,671,002 09
Legal-tender notes ..	2,482,770 00	2,667,646 00	2,552,562 00	2,279,216 00	2,850,541 00
U. S. cert's of deposit	5,000 00	5,000 00	5,000 00		
Due from U. S. Treas.	697,276 03	714,892 13	682,362 48	658,656 88	727,793 48
Total..........	74,576,630 40	75,562,044 84	74,197,427 78	74,467,197 74	75,796,799 55

CITY OF CINCINNATI.

	12 banks.	12 banks.	12 banks.	12 banks.	12 banks.
Loans and discounts	$17,469,746 87	$17,900,738 35	$18,645,664 08	$18,280,358 87	$18,666,706 62
Bonds for circulation	6,084,000 00	6,084,000 00	6,084,000 00	6,084,000 00	5,585,000 00
Bonds for deposits ..	1,013,000 00	1,013,000 00	1,013,000 00	1,188,000 00	1,188,000 00
U. S. bonds on hand..	627,050 00	436,950 00	448,650 00	285,500 00	304,500 00
Other stocks and b'ds	522,851 05	900,315 80	984,235 80	1,070,390 89	1,027,125 32
Due from res've ag'ts	2,023,765 51	2,305,430 05	1,514,393 78	1,818,066 85	2,235,212 19
Due from nat'l banks	1,369,486 88	1,173,239 51	1,189,388 96	1,173,025 73	1,323,634 90
Due from State banks	703,501 87	837,159 13	756,371 85	660,654 68	701,747 27
Real estate, &c......	229,670 25	219,961 63	228,101 92	227,913 42	228,033 56
Current expenses....	147,224 95	170,005 25	99,578 17	88,383 04	182,777 06
Premiums paid	471,964 08	474,718 53	492,592 81	487,372 94	451,361 64
Cash items	72,301 46	53,614 10	85,379 22	67,418 47	63,720 63
Clear'g-house exch'gs	348,601 92	291,659 58	328,049 92	302,343 58	331,509 51
Bills of other banks..	289,348 00	470,666 00	274,411 00	227,343 00	355,412 00
Fractional currency .	1,908 41	3,334 65	2,188 12	2,862 52	3,441 27
Trade dollars					13,471 00
Specie	450,197 55	624,738 00	524,828 90	446,406 00	1,048,087 00
Legal-tender notes ..	1,163,956 00	1,455,735 00	1,269,289 00	1,160,122 00	1,970,285 00
U. S. cert's of deposit	805,000 00	1,060,000 00	1,190,000 00	815,000 00	1,410,000 00
Due from U. S. Treas.	291,375 00	285,275 00	310,175 00	281,875 00	254,670 00
Total..........	34,088,039 80	35,760,540 58	35,440,298 58	34,665,936 99	37,350,754 97

by States and reserve cities—Continued.

TENNESSEE.

Liabilities.	DECEMBER 29. 33 banks.	MARCH 10. 33 banks.	MAY 6. 32 banks.	JULY 1. 33 banks.	OCTOBER 1. 32 banks.
Capital stock	$5,035,300 00	$5,110,300 00	$4,942,500 00	$5,00,000 00	$5,007,500 00
Surplus fund	1,066,106 75	1,079,920 39	991,904 89	1,006,264 24	998,499 82
Undivided profits	634,338 40	512,780 71	547,740 07	387,122 17	473,495 19
Nat'l bank circulation	2,259,350 00	2,257,150 00	2,227,850 00	2,214,750 00	2,114,010 00
State bank circulation					
Dividends unpaid	1,966 00	24,733 50	1,276 00	11,864 00	1,470 00
Individual deposits	8,462,532 01	9,180,403 76	8,521,668 41	8,448,358 05	7,783,995 25
U. S. deposits	207,861 62	187,621 86	215,987 08	208,314 37	212,754 53
Dep'ts U.S.dis.officers	108,979 20	91,200 83	72,474 21	71,799 07	53,048 19
Due to national banks	540,086 01	630,505 50	671,380 25	511,279 40	850,234 52
Due to State banks	295,704 34	543,217 48	517,943 01	380,378 10	418,884 32
Notes re-discounted	195,074 71	61,335 83	127,359 63	152,030 63	447,885 52
Bills payable	12,000 00	12,585 50	12,585 50	26,585 50	6,000 00
Total	18,818,399 13	19,691,755 36	18,850,669 05	18,418,745 53	18,397,783 34

OHIO.

	183 banks.	184 banks.	183 banks.	183 banks.	183 banks.
Capital stock	$22,014,000 00	$22,044,000 00	$21,964,000 00	$21,964,000 00	$21,909,580 00
Surplus fund	4,546,232 83	4,510,812 36	4,480,777 39	4,553,031 44	4,562,511 02
Undivided profits	1,877,033 25	1,918,919 13	1,635,801 97	1,418,402 62	1,962,587 57
Nat'l bank circulation	13,861,330 00	13,743,255 00	13,619,780 00	13,665,624 00	13,471,579 00
State bank circulation	4,386 00	4,376 00	4,376 00	4,376 00	4,376 00
Dividends unpaid	32,181 60	17,845 60	54,191 60	109,910 20	31,660 30
Individual deposits	29,825,168 96	30,778,960 31	29,833,708 73	30,360,771 80	31,594,912 37
U. S. deposits	373,512 48	347,917 94	441,896 05	394,806 04	431,581 09
Dep'ts U.S.dis.officers	72,009 76	52,469 47	49,132 49	36,841 93	52,869 51
Due to national banks	1,080,539 83	1,252,689 10	1,267,914 17	1,064,006 09	1,094,983 03
Due to State banks	398,722 73	481,162 01	438,183 03	422,874 06	480,119 28
Notes re-discounted	365,605 06	322,637 92	269,683 30	324,220 23	163,706 15
Bills payable	125,908 02	87,000 00	137,893 05	98,333 33	33,333 33
Total	74,576,630 40	75,562,044 84	74,197,427 78	74,467,197 74	75,796,799 55

CITY OF CINCINNATI.

	12 banks.	12 banks.	12 banks.	12 banks.	12 banks.
Capital stock	$8,800,000 00	$8,600,000 00	$8,600,000 00	$8,600,000 00	$8,600,000 00
Surplus fund	1,110,500 00	1,170,500 00	1,180,000 00	1,206,000 00	1,208,000 00
Undivided profits	749,196 18	637,705 73	552,936 37	452,104 90	714,100 61
Nat'l bank circulation	5,455,600 00	5,392,000 00	5,366,800 00	5,430,600 00	4,947,120 00
State bank circulation					
Dividends unpaid	22,807 00	3,518 00	46,671 00	94,014 00	19,125 00
Individual deposits	11,319,355 40	11,939,098 42	12,438,700 50	12,207,578 08	14,060,803 82
U. S. deposits	870,000 00	870,000 00	870,000 00	957,991 09	1,033,000 00
Dep'ts U.S.dis.officers					
Due to national banks	3,895,077 99	4,711,978 49	4,581,388 34	3,724,572 95	4,691,568 97
Due to State banks	1,638,503 23	2,032,739 94	1,495,802 32	1,600,075 91	1,681,646 57
Notes re-discounted					
Bills payable	403,000 00	403,000 00	398,000 00	393,000 00	393,000 00
Total	34,088,039 80	35,760,540 58	35,440,298 53	34,865,936 99	37,350,754 97

Abstract of reports since September 30, 1884, arranged

CITY OF CLEVELAND.

Resources.	DECEMBER 20. 8 banks.	MARCH 10. 8 banks.	MAY 6. 8 banks.	JULY 1. 8 banks.	OCTOBER 1. 8 banks.
Loans and discounts	$11,284,268 29	$11,193,507 16	$11,549,466 44	$11,529,982 28	$11,538,040 70
Bonds for circulation	555,000 00	655,000 00	655,000 00	655,000 00	655,000 00
Bonds for deposits	550,000 00	500,000 00	500,000 00	500,000 00	500,000 00
U. S. bonds on hand	2,300 00	2,300 00	2,300 00	2,400 00	2,400 00
Other stocks and b'ds	485,376 62	487,469 12	473,331 62	467,119 12	462,469 12
Due from res've ag'ts	1,344,348 33	1,519,466 68	1,023,616 42	1,325,567 34	1,169,641 01
Due from nat'l banks	903,027 33	809,273 82	1,016,665 46	1,167,609 14	1,041,905 97
Due from State banks	346,694 78	288,951 14	265,913 57	387,406 76	416,269 71
Real estate, &c	726,948 49	717,407 91	715,752 48	715,515 73	714,811 39
Current expenses	39,672 30	118,691 87	964 59	36,666 71	121,688 98
Premiums paid	47,158 75	33,153 75	25,125 00	25,125 00	25,125 00
Cash items	43,993 44	45,346 73	55,853 61	31,038 91	45,916 41
Clear'g-house exch'gs	97,308 05	100,999 14	97,687 44	143,711 63	143,657 17
Bills of other banks	192,348 00	263,452 00	346,958 00	145,329 00	446,734 00
Fractional currency	4,677 25	8,884 60	12,694 59	6,871 70	3,583 66
Trade dollars					1,100 00
Specie	465,169 55	771,454 21	753,694 13	787,112 81	911,225 41
Legal-tender notes	1,122,000 00	877,000 00	1,038,500 00	857,000 00	945,000 00
U. S. cert's of deposit	15,000 00	15,000 00	15,000 00	15,000 00	15,000 00
Due from U. S. Treas	24,474 50	30,375 00	35,075 00	29,575 00	31,574 62
Total	18,249,765 73	18,437,733 13	18,583,528 35	18,831,031 13	19,221,243 15

INDIANA.

	93 banks.	89 banks.	90 banks.	90 banks.	90 banks.
Loans and discounts	$24,792,943 31	$22,393,136 18	$22,858,325 93	$23,276,767 07	$23,357,584 51
Bonds for circulation	8,197,800 00	6,995,800 00	7,150,800 00	7,146,800 00	7,546,800 00
Bonds for deposits	850,000 00	850,000 00	850,000 00	850,000 00	1,050,000 00
U. S. bonds on hand	372,050 00	323,350 00	323,200 00	323,350 00	345,350 00
Other stocks and b'ds	1,756,847 23	1,504,658 01	1,498,675 10	1,521,904 60	1,515,050 00
Due from res've ag'ts	3,003,020 93	2,747,334 31	3,190,579 84	3,105,037 29	3,450,208 05
Due from nat'l banks	1,740,838 24	1,702,725 34	1,943,683 23	1,407,797 32	1,768,900 92
Due from State banks	240,518 90	256,647 97	267,756 70	327,670 08	297,501 35
Real estate, &c	1,270,102 83	1,063,459 56	1,083,470 66	1,091,046 49	1,106,061 09
Current expenses	272,356 62	125,425 00	250,275 15	67,152 32	179,941 98
Premiums paid	179,018 86	172,102 90	224,248 40	210,927 18	241,796 41
Cash items	222,894 47	242,588 11	203,710 32	197,416 76	268,284 65
Clear'g-house exch'gs	78,310 71	69,495 93	59,248 91	55,692 56	46,859 43
Bills of other banks	846,335 00	776,733 00	1,064,254 00	937,366 00	976,396 00
Fractional currency	14,573 59	14,866 69	16,070 93	16,055 76	13,491 78
Trade dollars					16,299 40
Specie	1,693,564 10	1,781,824 86	2,062,377 55	1,979,703 05	2,007,272 27
Legal-tender notes	1,826,091 00	1,859,134 00	1,860,000 00	1,623,862 00	1,598,277 00
U. S. cert's of deposit	10,000 00	10,000 00	10,000 00	10,000 00	10,000 00
Due from U. S. Treas	358,052 71	303,774 79	308,066 70	306,359 07	335,616 42
Total	47,726,218 50	43,193,006 65	45,234,743 42	44,545,988 15	46,191,676 26

ILLINOIS.

	152 banks.	150 banks.	151 banks.	151 banks.	153 banks.
Loans and discounts	$29,122,450 70	$29,214,179 49	$30,059,644 45	$30,277,363 22	$30,447,481 90
Bonds for circulation	7,223,750 00	7,017,950 00	7,108,250 00	7,033,250 00	6,912,750 00
Bonds for deposits	845,000 00	845,000 00	845,000 00	845,000 00	845,000 00
U. S. bonds on hand	420,950 00	443,450 00	363,950 00	401,000 00	333,450 00
Other stocks and b'ds	2,089,093 85	2,152,914 75	2,043,305 12	2,040,805 87	2,145,262 04
Due from res've ag'ts	4,808,305 60	5,825,305 40	6,248,238 60	6,908,593 14	5,348,092 49
Due from nat'l banks	1,845,786 97	1,399,690 46	1,454,505 09	1,170,392 43	1,321,354 11
Due from State banks	211,278 77	161,906 70	226,567 69	225,346 30	176,321 37
Real estate, &c	1,228,618 58	1,236,953 60	1,244,041 84	1,250,265 42	1,201,632 46
Current expenses	256,781 44	198,581 95	279,432 79	145,705 48	193,302 27
Premiums paid	352,496 21	385,010 78	365,297 78	366,736 37	367,663 85
Cash items	296,205 65	327,510 76	279,818 09	327,221 30	312,612 51
Clear'g-house exch'gs	29,671 31	47,791 40	54,146 54	57,312 92	63,530 28
Bills of other banks	773,825 00	1,137,685 00	955,377 00	931,832 00	814,668 00
Fractional currency	16,525 90	16,546 51	16,207 66	16,744 44	15,917 37
Trade dollars					2,785 20
Specie	1,974,944 19	2,147,439 67	2,351,394 88	2,401,802 76	2,440,263 49
Legal-tender notes	1,642,101 00	2,214,251 00	1,917,635 00	1,781,488 00	1,637,231 00
U. S. cert's of deposit	10,000 00	20,000 00	10,000 00	10,000 00	10,000 00
Due from U. S. Treas	334,517 46	326,711 57	333,265 77	342,763 12	349,492 07
Total	52,691,213 95	55,118,829 04	56,156,078 30	56,533,622 77	55,519,810 41

by States and reserve cities—Continued.

CITY OF CLEVELAND.

Liabilities.	DECEMBER 20. 8 banks.	MARCH 10. 8 banks.	MAY 6. 8 banks.	JULY 1. 8 banks.	OCTOBER 1. 8 banks.
Capital stock	$5,664,100 00	$6,200,000 00	$6,200,000 00	$6,200,000 00	$6,200,000 00
Surplus fund	705,000 00	545,000 00	629,000 00	629,000 00	629,000 00
Undivided profits	437,545 79	416,270 92	115,358 40	229,252 28	417,627 67
Nat'l bank circulation	494,460 00	489,410 00	589,410 00	579,510 00	589,410 00
State bank circulation					
Dividends unpaid	1,753 00	394 00	79,008 00	3,174 00	205 00
Individual deposits	8,225,299 55	8,482,996 98	8,654,763 16	9,034,949 86	8,998,619 71
U. S. deposits	447,112 93	438,730 23	514,165 07	466,632 09	472,566 60
Dep'ts U.S.dis.officers	70,272 45	53,931 38	16,372 17	14,755 16	12,315 36
Due to national banks	1,076,394 77	793,185 04	771,562 24	719,134 97	889,651 02
Due to State banks	763,489 57	772,814 58	740,873 07	724,622 77	881,847 79
Notes re-discounted	151,337 67		17,016 24		
Bills payable	213,000 00	245,000 00	256,000 00	230,000 00	130,000 00
Total	18,249,765 73	18,437,733 13	18,583,528 35	18,831,031 13	19,221,243 15

INDIANA.

	93 banks.	89 banks.	90 banks.	90 banks.	90 banks.
Capital stock	$13,299,500 00	$11,734,500 00	$11,869,500 00	$11,889,500 00	$12,189,500 00
Surplus fund	3,649,288 88	2,964,715 50	2,966,797 45	3,003,929 85	3,031,907 59
Undivided profits	1,803,963 53	1,061,974 02	1,230,273 57	951,393 44	1,478,693 51
Nat'l bank circulation	7,317,430 00	6,229,120 00	6,357,080 00	6,359,280 00	6,734,150 00
State bank circulation					
Dividends unpaid	12,160 37	15,764 49	14,261 49	90,466 87	5,529 39
Individual deposits	18,908,009 08	18,401,854 44	19,523,522 11	19,430,240 77	19,845,317 11
U. S. deposits	494,702 45	572,737 81	590,048 01	566,031 63	680,411 34
Dep'ts U.S.dis.officers	200,540 20	163,811 07	243,588 69	116,324 07	103,122 26
Due to national banks	1,273,855 02	1,101,739 66	1,378,200 10	1,288,228 93	1,258,344 84
Due to State banks	657,759 53	797,304 84	924,726 73	711,308 72	763,276 47
Notes re-discounted	81,000 00	136,164 00	81,745 27	112,283 87	97,423 75
Bills payable	28,000 00	13,320 82	35,000 00	18,000 00	4,000 00
Total	47,726,218 50	43,193,006 65	45,214,743 42	44,545,988 15	46,191,676 26

ILLINOIS.

	152 banks.	150 banks.	151 banks.	151 banks.	153 banks.
Capital stock	$13,484,600 00	$13,296,500 00	$13,546,500 00	$13,579,600 00	$13,673,600 00
Surplus fund	4,202,531 11	4,086,917 38	4,131,302 56	4,199,685 02	4,195,183 27
Undivided profits	2,071,623 46	1,703,244 97	1,884,644 38	1,650,127 76	1,788,800 71
Nat'l bank circulation	6,465,483 00	6,139,445 00	6,322,515 00	6,244,015 00	6,154,525 00
State bank circulation					
Dividends unpaid	22,987 67	22,710 00	56,681 67	124,847 00	28,994 50
Individual deposits	24,604,291 84	27,806,540 40	28,147,818 49	28,462,967 44	27,693,719 52
U. S. deposits	711,661 63	743,133 68	755,746 59	676,660 32	710,460 48
Dep'ts U.S.dis.officers	45,981 15	30,124 08	40,623 67	62,873 74	62,715 16
Due to national banks	393,388 13	580,231 36	552,229 28	727,587 22	556,527 09
Due to State banks	377,226 54	511,017 39	557,859 89	566,313 17	452,537 75
Notes re-discounted	276,437 42	188,964 78	150,156 77	143,946 10	152,746 93
Bills payable	35,000 00	10,000 00	10,000 00	95,000 00	50,000 00
Total	52,641,211 95	55,118,829 04	56,156,078 30	56,533,622 77	55,519,810 41

Abstract of reports since September 30, 1884, arranged

CITY OF CHICAGO.

Resources.	DECEMBER 20. 12 banks.	MARCH 10. 12 banks.	MAY 6. 12 banks.	JULY 1. 12 banks.	OCTOBER 1. 12 banks.
Loans and discounts .	$39,944,425 46	$43,045,047 04	$42,580,177 82	$43,659,503 65	$46,018,905 81
Bonds for circulation.	933,500 00	933,500 00	933,500 00	1,183,500 00	1,183,500 00
Bonds for deposits ..	100,000 00	100,000 00	200,000 00	200,000 00	200,000 00
U. S. bonds on hand..	821,550 00	1,051,100 00	1,576,000 00	1,413,950 00	1,438,650 00
Other stocks and b'ds	2,071,633 07	1,615,614 30	1,801,345 91	1,637,346 02	1,934,031 65
Due from res've ag't's.	4,822,909 20	6,086,358 42	5,391,445 16	6,269,497 55	6,622,633 64
Due from nat'l banks.	2,181,497 55	3,443,015 17	3,347,105 28	4,004,195 33	3,912,173 94
Due from State banks	1,643,829 70	1,926,784 62	1,922,292 90	1,973,849 27	1,704,323 49
Real estate, &c......	246,530 42	199,573 58	200,637 37	684,898 87	681,159 61
Current expenses...	50,919 09	49,666 04	52,601 62	6,702 99	31,114 85
Premiums paid ...	61,561 10	51,199 51	29,500 00	140,103 20	110,875 95
Cash items	52,373 55	19,906 06	21,949 37	26,240 04	18,484 70
Clear'g-house exch'gs	2,557,568 98	2,764,869 94	3,279,547 65	4,994,571 28	4,045,655 05
Bills of other banks..	1,078,273 00	1,169,242 00	2,610,816 00	2,028,772 00	996,495 00
Fractional currency.	3,193 24	10,473 85	5,736 56	5,747 66	5,363 16
Trade dollars					2 40
Specie	7,446,475 15	7,479,301 60	8,487,355 78	9,403,694 05	9,673,253 80
Legal-tender notes ..	5,747,074 00	5,625,812 00	8,202,945 00	7,171,042 00	5,191,100 00
U. S. cert's of deposit.	530,000 00	820,000 00	760,000 00	960,000 00	720,000 00
Due from U. S. Treas.	120,007 50	124,307 50	114,807 50	80,257 50	102,757 50
Total	70,413,321 01	76,515,771 63	81,517,793 92	85,843,871 41	85,190,480 55

MICHIGAN.

	97 banks.	97 banks.	97 banks.	97 banks.	97 banks.
Loans and discounts	$20,765,052 39	$21,035,561 07	$21,953,440 60	$21,801,433,73	$21,465,802 85
Bonds for circulation	4,210,000 00	4,105,000 00	3,985,500 00	3,935,500 00	3,958,000 00
Bonds for deposits ..	50,000 00	50,000 00	50,000 00	50,000,00	50,000 00
U. S. bonds on hand	61,550 00	80,150 00	75,150 00	78,000 00	352,550 00
Other stocks and b'ds	628,773 26	520,526 24	529,113 09	477,987 23	607,339 69
Due from res've ag'ts	2,979,239 53	3,260,556 81	2,362,161 74	2,885,722 68	4,161,874 90
Due from nat'l banks	487,422 23	705,851 25	562,474 54	513,539 67	508,185 47
Due from State banks	133,040 69	102,777 42	119,302 92	100,406 30	108,708 11
Real estate, &c	974,860 47	898,740 20	914,286 66	929,864 85	934,005 50
Current expenses....	210,061 22	119,846 83	184,207 68	42,181 02	156,082 99
Premiums paid	150,452 43	149,574 79	165,760 43	161,770 75	218,441 62
Cash items	195,984 15	190,525 23	190,816 09	182,653,98	218,987 32
Clear'g-house exch'gs					
Bills of other banks..	525,014 00	425,031 00	539,064 00	518,716 00	498,361 00
Fractional currency	11,020 70	15,777 70	16,275 30	11,817 56	11,544 75
Trade dollars........					3,638 60
Specie	1,461,587 64	1,579,843 15	1,586,474 54	1,507,978 36	1,616,226 24
Legal-tender notes ..	873,163 00	755,545 00	777,263 00	752,615 00	793,222 00
U. S. cert's of deposit					
Due from U. S. Treas	199,165 89	192,473 64	190,386 44	195,123 09	185,908 24
Total..........	33,916,387 60	34,181,780 33	34,206,776 63	34,195,310 22	35,930,879 37

CITY OF DETROIT.

	5 banks.	5 banks.	5 banks.	5 banks.	5 banks.
Loans and discounts.	$7,922,684 32	$8,170,644 25	$8,406,422 34	$8,205,541 74	$8,513,281 77
Bonds for circulation.	883,400 00	883,400 00	833,400 00	733,400 00	500,000 00
Bonds for deposits ..	500,000 00	500,0 0 00	500,000 00	800,000 00	500,000 00
U. S. bonds on hand..	35,000 00	35,000 00	35,000 00	35,000 00	100,000 00
Other stocks and b'ds	64,175 00	63,942 80	63,942 80	52,075 00	3,425 00
Due from res've ag'ts.	1,593,443 17	1,497,902 49	1,039,727 32	1,180,586 82	1,651,337 90
Due from nat'l banks.	1,137,829 04	1,097,762 36	785,212 92	678,737 82	1,331,389 73
Due from State banks	163,147 90	200,641 00	167,889 63	164,640 27	223,663 36
Real estate, &c	90,664 73	90,664 73	90,664 73	90,664 73	90,664 73
Current expenses....	38,071 80	42,737 93	20,566 00	10,425 01	18,609 29
Premiums paid	100,000 00	95,000 00	92,000 00	159,125 00	125,375 00
Cash items	22,133 42	39,663 24	19,770 38	52,798 67	43,853 94
Clear'g-house exch'gs	169,054 98	183,829 72	122,916 23	262,168 45	218,843 89
Bills of other banks..	162,468 00	77,280 00	162,624 00	131,088 00	100,825 00
Fractional currency	17,647 70	13,377 76	8,548 14	7,133 27	14,189 15
Trade dollars					
Specie	895,199 20	874,052 37	911,314 75	922,251 16	987,487 75
Legal-tender notes ..	594,283 00	573,670 00	650,531 00	466,665 00	662,260 00
U. S. cert's of deposit					
Due from U. S. Treas.	60,988 37	54,349 40	52,498 80	40,450 00	34,500 00
Total..........	14,450,190 63	14,493,899 15	13,963,032 04	13,992,750 94	15,119,802 51

by States and reserve cities—Continued.

CITY OF CHICAGO.

Liabilities.	DECEMBER 20. 12 banks.	MARCH 10. 12 banks.	MAY 6. 12 banks.	JULY 1. 12 banks.	OCTOBER 1. 12 banks.
Capital stock	$10, 550, 000 00	$11, 150, 000 00	$11, 725, 400 00	$11, 750, 000 00	$11, 750, 000 00
Surplus fund	3, 040, 000 00	2, 890, 000 00	2, 640, 000 00	2, 656, 600 00	2, 691, 600 00
Undivided profits	1, 884, 898 75	858, 930 39	737, 953 99	576, 814 03	692, 660 39
Nat'l bank circulation	745, 350 00	674, 150 00	658, 550 00	623, 450 00	722, 850 00
State bank circulation					
Dividends unpaid	1, 399 00	2, 809 50	4, 430 00	209, 029 00	64, 002 00
Individual deposits	32, 222, 828 75	34, 311, 167 40	36, 826, 970 86	39, 518, 157 28	40, 970, 738 93
U. S. deposits	66, 966 71	58, 900 87	144, 595 09	124, 822 54	145, 079 72
Dep'ts U.S.dis.officers					
Due to national banks	13, 215, 712 71	15, 452, 172 23	17, 061, 545 32	17, 918, 261 73	17, 039, 310 66
Due to State banks	8, 686, 225 09	11, 117, 641 24	11, 718, 348 66	12, 466, 736 83	11, 114, 238 85
Notes re-discounted					
Bills payable					
Total	70, 413, 321 01	76, 515, 771 63	81, 517, 793 92	85, 843, 871 41	85, 190, 480 55

MICHIGAN.

	97 banks.	97 banks.	97 banks.	97 banks.	97 banks.
Capital stock	$9, 997, 100 00	$10, 075, 100 00	$10, 174, 200 00	$10, 167, 200 00	$10, 194, 600 00
Surplus fund	2, 174, 581 24	1, 962, 894 31	1, 860, 894 31	1, 882, 530 79	1, 864, 192 87
Undivided profits	1, 481, 294 01	1, 013, 900 17	1, 225, 060 68	816, 116 52	1, 107, 596 81
Nat'l bank circulation	3, 715, 215 00	3, 542, 240 00	3, 475, 490 00	3, 510, 440 00	3, 479, 715 00
State bank circulation					
Dividends unpaid	10, 235 47	20, 065, 17	16, 403 00	217, 285 70	24, 038 60
Individual deposits	15, 989, 288 00	16, 665, 842 35	16, 504, 363 55	16, 716, 337 61	18, 575, 061 34
U. S. deposits	31, 132 37	33, 261 86	48, 426 14	35, 962 54	30, 200 99
Dep'ts U.S.dis.officers	2, 886 85	5, 834 01	3, 463 21	1, 000 30	4, 026 37
Due to national banks	189, 739 36	496, 235 32	272, 798 26	251, 509 78	263, 085 50
Due to State banks	200, 713 46	316, 673 09	331, 349 20	264, 714 01	272, 791 74
Notes re-discounted	119, 200 78	49, 674 05	283, 328 28	326, 846 97	114, 970 15
Bills payable	5, 000 00		5, 000 00	5, 000 00	
Total	33, 916, 387 60	34, 181, 780 33	34, 200, 776 63	34, 195, 310 22	35, 930, 879 37

CITY OF DETROIT.

	5 banks.	5 banks.	5 banks.	5 banks.	5 banks.
Capital stock	$2, 650, 000 00	$2, 650, 000 00	$2, 650, 000 00	$2, 900, 000 00	$2, 900, 000 00
Surplus fund	240, 000 00	200, 000 00	203, 000 00	325, 000 00	390, 000 00
Undivided profits	484, 175 80	434, 779 42	416, 447 51	340, 934 24	211, 216 95
Nat'l bank circulation	719, 700 00	678, 300 00	655, 400 00	601, 665 00	371, 265 00
State bank circulation					
Dividends unpaid	187 50	75 00	542 50	51, 550 00	25, 075 00
Individual deposits	7, 210, 239 79	6, 999, 066 34	6, 784, 267 54	6, 154, 142 12	7, 313, 737 43
U. S. deposits	254, 213 55	235, 845 35	276, 451 15	241, 428 80	220, 365 86
Dep'ts U.S.dis.officers	215, 251 55	221, 950 91	255, 024 96	231, 107 46	169, 537 57
Due to national banks	1, 192, 066 82	1, 372, 484 33	1, 125, 120 34	1, 564, 038 91	1, 658, 864 01
Due to State banks	1, 484, 405 62	1, 641, 397 80	1, 536, 778 04	1, 573, 884 41	1, 919, 740 69
Notes re-discounted					
Bills payable					
Total	14, 450, 190 63	14, 493, 899 15	13, 963, 032 04	13, 992, 750 94	15, 119, 802 51

Abstract of reports since September 30, 1884, arranged

WISCONSIN.

Resources.	DECEMBER 20. 47 banks.	MARCH 10. 47 banks.	MAY 6. 47 banks.	JULY 1. 46 banks.	OCTOBER 1. 47 banks.
Loans and discounts.	$9, 096, 421 14	$9, 047, 146 14	$9, 366, 081 59	$9, 520, 956 27	$9, 668, 255 60
Bonds for circulation.	1, 821, 750 00	1, 815, 750 00	1, 815, 750 00	1, 775, 750 00	1, 753, 250 00
Bonds for deposits ..	100, 000 00	100, 000 00	100, 000 00	100, 000 00	100, 000 00
U. S. bonds on hand..	32, 700 00	41, 250 00	37, 600 00	18, 950 00	128, 400 00
Other stocks and b'ds	488, 018 55	481, 755 44	548, 583 92	565, 749 04	575, 517 90
Due from res've'ag'ts	1, 658, 507 58	2, 317, 120 05	2, 142, 106 73	1, 895, 996 08	1, 853, 155 20
Due from nat'l banks	318, 914 43	369, 104 37	333, 480 41	330, 980 09	595, 180 31
Due from State banks	88, 318 50	107, 608 81	105, 877 02	102, 590 67	166, 899 00
Real estate, &c	317, 932 38	341, 777 15	341, 704 80	340, 793 96	345, 703 58
Current expenses....	111, 682 21	49, 382 83	78, 968 80	16, 023 74	55, 251 48
Premiums paid	104, 250 42	104, 741 87	103, 556 20	80, 359 97	90, 063 96
Cash items	65, 393 94	51, 960 70	69, 593 92	81, 402 30	64, 660 92
Clear'g-house exch'gs					
Bills of other banks..	259, 031 00	221, 281 00	249, 049 00	228, 316 00	185, 111 00
Fractional currency	7, 960 38	7, 766 50	7, 711 00	7, 463 80	7, 696 92
Trade dollars......					1, 198
Specie	817, 907 21	888, 018 68	910, 514 82	859, 233 85	998, 845 05
Legal-tender notes ..	442, 669 00	410, 870 00	429, 174 00	385, 185 00	384, 582 00
U. S. cert's of deposit.					
Due from U. S. Treas.	85, 725 07	82, 697 00	86, 439 10	77, 857 65	94, 295 70
Total.	15, 817, 182 41	16, 438, 230 54	16, 731, 791 31	16, 390, 608 42	16, 967, 066 62

CITY OF MILWAUKEE.

	3 banks.	3 banks.	3 banks.	3 banks.	3 banks.
Loans and discounts	$3, 074, 550 24	$3, 207, 948 40	$3, 173, 605 66	$3, 379, 084 35	$3, 956, 083 25
Bonds for circulation	610, 000 00	500, 000 00	500, 000 00	503, 000 00	590, 000 00
Bonds for deposits ..	550, 000 00	550, 000 00	550, 000 00	550, 000 00	550, 000 00
U. S. bonds on hand	4, 000 00	11, 750 00	5, 900 00	2, 050 00	1, 000 00
Other stocks and b'ds	327, 933 25	428, 821 68	281, 836 81	434, 380 25	491 442 55
Due from res've'ag'ts	642, 438 20	581, 192 09	579, 313 04	709, 354 88	767, 759 20
Due from nat'l banks	416, 013 04	515, 700 00	885, 783 50	1, 015, 833 76	604, 466 84
Due from State banks	49, 488 35	76, 744 06	117, 728 44	53, 595 35	46, 596 59
Real estate, &c	120, 000 00	120, 000 00	120, 000 00	120, 000 00	120, 000 00
Current expenses....	10, 488 13	10, 852 27	8, 691 35		6, 207 50
Premiums paid......			1, 119 43	261 03	224 50
Cash items	1, 993 60	443 52	1, 134 79	1, 062 03	5, 135 29
Clear'g-house exch'gs	161, 340 83	114, 043 98	99, 535 71	360, 500 65	398, 700 90
Bills of other banks..	40, 508 00	21, 225 00	36, 550 00	34, 065 00	17, 307 00
Fractional currency	1, 410 30	2, 498 71	2, 184 11	2, 987 04	2, 258 80
Trade dollars					
Specie	583, 463 00	726, 364 00	858, 677 37	700, 460 00	616, 450 00
Legal-tender notes .	518, 972 00	405, 377 00	387, 490 00	400, 317 00	472, 621 00
U. S. cert's of deposit					
Due from U. S. Treas	40, 750 00	27, 500 00	22, 500 00	25, 500 00	28, 500 00
Total......	7, 153, 414 94	7, 300, 460 71	7, 631, 997 81	8, 289, 465 24	8, 614, 753 60

IOWA.

	122 banks.	124 banks.	126 banks.	125 banks.	125 banks.
Loans and discounts	$20, 192, 578 74	$19, 954, 025 65	$20, 260, 713 75	$20, 185, 236 51	$21, 321, 486 47
Bonds for circulation	4, 516, 000 00	4, 506, 000 00	4, 523, 000 00	4, 393, 500 00	4, 391, 000 00
Bonds for deposits ..	350, 000 00	350, 000 00	350, 000 00	350, 000 00	350, 000 00
U. S. bonds on hand	35, 350 00	36, 000 00	36, 700 00	37, 000 00	33, 200 00
Other stocks and b'ds	1, 059, 863 31	1, 151, 154 33	1, 155, 265 82	1, 101, 084 24	1, 668, 484 33
Due from res've'ag'ts	2, 256, 935 84	3, 097, 951 47	3, 409, 311 07	3, 118, 232 07	2, 739, 833 63
Due from nat'l banks	910, 007 29	1, 550, 498 75	1, 705, 895 16	1, 801, 947 62	1, 491, 403 73
Due from State banks	238, 170 00	228, 093 78	213, 727 61	241, 020 31	249, 616 78
Real estate, &c......	1, 422, 498 15	1, 420, 983 80	1, 455, 061 80	1, 462, 280 66	1, 483, 858 09
Current expenses....	258, 549 96	174, 155 32	277, 283 42	142, 556 50	223, 983 37
Premiums paid......	253, 800 84	240, 925 48	244, 136 25	287, 476 00	224, 450 96
Cash items	217, 427 49	267, 017 76	237, 645 73	256, 717 82	274, 180 85
Clear'g-house exch'gs					
Bills of other banks..	521, 533 00	687, 737 00	669, 1-3 00	556, 169 00	600, 040 00
Fractional currency	11, 974 28	12, 565 34	14, 036 52	12, 635 66	11, 619 51
Trade dollars					1, 373 15
Specie	887, 097 24	1, 283, 455 79	1, 449, 417 92	1, 304, 812 98	1, 248, 851 00
Legal-tender notes	1, 223, 150 00	1, 353, 505 00	1, 291, 641 00	1, 153, 810 00	1, 166, 617 00
U. S. cert's of deposit					
Due from U. S. Treas	212, 684 66	218, 551 28	214, 742 93	211, 019 83	202, 480 33
Total	34, 597, 680 80	36, 534, 220 75	37, 512, 731 98	36, 615, 460 20	36, 844, 922 70

by States and reserve cities—Continued.

WISCONSIN.

Liabilities.	DECEMBER 20. 47 banks.	MARCH 10. 47 banks.	MAY 6. 47 banks.	JULY 1. 46 banks.	OCTOBER 1. 47 banks.
Capital stock	$3,780,000 00	$3,795,000 00	$3,770,000 00	$3,735,000 00	$3,785,000 00
Surplus fund	874,489 18	875,859 47	879,782 53	808,578 13	921,607 63
Undivided profits....	549,572 08	357,475 44	456,516 63	305,198 82	410,182 11
Nat'l bank circulation	1,619,633 00	1,504,393 00	1,602,228 00	1,562,128 00	1,517,078 00
State bank circulation					
Dividends unpaid....	1,628 30	845 30	1,921 30	12,645 30	835 30
Individual deposits..	8,771,480 86	9,594,174 58	9,766,000 93	9,685,958 63	10,132,395 94
U.S. deposits ..	79,106 77	85,367 71	113,603 66	86,081 95	80,063 55
Dep'ts U.S. dis. officers	7,480 72	6,608 72	5,787 65	5,162 71	6,046 01
Due to national banks	29,991 68	15,556 85	32,685 85	21,905 54	31,651 00
Due to State banks ..	27,562 16	70,451 01	72,764 30	65,099 34	55,072 80
Notes re-discounted.	73,177 70	42,498 46	30,498 46	12,850 00	27,134 28
Bills payable					
Total ...	15,817,182 41	16,138,230 51	16,734,791 31	16,390,608 42	16,967,066 62

CITY OF MILWAUKEE.

	3 banks.	3 banks.	3 banks.	3 banks.	3 banks.
Capital stock	$450,000 00	$650,000 00	$650,000 00	$650,000 00	$650,000 00
Surplus fund	340,000 00	340,000 00	340,000 00	340,000 00	340,000 00
Undivided profits ...	132,168 15	105,672 96	124,995 05	109,416 41	149,246 45
Nat'l bank circulation	544,000 00	447,000 00	447,000 00	446,000 00	418,400 00
State bank circulation					
Dividends unpaid ..					
Individual deposits	3,987,063 35	3,874,631 81	4,251,991 62	4,856,122 77	5,140,354 90
U.S. deposits	303,343 47	307,109 64	354,515 52	271,909 86	264,657 61
Dep'ts U.S. dis. officers	143,084 90	145,627 31	174,611 49	210,700 73	221,800 27
Due to national banks	678,392 85	953,843 31	831,978 56	916,343 98	983,779 12
Due to State banks...'	355,421 22	413,275 71	436,905 57	488,969 49	414,515 25
Notes re-discounted					
Bills payable ...					
Total	7,153,414 04	7,300,460 71	7,631,097 81	8,289,465 24	8,614,753 60

IOWA.

	122 banks.	124 banks.	126 banks.	125 banks.	125 banks.
Capital stock	$10,105,000 00	$10,167,400 00	$10,290,000 00	$10,155,000 00	$10,155,000 00
Surplus fund	2,203,120 46	2,278,090 17	2,300,200 17	2,208,542 98	2,290,504 47
Undivided profits ...	1,331,457 04	1,007,795 71	1,247,870 41	1,073,241 14	1,144,696 56
Nat'l bank circulation	4,019,131 00	3,999,790 00	4,007,591 00	3,876,776 00	3,813,858 00
State bank circulation					
Dividends unpaid....	18,859 82	27,543 43	26,637 42	100,174 53	19,516 13
Individual deposits..	14,800,837 78	16,439,981 57	17,070,790 59	16,505,386 42	17,053,775 48
U.S. deposits	248,465 37	277,391 03	234,702 17	264,251 82	275,500 21
Dep'ts U.S. dis. officers	62,377 32	44,169 02	44,203 71	61,102 49	58,933 50
Due to national banks	473,757 01	769,645 62	775,679 63	799,441 47	651,624 92
Due to State banks ..	721,834 87	1,266,470 59	1,398,473 92	1,271,523 54	1,110,999 35
Notes re-discounted	434,834 13	148,334 75	93,203 40	128,739 25	210,024 08
Bills payable.	88,000 00	47,500 86	20,280 56	20,280 56	30,000 00
Total	34,597,689 80	36,554,220 75	37,512,731 93	36,615,469 20	36,844,522 70

Abstract of reports since September 30, 1884, arranged

MINNESOTA.

Resources.	DECEMBER 20. 44 banks.	MARCH 10. 44 banks.	MAY 6. 44 banks.	JULY 1. 43 banks.	OCTOBER 1. 43 banks.
Loans and discounts	$13,173,807 43	$13,323,478 30	$13,357,958 31	$13,782,997 27	$14,697,450 75
Bonds for circulation	1,568,000 00	1,568,000 00	1,520,500 00	1,563,000 00	1,563,000 00
Bonds for deposits					
U. S. bonds on hand	5,000 00	5,100 00	5,100 00	5,300 00	5,200 00
Other stocks and b'ds	231,744 60	225,847 18	229,972 80	270,023 36	272,978 60
Due from res've ag'ts	1,243,128 77	1,122,505 98	1,124,158 74	1,354,938 53	1,420,290 97
Due from nat'l banks	743,747 40	822,548 36	974,130 44	1,380,749 83	1,107,652 05
Due from State banks	161,500 29	142,080 53	170,078 32	203,850 46	195,625 67
Real estate, &c	549,009 57	562,323 07	548,758 84	531,388 60	585,898 34
Current expenses	134,343 75	124,366 70	178,112 35	37,439 70	90,627 25
Premiums paid	79,526 59	78,876 47	81,198 08	76,150 86	76,963 16
Cash items	218,029 17	156,682 53	204,662 96	256,441 15	458,446 20
Clear'g-house exch'gs					
Bills of other banks	430,504 00	277,295 00	184,186 00	290,766 00	284,985 00
Fractional currency	3,344 06	4,750 50	3,388 14	2,342 97	3,509 87
Trade dollars					313 60
Specie	580,654 89	688,736 80	745,589 68	675,439 00	794,336 83
Legal-tender notes	565,825 00	481,499 00	325,605 00	619,026 00	511,951 00
U. S. cert's of deposit					
Due from U. S. Treas	80,821 69	76,296 70	75,866 00	74,979 00	72,980 30
Total	19,770,987 30	19,660,531 12	19,788,465 66	21,134,773 57	22,141,112 79

CITY OF ST. PAUL.

	6 banks.	6 banks.	6 banks.	6 banks.	6 banks.
Loans and discounts	$11,283,356 49	$11,255,604 73	$12,301,391 27	$12,849,172 09	$13,474,671 98
Bonds for circulation	550,000 00	550,000 00	550,000 00	550,000 00	550,000 00
Bonds for deposits	500,000 00	500,000 00	500,000 00	500,000 00	500,000 00
U. S. bonds on hand	100 00	100 00	100 00	200 00	
Other stocks and b'ds	554,680 31	670,827 28	488,515 33	485,336 00	331,548 89
Due from res've ag'ts	1,229,602 70	1,757,674 19	1,478,398 74	1,551,503 51	1,095,283 38
Due from nat'l banks	217,495 96	113,201 51	209,674 93	152,742 73	253,708 00
Due from State banks	145,012 32	192,826 69	134,084 13	156,103 36	292,443 53
Real estate, &c	428,556 15	454,120 10	517,533 23	545,180 09	554,148 71
Current expenses	58,681 37	57,989 53	80,045 04	252 08	34,712 27
Premiums paid	32,497 46	31,502 46	22,262 46	22,283 41	22,390 96
Cash items	24,630 08	19,041 56	10,427 85	43,573 46	41,674 57
Clear'g-house exch'gs	152,371 56	114,163 45	265,328 52	262,273 90	305,966 89
Bills of other banks	359,493 00	136,111 00	119,826 00	231,495 00	197,561 00
Fractional currency	2,597 73	3,883 36	4,191 07	3,657 40	5,147 73
Trade dollars					
Specie	773,031 41	780,364 19	810,199 71	831,819 32	756,837 50
Legal-tender notes	334,140 00	138,479 00	125,736 00	215,417 00	390,502 00
U. S. cert's of deposit					
Due from U. S. Treas	34,905 42	41,299 42	24,998 82	23,793 42	32,326 22
Total	16,681,151 96	16,826,418 47	17,642,713 10	18,424,902 77	18,838,923 81

MISSOURI.

	34 banks.	35 banks.	35 banks.	35 banks.	36 banks.
Loans and discounts	$6,846,265 83	$7,162,797 30	$7,106,357 70	$6,866,992 49	$7,269,131 59
Bonds for circulation	1,358,600 00	1,401,100 00	1,334,150 00	1,363,600 00	1,428,600 00
Bonds for deposits	100,000 00	100,000 00	100,000 00	100,000 00	100,000 00
U. S. bonds on hand	61,250 00	57,400 00	60,750 00	58,900 00	35,950 00
Other stocks and b'ds	827,079 08	768,715 47	711,265 43	663,749 61	601,057 10
Due from res've ag'ts	788,929 02	878,144 37	957,091 03	1,289,645 21	1,044,343 38
Due from nat'l banks	228,502 66	342,736 02	297,635 02	382,394 00	204,685 32
Due from State banks	204,721 17	221,673 72	235,830 72	321,678 97	288,667 63
Real estate, &c	305,958 95	357,581 25	342,002 18	321,106 94	353,213 94
Current expenses	91,629 96	71,282 30	83,760 00	33,442 96	54,267 90
Premiums paid	75,423 03	82,196 34	84,990 63	100,981 98	94,194 73
Cash items	67,969 04	79,259 93	70,180 79	77,750 22	55,416 48
Clear'g-house exch'gs	75,584 70	82,908 68	93,270 20	143,063 20	135,924 02
Bills of other banks	216,355 00	260,237 00	358,843 00	248,003 00	263,212 00
Fractional currency	2,173 12	2,603 37	2,326 80	2,211 71	2,345 43
Trade dollars					497 55
Specie	424,743 30	421,226 32	516,988 57	576,881 95	484,168 96
Legal-tender notes	404,858 00	429,397 00	427,556 00	399,597 00	377,050 00
U. S. cert's of deposit					
Due from U. S. Treas	69,355 20	67,146 00	65,832 40	62,558 00	66,393 00
Total	12,149,308 24	12,785,865 07	12,846,831 37	13,012,557 38	12,949,059 03

by States and reserve cities—Continued.

MINNESOTA.

Liabilities.	DECEMBER 20. 44 banks.	MARCH 10. 44 banks.	MAY 6. 44 banks.	JULY 1. 43 banks.	OCTOBER 1. 43 banks.
Capital stock	$6,060,000 00	$6,083,181 00	$6,137,742 00	$6,090,000 00	$6,190,000 00
Surplus fund	750,811 06	813,758 87	814,903 87	830,933 87	850,233 87
Undivided profits....	899,055 36	600,193 95	744,870 41	477,659 48	657,904 26
Nat'l bank circulation	1,404,349 00	1,401,049 00	1,415,616 00	1,401,576 00	1,405,176 00
State bank circulation					
Dividends unpaid....	6,102 19	11,865 83	8,159 95	140,682 36	6,553 34
Individual deposits...	9,036,070 15	9,372,963 02	9,556,896 95	10,982,407 21	11,385,970 65
U. S. deposits					
Dep'ts U.S.dis.officers					
Due to national banks	446,385 76	510,962 31	482,564 30	609,946 33	649,033 10
Due to State banks ..	636,926 22	294,820 18	282,805 83	385,772 71	709,978 52
Notes re-discounted ..	611,287 53	559,736 96	330,833 20	207,795 61	252,173 05
Bills payable........	10,000 00	12,000 00	5,000 00	5,000 00	34,000 00
Total	19,770,987 30	19,660,531 12	19,788,465 66	21,134,773 57	22,141,112 79

CITY OF ST. PAUL.

	6 banks.	6 banks.	6 banks.	6 banks.	6 banks.
Capital stock	$5,200,000 00	$5,200,000 00	$5,200,000 00	$5,200,000 00	$5,200,000 00
Surplus fund.........	974,000 00	986,000 00	989,200 00	1,000,500 00	1,001,600 00
Undivided profits....	602,994 64	411,629 95	560,554 45	361,369 67	546,224 32
Nat'l bank circulation	495,000 00	490,100 00	487,600 00	483,300 00	479,400 00
State bank circulation					
Dividends unpaid....	435 00	1,742 00	1,435 00	102,192 00	8,163 00
Individual deposits ..	7,078,367 06	6,963,159 40	7,409,748 58	7,285,396 08	8,265,325 80
U. S. deposits........	97,124 14	134,644 72	144,824 55	88,372 80	118,513 62
Dep'ts U.S.dis.officers	387,734 54	261,810 88	296,879 93	322,914 05	261,685 54
Due to national banks	866,803 30	1,044,410 87	1,207,839 96	1,702,005 64	1,382,332 77
Due to State banks...	946,493 74	1,139,914 60	1,092,848 78	1,614,249 62	1,314,756 54
Notes re-discounted..	28,812 90	193,006 05	131,781 85	264,602 91	260,922 22
Bills payable........	3,386 64				
Total	16,681,151 96	16,826,418 47	17,642,713 10	18,424,902 77	18,838,923 81

MISSOURI.

	34 banks.	35 banks.	35 banks.	35 banks.	36 banks.
Capital stock	$3,065,000 00	$3,265,000 00	$3,265,000 00	$3,277,000 00	$3,311,000 00
Surplus fund.........	604,000 15	637,748 10	604,498 16	601,054 39	623,425 08
Undivided profits....	487,693 92	381,937 99	446,740 73	279,618 95	320,412 29
Nat'l bank circulation	1,215,673 00	1,248,598 00	1,171,908 00	1,198,658 00	1,251,648 00
State bank circulation					
Dividends unpaid....	650 50	959 50	4,639 69	21,649 00	19,994 00
Individual deposits...	5,376,075 84	5,927,607 65	5,917,536 39	6,012,663 89	5,972,242 24
U. S. deposits........	72,846 87	62,627 07	107,502 48	65,492 87	81,582 35
Dep'ts U.S.dis.officers	18,518 94	18,739 32	17,590 96	16,209 45	4,756 95
Due to national banks	225,922 92	237,618 08	325,081 06	427,872 88	385,402 37
Due to State banks...	656,110 25	761,549 97	831,833 90	1,029,777 90	809,995 75
Notes re-discounted..	367,045 85	193,479 33	129,500 00	47,500 00	113,600 00
Bills payable........	59,000 00		25,000 00	35,000 00	55,000 00
Total	12,149,398 24	12,735,865 07	12,846,831 37	13,012,557 33	12,949,059 03

Abstract of reports since September 30, 1884, arranged

CITY OF ST. LOUIS.

Resources.	DECEMBER 20.	MARCH 10.	MAY 6.	JULY 1.	OCTOBER 1.
	6 banks.	6 banks.	6 banks.	6 banks.	6 banks.
Loans and discounts	$8,548,587 30	$8,630,444 98	$8,380,094 33	$8,488,775 89	$9,202,786 11
Bonds for circulation	760,000 00	760,000 00	760,000 00	860,000 00	860,000 00
Bonds for deposits ..	250,000 00	500,000 00	500,000 00	500,000 00	500,000 00
U. S. bonds on hand	6,050 00	3,350 00	4,600 00	9,250 00	2,650 00
Other stocks and b'ds	364,861 93	403,825 94	451,465 76	567,040 29	569,187 95
Due from res've ag'ts	837,381 99	966,506 95	1,191,188 98	1,123,645 01	1,263,818 95
Due from nat'l banks	680,892 36	629,800 31	915,265 91	749,387 79	414,136 52
Due from State banks	273,785 64	293,867 26	161,172 03	137,831 83	170,295 11
Real estate, &c	199,280 48	199,280 48	214,280 48	212,621 73	213,020 74
Current expenses....	108,105 38	66,108 55	76,729 18	19,387 43	118,241 30
Premiums paid	17,832 93	71,270 43	71,270 43	33,939 18	33,839 18
Cash items	36,008 76	24,256 45	77,565 80	61,771 72	29,132 45
Clear'g-house exch'gs	559,826 36	475,445 13	500,965 80	696,069 53	557,022 01
Bills of other banks..	168,700 00	234,762 00	578,401 00	214,203 00	117,811 00
Fractional currency.	5,505 80	3,132 46	2,112 81	1,676 81	1,948 22
Trade dollars........					
Specie	936,979 15	1,033,207 55	1,210,185 95	1,485,303 60	962,172 21
Legal-tender notes ..	901,881 00	712,536 00	1,586,915 00	998,830 00	641,629 00
U. S. cert's of deposit.	120,000 00	120,000 00	210,000 00	250,000 00	120,000 00
Due from U. S. Treas	41,195 00	40,195 00	47,695 00	34,195 00	39,695 00
Total..........	14,816,964 08	15,167,989 49	16,939,908 46	16,443,928 81	15,847,385 75

KANSAS.

	60 banks.	62 banks.	64 banks.	67 banks.	74 banks.
Loans and discounts.	$8,548,316 19	$8,731,074 72	$9,135,427 71	$9,724,591 64	$10,730,627 16
Bonds for circulation	1,467,500 00	1,471,300 00	1,533,300 00	1,589,350 00	1,702,300 00
Bonds for deposits ..	350,000 00	350,000 00	350,000 00	350,000 00	350,990 00
U. S. bonds on hand	3,100 00	3,200 00	3,100 00	2,100 00	3,100 00
Other stocks and b'ds	171,323 10	125,546 23	102,821 90	175,054 93	170,817 91
Due from res've ag'ts	690,648 88	907,899 47	1,084,605 04	1,118,664 16	1,372,090 15
Due from nat'l banks	384,284 28	514,706 27	691,342 14	730,435 12	706,424 24
Due from State banks	453,926 56	300,312 82	564,432 44	617,126 28	553,616 87
Real estate, &c	500,912 86	531,428 00	540,543 14	576,602 31	636,679 98
Current expenses....	146,002 37	83,061 05	111,513 66	78,364 50	105,713 99
Premiums paid	85,620 49	105,898 92	111,068 48	110,482 03	126,289 16
Cash items	133,624 86	122,984 18	114,871 54	141,807 43	130,039 24
Clear'g-house exch'gs					
Bills of other banks..	432,018 00	464,600 00	593,750 00	529,186 00	474,333 00
Fractional currency	4,048 09	4,489 40	5,320 91	5,983 74	5,441 61
Trade dollars........					1,000 00
Specie	439,249 64	500,351 12	558,971 94	689,460 69	899,754 65
Legal-tender notes ..	743,085 00	832,484 00	903,136 00	868,250 00	713,148 00
U. S. cert's of deposit					
Due from U. S. Treas.	67,658 61	63,178 23	76,577 00	73,235 01	77,654 49
Total	14,621,328 93	15,181,514 41	16,483,599 00	17,386,913 86	18,818,431 45

NEBRASKA.

	63 banks.	65 banks.	65 banks.	70 banks.	75 banks.
Loans and discounts	$12,652,008 54	$13,011,330 46	$13,347,102 12	$13,596,336 71	$15,432,741 80
Bonds for circulation	1,870,250 00	1,895,250 00	1,887,750 00	1,951,500 00	2,014,000 00
Bonds for deposits ..	450,000 00	450,000 00	450,000 00	450,000 00	450,000 00
U. S. bonds on hand.	50 00	150 00			600 00
Other stocks and b'ds	278,560 82	227,545 18	284,419 03	278,098 56	267,216 19
Due from res've ag'ts	1,433,638 01	1,367,471 80	1,733,288 37	2,394,677 60	2,096,998 07
Due from nat'l banks	664,780 74	832,518 95	1,160,961 01	1,268,973 56	1,018,346 81
Due from State banks	377,448 94	492,177 32	504,354 95	592,270 21	628,086 73
Real estate, &c	785,379 98	805,842 70	836,830 01	860,632 03	935,867 25
Current expenses.....	178,077 05	150,834 38	138,575 29	95,906 19	135,657 72
Premiums paid	99,165 83	95,824 34	93,959 98	98,766 71	101,774 85
Cash items	486,744 26	270,107 07	227,830 07	348,151 63	419,319 12
Clear'g-house exch'gs					
Bills of other banks	248,929 06	324,711 00	321,062 00	228,767 00	274,727 00
Fractional currency	4,735 47	6,890 98	6,428 08	6,508 17	7,672 56
Trade dollars........					851 00
Specie	779,704 85	999,561 76	1,238,738 11	1,148,700 86	1,038,439 18
Legal-tender notes	579,378 00	524,224 00	510,234 00	424,833 00	545,699 00
U. S. cert's of deposit					
Due from U. S. Treas	89,771 00	87,651 00	93,738 00	93,825 50	90,691 50
Total	20,979,623 35	21,542,090 94	22,704,771 65	23,843,387 13	25,458,141 08

by States and reserve cities—Continued.

CITY OF ST. LOUIS.

Liabilities.	DECEMBER 20. 6 banks.	MARCH 10. 6 banks.	MAY 6. 6 banks.	JULY 1. 6 banks.	OCTOBER 1. 6 banks.
Capital stock	$3,250,000 00	$3,250,000 00	$3,250,000 00	$3,250,000 00	$3,250,000 00
Surplus fund	845,517 75	842,874 15	842,874 15	852,928 03	856,128 29
Undivided profits	363,026 86	320,780 55	356,251 90	264,789 35	438,891 69
Nat'l bank circulation	681,950 00	676,550 00	668,650 00	658,450 00	766,400 00
State bank circulation					
Dividends unpaid	17,989 18	15,962 68	39,274 18	49,363 18	17,132 18
Individual deposits	5,288,797 41	5,665,874 14	6,126,649 17	5,815,866 33	5,634,622 84
U. S. deposits	198,644 58	196,379 15	386,767 22	411,064 07	401,163 70
Dep'ts U.S.dis.officers					
Due to national banks	1,955,205 48	2,032,405 73	2,480,991 79	2,373,968 61	1,988,845 34
Due to State banks	1,916,332 82	2,302,663 09	2,780,356 99	2,767,499 24	2,203,519 15
Notes re-discounted	90,500 00	375,000 00			90,682 56
Bills payable	200,000 00				200,000 00
Total	14,816,964 08	15,167,989 49	18,939,968 46	16,443,928 81	15,847,385 75

KANSAS.

	60 banks.	62 banks.	64 banks.	67 banks.	74 banks.
Capital stock	$3,995,000 00	$4,088,905 00	$4,324,780 00	$4,605,350 00	$4,995,720 00
Surplus fund	464,262 73	507,378 46	506,378 46	616,435 33	698,971 56
Undivided profits	668,134 38	463,092 11	588,930 98	457,373 38	572,595 73
Nat'l bank circulation	1,301,680 00	1,283,695 00	1,360,530 00	1,352,500 00	1,435,705 00
State bank circulation					
Dividends unpaid	816 50	5,313 00	6,039 37	37,381 77	7,489 71
Individual deposits	7,155,963 56	7,683,642 98	8,670,519 93	9,230,679 98	10,089,936 99
U. S. deposits	174,960 21	206,929 73	207,284 12	148,541 42	145,751 36
Dep'ts U.S.dis.officers	168,649 25	78,392 56	100,530 11	152,080 37	116,632 49
Due to national banks	101,916 62	176,654 25	280,508 66	285,233 83	213,274 17
Due to State banks	107,859 83	158,976 50	196,164 51	268,082 78	218,176 05
Notes re-discounted	401,294 85	290,062 32	213,927 76	233,255 00	346,208 39
Bills payable	80,845 00	38,472 50	10,000 00		8,000 00
Total	14,621,328 93	15,181,514 41	16,483,599 90	17,386,913 86	18,818,431 45

NEBRASKA.

	63 banks.	65 banks.	65 banks.	70 banks.	75 banks.
Capital stock	$4,755,000 00	$4,815,000 00	$5,142,500 00	$5,627,500 00	$5,949,250 00
Surplus fund	648,501 98	760,947 93	785,797 93	884,789 08	944,773 77
Undivided profits	872,605 66	673,260 85	659,295 52	547,783 97	567,803 22
Nat'l bank circulation	1,681,730 00	1,689,310 00	1,695,890 00	1,689,990 00	1,774,330 00
State bank circulation					
Dividends unpaid	395 00	273 00	1,072 00	20,356 95	260 00
Individual deposits	8,932,567 50	9,766,711 32	10,330,957 85	10,880,841 07	11,316,796 75
U. S. deposits	251,753 62	248,406 20	209,901 27	183,249 06	187,953 09
Dep'ts U.S.dis.officers	188,292 03	147,214 80	199,179 94	215,623 02	164,915 59
Due to national banks	1,230,221 39	1,302,360 21	1,501,147 37	1,774,302 48	2,126,700 73
Due to State banks	1,075,649 03	1,174,395 79	1,570,112 03	1,708,379 03	1,498,908 36
Notes re-discounted	1,261,577 49	910,677 95	580,540 43	290,072 47	878,190 07
Bills payable	78,234 25	45,533 30	28,376 71	21,000 00	48,318 90
Total	20,979,623 95	21,542,090 94	22,704,771 05	23,843,887 13	25,456,111 08

Abstract of reports since September 30, 1884, arranged

COLORADO.

Resources.	DECEMBER 20. 24 banks.	MARCH 10. 24 banks.	MAY 6. 24 banks.	JULY 1. 24 banks.	OCTOBER 1. 25 banks.
Loans and discounts	$6, 695, 529 78	$6, 908, 629 11	$7, 304, 609 62	$7, 560, 811 18	$7, 608, 986 99
Bonds for circulation	1, 140, 000 00	1, 085, 000 00	1, 047, 500 00	1, 052, 500 00	1, 032, 500 00
Bonds for deposits	400, 000 00	400, 000 00	400, 000 00	400, 000 00	400, 000 00
U. S. bonds on hand	500 00	500 00	12, 000 00	....	....
Other stocks and b'ds	588, 222 04	607, 822 65	681, 560 52	628, 284 17	702, 159 44
Due from res'veag'ts	1, 728, 421 07	1, 862, 010 12	1, 755, 641 55	1, 843, 677 38	2, 453, 997 17
Due from nat'l banks	1, 065, 048 44	1, 224, 017 78	1, 011, 579 27	1, 191, 180 14	1, 050, 589 00
Due from State banks	433, 245 37	400, 474 32	390, 761 83	356, 038 93	490, 882 11
Real estate, &c	340, 104 80	331, 763 01	362, 163 95	359, 343 52	351, 126 86
Current expenses	84, 411 37	80, 881 30	76, 680 58	39, 782 63	37, 429 85
Premiums paid	86, 346 24	86, 393 74	79, 037 49	79, 532 80	78, 539 05
Cash items	234, 618 6C	309, 610 72	223, 713 39	259, 423 22	232, 062 43
Clear'g-house exch'gs	....	....	....	....	....
Bills of other banks	293, 985 00	170, 680 00	166, 995 00	198, 309 00	210, 254 00
Fractional currency	1, 156 94	1, 489 52	1, 381 85	1, 319 98	3, 296 13
Trade dollars	....	....	....	....	....
Specie	674, 907 64	877, 551 03	1, 005, 016 29	1, 005, 739 32	977, 646 92
Legal-tender notes	846, 275 00	711, 587 00	705, 720 00	673, 622 00	738, 561 00
U. S. cert's of deposit	....	....	....	....	....
Due from U. S. Treas	54, 640 54	58, 505 12	62, 022 62	53, 443 37	72, 981 37
Total	14, 668, 413 49	15, 206, 909 42	15, 286, 383 96	15, 723, 007 64	17, 061, 012 32

NEVADA.

	1 bank.	1 bank.	1 bank.	1 bank.	1 bank.
Loans and discounts	$240, 040 20	$220, 311 52	$183, 243 19	$183, 816 83	$248, 248 38
Bonds for circulation	40, 000 00	40, 000 00	40, 000 00	40, 000 00	40, 000 00
Bonds for deposits	....	....	....	....	5, 000 00
U. S. bonds on hand	....	....	....	....	....
Other stocks and b'ds	9, 430 90	8, 164 60	8, 579 74	8, 619 41	13, 624 98
Due from res've ag'ts	4, 277 86	3, 524 29	5, 864 29	6, 495 36	3, 042 00
Due from nat'l banks	737 46	1, 300 89	53, 134 78	27, 900 27	....
Due from State banks	1, 408 15	15, 092 74	2, 397 30	8, 862 15	2, 303 17
Real estate, &c	3, 375 00	3, 400 00	3, 400 00	4, 508 18	8, 303 18
Current expenses	4, 288 00	1, 863 07	3, 555 60	....	2, 595 58
Premiums paid	3, 225 00	3, 225 00	3, 225 00	3, 225 00	4, 343 75
Cash items	494 56	350 71	354 02	500 00	502 25
Clear'g-house exch'gs	....	....	....	....	....
Bills of other banks	875 00	....	1, 740 00	1, 750 00	4, 600 00
Fractional currency	....	....	....	40 50	47 20
Trade dollars	....	....	....	....	....
Specie	31, 943 12	36, 840 87	49, 187 40	64, 010 73	46, 380 50
Legal-tender notes	763 00	386 00	1, 265 00	1, 150 00	2, 476 00
U. S. cert's of deposit	....	....	....	....	....
Due from U. S. Treas.	1, 800 00	1, 800 00	1, 800 00	1, 800 00	1, 800 00
Total	351, 667 31	336, 349 69	357, 776 32	352, 678 43	383, 177 08

CALIFORNIA.

	14 banks.	14 banks.	15 banks.	16 banks.	16 banks.
Loans and discounts	$5, 875, 700 35	$5, 740, 420 33	$5, 918, 517 55	$5, 994, 747 58	$6, 051, 487 19
Bonds for circulation	910, 500 00	910, 500 00	935, 500 00	948, 000 00	900, 500 00
Bonds for deposits	....	....	....	....	....
U. S. bonds on hand	13, 400 00	15, 000 00	20, 600 00	22, 950 00	22, 650 00
Other stocks and b'ds	373, 452 37	307, 976 20	306, 433 91	337, 906 09	373, 743 76
Due from res'veag'ts	388, 340 65	377, 446 55	346, 953 93	456, 197 72	554, 114 48
Due from nat'l banks	94, 673 67	108, 045 46	119, 788 35	114, 336 55	94, 885 66
Due from State banks	73, 128 36	207, 144 29	149, 829 82	138, 786 43	248, 963 49
Real estate, &c	316, 053 61	316, 106 35	322, 877 51	338, 896 04	344, 981 87
Current expenses	52, 597 13	41, 196 23	42, 572 61	26, 952 81	29, 664 23
Premiums paid	83, 159 47	82, 517 02	83, 503 52	86, 923 37	89, 149 55
Cash items	126, 297 63	73, 662 09	70, 072 64	44, 619 83	86, 977 36
Clear'g-house exch'gs	....	....	....	....	....
Bills of other banks	35, 440 00	32, 905 60	30, 697 00	23, 216 00	41, 428 00
Fractional currency	636 04	252 79	269 40	342 47	423 23
Trade dollars	....	....	....	....	....
Specie	1, 160, 074 76	1, 220, 937 92	1, 014, 873 51	852, 243 13	910, 083 70
Legal-tender notes	21, 884 00	126, 117 00	61, 491 00	43, 252 00	48, 004 00
U. S. cert's of deposit	....	....	....	....	....
Due from U. S. Treas	39, 172 00	40, 972 00	39, 872 00	51, 707 00	52, 722 50
Total	9, 574, 401 04	9, 601, 193 23	9, 463, 852 75	9, 481, 167 02	9, 909, 729 02

by States and reserve cities—Continued.

COLORADO.

Liabilities.	DECEMBER 20, 24 banks.	MARCH 10. 24 banks.	MAY 6. 24 banks.	JULY 1. 24 banks.	OCTOBER 1. 25 banks.
Capital stock	$1,990,000 00	$1,965,000 00	$1,965,000 00	$1,965,000 00	$2,025,000 00
Surplus fund	907,500 00	984,500 00	985,000 00	996,400 00	1,003,100 00
Undivided profits....	679,120 57	452,730 46	468,671 96	429,376 91	453,549 63
Nat'l bank circulation	972 510 00	961,190 00	933,340 00	929,840 00	926,540 00
State bank circulation					
Dividends unpaid ...	2,240 00	570 00	306 00	9,211 85	2,592 00
Individual deposits ..	8,357,232 22	8,923,556 22	9,096,065 09	9,406,017 81	10,281,552 99
U. S. deposits.......	236,989 24	286,099 44	258,125 26	237,648 10	248,074 64
Dep'ts U.S.dis.officers	124,254 82	117,065 36	148,523 85	122,646 75	77,954 93
Due to national banks	766,474 22	784,714 65	634,328 95	865,556 15	1,063,023 80
Due to State banks ...	619,592 42	778,515 51	779,134 12	750,438 55	979,624 33
Notes re-discounted..	12,500 00	12,967 78	17,888 74	10,871 52	
Bills payable.......					
Total	14,668,413 49	15,206,909 42	15,286,383 96	15,723,007 64	17,061,012 32

NEVADA.

	1 bank.	1 bank.	1 bank.	1 bank.	1 bank.
Capital stock	$75,000 00	$75,000 00	$75,000 00	$75,000 00	$75,000 00
Surplus fund.......	25,000 00	25,000 00	25,000 00	25,000 00	25,000 00
Undivided profits....	14,984 44	7,372 08	10,649 52	11,8.9 13	10,664 72
Nat'l bank circulation	36,000 00	35,960 00	34,560 00	34,220 00	35,380 00
State bank circulation					
Dividends unpaid ...					
Individual deposits ..	138,048 88	189,858 66	212,308 30	206,636 16	214,700 56
U. S. deposits.......					
Dep'ts U.S.dis.officers					
Due to national banks	10,073 22				678 49
Due to State banks...	52,560 77	3,158 95	258 50	22 14	21,753 31
Notes re-discounted..					
Bills payable.......					
Total	351,667 31	336,349 69	357,776 32	352,678 43	383,177 08

CALIFORNIA.

	14 banks.	14 banks.	15 banks.	16 banks.	16 banks.
Capital stock	$2,050,000 00	$2,050,000 00	$2,150,000 00	$2,175,000 00	$2,345,000 00
Surplus fund	463,791 52	499,779 96	501,770 96	500,779 90	548,414 87
Undivided profits....	468,803 31	353,400 46	389,181 96	393,602 53	339,671 69
Nat'l bank circulation	818,200 00	818,470 00	815,190 00	837,350 00	855,720 00
State bank circulation					
Dividends unpaid	2,304 75	2,200 25	1,705 00	15,750 00	2,169 50
Individual deposits...	5,617,193 67	5,605,721 92	5,412,674 08	5,313,246 25	5,620,030 24
U. S. deposits.......					
Dep'ts U.S.dis.officers					
Due to national banks	46,370 23	64,034 04	93,303 51	85,724 16	68,508 72
Due to State banks...	167,787 56	207,586 60	100,078 24	153,714 12	130,814 00
Notes re-discounted..					
Bills payable.......					
Total	9,574,401 04	9,601,193 23	9,463,852 75	9,481,167 02	9,909,729 02

Abstract of reports since September 30, 1884, arranged

CITY OF SAN FRANCISCO.

Resources.	DECEMBER 20. 1 bank.	MARCH 10. 1 bank.	MAY 6. 1 bank.	JULY 1. 1 bank.	OCTOBER 1. 1 bank.
Loans and discounts	$1,921,822 64	$1,746,760 81	$1,799,303 50	$1,766,670 93	$2,146,771 56
Bonds for circulation	600,000 00	600,000 00	600,000 00	600,000 00	600,000 00
Bonds for deposits					
U. S. bonds on hand					
Other stocks and b'ds					
Due from res'v ag'ts	23,220 29	29,381 34	17,699 68		
Due from nat'l banks	87,027 43	90,009 78	96,087 62	102,178 14	100,302 34
Due from State banks	322,755 50	207,666 05	171,710 79	193,613 58	176,515 55
Real estate, &c	92,598 75	92,598 75	92,598 75	92,598 75	92,598 75
Current expenses	2,371 84	801 90	542 90	510 33	440 20
Premiums paid	7,200 00	6,900 00	6,700 00	6,500 00	6,200 00
Cash items					
Clear'g-house exch'gs	56,344 51	37,618 23	45,691 19	67,259 28	115,058 48
Bills of other banks	2,445 00	1,510 00	6,178 00	3,195 00	2,965 00
Fractional currency	5 48	7 07	6 95	10 20	7 82
Trade dollars					
Specie	276,500 00	513,110 00	565,673 00	312,195 00	458,435 00
Legal-tender notes	2,770 00	2,279 00	3,246 00	6,960 00	2,589 00
U. S. cert's of deposit					
Due from U. S. Treas	24,500 00	26,972 50	27,000 00	27,000 00	27,000 00
Total	3,419,561 44	3,355,558 43	3,432,438 28	3,378,691 21	3,728,883 70

OREGON.

	8 banks.	8 banks.	9 banks.	9 banks.	9 banks.
Loans and discounts	$2,028,208 88	$1,921,312 59	$2,013,893 34	$2,100,107 93	$2,202,226 30
Bonds for circulation	410,900 00	410,900 00	423,400 00	423,400 00	423,400 00
Bonds for deposits	500,000 00	500,000 00	500,000 00	500,000 00	500,000 00
U. S. bonds on hand	38,500 00	39,000 00	39,700 00	39,700 00	40,900 00
Other stocks and b'ds	438,258 23	444,387 19	418,231 64	420,828 40	441,437 59
Due from res'v ag'ts	117,387 65	176,605 29	147,707 90	319,770 86	253,262 52
Due from nat'l banks	54,296 01	125,761 53	141,120 78	173,494 65	188,627 94
Due from State banks	86,325 45	233,818 44	205,398 46	96,592 99	144,426 43
Real estate, &c	147,888 19	158,009 41	160,073 23	163,849 92	169,802 77
Current expenses	55,115 53	30,375 03	41,200 57	21,389 18	20,625 72
Premiums paid	23,549 50	18,733 50	21,644 12	21,196 12	21,459 62
Cash items	11,107 26	31,187 18	18,965 33	15,887 76	24,370 35
Clear'g-house exch'gs					
Bills of other banks	12,373 00	9,291 00	12,810 00	18,580 00	12,805 00
Fractional currency	661 11	424 35	297 42	776 39	634 93
Trade dollars					
Specie	424,554 75	468,647 52	505,249 45	306,074 30	508,700 80
Legal-tender notes	9,957 00	8,462 00	11,439 00	20,786 00	28,761 00
U. S. cert's of deposit					
Due from U. S. Treas	18,620 00	19,688 00	20,450 50	20,150 50	20,050 50
Total	4,377,705 56	4,596,605 97	4,681,575 83	4,662,584 40	5,031,641 47

ARIZONA.

	2 banks.	1 bank.
Loans and discounts	$134,624 37	$59,473 07
Bonds for circulation	37,500 00	12,500 00
Bonds for deposits		
U. S. bonds on hand		
Other stocks and b'ds	63,194 22	22,803 71
Due from res'v ag'ts		
Due from nat'l banks	1,183 46	260 02
Due from State banks	14,496 77	
Real estate, &c	7,047 48	2,288 64
Current expenses	1,068 80	
Premiums paid	3,593 75	125 00
Cash items	729 80	360 28
Clear'g-house exch'gs		
Bills of other banks	24,972 00	5,707 00
Fractional currency	250 08	
Trade dollars		
Specie	62,203 65	30,496 70
Legal-tender notes		
U. S. cert's of deposit		
Due from U. S. Treas	1,687 50	562 50
Total	353,451 88	125,576 92

by States and reserve cities—Continued.

CITY OF SAN FRANCISCO.

Liabilities.	DECEMBER 20. 1 bank.	MARCH 10. 1 bank.	MAY 6. 1 bank.	JULY 1. 1 bank.	OCTOBER 1. 1 bank.
Capital stock	$1,500,000 00	$1,500,000 00	$1,500,000 00	$1,500,000 00	$1,500,000 00
Surplus fund	228,309 90	228,850 49	231,850 49	231,850 49	234,520 48
Undivided profits....	98,183 54	101,691 21	75,505 73	100,281 97	99,131 30
Nat'l bank circulation	495,000 00	538,150 00	539,850 00	533,000 00	539,200 00
State bank circulation					
Dividends unpaid....	872 00	1,222 00	1,656 00	956 00	1,144 00
Individual deposits...	945,968 34	803,936 15	885,981 54	809,690 74	1,090,089 14
U. S. deposits........					
Dep'ts U.S.dis.officers					
Due to national banks	84,468 43	126,744 13	96,406 05	108,818 83	183,409 66
Due to State banks...	66,759 23	54,964 45	101,098 47	94,084 18	81,389 12
Notes re-discounted..					
Bills payable					
Total..........	3,419,561 44	3,355,558 43	3,432,438 28	3,378,691 21	3,728,883 70

OREGON.

	8 banks.	8 banks.	9 banks.	9 banks.	9 banks.
Capital stock	$710,000 00	$710,000 00	$695,000 00	$705,000 00	$710,000 00
Surplus fund	73,806 77	76,000 00	78,900 00	80,500 00	81,600 00
Undivided profits....	602,178 12	580,786 74	601,846 15	587,944 83	618,659 63
Nat'l bank circulation	364,310 00	358,950 00	351,805 00	346,850 00	346,740 00
State bank circulation					
Dividends unpaid....			150 00	7,000 00	15,000 00
Individual deposits.	2,001,907 12	2,269,527 62	2,243,032 85	2,295,858 54	2,555,552 41
U. S. deposits	227,933 47	192,629 23	234,854 53	242,235 12	238,233 66
Dep'ts U.S.dis.officers	227,306 86	229,062 19	270,713 86	212,008 53	176,344 28
Due to national banks	46,347 02	86,082 86	115,334 51	84,588 01	112,583 21
Due to State banks...	123,826 20	94,167 33	89,938 93	97,599 37	156,818 68
Notes re-discounted.					
Bills payable.......				3,000 00	20,109 60
Total..........	4,377,705 56	4,596,605 97	4,681,575 83	4,662,584 40	5,031,641 47

ARIZONA.

	2 banks.	1 bank.			
Capital stock	$150,000 00	$50,000 00			
Surplus fund	2,842 19				
Undivided profits....	6,613 15	591 67			
Nat'l bank circulation	30,650 00	11,250 00			
State bank circulation					
Dividends unpaid....					
Individual deposits...	144,509 68	61,186 55			
U. S. deposits					
Dep'ts U.S.dis.officers					
Due to national banks	4,017 61	82 61			
Due to State banks...	11,819 25	2,466 09			
Notes re-discounted..					
Bills payable					
Total	353,451 88	125,576 92			

Abstract of reports since September 30, 1884, arranged

DAKOTA.

Resources.	DECEMBER 20.	MARCH 10.	MAY 6.	JULY 1.	OCTOBER 1.
	35 banks.	36 banks.	38 banks.	40 banks.	41 banks.
Loans and discounts.	$3,370,856 60	$3,440,795 04	$3,525,874 60	$3,764,719 97	$4,000,272 60
Bonds for circulation.	654,250 00	678,750 00	696,000 00	721,500 00	736,500 00
Bonds for deposits	175,000 00	175,000 00	175,000 00	175,000 00	175,000 00
U. S. bonds on hand.	300 00	300 00			
Other stocks and b'ds	262,761 78	258,528 92	291,755 75	333,256 96	294,681 95
Due from res've ag'ts	270,298 72	318,207 74	303,702 21	300,022 23	414,411 74
Due from nat'l banks	407,512 28	452,724 48	466,488 78	532,630 66	700,994 33
Due from State banks	107,568 20	163,273 69	202,806 24	162,659 51	168,102 65
Real estate, &c	444,122 57	456,406 77	460,845 63	478,292 00	500,515 10
Current expenses.	114,907 37	66,082 64	89,210 20	45,928 27	79,085 99
Premiums paid	58,821 40	67,387 83	67,606 05	65,493 07	65,305 95
Cash items	57,476 13	47,233 08	62,880 56	48,778 35	54,019 39
Clear'g-house exch'gs					
Bills of other banks.	185,357 00	83,922 00	103,047 00	109,301 00	242,905 00
Fractional currency	1,931 07	2,035 03	2,328 44	3,169 81	3,318 93
Trade dollars					
Specie	154,051 27	176,472 51	193,820 45	199,049 02	211,004 30
Legal-tender notes	307,992 00	290,142 00	306,704 00	269,330 00	373,821 00
U. S. cert's of deposit					
Due from U. S. Treas	30,536 39	30,071 44	34,359 50	31,775 59	37,107 20
Total	6,693,756 78	6,733,417 17	6,982,429 50	7,240,306 44	8,055,946 22

IDAHO.

	4 banks.	4 banks.	4 banks.	4 banks.	4 banks.
Loans and discounts.	$336,842 14	$355,257 45	$359,726 74	$345,295 34	$350,795 03
Bonds for circulation	67,800 00	67,800 00	67,800 00	67,800 00	67,800 00
Bonds for deposits					
U. S. bonds on hand.	50,000 00	50,000 00	50,000 00	50,000 00	
Other stocks and b'ds	108,866 00	103,884 30	137,603 56	116,032 21	114,888 54
Due from res've ag'ts	14,374 16	2,942 39	4,637 53	3,920 27	23,143 82
Due from nat'l banks	11,450 50	22,758 37	39,517 86	50,698 84	62,775 26
Due from State banks	111,895 74	46,381 47	53,368 07	22,470 38	53,543 41
Real estate, &c	16,231 11	20,715 11	20,708 36	21,458 36	20,960 61
Current expenses.	14,012 77	7,218 40	7,894 22	9,776 89	10,907 48
Premiums paid	16,504 92	16,582 66	16,457 66	16,457 66	10,943 49
Cash items	8,143 17	6,378 63	3,134 09	12,523 33	21,738 49
Clear'g-house exch'gs					
Bills of other banks.	19,175 00	25,690 00	8,625 00	15,527 00	17,010 00
Fractional currency.	2 21	12 32	7 59	9 39	12 49
Trade dollars					
Specie	38,410 50	32,570 50	16,788 00	33,996 50	42,101 80
Legal-tender notes	64,441 00	78,021 00	35,976 00	52,010 00	54,291 00
U. S. cert's of deposit					
Due from U. S. Treas.	3,049 50	3,049 50	3,049 50	4,049 50	3,049 50
Total	881,265 32	837,262 19	825,294 18	822,025 67	853,961 82

MONTANA.

	13 banks.	14 banks.	14 banks.	14 banks.	15 banks.
Loans and discounts.	$5,124,069 30	$5,271,686 26	$5,404,216 99	$5,603,177 12	$5,515,195 02
Bonds for circulation.	399,350 00	424,350 00	424,350 00	424,350 00	439,350 00
Bonds for deposits	200,000 00	200,000 00	200,000 00	200,000 00	200,000 00
U. S. bonds on hand.					
Other stocks and b'ds	399,755 52	386,258 90	416,780 14	431,030 49	492,330 51
Due from res've ag'ts	246,719 82	214,744 51	195,649 27	282,748 26	407,898 27
Due from nat'l banks	293,020 54	255,023 18	209,307 93	285,694 82	521,058 70
Due from State banks	206,072 19	209,548 92	214,426 89	189,783 25	271,296 42
Real estate, &c	242,475 89	271,891 36	268,273 89	270,092 94	294,903 56
Current expenses.	75,397 60	40,522 34	61,659 86	10,183 60	39,815 19
Premiums paid	52,759 97	54,170 62	53,125 21	52,914 32	52,894 01
Cash items	78,851 15	70,548 99	40,034 88	69,381 03	52,054 98
Clear'g-house exch'gs					
Bills of other banks.	112,438 00	118,838 00	81,920 00	111,039 00	74,636 00
Fractional currency.	994 34	1,062 07	740 74	556 81	396 59
Trade dollars					
Specie	454,211 80	521,447 90	519,790 37	520,760 41	574,460 45
Legal-tender notes	239,845 00	342,103 00	297,743 00	352,670 00	327,458 00
U. S. cert's of deposit					
Due from U. S. Treas	23,495 36	21,892 87	20,120 87	20,283 87	23,866 87
Total	8,056,456 48	8,404,688 92	8,408,150 01	8,824,665 89	9,287,524 57

by States and reserve cities—Continued.

DAKOTA.

Liabilities.	DECEMBER 20. 35 banks.	MARCH 10. 36 banks.	MAY 6. 38 banks.	JULY 1. 40 banks.	OCTOBER 1. 41 banks.
Capital stock	$2,140,000 00	$2,240,000 00	$2,300,000 00	$2,332,500 00	$2,402,100 00
Surplus fund	438,424 67	467,923 35	456,523 35	490,073 35	500,573 35
Undivided profits....	361,825 27	217,348 89	285,628 50	209,964 92	279,028 82
Nat'l bank circulation	573,485 00	584 025 00	605,700 00	620,900 00	646,630 00
State bank circulation					
Dividends unpaid....	135 00	7,790 00	275 00	20,138 00	1,240 00
Individual deposits ..	2,791,030 66	2,863,802 40	2,945,616 60	3,170,700 40	3,725,521 66
U. S. deposits.......	119,715 95	130,047 85	122,727 66	114,607 92	113,195 75
Dep'ts U.S.dis.officers	26,193 71	17,628 54	18,696 36	29,233 88	37,921 12
Due to national banks	37,887 04	24,701 93	21,267 32	53,186 12	44,077 78
Due to State banks...	80,639 33	97,077 14	107,198 77	79,269 23	154,782 47
Notes re-discounted..	92,360 15	65,072 07	95,795 85	104,142 62	136,975 27
Bills payable	32,000 00	18,000 00	23,000 00	15,500 00	13,000 00
Total	6,693,756 78	6,733,417 17	6,982,429 50	7,240,306 44	8,055,916 22

IDAHO.

	4 banks.	4 banks.	4 banks.	4 banks.	4 banks.
Capital stock	$250,000 00	$250,000 00	$250,000 00	$250,000 00	$250,000 00
Surplus fund	20,000 00	20,000 00	20,000 00	20,000 00	20,000 00
Undivided profits....	68,444 29	37,167 96	39,931 44	50,400 97	62,516 34
Nat'l bank circulation	59,290 00	58,090 00	60,040 00	59,740 00	60,140 00
State bank circulation					
Dividends unpaid ..					
Individual deposits..	458,866 71	454,826 01	426,084 30	423,388 98	416,654 59
U. S. deposits					
Dep'ts U.S.dis.officers					
Due to national banks	1,385 27	256 20	65 94	3,221 25	45 59
Due to State banks ..	23,279 05	16,922 02	29,172 50	15,274 47	44,575 30
Notes re-discounted..					
Bills payable					
Total	881,265 32	837,262 19	825,294 18	822,025 67	853,961 82

MONTANA.

	13 banks.	14 banks.	14 banks.	14 banks.	15 banks.
Capital stock........	$1,650,000 00	$1,735,000 00	$1,750,000 00	$1,750,000 00	$1,810,000 00
Surplus fund	264,500 00	292,500 00	292,500 00	203,500 00	208,000 00
Undivided profits ...	641,828 37	629,881 56	605,316 42	649,105 28	740,678 17
Nat'l bank circulation	355,950 00	378,750 00	378,250 00	378,550 00	378,250 00
State bank circulation					
Dividends unpaid...				10,000 00	
Individual deposits ..	4,622,744 69	4,854,587 24	4,858,381 76	5,247,476 67	5,320,503 13
U. S. deposits	61,241 17	50,852 44	110,759 01	69,801 16	136,328 47
Dep'ts U.S.dis.officers	140,832 80	102,021 44	15,892 68	80,733 93	26,293 81
Due to national banks	183,272 75	200,398 73	118,770 70	178,447 91	413,987 42
Due to State banks...	60,312 66	52,919 87	76,990 71	50,361 52	45,133 20
Notes re-discounted..	66,714 04	98,177 64	111,288 73	116,689 42	109,322 02
Bills payable........					28 35
Total	8,056,456 48	8,404,088 92	8,408,150 01	8,824,665 89	9,287,524 57

Abstract of reports since September 30, 1884, arranged

NEW MEXICO.

Resources.	DECEMBER 20.	MARCH 10.	MAY 6.	JULY 1.	OCTOBER 1.
	8 banks.	8 banks.	8 banks.	8 banks.	8 banks.
Loans and discounts	$1,278,031 22	$1,322,069 31	$1,426,003 14	$1,443,714 49	$1,423,513 01
Bonds for circulation	450,000 00	450,000 00	450,000 00	412,500 00	412,500 00
Bonds for deposits	210,000 00	210,000 00	210,000 00	210,000 00	210,000 00
U. S. bonds on hand					
Other stocks and b'ds	38,529 49	45,661 28	47,381 06	46,848 44	60,597 91
Due from res've ag'ts	125,715 62	155,560 70	217,592 14	205,493 55	324,626 24
Due from nat'l banks	382,929 60	304,031 12	284,433 32	331,166 49	308,296 77
Due from State banks	133,396 97	100,304 60	61,274 30	97,820 12	67,379 52
Real estate, &c	122,691 70	146,959 09	172,497 73	174,429 73	159,906 98
Current expenses	40,002 41	25,968 08	29,835 14	28,778 22	28,714 53
Premiums paid	4,687 66	5,567 71	5,143 41	6,513 25	7,935 13
Cash items	26,306 16	12,263 84	22,962 72	25,287 90	11,977 29
Clear'g-house exch'gs					
Bills of other banks	29,950 00	24,166 00	24,603 00	21,307 00	23,121 00
Fractional currency	781 56	1,215 53	1,286 48	987 90	942 61
Trade dollars					
Specie	147,951 05	174,256 35	173,385 78	125,807 57	141,583 65
Legal-tender notes	80,185 00	83,107 00	77,248 00	60,178 00	70,816 00
U. S. cert's of deposit					
Due from U. S. Treas	20,470 00	23,737 50	19,757 50	20,550 00	17,850 00
Total	3,091,638 44	3,084,868 11	3,223,403 72	3,220,382 66	3,269,710 64

UTAH.

	5 banks.	5 banks.	5 banks.	6 banks.	6 banks.
Loans and discounts	$1,322,922 13	$1,214,142 91	$1,197,815 62	$1,344,386 33	$1,365,239 07
Bonds for circulation	387,500 00	387,500 00	387,500 00	437,500 00	437,500 00
Bonds for deposits	100,000 00	100,000 00	100,000 00	100,000 00	100,000 00
U. S. bonds on hand					
Other stock and b'ds	192,154 25	192,094 34	192,004 34	296,809 60	247,880 35
Due from res've ag'ts	50,588 40	53,954 27	66,498 17	170,846 76	135,390 20
Due from nat'l banks	237,290 66	163,822 97	143,041 42	205,465 04	357,426 67
Due from State banks	84,155 14	92,105 25	88,851 73	106,579 16	101,631 27
Real estate, &c	84,495 04	83,745 04	84,691 04	110,827 77	111,183 24
Current expenses	12,852 49	13,292 09	5,375 96	4,921 11	17,639 77
Premiums paid	35,109 56	33,453 31	33,453 31	28,367 73	27,805 23
Cash items	4,822 13	6,462 41	5,477 30	13,035 87	8,719 27
Clear'g-house exch'gs					
Bills of other banks	34,864 00	2,045 00	4,717 00	5,476 00	28,174 00
Fractional currency	74 44	195 08	468 85	375 75	160 00
Trade dollars					
Specie	320,890 75	237,278 90	222,386 00	182,113 64	215,577 62
Legal-tender notes	21,391 00	12,239 00	9,046 00	23,600 00	35,040 00
U. S. cert's of deposit					
Due from U. S. Treas	17,437 50	16,937 50	17,437 50	19,687 50	19,687 50
Total	2,906,547 49	2,609,268 07	2,55?,854 24	2,990,055 86	3,209,054 28

WASHINGTON.

	15 banks.	15 banks.	15 banks.	15 banks.	15 banks.
Loans and discounts	$1,854,265 86	$1,865,373 62	$1,878,240 38	$1,933,331 65	$2,035,383 91
Bonds for circulation	317,500 00	310,000 00	310,000 00	310,000 00	380,000 00
Bonds for deposits					
U. S. bonds on hand	100 00	10,100 00	100 00	100 00	
Other stocks and b'ds	90,463 28	88,015 31	87,297 95	73,738 58	79,152 06
Due from res've ag'ts	73,136 97	78,572 96	100,856 75	172,817 44	154,355 17
Due from nat'l banks	24,841 27	57,327 27	41,917 97	74,768 90	84,491 39
Due from State banks	56,761 06	42,449 32	57,662 08	53,781 47	110,245 01
Real estate, &c	170,527 76	175,411 81	183,939 50	182,162 90	148,075 20
Current expenses	30,047 62	18,258 38	25,510 02	17,995 94	19,435 70
Premiums paid	21,299 91	25,958 64	35,953 64	35,647 49	51,452 49
Cash items	14,324 43	15,880 79	15,606 90	20,366 32	26,377 54
Clear'g-house exch'gs					
Bills of other banks	9,379 00	9,296 00	10,942 00	11,278 00	22,746 00
Fractional currency	125 31	156 78	247 40	270 78	235 04
Trade dollars					
Specie	286,290 42	303,632 07	263,183 54	269,067 71	265,365 44
Legal-tender notes	7,069 00	17,846 00	21,088 00	13,844 00	15,109 00
U. S. cert's of deposit					
Due from U. S. Treas	15,225 00	15,987 50	14,650 00	14,048 50	17,200 00
Total	2,971,346 89	3,034,266 45	3,047,196 13	3,188,154 68	3,409,643 95

by States and reserve cities—Continued.

NEW MEXICO.

Liabilities.	DECEMBER 20.	MARCH 10.	MAY 6.	JULY 1.	OCTOBER 1.
	8 banks.	8 banks.	8 banks.	8 banks.	8 banks.
Capital stock........	$645,000 00	$650,000 00	$650,000 00	$650,000 00	$650,000 00
Surplus fund........	165,888 03	137,575 88	139,287 85	157,287 85	153,209 75
Undivided profits....	86,298 22	64,627 48	63,727 33	51,020 48	50,474 70
Nat'l bank circulation	400,097 00	400,237 00	401,160 00	369,590 00	369,770 00
State bank circulation					
Dividends unpaid....	40 00	40 00	844 00	200 00	240 00
Individual deposits.	1,430,297 08	1,468,668 12	1,585,215 21	1,587,844 57	1,750,475 14
U. S. deposits....	82,653 27	74,346 73	99,617 35	85,471 83	77,999 07
Dep'ts U.S.dis.officers	124,942 50	108,547 39	103,270 05	100,174 52	99,279 70
Due to national banks	77,918 11	116,796 19	144,160 22	162,570 50	96,031 43
Due to State banks...	68,504 23	54,029 32	24,121 71	46,222 91	22,230 85
Notes re-discounted..					
Bills payable	10,000 00	10,000 00	10,000 00	10,000 00	
Total..........	3,091,638 44	3,084,868 11	3,223,403 72	3,220,382 66	3,269,710 64

UTAH.

	5 banks.	5 banks.	5 banks.	6 banks.	6 banks.
Capital stock........	$600,000 00	$600,000 00	$600,000 00	$800,000 00	$800,000 00
Surplus fund........	243,750 00	266,250 00	266,500 00	274,000 00	274,500 00
Undivided profits....	83,773 86	55,409 17	54,575 98	37,880 62	67,097 89
Nat'l bank circulation	319,150 00	306,900 00	298,800 00	299,750 00	324,930 00
State bank circulation					
Dividends unpaid....	642 00	856 00	2,626 00	6,471 00	3,171 00
Individual deposits..	1,507,479 82	1,206,735 50	1,207,693 59	1,452,188 79	1,626,610 92
U. S. deposits	20,327 63	47,459 32	41,322 02	51,389 02	17,682 88
Dep'ts U.S.dis.officers	64,810 92	41,587 77	39,221 72	20,925 84	45,904 58
Due to national banks	38,031 98	27,954 78	26,775 59	15,861 49	21,836 61
Due to State banks ..	21,901 28	49,435 53	16,339 34	26,589 10	27,290 40
Notes re-discounted..	1,680 00	1,680 00			
Bills payable	5,000 00	5,000 00	5,000 00	5,000 00	
Total..........	2,906,547 49	2,609,268 07	2,558,854 24	2,090,055 86	3,209,054 28

WASHINGTON.

	15 banks.	15 banks.	15 banks.	15 banks.	15 banks.
Capital stock........	$960,000 00	$980,000 00	$980,000 00	$1,005,000 00	$1,005,000 00
Surplus fund	90,429 49	114,529 82	135,529 82	137,423 50	140,091 26
Undivided profits ...	050,058 00	312,688 10	349,907 99	379,057 40	375,375 60
Nat'l bank circulation	284,450 00	277,600 00	277,600 00	264,950 00	322,560 00
State bank circulation					
Dividends unpaid....	4,620 00	1,270 00	790 00	2,165 00	575 00
Individual deposits...	1,139,626 48	1,221,513 01	1,207,010 25	1,343,740 24	1,450,206 17
U. S. deposits.......					
Dep'ts U.S.dis.officers					
Due to national banks	46,125 65	51,023 55	43,546 86	20,205 70	48,298 90
Due to State banks...	83,036 47	75,041 97	52,811 32	18,612 84	67,537 02
Notes re-discounted..					
Bills payable........	10,000 00			10,000 00	
Total..........	2,971,346 89	3,034,266 45	3,047,196 13	3,183,154 68	3,409,643 95

Abstract of reports since September 30, 1884, arranged

WYOMING.

Resources.	DECEMBER 20.	MARCH 10.	MAY 6.	JULY 1.	OCTOBER 1.
	4 banks.	5 banks.	5 banks.	5 banks.	5 banks.
Loans and discounts	$1,593,362 45	$1,549,736 66	$1,610,460 15	$1,637,800 47	$1,860,906 47
Bonds for circulation	142,500 00	155,000 00	155,000 00	155,000 00	155,000 00
Bonds for deposits	75,000 00				
U. S. bonds on hand					
Other stocks and b'ds	56,638 14	60,105 30	60,042 29	68,411 44	74,153 30
Due from res've ag'ts	333,790 35	244,627 31	200,216 88	337,611 88	244,907 72
Due from nat'l banks	201,971 57	201,650 27	117,383 30	258,652 77	295,693 93
Due from State banks	5,726 77	84,447 54	45,547 02	29,924 53	44,863 77
Real estate, &c	37,169 61	38,624 07	38,647 57	38,679 92	38,821 34
Current expenses	29,854 54	11,322 79	19,234 04	13,668 13	26,352 63
Premiums paid	32,382 50	16,925 01	16,941 23	16,614 75	16,577 23
Cash items	11,454 31	8,747 96	15,565 25	13,101 09	9,683 42
Clear'g-house exch'gs					
Bills of other banks	16,770 00	18,566 00	23,981 00	19,014 00	17,763 00
Fractional currency	289 13	299 32	426 84	265 16	154 65
Trade dollars					
Specie	108,330 75	138,561 60	164,027 23	170,576 76	209,694 85
Legal-tender notes	64,134 00	87,417 00	86,790 00	72,510 00	64,416 00
U. S. cert's of deposit					
Due from U. S. Treas	7,125 43	10,412 50	6,975 00	6,975 00	7,675 00
Total	2,719,499 55	2,626,443 33	2,561,084 80	2,829,835 89	3,006,613 44

*by States and reserve cities—*Continued.

WYOMING.

Liabilities.	DECEMBER 20. 4 banks.	MARCH 10. 5 banks.	MAY 6. 5 banks.	JULY 1. 5 banks.	OCTOBER 1. 5 banks.
Capital stock.......	$525,000 00	$800,000 00	$800,000 00	$800,000 00	$800,000 00
Surplus fund.........	80,000 00	134,000 00	134,000 00	139,000 00	140,000 00
Undivided profits....	142,535 27	98,803 17	130,327 27	103,917 43	151,593 32
Nat'l bank circulation	125,950 00	127,450 00	137,700 00	136,500 00	139,500 00
State bank circulation	....	....	....	....	....
Dividends unpaid....	....	....	....	....	....
Individual deposits...	1,708,042 44	1,429,881 56	1,340,956 04	1,595,710 87	1,744,352 95
U. S. deposits	17,135 92	....	....	....	....
Dep'ts U.S.dis.officers	49,908 03	....	....	....	....
Due to national banks	21,357 47	31,461 69	15,461 79	28,442 42	61,258 07
Due to State banks...	6,906 76	4,846 01	2,639 70	26,265 17	29,909 10
Notes re-discounted..	42,663 66	....	....	....	....
Bills payable.........	....	....	....	....	....
Total	2,719,499 55	2,626,443 33	2,561,084 80	2,829,835 89	3,066,613 44

INDEX.

TABLES CONTAINED IN THE APPENDIX.